DIMENSIONS OF HUMAN SOCIETY AND CULTURE

Essays in Honour
of
Professor Prabodh Kumar Bhowmick

Edited by
MANIS KUMAR RAHA

GYAN

Dimensions of Human Society and Culture
(Anthropology, Sociology, Behavioural Science))

ISBN: 81-212-0520-4

Reprinted in 2013 in India by
Gyan Publishing House
23, Main Ansari Road, Daryaganj,
New Delhi - 110002
Phone : 23282060, 23261060
Fax : (011) 23285914
E-mail : books@gyanbooks.com
Website: gyanbooks.com

Printed at: G. Print Process, Delhi

PROLOGUE

This planet, this home of ours, is millions of years old and has accommodated a very big number of 5,505,914,000 human souls, as estimated in the mid-year of 1993 and referred to by Britannia Book of the Population Reference Bureau, 1994. This huge human populations are found in almost every nook and corner of the world. While they are found in the snowy arctic region, they also inhabit on the sands of the desert. While they live in the extreme cold of the high altitudes, they are also found to dwell in the coastal region or in the islands. They live in the plains as well as in the forests. While some of them live in the cities, towns and industrial belts, a very large number of them lead their life in the rural areas. Many of these God's best creatures enjoy a very sophisticated life in the cities and again some others lead a so called very 'backward' life in the very remote or inaccessible areas. That means humankind are found to live in varied ecological set ups and get themselves adjusted to these.

While hunters and gatherers are still found to roam in the forest clad areas and to depend mostly on the hunted animals and fishes and collected roots and tubers, others are involved in highly sophisticated professions mostly in the urban centres. Again in between these two extreme life styles rest millions of people who have varied livelihood patterns. Similarly, they have different social structures, different life cycle complexes and different types of interactions. The customs, manners and norms of the society also vary from one group to another and from one area to another. They have been found to have embraced different religions, with numerous beliefs and practices and also have different world views. But inspite of the presence of these multiple variability of the cultural pattern of the human being living in different continents and other areas some similarity among many groups could also be traced. Another interesting feature of the diverse human cultures is that due to the constant action of various internal and/or external forces the human culture everywhere is changing which is quite rapid somewhere but quite slow in some other places depending upon the contact situation prevailed there and the intensity of the forces acting on the culture.

Everywhere tradition and modernity are being shared by every human culture. In every place on this earth the human being like to live in the society which has its own traditions, institutions and collective activities and interests. Here the members interact with one another and these interactions have helped them to develop an organised patterns of relationship. A marked variations are found in the types of societies which depend on the life style of the members, socio-economic activities, socio-political set up and ecological conditions of their habitat. But whatever may be the type the human societies are always subjected to constant change.

When I planned to publish a book on human societies and cultures I had some idea about how big is the world and how much are the constrains and how low is my capability to take up this project. I also had some idea about the great diversities present in human culture, and the variability and drift that characterise innumerable number of human societies and cultures present on this earth. No doubt the whole world is at present quite close to one thanks to the modern communication systems, but it is never that close which would make a scholar easy to study the human culture all over the world. So I never had any intention to capture the whole human societies and cultural patterns in my book, as I had enough idea about my capability. I had no intention to do what is not humanly possible. With the limited strength, that I had, I thought of highlighting aspects of some human societies and cultures existing in different parts of the world including India. So the readers may have glimpses of only some aspects of the some human societies and cultures surviving in far and near.

It is true that we do not have much idea about all the people living on different land masses of the world as not many human societies and cultures have been anthropologically studied. There are many groups living in far inaccessible areas, who have not been touched upon by the social scientists. Even we know very little of many people who live in our neighbourhood. The totality of culture has not even been rightly focussed through any study on any particular human group. In this regard no doubt our knowledge is very much limited. As a result even with the development of communication channel, we have failed to come closer to our own congeners in the true sense. The **Home Sapien Sapien** is one of the largest and most important members in the animal kingdom. Some members of this species have achieved golden success in many fields, both science and arts. Even some during scientists and technologists have sat out to the outer space beyond this earth, to discover what was so long mystery to us. They are revolving round the earth in the sky above to know the unknown. They have even landed on the moon. But in one sphere where the distinct failure is noticed, is that we have learnt very little of us in the thousands of years of human history. Even then whatever we get from the writings of the scholars and others about humankind is for the positive benefit of us. And here lies the importance of this study. From this book our readers will come to know something new about some of our brethren inhabiting different parts of this earth.

As already stated I have included articles on some aspects of a few human societies and cultures of the people of different parts of the world other than India and some general articles in Part—I of this book whereas Part—II is specially meant for India. In Part—I I have incorporated sixteen articles. Of these sixteen articles two have been written on the people of Africa, five on the people of America, one on the tribal people of Australia, one on the people of Europe, one on the people of Maxico and two on the people of Jordan. The rest four articles are general in nature.

In Part—I I have included articles covering varied aspects of the society and culture of the people of different parts of globe, as already stated. The articles include from urban studies to tribal studies, from state policies to ethnicity, from economic situation to human values, from status of students to the status of women, from human habitat to delinquency and so on. It is expected that scholars of different disciplines will be interested of this book because of the varied nature of articles.

Considering the diversity of the themes of the articles I have arranged these countrywise, keeping the articles of general nature at the beginning.

PART—II

As already stated Part—II of this book includes articles on society and cultures of some people of India, that is Bharat, is a big country spread over an area of 3,287,263 sq. kms. and has accommodated a total of 844,324,222 souls according to 1991 Census. Of these population males consist of 437,005,005 while the fair sex has a population of 406,518,417. From the Himalayas to Indira Point all these people are found to live in varied numbers. They have constructed their settlement in all the twenty-five States and seven Union Territories of India. They have different ethnic affinities and belong to different castes, creeds, sects, and religious groups. They have different social systems, languages, and cultural patterns. They survive with different livelihood pattern, different social orders, world views and with multiple religious faiths. Even with all these diversities the Indians are found to live one beside the other interacting with one another for centuries. Their centuries long contact with one another have enable them to establish a strong network of relation and develop a deep feeling for them. They live in different ecological zones and adopted themselves accordingly for their survival. The invasions on India in different phases of history by the external forces have added further diversities to already highly diverse Indian societies and cultures. Possibly these unique and marked diversities prompted Pandit Jawaharlal Nehru to remark,

> The diversity of India is
> tremendous; it is obvious; it
> lies on the surface and anybody
> can see it. If concerns itself
> with physical appearances
> as well as with certain mental
> habits and traits.

No doubt these unmatched diversities have made India a unique one in the global arena; but these diversities are superficial as there lies an undercurrent of unity everywhere. Here inspite of the great diversities the Indians are found to live in the midst of harmony having both cohesions and conflicts. Here diversities are found to co-exist with unities.

In Part—II of this book, I have incorporated fourteen articles, all on Indian societies and/or cultures. That means, while Part—I is devoted to the societies and/or cultures of some people living outside India, Part—II is exclusively on some Indian societies and cultures.

India, as we all know, is a vast country with innumerable

number of societies and cultures. My limitations have allowed me to cover only some small parts of it, a few societies and a few cultures, I could not go beyond that.

All the fourteen articles I have incorporated in Part—II are diverse in nature. The first six articles are general in nature covering different aspects of Indian society and culture. Various themes like the levels of socio-cultural integration, conception of the self, origin and development of Scheduled Castes, status of women and development and integrations of slum dwellers have been discussed in the first six articles. The seventh article deals with the Devadasi system. The life of the rural poor and the impact of land reforms on them has been described in another article. Tribal development planning is an interesting topic and through one article some new light has been thrown on this topic. The Lepcha of Darjeeling and Sikkim have attracted many anthropologists. Their life and activities have been shown in one article. One of the articles has discussed on the Bauls—a singer community of West Bengal. In the North East India the problem of ethnicity has created headache to many scholars, politicians and commoners. This problem has been discussed in one article. The Himalayan environment, for centuries remained free from the pollution of the modern world. But ultimately human activities have changed much of it. The last but one article has revealed this problem. The last article of this volume deals with the economy of the tribal people inhabiting the Great Himalayas.

I firmly believe that scholars and academicians belonging to the disciplines of Social and Environmental Sciences and also the planners and administrators who are interested on the human society and culture, will consider this book very interesting and useful as this book I believe, will be able to feed them back with many information about the societies and cultures of the people of our good earth.

This book distributed in two parts is meant for honouring Professor Probodh Kumar Bhowmick who has recently retired from his teaching profession. I was one of his senior students and had the opportunity of understanding him not only as teacher but also as man. I think this is the proper way to pay homage to a teacher, educationist and an anthropologist.

Professor Bhowmick was born in 1926 in an affluent landholding caste in coastal Midnapur, West Bengal where he had his early education upto matriculation standard in a National School. While he was a student he participated in the 'Quit India Movement' and was put in jail for about two years. Then he came to Calcutta to read Intermediate of Science in Bangabasi College but again involved in a movement against partition of India. He went upto Sylhet (now in Bangladesh) and stayed there for about a month even after the riot. During Gandhiji's visit to Midnapore he led the volunteers. Later on he received his Honours Degree in Anthropology. He got his M.Sc. Degree in Anthropology from the University of Calcutta in 1951 and became a teacher in Bangbasi College in 1952. Prof. N.K. Bose encouraged him to prepare a monograph on the Lodhas who were at that time treated as a 'criminal' tribe. His monograph The *Lodhas of West Bengal—A socio-economic study* earned his Doctor of Philosophy in which he expressed that :

> territorial and economically displaced Lodhas could not adopt themselves to the changing situations which further drove them towards a precarious existence and the growing need of an expanding family clamped in a small territory, could not be met with hewer's income. Enduring frustration and lack of self reliance brought in its terrain a perpetual stagnation in their collective life and subsequently turned them into inveterate criminals with every knock of the waves of changing circumstances.

Professor N.K. Bose suggested to him to organise one centre to change the habit of the Lodhas, i.e., to mould the criminals into friends of the society. An organisation named Samaj Sevak Sangha, was started by Professor Bhowmick at Narayangarh, Midnapore where many scholars and teachers joined. This place is popularly known as Bidisa, i.e., 'diffusing light'. It is considered to be the centre of Action Anthropology. This place has been visited by many scholars administrators and planners not only from this country but also from abroad.

His another contribution *Socio-cultural Profile of Frentier Bengal* earned for him the Degree of Doctor of Science in Anthropology. His another book '*The Chenchus of the Forests and Plateaux—a gatherings hunting tribe in transition*' earned good reputation as a tribal study, and was rewarded as the best book (1994) on Dravidian speaking tribe. He retired from his teaching profession in 1994. During the course of his teaching carrier he has produced hundreds of students and guided a large number of them for their research work. Many of them are well placed in their life and are new holding prominent positions. Professor Bhowmick is not an arm-chair anthropologist. He is the man who loved to stay very close to the soil of the earth where the down-trodden and the weaker sections live. He often tells "don't treat the tribals as cultural guineapig—they are our fellow friends, do something for them as they have given you the opportunity of learning of your subject." Thus Bidisa has been organised and it is a growth centre—a model of development.

Professor Bhowmick is attached to many organisations and learned societies and had the advantage of participating in various capacities to the different Universities and Government Departments of this country. He is the founder member of the Institute of Social Research and Applied Anthropology and editor of the journal, *Man and Life*. Two dozen or so books and about 600 papers in English and Bengali have been written by him.

Another important contribution of Professor Bhowmick is to take anthropology from University to college and school levels. For his efforts anthropology is now taught as a subject in different colleges and schools of West Bengal. As a member of U.G.C. he also tried to open anthropology in some other universities of India and abroad and became successful also.

Apart from his professional carrier Professor Bhowmick is an extraordinary man. He is the man with many noble ideas, vision and compassion, a philanthropologist and a man who spent almost whole of his life for the well-being of the tribals. He is also a man of much controversy. He is an outspoken man who is never afraid of speaking frankly what he thinks as true. For this no doubt, some people misunderstood him.

I have the chance to come very close to him. He is not only my teacher, but like my elder brother. The most precious thing was I got from him is his affection. It is difficult to repay this in any possible way. But even then I have thought that the most humble way to repay his debt, is to offer my respect and regards in the form of this felicitation volume which is, I consider a symbol of my deep sense of gratitude and respect to this many-sided man.

To finalize this volume I have taken help of many people. I shall deliberately retreat from performing my duties, if I do not acknowledge my debt to those who spontaneously came forward to help me to successfully complete this book. At first I remember the contributors of this volume. They are very kind, sympathetic and co-operative. Some of them are very good friends of Professor Bhowmick also. Without their cooperation and contribution I could not have launched this project. I express my heartfelt gratitude to all of them. I am also thankful to Miss. Suparna

Sanyal, a scholar who helped me much in checking the typescripts, I am indebted to Miss Anima Pal, Miss Mala Mukherjee, Shri Nandanwar, Shri Prafulla Mozarkar and Miss S.V. Rajam for their untiring typing work. Some of my colleagues have also helped me in one way or the other, I have no hesitation to acknowledge them.

Finally I express my sincere gratitude to Gyan Publishing House, New Delhi, publishers of a number of my books, who has so kindly agreed to publish this book also.

—Manis Kumar Raha

CONTRIBUTORS

Professor Fernando Poyatos — Professor
Deptt. of Anthropology, Sociology and Psychology
University of New Brunswick
Fredericton
New Brunswick
Canada.

Professor Irwin Deutscher — Professor Emeritus
Deptt. of Sociology
The University of Akron
Buchtel College of Arts and Science
Akron, U.S.A.

Dr. Julius O. Ihonvbere — Associate Professor
Deptt. of Political Science
Bendel State University
Ekpoma, Nigeria.

Dr. Darlington Iwarimie-Jaja — Assistant Professor of Criminology
Department of Sociology
Faculty of Social Sciences
University of Port Harcourt
Port Harcourt, Nigeria.

Dr. Robert J. Fornaro — Director
International Programs and Development and
Professor
Deptt. of Anthropology

University of South Alabama
Mobile, Alabama
U.S.A.

Professor Marion J. Rice — Professor Emeritus
Social Science Education
University of Georgia
Athens, Georgia
U.S.A.

Professor John van Willigen — Professor
Department of Anthropology
University of Kentucky
Lexington, Kentucky
U.S.A.

Professor Harsha N. Mookerjee — Professor
Department of Sociology and Director
Alcohal Safety Education Programme, Tennessee Technological University
Cookevile, Tennessee
U.S.A.

Dr. Magdalena Villarreal — Deptt. of Sociology and Rural Development
Wageningen Agricultural University
Wageningen
The Netherlands.

Professor Rishikeshab Regmi — Former Head
Deptt. of Sociology and Anthropology
Tribhuvan University
Kathmandu, Nepal.

Dr. Muhanna Haddad — Associate Professor
Deptt. of Anthropology
Institute of Archaeology and Anthropology
Yarmouk University
Yarmouk, Jordan.

Dr. Faisal Al-Matalka	Research Scholar Deptt. of Sociology University of Rajasthan Jaipur.
Professor Kenneth Maddock	Professor of Anthropology School of Behavioural Sciences MacQuarrie University Sydney, New South Wales Australia.
Professor Peter T. Suzuki	The Frederick W. Kayser Professor Department of Public Administration University of Nebraska at Omaha Omaha, Nebraska U.S.A. Editor, *European Studies Journal* Editor, *Internationa, Third World* Studies *Journal.*
Professor J.B. Ganguly	Former Vice-Chancellor Tripura University Tripura.
Professor N.K. Behura	Former Professor and Head Deptt. of Anthropology Utkal University Vani Vihar Bhubaneswar Orissa.
Professor Edward J. Jay	Professor Emeritus California State University Hayward California, U.S.A.
Professor Brian Morris	Professor Deptt. of Anthropology and Community Studies Goldsmith College University of London London.

Sri S.K. Chatterjee	Former Deputy Inspector General of Police, Bureau of Investigation
Dr. Horst F. Rolly	Associate Professor Social and Behavioural Sciences and Head Deptt. of Development Studies and Social Service, Spicer Memorial College Pune, India.
Dr. (Mrs.) Dipali G. Danda	Superintending Anthropologist Anthropological Survey of India 27, Jawaharlal Nehru Road Calcutta 700 016 India.
Dr. D.K. Behera	Reader and Head Department of Anthropology Sambalpur University Burla, Sambalpur India.
Professor Jaan Valsiner	Professor and Director Developmental Psychology Program Department of Psychology College of Arts and Science University of North Carolina Chapel Hill North Carolina, U.S.A. Editor, *Culture and Psychology*.
Professor Ajit Kumar Danda	Former Professor Department of Sociology and Social Anthropology North Bengal University Darjeeling Professor of Research, Asiatic Society, Calcutta Editor *Journal of Indian Anthropological Society*.

Dr. Prasanna K. Samal	Scientist G.B. Pant Institute of Himalayan Environment and Development Kosi-Katarmal, Almora India.
Dr. R.V. Ramarao	Department of Geo-Engineering and Resource Development Technology Andhra University.
Dr. R.C. Prasad	Scientist G.B. Pant Institute of Himalayan Environment and Development Kosi-Katarmal, Nainital India.
Dr. Amal Kumar Das	Former Director Cultural Research Institute Govt. of West Bengal and Presently Member, Other Backward Classes Commission, West Bengal, Calcutta India.
Dr. R.M. Sarkar	Head Deptt. of Anthropology Bangabasi College and Editor, *Man-in-India* Calcutta India.
Dr. B.N. Bordoloi	Former Director and Ex- Consultant Assam Institute of Research for Tribals and Scheduled Caste, Guwahati, Assam India.
Dr. Mamata Desai	Professor and Head Deptt. of Ecology Netaji Institute for Asian Studies Calcutta India.

Dr. Manis Kumar Raha	Former Joint Director Anthropological Survey of India Govt. of India Calcutta. President Anthropology and Archaeology Section 83rd Indian Science Congress Editor *Journal of Human and Environmental Sciences.*
Sri Sumitabha Chakravarty	Junior Research Fellow Anthropological Survey of India Nagpur, India.

CONTENTS

PART—II

Part—I

Fernando Poyatos

COUGHING AND THROAT-CLEARING, SPITTING AND SNEEZING : FOUR SAMPLES FOR CULTURAL AND CROSSCULTURAL RESEARCH

Introduction

After visiting many cultures throughout the world in the last twenty years, I have learned to observe the fascinating, though at times subtle, differences and similarities in the use of non-verbal communication and, within this broad interdisciplinary field—which has engaged my interest all this time—the social handling of what I have termed *paralinguistic differentiators*, that is, truly quasilexical utterances that characterize and 'differentiate' physiological reactions (many of a reflex nature) as well as psychological states and emotional reactions. Elsewhere (Poyatos, 1993) I have studied the following : laughter, crying, shouting, sighing, gasping, panting, yawning, coughing, spitting, belching, hicuping, and sneezing. The four chosen here, coughing, throat-clearing, spitting and sneezing, are presented as samples of what should constitute a much broader systematic research across cultures, even subcultures, as is the case in a rich, large country like India.

1. Coughing and Throat-Clearing as Communicative Activities

Although no systematic research seems to have been attempted to identify the potential interactive and communicative functions of these two audible-visual activities, they are much more than mere physiological reactions, since we can imitate them voluntarily and use them as a communicative message-conveying vehicle and interpret them quite accurately if others use them in non-spontaneous, non-physiological language-like ways. Also, the narrative and dramaturgic literatures of the various cultures are rich and eloquent sources of data. What sets throat-clearing apart from actual coughing is that it is a controlled act (though not always voluntary), that it cannot be subject to the unwitting behaviors a cough can (i. e., uncontrollable face and body movements, choking, etc.), and that therefore it is used as a conscious communicative behavior much more than coughing.

1.2. The Morphology of Coughing and Throat-Clearing

The researcher must differentiate the following morphological features in a cough or throat-clearing : the *paralinguistic leader*, which can be a conspicuous breath intake, its *onset*, which can be, for instance, a whooping cough; *duration* will almost always refer to the second (more important) phase of a cough, during which expiration words are perhaps brokenly articulated; *loudness:* soft-forte-fortissimo; *pitch:* low, mid and high; *resonance :* markedly pharyngeal or oral, mainly; a cough can be *qualified* mainly be hoarseness and whizziness; and, if it alters respiration repeatedly, it shows an audible (and visible in a heaving chest) intake of breath as its *paralinguistic aftermath*. As for a cough's *kinesic leader*, which blends with its *onset*, and the behaviors of the *face, hands* and whole *body*, they depend very much on whether coughing is abruptly triggered, voluntarily elicited (though still natural) or calculated and feigned; certain *contextual* and *concomitant* activities that are typical of spontaneous coughing, such as reddening of the face, gorged veins, and choking; the *cultural background* and the *socioeducational status* of the cougher, as they are always subject to cultural display rules that, within the same culture, exist in certain classes and not in others and, ultimately, to individual norms according to one's upbringing and sensitiveness; the *situational context*, such as with the anxiety, perhaps part of a *clinical configuration*, as with a patient's attention-getting cough; finally, awareness of the *cointeractants' behaviors* (e.g., triggering the cough, or acting upon it).

1.3. A Functional Classification of coughing and throat-clearing

(a) *Interaction Regulation*. There are a series of versatile and eloquent instances of coughing in interaction.

Announcement of self, typically done through either a 'polite' throat-clearing or a loud, intentionally disrupting cough or throat clearing, depending on whether we just intend to make our presence acknowledged or must also allow others to change their present behavior. "She coughed elaborately at the door so that Philip should have time to compose himself (...), then she rattled the door handle" (Maugham *OHB*, IX). A similar behavior is the attention-getting cough or throat-clearing, to attract someone's attention for various purposes, often preparatory to calling out or speaking to the person. "She tapped softly with the key at one of the cell-doors, and listened (...) she coughed and listened again" (Dickens *OT*, XIII).

The *prespeech* cough or throat-clearing, which can even be accompanied by the typical prespeech (apicoalveolar) click and/or the prespeech breath intake (both included later under 'alternants'), can be an unconscious anxiety-based behavior (therefore identified below within that category), or a conscious preparatory and effect-seeking opener which is even used consciously in informal as well as formal oratory. This prespeech cough, or rather throat-clearing—traditionally used in formal oratory—may be a louder cough when it must also request silence and/or attention, but otherwise it is a throat-clearing, even though it may be referred to as cough. "(Dorothea after preparing herself) by coughing and other mannerisms, began to say very gracefully (...)" (Cervantes DQ, 1, XXX, trans. mine). A similar type is, of course, a *pre-singing:* "(after being asked to sing) he was clearing his throat, pulling his clean handkerchief farther out of his breast pocket, and thrusting his fingers between the buttons of his vest" (Lewis *MS*,VI).

The *prompting* cough or throat-clearing is familiar and important regulatory behavior, as it serves to induce someone to, or prevent him from, saying or doing something (typically acknowledging someone else's presence), acquiesce with what someone says, avoid making a social blunder, etc., usually accompanied by meaningful eye contact, perhaps even a postural shift as a signal to the person we are trying to cue. "The old gentleman was just going to say that Oliver should not go out (...) when a most malicious cough from Mr. Grimwig determined him that he should" (Dickens *OT*, XIV). One can find interesting crosscultural occurrences of this cough, such as the throat-clearing that means 'Let's stop eating and let's go', traditionally given in Saudi Arabia by the guest of honor at a meal in a house in order to leave enough food for those who have not eaten yet, a practice less common now as living standards rise and most families can afford an abundance of food.

A cough or throat-clearing can also act as a *stalling* tactic, or as a *thinking pause*, often combining both : "The audience cleared their throats and tossed a few stalks into the fire, not because these deeds were urgent, but to give themselves time to weigh the moral of the story" (Hardy *RN*, 1, III).

An intentionally conspicuous cough is a typical cover-up

behavior to *muffle* an inopportune comment or statement or distract from inappropriate audible or visual conduct : " Mr. Dedalus' cup had rattled noisily against its saucer, and Stephen had tried to cover that shameful sign of his father's drinking bout of the night before by moving his chair and coughing" (Joyce *PAYM*, II).

Naturally, as a conversational or non-conversational regulatory behavior in interaction, a cough or throat-clearing can typically act as a *feedback* behavior, but this function is implied in many of the instances discussed in article (e.g., showing anger, impatience, disinterest).

(b) *Satisfaction*. A little cough or a pensive throat-clearing can be sometimes a subtle and eloquent proof of self-satisfaction, mostly moral but sometimes physical too, as witnessed in someone who just donned an elegant suit and walks out of his house on a fine morning as if the world were a mirror, or who received a compliment, or performed a good deed. "He cleared his throat as he looked himself up and down (in the mirror, at the barbershop, after a manicure girl finishes her job)" (Dos Passos *MT*, 3, I).

(c) *Uncertainty*. This is the general feeling with which we tend to associate nonreflex coughing and throat-clearing and with which we pretend to experience doubt, hesitation, confusion, etc.: *doubt and incredulity* and *dubious acquiescence* can be tacitly expressed by throat-clearing : '(the lawyer, tole by Mr. Pickwick that he will not call any witnesses) coughed dubiously. These tokens (...) were not lost on Mr. Pickwick" (Dickens *PP*,s XXXI); *puzzlement and confusion* elicit often conscious or unconscious throat-clearing : "(he) professed to be puzzled. 'Hem!' said he" (C. Bronte *JE*, XXIV).

(d) *Embarrassment*. This category should be set apart, although it includes various nuances, depending on the situation or personality characteristic that causes the feeling, for instance, of sheer *shyness* : "one of those little things that goes around higher up"/'You mean the little silk pockets on a string?'/ 'Yes (...)' (...). He coughed to clear his throat" (Steinbeck *TF*, IV). Often the person makes and effort to overcome shyness, but the nonverbal behavior of embarrassment is present nevertheless. Realizing a silly *error* causes embarrassment : "(after mistaking a heap of dead rabbits for a dog) I hemmed once more" (E.Bronte *WH*, II). Embarrassment and a desire to prevent someone from *exposing our weaknesses* elicits a word-like throat-clearing. A shy person must sometimes make an *effort to participate* in an interaction.

(e) *Social Anxiety*. Although embarrassment is often caused by social tension in interaction, the tension itself triggers in us coughing and throat-clearing, even as an *a priori reaction*. Tension in the face of a difficult decision can also make us be *at a loss for words* : "He stands there awkwardly (...) clears his throat, swallows, but fails to speak" (Laurence *SA*, II). Other times it is a *sense of propriety* that triggers the behavior : "Tom (after kissing the shy Laura) *coughs decorously*" (Williams *GM*, VII). A most typical instance of social tension arouses when a subordinate is in front of a superior in a difficult situation, as in fact the superior-subordinate or dominance-submission situation relationship is often inferred precisely from this behavior (e.g., police officer-law breaker): "O' Keefe (in front of his boss) cleared his throat and shuffled his feet" (Dos Passos *MT*, 2, III). *Not being on speaking terms* typically causes throat-clearing between silent interactants. Coughing and throat-clearing can act also as *silence fillers* when no other audible behavior is displayed, a compulsive attitude that responds to the different ways in which different cultures cope with interactive silences (e. g., longer and better accepted in general among Orientals and North-American Native Indians), at the point in which the silence creates anxiety. But the most intriguing and most elusive of all the anxious coughs and throat-clearings is, in my opinion, and after observing it for many, many years (not just in others, but when I catch myself doing it), the loud cough or subdued throat-clearing which, perhaps for lack of a better term, I will call the *solitary dyadic cough* or throat-clearing, for instance : two solitary pedestrians pass each other on both sides of an ordinary empty street in the middle of the night and their only mutual acknowledgement is their throat-clearing if they walk on the same sidewalk or along a narrow street. There is definitely a mutual acknowledgement of our presence, though at times reluctant perhaps. In a dark street at night or in an empty New York subway platform or car (rarely in its Tokyo counterpart, though) it can easily be interpreted as a signal of assurance that we are both safe people in an unlikely place.

(f) *Disinterest and Rejection*. Coughing and throat-clearing are used to more or less intentionally signify our negative attitude toward the situation, as a verbal statement to that effect would be most of the time inappropriate. They are the typical behaviors of *boredom* at a gathering : "People cleared their throats, tried to choke down yawns. The men shot their cuffs and the women stuck their combs more firmly into their back hair" (Lewis *MS*, IV). Boredom can soon grow out of *disinterest*, with different manifestations, signifed also through the same behavior, as when we use it *to avoid acknowledging someone* verbally : "Hurstwood only cleared his throat by way of acknowledgement (talking to another street bum like him when he is reduced to beggary)" (Dreiser *SC* XLI). The disinterest of *reluctant acceptance* can be clearly stated in word-qualifying throat-clearing : "Merivale cleared his throat. 'Very well', he said dryly (disliking the idea, but obliged to do it)" (Dos Passos *MT*, 3,II). And, of course, there is disinterest and rejection in *disagreement* :"Some people think so, I know,' (...) 'But personally...' He cleared his throat with violence. That was *his* personal opinion" (Huxley *PCP*, VII).

(g) *Impatience, Reproach, and Anger*. Impatience, reproach and anger denote various forms of annoyance : "Joe gave a reproachful cough, as much as to say, 'Well, I told you so' (Dickens *GE*, II, 12).

2. Spitting as a Voluntary Paralinguistic-Kinesic Behavior

Spitting is a paralinguistic-kinesic behavior (i.e., audible-visual) with both physiological and communicative functions, but mainly a voluntary act that can qualify words and even replace them, possessing in addition an extraordinary historical and crosscultural relevance, trivial as it may seem at first sight. We know that physiologically it is a very simple action, expelling phlegm an nasal mucus—usually preceded by ordinary throat-clearing or its tenser form, 'hawking'—and also to spit out any other unwanted matter from the mouth; but even these two stages of spitting can be meaningfully modified by paralinguistic and kinesic qualifiers and add to the expulsion of saliva or any other matter any of a series of emotional and interactive messages, as when someone spits at another person directly or in front of him with a look of contempt, or spits out dusty saliva naturally but with an attitudinal 'paralinguistic' loudness that expresses disgust or weariness, or a final prolonged and harsh (velopharyngeal) voiced friction as a reaction of repugnance.

2.2. The Morphology of Spitting

It would be a mistake to shun a more systematic, scientific way of documenting, for instance spitting behaviors across cultures, for any kinesic or paralinguistic behaviors may reveal subtle (or not so subtle) variations that betray precisely attitudinal and culural or social differences; anyone may, for instance, spit at someone in contempt or as an angry act of humiliation, but the 'slowness' or 'quickness' of the facial gesture and actual spitting may betray cultural background, the spitter's social status and perhaps the exact meaning put in that aspect of the behavior which, otherwise, we might just regard as spitting 'in anger' or 'as a punishment'. The *paralinguistic leader* can be an audible deep inspiration to gather strength for the hawking and/ or spitting itself; thus, *the two stages*, hawking and the actual spitting, are important; the audible inspiration that may follow the actual spitting (when, for instance, a man spits on his hands before grabbing a pick) could be taken as a *paralinguistic aftermath* of as a leader for the ensuing task; the *loudness* of the two possible stages, as well as their *duration* (the latter more for the hawking) can also be significant; the possible *paralinguistic qualifiers* are, of course, velarization, pharyngealization and velopharyngealization; the *kinesic leader* is shown mainly on the face, as the spitter prepare himself, but it can blend with an emotional expression, such as contempt, the movement of mouth and cheeks being then more of an *onset;* the behavior of the *face* may be relevant, as when the spitter approaches his victim with puffed-up cheeks; a general *body behavior* may include bending toward the victim slowly or abruptly, as in tense and premeditated anger or in a sudden outburst; the *kinesic aftermath* can be again the angry expression or the gesture of contempt; we should acknowledge also the *spittle* in the general configuration, for its mere presence on the face, body or clothes of the victim (if not just on the ground) adds a powerfully humiliating element to the equally abasing spitting sound; his or her *cultural background* and *socioeducational status* as a spitter are essential, as are the *situational context* and the *cointeractants' behaviors*, particularly when the latter may have triggered the spitting or they are a response to it.

2.3. Physiological and Social Functions of Spitting

(a) *Physiological Functions*. Leaving aside the pathological motivated instances of spitting, the term should still be applied to those occasions when it is elicited by the need to reject *dirtied saliva*, for it may happen that the foreign observer in a foreign culture or an unfamiliar environment or situation may misjudge it as merely an unnecessary unrefined act, for instance: pedestrians and bicycle riders returning to New Delhi along a tributary dusty dirt road late in the afternoon; people at a threshing floor or while winnowing grain avoiding to swallow its dust. What would make the difference is—and that must be weighed very carefully—whether they do it in the presence of others, how close to them, and how necessarily or unnecessarily they make the 'paralinguistic' part of it conspicuously loud, that is, hawking and the sound of spitting. What presumably would be physiological spitting is, however, condemned in many different cultures when done in public places, particularly while walking in the street—as so many Spanish men do from middle class down—visibly and audibly enough, the hawking sound being considered as offensive as the spitting itself. I have seen looks of disgust in pedestrians in European cultures as well as in North America. In Nigeria, where audible and visible spitting seems to be a habit among one of the three ethnic groups, but strongly looked down upon by the other two, the latter look away or throw a disapproving look at the spitter, as they do in Ghana, for spitting, if necessary, must be silent, shielding one's mouth and away from others.

(b) *Social Spitting*. This category certainly blends with the first, as they are both subject to social norms and personal sensitiveness, which obviously vary crossculturally just as they have changed historically. Wildeblood (1965:205) reports from Samuel Pepys' *Diary*, that he did not object at all when a pretty lady in the darkness of a theater box spat" 'backward upon me, by mistake'". Today, middle-class male teenagers in the more 'spitting cultures' are observed, when outdoors, to hawk-and-spit 'like men' in front of other male peers to gain approval as a form of *affiliative* behavior during a conversation or while playing a game (e.g., the soccer goalkeeper ready to stop the ball), or during a spitting contest, seeing who gets the farthest. The outdoors spitting of North-American or English males, or the tobacco chewer, or Indian or Pakistani chewers of betel or a kola chewer in Ghana is also seen done quite commonly as a social activity in the company of others and we certainly appreciate the difference between higher and lower class in various aspects of the behavior (e.g., who would leave the red mark of betel on automobiles parked along the street, as I have observed in India, or how the Ghanaian night security officer, who chews his kola-nut to keep more alert, typically throws his clay-red spittle describing a wide curve on walls, with an audible, skillful spitting movement). But sometimes 'social spitting' is an unspoken expression of togetherness, as with the reported spitting of the Navajo Indians around the fire : the men spitting right into the fire, the women on the ground, a singer doing it intermittently and continuing the song "on a humming note" while getting ready to do it by (Key, 1975). Spitting always possesses that quasiparalinguistic quality that can certainly fill a silence or blend significantly in the conversation, often with what La Barre (1964 :217) perceptively calls "punctuational and editorial-comment" characteristics.One particularly bizarre form of spitting is practiced among the Turkana men of Northern Kenya, who pierce the lower lip with a hollow metal tube or stick and spit through it at a distance.

(c) *Random Spitting and Task-Performing Spitting.* The most interesting cultural form of noninteractive spitting—although a possible intentionality in its performance could certainly be considered interactive when in co-presence, as when done with a 'watch-this' sort of attitude—is the *task-performing* function of spitting : "he spat on his hands. The pick arose into the air and flashed down. Tom grunted softly (...) the grunt came at the moment it sank into the ground" (Steinbeck 1931 : XXII). I have always observed this kind of spitting among Spanish peasants and labourers and in other cultures, before grabbing the smooth wooden handle of a hoe or pick, which, beyond its practicality, may communicate quite eloquently the person's disposition (i.e., enthusiastic, frustrated, tired, angry, etc.) through the loudness of his hawking and spitting, the audible inspiration while 'looking at' the job to be tackled, the facial expression qualifed by grunting, etc.

(d) *Rejection.* Spitting is observed in many cultures as a sign of rejection, whether specifically addressed to a person or to an idea or attitude, as when spitting in *disgust:* "EBEN *(spitting with disgust)*" (O' Neill, 1924 : I, iii); *contempt* is another common elicitor, whether the object is present or not, and Darwin (1872 : 260) documented spitting as "an almost universal sign of contempt or disgust", citing various sources and personal communications; *anger* can trigger spitting also on a habitual impulse : "the policemen (who could not stop the religious procession) swearing and spitting (Rao, 1938 : XVIII).

(e) *Aggression. Challenge* is expressed in some cultures through ritualized spitting, as when a youth spits at another as an exploratory challenge). One of the most picturesque forms is seen among young Ghanaians trying to pick a fight : the challenger spits on the palm of his right hand and shows it to his opponent who, if he accepts the challenge, slaps it with a slap-and-retract motion; *bodily aggression,* out of contemptuous and angry rejection can be done through spitting : "I spit upon him, whilst I say h lies" (Shakespeare 1595-96, IV,i), and is documented also Indian novels : "and now the police (...) spit on them and bi them with ropes (...) and beat them, and spat into their mouth (Rao, 1938, X). My own recollections are of 'the older ones' in t school playgrounds spitting at each other, as well as of bulli doing it as an intimidating behavior.

(f) *Ritual Spitting.* This function should be seen as a separa category for its cultural and historical significance and for t striking similarities found crossculturally and in different period

To further spur systematic research on paralinguistic-kinesic differentiators, the following modalities could be mentioned. *Rejection ritual,* such a primitive behavior of aggression and rejection, of which the Bible offers instances of ritual forms : "then his brother's wife (if he refuses to marry his brother's widow) shall (...) remove his sandal from his foot, spit in his face, and answer and say 'So shall it be done to the man who will not build up his brother's house" *(Deuteronomy* 25:9*).* In India, where social life is pervaded by ritual, this type of spitting is reported in its rich realistic novel : "standing at the village gate, she spat once toward the east and once toward the west, once toward the south and once toward the north, and then spitting again thrice at the Pariah huts" (RAO, 1938, IV). *Healing,* since from ancient times on saliva has been thought to have healing properties (easy to verify by applying it to a small bleeding scratch), and the practice of spitting on the sick person seems to be common to many cultures throughout history and across continents. Spitting during *play* is something most of us have witnessed during our childhood, that 'spitting prowess' of some schoolmates engaged sometimes in real spitting contests, or as young girls do in Ghana, a sort of 'distance-spit', between their teeth and producing only a slight interdental hissing sound (and no hawking, which would not be feminine at all).

3. Sneezing as a Cultural Communicative Behavior

Sneezing, as a natural spontaneous reflex, it is usually initiated by irritation in the nasal lining, in response to which (unless it happens very suddenly with no warning) there is a first stage in the form of a silent or audible inhalation; an abundant and spasmodic blast of air forced through the glottis follows and rapidly goes either through the nasal passages or both through the nasal passages and the mouth, through the latter often as a third stage during which a strained voiced expulsion prolongs itself if the mouth is kept shut. In other words, the first stage is the 'atchoo !' sound, and the second, not always present, the vowel-like continuous one. But the presence or absence of this second part, and the possible paralinguistic and kinesic qualifiers of the whole act, give it enough audible-visual and socio-semantic complexity to deserve a detailed description of its features. "With gaping mouth and head far back he stood still and, after an instant, sneezed loudly. —Chow ! he said. Blast you ! (...) Chow !" (Joyce 1922, 231-232).

3.1. The Morphology of Sneezing

The following components of a sneeze should be observed

for research : its *paralinguistic leader* (not always present), consisting of the prolonged audible pharyngeal ingression, which may not lead to the sneeze proper if we check it or it does not happen naturally; the *first, second third stages* of the sneeze, including its *vowel type* and its overall *duration* or that of the first and third stages; then the paralinguistic *aftermath;* the *kinesic leader* or first stage, shown on the *face*, typically eye-closing and the nasolabial furrowing of the first stage or leader, the *hand* that may pinch the nose or press under the nostrils to minimize it or repress it, the whole *body* when someone staggers, twists, swirls around; and the *aftermath*, sometimes still pinching the nose, mouth open and looking downward; the *concomitant activities*, whether verbal or nonverbal, mostly those prescribed by good manners, like using one's handkerchief instead of the hand; the *cultural background and socioeducational status*, which can vary also according to the *situational context* e.g., displaying the three-stage sneeze in a very conspicuous way among friends, but repressing it in a formal setting).

3.2. Social Sneezing and its Associated Behaviors

In some cultures, as in North America and England, where sneezing may be responded to with 'God bless you!' or 'Bless you !', the average well-mannered middle-class sneezer apologizes with 'Excuse me!', typically (seriously or not) emphasizing the apology by putting a major stress and drawling on 'me' ('Excuse-me!') when the sneeze was unexpectedly abrupt or loud, even when not in true interaction (e.g., while reading a magazine at a doctor's waiting room, as I observed recently). In fact those same people apologize after coughing or just clearing the throat mildly, not only in a noninteractive gathering, but by a regional television newsperson 'facing' an audience.

A simple *social courtesy* is, for instance, German *Gesundheit!* ('Health!'), French *A vos souhaits !* ('Good wishes !*), Greek *Hygeia sou* ("To your health !'), Trinidad's rather humorous 'Marche, dog !' (pronounced *mash* by many, from F. *marche*, march), Hong-Kong's *Tai carc lei shi!* ("Good things will happen !'), Russian *Za zdarovye!* ('To your health!'), Hungarian *(Kedves,) ege'sze'gere!* ('Dear,) health !'), South India's *Chiringeer !* ('May you live long !) in Telegu language, the *No obo !* of Nigeria's Edo people, or the *Salud !* ('Health') in many Latin American cultures (Colombia, EL Salvador, Nicaragua, Mexico), in some of which, however, it competes with Spain's *Jesus !*.

Superstitious responses to a sneezer are common in some cultures. In Ghana, if someone sneezes in the morning toward the right side of another it is an omen of good luck, but if something bad befalls that person it would be associated with someone having sneezed toward his left that morning. In Niger, if two people are engaged in a discussion and a third party (outside their group) sneezes, both conversants will bless him, as the sneeze sanctions what one of them was trying to prove.

Finally, the *religious character* of the responses to sneezing is seen in many cultures and in different religions, particularly Christian and Muslim, on the part of both sneezer and listener, for instance : in English many Christians believers respond with 'God bless you !' or 'Bless you !' (although for most without a true religious connotation). Icelandic males say *Blessadur !*, while females say *Blessod*, both meaning 'God bless you !' In Spain the listener has, if used at all, only one response, *Jesus !* In Lebanon Catholics invoke the name of the Virgin Mary, *Ya, Adra!*, the Muslims that of Mohammed, but those who are neither simply say *Siha !* ('Health !'). The Yoruba of Nigeria respond *Pele!* (otherwise a greeting), which means "God bless you !'. A very interesting variety is found across Muslim cultures. In some the sneezer is the only one who is obliged to respond to his own sneeze, as with Egyptian *Yarhamukum Allah !* ('May Allah have mercy !') or Malaysian *Al-hamdilil-Lah !* ('All praise be to God !'). In other cultures sneezing may be the occasion for a more elaborate ritual between the sneezer and his listeners : among the Muslims of Malaysia the sneezer must say *Alhamdu lil-Lah !* ('Thank God!'), and the listeners answer *Yarhamukum Allah !* ('God bless you !'); but in Saudi Arabia this socioreligious observance becomes more elaborate : the sneezer says *Alhamdu lil-Lah !* ('Thank God !'), the others respond *Yarhamukum Allah !* ('God bless you !'), to which he must add *Yahdina wa yahdikum Allah* ('God shows us and you the right path'), but if he fails to thank God first the listeners express God's blessing anyway, which obliges him to thank God, and this exchange can happen up to three times. Obviously, the most important aspect of sneezing is the religious one, as it helps to understand the character of a culture through the degree in which spiritual values and beliefs permeate its daily life and, on a more individual level, to gauge a person's or family's religious makeup and the likely relationship between their religious responses to sneezing and their general attitudes and behaviors (although many otherwise 'religious' or 'spiritual' persons may never respond to a sneeze in cultures where it is not rigidly prescribed).

4. Conclusion

This has been just a preliminary approach to some of the socalled paralinguistic differentiators, trying to establish the profound psychological, social and cultural relevance—and suggesting the literary one as well—of what otherwise can be regarded as only incidental phenomena. But, aside from the social and crosscultural aspects, research should acknowledge their more hidden conscious and unconscious functions in interaction. Anyone, not just doing research,but even more when engaged in professional interaction (i.e., doctors, nurses, psychiatrists, counsellors, interviewers, etc.), need to be acutely aware of the subtle relationships between paralinguistic differentiators and other activities and nonactivities in personal encounters or in noninteractive situations. It is a matter of being able to relate what is said as well as what remains unsaid, what is done and what is not done, with other verbal and nonverbal interaction components, when a simple clearing of the throat or a sigh (another important differentiator) can be an eloquent comment which otherwise would be missed altogether or misinterpreted, the former being usually more common because one does not even suspect that it might serve any specific purpose in the encounter. When we consider differentiators as dynamic components of personal interaction as well as of situations of interaction with our personal environment and the environment at large, be begin to discover that nothing can be said not to communicate until proven otherwise, and that such nonverbal signs often express what otherwise would not, or could not, be expressed with words.

References

Anonymous 1983 *The Holy Bible. The New King James Version.* Nashville. Thomas Nelson.

Bronte, Charlotte 1847 *Jane Eyre* (New York : Washington Square Press, 1973) *JE.*

Bronte, Emily 1874 *Wuthering Heights* (New York : W. Norton, 1963) *WH.*

Cervantes, Miguel de 1605 to *1615* *Don Quijote be la Mancha* (Barcelona : Editorial Juventud, 1965) *DQ.*

Darwin, Charles 1872 *The Expression of the Emotions in Man and Animals :* Report Chicago : University of Chicago Press, 1965.

Dickens, Charles 1860 *Great Expectations* (New York : Washington Square Press, 1970) *GE.*

	1838	*Oliver Twist* (New York : Holt, Renehart and Winston, 1962) *OT.*
	1836 to *1837*	*Pickwich Papers* (New York : Dell, 1964) *PP.*
Dos, Passos	1925	*Manhattan Transfer* (New York : Bantam Books, 1959) *MT.*
Dreiser, Theodore	1900	*Sister Carrie* (New York : Dell, 1960) *SC.*
Hardy, Thomas	1878	*The Return of the Native* (London : Macmillan, Pocket Papermacs) *RN.*
Huxley, Aldous	1928	*Point Counterpoint* (New York : Avon Books) *PCP.*
Joyce, James	1922	*Ulysses* (New York : Vintage Books, 1961). *U.*
Joyee, James	1916	*A Portrait of the Artist as a Young Man* (Harmondsworth : Penguin, 1976). *PAYM.*
Key, Merry R.	1917	*Paralanguage and Kinesics.* Metuchen, N. J. Scarecrow Press.
La Barre, Weston	1964	Paralinguistics, Kinesics, and Cultural Anthropology. In *Approaches to Semiotics Cultural Anthropology, Education, Psychiatry, Psychology,* Ed. by R. A. Sebeok, A. Hayes, M. Bateson. 198-220. The Hague: Mouton.
Laurence, Margaret	1968	*The Stone Angel* (Toronto : McClelland and Stewart, 1968) *SA.*
Lewis, Sinclair	1920	*Main Street* (New York : New American Library, Signet Bavailableooks, 1961)*MS.*
Maugham, Somerset	1915	*Of Human Bondage* (New York : Random House, Modern Library, 1942) *OHB.*
O'Neill, Eugene	1924	*Desire Under the Elms (Masterpieces of the Drama.* New York : Macmillian, 1974) *DUE.*
Rao, Raja	1938	*Kanthapura* (New York : New Directions, 1963) K.
Shakespeare, William	1595 to 1596	*Richard II (The Complet Works of William Shakespeare.* London : Spring Books) *R-II*
Steinbeck, John	1931	*The Grapes of Wrath* (New York : Bantam Books, 1964) *GW.*
Steinbeck, John	1935	*Tortilla Flat* (The Short Stories of John Steinbeck. New York : Viking Press, 1953) *TF.*
Wildeblood, Jane P.	1965	*The Polite World.* London : Oxford University Press.
Williams, Tennessee,	1945	*The Glass Menagerie* (New York : New Directions, 1966) *GM.*

Irwin Deutscher

NATIONAL POLICIES AND CULTURAL MINORITIES : WHAT IS POSSIBLE ?

1. Biography, History, and A Change in Research Interests

The convergence of personal biography and world history has resulted in a new area of research for me. Without P. K. Bhowmick this would not have happened. In March, 1989, my friend and former student, Professor Simhadri Yedla, invited me to participate in an international conference at Visakhapatnam University. There I met P. K. Bhomick who not only provided me with graduate students as excellent guides on my long train trip to Calcutta, but also invited me to lecture to his graduate seminar at the University of Calcutta. The personal stimulus for my shift in research interests originated during that anthropology seminar.

I was greatly impressed by the ethnographic evaluations of tribal peoples and villages which these students were doing for their dissertations and the relationships to policy makers, administrators, and practitioners which their professor, P.K. Bhowmick, had developed. It was my intention to use the seminar to explore their work and to compare it with my own evaluation research on social programs in the United States. But the students had a different agenda. They preferred to exploit my "Americanness" with a discussion of what they viewed as the great American melting pot. They were committed to an Indian assimilationist policy which seemed to them the only way to unify their large, culturally, and linguistically diverse nation. They were appalled when I suggested that the American melting pot was no longer fashionable. For two hours we discussed ethnicity in America as best I could from my limited familiarity with the literature and my own knowledge.

As thought provoking as that seminar was, my interests did not really begin to crystallize until I found myself in Ottawa a few months later (May, 1989) listening to Delahanty's scholarly review of Canada's failing pluralistic minority policy (Delahanty, 1990). It was the contrast that struck me ! Here were two cases of nations struggling for humane solutions to problems resulting from the existence of national minorities within their borders and they appeared to move in opposite directions. Furthermore, neither the assimilationist nor the pluralist policy seemed to be succeeding.

History was about to provide the final catalyst, for at the very moment of the Ottawa conference on 'sociotechnics" (a term coined by Adam Podgorecki (1989) which could be used to describe this paper), bits of souvenir barbed wire were being sold in Budapest.The iron curtain had begun to crumble. Poland removed its communist leadership and one by one the authoritarian regimes of Eastern Europe fell apart to be replaced, hopefully, by democratic governments. By the Spring of 1990 even isolated Albania was seeking to establish relations with the rest of the world. That summer East Germany disappeared from the map of Europe.

When I spoke with some of the Hungarian sociologists at that conference, I expected them to be elated with recent events at home. To my surprise, I discovered that they had reservations. Their concern, it turned out, was with some of the possible consequences of peasant populist movement. They anticipated a resurgence of religion, of nationalism, and of anti-minority feelings such as antisemitism, all of which had been suppressed under the authoritarian communist regime. There have, in fact, been increased signs of such phenomena, not only in Hungary but throughout Eastern Europe and in the former Soviet Union as well. A terrible and tragic ethnic bloodbath developed in the former Yugoslavia. The Baltic states provide a purely nationalistic instance, while the conflict in Azerbaijan with Armenians has strong religious undertones. I have reviewed some of the unintended consequences of democratization in another paper (Deutscher 1991). On the other hand it is possible that democracy has improved conditions for ethnic Turks in Bulgaria and ethnic Hungarians in Romania.

So it is that the seed which was planted in Calcutta germinated in Ottawa and has since born the fruit of several articles and lectures. I must confess, however, that this is a matter in which I have always had great interest in spite of my failure to address it professionally. It seemed to me that in my country, ethnic and especially racial equality was an issue of morality and politics. It had nothing to do with scientific research, since no matter what the findings of studies comparing, say African Americans and European Americans, all people in my country were supposed to be equal in the eyes of the law. Why would I engage in research when I could not take its findings seriously ?

These were matters which should have been settled in the courts and not in scientific journals. When they were not settled in the courts, then, beginning in 1950, my wife and I (and later our children) took to the streets engaging in sit-ins and demonstrations and parades to protest the injustice. That seemed more appropriate than studying race relations even though I was twice arrested and jailed during those turbulent times. I remain unable to consider American race relations with any degree of scientific detachment. What I began to realize during that seminar in Calcutta was that I might learn more about my own nation's racial problems if I could better understand how other nations deal with these issues.

A final personal vignette will complete my weaving between biography and history. In 1966 I found myself on a stage at Syracuse University attempting to defend Martin Luther King's unpopular dream of an erosion of racial distinctions as all peoples were assimilated into one people. My principle opponent was an angry and articulate Stokely Carmichal (later, Kwame Toure) proclaiming the dogma of "Black is beautiful."

There was a profound truth to Carmichal's arguments and the audience, both Black and White were clearly with him. Even I, sitting with my lonely and archaic assimilationist notions, felt that truth and was sadly uncertain about the dream I shared with King. I was saddened by the knowledge that as long as one group defines itself as collectively "different" from another group, that difference will become an invidious one. I had a similar experience while working with young radical Native Americans who demanded for their small isolated tribes a return to their own languages and cultures. How, I wondered, could the Cherokee children who were educated in the Cherokee language about the Cherokee things, hope to prosper in an industrial society dominated by English speaking whites ? Nevertheless, Carmichal was to begin a movement that brought about a resurgent pride of ancestry and culture among many American ethnic groups. If it ever had existed, the American melting pot was no longer. We were, as Glazer and Moynihan (1963) put it, "beyond the melting pot". And there I let the matter drop—until it surfaced again in Calcutta in March, 1989. Let us get on with it.

2. First Step : Getting and Clarifying Information

Where does the search begin for problems and solutions which appear everywhere and in all times ? Wherever in the world one may look, there are people living within the bounds of a nation who are despised by the dominant group in that nation. This has been true throughout human history and it remains true today—in Europe, in Asia, in Africa, and in North and

South America. In this paper I shall refer to such minorities as "ethnic" for want of a better word. They are thought by the dominant group to be "different" in some important respects. Such differences may be based upon language, religion, social class, national origins, tribalism, apparent physical differences, historical events, or myths about any of these criteria.

To explore such phenomena comparatively in the contemporary world alone would require an enormous staff as well as great amounts of money. With neither of those resources available, I found a procedural clue in the work of the Chicago sociologists early in this century. At the turn of the last century, a newspaper reporter who was to become one of the founders of American sociology, described sociology as a quest for the "big news". During his years as a newsman, Robert E. Park had pursued his particular stories wherever and whenever they occurred. As a sociologist he asked what lay behind these stories which could inform us on human behavior and social processes in a more general way (Park, 1940). This paper is based in large part on particular stories in the contemporary press. The question it addreses in, is there big news here which can provide useful insights to other peoples in other places at other times ?

There is no scarcity of the kinds of little stories from which the Big News must be built. In this section I will review the scope and seriousness of national and ethnic conflict mostly as reported in the Washington Post during 1990 and into 1991. I selected that newspaper for no better reason than that it is a reputable one with broad international coverage and I read it everyday. The dates are from the time of my renewed interest in these issues until about a year later when I could no longer spend the time systematically reading and clipping. This remains my major source of data although the collection is no longer systematic. I have discussed the methodological rationale for this procedure elsewhere (Deutscher, 1993).

What follows is a loose and arbitrary typology of the kinds of events which are reported and which can inform us on ethnic issues. Because events move rapidly in the contemporary world, I have made an effort to update these materials. Some instances are so commonplace and persistent that they are taken for granted by the world. This includes the everyday reports of the deadly and violent tribal conflicts in Sri Lanka, the continuing demands of Palestinians for rights in their own country, the endless conflict in South Africa, not only between blacks and whites but also tribal based violence among black groups. The enduring war between Catholic and Protestant in Northern Ireland has become so commonplace that it is hardly noted in the daily press. Continuing efforts to keep the Canadian federation from falling apart also belong in this category of the commonplace.

Other instances of such intergroup conflict are so obscure as to be hardly recognizable by most of the world. Although Iraq'a treatment of its Kurdish minority is familiar enough, who is familiar with that country's militant repression of its Assyrian minority. We all recognize the persistent violence in Kashmir and the ongoing conflict between Pakistan and India in that region but the violence in Hyderabad and clashes between rival ethnic groups in Karachi is less familiar. That conflict is blamed on descendants of Moslem migrants from India following the 1947 partition. They are demanding official recognition as Pakistan's fifth nationality group.

Falling somewhere between these extremes of journalistic notoriety and obscurity is a broad set of widely scattered events which occurred during this short period of history. The Kashmir troubles are one such event as are the ethnic disturbances reported in Kashgar, China's westernmost city, populated mostly by Moslem Uighurs.The government of Liberia has collapsed after a long and bloody struggle between two tribal coalitions : the Krahns and Mandigos fighting the Gios and Manos. Turkey's ten million Kurds continue to wage their ten year war for independence, unlike Iraq's Kurds who are fewer in number and ask only for a degree of autonomy within the Iraqi state. Tens of thousands of Muslim women and children have fled from Myanmr (formerly Burma) to neighboring Bangladesh, already one of the poorest countries in the world. They accuse Myanmr's Buddhist military junta of "launching an indiscriminate campaign of violence and intimidation aimed at driving Muslims of the ethnic Rohingya minority out...to make room for (ethnic) Buddhist settlers" (Coll, 1992). As pathetic as it may be to consider people seeking refuge in the poverty of Bangladesh, it is not unique. By the first of the following year 60,000 Tajiks had fled their civil war into Afghanistan where many froze to death (Moore, 1993).

The former Communist controlled countries of Eastern Europe provide a dramatic set of cases. Romania was the only country where the military resisted the rebellious people. At first Romanians and ethnic Hungarians joined together to overthrow Nicolae Ceasescu who had embarked on a policy of systematically destroying all traces of Hungarian culture in Romania. But contemporary Transylvania is described as a place of fear, tempers, and violent nationalism. One Romanian writer reminds us that "The miners savage attack on demonstrating students in Bucharest last June 14 and 15 was well covered in the Western media...But not much was written about the miners gratuitous assault on the Gypsies" (Pavel, 1991). In the new "democratic" Romania, ethnic Hungarians, Gypsies, and Germans find themselves constantly under threat.

Yugoslavia consisted of six republics, two autonomous provinces, more than a dozen nationalities, three major religions and two alphabets. In free elections, both Slovenia and Croatia threw out their communist officials and declared themselves independent states. Slovenia got away with it but it was not so easy for Croatia with its ethnic Serbs, its border with Serbia, a largely Serbian national army, and an expansionist Serbian government, all fighting to prevent Croatian autonomy. Bosnia, with local Serbs and Croats both fighting for most of that region, had little hope for survival without outside help. But the world only watched. Czechoslovakia and Hungary, both with long standing democratic traditions also had their troubles. Czechs and Slovaks, although so far without violence, have their extreme nationalists who succeeded in splitting the country in two and ethnic Hungarians, Gypsies, and Jews are unlikely to fare well in Slovakia. The new Hungarian government elected in the Spring of 1990 ran on a nationalist platform of "Hungarian-ness" while its defeated opponents had stood for "European-ness." Public antisemitic and anti-Gypsy statements surfaced almost immediately.

All of these differences seem to pale besides the mass of nationality issues confronting the former Soviet Union. I will not review the litany of former Republics which have or are in the process of declaring their independence from the old Union as well as from Russia. But the fact that the Baltic states have become nations again, leaves as many nationality and ethnic issues unsolved as it solves. According to the Estonian government, the Russians make up 40 percent of Estonia's population and are a majority in the Capital (Battiata, September 30, 1991). The Latvians too are a minority in their own capital (Lee, 1991). About a third of the population of Latvia and Estonia is the Russian. There are also sizeable Polish and German minorities, but the potential problem with the Russian ethnics lies in their total isolation from the Baltic peoples. They live in the cities, work in former Soviet industries, have their own residential areas, schools, entertainment, etc. These Russian-Balts have been more prosperous than their hosts and few have managed to learn any of the Baltic languages.

It was estimated in 1990 that "One out of every four Soviet citizens—including about 24 million ethnic Russians—live outside their titular republic" (Dobbs, 1990). Because of the settlement policy instituted by Stalin, there are Russian ethnics fleeing or living in fear in all of the far reaches of the former Soviet Union. Add this to the fact that political boundaries can never conform to national or ethnic ones and it seems clear that unless strong preventive measures are taken, there will be nationalist and ethnic trouble in the former Soviet Union for a long time. There has been rioting between Kirghiz and Uzbeks in Kirghizia and between Uzbecks and Meskhetial Turks in Uzbekistan. There has also been ethnic violence in central Asia in Turkmenistan and Tajikistan. In Azerbaijan there is no peace between warring Azeris and Armenian ethnics. Only three of the five million people living in Georgia are the Georgians and there has been constant ethnic conflict before and after Georgia's declaration of independence.

Barber (1992) tells us that in 1991 there were more than thirty wars in progress, "most of them ethnic, racial, tribal, or religious in character..."Nation states have had to deal with problems of minority peoples everywhere in the world and from time immemorial. The dissolving of oppressive totalitarian regimes into more democratic ones results in a new rash of national and ethnic problems. What kinds of policies have been attempted and what kinds are emerging in the contemporary world and what in all of this appears useful ?

3. The Historic Range of Minority Policies : What is Possible?

On humanitarian grounds, certain possible policies must be dismissed as inadmissible. One can eliminate minority problems by eliminating the minority. Hitler's final solution almost succeeded with both the Jews and the Gypsies. The interference of the native Americans with the "progress" of European colonists and, later, the Euro-Americans, was dealt with in a similarly efficient manner. Genocide has been an effective solution to the minority problem (Chalk and Jonassohn, 1990; Walliman and Dobkouski, 1987; Fine, 1992; Porpora, 1990). On purely moral grounds, we cannot admit it as a possible solution.

Only slightly less noxious than genocide as a minority policy is the use of forced labor, slavery, or some form of serfdom. This solution may be tempting when the dominant powers view the minority as a source of cheap labor. Prior to the First World War, the Hungarian landlords found this a useful device in Slovakia and it was employed by the British in Ireland well into the 20th Century. Chattel slavery (the total ownership of one person by another) continues to exist in the contemporary world. It remained legal on the Arabian Peninsula until the early 1970's and may be expanding in parts of Northern Africa, particularly Sudan. Far more common is debt bondage where, in effect, one rents a slave,, rather than taking on the expense of owning one. It is a form of forced labor found among the Haitians living illegally in the Dominican Republic. Probably unrelated to minority problems is the selling of children for abusive purposes whether as labor in Indian rug factories or prostitutes in Thailand (Will,

1990; Ennew, 1981; 1989). Again, on purely moral grounds we cannot admit slavery in any form as a possible solution.

It is also inhumane for a government to encourage, force, and possibly even permit, the mass exodus of whole communities. The image of hoards of the Kurdish peoples miserably huddled in fear in the mountain or desert wastelands that border Iraq, remains vivid. The memory of the mass migrations in both directions that occurred with the partition of India may have faded but is no less tragic. Bulgaria's problems with its Turkish minority would indeed be solved by expelling over a million people who have lived in Bulgaria for centuries. In fact, at the time of his overthrow, communist dictator Todor Zhivkov had already forced hundreds of thousands of the Turkish ethnics to leave Bulgaria (Battiata, Oct. 17, 1991). It is not an acceptable solution to the Irish problem to dispatch the Protestants back to Scotland and England.

These problems usually are a consequence of the policies of former authorities, sometimes invaders or occupiers, to settle loyal peoples in alien territories under their control. The Ethnic Serbs in Croatia are the result of such a policy as are the Hungarians in Slovakia, the Turks in Bulgaria, and the ethnic Russians everywhere in the former Soviet Union. Expulsion of peoples seeking a better life for themselves at great personal sacrifice, persists under the less ugly term "re-patriation". It happens to the Vietnamese who manage to reach Hong Kong, to the Haitians and the Chinese who attempt to reach the United States, and is likely to happen to the Salvadorans already in the United States.

A more common contemporary policy might be called "dumping and containing". It is most likely to occur when slavery or forced labor loses its economic viability. These "used up minorities" are then relegated to ghettos or otherwise isolated physically from the dominant group, identified as second class people, and then denied access to housing, work, education, other societal rights and privileges and to the same civil rights enjoyed by the dominant group. This was the fate of most former slaves in the Americas and is the fate today of the descendants of forced Korean laborers imported to Japan during the Second World War (Asiaweek, 1990). A Norwegian anthropologist has argued that there are two role choices open to minorities : they may be either "mute" or "cute (Woon, 1993). The isolation of dumping and containing is one way to keep a minority mute. What of "cute" ?

A final policy which sometimes, but not always, evolves in this line from forced labor to dumping and containing, is a protected reserve or theme park policy. The result is what Woon described as a "cute" minority. This happens when a government decides to protect those among the remaining fragments of a people who wish to preserve their traditional culture. Usually this involves a protected area, heavily subsidized by the dominant group, sometimes economically viable as a result of a tourist economy. Cases of this type include some native Americans, the Ainu of northern Japan, possibly the Laplanders (Sami) of northern Scandinavia and perhaps the Australian aborigines. The Brazilian government appears to be moving in this direction.

In its 1991 effort to preserve and protect the remaining native peoples of the upper Amazon, the Brazilian administration expelled the 20,000 miners who had invaded the area in search of gold. A study commission is trying to decide whether to make the area a permanent preserve, a policy derisively referred to by Robinson as "artificial isolation as a kind of theme park exhibit" (Robinson, 1991). As we shall see, it is possible that not all native peoples wish to be preserved and protected. Nevertheless, this is a less tragic policy than those mentioned so far, only because it may be the last hope for survival of those minority peoples who prefer to retain their traditional ways.

There is no place among civilized nations for such painful minority policies as extermination, slavery, expulsion, or dumping and containing. No society ought to let matters evolve to the point where the only choice for survival of the minority culture lies in a theme park policy where they become a living museum protected by the state and prospering from the tourists. In most of this paper, I have focused on the "downside"—the kinds of minority policies to be avoided. What of more positive policies which do not leave a legacy of destruction, fear, hatred, suspicion and a lust for vengeance ? Such policies do exist. Let us examine a few of the possibilities.

4 Toward More Hopeful Policies

The policy issue boils down to this : under what conditions can nations adopt which kinds of policies with the least harm resulting to the most people ? Does pluralism necessarily result in a nation characterized by hostile camps populated by peoples who despise one another ? Does assimilation necessarily result in a bland sameness—a lack of diversity ? If we attempt to put together the "Big News" what do we learn that helps us approach these questions ?

There are both discouraging and encouraging clues in the little stories. On the one hand it is discouraging that after seventy years of state nurturing of cultural pluralism in the Soviet Union, archaic ethnic and national animosities should suddenly resurface in 1990. It is also true that such feelings were largely repressed in most of Eastern Europe for forty years only to return with the demise of Communism. In fact the Poles inform us that it is not even necessary to have Jews in order for antisemitism to flourish. In spite of the absence of Jews in contemporary Poland, antisemitism is widespread with desecration of abandoned Jewish cemeteries and anti-semitic graffiti observed on walls and elsewhere. It is clear that obsolete beliefs and enmities die hard. But there are success stories too.

Enclaves. The Swiss have survived a territorial and linguistic based pluralism for centuries without internal violence. Cantonization is not a peculiarly Swiss adaptation. A more modern version of that solution appears to have emerged successfully in Ghana. In an interview with sociologist J. Max Assimeng, Neil (Henry, 1990) reports that the Chieftaincy Act of 1971 has enabled "Ghana's more than 75 distinct languages and major ethnic groups to be bound peacefully together with the help of some imaginative Government policy". Local culture is preserved by locally elected chieftains while national and international affairs are the concern of the central government. We are told that the Act has unified Ghana's once war-prone ethnic groups in an officially recognized national forum. The Ghanian students I have spoken with in the U. S. and Ghanian exiles in Britain confirm this impression.

More careful analysis of this apparently successful effort to unify a multicultural society, may provide useful clues for policy in other societies. This is a model designed to reduce inter-ethnic conflict in nations which have enclaves, which are homogeneous and which are somewhat isolated from other enclaves of different homogeneous peoples. Such a model was proposed as a solution to the Bosnian conflict and it was an appropriate one. Sadly, no serious effort was made to implement it until the violence had progressed beyond the point of peaceful solution.

Immigrants. Very different kinds of solutions are required when the minority groups do not reside in homogeneous communities in relative isolation from one another. Permanent cantonization is certainly less than appropriate in the case of foreign immigrant minorities. Immigration is a complex phenomenon which encompasses a number of different types, but it is so widespread and so troublesome in the contemporary world that it cannot be ignored. I will bypass such disturbing inconsistencies as a United States policy which welcomes Cubans but not Haitians. In contemporary Germany we find that a generous open border policy, in effect since the end of World War II, leads ultimately to resentment and conflict. That policy was rescinded in mid-1993. There are, for example, third generation people of the Turkish decent who remain ineligible for citizenship. The Germans might have taken a lesson from the equally homogeneous and nationally older Swedes who were far more successful with an immigrant policy which not only did not deny citizenship to immigrants but encouraged their ethnic identity and the maintenance of their cultural heritage.

Let us consider this second successful policy and its consequences.[2] The Swedish Home Language Reform Act made it the responsibility of municipalities "to provide home language instruction for all students who desire it and for whom the home language represents a living element in the child's home environment (Hyltenstam, 1988 :488 (cited by Paulston, 1988:22)." According to Paulston this policy was rigorously adhered to. It would be difficult to imagine any policy better designed and implemented for the purpose of preserving the integrity of immigrant and ethnic cultures. "In fact, it is not happening" (Paulston, 1988:22). The evidence suggests (as the Chicago sociologists predicted) that a pluralist policy benignly administered leads ultimately to assimilation. This is a matter to which I shall return.

Just as there were conditions under which a policy modeled upon Ghana's Chieftaincy Act would be inappropriate, so too certain caveats are required when considering Sweden's Pluralist policy. Paulston notes that there are two important exceptions to the trend toward assimilation. Neither the Swedish Gypsies nor the Swedish Finns follow this pattern. Since the Gypsies are found nearly everywhere in the world, and they are likely to be despised by dominant groups wherever they are found it is important to understand why these people remain apart. Paulston confesses that "I believe the Gypsies will remain Gypsies, just as I believe the great-grandchildren of the Estonians and the Hungarians will become Swedes" (1988:23).

Paulston attributes the failure of rapport between the Swedes and the Gypsies to the limits of Swedish tolerance. The Gypsies are free to choose, but only among alternatives that are acceptable to the Swedes : "To choose not to send children to compulsory school is simply not an acceptable choice, however appropriate to Gypsy culture"(1988:23). It may also be that the Gypsies see themselves as sojourners in a foreign world. But, unlike other sojourners, they have no "home" to return to. This brings us to the Swedish Finns.

Almost half of the pupils with a home language other than Swedish are Finns. Paulston compares the Swedish Finns to the Puerto Ricans in the United States because of the frequent back and forth movement between the original community and the new one. Note that the Finns are not far from home and are free to migrate and to return at will. It is this constant renewal of ties with their homeland that seems to make the Finns different and unlikely to assimilate to Swedish culture. If the Swedish policy fails in all respects for the Gypsies who have little use for the concept of formal schooling, it succeeds in its original pluralist intent for the Finns who insist on maintaining their Finnishness.

The sojourner concept may be relevant here, but its more complete treatment will have to await further consideration.[3] What can be said of the Swedish pluralist policy is that it is an effective device for ultimately assimilating minority peoples who have no intention of returning "home". For sojourners it appears to provide a temporary pluralist haven. Note that even the Gypsies, of whom the Swedes disapprove, are not persecuted in that country. The conclusion of Paulston's research is that, "Voluntary migration results in much faster (assimilation) than does annexation or colonization" and "Voluntary migration, access to public schools and thus to the national language, and economic incentives in the form of available jobs all contribute to assimilation and language shift" (Paulston, 1988 : 31). If we did not know she was writing of Sweden in the last half of the twentieth century, we might think Paulston was describing the United States in the last half of the nineteenth century.

New Borders and New Nations. The most extreme pluralist solution occurs when one nation becomes two or part of a nation separates itself into a new nation. As the example of the Czech and Slovak division suggests, it is possible to accomplish this peacefully and to the mutual satisfaction of both parties. Reports from Czechoslovakia were devoid of signs of violence, with words like "feud" being employed to describe the differences between the two major regions that made up that country.

From the American press one got the impression of a younger sibling (Slovokia) attempting to express its independence from a domineering and protective older brother (The Czechs). In fact, much of the competitiveness between the two was described at first as related to changing the name of the country to emphasize their separateness. Protesters in Bratislava complained of the "arrogance" of the Czech majority. When one talked to people in Bratislava about these matters, they did not seem trivial. Yet the "velvet revolution" brought with it a sense of warmth and good feeling.

Although it is probable that the anti-Hungarian, Jewish, and the Gypsy feelings persist in the Slovak Republic, there have not been press reports of overt public expressions of prejudice.[4] Of immediate importance is the fact that when a border is defined in terms of linguistic and ethnic differences and when it is accepted by both sides; when there is a common tradition of joint action against common enemies; when there is no history of mutual violence; when it is the less economically viable of the two parties which is most adamant in demanding separation; and when there is a history of democratic ideology among the peoples of the more powerful group ......when all of these factors are present, a peaceful division into two national entities can result. Whether all of these factors are necessary is not clear.

Slovenia managed to achieve its independence from Yugoslavia with little more than a symbolic protest from the dominant Serbian government. Most of the above conditions were present there. Events were much more unpleasant in Croatia and Bosnia where most of these conditions were not present. What is clear is that we have three models for successful solution of ethnic differences in the contemporary world. Each of these models applies to a different sort of problem with a different sort of solution. Further analysis will surely reveal other conditions under which other sorts of solutions are possible.[5]

Notes

1. *Chapter prepared in July, 1993 for inclusion in a volume honoring Professor P.K. Bhomick of the University of Calcutta to be edited by Dr. M. K. Raha and tentatively titled, Man in the Contemporary World.*
2. *Unlike Ghana's Chieftaincy Act, I have extensive documentation of Swedish policy provided by Christina Bratt Paulston in a paper (1988) and a report (1982). The following observations are derived from Paulston's work.*
3. *The definitive piece on the sojourner is Siu (1952). A recent analysis is found in Karpathakis (1991).*
4. *Under the volatile conditions posed by inter-ethnic relations, it is necessary to date such statements. This one was written in July, 1993.*
5. *I am currently attempting to expand on the possibility for positive solutions in a paper I am preparing for a conference on the Balkans to be held in Athens in October, 1994. I intend to incorporate much of what has been said in the present paper into that one and extend it from there.*

References

Anti-Slavery Society 1989 *Anti-Slavery Reporter 13 (5)*. Brixton, South London.

Asiaweek 1990 *Strangers In Their Native Land.* May 4, 18-20.

Barber, B. R. 1992 Jihad Vs. Mc World. *The Alantic*, March, 53-63.

Battiata, M. 1991 (a) Bulgaria's Democrats Face Dilemma Over Turkish Party's Role. *The Washington Post*, October 17, A 41.

Battiata, M. 1991 (b) *The Washington Post*, September 30.

Chalk, F., and *K. Jonassohn* 1990 *The History and Sociology of Genocide : Analyses and case Studies*. New Yaven : Yale University Press.

Coll, E. 1992 Flood of Minority Muslims Flees Repression by Myanmr's Junta. *The Washington Post*. February 6.

Delahanty, C 1990 Multiculturalism : Policy or Myth ? Revision of paper presented May 10, 1988 at the Ottawa conference on sociotechnics. Annual Meeting of the Society For Applied Sociology. Cincinnati, November.

Deutscher, I. 1990 The Downside of Democracy : What can the Third World Learn From The Rest of the World?" Paper presented at a Conference on Democracy and Democratization in the Third World : Prospects for the 1990's. Sponsored by the Association for the Advancement of Policy, Research and Development in the Third World. Nassau, The Bahamas, November.

Deutscher, I. 1993 Using Secondary Data in Applied Comparative Research: The Case of Cros-National Comparisons of Ethnic and Minority Policies. In *Between Sociology and Sociological Practice: Essays on Social Policy Research*. K. M. Schultz, J. T. A. Koster, F. L. Leeuw and B. M.J. Wolters, eds. P. 63-71. The Netherlands : Catholic University of Nijmegen.

Dobbs, M. 1991 The Empire of Ethnic Russians Retrenches. *The Washington Post*, October 7 : Al &A 19.

Ennew, J. 1981 *Bebt Bondage: A Survey*. Bixton, South London: Anti-Slavery Society.

Fine, H. 1992 *Genocide Watch*. New Haven : Yale University Press.

Glazer, N. and D. P. Moynihan 1963 *Beyond the Malting Pot : The Negroes, Puerto Ricans, Jews, Italians and Irish of New York City*. Cambridge, Mass : M. I. T. Press.

Henry, N. 1990 *The Washington Post*, July 27.

Hyltenstam, K. and L. Arnberg 1988 Bilingualism and Education of Children and Adults in Sweden in C. B. Paulston (ed.) *International Handbook of Bilingualism and Bilingual Education*. New York : Greenwood Press.

Karpathakis, A. 1991 To Return or to Stay ? Factors of Sojourning Among Greek Immigrants of Astoria, New York. Paper presented at the annual meetings of the American Sociological Association. Cincinnati, Ohio, August.

Lee, G 1991 *The Washington Post, 30 September,*

Liljegren T. 1981 Compulsary School Leavers in 1979 With Home languages other than Swedish. Interim Report 3. Stockholm : National Swedish Board of Education.

Moore, M. 1993 Tajiks Trade One Nightmare For Another. *The Washington Post,* January *19.*

Park, R. E. 1940 News as a Form of Knowledge : A Chapter in the Sociology of Knowledge. *American Journal of Sociology* 45 : 669-686.

Paulston, C. B. 1982 Swedish Research and Debate About Bilingualism : A Report to the National Swedish Board of Education. Stockholm : National Swedish Board of Education.

Paulston, C. B. 1988 International Perspectives on Multilingualism and Language Policies. Paper read at Conference on Language and Ethnicity. Baku, Azerbaijan, June.

Pavel, D. 1991 *Wanderers.* The New Republic, March 4.

Podgorecki, A. and R. Shields 1989 Sociotechnics : A Paradigm for Efficient Social Action. *Journal of Applied Sociology* 6.

Porpora D. V. 1990 *How Holocausts Happen : The United States in Central America.* Philadelphia : Temple University Press.

Robinson, E. 1991 *The Washington Post,* June 23.

Siu, C. P. 1952 The Sojourner. *American Journal of Sociology* 58 : 34-44.

Walliman, I., and N. Dobkouski editors 1987 *Genocide and the Modern Age : Etiology and Case Studies of Mass Death.* New York : Greenwood Press.

Will, G, 1990 *The Washington Post,* June 21.

Woon, L. L. 1993 The European Tribes : A Question of Identity. Conference Report. In K. Ahmed, ed. Pp. 27. Birmingham, England : Birmingham City Council Race Relations Unit, December 3-6, 1991.

Julius O. Ihonvbere

THE 'IRRELEVANT STATE', ETHNICITY AND THE SUBVERSION OF THE GOALS OF NATIONHOOD IN AFRICA

African ruling classes, unlike their metropolitan counterparts, have no faith in the future of their respective nations, let alone in the future of the continent. (Gana, 1985 : 129)

...the ruling classes in Africa are an integral part of the structure of imperialism and of the syndrome of imperialist exploitation. (Ake, 1978 : 65)

Africa is unable to point to any significant growth rate, or satisfactory index of general well-being, in the past 20 years. (OAU, 1981 : 5)

Introduction

The debate on the nature of the state in Africa seemed to have ended abruptly.[1] Yet, no clear political positions were adopted in terms of understanding the specifics of state power and their implications for growth, development, stability and progress in the continent. There is no doubting the fact that as a precipitate of the continent's historical experiences and the realities of dependence and underdevelopment, the state has come to play a major role in the political economy of African social formations. It should have been expected therefore, that in the struggle to reverse underdevelopment, mobilise the masses, lay a viable foundation for self-reliance and self-sustainment and provide for the basic human needs of the vast majority, the state would play a *positive* role.[2]

The African experience has been radically different from the experiences in Europe and North America. The state has become a tool in the hands of a largely decadent, unproductive, corrupt and dependent dominant class. The state is used for accumulation as against legitimation purposes. Its structures, institutions and instruments are easily employed by the dominant forces to repress, exploit, suppress and marginalise the masses. The limited autonomization of the state makes it not only unhegemonic but also incapable of resisting the penetration, manipulation, exploitation and peripheralisation of the social formation in world capitalism by forces of imperialism. Thus, the masses in Africa, relate to the state as an exploitative, coercive and alien structure. Its custodians lack credibility and legitimacy and are thus incapable of mobilising or leading the people. Given the violent, coercive and exploitative nature of the state, the masses turn to ethnic, religious and philanthropic organisations for hope, leadership, self expression and support. The state becomes largely "irrelevant" in their consciousness and existential conditions. It is at this level that we speak of the "irrelevant state" i.e. a state which has virtually lost its capacity to provide leadership and direction, mobilise human and material resources and effectively mediate class contradictions and conflicts.[3]

In this paper, we begin by examining the notion of the "irrelevant" state in order to put the study in proper perspective. Next, we examine the material basis or dimension the socio-economic crisis in Africa with special reference to the ethnic factor. We also highlight how the irrelevant state and the social crisis combine to subvert the goals of nationhood in the continent. The third section of the paper is the conclusion.

The 'Irrelevant' state and the antinomies of a periphery continent

In Antonio Gramsci's discussion of hegemony in *Selections from Prison Notebooks* (Gramsci, 1981) he argued that a state can be dominant at two levels. The first is what he refers to as *political* domination. This is where a state relies on force, violence, coercion and other extra-legal methods to retain control or dominance over society. In this case, the state creates, services and relies heavily on a well armed military machine (Thomas, 1984). The second level of state dominance is at the level of *civil society*. Here, the state does not rely on violence; at least, not in the first instance. Rather, it relies on moral, intellectual, spiritual and emotional manipulation and leadership. The prevalent ideas and consciousness are those "sponsored" of "released" into society by the state, its agents and agencies (Williams, 1970). While both levels of domination are what Gramsci calls *hegemony* he notes that domination at the *political* level is tenuous while domination in civil society, tends to be more permanent.

If we apply this mode of analysis to Africa, we find the state is not dominant in civil society. Rather, African states are only dominant at the political level. There is an extensive reliance on the police, secret service, and the armed forces to maintain order, discipline and control.

To be sure, this situation is not a natural or God created condition. It is the direct precipitate of Africa's historical experiences i.e. the contact between the previously *pre-capitalist* societies and the forces of western imperialism. (Rodney, 1974). This contact culminated in the monetization of the economy; structural deformations, distortions and disarticulations; a partial revolutionization of pre-capitalist modes relations of production and exchange; ruthless exploitation; underdevelopment and dependence and peripheralisation in a highly exploitative world capitalist system. Of course, the contact with the forces and agents of imperialism specifically ensured that foreign capital gained a dominant foothold in Africa; that an unproductive, corrupt and dependent foster elite was created to service the colonial and neo-colonial societies and that the state structure bequeathed at political independence had to rely on violence and force to reproduce itself. This is because of the limited commodification of production forces; the non-autonomization of the state; and the general degree of consciousness, organisation and action amongst factions and fractions of non-bourgeois forces.

Perhaps, equally important in determining the weakness, instability and mediated hegemony of state structures in Africa is the fact that it is not used for legitimation or development purposes. Rather, the state and its institutions just like *politics* are consistently manipulated for accumulation and other extra-legal purposes. (Ake, 1985 : 105-114). This, of course, creates the impression that the state is a class state: it caters for the privileged, it is manipulated by the privileged and its resources, especially its ideological apparatuses and instruments of coercion service the privileged with only occasional concessions to the poor.

The combination of the tendencies, limitations and contradictions highlighted above in the epoch of monopoly capital underscores the crisis, instability and irrelevance of the state in Africa. The continent is extremely vulnerable to imperialist penetration, manipulation and exploitation. The indigenous elites who have unrestricted access to the institutions and resources of the state are largely content to serve as agents, share holders, major representatives, distributors, legal and political advisers to transnational corporations. Since, these indigenous forces dominate the state, the state in Africa is used to service the needs of imperialism at the expense of non-bourgeois forces.[4] Thus, politics; development (growth) planning; resource allocation; foreign trade, sources of foreign aid and military supplies and other policies aimed at systemic reproduction come under the direct and/or indirect influence of transnational forces. *(ibid).* Under these conditions, the state virtually looses control of the social formation; its structural coherence dissolves into ad-hoc and post-hoc responses to developments and crises and the character and accumulative bases of the dominant classes come to determine its role and relevance in society :

> In Africa, there are few social formations that are capitalist enough or socialist enough to be identifiable as clearly boasting the state form of domination. The unique feature of the socio-economic formations in post-colonial Africa is that the state, if we can properly talk of such an existence at all, has extremely limited autonomy. The state is composed in such way that it enjoys limited independence from the social classes-particularly the hegemonic social class- and is immersed in the class struggle. Because autonomization is the essence of the state as a modality of domination, it is not clear whether we can properly talk of the state in post-colonial Africa. That is not to say that government does not exist. (*ibid* : 108).

This issue of "limited independence" is very crucial to our analysis. Because the state is not hegemonic and lacks autonomy, its full immersion in the class struggle not only increases its vulnerability and manipulability but marks it out as a biased and class state. The state is thus unable to plan effectively for development. It is unable to mobilise for self-reliance. It is unable to regulate the activities of profit and hegemony-seeking transnational corporations. It is unable to withstand or mediate the pressures and impact of the deepening crisis of world capitalism and it is unable to effectively mediate intra-and inter-class contradictions and conflicts. Social forces, in their struggle for dominance and accumulation confront each other with restraint. Politics loses all its norms. Corruption reaches unprecedented proportions. Scarce resources are looted by factions or fractions of the bourgeoisie. Defence expenditure increases and the masses are pauperised, marginalised, exploited and suppressed. The major preoccupation of the state and its custodians become survival; not the provision of basic needs. This preoccupation deepens with increasing systemic crisis culminating in border clashes, civil wars, coups and counter coups and the ruthless implementation of harsh IMF and World Bank inspired monetarist programmes. Claude Ake explains the context and implications of these conditions thus:

> Non-autonomization of class domination means among other things that the state is immersed in class struggle and cannot mediate it, that the rule of law is not properly instituted with the result that political competition is without norms and unrestrained. All this places a high premium on political power and makes the struggle for power Hobbesian. The state of affairs in turn tends to block the development of productive forces generally and economic development in particular...because the power struggle is so intense, politics becomes an absorbing pursuit to the detriment of everything else including economic development. (*ibid* : 112).

The general precipitate of this unfortunate development or condition in which the development of society is sacrificed on the alter of personal political interests and expediency is that :

> Those in power develop a siege mentality and see everything in terms of increasing their power. A tradition of authoritarianism and brutality has made mobilisation for development impossible. Repression is such a prominent feature of the social formations of Africa that there can now be no question of the people being the end of development : there is now no question of any meaningful pursuit of self-reliant strategy of development that is so badly needed (*ibid*).

Of course, where the state is so visibly repressive and used by a corrupt and dependent elite for personal accumulation, the question of its being relevant to non-bourgeois forces as a mobilising force does not arise. Once an underdeveloped, dependent, distorted and foreign dominated social formation abandons development and self-reliance as priority areas or where the confrontation within and between social classes created hostile conditions for the attainment of mass-based goals, then anarchy, alienation and class contradictions and struggles are bound to become dominant features of society and social relations. Ironically, in many parts of Africa, the responses by the state and bourgeoisie to such situations have been increased depoliticisation, ideological containment, diversions, divide-and-rule tactics, intimidation and bribery.[5] These in themselves only make the state relevant *politically* but not in civil society :

> Because of the non-autonomization of class domination, the ruling class in undisciplined and vulnerable despite its political authoritarianism. One expression of this lack of discipline is the unrestrained exploitation of the subordinate classes. Sometimes the exploitation is so extreme that the working class is not really able to reproduce itself... Exploiting the subordinate classes can neither be in the interest of social capital nor the development of the productive forces. (Ake, 1985 : 113; 1981).

What we begin to witness in Africa therefore, is that the character of the dominant forces, the ruthless exploitation and impoverishment of non-bourgeois forces and the non-autonomization of the state combine within conditions of underdevelopment, dependence and marginalization in the international division of labour not only to heighten reliance on *particular* (as against social or collective) interests but also to subvert the goals of nationhood in all its ramifications. We can thus understand A.T. Gana's lament that

> ...25 years after independence, African economies, have exhibited no substantial change from their colonial antecedents. The post-colonial state has been critical in maintaining this state of affairs. (1985 : 120).

The state is able to perform the role of maintaining inherited conditions of poverty, corruption, ethnic antagonisms, foreign domination and instability because, according to Gana.

> The state in contemporary Africa...remains primarily the instrument of the metropolitan bourgeoisie for the reason that the internal process of capital accumulation is subordinated to the requirements of external, primarily metropolitan interest...The state has functioned as the conduit for the transfer of Africa's surplus abroad, generating the crisis of underdevelopment with few historical parallels. (*ibid* : 129)

It is not only the conditions above that makes the state"irrelevant" in Africa. In fact, in some cases, the conditions above make the state the more "relevant" albeit, politically. It seems that the more "politically relevant" a state is, the less relevant it becomes at the level of civil society. This is because people who are subjected to violent repression and all sorts of social, economic and cultural abuses and deprivations, easily become alienated from the state, even the society. It means that reliance or force, subverts the goals of civil society. However, it is more the interplay of power and politics within African states that makes the state "irrelevant".

Political independence in Africa as Gana has pointed out, did not see the structural transformation of society. This was more so where in the majority of cases, political independence was not won on the battlefield. In fact, in most of Africa, political independence witnessed concrete and strenuous efforts by local elites (itself largely a creation of colonialism) to rationalise and legitimise even extend the presence and participation of foreign capital in their respective states. Generous incentive were granted and "Africanization" or "indigenization" programmes were aimed at Africanizing or indigenizing inherited unequal and exploitative relations of power, production and exchange. The patterns of dependence on the metropole were infact strengthened and at times multilateralised. Thus, the African elites joined hands with transnational firms and interests to exploit the continent. Of course, the pressures of dependence and underdevelopment culminated in deepening contradictions between the rich and poor. The responses varied from diversions, through brands of populism to open repression. Given the condition of internal and external marinalization, the post colonial state remained unable to respond to the needs of the mass majority. Programme after programme, development plan after development plan and diversion after diversion failed to cover up the glaring realities of poverty, crisis and conflicts. The legitimacy of the bourgeoisie, the stability of the state and the expectations that the post-colonial state and its custodians will make a substantial difference from the colonial period were dashed by increasing poverty, disease, illiteracy and repression.[6]

> Economic stagnation and desperate poverty deprive the ruling classes of Africa of the chance of maintaining even a veneer of legitimacy. They reveal capitalism in all its grotesqueness and wickedness and compel attention to the necessity of equitable distribution. (Ake, 1978 : 30).

The inability of the state and bourgeoisie to respond to the crisis of economic stagnation or underdevelopment compels non-bourgeois forces to seek alternative legal and extra-legal means of survival. They turn to churches, mosques, traditional healers and diviners, ethnic organisations, community development associations, only boys' associations; individual members of the bourgeoisie; secret societies, philanthropic organisations like Rotary

Club and armed robbery and prostitution. People begin to realise that government does not care for the poor as education, housing, transportation, health services, food and other basic needs go beyond the reach of the poor. The conditions (strengthening the view that the state is for the rich alone) are not helped when economic mismanagement, criminal corruption, ruthless exploitation and drain of scarce resources abroad culminatebecause people who are subjected to violent repression and all sorts of social, economic and cultural abuses and deprivations, easily become alienated from the state, even the society. It means that reliance or force, subverts the goals of civil society. However, it is more the interplay of in spiralling inflation, closure of factories, mass unemployment, retrenchment of able-bodied workers and capital flight. Given its desperate poverty, the state is unable to respond concretely to these problems. Most African states often opt for harsh monetarist policies with the encouragement of bourgeois economists, the World Bank and the IMF. The policies which follow pay cuts, retrenchment, emphasis on individualism, imposition of taxes, levies and user-fees for social facilities, privatisation of public parastatals, devaluation of the currency, harassment of trade unions etc.-only furthers the irrelevance of the state. Loyalties are then easily transferred to those bodies and interests identified above. Thus, in spite of the military strength of the state and the expansion of its security services, it remains completely incapable of providing leadership and direction towards the creation and nurturing of values, interests, aspirations, institutions and processes which would support the cause of nationhood. People just dissolve directly and/or indirectly into their respective particular orgnisations which begin to compete with the state for the loyalty, support, emotions and patriotism of the citizens. This has been the case in virtually all African states and at this level people no longer believe in or have faith in the state.

I SOCIO-ECONOMIC CRISIS, ETHNICITY AND THE STATE

There is no gain saying the fact that the quest for development, self-reliance, unity, stability, peace and progress in Africa has consistently been undermined by the depth and dimensions of the economic crisis as well as the potency of ethnicity among other factors and forces.[7] Of course, both the economic crisis and the contemporary role of ethnicity are precipitates of the continent's historical experiences. Yet, inspite of post-colonial alignments and re-alignments of class forces as well as other programmes initiated at national, sub-regional and continental levels, the *African Predicament* (Ihonvbere, n.d.) continues to threaten the world.

The crisis of world capitalism (Sweezy, 1978; Ihonvbere, 1987) evidenced in double digit inflation, mass unemployment, bankruptcies, retarded growth, increasing amounts of idle productive capacity, lower levels of investment in plant and equipment and militarism have been reproduced in Africa in greater proportions. This is largely because, Africa is today the least developed, least industrialised, most vulnerable, exposed and crisis-ridden continent in the world. (Arnold, 1980). The continent's contribution to global GDP and industrial output is infinitesimal. Its Physical Quality of Life Index (PQLI) and other indicators of development are far below the standards of other regions. In fact, the desperate nature of the *African Condition* (Mazrui, 1980) is attested to in the admission of African leaders is the 1981 *Lagos Plan of Action.*[8] Even more than that, the dangerous implications of the African crisis, which has generated severe tensions, conflicts and fascistic tendencies in the continent are evidenced in the fact that in 1986, the United Nations for the first time in its history held a special session on the problems of the African continent.[9] Problems of declining or stagnating growth rates, deindustrialisation, high mortality rates, hunger and disease, drought, refugees, civil wars and massive extraction and repatriation of surplus by transnational corporations and finance institutions continue to plague the continent. Added to these we can mention the heavy debt burden of the continent—over $ 200 billion in 1989; rising interest rates and debt service ratios; declining terms of trade; fall in commodity prices—this fell by 32% in 1986; massive drain of resources-resources flow into Africa in 1986 was $18 billion, resource outflow for the same year was $34 billion-; and crisis in the agricultural sector.[10]

In the face of these numerous and debilitating predicaments and problems, African states opted for IMF and World Bank adjustment and recovery programmes. In country after country, this approach to recovery has spelt death, disease, alienation riots and crisis. The political tensions that have accompanied monetarism have furthered repression, human rights abuses, riots and national disintegration. (Lone, 1987; Ekekwe and Ihonvbere : n.d.) It is now only being recognised that :

> Such measures do not necessarily work in low-income countries where unemployment and malnutrition are already high and which do not have a resilient industrial base...adjustment programmes have reduced balance of payments deficits but not led to economic revitalization.[11]

The very high degree of human suffering, disillusionment, anger, alienation, rural decay, urban dislocation, suicides, marital crisis, prostitution and crime which have accompanied monetarist responses to the African economic crisis, hold major implications for the potency of ethnicity and the subversion of the goals of nationhood. The point is that the poor majority, have no option but to find solace, support and security in ethnic or communal associations where the state has failed woefully. Such conditions where loyalty and support for the state are mediated by loyalty to and support for ethnic associations, clubs and other interests, mean that the questions of patriotism, nationalism, sacrifice and unity become secondary. This is the situation in virtually all African states today.

II THE MATERIAL BASIS OF ETHNIC CONSCIOUSNESS[12]

It is all too easy to dismiss the problem of ethnicity in the quest for nation-building. It is even easier, in the analysis of African politics to see ethnicity as the primary, indeed most important contradiction: a variable which explains everything. Both positions would be doing a lot of disservice to the study of politics and society in Africa. All Africans necessarily belong to ethnic groups; if we take ethnicity to mean "a social phenomena associated with interactions among members of different ethnic groups". (Nnoli; 1978 : 5) Furthermore

> Ethnic groups are social formations distinguished by the communal character of their boundaries. The relevant communal factor may be language, culture or both. In Africa, language has clearly been the most crucial variable. As social formations, however, ethnic groups are not necessarily homogeneous entities even linguistically or culturally. (*ibid* : 9)

Thus, there is nothing intrinsically bad in belonging to an ethnic group. Infact, prior to the advent of colonial domination, ethnic groups in Africa fought violently between and within themselves. They also coexisted peacefully, traded and intermarried among themselves. However, with colonialism, religion, region and ethnic identity took completely new forms. They were manipulated as part of the divide-and—rule tactics of the colonial powers. Certain ethnic groups were favoured at the expens of others. Some were barred completely from holding certain positions, enjoying certain facilities, cultivating certain crops and so on. The ethnic groups were instigated against one another and emerging leaders were given ethnic labels and regarded as ethnic leaders. These measures were taken as part of the grand imperialist programme of subjugation, domination and exploitation of the colony. It is precisely for this reason that ethnicity cannot be "made a decisive independent variable". *(ibid)*. Left on its own, it poses no problem to the quest for nationhood in Africa. But ethnic consciousness is carried by social actors with varying social, economic and political interests and aspirations. It is therefore the socio-economic and political purposes to which ethnicity is put that holds implications for the quest for rational politics, stability and national unity in Africa.

It is important that we always bear in mind therefore that the politics of ethnicity was promoted in the colonial period. The proto-bourgeoisie in the early periods of colonialism imbibed this as part of the politics of resource generation and allocation and it became a very useful tool in the post independence period for mobilising regional (ethnic) support for personal or class based ambitions and goals. This became the more important in view of the marginalization of indigenous elites from the production process and the dominant role of foreign capital. The local elites found ethnicity a very potent force in their competition for favoured positions in transnational coroporations. As well, given their largely unproductive location in the social formation, the state became the means to rapid capital accumulation and power. Again, ethnicity, just like religion was an available tool employed to whip up support, antagonism, suspicion and emotions in the struggles to win access to the state and preside over the collection and allocation of scarce resources. As Eme Ekekwe points out:

> It is in the competition for control of and/or access to the state that a...component of the ideology of development comes in. This component is ethnicity. Conflict between ethnic groups can be manifestations of class struggles and competitions. In the Nigerian situation this appears to have been the case; explanations of ethnic conflict there would be incomplete without references to the class situation. As Amilcar Cabral pointed out, it is usually those persons who are detribalized and well off-such as those who comprise the governing class-who resort to an appeal to ethnicity. There exists a certain dialectic between ethnicity and class that has to be appreciated in the search to understand politics in many post-colonial societies. (Ekekwe, 1986 : 10).

Furthermore, the ethnic fator is so strong and effective not only because of the poverty of the masses who are easy victims of ethnic manipulations especially within a patron-client context but also because of the limited development of production relations. This is well explained by Claude Ake :

> The bulk of the subordinate classes consists of peasants, workers and petty commodity producers

> but mainly of peasants. The peasants are still deeply involved in the production of use value and their involvement in commodity relations is limited. In the essential pre-capitalist social relations in which they find themselves there in little social atomisation and individualism, and the differentiation of interests is rudimentary. In short, the legal form is as under-developed as the commodity form, the person has not yet fully emerged as a legal subject. (Ake, n.d. : 6).

The above is very crucial for it continues to provide a fertile ground for the elite to play ethnic politics by manipulating the fears of the peasants, capitalising on their largely pre-capitalist environment and manipulating their aspirations and fears.

Thus, ethnicity within the context of neo-colonial politics and production relations subverts the goals of nationhood at two main levels. The first, is that the dominant elites exploit the ethnic factor to carve out and retain spheres of interest while advancing their personal, class and occasionally community interests. In this case, "ethnicity becomes a mask for class privileges". (Nnoli, *op. cit.* : 10). In addition,

> By diverting attention away from imperialist exploitation and the resultant distortion of African economic and social structures, ethnicity performs the function of mystification and obscurantism. Consequently, it helps to perpetuate imperialism, and militate against the imperative of revolutionary struggle by hampering the development of a high level of political consciousness by its victms. (*Ibid* : 13).

Thus, it is the politicisation of ethnicity by the bourgeoisie in furtherance of their respective inter and inter class struggles that has generated contradictions which subvert the goals of nationhood in Africa. This position is supported by Ekekwe when he notes that the pattern of ethnic politics "is directly related to the struggle within the (petty) bourgeois class for control of state apparatuses". (Ekekwe, *op. cit.* : 40). Of course this politicisation of ethnicity all over the continent has never been a basis for effective mobilisation and national unity. It has generated deep-rooted suspicions, massacres, wastage of resources and general insecurity and confusion. At the end of it all, the quest for nationhood suffers.

The other level at which the ethnic factor subverts the goal of nationhood arises from the economic crisis discussed earlier on. Either at the national or continental levels, deep-rooted economic crisis, desperate poverty, repression and harassment lead people to rely less on the state, its institutions and agents and leads to the transfer of loyalty from the state to ethnic and other associations. Thus, most Africans confront the state as a wicked, exploitative and coercive force. Claude Ake explains this in the Nigerian case:

> Most Nigerians confront the state not as a public force but as an alien and hostile coercive power. This is all more so because the Nigerian state, lacking autonomy, is immersed in the class struggle and is conspicuously a state for the few against the many, because the Nigerian state tendentially appears as irrelevant or hostile, a critical condition for the transfer of loyalties to ecumenical levels is removed. Nigerians embraced ethnic identity all the more. The ethnic groups have been emotionally and materially supportive of their members, and do not rely on coercion. (Ake : *op. cit.* : 7-8).

The above then is the crux of the matter. Ethnic or community unions all over Africa do not rely on coercion. They provide "entry points" into the urban systems. They provide support in cases of unemployment or ill health. They take care of families in cases of accidents and transport corpses to villages for burial. They run scholarship schemes, serve as sources of information and provide refuge and hope in times of crisis. They also have political functions. In all these areas, the state in Africa has proved irrelevant. Infact, the state not only imposes new taxes, tolls and levies, it also retrenches able-bodied workers on a massive scale and gives open protection to the corrupt, rich and powerful. Since it is incapable of meeting the yearnings of the poor it resorts to diversions—War Against Filth, War Against Indiscipline, War Against Rats and Snakes, Mass Mobilisation Programmes of all sorts, Ethical Revolution etc. It also employs repression to contain popular pressures. These pressures become politically dangerous and threatening to the dominant classes as "rising expectations gave way to the revolution of rising frustrations." (Gana, 1985 : 129).

> As soon as political independence was won, the nationalist movement had to be deradicalized quickly and politics democratized by a bourgeoisie which was intent on a bourgeois revolution all along but had given the impression of wanting to effect radical transformation. Disappointed popular aspirations could not be bought off for lack of resources; they had to be contained by repression. (Ake : n.d. : 7).

It is obvious therefore that where the post-colonial state had failed to provide hope, support and direction to the masses, ethnic associations have tended to succeed. To be sure, these associations are easily "captured" by ethnic notables and used to advance narrow interests. This is, of course, largely due to the "limited development of commodity relations and on a more fundamental level,...the (limited) development of productive forces". (Ake, 1981 : 11). In any case, the ability of ethnic notables to manipulate ethnic associations also reflect the degree to which the members of the association have transferred their loyalties to the notables via the association. Again Ake, reflecting on the Nigerian situation notes the insensitivity and indifference of the state to the welfare of the vast majority who are usually the worse victims of so-called adjustment programmes. The observation is valid for the rest of Africa :

> The tenuous relationship between the Nigerian state and its subjects implied by these conditions is underscored by the indifference of the Nigerian state to social welfare. For the urban population there are some programmes which are no more than a notional concession to the idea of welfare. For the rural population there is virtually nothing. More often than not it is not only welfare schemes that are lacking but any visible sign of government presence besides the coercive personnel. *Voluntary associations mainly ethnic associations, religious groups, cooperatives, free masonry have mushroomed in Nigeria filling the gap left by the state's indifference to social welfare.* A good part of the amenities and intrastuctures in the villages have been provided by self-help projects or ethnic associations. (Ake, n.d. : 6-7).

Under the conditions described thus far, how can we expect the goals of national integration, unity, stability, growth and development to be attained ?

III CONCLUSION: ATTAINING THE GOALS OF NATIONHOOD IN AFRICA

From our discussion so far, we have identified four major obstacles to the quest for nationhood in Africa: (i) the unhegemonic, "irrelevant" and unstable post-colonial state; (ii) the decadent, corrupt, unproductive and subservient dominant classes, (iii) the conditions of poverty, ignorance, disease, marginalization, exploitation and repression of the poor majority and (iv) the internally dominant role of foreign capital and the structured incorporation of Africa into and peripheralisation in a hostile and ruthlessly exploitative international division of labour. Other problems of natural disasters, debts, falling commodity prices, technology backwardness etc. as well as the crisis of world capitalism are given concrete expression (in greater detail) due to the existing distortions, deformations and disarticulations within the continent.

The contradictions and conditions identified above have combined at various levels to generate insecurity, tensions, wars, conflicts, the transfer of resources abroad, waste and backwardness. The insecurity of the elites who dominate the state and control the means of coercion has compelled them to rely on violence, human rights abuses, intimidation and depoliticization. This way, they promote alienation, distrust, instability and subvert possibilities for nationhood. As well, the gross mismanagement of scarce resources, flirtations with monetarist policies, commitment to the indigenization of unequal exchange and emphasis on exchange or distribution as against production, have made life worse for non-bourgeois forces. Thus, they too have been compelled, especially with increasing repression to withdraw their loyalties from the state which they see as biased (in favour of the privileged), exploitative and coercive. They now seek support, refuge and direction from ethnic and religious associations. This, again, subverts the goals of nationhood.

It would appear therefore that existing internal and external relations of power, production and exchange in Africa cannot support the quest for nationhood in Africa. Ethnicity as well cannot be "the basis for explaining and changing society. (Nndi, *op. cit.* : 12). Ethnic positions, consciousness and actions have to be confronted with class consciousness. With increasing commodification of labor and the integration of rural producers into world capitalism, the strangle-hold of ethnic consciousness is withering away. Nonetheless, given the "irrelevance" of the state it is still a potent force. The quest for nationhood in a colonised, dominated, distorted, disarticulated, peripheralised, under-developed and dependent Africa cannot be sought or attained outside a popular and collective resolution of the African crisis. The fundamental obstacles to the quest for stability, national integration, peace and development in Africa are fast generating fascistic tendencies all over the continent. Decades of tinkering with inherited contradictions, alliances and problems have not in any way improved the *African Condition*. Accelerated capitalist development is not taking place. Rapid *growth* in a few countries—the Ivory Coast, Nigeria, Kenya and Egypt—have only increased foreign domination, widened the gap between the rich and the poor, furthered integration into the orbit of world capitalism and furthered existing crisis. Though Ake is of the view that in the context of deepening crisis in Africa, the choice is not between capitalism and socialism but between socialism and barbarism, (Ake, 1978 : 107) it would seem that the situation has so deteriorated since 1978 that the choice today is between a radical and popular restructuring in favour of the majority and extinction. Nationhood cannot be attained within the context of imperialist domination and exploitation. The task before all patriotic Africans is to organize, mobilise and struggle for the termination of neocolonial domination and exploitation.

Note

1. *The works of Issa Shivji, M. Mamdani, Colin Leys, John Saul, Terisa Turner, Michela von Freyhold, R. Kaplinski, S. Langdon and a host of others who made useful contributions to the debate.*
2. *By "positive role" we assume that the role a state plays in any social formation can either be "nagative" or "positive." If it is a popular state i.e. one which acts in the specific and general interest of the majority, then such a role is positive and vice versa.*
3. *For detailed discussions of the "irrelevant state" Julius Ihonvbere and Eme N. Ekekwe, "The Irrelevant State, the National Question and the Future of Dependent Capitalism in Nigeria" in Julius Ihonvbere (ed.) Dependent Capitalism and Crisis in Nigeria (Benin-City : Jodah Publishers, 1988). Also Claude Ake "Theoretical Notes on the National Question in Nigeria" (Mimeo : Uniport, n. d.) I owe the use of this concept to Professor Ake.*
4. *Ake has argued that the African bourgeoisie and the respective state structures they dominate, are obstacles to development in the continent. His Revolutionary Pressures in Africa (London : Zed Press, 1978) pp. 65-77.*
5. *These mechanisms and the ways in which they are employed are discussed in Claude Ake, Revolutionary Pressure...Op. cit. and Clive Thomas, The Rise of the Authoritarian State...Op. cit.*
6. *For detailed discussions of how the respective dreams for a democratic, stable and united Africa have been effectively shattered by the realities of neo-colonial capitalism and politics. John Hatch, Africa's Problems Since Independence : Africa Emergent (Chicago : Holt Regnery 1974).*
7. *For details on the causes, dimensions and implications*

for the African crisis Timothy M. Shaw, Towards a Political Economy for Africa : The Dialectics of Dependence (London : Macmillan, 1986); Centre for African Studies, Dalhousie University, Canada, Briefing Paper on Africa's Economic Crisis Number 1, January, 1985 and Julius Ihonvbere, "The African Economic Crisis : Responses and options" Development and Peace (Autumn 1988).

8. OAU, Lagos Plan 01 Action for the Economic Development of Africa, 1980-2000 (Geneva : International Institute for Labour Studies, 1981). For a critique Timothy M. Shaw, "Debates about Africa's Future; The Brandt, World Bank and Lagos Plan Blueprint" Third World Quarterly 5 (2) (April, 1983).

9. This was in June 1986 when the OAU presented its African Priority Programe for Economic Recovery (APPER) asking the developed nations to contribute $128 billion needed to address the African crisis.

10. Data drawn from Africa Recovery No. 3. November 1987, (Published by the Office of the Secretary General to the United Nations).

11. Salim Lone, " African Reforms Fail to Stem Slide" African Recovery (3) (Nov. 1987) and Eme Ekekwe and Julius O. Ihonvbere Economic Crisis and Human Rights Violations in Africa" (Forthcoming).

12. For other works which have dealt with the problem of ethnicity see Okwudiba Nnoli, Ethnic Politics in Nigeria (Enugu : Fourth Dimension 1978); Mamood Mamdani, Politics and Class Formation in Uganda (New York : Monthly Review 1976); Archie Mafeje, "The Ideology of Tribalism" Journal of Modern African Studies IX (2) (1971); B. Magubane, "Pluralism and Conflict Situations in Africa; A New Look" African Social Research VII (2) (June 1969).

References

Ake Claude	1978	*Revolutionary Pressures in Africa* London : Zed Press. p. 65.
	1981	A *Political Economy of Africa.* (London : Longman).
	1985	"The Future of the State in Africa *International Political Scienc Review* 6 (1) pp. 105-114.
	n.d.	Theoritical Notes in the National in Nigeria. (Mimeo) University of Port Harcourt, Nigeria.
Arnold Hugh M.	1980	"Africa and the New International Economic

		Order" *Third World* Quarterly Vol. 11(2) (April, 1980).
Brett E. A.	1973	*Colonialism and Underdevelopment in East Africa* (London : Heinemann).
Ekekwe, Eme.	1986	*Class and State in Nigeria* Lagos and London : Longman.
Ekekwe, E. and Julius O. Ihonvbere	n.d.	Economic crisis and Human Rights violations in Africa (Forth coming).
Gana Aaron T.	1985	"The State in Africa : Yesterday, Today and Tomorrow" *International Political Science Review* 6 (1) p. 129.
Fanon Frantz	1978	*The Wretched of the Earth* (New York, Grove Press.
Gramsci Antonio	1981	*Selections From Prison Notebooks.* New York : International Publishers.
Ihonvbere Julius O. (Ed.)		*The African Predicament : Essays on Crisis, Poverty and Dependence* (forthcoming).
	1987	"The International Environment and Africa's Deepening Crisis." Paper prepared for the 1987 Conference of the African Political Science Association, Yaounde, Cameroun, May, '87.
Lone, Salim	1987	African Reforms Fail to Stem Slide. *African Recovery* : 3.
Mazrui Ali A.	1980	*The African Condition : A Political Diagnosis* (London : Heinemann)
Nnoli, Okwudiba	1978	*Ethnic Politics in Nigeria.* Enugu : Fourth Dimensions.
OAU	1981	*Lagos Plan 01 Action for the Economic Development in Africa, 1980-2000.* Geneva, International Institute for Labour Studies.
Rodney Walter	1974	*How Europe Underdeveloped Africa.* (Washington, D. C. : Howard University Press).
Sweezy Paul M.	1978	"The Present Global Crisis of Capitalism" *Monthly Review* 29 (11) (April, '78).
Thomas, Clive.	1984	*The Rise of the Authoritarian State in Peripheral Societies,* New York and London, Monthly Reveiw Press.
Williams, Gwyn.	1970	The concept of 'Egemonia' in the Thought of Antonio Gramsci. *Journal of History of Ideas* : 2.

Darlington Iwarimie-Jaja

SOCIO-ECONOMIC ENVIRONMENT OF CRIME : THE CASE OF A PERIPHERAL STATE (1970-1989)

The Socio-economic environment of crime refers to the social milieu where criminal activities strive under certain limitations imposed by law enforcement controls. However, most criminal activities have continued unabated despite all efforts by federal, state and local governments to reduce the crime rate in every peripheral or advanced capitalist states.

The phenomenon of crime in the context of economic conditions reflect the constraints man finds himself in any given social formation. Guerry (1833) and Quetelet (1835) authenticate this fact when a century and half ago, they claimed that crime rates were significantly related to economic conditions of social areas. Their assertions raised a critical question which renewed the controversy (Blau and Blau, 1982; Messner, 1982; O' Brien, 1983; Sampson, 1985; Williams, 1984).

In the 1900s, criminologists such as Kornhauser (1978), Cohen, *etal.* (1980), and Cantor and Land (1985) opined that differentiation in the spatial distribution of crime are mainly due to the degree of poverty characterizing an area. Vold and Bernard (1986) support this claim when they asserted that the lack of certain fixed level of material goods necessary for human minimum existence and well-being create opportunity for criminality to flourish in an area. However, studies by Decker (1980), Blau and Blau (1982) and Messner (1983) contradicts this notion by contending that poverty has little or no relationship (if any) with criminal tendency.

Some studies on socio-economic environment and crime have shifted attention to unemployment per se as a causal factor of criminality. Such studies include Box (1985), Danzigar (1976) and Stack (1978).

Other studies contributing to the debate on socio-economic environment of crime have focused on economic inequality rather than poverty or unemployment. Among these include Carroll and Jackson (1983), Sampson (1985) and Rosenfeld (1986).

The study is a contribution to existing literature on the socio-economic environment of crime within the context of Nigeria which has experienced cyclical fluctuations in its economy. It has been observed that previous studies have not studied crime to determine the critical factor which necessitate it in the periods of economic boom and crisis. Previous studies have also not compared crime rates within these periods, especially in West African subregion and Nigeria in particular. This vacuum is what the present study intends to fill.

To explain the socio-economic environment of crime in the Nigerian context and explanation of the cyclical fluctuations is imperative.

Cyclical Fluctuation of the Nigeria Economy

Post-colonial Nigeria experienced cyclical fluctuations between 1970 and beyond. For analytical purposes, two major periods—the boom era which Spanned 1970-1979 and the slump or crisis period which covered 1980 to the present are conceived.

There is a general consensus that the major source of the boom in the 1970s was the guadrupling of oil revenue during that period compared with the preceding decade. This phenomenal rise in the Nigeria oil revenue was due to the Arab-Israeli war in 1973 which sent the price of oil in the international market skyrocketing. According to The Economist (1984 : 3), "wealth beyond the dreams of avarice" is the best description of the scene as it appeared to Nigeriain leaders after the oil price rise. Oil production quickly climbed out of the civil war trough from a 1968 low of 0.14 million barrels a day (B/D) to 1.08 million b/d at the start of the decade. By 1973 it had reached the level that has been roughly the government's target ever since : 2 million b/d.

With this rise, Nigeria's crude oil production and exports have made some significant contributions to the country's ability to earn foreign exchange over time. For example, between 1958 and 1974, the amount of foreign exchange earned by petroleum exports rose from N 2 million to N 5, 366 million (Fos, Annual Abstract of Statistics, Lagos, 1950 : 74).

Another source of economic boom was the petroleum industry which contributed significantly to government revenue in the form of royalties, rents,license fees and petroleum profits tax. This increased government revenue from a 1970-3 average of N1.15 billion to N13.8 billion by 1979-80 (The Economist, 1984:16). On the economic front, the main effect of prosperity has been a massive public investment programme that has, simultaneously, stimulated growth in many sectors and created several distortions.

Given the phenomenal rise in revenue accruing from the oil sector, government was able to embark on a number of projects which in turn led to the creation of jobs, increase in the volume of purchasing power, massive importation of goods, especially consumer items. Public investment also concentrated on traditional targets : physical infrastructure (especially transport and, to a small extent, heavy industry) and social infrastructure (particularly education facilities). A quarter of capital spending under the third plan (1975-1980) was in transport, and a further 13 percent was in manufacturing, while education received 8 percent. Over half of the existing road network was widened, strengthened or improved, power output rose by 15 percent per annum, new port facilities were created, and universal primary eduction introduced. So rapid was the growth of public investment that it outgrew the governments' management capacities. The projected level of total investment, in the Third Plan (1975-1980) was ten times higher than in the second plan, on the assumption that money was no longer a constraint (The Economist, 1984 : 17).

But in the early 1980s, money became the major constraint to the economic development of the country. In 1982, the country plunged into a period of economic crisis—"a situation whereby the level of economic resources was not able to sustain the majority of her people. This condition implied that the composite Units of production process no longer contributed to systematic reproduction that yielded poduction output large enough to increase the well-being of the majority. By 1983, there was a declining level of production, on set of recession, rising cost of living, heightening unemployment level, falling rate of profit, exchange rate fluctuation, increasing scarcity of goods and services, including the privatization of public companies" (Iwarimie-Jaja, 1992 : 2-3).

Neo-classical scholars and Nigerian officials explain that Nigeria's economic crisis was caused by the world oil glut and Nigeria's dependence on a single commodity; the general world-wide recession; low savings and low investments coupled with lack of sectoral linkages; low productivity of workers and high wages; unregulated and excessive government expenditure (Usman and Banqura, 1984 : 37).

Contrary to the Neo-classical explanations, Marxists contend that since Nigerian economy is an integral part of the capitalist world economy, it is susceptible to crisis and fluctuations in the capitalist world economy which leads to contradictions between social surplus and investment problem. According to Bangura,

> "most of the social surplus has not been utilised in the economy; the various arms of capital have either transferred large amounts of such surplus overseas by way of dividends, corrupt import practices that are a cover for capital transfers, and the actual importation of manufactured commodities, raw materials and capital inputs" (1984 : 44).

Thus, in spite of the enormous sums of profit generated in all sectors of the Nigerian economy such as oil, banking, manufacturing and industry, the level of development remains abysmally low because a big chunk of the surplus is either spent in conspicuous consumption or in overseas investments.

Nigeria's former Head of State, General Obsanjo has shed more light on the extent of surplus transfer out of the Nigerian economy. According to him,

> "experience has shown that most of the so called foreign investors come in with little or nothing in finances; they raise internal loans from the savings of ordinary Nigerians and within months, they are devising all means (of) repatrating huge sums out of Nigeria in terms of dividends, profits, management fees, loaded invoices, etc." (Bangura, 1984 : 45-46).

According to Marxists, therefore, the current crisis can be attributed not so much to the so called oil glut or global recession but rather to the fact that surplus from the oil sector has not been creatively and productively invested in the Nigerian economy but has instead been siphoned out of the country by powerful clients, agents, partners and servants of neo-colonialism and imperialism. Thus the country is being denied the multiplier and other spin-off effects arising from such reinvestment. By this fact, the Nigarian masses have continued to suffer from poverty, misery and helplessness. Thus persons who suffer under these conditions of deprivation engage in parasitic criminal behavior, including burglary, robbery, drug dealing and prostitution. In the bid to survive, criminal and delinquent gang activities are initiated in both rural and urban areas. However, such gang activities are relatively limited in the hinterlands than in township.

Having set the background for the study, an analysis of crime within the context of cyclical fluctions in Nigeria follows.

Table 1. Nigeria's crime profile, 1974-1984

Year	*Person N (%)*	*Property N (%)*	*Miscellaneous N (%)*	*Total N (%)*
1974	53,646 (27.54)	111,056 (57.00)	30,108 (15.46)	194,810 (100.00)
1975	56,197 (29.02)	108,282 (55.92)	29,154 (15.05)	193,633 (99.99)
1976	58,555 (27.33)	115,688 (53.99)	40,043 (18.69)	214,286 (100.01)
1977	72,404 (33.05)	100,416 (45.83)	46,272 (21.12)	219,092 (100.00)
1978	66,359 (32.22)	99,766 (48.45)	39,805 (19.33)	205,930 (100.00)
1979	64,726 (32.98)	101,815 (51.88)	29,699 (15.13)	196,240 (99.99)
1980	55,875 (26.49)	140,625 (66.68)	14,408 (6.83)	210,908 (100.00)
1981	64,346 (30.54)	91,856 (43.59)	54,515 (25.87)	210,717 (100.00)
1982	88,433 (30.19)	131,408 (44.86)	73,076 (24.95)	292,917 (100.00)
1983	93,752 (30.08)	145,607 (46.71)	72,367 (23.21)	311,726 (100.00)
1984	112,116 (30.34)	187,610 (50.77)	69,796 (18.89)	369,522 (100.00)

Source : Data was obtained from the Annual Report of the Nigeria Police Force, 1970-1980 and deduced from Tables 9,10,11, 12 in crime prevention for Freedom, Justice, Peace and Development in Nigeria, *The Nigeria National Paper for the 7th United Nations Congress on crime prevention and treatment of Offenders*, held at Milan Italy, between 26th August and 6th September, 1985.

Economic Boom and Crime

During economic boom crime rate decreases for these reasons (a) the major macro-economic variables of the country such as income, employment, aggregate demand, prices, etc. often go up. The number of unemployed persons is often very marginal and hence very few persons feel deprived and frustrated. Given that most pople are gainfully employed, a few members of the society are therefore prone to committing crime; (b) government often has sufficient funds to embark on public

Table 2. General Crime Figures (1967-1977)

Year	Crimes known to the police				True Cases			
	Figures	Percentages	Rates Per 100,000 of Population	Annual % Increase/ Decrease	Figures	Percentages	Rate per 10,000 of Population	Annual % Increase/ Decrease
1967	68,535	—	112.25	—	55,957	81.65	91.65	—
1968	71,423	—	114.06	+4.21	57,984	81.18	92.60	+3.62
1969	85,958	—	133.87	+20.35	70,249	81.73	107.40	+21.15
1970	137,021	—	208.09	+59.41	112,943	82.43	171.52	+60.78
1971	169,084	—	250.39	+23.40	139,526	82.52	206.62	+23.54
1972	176,124	—	254.32	+4.16	146,331	83.08	211.30	+4.88
1973	187,514	—	264.03	+6.47	156,696	83.57	220.64	+7.08
1974	211,557	—	290.47	+12.82	182,832	86.42	251.03	+16.68
1975	209,213	—	280.10	—1.11	181,334	86.67	242.77	+0.82
1976	222,496	—	290.46	+6.35	194,063	87.22	253.34	+7.02
1977	219,769	—	279.76	—1.23	194,196	88.36	247.21	+0.07

Soruce : Crime and the Quality of Life in Nigeria, *The Nigerian National Paper for the Sixth United Nations Congress on Crime Prevention and Treatment of Offenders*, held at Caracas, Venezula, August 25 to September 5, 1980.

investment projects, particularly the provision of qualitative social services for the masses of the country and also at cheaper rates; (c) government undertakes the subsidisation of the cost of the social services it provides. This is particularly true of social services such as education, health services, petrol and kerosine. With subsidized cost of social services, very few persons are thus deprived marginalised and frustrated.

Based on the assertions above, a conclusion can easily be drawn from the analysis : we expect crime rate to be generally low within the period of ecomomic boom in Nigeria. We now critically examine Nigeria's crime statistics in order to see whether they support our theoretical expectations. Table 1 shows Nigeria's crime profile between 1974 and 1984.

It can be easily observed from Table 1 that there was no significant decrease in the rate of crime during the period of economic boom. Although the number of crimes slightly fell from 194, 810 in 1974 to 193,633 in 1975 (by 0.01 percent), the figure quickly jumped to 214, 286 in 1976 (by 0.02 percent) and rose to an all-time high of 219,092 in 1977 (by 0.01 percent). At the time the economic boom effectively terminated in 1979, the crime rate had reached 196,240, which was higher than the 1974 figure.

Table 3. Total Reports to the Nigeria Police by Type

Year	*Cases Reported to the Police (Excluding Traffic Offences)*			*Cases for which prosecutions have been instituted*		
	Serious Crime	*Minor Crime*	*Minor Offence*	*Serious Crime*	*Minor Crime*	*Minor Offence*
1970	82,082	41,714	11,202	68,268	33,432	5,546
1971	98,332	54,365	11,816	83,406	40,677	9,838
1972	89,387	60,760	15,392	89,603	45,877	13,456
1973	114,887	64,598	23,586	94,860	50,467	21,372
1974	120,308	70,765	15,217	107,068	54,678	13,318
1975	118,270	70,516	14,398	98,169	55,164	10,819
1976	125,117	77,045	16,580	114.073	62,980	11,791
1977	109,355	86,769	16,428	100,543	73,238	14,832
1978	119,129	82,470	16,311	109,769	68,295	14,810
1979	120,825	79,524	16,760	109,490	65,490	14,840

Source : The Nigeria Police. Also see *Annual Abstract of Statistics*, 1982 edition, Federal Office of Statistics. Lagos.

Indeed, if compared with the pre-economic boom era, it would seem as if the crime rate was on the increase during the period of economic boom. Table 2 vividly illustrates this point.

In the late 1960s, the total number of crimes committed was far less than 100,000 throughout the period. However, the number jumped sharply to 137,021 at the beginning of the period of economic boom in 1970 and further peaked at 211,557 in 1974 when the oil boom became stronger.

The extent of crime during the economic boom period becomes glaring if one takes a critical look at the severity of the crimes committed. Table 3 shows the total reports made to the Nigeria Police according to the severity of the crime.

In Table 3, 82,082 cases of serious crimes (armed robbery, murder, manslaughter, etc.) were reported to the police at the beginning of the economic boom in 1970. However, by the time economic boom peaked in 1973, the number of cases of serious crime reported had reached an alarming figure of 114,887. Serious crimes figure continued to increase throughout the economic boom period. For instance, it rose to 120, 308 in 1974, hit 125, 117 in 1976 and later stabilized at 120,825 in 1979.

Cases of minor crimes reported to the police such as assault, affray, etc., also showed similar trends during the economic boom period. At the beginning of the boom era, 41,714 cases of minor crimes were reported. As usual, the number rose phenomenally to 64,498 during the peak of the oil boom in 1973. This increase continued steadily for the rest of the 1970s and indeed reached an all-time high of 86,769 in 1977. Cases of minor offences such as idleness, disorderly conduct, trafic offences, etc., reported were also on the increase during the period under consideration. From 11,202 in 1970 the number increased to 23,586 in 1973. Although the number of cases reported later dropped to 14,398 in 1975, it should be noted that the number did not show any appreciable decrease throughout the economic boom era.

Crimes in Nigeria have been classified into various categories. For example, offences agains personst, offences against property, other offences against local acts. A general picture that emerges from Tables 4-7 is that the number of offences in each category was on the increase during the "core" period of the economic boom which is normally regarded as the mid - 1970s.

Table 4. Offences Against Persons (1975 - 1979)

Year	Figures	% of Total Criminality	Rates Per 100,000 of Population	Annual % Increases/ Decreases
1975	56,197	29.24	75.41	+ 0.59
1976	58,555	27.33	76.63	+ 4.19
1977	72,424	33.05	92.78	+ 23.68
1978	68,521	31.07	85.02	- 5.38
1979	64,726	29.35	77.78	- 5.53

Table 5. Offences Against Property (1975 - 1979)

Year	Figures	% of Total Criminality	Rates Per 100,000 of Population	Annual % Increases/ Decreases
1975	108,282	52.82	145.30	- 5.35
1976	115,688	53.98	151.41	+ 6.84
1977	100,416	45.82	128.64	- 13.20
1978	107,879	48.93	133.85	+ 7.43
1979	109,308	53.65	131.35	+ 1.32

Table 6. Other Offences - Social Disorganisation Crimes (1975 - 1979)

Year	Figures	% of Total Criminality	Rates Per 100,000 of Population	Annual % Increases/ Decreases
1975	16,502	8.52	22.14	+ 29.65
1976	19,820	9.24	25.94	+ 20.11
1977	20,847	9.51	26.71	+ 5.18
1978	19,541	8.86	24.25	- 6.26
1979	15,323	7.52	18.41	- 21.58

Table 7. Offences Against Local Acts (1975 - 1979)

Year	*Figures*	*% of Total Criminality*	*Rates Per 100,000 of Population*	*Annual % Increases/ Decreases*
1975	12,652	6.53	16.98	+ 8.23
1976	19,820	9.24	25.94	+ 56.66
1977	25,425	11.60	32.57	+ 28.28
1978	24,534	11.12	30.44	- 3.50
1979	14,376	7.05	17.28	- 41.40

Source : Crimes prevention for Freedom, Justice, Peace and Development in Nigeria, *The Nigeria National Paper for the 7th United Nation's Congress on Crime Prevention and Treatment of Offenders,* held at Millan, Italy, 26th August—6th September, 1985.

An interesting observation from Table 4-7 which has implication for our conclusions, is that the rate of crime committed under each category of offences tended to decrease towards the tail end of the economic boom i.e. 1978 and 1979. This is particularly true of : offences against persons, social disorganisation crimes and offences against local Acts.

At the beginning of this paper, it was proposed that *a priori*, we expect the rate of crime to be lower during a period of economic boom than during an era of economic crisis. Our analysis so far is instructive : how come the rate of crime was decreasing for most of the offences at a period when the economic boom was fizzling out ? This has indeed raised a fundamental issue concerning the relationship between economic boom and criminality. The question now is : can orthodox notions about the relationship between boom and crime be sustained in the light of available empirical evidence ? This study has shown that crime is increasing during economic boom. This observation contradicts the expectation that there is a negative correlation between economic boom and the rate of crime. We had expected to find a situation whereby the crime rate would decrease significantly during the era of boom. The result of our empirical analysis has been the contrary : crime rate in Nigeria has tended to rise peripasu with economic boom. In other words, contrary to popular opinion, there is rather a positive correlation between economic boom and crime rate in Nigeria.

Economic Crisis and Crime

Conceptually speaking , there is a positive correlation between economic crisis and crime. Generally, economic crisis generates poverty amongst the majority of the populace. And in developing countries, it seems logical to associate their poverty with their criminality or to attribute their increasing criminality to their poverty (Clinard and Abbott, 1973 : 172). Indeed, the Economic and social Council and the Secretariate of the United Nations have observed that "crime problems lie deep in the processes of economic and social development and must be resolved within them" (United Nations, 1966 and 1977).

Poverty and social inequality have been assumed by some scholars to explain the general increase in rates of crime and delinquency in developing countries, in view of the fact that economic deprivation has long been considered a basic cause of the social problems in the more developed societies (Ferman, *etal,* 1965 : 5). Economic writers and social workers, including earlier writers like Henry George, Karl Marx, Charles Booth, Jane Addams, and William Bonger, have recognised the significance of economic factors in social life. According to these scholars, society's failure to provide adequate goods, services, and housing for everyone precipitates crime and allows other forms of deviant behavior to develop, while economic fluctuations and the maldistribution of wealth contribute to these deviations (Clinard and Abbott, 1973 : 173).

That there is a relationship between socio-economic conditions and crime is not very much in doubt. Most persons arrested, prosecuted and imprisoned for crimes are from the lower socio-economic groups. For instance, an average distribution of a sample of offenders arrested in Port Harcourt Metropolis, Nigeria, revealed that about 87.5 percent were very poor, 8.5 percent were poor, 2.5 percent were fairly well off, and 1.5 percent were very well off (Iwarimie - Jaja, 1992).

One implication of our analysis so far is that crime rate is likely to be higher during a period of economic crisis than during boom era. This is because economic crisis is usually accompanied by the impoverishment of a good number of the populace. This impoverishment may result from a rise in the rate of unemployment, drastic fall in real income, frustration, reduced access to basic social services such as health, education, housing etc. Given the one-to-one relationship between poverty and crime pointed out earlier, it therefore means that the problems of crime are likely to worsen during of economic crisis.

But there is a contrary opinion in the literature which argues that crime is not very much related to poverty. For instance, it has been observed that the crime rates of many highly developed countries negate the hypothesis that an increasingly high standard of living and the provision of a variety of social services diminished crime. Infact, a stronger case can be made for the relation of affluence to crime (Galbraith, 1958). Crime rate has increased tremendously over the last century, inspite of a constant rise in the living standards, in countries such as Sweden the United Kingdom, and Germany. Indeed—the two countries with the highest per capita income—Sweden, and the United States—have particularly serious crime problems, Supporting this line of argument, Middendorff (1960 : 41) has equally observed that "improvement in living conditions, or what is called a better standard of living, does not necessarily, by itself, reduce juvenile delinquency." Bergali (1972 : 66) has also argued that if poverty was a cause of crime then all states in Latin America should have a much higher crime rate than the United States, whose income per capita is much greater than any Latin American country. Clearly, poverty, including unemployment and income inequality is neither an excuse nor a justification for committing conventional crimes, such as murder, forcible rape, robbery, aggravated assault, burglary, illegal trafficking and smuggling, etc. During a period of economic crisis, there is usually a long period of seriously reduced business activity and high unemployment. Therefore in capitalist societies, whether in developed or underdeveloped ones, people compete seriously for survival and economic security. In that case, people ignore legitimate means, the right path way and choose to act criminally to obtain their respective social goals—such as material needs. Our argument is supported by Gordon's claims which has been quoted by Box (1985 : 32).

> Capitalist societies depend on basically competitive forms of social and economic interaction and upon substantial inequalities in the allocation of social resources... Driven by the fear of economic insecurity and by a competitive desire to gain some of the goods unequally distributed throughout the society, many individuals will eventually become criminals...

One major conclusion from our analysis so far is that crime is a very complex phenomenon. It is not particularly easy to identify one factor as the sole cause of crime. The argument that economic deprivation leads to crime has been challenged by other scholars (e.g. Stack, 1978; Box, 1985). At this point, we want to examine the nature of the relationship between economic crisis and crime in Nigeria in the light of available statistics. But a priori, we expect a positive correlation between economic crisis and crime. To determine whether statistical data support this expectation. Tables 8-10 are considered.

Table 8 shows general crime figures in Nigeria between 1980-1984.

Table 8. General Crime Figures-True cases (1980-1984)

Year	*Figures*	*% of Total Criminality*	*Rates Per 100,000 of Population*	*Annual % Increases/ Decreases*
1980	210,908	100	245.46	+ 3.52
1981	253,952	100	286.25	+ 20.40
1982	271,240	100	296.11	+ 6.80
1983	311,961	100	329.84	+ 15.01
1984	372,558	100	381.50	+ 19.42

Source : Crime Prevention for Freedom, Justice, Peace and Development in Nigeria, *The Nigeria National Paper for the 7th United Nations Congress on Crime Prevention and Treatment of Offenders*, held at Milan, Italy, 26th August—6th September, 1985.

From Table 8, it can be seen that the rate of crime was on the increase throughout the period. For instance, in 1980 (the beginning of the crisis period) there was 210,908 cases of crime. By 1983, the figure had climbed up to 311,961 and reached an all time high of 372,558 in 1984. The high crime rate recorded during the period of economic crisis would become more glaring if crime are disaggregated into crimes against persons and property as shown in Table 9.

Table 9. Nigeria's Crime Profile (1980-84)

Year	*Person N (%)*	*Property N (%)*	*Miscellaneous N (%)*	*Total N (%)*
1980	55,875 (26.49)	140,625 (66.68)	14,408 (6.83)	210,808 (100)
1981	64,346 (30.54)	91,856 (43.59)	54,515 (25.87)	210,717 (100)
1982	88,433 (30.19)	131,408 (44.86)	73,076 (24.95)	292,917 (100)
1983	93,752 (30.08)	145,607 (46.71)	72,367 (23.21)	311,726 (100)
1984	112,116 (30.34)	187,610 (50.77)	69,796 (18.89)	369,522 (100)

Source : Data were obtained from the Annual Report of the Nigeria Police Force, 1970-1980 and deduced from Tables 9,10,11 and 12 in crime Prevention for Freedom, Justice, Peace and Development in Nigeria, *The Nigeria National Paper for the 7th United Nations Congress on crime Prevention and Treatment of Offenders*, held at Milan, Italy, between 26th August and 6th September, 1985.

Crime against persons was on the increase throughout the period 1980-1984. From 55,875 or 26 percent of the total figure in 1980, the figure for crime against persons increased to 93,752 or 30 percent of the total figure in 1983 and jumped to 112,116 in 1964. Although the figure for crime against property fell in 1981, and 1982 it rose astronomically to 187,610 in 1984. However, there has been generally more crime against property than the person. Between 1980 and 1984, the volume of crime against property (697,106) exceeded that for crime against person (414,522) by 282,584 cases. It is evidenced from Table 9 that crime against property, are frequently committed, despite law enforcement control measures than crime against persons in Nigeria.

Between 1982 and 1986, the number of serious crimes cases reported was greater than that of minor crimes/offences as shown in Table 10.

Table 10. Total Crimes Reported to the Nigeria Police by Type ((1982 - 1986)

	Cases Reported to the Police (Excluding Traffick Offences)		*Cases from which Prosecutions have been instituted*	
Year	*Serious crimes*	*Minor crimes/ Offences*	*Serious crimes*	*Minor crimes/ Offences*
1982	153,221	101,564	90,523	60,005
1983	140,818	118, 192	87,251	73,232
1984	185,548	169,281	91,772	83,726
1985	172,249	157,148	90,401	82,475
1986	160,926	146,818	78,006	71,167

Source : The Nigeria Police Force.

One general conclusion that can be drawn from our overall analysis is that in Nigeria, the crime rate has tended to rise with the severity of economic crisis. A comparison between Tables 3 and 10, for the years 1972-76 and 1982-1986 show that the problems of serious crimes became more acute during the era of economic crisis. When total crime figures for crimes against persons is compared for the periods 1975-1979 and 1980 - 1986 (see Tables 4 and 9), it appears that crimes against persons have higher rates during economic crisis than economic boom period. The same trend applies to crimes against property (see Tables 5 and 9).

One major scenario that has emerged from our discussion so far is that of discerning a correlation between economic crisis/boom and crime. The study has demonstrated with statistical evidence that the rate of crime tended to be quite substantial during the period of economic boom in Nigeria. It was observed that crime rate was invariant with respect to boom and crisis periods. Thus, irrespective of whether there is crisis or boom, the crime rate has tended to be quite high in Nigeria.

This raises a fundamental question : what accounts for the high crime rate in Nigeria during boom and crisis periods ? This question can be resolved within the context of the country's neo-colonial socio-economic structures. The study contends that the rate of crime in Nigeria has remained high because the country's socio-economic arrangement is not only irrational, it is also exploitative and oppressive. For instance, while majority of Nigerians participate in the generation of economic surplus, only a few appropriate a great proportion of this surplus. Consequently, criminality in Nigeria can be properly understood within the context of surplus generation, appropriation and use in the neo-colony. The neo-colonial Nigerian political economy was, and is still, the product of colonial incursion into the Nigerian socio-formation. With the colonial incursion, social inequality which is a legacy of British colonial political economy was introduced and crystallized in post-colonial Nigeria. Social inequality became accentuated as a result of the role which the post-colonial state and its custodians came to play in the neo-colonial political economy. Social inequality made it possible for the society to be divided into the rich and poor, or upper, middle and lower classes. With this arrangement, the subject classes became deprived of their legitimate earned surpluses. Economic deprivations caused by inequality have the implication for the prevalance of crime and criminal tendencies in Nigeria.

Economic inequality breed disharmony, misunder- standing and aggression amongst social classes in post- colonial Nigeria. It generates antagonism within the rank and file of the peasants and workers who are denied access to socially generated surplus. Some of these low ranked persons in the social structure of Nigeria express their resentment in the form violent crimes : armed robbery, arson, etc. This is in conformity with the argument advanced by sociologists such as Schur (1969) and Radzinowicz (1977) to the effect that

> "pronounced differences in the allocation of resources cause less fortunate men to compare their life choices with others and decide that legitimate avenues to material reward must be supplemented by property crime."

Earlier the study discovered that there was no fundamental variation between the rates of crime in the boom and crisis periods. Indeed, the rates remained quite substantial during these periods. This, therefore, suggests that there is an intrinsic causative factor responsible for high crime rate be it during boom or crisis period. What then is this intrinsic causative factor ? The identification of this factor has important policy implications. For instance, policy makers concerned with crime prevention have to tinker with this factor if a lasting solution would be found for the problem of crime in Nigeria.

Some observers have attributed the high rate of crimes in Nigeria during economic boom and crimes to the aftermath of the Civil War (1967-70). However, the scientific status of this argument is questionable. We, therefore, consider the civil war argument as very superficial and pedestal. At any rate, further research is required to determine the relationship between the civil war and the incidence of crime in Nigeria.

Having rejected the civil war thesis, we contend that the pattern of socio-economic inequality which became institutionalized in the post independence era, which was not only reproduced in the post-civil war era, but which became exacerbated, is the critical/causative factor responsible for the high crime rate observed in the 1970s and 1980s. Since independence, Nigeria has been operating in irrational, exploitative and inhumane socio-economic arrangement. The country has been operating a system whereby socially generated economic surplus is privately appropriated by a minority of the population at the exclusion of the toiling majority. This private appropriation of economic surplus is being carried out in the post-civil war era iin the same manner with which it was done in the 1960s.

Thus, although there was economic boom in the 1970s the fruits of that boom were not equitably distributed amongst members of the Nigerian society. The unequal distribution of economic resources continued into the period of economic crisis. The unequal distribution of economic resources was skewed against the subject classes. The majority of the Nigerians who constituted members of the subject classes were denied access to the national economic surplus. This majority were not only deprived of their fair share of the economic surplus, they were forced to live in poverty amidst affluence. They found themselves living in environment where ill-gotten wealth is publicly displayed. In Nigeria, most underprivileged persons believe that the privileged group in society acquired their wealth illegally and through dubious means. The underprivileged, therefore, do not see any reason why he should aspire to acquire wealth through legal and legitimate means.

The implication of our analysis is that whether there is boom or crisis, the crime rate will continue to be high as long as the system of distributing economic surplus remains irrational and unjust.

References

Abba, A. *etal* 1985 *The Nigerian Economic Crisis : Causes and Solutions*, Academic Staff Union of Universities of Nigeria.

Bangura, Y. 1984 "Overcoming some Basic Misconceptions of the Nigerian Economic Crisis." *Studies in Politics and Society*, Issue No. 2 October, 1984.

Bangura, Y. *et al* 1986 "The Deepening Economic Crisis and its Political Implications,"in Saddique Mohammed and Tony Edoh (eds), *Nigeria : A Republic in Ruins.* Dept. of Political Science, ABU, Zaria.

Bergalli, R. 1972 *Criminologica on America Latina* Edicieones Pannedille, Buenos Aires.

Blau, J. and P.M. Blau 1982 The cost of Inequality : Metropolitan Structure and violent Crime,"*American Sociological Review* 47 : 114-129.

Benger, W. 1969 *Criminality and Economic Conditions*, Bloomington Indian a University Press.

Box, S. 1985 *Recession. Crime and Punishment*, Birmingham: University of Birmingham.

Cauter, D. and K.C. Land 1985 "Unemployment and crime rates in the post world War II United States : A theoretical and empirical analysis, "*American Sociological Review* 50 : 317-332.

Carroll, L. and P. Jackson 1983 "Inequality, Opportunity and crime rates in Central Cities, "*Criminology* 21 : 178-194.

Clinard, M.B. and 1990 *Crime in Developing Countries*, New York :

and D.J. Abott		Wiley - Interscience.
Cohen, R.	1990	"Hidden Forms of Workers Consciousness" *Review of African Political Economy No. 19.*
Cohen, L.E., M. Feison and K.C. L.I. and	1980	"Property crime rates in the United States : A Macrodynamic analysis, 1947 - 1977, with ex ante forecasts for the mid—1980s *American Journal of Sociology* 86 : 90-118.
Danziger, S.	1976	"Explaining Urban crime Rates, "*Criminology* 14 : 291-295.
Decker, S.H.	1980	*Criminalization, Victimization and Structural Correlates of Twenty-six American Cities,* Saratega : Century Twenty-one Publishing.
Ferman, L.A. et al	1965	*Poverty in America : A Book of Readings,* Ann Arbar : University of Michigan Press.
Galbraith, J.K.	1958	*The Affluent Society, Boston* : Houghton Mifflin.
Gordon, D.	1981	"Class and Economics of Crimes, "*Review of Radical Political Economy,* (Summer) 1981 : 51-75.
Guerry, A.	1883	*Essai Sur Is statistidue Morale de la France.* Paris : Crechard.
Ileabachie, N.B.	1986	"Salient Features in the Structure of the Nigerian Economy,"in Saddique Mohammed and Tony Edoh (eds), *Nigeria : A Republic in Ruins,* Dept. of Political Science, ABU, Zaria.
Iwarimie-Jaja, D.\	1992	"Unemployment and Armed Robbery, "*Ph.D. Dissertation Memo. Uniport.*
Jacobs,D.	1981	"Inequality and Economic Crimes," *Sociology and Social Research,* Vol. 66. October, 1981 No. 1.
Kornhauser, R.R.	1978	*Social Sources of Delinquency,* Chicago : University of Chicago Press.
Keynes, J.M.	1936	*The General Theory of Employment, Interest and Money.*
Marx, K.	1986	*Capital,* Vol. II Moscow : Progress Publishers.
Messner, S.F.	1982	"Poverty, ineduality and the Urban homicide rate." *Criminology* 20 : 103-114.
Messner, S.F.	1983	"Regional and Racial effect on effect on the Urban homicide rate : The Structure of violence" revised. *American Journal of Sociology* 88: 997-1007.
Middendorff, W.	1960	"The Origin of the New Forms" of Juvenile Delinquency," *in New Forms of Juvenile Delinquency : Their Origin, Prevention and Treatment,* United Nations Publication (A/Conf. 17/7).
Mitchell, W.C.	1997	Business Cycle : The Problem and its Setting, *N. NBER.*

Nwankwe, A.A. 1981 *Can Nigeria Survive ?* Enugu : Fourth Dimension Publishers.

Nweke, A.A. 1981 "Inequality and Instability in Nigeria : The Political Economy of Neo-Colonial Development", "*The Nigerian Journal of Development Studies* Vol. I, No. 1, April 1981.

O'Brien, R.M. 1983 "Metropolitan Structure and Violent Crime, Wich measure of crime ?" *American Sociological Review* 48 : 434-427.

Odife, D. 1989 *Structural Adjustment and Economic Revolution in Nigeria*, Heinemann Educational Books.

Offion, D.A. 1980 *Imperialism and Dependency*, Enugu : Fourth Dimension Publishers.

Quetelet, A. 1835 *Research on the Propensity for Crime* at Different Ages, Trans. S.F. Sylvester, Cincinnati : Anderson (1984).

Radzinowicz, L. 1971 "Economic Pressures, "In Leon Radzinowicz and Marvin E.Wolfgang (eds.) *The Criminal in Society*. New York : Basic Books.

Rosenfeld, R. 1986 "Urban crime rates : Effects of inequality, Welfare dependency, region, and race, "In J.M. Byrne and R.J. Sampson (eds.) *The Social Ecology of Crime*. New York : Spring-Verlag.

Sampson, R.J. 1985 "Neighbourhood and Crime : The Structural determinants of Personal Victimization, "Journal *of Research in Crime and Delinquency* 22 : 7 - 40.

Schur, E.M. 1969 *Our Criminal Society*, New Jersey : Prentice Hall.

Stack, S. 1978 "Macro Sociology, and the Analysis of Suicide Rates, "*Proceedings of the American Association of Suicidology*, 1978 Annual Meetings, New Orleans, Louisiana.

The Economist, 1984 *The Political Economy of Nigeria*, England : The Economist Newspaper Limited.

Usman, Y.B. 1984 "Middlemen, Consultants, Contractors and the Solutions to the Current Economic Crisis, "Studies in Politics and Society : Issues No. 2. October, 1984.

Vold, G.B. and T.J. Bernard 1986 "*Theoretical Cariminology*, New York : Oxford University Press.

Williams, G. 1981 "Nigeria : The Neo-Colonial Political Economy " in Dennis L. Cohen and Jhon Daniel (eds), *Political Economy of Africa*, London :Longman.

Williams, K. 1984 "Economic Sources of Homicide : Reestimating the effects of Poverty and inequality" *American Sociological Review*, 49 : 283-289.

Robert J. Fornaro

SEXUAL PREFERENCE IN AMERICA : A SOCIAL AGENDA DEFERRED

Homosexuality is not new to human culture. Cultural myths and legends are replete with conscious and unconscious references to it. However, despite cultural mythology there exists no unassailable proof that what is understood in the West as homosexual behavior exists in all human cultures and at all stages of human development. Therefore, the phenomena where it does exist should be studied with in its cultural context.

In the United States American homosexuals have become agents of cultural change. They have articulated a social agenda that would radically change the norms and values most Americans live by. The popular press refers to the homosexual social agenda as the "gay rights movement." There has been at least two decades of struggle on the part of homosexuals to end legal and social discrimination. An examination of certain variables, vis a vis the homosexual agenda, reveals that there are regressive forces at play that have the potential of stifling the whole gay rights movement. To support this, contention data on social change was obtained from the life history interviews of forty male and female homosexuals and a review of historical and popular literature. This inquiry began with a study of the homosexual community of Mobile, Alabama in 1981 (Curry and Fornaro, 1981) and continued for ten years. The forty individuals selected for the study, 10 females and 30 males ranged in age from seventeen to forty five. All of the informants were actively engaged in the homosexual life style. During the study all of the informants resided in Mobile, Alabama[1], though many originally came from other parts of the country. Mobile's homosexual community reflects the social realities of most medium size American cities. Variables of social change when they appear in cities like Mobile indicate a significant degree of social acceptance by American culture and society.

Sex Revolution

It has been said that the American culture is preoccupied with sex; its repression and exploitation are powerful themes in American Life (Schur, 1988). Burdened by the Puritan Ethic, the Americans have great difficulty publically discussing sex and sexuality. In the late sixties and early seventies, there was much talk about a "sexual revolution" that on the surface brought a relaxation of sexual norms and growing toleration of "alternate" lifestyles. The political climate, however, was tense with minority unrest and the growing anti-war movement. American homosexuals in their turn were galvanized by an event that took place on June 28, 1969 in New York's Greenwich Village. On the night of June 28 in a series of harassing raids the police entered several homosexual bars, among them the Stone Wall Inn. Traditionally homosexuals accepted the indignities of being questioned and searched by the authorities but this time they reacted violently : "Before the night was over four policemen were hurt as rioters bombarded them with cobblestone bricks from the Village streets, as well as bottles, garbage, pennies and an uprooted parking meter...to many homosexuals, male and female alike, the Stone Wall Rebellion was the shot heard round the world" (Faderman, 1991 :194-5). The Stone Wall Rebellion more than any one even brought into being the "gay liberation movement." Police and city governments throughout the country faced with the possibility of violence began to reassess their relations with the homosexual community.

All of the respondents in this study were aware of the "Stone Wall Rebellion" and seemed to agree that it was both a turning point and an indicator of social change. As one stated "It's funny, that in America you have to get violent to get justice-to get acceptance."

Social Agenda

For many in the homosexual community there was hope that if homosexuals organized and stood up for their rights, like other groups, they could achieve a degree of social acceptance. True social acceptance would signal significant social change and gay men and women could begin to engage in "culture building", e.g. to form same sex family units, to revoke the sodomy laws, to win minority status and to end discrimination in jobs and housing.

It has been over two decades since the Stone Wall

Rebellion and the exposition of the homosexual social agenda. In that time, how has the gay rights movement changed the social landscape of America ? Is there a story of significant gains or are we withnessing a social agenda deferred ?

Religion

Acceptance of the homosexual social agenda poses a problem for America's religious establishment. As of this date no "mainstream" American religious denomination has accepted homosexuality. A "repentant" homosexual may find shelter in some Churches but homosexuality is still condemned as it was during the Inquisition when "a more violent hostility appeared in popular literature and eventually spread to theological and legal writings...all testify to increasing intolerance of deviation from the standards of the majority" (Boswell, 1980 : 334), The Roman Catholic Church and its major Protestant offshoots have not repudiated those "theological and legal writings." Openly homosexual priests and ministers are still removed from their congregations. In addition, recent suits against homosexual priests and ministers for sexual misconduct with children has fed homophobia in America's Churches.

The most virulent opposition to any societal accommodation with homosexuality comes from America's fundamentalist churches. These churches rely on the literal interpretation of the Bible and preach vigorously against the gay lifestyle. In the South and in cities like Mobile their "missionary representatives" set up "rescue missions" in areas frequented by homosexuals : "Nevertheless most churches remain hostile to homosexuality; and this antipathy is probably the major impediment to gay peoples integration into the Mobile community. Two churches maintain missions in the downtown area with the explicit goal of "curing" homosexuals by means of conversion to fundamental Christianity" (Curry and Fornaro, 1981 :83). The homosexuals interviewed expressed universal antipathy toward the fundamentalists, especially those that shouted at them from street corners. Several informants have had violent confrontations with the "missionaries." These confrontations have led to a hardening of religious opposition in Mobile to the homosexual agenda.

In Alabama, in 1992, the Religious Right was instrumental in passing legislation restricting the use of state funds by homosexual organizations in the State's colleges and universities. The constitutionality of the new law is now being tested in the courts. The fact that the new law was passed almost unanimously in the legislature is an indication of the depth of public opposition to "gay rights" in the state.

Misogyny

On a deeper psychological level the identification of male homosexuality with feminine traits is perceived as a threat to male socialization. American men view themselves as highly masculine, and American socialization still strongly differentiates between male and female role. Boys are still taught to disparage female traits and to avoid female behavior. American cultural norms support the latent antifeminism or misogyny historically present in Western Culture and : "Homophobia, many theorists hold is driven by misogyny, by the perception that gays are like girl (hence "fairly" "pansy" "sissy" "queen" and even "faggot" all words that relate, if only in their derivation, to degraded states of femininity)" (Solomon, 1993 :25). Homosexuality has no place in the John Wayne/Rambo milieu of American maleness. The American male cultural image is a product of America's frontier past. A past that lionizes the hunter, explorer, scout, cowboy and military hero. Women play only a minor role and homosexuals no role at all in America's frontier mythology.

It is interesting to note that most of the male homosexuals interviewed, 70% rated themselves slightly higher in so called feminine, characteristics, e.g. being affectionate, compassionate, gentle, loving, sensitive, sympathetic, tender, understanding and warm. However, several subjects mentioned that while they identified with the above traits they did so only in the confidential atmosphere of the interview. Publicly they would not "admit" to having characteristics so detrimental to their maleness. The continued identification of male homosexuality with female traits by the general public remains an impediment to social change. Also, in the homosexual community the antipathy toward women among male homosexuals pointed to the fact that "connections between the gay male and lesbian communities had been problematic over the years...A major cultural gap existed" (Miller, 1989 :153) In Mobile, "Gay men occasionally expressed an exaggerated spirit of male superiority in statements of social preference for males or more blatantly in assertions of distaste for women. Many gay males find lesbian rhetoric inspired by the women's movement condemning male behavior offensive since the last thing male homosexuals feel they are capable of doing is to exploit women" (Curry and Fornaro, 1981 : 82).

For their part radical lesbian-feminists view males including homosexual males with anger and suspicion. Some felt that "American culture was in deep trouble and drastic measures were required to reverse its unwise course. Since they were convinced through feminism that the root of the problem was male-caused by the greed, egocentrism and violence that came along with testosterone or male socialization—" (Faderman, 1991 : 216). Male-female antipathy within the homosexual community, while in keeping with dominant cultural themes, has the potential of seriously weakening the gay rights movement. However, for the moment, lesbians and gay males in America still support the homosexual social agenda.

Sodomy Laws

It is not against the law in the United States to be a homosexual; however, in forty two states there are "sodomy laws" that make oral and anal intercourse criminal acts. Only seven states have removed criminal penalties for any private consensual sex acts, and every state has laws prohibiting sexual acts in public. Generally there has been little change in the sodomy laws and a recent Supreme Court case upheld the constitutionality of Georgia's sodomy statute. The effort to repeal the sodomy laws, an important variable in the homosexual social agenda, is for the time being dead in the water. Most homosexuals feel that the existence of these laws poses a latent threat to the social changes homosexuals desire.

Same Sex Families

Same sex families exist in every American community but none enjoy the legal sanction or protections of heterosexual marriage. In the United States no same sex bonding or homosexual marriages are legally recognized. So far every attempt at legal recognition has failed. Homosexual couples cannot sue for divorce, alimony, or child support. In Mobile lesbian family units were studied in depth and not surprisingly they manifested characteristics present in traditional family units. While lesbian family units are more likely to have children present, there was a growing number of male units with children. Children in lesbian families were usually present as a result of heterosexual divorce or in rare cases invetro-fertilization.

The Lesbian family units in Mobile functioned in much the same way traditional families did. As one respondent noted "the meals have to be made—the garbage taken out—the bills paid—regardless of your sexual preferences." (Curry and Fornaro, 1981 : 80). There were no gender identification problems. Children were fully aware of their male or female identities. The lesbian mothers interviewed were anxious to pass on traditional roles to their children and not predetermine sexual preference. Pre-adolescent children identified with their biological mothers and seemed to accept their mother's "companion" as a member of the family. The children were fully aware that they had fathers and that they, like many other "divorce children" just did not live with them. There was no evidence that any of the women involved in these relationships tried to be a father substitute. Tension usually developed as male children reached puberty. The pressures of male sex role identification brought in external variables that undermind the lesbian mother's authority. Many boys chose to live with their fathers at this juncture if they had the option.

Another threat to the homosexual family unit is adolescent peer pressure. Children of homosexual family units, when publically identified, can face substantial peer harassment which disrupts family life. The fact that homosexual families have no legal status makes them vulnerable to destructive social pressures. Until same sex marriage is legally recognized there is little hope that such family units will achieve social acceptability.

Employment

Homosexuals hold a variety of jobs throughout the American economy, but many risk being terminated if their sexual preference becomes public knowledge. Only 10% of the homosexuals inerviewed acknowledged being gay in their work place. Most felt that if their employers knew they were gay they would be fired. In a recent case a lesbian waitress was fired from a national chain restaurant. The Mobile homosexual community joined a nationwide "sit in" to protest the restaurant's policy. The case in now in the courts. Homosexuals who held professional or semiprofessional jobs were less concerned about being fired than those holding jobs at the lower end of the employment spectrum.

The Military

The subject of gays in the military has recently received much attention. Historically the American military has vigorously pursued exclusionary policies to prevent the enlistment or retention of homosexuals in all branches of the armed services. The attitude of the military is expressed by Navy instruction

1900. 9A "Members involved in homosexuality are military liabilities who cannot be tolerated in a military organization. In developing and documenting cases involving homosexual conduct, commanding officers should be keenly aware that members involved in homosexual acts are security and reliability risks who discredit themselves and the naval service by their homosexual conduct. Their prompt separation is essential". (Boggan and Haft, 1975 : 44-5).

Thousands of homosexuals have and do serve in the American military but over the past decade the armed services have spent 500 million dollars to remove them. Recently the newly elected President William Clinton proposed lifting the ban on homosexuals in the military. Clinton stated : "The issue is not whether there should be homosexual in the military. Everyone concedes that there are. The issue is whether men and women who can and have served with real distinction should be excluded from military service solely on the basis of their status...and I believe they should not." (Ridgeway, 1993, p. 21) Clinton's announced intention to use his executive authority to remove the ban on homosexuals caused a firestorm of opposition. The Joint Chiefs of Staff unanimously opposed the lifting of the ban as "detrimental to troop morale" and "military preparedness." Key members of Congress from both Parties refused to support Clinton and the President was forced to accept a six month moratorium on the question.

The armed services traditionally has served American culture as a vehicle of social change. Integration of American Blacks was ordered in the military before it became the law of the land. Women in the military have been instrumental in breaking down the occupational barriers that mandated "male only" jobs. The Dutch and Canadian armies have successfully integrated both women and homosexuals with no perceivable loss in moral or efficiency. However, in the United States the opposition to admitting homosexuals to the military has strong public support and the issue is destined to be fought out in the courts. As it stands now homosexuals in the military and in most occupations are still being discriminated against.

A.I.D.S.

A.I.D.S. has been called "the plague of the twentieth century" "the gay disease." In the United States it first appeared in the homosexual community and has since killed thousands of homosexuals and according to one author, "It was quite possible that the progress and increasing options gays and lesbians were beginning to enjoy would eventually be overwhelmed by the magnitude of the A.I.D.S. epidemic". (Miller, 1989 : 307). The relentless progression of the disease is a clear and present danger to the homosexual social agenda : "Hand in hand with A.I.D.S. came the threat of repression, the growing power of the anti-gay religious right...reports of delegates to the 1988 Republican National Convention in New Orleans physically attacking gay protesters, shouting, 'A.I.D.S. in not a disease-it's a cure !' vividly illustrated the extent of homophobia that the epidemic had brought to the surface" (Ibid : 308), Recent statistics show that the epidemic is slowing in the homosexual community but is on the rise among Blacks and Hispanics. Many homosexuals feel that because the disease disproportionally effects homosexuals and certain minorities the government is dragging its feet in trying to find a cure. In fact, the Senate, on February 18, 1993, reflecting a fear of A.I.D.S., voted 76 to 23 to prevent people with the A.I.D.S. virus from immigrating to the United States. The House endorsed the Senate vote to keep AIDS-infected immigrants out of the country and the "Lawmakers voted 278-139 Thursday to bar further funding of Project Aries, a national project that provides free anonymous telephone counseling to men...gay and bisexual men on how to avoid unsafe sex...the debate came as the National Gay and Lesbian Task Force said violence against gay, lesbian and bisexual Americans rose to record highs...the group also concluded that violence against homosexuals in the military is on the rise" (*Mobile Press* March 13, 1993) Fear of A.I.D.S. within and without the homosexual community is having a detrimental impact on the homosexual social agenda. Its effects are certainly evident in the informant interviews taken since 1987. The optimism of the early respondents about the prospects of social change has given way to fear and a morbid preoccupation with the disease. As one respondent stated : "This (AIDS) gives them one more reason to hate us and it will probably wipe us out anyway...I don't think they will ever find a cure, and if they do it will come too late for me." One respondent recently died of the disease at the age of 28 and at least three more have tested H.I.V. positive. The feeling among many homosexuals is that finding a cure for A.I.D.S is a question of survival, and as such supercedes any other aspects of the homosexual social agenda because "In every branch of culture—dance, theatre, literature, music, design, fashion, and television, movies—the devastation from A.I.D.S. continues (David Ansen, 1993 :16).

Current Regressive Trends

President Clinton's attempt to remove the gay ban in the military has galvanized right wing opposition : "in a dozen states around the country organizers are preparing ballot measures patterned after an initiative in Colorado last November (1992) repealing gay rights laws in Denver, Aspen and Boulder and preventing any other such laws at the state or local level...'we are trying to defeat the homosexual agenda' says Ms. Mullins of the Traditional Values Coalition, an Anaheim California-based organization with a lobbying office in Washington, D. C. that represents about 25,000 churches in the United States: (Knickerbocker Feb. 1993 : 4). According to the "agenda" opponents gay rights laws create a special protected status under civil rights that allows homosexuals to establish the acceptability of homosexuality. Scott Lively of the Oregon Citizen's Alliance states : "Homosexuality is not a healthy thing, not something we want to allow to be legitimized by our public institutions" (1993), Lively and the O.C.A. tried unsuccessfully to pass an anti-gay measure that "linked homosexuality with pedophilia, sadism, and masochism, and it would have required schools and state agencies to label such behavior as 'abnormal, wrong, unnatural and perverse...to be discouraged and avoided" (1993). In addition, since homosexuals engage in high risk sexual practices and have a greater potential for contracting sexually transmitted diseases like A.I.D.S. they should not be allowed to work around children, the sick or the elderly.

Minority Status

Being recognized as a minority is a goal of the homosexual social agenda. Homosexuals are "beginning to think of themselves as constituting a minority, sharing problems similar to those of other oppressed minority groups and having to struggle for their rights against the dominant heterosexual majority.: (Karina Walters and Jane Simoni, 1993 : 94).

However, many minority groups resent the attempts by homosexuals to be declared a "minority" worthy of government protection and aid. With a per-capita income estimated at over $40,000 per year the minorities feel that gays do not need government assistance. With social welfare money so limited establishing homosexuals as a recognized minority would deprive the "real" minorities of needed resources.

Conclusion

Considering the regressive variables present in the

American social paradigm the changes homosexuals have been hoping for still seem remote. Internal and external variables make the process of acceptance slow and agonizing. There are even signs of regression as powerful groups single out the homosexual social agenda as a threat to morality and family values. If enacted, the laws recommended by these groups could expose homosexuals to increased discrimination. Data collected from the informant interviews suggests that over the decade individual homosexuals are more aware of the social and political difficulties they face and that at the present time the changes in attitude norms and values they hoped for are not coming to fruition. The homosexual social agenda has been deferred, stalled by A.I.D.S. and growing social and political opposition. However, it would be inappropriate to underestimate the intellectual and political resources of the homosexual community. Homosexuals have learned how to politically organize and the United States now has a President committed to ending discrimination against them. In Congress 140 members of the House are poised to amend the Civil Rights Act to include homosexuals so change is still possible. (Knickerbocker, p.4). However, in light of the variables cited in this study, true social change is still a long way off. But, for America's homosexuals "there is no going back;" social change can be temporarily deferred but not ultimately stopped.

References

Ansen, David	1993	"The Lost Generation." *Newsweek*, Jan. 18, pp. 16-20.
Bogan, E. Carrington, Marilyn G. Haft, Charles Lister and John P. Rupp	1975	*The Rights of Gay People : The Basic ACLU Guide to a Gay Person's Rights.* New York : Avon Press.
Boswell, John	1980	*Christianity, Social Tolerance, and Homosexuality : Gay People in Western Europe from the Beginning of the Christian Era to the Fourteenth Century.* Chicago : The University of Chicago Press.
Curry, G. David and Robert J. Fornaro	1981	"The Issue of Sexual Preference in Mobile. South Alabama Toward 2000." Howard F. Mahan, ed. Mobile : *The South Alabama Review*, pp. 78-84.
Faderman, Lillian	1991	*Odd Girls and Twighlight Lovers : A History of Lesbian Life in Twentieth Century America*, New York : Penguin Books, pp.

		194-195.
Miller, Neil	1989	*In Search of Gay America : Women and Men in a Time of Change.* New York : Harper and Row, pp. 109, 153, 248-249.
Muller-Christiansen, Konrad	1993	New Findings Bring New Questions. "Stymied in the AIDS Struggle." Frankfurter Rundshau in *World Press Review*, Feb. pp. 24-25.
	1993	"Safe sex program gets ax. "*Mobile Press*, Mobile : March 12 pp. 8-A.
Schur, Edwin M.	1988	*The Americanization of Sex.* Philadelphia : Temple University Press.
Solomon, Alisa	*1983*	"An Army of Others :Why the Gay Ban Makes the Man." *The Village Voice, Feb.9, 38 : 25.*
Walters, Karina L. and Jane M. Simoni	*1993*	"Lesbian and Gay Male Group Identity Attitudes and Self-Esteem : Implications for Counseling." *Journal of Counseling Psychology, 40; 94-99.*

Marion J. Rice

DEVELOPING NATIONS AND ECONOMIC STEREOTYPING

In the post World-War II years, an academic and economic explosion occurred in the theory and practice of development. The elaboration of models and recommendations and descriptions of field practices have spawned a vast literature. The pursuit of development, the granting and administration of loans, the design and implementation of projects, and the institutionalization of international and national development agencies have created what might be termed a development industry. This development industry has its own political agenda, bureaucracies, and career personnel, sometimes trained in degree programs in development, who migrate from one project to another.

The particular vocabulary of modern development arose with Western proposers of aid and accepted by nations with weaker economies who hoped to benefit from Western largesse. The concept of development implies both a process and a desired condition, and thus involves a dichotomy of an imperfect with an ideal or desired condition. Over time, the concept itself developed, from the emphasis on a condition, such as President Truman's use of the term "underdeveloped areas" In initiating the Point Four Program in 1949;[1] to that of the Third World and non alignment emerging from the 1955 Bandung Conference in Indonesia (Balandier, 1956 :369) and then to the more politically correct appellation of "developing country" by the 1970s. (Myint, 1964). Some Latin American economists showed an independent streak in interpreting development in terms of dependency relationships (Cardoso & Faletto, Ho, 1964).

But whatever the terms in vogue, they became shorthand for all the defects alleged to accompany a non-industrialized world and a synonym for agrarian economies characterized by poverty, ill health, low educational level, an abuse or misuse of resources, and a maldistribution of wealth. At the same time, the experts, either Western or Western-trained, also made the value assumptions that poverty and its accompanying indicators reflected the neglect of market economy and the absence of democratic political processes.

Dichotomization of the world into developed—industrialized—and developing—agricultural—countries carried some implicit value assumptions that often went unexamined. The first assumption was that industrialization and participation in international trade, driven by a market economy, was a good in itself. Derivative subsidiary advantages would naturally follow—an increase in the standard of living, higher consumption of goods and services, increasing levels of education, and better access to health services. A second assumption was that the cultural values and practices of nations and areas, not in harmony with the Western capitalist development ethic, should be modified or adapted to those of the lending or aiding country, such as the United States, or agency, such as the World Bank (International Bank for Reconstruction and Development) or IDA (International Development Association). The latter was established to extend loans to the poorest countries on more generous terms than to World Bank-funded countries, whose loan terms are shorter and at the prevailing market rates of interest.

The development literature is replete with studies of development projects which have not succeeded. The question of critical importance for the Western model of development is not the record of development in various countries as much as the extent to which the so-called developed nations have been able to achieve development goals for themselves which they recommend for undeveloped countries, such as full employment, reduced poverty, and increasing levels of health, education, and general living. The usual development literature takes the gross country indicators for countries designated developed and compares those indicators with those of developing countries. Such country-wide data inevitably show the superiority of the developed to the developing country, with the implication that all developing countries have to do is to follow the model of the developed countries. When within country variation—by area, ethnic group, or producing sector—is examined,however, it is often found that developed countries have problems of unequal development that have existed for decades. This is true of the United States, which is often pictured as at the apogee of development, an exemplar to be emulated by developing countries.

Within the United States, the South continues to be most depressed economic area of the country; the African American, hereafter referred to as Black, continues to be the largest underprivileged minority within the nation and the South; and within the nation and states, rural counties continue to decline in population and prosperity. My home state of Georgia reflects a phenomenon becoming all too common—of job-generating, wealth-producing metropolitan counties, satellite to a core city, which prompt in-migration, and of job-losing rural counties with an almost extinct agricultural base which encourages out-migration (Wheelers, 1986). This has led to a discussion of Two Georgias—of prosperous urban areas, with all the privileges that high income implies; and poor rural areas, with all the shortfalls in health, education, housing, and depressed living standards that low income entails.[2]

This paper is about the importance of considering within-country data in development studies and comparisons rather than relying on the macro-country data which are common to international reporting, such as in the country data of the United Nations, United Nations Children's Fund, International Bank for Reconstruction and Development (World Bank), and other organizations. In any country there exists regional variation. A cursory look at physical maps of the world—topography, climate, soils, minerals, vegetation—shows that not only within large but even within small countries there is considerable variation; resources are not evenly distributed. Physical resource differences are directly related to population distributions, and pre-industrial areas of high population density, described in the sixteenth century, such as the alluvial plains of China and India, continue to be areas of high density.

Then there is the matter of history and culture of different groups within countries. While all human beings everywhere appear to do similar things—live in families, care for the young, conduct rites for the dead, provide for the fundamental needs of food, shelter, and clothing—they do not do these things in the same ways. Ethnic and racial differences, which become preserved in cultural differences, persist over time.

The theme of this paper will be developed by showing the long effects of ethnicity, history, and culture on the development of the South within the United States. Next to Whites of European origin, Blacks of African origin have been the largest ethnic group in the country. Throughout its history, first as colonies of Britain and then as an independent country, the United States has had a large Black population with a regional distribution which concentrated them in the rural economy of the South. It is only since 1960 the Blacks have become legally integrated throughout the country, a short time to overcome handicaps of status, prejudice, and lower income.

Black Population Distribution. Blacks have always been found throughout the territory of the United States. While their percentage distribution in the South has declined, the early nineteenth century area in which they were concentrated still has over of the Black population, as shown in Table 1.

Table 1a. **Percentage of Black Population by Region in the United States, 1860 and 1991.**

Region	*1860*[1]	*1991*[2]
South	87.5	55.1
Northeast	8.2	18.0
Midwest	4.2	19.5
West	0.1	7.4
U.S.	14.1	12.0

Table 1 b. **Total Population of United States and Percent Black**

	1860 *x 1,000*	*1991* *x1,000*
Total Population	31,443	248,710
Black	4,442	29,986
U.S. % Black	14.1	12.0
Georgia % Black	44.0	27.0

Sources :

1. Compiled from 1860 Population of the United States, Population of States and Territories by Color, pp. 598-599.
2. Bureau of the Census, Current Population Reports, P-20, 464, The Black Population in the United States, March 1991.

Push-pull factors have contributed to substantial out-migration from the South of both Blacks and Whites. For both the underlying causes were economic—the collapse of cotton culture and the attraction of better salaries and jobs outside the region. In the case of Blacks there was the added incentive of more personal freedom. The historical legacy as well as continuation of a large Black presence in the South helps to set off the South from other sections of the country. Prior to 1865, the status of most Blacks in the South was that of slaves. But for another 100 years, racial separation was maintained by a system of legal restraints, while outside the South prejudice and custom were handicaps to Black advancement. Only in the latter part of the 20th century has the American Black citizen begun to achieve equity in a White-dominated society. But there was intermingling of Blacks and Whites in the South, and much that is regarded as distinctively Southern—in speech, food, human relations, cultural values, and religiosity—is a product of Black-White interaction.

Urbanization. Throughout the world, as well as the United States, there is a tendency for more people to live in cities and their suburbs. Urbanization does not imply a mere change of residence for human beings, but a change in their styles of work, play, and general living. In the past sixty years, the urban-rural distribution for Georgia and the Southeast has reversed as shown in Table 2.

Table 2. Percentage of Urban and Rural Population

	1930		*1990*	
	Urban	*Rural*	*Urban*	*Rural*
United States	56.2	44.8	75.2	24.8
Southeast	29.4	70.6	68.6	31.4
Georgia	30.8	69.2	63.2	36.8
Rural Farm		43.9		1.2
Rural		25.3		35.5

Source : *Statistical Abstract of the United States*, 1933, 1993; *The Georgia Country Guide 1993*, Extension Service, University of Georgia.

The shift in Georgia from a rural to an urban state is indeed dramatic, but even more telling is the loss of rural farm population, one might say, collapse. This is a sorely neglected subject in the United States, where agricultural economists emphasize the total contribution of agribusiness to the economy—the processing of farm materials as well as all the manufacturing and processing of goods destined for and relating to farm production. This only serves to inflate the role of agriculture in the economy, and to divert attention from the human as well as economic costs of the abandonment of people-based agriculture for machine-pesticide-insecticide-fertilizer field factories.

Table 2 indicates that there is still a large rural population in Georgia, but it no longer derives sustenance from an agricultural economic base as much as it does from jobs related to government, military bases, scattered industry, and welfare and Social Security payments. The result is a very fragile economic base for the thousands of people who live in a rural, non-farm Georgia. The people who still live in the country are not dependent on a country economy and are no longer country oriented, but looking for a means of escape. This is one of the reasons why development and stimulus packages, worked out in cooperation with various government agencis, rarely succeed; the local people involved are no longer looking to the land for sustenance.

Sectorial Economic Collapse : Agriculture. Sixty years ago almost one half of Georgia's population was rural farm; today it is one percent. Even then farm prices were so low that farm income was only 17.5 percent of Georgia personal income. While net fram income in 1990 was six times what it was in 1930, net fram income has been dwarfed by the tremendous increase in Georgia personal income. It is now less than one percent, as shown in Table 3.

Table 3. Changes in the Agricultural Sector, 1930-1990, Georgia (1987 Census of Agriculture Figures*

	1930	*1990*
Georgia Population	3,000,000	6,500,000
Rural Farm Population	1,418,500	80,083*
% Rural Farm	48.8	1.2
Number Farm Operators (Owners, Managers, Croppers, and Tenants)	255,598	43,552*
% Croppers and Tenants	68.2	—
*Georgia Personal Income (Millions)	889	110,860
Farm Income (Cash)	156	1,076
Per Capita Farm Income (dollars)	110	13,436
Personal Income (dollars)	306	14,354
Per Capita U.S. Personal Income ($)	619	15,898

Sources : U.S. Bureau of the Census, *Statistical Abstract*, 1933, 1993 Tables No. 66, 438, 1086; Georgia *County Data Book*, 1993; Bureau of Economic Analysis, U. S. Department of Commerce, State Personal Income : 1929-1982.

Today farm problems and farm concerns receive little attention in the United States and in Georgia. Loss of population indicates a loss of political clout; decline in income share has meant declining political importance. But these figures conceal the human dimensions of the problem. During the period 1930 to 1990, the population increased 123 percent, from three to six and a half million. But during this period, mainly since 1960, a million and a half farm people had to be absorbed by other economic activities. This meant that Georgia growth has been very uneven—booming cities, abandoned farm houses and hamlets. From 1930 to 1990, 53 Georgia counties lost population, and today one out of three of Georgia's 159 counties had more people in 1900 than in 1990.

Urban as well as rural problems have arisen from the collapse of Georgia agriculture as an important employment sector. Historically, rural counties in the South and in Georgia have had an educational system that has not been as good as those of urban areas. Rural migrants to towns, White as well as Black, carried with them a low level of education and a lack of job skill adaptability. The tremendous expansion in urban social disargamization in the South and in Georgia is a by-product of the lack of a rural infrastructure to provide for the welfare of its people. As both Whites and Blacks in metropolitan areas improve their status, move to the suburbs, and leave the inner city, the people left behind in urban Georgia are some of the nation's poorest and least educated. (Bachtel, 1992 : P,51);

The 53 counties losing population have been characterized by Bachtel as "declining rural Georgia." The problems characteristic of these counties read like a litany for Third World countries : lack of jobs, low levels of education and technical knowledge, poor health services and lack of access to health facilities, an inadequate infrastructure, and low incomes. The continued out-migration of the rural working-age population leaves behind a disproportionate number of people in their dependent years—the very young and the old. In an agricultural society, such people are able to make an economic contribution to the well being of their families, but in a "developed" economy the only role the young and old fill is that of dependents. In eighty of Georgia's countries-half-twenty percent or more of personal income depends on transfer payments, mainly government pensions assistance, and direct welfare. However, the overall Georgia transfer payment rate of thirteen percent is less than the United States transfer rate of fifteen percent.

The social costs of permitting the family farm to disappear in most of the South has been only indirectly examined (Fite, 1984 : 222). But the emphasis mainly on productivity and the neglect of people in the equation ill fits the United States to be a model for agricultural development in the world. It emphasizes large, mechanized producing units, and where labor is involved for vegetable and fruit crops, the use of low-paid, migrant workers. While the image of the independent farmer has been extolled in the history of the United States, this image has all too often obscured the role of farm laborers who existed at the mere subsistence level—of indentured laborers and transported convicts, of Black slaves brought from Africa, of lowly European immigrants, and, more recently, the Hispanic migrant worker.

While most Hispanics, mainly of Mexican origin, head for the urban areas where there are greater job opportunities, large numbers of the less skillful, legal as well as illegal, are recruited as migrant laborers in vegetable fields and orchards where a large amount of hand labor is still required. Whether in urban or rural counties, they tend to be concentrated in lower paying wage brackets. Prior to 1990, Hispanics in Georgia fell into the amorphous "Other" category, not White or Black, but in 1990 were separately identified, as shown in Table 4.

Table 4. Persons of Hispanic Origin, 1990, in Georgia.

	Number	Percent
Total	108,922	100.0
In 41 Metropolitan Statistical Area Counties	70,948	65.1
Rural	37,974	34.9

Source : Compiled from *The Georgia County Guide, 1993*, pp. 149-150.

The dynamics of job replacement is not well understood, but Hispanics now carry out jobs which once were filled by Black workers. It is not known to what extent Hispanic immigration and employment have contributed to unemployment among Blacks.

Ethnicity and Income. Many countries have ethnic groups, which, despite their long presence, have not attained the level of income enjoyed by a dominant population. Some disadvantaged populations are indigenous to a country, scuh as the Ainu in Japan and the scheduled castes and tribes of India. Others are mixed populations, as in Mexico, where in 1970 55 percent of the population was mestizo, 29 percent Indian, and 15 percent of European origin. Others have been imported, such as Black slaves to the New World to replace the heavy losses in Indian workers resulting from the diseases of White contact. Although the Black slave population of the southern United States has been emancipated since the Civil War, the living and educational condition of Blacks was not perceived as a national Problem until President Roosevelt's New Deal policies of the 1930s. Interest was revived with the Civil Rights movement of the 1960s and President Johnson's Great Society programs. While much has been achieved in favor, of blacks since desegregation in the armed services, school, and the work place, it has been difficult to maintain a sustained government thrust to improve the economic status of the Negro because special compensatory efforts, called "affirmative action" have often been met with White charges of reverse discrimination.

Instead of the racial reconciliation that was advocated by Martin Luther King, Jr. in the 1960s, the 1990s are marked with reports of growing tension. Sometimes these are greatest in large cities outside of the South, where there are large concentrations of Blacks. But racial conflicts have occurred on college campuses where traditionally it is expected that education and social background ameliorate racial attitudes. On the part of Whites, there is a growing weariness with the idea of responsibility for Black improvement, a spirit not unlike that which took over in the 1870s and left the South alone to "handle" its racial problem. On the part of the Blacks, there is a growing tendency to blame Whitey for their problems and to embrace the confrontational policies of Malcolm X in preference to the more moderate social change policies advocated by Martin Luther King, Jr. Prejudice and discrimination toward Blacks is not a monopoly of the South; it is found throughout the United States.

One of the most important indicators of the status of an ethnic group in a country is the income for that population, compared to that of the dominant population. Money is necessary to provide both the material and social amenities of life, from good housing and food to education and recreation, and thus a low income level is normally associated with everything from infant mortality and longevity rates to educational attainment.

Historically, in slavery times Blacks were maintained at a subsistence level, a condition that existed until fairly recent times through a combination of low productivity in a rural economy and discriminatory economic practices. There are no good longitudinal census data comparing per capita income data of Blacks and Whites until 1947 for the United States. In that year, 81.1 percent of the Black population had incomes of under $3,000 a year compared to 46.2 percent for Whites.[3]

A 1938 Georgia report gave comparative wage data by sex and race for 36 establishments for males and 18 for females. A compilation is summarized in Table 5a and 5b.

Table 5a. Weekly Wages in Cotton Textiles in Dollars, c. 1937, Georgia

Sex	White $	F % of White Male	Black $	F % of White Male	Black % of White
Male	$ 17.56		$ 11.58		66.0
Female	14.90	84.9	8.42	47.9	57.0

Table 5b. Weekly Wages by Race for 36 Establishments Male and 18 female, Georgia, c. 1937

Male	$ 23.51		$ 12.40		52.7
Female	14.82	63.0	8.36	35.6	57.5

Source : Georgia, *Second Annual Report of the Department of Labor*, Atlanta, 1938.

These data show that there was a substantial difference in salaries—females by race made less than males of the same race and Blacks of both sexes made only a little over half as much as Whites. These employment data do not take into consideration the wages or incomes received by Blacks on the farm or in domestic work, where most were employed. In the 1930s, Black female domestics generally were paid from $ 2.50 to $3.00 a week, and, in many cases, women the most stable earners in a Black family or household. The Black female domestic, once common in White households, has now practically disappeared from the South, a casualty of low wages as well as Black perception of economic exploitation by White employers and unwillingness to work for payments which were often less than income offered by government welfare.

In the 1930s, Black farm laborers were underemployed seasonal workers, making fifty to seventy-five cents a day, sometimes with board. Because of low ten-year cotton prices, cropper income on half-shares netting five bales meant gross incomes of about $275, a per capita income for a family of 4.5 of $ 62.0, ten percent of United States per capita income in 1930 (Table 3), for 1930-1939. No wonder President Roosevelt in 1938 characterized the South as "the nation's No. 1 economic problem."[4]

Statistical comparisons of Black and White income by state and region do not begin until 1947, but the figures of personal income by state (which include all races) show an astronomical increase in per capita personal income on 1990, as shown in Table 6.

Table 6. Per Capita Income, U.S. and Georgia, 1930-1990, in Current Dollars.

	1930	*1990*	*Pop. % Black of Area*
United States per capita ($)	$ 619	$18,639	12.0
Southeast	—	16,057	
Georgia	306	17,436	27.0
Connecticut (highest)	919	26,022	8.3
Mississippi (lowest)	202	12,709	36.5

Sources : Bureau of the Census, *Consumer Personal Income, 1929-1982; Consumer Income, 1990,* Current Population Reports, Series p-60.

Generally speaking, states which have a high percentage of Black population have a lower per capita income than states which have a small percentage of Blacks. Connecticut, the highest per capita income state, and Mississippi, the lowest, present two extremes : Connecticut is a bedroom state to the New York Metropolitan area while Mississippi has the largest percentage of Blacks of any of the states in 1990.

Blacks as well as Whites have shown income increases since 1967 in family median income.

Table 7. U.S. Median Family Income, 1967 and 1990, by Race, in Current and Consumer Price Index (CPI) Adjusted 1990

	1967			1990		
	Current	*%Black of White*	*CPI*	*Current*	*% Black of White*	*CPI*
White	8,234		29,647	36,915		36,915
Black	4,875	59.1	17,553	21,423	58.0	21,423

Source : *Consumer Income*, 1990, Series P-60, No. 174, Table B-14.

While incomes increased for both races as shown in Table 7, the relative standing of the percentage of Black income remained at below 60 percent of White income over the 23-year period. This percentage differential in 1990 is very similar to that in weekly wage rates for Blacks and Whites in Georgia in 1930 (Tables 5a and 5b). Table 8 compares family mean and aggregate income distribution by fifths for Blacks and Whites.

Tables 8. Family Mean and Aggregate Income by Fifths, 1974 in Current Dollars, 1990 in Current Price Index Adjusted Dollars (CPI).

		Dollar Mean Income (Current)						
		First Fifth	*Second Fifth*	*Third Fifth*	*Fourth Fifth*	*Fifth Fifth*	*Top 5%*	*Total*
1947	White	1,004	2,267	3,159	4,237	7,917	12,935	3,717
	Black	433	1,038	1,612	2,398	4,594	6,932	2,015
		1991 CPI Adjusted Dollars						
1990	White	11,834	85,778	38,568	54,723	101,161	159,o82	46,406
	Black	4,721	12,325	23,394	36,295	67,860	99,563	28,714
		Percent Distribution of Aggregate Income GINI Ratio						
1947	White	5.4	12.2	17.0	22.8	42.6	17.4	
	Black	4.3	10.3	16.0	23.8	45.6	17.2	
1990	White	5.1	11.1	16.6	23.6	43.6	17.1	0.384
	Black	3.3	8.6	15.6	25.3	47.3	17.3	0.445

Source : Historical Statistics, 1970, Series G, 31-138; *Consumer Income 1992*, Table B-7.

In terms of mean income, the Black percentage of White increased from 54.2 percent to 61.9 percent, but at the expense of the lowest three quintiles, which had less of aggregate Black income in 1990 than in 1947. The GINI ratio, a measure of inequity in income distribution, rose for both Whites and Blacks from 1967 to 1990, but was greater for Blacks.

While considering aggregate income percentages by quintile, it might be useful to compare United States distribution with that which prevails in some other countries. It is common in geography or social studies school texts in the United States to characterize a developing country as one "whose wealth is in the hands of only a few and in which there are many poor people."[5] A comparison of income distribution by country indicates that some highly industrialized countries, such as Japan and the United States, have income distributions which are not unlike those of some poor, developing countries, as shown in Table 9, taken from Table 8 for U.S. data and from the world Development Report, 1989 for other countries. Brazil in 1972, however, showed the classic pattern of extreme wealth concentration.

Table 9. Family Aggregate Income, Various Years, by Quintile, for Selected Industrialized and Developing Countries, Various Years

Year	*Sub Group*	*Country*	*First Fifth*	*Second Fifth*	*Third Fifth*	*Fourth Fifth*	*Fifth Fifth*
1990	White	U.S.	5.1	11.1	16.6	23.6	43.6
	Black		3.3	8.6	15.6	25.3	47.3
1979		Japan	8.7	13.2	17.5	23.1	37.5
1976		Indonesia	6.6	7.8	12.6	23.6	49.4
1975-76		India	7.0	9.2	13.9	20.5	49.4
1981-82		Bangladesh	6.6	10.7	15.3	22.1	45.3
1972		Brazil	2.0	5.0	9.4	17.0	66.6
1973		Panama	2.0	5.2	11.0	20.0	61.8

Sources : U.S., *Consumer Income*, 1992, Table B-7; World Bank *Development Report*, 1989. Note : Because of the lack of comparability of data and years, these comparisons are rough and not exact comparisons.

Notwithstanding higher incomes in developed countries, there neverthelss remain great inequities in the distribution of wealth. In Georgia in 1989, 20.3 percent of White and 41.8 percent of Black families were below or bordering on the family poverty level. The problem is exacerbated because of the increase in the number of female families with dependent children. In 1990, 13.2 percent of all Georgia families with children under 18 were headed by females. Part of the problem lies with the tremendous increase in births to unwed mothers. The overall Georgia rate is 23.4 births per 1,000 women aged 10-44, but is much more pronounced for Blacks, 55.7, than for Whites, 9.5.[6] Since female income in 1990 still lags behind male income by race, as it did in the 1930s (Cf. table 4b), lower income of female-headed families has immense consequences for all other social indicators. Table 10 shows the differences in mean personal income by sex and race in 1990.

Table 10. U. S. Mean personal Income by Sex and Race, 1990, in Cost price Index Adjusted Dollars

	White	*% of Male*	*Black*	*% of Male*	*% Black of White*
Male	27,142		16,985		62.9
Female	14,138	52.08	12,049	70.9	85.2

Source : *Consumer Income 1990,* Series P-60, No. 174.

Infant Mortality. One measure of the relationship of income to the health of a population is the Infant Mortality Rate (IMR). Inadequate diet and poor prenatal and postnatal care are all too often associated with low income. Many harmful practices by prenatal and nursing mothers, such as smoking, alcohol drinking, and drug usage, which contribute to low birth weight and premature birth, are especially exacerbated in low-income mothers, who tend to be poorly educated and do not avail themselves of the public health care and assistance available.

Table 11. Infant Mortality Rates in the United States, 1930, 1970, and 1989, by Race

	1930[1]	*1970*[2]	*1982*[2]	*% Improvement*
United States	64.6	20.0	9.8	84.8
White	60.1	17.8	8.2	86.3
Black	99.9	32.6	17.7	82.3
% Black of White	166.2	183.1	215.8	

Sources : (1) *Historical Statistics of the United States...to 1870,* Series B-136.14.

(2) Statistical Abstract of the United States, Tables 109 and 112.

Although the rates have declined for both Blacks and Whites, the improvement of IMR rates for Whites has actually been greater than for Blacks. Part of the explanation undoubtedly lies in the much higher rate of births to Black teenage unwed mothers to Whites, almost six times greater (586 percent), as discussed in the previous section. Lack of proper prenatal health care of foetus and mother is much more likely in the case of unwed than wed mothers, and carries a social welfare cost that does not end, but rather begins, with birth.

Regional variation in infant mortality by ethnic group is another characteristic of the United States, and for both Blacks and Whites is higher in the Southeast and in Georgia than for the United States as a whole, as shown in Table 12.

Table 12. Infant Mortality by Region, 1988 S.E. and Ga., 1989 U.S., and Race

	U.S	*S.E.*	*Georgia*
White	8.2	8.8	9.2
Black	17.2	18.5	18.9

Source : Statistical Abstract of the U.S., 1993.

As noted previously, the Southeast has the highest ratio of Black to Whites in the country, while 27 percent of Georgia's population is Black. But the South has less income than the United States and has always had a comparatively poor health infrastructure delivery system. The poorer showing of the South and Georgia are thus in the expected direction for Whites as well as Blacks.

Education is a social indicator characteristically associated with material as well as cultural well being—the higher the level of education the greater the personal income. Within the United States in education, there have existed both regional and racial variations in level of educational attainment.

Table 13. Percent of Illiteracy, 10 Years and Over, U.S., by Regions and Urban Rural and Race

	1930		
	Area	*Urban*	*Rural*
United states	4.3	3.2	6.9
White	1.8	1.4	5.3
Black	16.3	9.2	23.2
Southeast	11.1	5.7	12.7
White	4.9	1.7	6.7
Black	21.3	14.4	24.5
Georgia	9.4	6.4	11.6
White	3.4	1.5	5.0
Black	19.9	15.1	22.1

Sources : Biennial Survey of Education, 1933-1934, Bullet in No.2, U.S. Department of Education, p. 73; Fifteenth Census of the United States, 1930, Vol. II,pp. 1256-1271.

The higher levels of illiteracy in the Southeast and in Georgia reflect lower levels of expenditure for pubic school education, as shown in Table 14.

Table 14. Educational Expenditures by All Government Divisions, by Pupils Enrolled and Per Capita

	1931-1932	
	Per Pupil	*Per Capita*
United states	$74.22	$17.31
Southeast (1933-34)	27.61	6.84
Georgia	25.27	6.59

Source : *Contemporary Georgia*, 1938, Univ. of Georgia Press, p. 15.

Expenditures for Black education, in the apartheid system then prevailing, was substantially less than for Whites. Figures from the Georgia State Department of Education's *Sixtieth and Sixty-First Annual Report for the Biennium Ending June 30, 1932* show systematic discrimination in every item compared, form pupil-teacher ratios and teacher salaries to number of high school teachers and pupils transported at public expense. In 1929-30, the year for which comparative data are available, per pupil in average daily attendance expenditures were $ 10.26 for Black pupils and $ 42.62 for White pupils, over four times as much. It must be recalled that in the Georgia of 1930, almost three quarters of the population was rural and that Georgia per capita income was only half that for the United States, probably only 10 percent for farm Blacks.

As early as 1821, Georgia had sought national aid to education, and beginning in 1877, after the reestablishment of public schools following the Civil War, Georgia led in an effort to obtain national aid to education. Georgia argued that the United States, which had freed the slaves, had a particular educational responsibility toward the Black population. (Opp, 1950 : 71, 229-237); But there was no national understanding of the Civil War destruction of Southern wealth and the problem of educating Blacks. It was a hundred years after Emancipation, in 1965, before the Elementary and Secondary

Education Act was passed. It began a program of national aid to education in which family income was considered in the allocation of funds. But even today there is no massive national equalization effort, with education still regarded primarily as a state and local responsibility. For example, in the school year 1990-91, only 4.1 percent of Georgia school revenue came from the national government, the equivalent of $ 165 per child dollars of an expenditure of $4,056 per child.[7] Since, as we have noted, Black family income continues to be lower than White family income, an income test for benefits indirectly amounts to a kind of equalization.

Education is not a quick means of overcoming social and economic differences because other, more advanced groups do not remain stagnant while deficient groups catch up. Thus, while the status of a backward group may improve, the overall relative gain may not be as dramatic.

For the United States, data for Black education show improvement over the years. Starting at an enrollment rate at 1.8 percent in 1850, when most of the Blacks were still in the South as slaves, by 1880 the rate had increased to 33.8 percent compared to 62 percent White. By 1970 the Black rate was almost as high as White, 85.3 compared to 88 percent.[8] For children 13 and under, it is now almost 100 percent for both Whites and Blacks, but in the high school years it is about 98 percent for Whites and 95 percent for Blacks.[9] Compulsory school attendance in many states does not extend beyond age sixteen, and the effect of lower school attendance is reflected in overall statistics for many years after drop-out. Thus, in 1991 only 66.7 percent of Black, compared with 79.9 for Whites 25 years or older, had four years of high school.[10] These data, however, do not address the extent to which Black students follow rigorous high school programs which will prepare them for mathematics, science, and engineering programs in college.

It is in the area of higher education that Blacks throughout the United States still lag substantially behind Whites. Recent enrollment in higher education, except for professional enrollment, actually shows a decline for both Whites and Blacks, as given in Table 15.

Table 15. Fall Enrollment in U.S Higher Education by Percent Distribution by Level of Study and Race, 1976-1990.

Level	*1976*	*1990*
Undergraduate		
Black	10.2	9.7
White	83.4	79.3
Graduate		
Black	6.3	5.9
White	89.2	86.7
First Professional		
Black	4.6	5.9
White	91.3	82.9

Source : National Center for Education Statistics, *Digest of Educational Statistics*, 1992, Table 194.

The cumulative effect of higher drop-out rates for Blacks and Whites depressing long-term educational chances is shown in the category "Not High School Graduate" in Table 16.

Table 16. Percentage Distribution by Highest Level of Education, Population 18 and over, by Race, in Spring 1987.

	Race	
Educational Level	*White*	*Black*
Not H.S. Graduate	21.0	33.0
H:S. Graduate	37.0	35.9
Some College, No Degree	17.8	15.9
Vocational Certificate	2.2	1.3
Associate Degree (2-year)	4.3	3.7
Bachelor's (4 Year)	12.4	7.5
Master's Degree	3.6	2.3
Professional Degree	1.1	0.2
Doctorate	0.6	0.

Source : Table 11, Natl. Cen. Ed. Stat., *Digest of Educational Statistics*, 1992, Table 11.

Over the period 1976-77 to 1989-90, the percentage of Blacks receiving master's and doctorates declined. Excluding non-resident aliens from the distribution, the small Black doctorate share declined from 4.3 to 3.9, while Hispanic and Asian group percentages increased from 1.8 to 2.7 and 2.2 to

4.4, respectively. In terms of 1989-90 field of study, Blacks were over-represented in education and social sciences, but under-represented in engineering, sciences, and business management. In contrast, persons of Asian origin were over-represented in engineering, physical sciences, and business management.[11] Since the majority of persons acquiring doctorates in these fields have bachelor's degrees in those fields, the technical and scientific training deficit for Blacks has deep roots that begin with elementary education.

This paper has shown the persistence of regional differences between the South and the United States, and differences between Blacks and Whites, notwith- standing increasing industrialization and urbanization. Inequity may thus persist even in advanced countries after years of sustained over-all growth. Country differences may not be understood merely be dealing with gross comparisons, but require careful attention to within country inequities. And despite the best intentions of government, they are often difficult to eliminate.

There is often a tendency to identify development with a Western tradition of progress, in contrast to a lethargic East. This often results from a myopic view of development and a short term view of history, culture, and civilization. Desert sands now blow which once were the seat of major civilizations and jungle tree roots entertwine the stones of cities which once flourished in the humid tropics. Western wealth and preeminence in technology is relatively new in emergence of human culture.

Mankind has always been involved in development, and began when men and women shaped stones into tools and began gathering and storing forest products for the lean months ahead. As governments emerged, either in the form of tribal domination, city states, or empires, the developmental initiative of some kind of central administration has been crucial, first to give stability and later to organize resources.

One might make the generalization that prior to the invention of joint stock companies, which permitted the sharing of risks with the raising of increased capital, the state was crucial in wide scale cultural and economic development : It had the ability to raise large amounts of revenue and to organize manpower and other resources to dig, till and build. This appears to hold true over space and time with such diverse cultures as that of classic Teotihuacan in Mexico; Sumerian Uruk; Cola Tanjore; or Khemer Angor Wat.

Much of the existing Chinese landscape dates from that

union of philosophic thought, and practical concerns in Han China of two thousand years ago which inspired a diversity of state projects. In India, the Mauryan empire under Asoka engaged in undertakings continental in scope, and found in Kautilya (Canakya) an Indian Machiavelli whose *Arthasastra* (C. 300 B. C.) became a manual for Mauryan statecraft.

Except for the poorest, it is probable that most countries have the capacity to generate the funds and to organize their own resources for development. Sometimes stimulus, internal or externals, in the form of a charismatic leader is helpful to development, especially in stimulating among people a desire to change and work for new goals in the context of their own cultural values. Instead of so much emphasis on underdevelopment, the refrain of so many development texts, is the need to examine the values inherent in cultures which may be harnessed to generate men, women, and children to aspire to a better life.

Having a better life does not have to be defined in terms of Western gadgets and goods, but how the ethics and values of a culture may be extended to all its people. The future task of development is not so much the diffusion of Western models as much as finding modes which reflect the particular ethos of a culture within the vision of a common humanity.

Notes

1. *Congressional Record*, 20 January, 1949, p. 478.
2. Eugene P. Odum, *In Defense of Two Georgias*, mss, nd.
3. Bureau of the Census, *Historical Statistics of the United States to 1970*. Table G1-15.
4. National Emergency Council, *Report to the President on the Economic Conditions of the South*,, p. 1. Others data from personal experiences and ten year cotton prices, 1930-1939, compiled from Continental Eagle Gin Co., "Production and Price Record of Lint Cotton for 160 Years," n.d.
5. *A World View*, Silver Burdette, 1985, p. 96.
6. Regent's Report, 1992, p. 47.
7. *The Georgia Country Guide Book 1993*, p. 61
8. Historical Statistics of the United States...to 1970, Table H-433-441.
9. *Statistical Abstract...1993*, Table No. 216.

10. *Statistical Abstract..1993*, Table 222.
11. National Centre for Educational Statistics, *Digest of Educational Statistics*, 1992, Tables 252, 255, and 203.

References

Balandier, G.	1956	*Tiers Mende*, p 478
Myint, N.	1964	The Economics of the Developing Countries.
Cardese H. Fernando and Enze Faletto	1979	*Dependency and Develepment in Latin America*, rev. ed.,
Wheeler, O. James	1986	"The Role of Metropolitan Areas in Employment Change," *Georgia Business and Economic Conditions*, V. 46, No. 6.
Bachtel, C. B Douglas et al	1992	*Growth and Change in Georgia's Social Economic and Demographic Environment*, P-51.
Fite, C. Gilbert	1984	*Cotton Fields No More : Southern Agriculture 1865-1980*, The University Press of Kentucky P-222 passim.
Orr, Dorothy	1950	*History of Education in Georgia*, University of north Carolina Press. pp. 71, 229-237.

John van Willigen

AGE AND GENDER DIFFERENCES IN VOLUNTARY ASSOCIATION MEMBERSHIP IN A RURAL AMERICAN COUNTY

This analysis addesses aspects of the relationship between age and participation in voluntary associations unsing an array of survey, historic and ethnographic data referenced to a rural Kentucky county. Over the past thirty years much research in social gerontology has focused on questions concerning the relationship between age and social participation (Atchley, 1975; Binstock & Shanas, 1976; Cumming & Henry, 1961; Hochschild, 1975; Rossow 1967; Shanas, 1962; Sill, 1980). A portion of this substantial research effort has focused on the relationship between age and voluntary association participation (Babchuk & Booth, 1969; Beyer & Woods, 1963; Cutler, 1981; Edwards et al, 1977; Hausknecht, 1962).

For the most part the voluntary association literature demonstrates a general age related pattern of participation. This pattern indicates a gradual increase in voluntary association participation from early in life through the teenage period. Following the teens and the completion of high school there is a dramatic decline in participation. The middle years are characterized by growth in participation, while the later years are often described as a period of decrease in participation (Edwards, et al, 1977;127).

There is some disagreement concerning the extent of the late life decline in voluntary association participation. For example, in a study of a national sample Hausknecht (1962) notes that there is a plateau of voluntary association participation between the ages of 30 and 59, and a small drop at age 65 and beyond. Beyer and Woods (1963) report a drop among those beyond the age of 80. In contrast, Neal Cutler (1981:127) notes that, "one of the most important findings derived from recent studies is the critical observation that older persons do not withdraw or disengage from voluntary association membership as a consequence of the aging process." (1981 : 127).

Age is just one of many variables studied in terms of voluntary association membership. Some factors which have been empirically related to participation rates include rural residence (Wright & Hyman, 1958), socio-economic status (Payne et al, 1972; Smith & Freedman, 1972), population density (Hougland, et al, 1979), length of residence (Bell & Force, 1956), ethnicity (Mayo, 1950); civil status (Hausknecht, 1962; Scott, 1957), community size (Babchuk & Edwards, 1965), and gender (Booth, 1972). This pattern indicates a gradual increase in voluntary association participation from early in life through the teenage period. Following the teens and the completion of high school there is a dramatic decline in participation. The middle years are characterized by growth in participation, while the later years are often described as a period of decrease in participation (Edwards, et al, 1977 : 127).

There is some disagreement concerning the extent of the late life decline in voluntary association participation. For example, in a study of a national sample Hausknecht (1962) notes that there is a plateau of voluntary association participation between the ages of 30 and 59, and a small drop at age 65 and beyond. Beyer and Woods (1963) report a drop among those beyond the age of 80. In contrast, Neal Cutler (1981 : 127) notes that, "one of the most important findings derived from recent studies is the critical observation that older persons do not withdraw or disengage from voluntary association membership as a consequence of the aging process."

Age is just one of many variables studied in terms of voluntary association membership. Some factors which have been empirically related to participation rates include rural residence (Wright & Hyman, 1958), socio-economic status (Payne et al, 1972; Smith and Freedman, 1972), population density (Hougland, et al, 1979), length of residence (Bell & Force, 1956), ethnicity (Mayo, 1950), civil status (Hausknecht, 1962; Scott, 1957), community size (Babchuk & Edwards, 1965), and gender (Booth, 1972).

Our analysis deals with the entire life span. Part of our reasoning for this is reflected in a statement made by Paul

Bohannan. "like studies in child development, studies in gerontology have limited themselves to one arc of the life span. Ultimately of course, these specialities must grow together. Aging after all, begins at conception. Growth, after all, stops only at death" (1980:viii). Further, research in the area of voluntary association participation is still characterized by Mayo's statements of over three decades ago, "There is a dearth of studies that have attempted to analyze the intensity of participation of all segments of the age structure within the same community" (1950:242). For the most part studies gather data on less than the entire age structure. Some studies which have addressed a greater array of ages are reported by Wright and Hyman (1958), Scott (1957), and Babchuk and Booth (1969).

Data Sources and Analysis

The basic data for this study was collected with a census survey of a rural Kentucky county. This survey collected information for a broad range of variables (household composition, sex, age, marital status, occupation, education, farming activities and others) in addition to the dependent variables, voluntary association membership and church affiliation. This research was part of a larger project dealing with the social relationships of older people (van Willigen, 1989; van Willigen, Arcury and Cromley 1985; Arcury, 1984, 1986). Data were collected on 2,103 persons residing in 741 households. The survey data are coupled with ethnographic and historical data from participant-observation, key informant interviewing, and reading both old and contemporary newspapers. A number of club meetings and church services were also attended. The survey asked respondents to provide the names of voluntary associations to which they and members of their households belonged. This resulted in the identification of memberships in about 110 different local, state and national organizations. There was no attempt to measure degree of participation. The measure of voluntary association participation used in this study is thus nominal membership.

The county is situated in the Outer Bluegrass region of central Kentucky. The dominant aspect of the economy is agriculture. Most farmers follow a mixed economic strategy based on raising burley tobacoo, beef cattle and forage crops like alfalfa and grasses for the market. Many households have a large kitchen garden during the summer months. In addition to farming many county residents work in industrial plants located in nearby towns. A large portion of the residents participate in the life of the local churches. All churches are evangelical and protestant.

Most residents belong to voluntary associations. These include sports teams, service clubs, secret lodges, professional associations, school associations, educational organizations and various others. Although different by their very nature churches also contribute to the organizational life of the community beyond that of the household and kin group. County residents are introduced to voluntary association membership early as many become affiliated with Sunday school[1] classes. There has been a proliferation of community organizations starting in the late 1930s as part of government economic and social development efforts. The goal of these organizations was to provide a means for the government to provide useful information to community members.

The analysis consists of reporting a single data array on life course changes (see Figure 1) and then interpreting this single array. The interpretation is expressed through a comparison at a general level with findings reported in the literature and a specific comparison with the results of a similar study done in a similar community. Interpretation is continued by decomposing the data array by sex and then adding a related data array on church attendance. The male-female comparison raised some analytical questions which were addressed by expanding the data under consideration. Additionally some ethnographic data are presented in order to better understand the interpretations developed.

Social Participation in Voluntary Associations

As noted above, our measure of voluntary association participation is nominal membership. Memberships reported were aggregated by age cohorts and rendered as the mean number of memberships for that age cohort. The mean number of memberships across the population is 0.40. A histogram by five year age cohorts is provided (Figure 1).

The pattern which emerged from the Kentucky County data set shows : (1) rapid growth membership during the pre-teen years; (2) highest participation during the high school years; (3) rapid and precipitious decline following the typical years for high school leaving; (4) gradual increase to a plateau

---

1. Sunday schools meet for about one hour before the Sunday worship service that is typically scheduled at 11.00 AM. There will be instruction and other activities that are intended to increase knowledge of the sacred texts of Christianity. These classes often have a club like organizational structure with officers and dues.

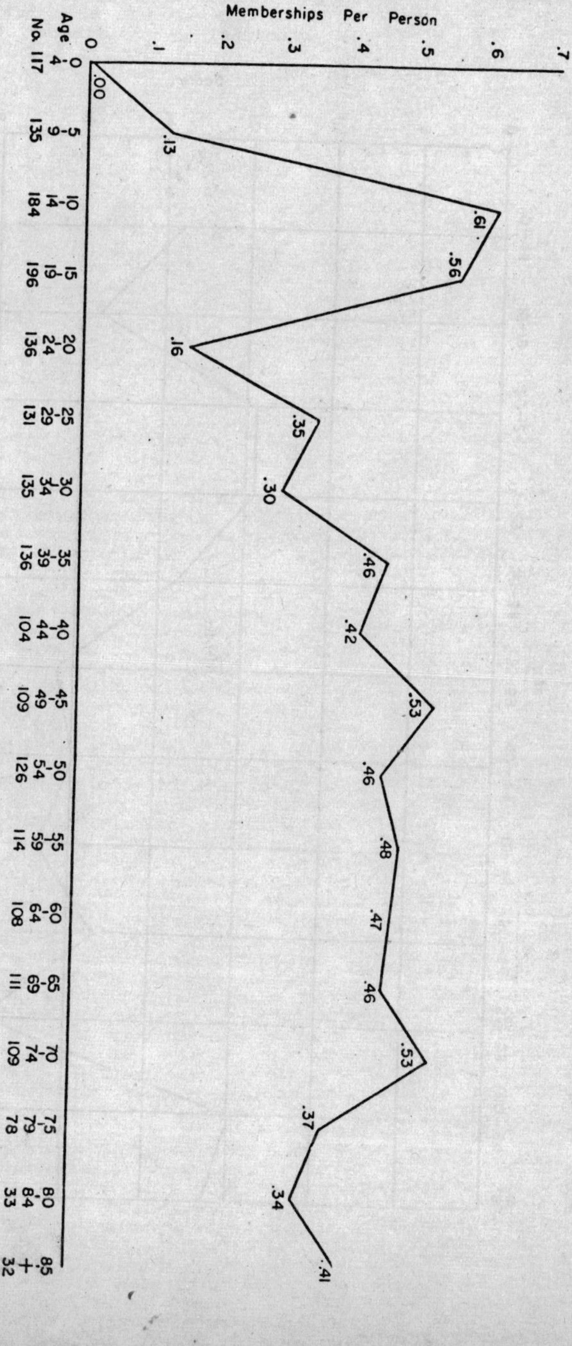

Figure 1: Voluntary Association Memberships per Person for Total Population by Age

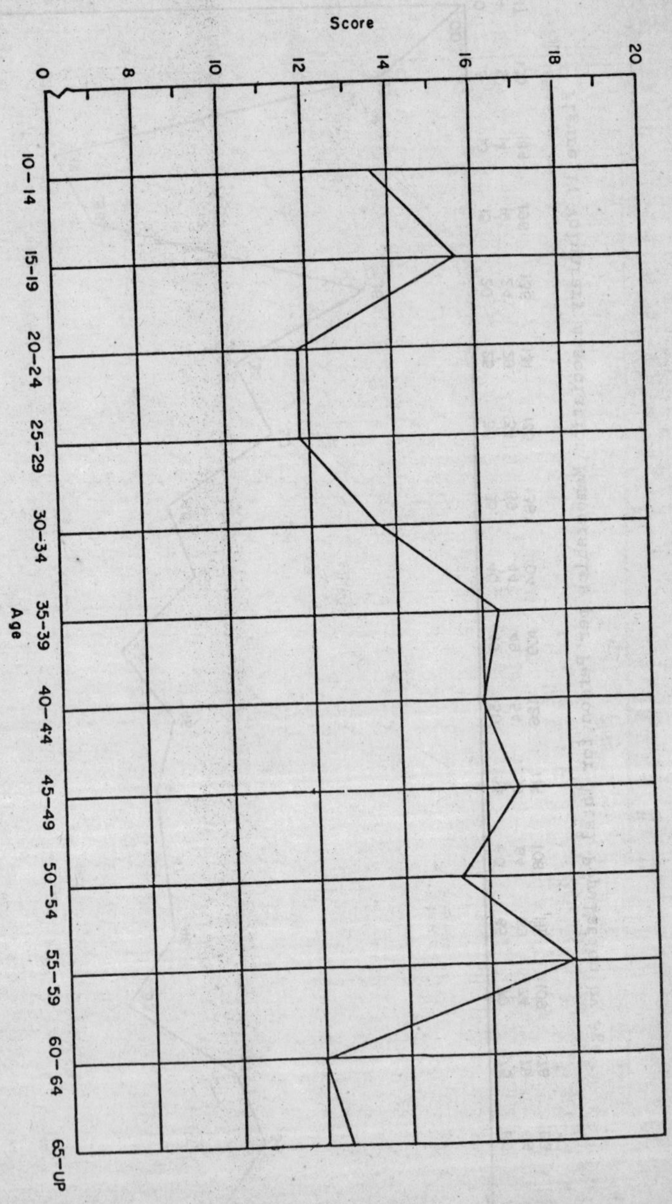

Figure 2: Average Individual Social Participation Score by Age, North Carolina Study, 1948

between the 45-49 and 70-74 age cohorts) (5) slow decline in membership in the years following and (6) a small rebound appears in the 85 plus group. The overall effect is one of a whale-backed curve with a pronounced fluke. It is worth emphasizing that the decline in membership following the years of high school graduation is greater than the decline following the midlife peak. The reader's attention is directed to the downward slope in the curve in the cohorts 45-49 and 70-74.

The pattern manifested for voluntary association membership is similar to the pattern described for social participation by age of an earlier study done in rural North Carolina (Mayo, 1950; Edwards, White and Owens, 1977;127). The similarity can be seen by examining figure 2.

Differences between Males and Females. Stratification by sex of the Kentucky County data shows both similarity and difference between males and females. Generally males show greater participation in voluntary associations than females. The average number of membership by sex and age (Figure 3) shows that males and females have essentially similar distributions up to the 45-49 cohort. Following this, females show a precipitous decrease whereas males show a slight increase. Later in life female membership increases and becomes more similar to males.

The frequency distribution (Figure 3) shows female membership decline from the 45-49 cohort to the 55-59 cohort. Simultaneous with this decrease is an increase in male membership. The female decrease is actually greater than all other declines save the substantial post-high school drop. The female participation rate decreases by almost half between the 45-49 and 50-54 cohorts. Female participation declines to less than 50 per cent of male in the 50-54 and 55-59 cohorts. It is apparent that much of the downward reflection in the curve of the entire population between the 45-49 ad 70-74 is due to the effect of the decrease in female participation.

The mid-life female membership decrease may be interpreted in a number of ways. Here we choose to examine the decline in terms of changes in employment and changes in household structure in those age cohorts. Our consideration of employment as a factor in the decline involved the examination of the rate of employment in a salaried or wage paying job. Analysis shows that employment for the two cohorts is relatively low, lower than all preceding cohorts. The percentage employed in a salaried or wage paying position in the 50-54 and 55-59 cohorts are 34.5 per cent and 39.3 per cent. This is lower than

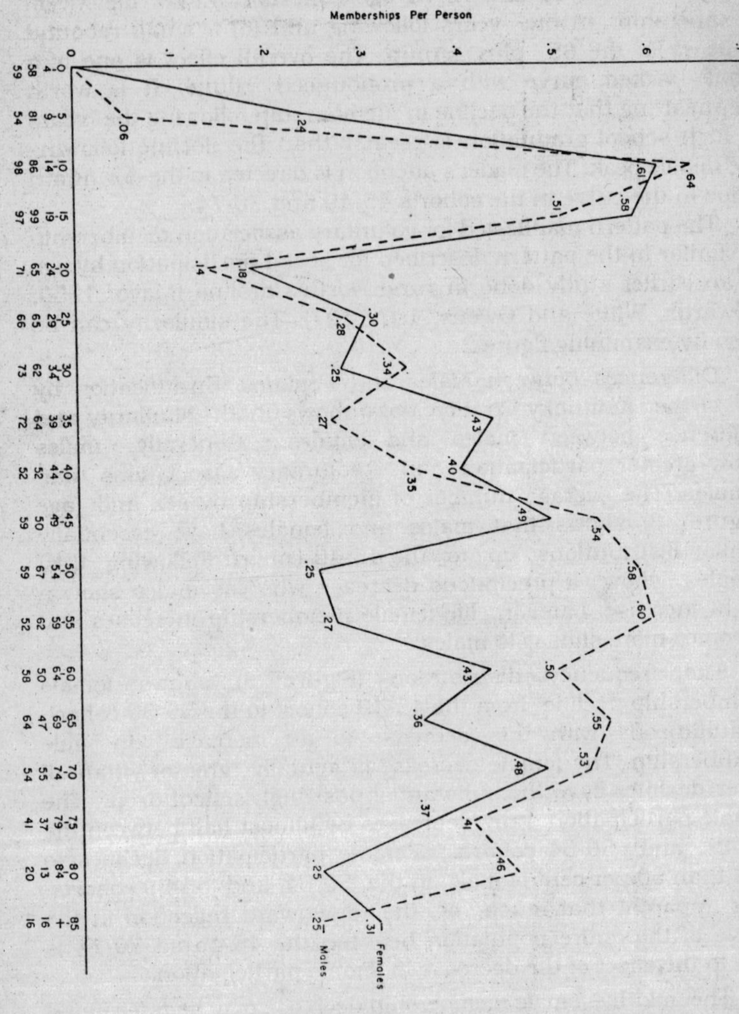

Figure 3: Voluntary Association Memberships per Person by Sex and Age

all preceding cohorts. The per cent employed in 40-44 and 45-49 cohorts is 51.4 and 46.0, respectively, and the following pre-retirement 60-64 cohort with 42.9 per cent employed. It is clear that the 50-54 and 55-59 female age cohorts which have low voluntary association participation rates also show a decline in employment as it is measured here.

Analysis of data on household structure (see Arcury 1984) indicates another important change occuring in homes containing women aged 50 to 59 years. The households of these women are characterized by a decrease in size and complexity. Of households with female householders aged 35 to 49 years, 84 per cent (135 of 160) contain at least one child of the householder. Only 56 per cent (75 of 134) of the households with female householders age 50 to 59 have a child of the householder present. Like those leaving their teens and entering their twenties, the employment and household data show a set of changes which indicate the transition of life phase for women in their fifties. A life transition is reflected in their degree of social participation through voluntary associations.

After the decline in participation among females aged 50 to 59, participation increases among women in their sixties only to rapidly decrease again among women over the age of 70 years. Male voluntary association participation begins a gradual decrease among those over the age of sixty which continues through the oldest cohort.

Church Attendance and Voluntary Association Membership. In addition to the data on voluntary association membership the Kentucky study included data on church attendance. In this social context church attendance was thought to be a better indicator of participation than church membership because of the variability associated with the concept of church membership. In most cases church membership is based on some idea of having achieved salvation. That is, many church participants would not technically be members because they had not been "saved". To further extend our analysis we considered a self-report of regular church attendance as another type of associational affiliation. The combination of voluntary association membership data and church attendance data provides another platform for understanding life course changes in social participation. Generally the frequency distribution for church attendance is higher and smoother than that of voluntary association membership.

Figure 4 displays the frequencies for the total, population for voluntary association membership, church attendance and these two variables combined. Average voluntary association membership is higher than average church affiliation in only one age cohort (10-14) and the difference in that case is quite small. Whereas the peak in voluntary association membership is in the 10-14 age cohort it is in the 65-69 age cohort for church affiliation. Although there is a downward deflection of the curve in the post-high school years for the church affiliated respondents in church attendance the drop is of a much smaller magnitude than that found in voluntary association membership. Overall the frequency distribution of the combined memberships is relatively smooth.

Figures 5 and 6 allow the comparison of men and women's overall participation. Comparison between male and female church affiliation shows less difference between males and females than is found in the comparison of the male and female voluntary association membership comparison. Note that in all cohorts except one, the female average church affiliation score is higher than that of males. Further, the maximum spread between males and females is smaller in this comparison that in than associated with the comparison of average voluntary association membership. Noteworthy is the effect of combining church affiliation with voluntary association membership on the male-female differences in participation in the 50-54 and 55-59 age cohorts. Clearly, the inclusion of church affiliation decreases the differences which exist between males and females in these combined sectors of social participation. While differences in male and female social participation are interesting our purpose analytically is to deal with life course changes. It is apparent from this analysis that in this community church affiliation softens the pattern of expansion and contraction found in these kinds of social participation. Both males and females maintain church affiliation levels with slight downward deflections during the precipitous post-high school drop in voluntary association membership. This serves as a kind of buffer in social relationships. Additionally, especially in the case of females the decreases in voluntary association membership found in the 50-59 cohort are largely compensated for by relative increase in church affiliation. Note especially the substantial upward pattern in the church affiliation of females in the 50-54 and 65-69 age groups both of which are associated with simultaneous decreases in voluntary association membership. In contrast late in life both male and female voluntary association and church affiliation rates move in parallel. Noteworthy is that as male rates decline in the last cohort female rates increase.

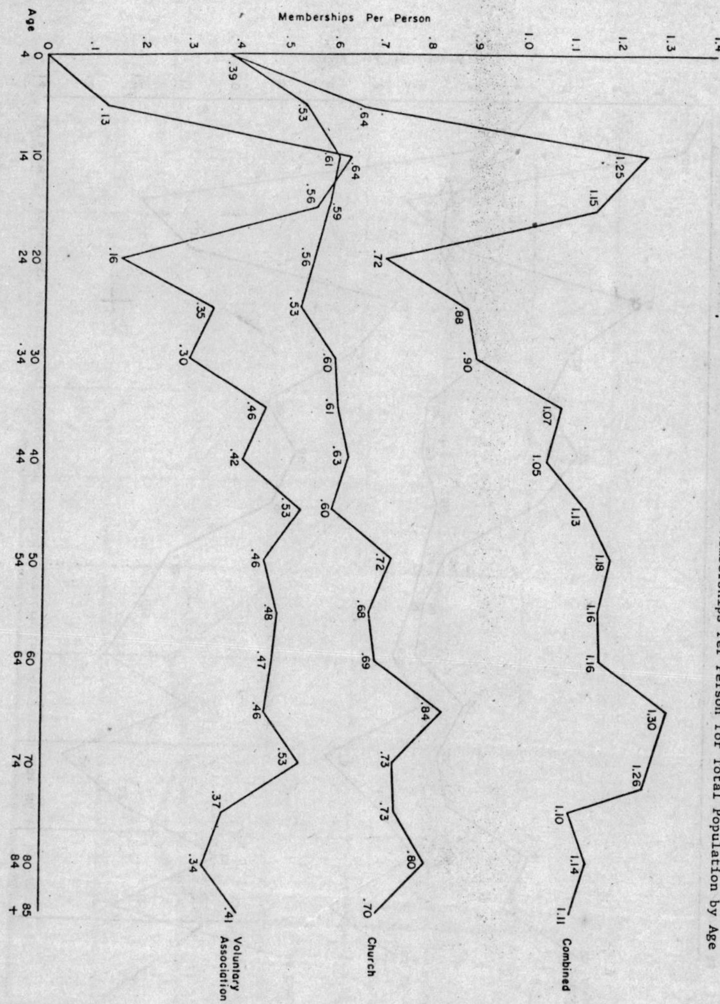

Figure 4: Voluntary Association, Church and Combined Memberships Per Person for Total Population by Age

Figure 5: Voluntary Association, Church and Combined Memberships per Person for Males by Age

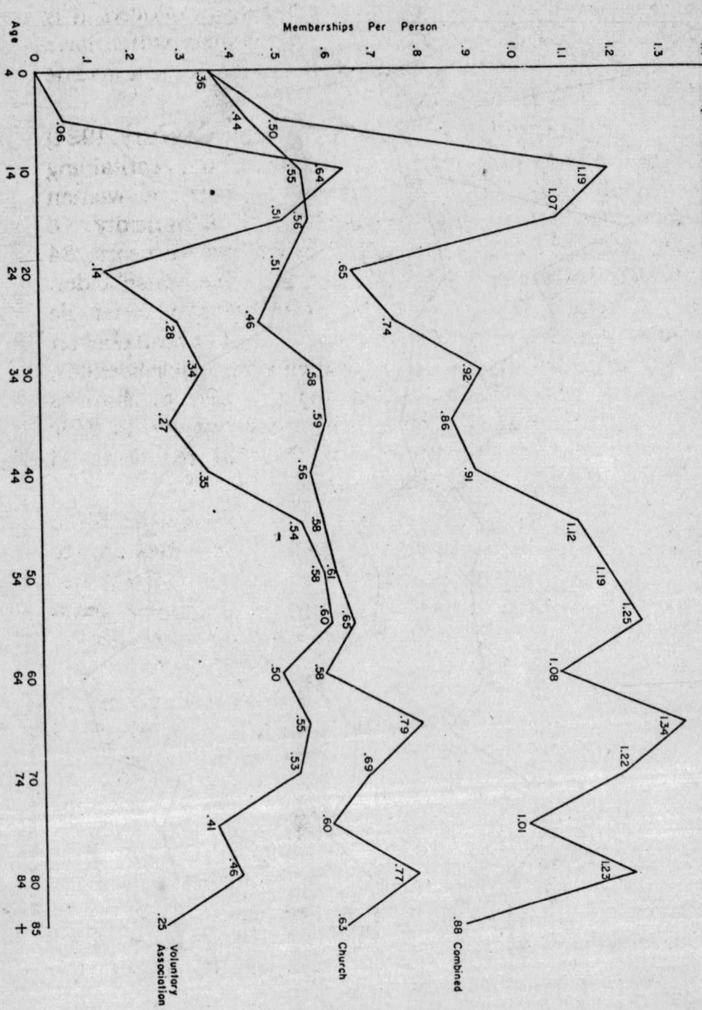

Aging and Voluntary Association Membership

Our analysis of voluntary association membership by age in a rural Kentucky county produced results which were consistent with previously reported research (Mayo, 1950; Edwards, White & Owens, 1977). That is, in the few cases where voluntary association membership is considered throughout the life span the pattern of distribution is best described by a fluked whale-backed curve. The similarity between the Kentucky and North Carolina study results was noted and thought to be substantial. The congruence with other studies allows us to tentatively suggest that it would be useful to think of life phases in voluntary association membership for American rural populations. The following phases are identified, I - Pre-adolescence Growth Phase (0-9) : II - Adolescence Peak Phase (10-19); III - Post-adolescence Collapse Phase (20-24); IV - Early Adult Growth Phase (25-49); Va - Female Middle Adult Decline Phase (50-69); Vb - Male Middle Adult Plateau Phase (50-69) and VI - Late Adult Decline Phase (70 plus). Three general points should be made concerning these phases and the curve frequency distribution upon which they are based. First, relative to the rest of the distribution the late life decline is not substantial, basically older people's membership levels drop to the mean of the entire population. Second, the decrease following the teenage years is precipitous, much more susbstantial than the decrease associated with the Late Adult Decline Phase. Third, there is a significant difference in the social aging pattern of males and females with the post-child rearing reduction in household complexity and size. This structural change apparently is more costly to females than to males.

Our ethnographic data show an apparent recent increase in age segregation in voluntary association membership. This is interpreted as an effect of increased industrial employment and the resulting increase in the complexity of the occupational structure of the community (van Willigen, et al, 1984). Put in simple terms, farmers and their wives and industrial workers participate in voluntary associations differently. Differential participation relates to different interests and different work scheduling patterns. This difference is expressed as age segregation because of the differences in mean age of the farmers and their wives and the industrially employed segment of the population. The intensity of the segregation is quite variable. It is most striking in the case of neighborhood homemaker clubs, where in some parts of the county both younger

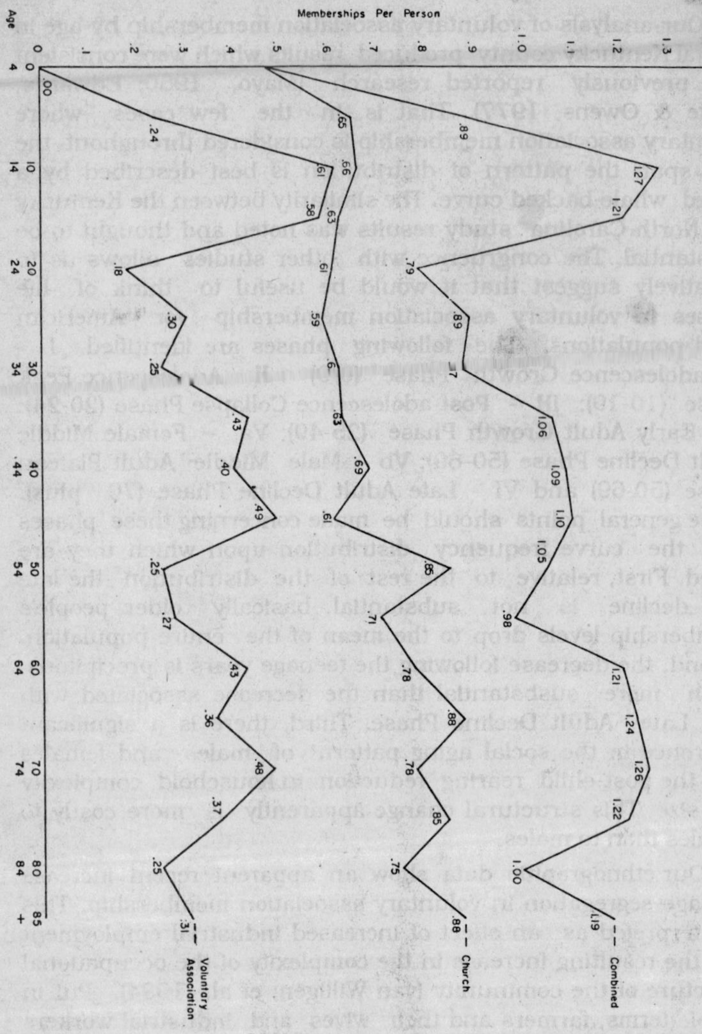

Figure 6: Voluntary Association, Church and Combined Memberships per Person for Females by Age

and older membership clubs exist side by side. The primary reason seems to be day time meeting preferences of the older, farm wives and the night meeting preferences of the younger industrially employed women.

Voluntary association age segregation takes a number of forms. First, it is important to recognize many associations are age segregated on a *de jure* basis. Among these some have both minimum and maximum ages while others have only minimum ages. Many of the adult minimum only associations are further segregated *de facto*. In this community the *de facto* age segregation occurs in two patterns. These are the quasi age grade of "pass through" type and the quasi age set or "die out" type. In associations of the quasi age grade type new members are continually recruited and older members are "passed through" on their own volition. In associations of the quasi age set or "die out" type few new members are recruited and the membership ages as a group. As the membership declines with the death of members "critical mass" can be lost and associations can shatter and become extinct. We are not able to ascertain the effect of this on the oldest cohorts. In any case because of shatter effects the array of associational alternatives for older people decline.

Much of the texture of difference in pattern of association membership of various age cohorts and sex strata is reduced when we add church affiliation as another measure of social participation. Three points are suggested by the effects of adding church affiliation to the voluntary association membership data analysis. First, it appears that unidimensional measures of social participation such as voluntary association membership will tend to exaggerate both age and sex differences. Yet it is difficult to combine measures. Second, the pattern of the relationship between voluntary association and church participation suggests that social aging is a process of change in type as much as amount of participation. While this statement seems obvious much social gerontology emphasizes amount of participation rather than type. One might hypothesize that high age differences in social participation are as much associated with simplicity of measurement as much as actual differences in social participation. Third, churches have a number of unique features which make them crucial resources for people as they age in society. Churches are the most free of age specificity in the potential to participate. New members are recruited continually at various age levels (although with a youth bias). Most churches have some type of programming relevant to older people such as home visitation, hospital calling and home communion service. Further the focal interest of church is relevant to all ages, while the content of voluntary association focus are of less broad interest.

References

Atchley, Robert C. 1975 The Life Course Age Grading and Age Linked Demands for Decision Making. In *Life Span Developmental Psychology : Normative Life Crises.* Detan and Ginsberg (eds.) New York : Academic Press.

Arcury, Thomas A. 1984 Household Composition and Economic change in a Rural Community, 1900-1980 : Testing Two Models. American Ethnologist 11 : 677-98.

1986 Rural Elderly Household Life-Course Transitions, 1900 and 1980 Compared. *Journal of Family History* 11 : 55-76.

Babchuk, Nicholas and Alan Booth 1969 Voluntary Association Membership : A Longitudinal Analysis. *American Sociological Review* 34 : 31-45.

Babchuk, Nicholas and J.N. Edwards 1965 Voluntary Associations and the Interaction Hypothesis. *Sociological Inquiry* 35 : 149-162.

Bell, W. and M.T. Force 1956 Urban Neighbourhood Types and Participation in Formal Associations. *American Sociological Review* 21 : 25-34.

Beyer, Glenn H. and Margaret E. Woods 1963 *Living and Activity Patterns of the Aged.* Research Report No. 6. Centre for Housing and Environmental Studies, Ithaca, N.Y.

Binstock, Robert H. *and Ethel Shanas (eds.)* 1976 *Handbook of Aging and the Social Sciences.* New York : Van Nostrand Reinhold Co.

Bohannan, Paul 1980 Foreword, In *Aging in Culture and Society, Comparative Viewpoints and Strategies.* J.F. Bergin (ed.) Brooklyn, New York.

Booth, A. 1972 Sex and Social Participation. *American Sociological Review* 37 : 183-192.

Chapin, F. Stuart 1937 *Social Participation Scale.* Minneapolis : University of Minnesota.

Cumming and W.E. Henry 1961 *Growing Old* Basic Books : New York.

Cutler, Neal E. 1981 Voluntary Association Participation and Life Statisfaction : Replication, Revision and Extension. *International Journal of Aging and Human*

Development 14 : 127-137.

Edwards, John N., Randall P. White and Arliss Owens — 1977 — Age and Social Involvement. *Journal of Voluntary Action Research* 6 :

Firth, Raymond — 1951 — *Elements of Social Organization.* Boston : Beacon.

Freedom, R. and M. Axelrod — 1952 — Who Belongs to What in a Great Metropolis ? *Adult Leadership* 1 : 6-9.

Hausknecht, M. — 1962 — *The Joiners : A Sociological Description of Voluntary Association Membership in the United States.* New York : Bedminster Press.

Hochschild, A. — 1975 — Disengagement Theory - Critique and Proposal. *American Sociological Review* 40 : 553-569.

Hougland, James G., Kyong-Dong Kim and James Christenson — 1979 — The Effects of Ecological and Socioeconomic Status Variables on Membership and Participation in Voluntary Organizations. *Rural Sociology* 44 : 602-612.

Long. L. and D. De Are — 1982 — Repopulating the Countryside : A 1980 Trend. *Science* 217 : 1111-1116.

Mayo, S.C. — 1950 — Age Profiles of Social Participation in Rural Areas of Wake Country, N.C. *Rural Sociology* 15 : 242-251.

Payne, Raymond, Barbara P. Payne and Richard D. Reddy — 1972 — Social background and Role Determinants of Individual Participation in Organized Voluntary Action. In *Voluntary Social Action.* David H. Smith, Richard D. Reddy and Burt R. Baldwin (eds.) Lexington, Massachusetts : Heath.

Ross. J. — 1972 — Toward A Reconstruction of Voluntary Association Theory. *British Journal of Sociology* 23 : 20-32.

Rossow, I. — 1967 — *Social Integration of the Aged.* New York : Free Press.

Scott, J.C. Jr. — 1957 — Membership and Participation in Voluntary Associations. *American Sociological Review* 22 : 315-326.

Shanas, E. — 1962 — *The Health of Older People : A Social Survey.* Cambridge, Massachusetts : Harward University Press.

Sill, J.S. — 1980 — Disengagement Reconsidered - Awareness of Finitude. The Gerontologist 20 : 457-62 Smith, Constance ad Anne Freedman. *Voluntary Associations : Perspectives on the Literature* Cambridge, Massachusetts: Harvard University Press.

Van Willigen, John 1983 Exchange Relationships in Social Networks of Older People in a Rural Kentucky Country. Paper presented at American Anthropological Association Meetings, Chicago.

Van Willigen, John 1989 *Gettin, Some Age on Me : Social Organization of Older People in a Rural American Community.* Lexington, Kentucky : University Press of Kentucky.

Van Willigen, John, Thomas A. Arcury and Robert G. Cromley 1985 Tobacco Men and Factory Hands : The Effects of Migration Turn around and Decentralized Industrialization on the Social Lives of Older People in a Rural Kentucky Country, *Human Organization* 44 : 50-57.

Wylie, Mary 1980 The Dying Community as a Human Habitat for the Elderly. In *The Dying Community,* Art Gallaher, Jr. and Harland Padfield (eds.) Albuquerque : University of New Mexico Press.

Wright, Charles R. and 1958 Herbert H. Hyman Voluntary Association Memberships of American Adults : Evidence from National Sample Surveys. *American Sociological Reveiew* 23 : 284-294.

Harsha N. Mookherjee

SOME CORRELATES OF FEMINISM AMONG COLLEGE STUDENTS

Introduction

Recent sex-role research generally reflects four main perspectives : (1) sex differences, (2) role differences, (3) minority-group differences, and (4) politics of caste (cf. Balbus 1992; Banton 1990; Block 1976; Blumberg 1989; 1988; Burleson & Samter 1992; Cowan, Mestlin and Masek 1992; Cubbins 1991; Davis and Robinson 1991; Fox and Ferri 1992; Hochschild 1973; Kristiansen 1990; Maccoby & Jacklin 1974; Marini 1984; Rossi 1985; Todd, Friedman & Kariuki 1990; Vanyperen & Buunk 1991). While the first perspective deals with sex *differenes*, the rest in different ways deal more with sex *equality* (cf. Rossi 1969).

The sex-role debate is essentially of two kinds : biological and sociocultural explanations for sex differences versus various socialization theories (Hochschild 1973 : 1015). Mischel (1970) believes children first learn to discriminate between "boy things" and "girl things" and later generalize to new situations. According to Kohlberg (1966), non-familial socialization stimulates or retards basic male and female modes of cognition, pretty much regardless of what parents do or say. These cognitive modes are based on how the young child categorizes himself or herself, with sex-linked values "develop*(ing)* out of the need to value things that are consistent with or like the self" (Maccoby 1966 : 165). But we have seen that girls as they grow up learn to value boys more and girls less (cf. Kitay 1940; Mendelsohn & Dobie 1970; McKee & Sherriffs 1959; Smith 1939), indicating the importance of socialization. Beyond the social differences, status differences, early socialization, and social change are important.

Research on sex difference behaviour in the United States further suggests that sex-role socialization may affect the relationship between people's satisfaction with an organization and their socially responsible orientation in it. Schopler and Bateson (1965) reported the tendency of American males to ignore the norm of social responsibility in order to optimize their own outcomes, whereas American females were more likely to adhere to the norm even without reciprocation. Empirical evidence indicates that men tend toward equity and women toward equality in their social relationship (Benton 1971; Leventhal & Anderson 1970; Leventhal & Lane 1970; Sampson 1975; Weinstein, DeVaughn & Wiley 1969). Funder, Block and Block (1983) argued that socialization for women emphasizes control and inhibition and behavioral impulses more so than for men. Women learn societal expectations and adjust their desires accordingly.

Studies of gender differences in achievement in science in terms of the effect of traditional feminine stereotypes on girls predict that differences would not develop before adolescence. The values and self-images involved would be expected to show greater gender differences during adolescence than during childhood, as they are related to traditional ideas of femininity embedded in conceptions of relations between the sexes (cf. Basow & Medcalf 1988; Licht & Dweck 1984; Licht, Stader & Swenson 1989; Ryckman & Peckham 1987a, 1987b; Sjoberg 1988; Smith 1992). Lamb (1982) found that traditional sex-roles were emphasized less and that daughters appeared more motivated to achieve in two-earner than in traditional families. An Australian study (Foon 1988) found that the mother's employment was associated with the daughter's performance in mathematics and school work. In addition, the effects of parental separation and maternal employment on academic achievement in general indicated that children in two-earner families place more value on competence of females than those in one-earner families (cf. Hunt & Hunt 1977; Mortimer & Sorensen 1984; Stephen & Corder 1985).

Hence, two questions are raised : (1) if values change as society develops technologically, to what degree values shared by males and females ? and (2) how does socialization influence changing values ?

To answer these questions with respect to sex-role stereotypes, an attempt was made in this study to examine the relationship of attitudes of college students toward women to thier personal characteristics and the characteristics of the student's parents.

It was assumed that the liberal ideas of appropriate sex-roles expressed by the students...particularly, attitudes toward feminine-roles...might have been conditioned by the socializing agents, especially family members. In addition, to examine the effect of socialization influences, we closely investigated the relationships of the students sex-role attitudes with their "traditional family ideology," "authoritarian attitudes," and "religious fundamentalism" attitudes and beliefs.

The stated objectives are based on the following assumptions : (1) traditionally feminine stereotypes are developed by parental influence through the socialization process, and (2) modeling after the mother will reduce the salience of traditionally feminine stereotypes. We therefore developed the following hypotheses :

1. The attitudinal variables of "authoritarianism," "traditional family ideology," "religious fundamentalism," and "feminism" are affected by socio-demographic variables.

On the assumption that these attitudinal variables are supported by sex-role stereotypes, which are developed through the socialization process, we further hypothesize that

2. Attitudes toward women (feminism) will be positively affected by "traditional family ideology" views which support the democratic end of the democratic-autocratic continuum.
3. Attitudes toward women (feminism) will be negatively related to authoritarian attitudes.
4. Attitudes toward women will be jointly influenced by attitudinal and socio demographic variables.

THE STUDY DESIGN

Data were collected in a structured questionnaire from a sample of 400 college students, randomly drawn from a rural college campus in middle Tennessee. Only 377 questionnaires completed by white students were used in the present study in order to control for race.

To measure the sex-role attitudes of the students, the 20-item Likert-type attitudinal scale titled "Open Subordination of Women scale" (OSW) was used (Nadler & Morrow 1959). This "Feminism Scale" measures for non-stereotyped attitudes toward women, attitudes denying their alleged inferiority, narrowness, offensiveness, and attitudes favoring the restriction of their freedom and equality. Scale scores may vary from 20 to 100, high scores indicating a more favorable attitude toward women.

The measure of "authoritarianism attitude" used was the 10-item "F-Scale" designed by the Survey Research Center, University of Michigan (cf. Robinson & Shaver 1969 : 268). The scale scores for this measure range from 10 to 50, with lower score suggesting less psychologically intolerant attitudes.

The "Traditional Family Ideology (TFI)" scale was designed by Levinson and Huffman (1925) to measure differences in family ideology along the democratic-autocratic and equalitarian-authoritarian continui of personality. The TFI is based on five personality factors: conventionalism, authoritarian submission, exaggerated masculinity and feminity, extreme emphasis on discipline and a moralistic rejection of impulsive life (cf. Robinson & Shaver 1969 : 295). As the TFI-scale is closely related conceptually to the F-scale, instead of using the TFI-scale in its entirely we only used that part of the scale which emphasizes the individual's personality as regards to masculinity and feminity. For the present study, therefore, we have used only two sections of the scale which deal with women; specifically, those relating to the "authoritarian submission" and "exaggerated masculinity and feminity." As adjusted, the TFI-scale presently used consists of 24-items, with the possible scores ranging from 24 to 48. High scores indicate greater "democratic" and "equalitarian" orientations.

The "Religious Fundamentalism" (RF-scale) used in this study was designed by Martin and Westie (1959). This is a 9-item scale, with possible scores varying from 9 to 36. This scale found to relate strongly with bigotry, authoritarianism, cognitive rigidity, intolerence of ambiguity, strict adherence to dogma and marked distinctions made between in-groups and out-groups (cf. Robinson & Shaver 1969 : 593).

Socio-demographic variables such as gender, age, and marital status were used as dummy variables, with "male", "single", "teens" scored as zero, while subjects' and their parents' religious preferences were coded separately into three categories (no religion=1, Protestant=2, and Other=3). Father's and mother's educations were coded separately into three categories (below high school=1, high school=2, and above high school=3). The socio-economic status variable was coded into three categories (Working class=1, Middle class=2, and Upper class=3), based on the subjects' perceived family social class background.

RESULTS

Results of analysis revealed a marked difference among the male and female students' attitude toward women (feminism). The mean difference between male and female feminism scores were statistically significant (F=58.91, df=1, 375, p<.00001). Among the personal characteristics (age, marital status, religious preference and self reported socio-economic status), age (F=9.46, df=1,375, p<.002), and religious preference (F=14.44, df=2,374, p<.00001) appeared to be the significant distinctive factors influencing feminism scores. While considering parental characteristics (father's and mother's religious preferences, and

Table 1. Means and standard deviation of feminism, authori-tarianism traditional family ideology, religious fundamenatalist scores by Socio-Demographic variables

Variables		*Scores on attitudinal variables*			
		Mean	*Standard deviation*	*F-values (df)*	*Significant level*
Feminism					
Gender :	Male	63.89	12.27		
	Female	73.68	12.43	58.91 (1,375)	.00001
Age :	Teens	66.80	12.94		
	Above teens	70.99	13.27	9.46 (1,375)	.002
Marital status :					
	Unmarried	69.11	13.66		not
	Married	69.10	12.27	0.0001 (1,375)	significant
Religion :	None	77.00	13.15		
	Protestant	67.37	12.64		
	Other	74.32	14.57	14.44 (2,374)	.00001
Father's religion :					
	None	72.80	11.51		
	Protestant	68.12	13.23		
	Other	75.86	14.61	5.45 (2,374)	.005
Mother's religion :					
	None	73.17	10.74		
	Protestant	68.34	13.14		
	Other	76.79	14.30	5.56 (2,374)	.004

Variables		Scores on attitudinal variables			
		Mean	Standard deviation	F-values (df)	Significant level
Father's education :					
Below high school		70.02	12.41		
High school grad.		68.07	13.25		not
Above high school		69.38	13.98	0.69 (2,374)	significant
Mother's education :					
Below high shool		68.41	12.15		
High school grad.		67.91	14.24		not
Above high school		71.37	12.58	2.50 (2,374)	significant
Socio-economic status :					
	Working class	69.66	12.14		
	Middle class	68.98	13.44		not
	Upper class	70.50	13.29	0.13 (2,374)	significant
Authoritarianism					
Gender :	Male	27.42	4.88		not
	Female	26.65	4.69	2.46 (1,375)	significant
Age :	Teens	27.67	4.68		
	Above teens	26.47	4.68	5.91 (1,375)	.02
Marital status :					
	Unmarried	27.01	4.72		not
	Married	27.71	5.00	.0004 (1,375)	significant
Religion :	None	23.73	5.04		
	Protestant	27.63	4.55		
	Other	26.18	4.22	16.29 (2,374)	.00001
Father's religion :					
	None	25.60	4.84		
	Protestant	27.32	4.7		
	Other	25.48	4.33	3.71 (2,374)	.03
Mother's religion :					
	None	25.94	5.01		
	Protestant	27.22	4.78		
	Other	24.83	4.19	3.29 (2,374)	.04
Father's education :					
Below high school		26.86	4.51		
High school grad.		27.45	4.68		not
Above high school		26.70	5.11	0.89 (2,374)	significant

Variables		Scores on attitudinal variables			
		Mean	Standard deviation	F-values (df)	Significant level
Mother's education :					
Below high school		28.03	4.55		
Below school grad.		27.06	4.60		
Above high school		26.07	5.09	4.56 (2, 374)	.01
Socio-economic status :					
	Working class	27.63	4.28		
	Middle class	27.03	4.86		
	Upper class	24.64	4.07	2.07 (2,374)	not significant
Traditional Family Ideology					
Gender :	Male	81.85	11.96		
	Female	87.49	12.95	19.12 (1,375)	.00001
Age :	Teens	82.07	12.17		
	Above teens	87.12	12.87	15.10 (1,375)	.0001
Marital status :					
	Unmarried	84.92	12.52		not
	Married	84.69	13.55	0.02 (1,375)	significant
Religion :	None	93.48	12.71		
	Protestant	83.00	11.99		
	Other	90.09	14.41	18.41 (2,374)	.00001
Father's religion :					
	None	88.64	12.10		
	Protestant	83.87	12.62		
	Other	91.38	13.96	5.77 (2,374)	.003
Mother's religion :					
	None	88.44	10.56		
	Protestant	84.12	12.75		
	Other	92.54	12.41	5.74 (2,374)	.004
Father's education :					
Below high school		85.03	12.26		
High school grad.		84.02	12.86		not
Above high school		85.54	13.19	0.48 (2,374)	significant
Mother's education :					
Below high school		83.49	10.32		
High school grad.		83.67	13.80		
Above high school		87.68	12.86	4.15 (2,374)	.02

Variables		Scores on attitudinal variables			
		Mean	*Standard deviation*	*F-values (df)*	*Significant level*
Socio-economic status :					
	Working class	83.59	11.34		
	Middle class	84.90	12.86		not
	Upper class	87.57	15.52	0.52 (2,374)	significant
Religious Fundamentalism					
Gender :	Male	25.99	7.94		
	Female	28.22	8.26	7.12 (1,375)	.008
Age :	Teens	29.24	7.25		
	Above teens	25.50	8.52	20.48 (1,375)	.00001
Marital status :					
	Unmarried	26.98	8.08		not
	Married	27.71	8.46	0.61 (1,375)	significant
Religion :	None	17.25	6.62		
	Protestant	29.13	6.99		
	Other	23.77	8.74	65.67 (2,374)	.00001
Father's religion :					
	None	21.42	8.07		
	Protestant	28.26	7.72		
	Other	23.52	9.14	17.35 (2,374)	.00001
Mother's religion :					
	None	18.74	7.41		
	Protestant	27.96	7.87		
	Other	22.52	8.19	16.00 (2,374)	.00001
Father's education :					
Below high school		27.48	7.81		
High school grad.		27.44	8.00		
Above high school		26.69	8.66	0.38 (2,374)	not significant
Mother's education :					
Below high school		28.62	7.19		
High school grad.		26.72	8.04		
Above high school		26.60	9.03	2.08 (2,374)	not significant
Socio-economic status :					
	Working class	27.46	7.91		
	Middle class	27.30	8.08		
	Upper class	23.64	10.74	1.37 (2, 374)	not significant

education), only the fathers' and mothers' religious preferences (F=5.45, df=2,374, p<.005 and F=5.56, df=2, 374, p<.004 respectively) were noted to have significant effects on feminism for both male and female students.

Similarly, significant differences were found between male and female attitudes toward "traditional family ideology" (F=19.12, df=1,375, p<.00001). Among other personal characteristics, age (F=15.10, df=1,375, p<.00001), and religion (F=18.41, df=2,374, p<.00001) were the most prominently significant characteristics. However, among parental characteristics, father's religion (F=5.77, df=2,374, p<.003), mother's religion (F=5.74, df=2,374, p<.004), and mother's education (F=4.15, df=2,374, p<.02) were also statistically significant. Although the results did not indicate any significant difference between the male and female students with respect to "authoritarian" attitudes, significant differences were noted in age (F=5.91, df=1,375, p<.02), and religion (F=16.29, df=2,374, p<.00001) among personal characteristics, and in father's religion (F=3.71, df=2,374, p<.03), mother's religion(F=3.29, df=2,374, p<.04) and mother's education (F=4.56, df=2,374, p<.01).

Regarding the "religious fundamentalism scale, gender (F=7.12, df=1,375, p<.008), age (F=20.48, df=1,375, p<.00001), and religion (F=65.67, df=2,374, p<.00001) were distinctively significant personal characteristics, whereas only father's religion (F=17.35, df=2,374, p<.00001), and mother's religion (F=16.00, df=2,374, p<.00001) were significant parental characteristics. These findings therefore strongly suggest the effect that such personal characteristics of the students as gender, age, and religion....in addition to parental religions and mother's education...may have in substantially influencing the development of social values.

The results of stepwise regression analyses clarified the above findings. Regarding authoritarianism, gender, age, religion, mother's religion and education were significant contributing variables, emphasizing the suggestion that women and older persons will be more tolerant of social change. Although the results indicated that mother's education and religious background may contribute to a child's understanding of social change, the child's own religious preference/participation may also inhibit a child's sense of tolerance.

TABLE 2. Regression models for effects of Socio-Demographic variables on authoritarianism, traditional family ideology, religious fundamentalism, and attitude toward women

Socio-Demographic variables	*Standardized Beta-values for regression models*				
	Authoritarianism	*Traditional Family Ideology*	*Reigious Fundamentalism*	*Feminism*	*Feminism*
Gender	-.110[a]	.266[e]		.414[e].	222[e]
Age	-.142[C]	.243[e]	-.209[e]	.224[e]	
Religion	.284[e]	-.248[e]	.371[e]	-.225[e]	
Father's religion			.150[b]		
Mother's religion	-.169[C]	.172[C]	-.219[C]	.156[C]	
Mother's education	-.174[d]	.147[e]-	.134[C]	.094[a]	
Traditional Family Ideology					.604[e]
Authoritarianism					-.172[e]
Adjusted R^2	.106	.166	.183	.227	.641
F-value	9.908	16.008	17.895	23.027	244.907
Significant level	.00001	.00001	.00001	.00001	.00001

[a]Significant at .05 level of probability.
[b] Significant at .01 level of probability.
[e] Significant at .005 level of probability.
[d]Significant at .0005 level of probability.
[e] Significant at .00001 level of probability.

Similarly, the results of regression analysis of "traditional family ideology" attitudes were consistent with the findings on "authoritarianism." Among all of the personal and parental characteristics considered in this study, only gender, age, religion, mother's religion and education contribute significantly in explaining both "authoritarianism" and "traditional family ideology."

Considering "religious fundamentalism," the results were consistent with earlier findings. Here, gender was not a significant contributing variable, but father's religion became an additional influencing variable. As expected, these were consistent with those of the analyses of "authoritarianism." These results also supported the assertion that women with higher education would be more tolerant of social change.

Consistent with the results of regression analyses on "authoritarianism," traditional family ideology," and "religious fundamentalism," the present regression model selected gender, age, religion, mother's religion and education as the significant personal and parental characteristics in explaining "feminism." These findings strongly support the effect of socialization influences on such social values as attitude toward sex role changes (feminism). The significant effect of mother's education on feminism is consistent with the result of earlier researchers (cf. Coser 1964 ; Kohn & Clausen 1956; Parsons 1954; Wylie 1942).

The present results thus clarified the hypothesis that the attitudinal variables...authoritarianism, traditional family ideology, religious fundamentalism, and feminism...are affected by the socio-demographic variables considered in this study. Among all of the socio-demographic variables, only gender, age, religion, mother's religion and education significantly affected "authoritarianism", "traditional family ideology", and "feminism". "Religious fundamentalism" was significantly affected by age, religion, father's and mother's religions, and mother's education.

The final stepwise regression analysis included all of the socio-demographic variables and attitudinal variables to explore their explanatory effects on "feminism", where, among all the socio-demographic variables, only gender, and, among the attitudinal variables, authoritarianism and traditional family ideology were retained in the regression equation. These three variables...gender, authoritarianism, and traditional family ideology...explained 64 percent of the total variations in "faminism." This result supports the hypothesis that positive attitudes toward women (feminism) is influenced by the combined effects of attitudinal and socio-demographic variables. Although gender was the only socio-demographic variable presently retained in the regression equation, the remaining socio-demographic variables...age, religion, mother's religion, mother's education....were observed to be the major contributing factors in "authoritarianism" and "traditional familiy ideology." In addition, the results also supported the remaining two hypotheses that

(1) attitudes toward women (feminism) would be positively affected by "traditional family ideology" (beta= +.604, p<.00001), and (2) attitudes toward women (feminism) would be negatively affected by "authoritarianism" (beta = .172, p<.00001).

SUMMARY

Principal purpose of this study was to test whether traditionally feminine stereotypes were developed by parental influence through the socialization process, and mother's influence would reduce the feminine sterotypes of the children. Data were collected with a structured questionnaire from 377 white students, randomly drawn from a rural college campus in middle Tennessee. To measure the effects of socialization influences the associations between students' sex-role attitudes (feminism) and "traditional family ideology," "authoritarian attitudes," and "religious fundamentalism" attitudes were examined. Results of analyses of variance revealed a marked difference among male and female students' attitudes toward women (Feminism scores). Age and religion were the significant personal characteristics influencing feminism scores. Parental religion had significant effect on feminism for both male and female students.

Attitudes of male and female students toward "traditional family ideology" were significantly different, where mother's education, in addition to student's age, religion, and parental religion, had significant effect on "traditional family ideology." Similarly, student's age, religion, parental religion, and mother's education were significantly effecting student's "authoritarian" attitude, while there was no difference between male and female students' "authoritarian" attitude scores. At the same time, student's gender, age, religion, and parental religion were significant characteristics affecting "religious fundamentalism" scale score. These findings, thus consistently suggested that student's gender, age, religion, parental religion and, mother's education had substantial influence in the development of students' social values.

The results of multiple regression analyses further clarified that the attitudinal variables ... traditional family ideology, authoritarianism, and feminism...were significantly affected by the socio-demographic variables, such as, student's gender, age, religion, mother's religion, and mother's education. Religious fundamentalism was significantly affected by student's age, religion, father's and mother's religions, and mother's education.

Thus, the results supported our proposed hypotheses that attitude toward women was positively affected by the combined effects of attitudinal and socio-demographic variables, and traditional family ideology, on the other land, attitude toward women was negatively influenced by the authoritarianism scores.

References

Balbus, Issac D. 1992 "De-Kleining feminist mothering theory ?" *Theory and Society*, 21 : 817-835.

Banton, Michael 1990 "Comparing inequalities of race and sex" *Social studies Review*, 5 : 157-161.

Basow, Susan A., and Kristi L. Medcalf 1988 "Academic achievement and attributions among college students: Effects of gender and sex typing." *Sex Roles*, 19 : 555-567.

Benton, A.A. 1971 "Productivity, distributive Justice and burgaining among children." *Journal of Personality and Social Psychology*, 18 : 68-78.

Block, Jeanne H. 1976 "Issues, problems, and pitfalls in assessing sex differences : A critical review of *The Psychology of Sex Differences*." *Merrill-Palmer Quarterly*. 22 : 283-308.

Blumberg, Rae Lesser. 1989 "A theoretical look at the gender balance of power in the American couple." *Journal of Family Issues*, 10 : 225-250.

Burleson, Brant R., and Wendy Samter 1992 "Are there gender differences in the relationship between academic performance and social behavior ?" *Human Communication Research*, 19 : 155-175.

Coser, Rose Laub. 1964 "Authority and structural ambivalance in the middle-class family." In Rose Laub Coser (Ed.) *The Family : Its Structure and Functions* (pp. 370-383). New York : St. Martin's Press.

Cowan, Gtloria, Monja Mestlin, & Julie Masek. 1992 "Predictors of feminist self-labeling." *Sex-Roles*, 27 :" 321-330.

Cubbins, Lisa A. 1991 "Women, men and the division of power : A study of gender stratification in Kenya." *Social Forces*, 69 : 1063-1083.

Davis, Nancy J., & Robert V. Robinson 1991 "Men's and women's consciousness of gender inequality : Austria, West Germany, Great Britain and the United States." *American Sociological Review*, 56 : 72-84.

Foon, Anne E.	1988	"Effect of mothers' employment status on adolescents' self perceptions and academic performance." *Educational Studies*, 14 : 265-274.
Fox, Mary Frank & Vincent C. Ferri.	1992	"Women, men and their attributions for success in academec." *Social Psychology Quarterly*, 55 : 257-271.
Funder, D.C.J.H. Block, & J. Block	1983	"Delay gratification : Some longitudinal personality correlates." *Journal of Personality and social Psychology*, 44 : 1198-1213.
Hochschild, Arlie R.	1973	"A review of sex role research." *American Journal of Sociology*, 78 : 1011-1029.
Hunt, Janet, & Larry Hunt.	1977	"Race, daughter and fathers loss : Does absence make the girl grow stronger ?" *Social Problems*, 25 : 90-98.
Kitay, P.M.	1940	"A comparison of the sexes in their attitudes and beliefs about women." *Sociometry* 34 : 399-407.
Kohlberg, L.	1986	"A cognitive developmental analysis of children's sex-role concepts and attitudes." In E.E. Maccoby (Ed.), The Development of Sex Differences. Standford, Calif; Stanford University Press.
Kohn, Melvin L., & John A. Clausen.	1956	"Parental authority behavior and schiezo-phrenia. "*American Journal of Orthopsychiatry*, 26 : 297-313.
Kristiansen, Connie M.	1990	"The role of values in the relation between gender and health behavior." *Social Behavior*, 5 : 127-133.
Lamb, Michael E	1982	"Parental behavior and child development in non-traditional families : An introduction." (Pp. 1-12). In Michael E. Lamb (Ed.) *Non-Traditional Families : Parenting and Child Development.*
Leventhal, G.S. & D. Anderson	1970	"Self-interest and maintenance of equity." *Journal of Personality and Social Psychology*, 15 : 57-62.
Leventhal, G.S., & D.W. Lane.	1970	"Sex, age, and equity behavior." *Journal of Personality and Social Psychology*, 15 : 312-316.
Levinson, D., & P. Huffman	1925	"Traditional family ideology and its relation to personality." *Journal of Personality*, 23 : 251-273.
Licht, Barbara G., & C. Susan Dweck	1984	"Determinants of academic achievement : The interaction of children's achievement orientation with skill area." *Developmental Psychology*, 20 : 628-636.

Licht, Barbara G., Sandra R. Stader, & Cynthia C. Swenson	1989	"Children's achievement-related beliefs : Effects of academic area, sex, and achievement level." *Journal of Educational Research*, 82 : 253-260.
Maccoby, Elenor E. (ed.)	1966	*The Development of Sex Differences.* Stanford, Calif. : Stanford University Press.
Maccoby, Elenor E., & Carol N. Jacklin	1974	*The Psychology of Sex Differences.* Stanford, Calif : Stanford University Press.
Marini, Margaret Mooney	1984	"Women's educational attainment and the timing of entry into parenthood." *American Sociological Review*, 49 : 491-511.
Martin, J., & F. Westie	1959	"The tolerant personality." *American Sociological Review* 24 : 521-528.
McKee, J.P.& A.C. Sherriffs	1959	"Men's and womens's beliefs, ideas and self-concepts." *American Journal of Sociology*, 64 : 356-363.
Mendelsohn, Robert, & Shirley Dobie	1970	"Women's self conception : A block to carrer development." Manuscript LaFayette Clinic, Department of Mental Health, Detroit, Michigan.
Mischel, W.	1970	"Sex-typing and socialization." In P.H. Mussen (Ed.) *Carmichaesls Manual of Child Psychology.* New York : Wiley.
Mortiner, Jeylan T., & Glorian Sorensen.	1984	"Men, women, work and family." (Pp. 139-167). In Kathryn M. Borman, Daisy Quarm, Sarah Gideonse (Eds.). Women in the *Workplace : Effects on Families.* Ablex.
Nadler, E.D. & W.R. Morrow	1959	"Authoritarian attitudes toward women and their correlates." *Journal of Social Psychology*, 49 : 113-123.
Parsons, Talcott	1954	"Certain primary sources and patterns of aggression in the social structure of the Western World." (Pp. 299-322). In Talcott Parsons, *Essays in Sociological Theory*, Glencoe, Illinois : Free Press.
Robinson, John P., & Phillip Shaver	1969	*Measures of Social Psychological Attitudes.* Ann Arbor, Michigan : Institute for Social Research, University of Michigan.
Rossi, Alice.	1969	"Sex equality : the beginnings of ideology." *Humanist* (September-October).
Rossi, Alice	1985	*Gender and The Life Course.* New York : Aldine Publ.
Ryckman, David B., & Percy D. Peckham	1987a	"Gender differences in attributions for success and failure." *Journal of Early Adolescence*, 7 : 47-63.
Ryckman, David B., & Percy D. Peckham	1987b	"Gender differences in attributions for success and failure across subject areas," *Journal of Educational Research*, 81 : 120-125.

Sampson, E.E. 1975 "On Justice as equality." *Journal of Social Issues*, 31 : 45-64.

Schopler, J., & N.Bateson 1965 "The power of dependency." *Journal of Personality and Social Psychology*, 2 : 247-254.

Sjoberg, Svein 1988 "Gender and the image" of science. *Scandinavian Journal of Educational Research*, 32 : 49-60.

Smith, S. 1939 "Age and sex differences in children's opinions concerning sex differences." *Journal of Genetic Psychology*, 54 : 17-25.

Smith, Thomas Ewin 1992 "Gender differences in the scientific achievement of adolescents : Effects of age and parental separation." *Social Forces*, 71 : 469-484.

Stephan, Cookie W, & Judy Corder 1985 "The effects of dual- career families on adolescents' sex role attitudes, work and family plans and choices of important others." *Journal of Marriage and the Family*. 47 : 912-929.

Todd, Judith, Ariella Friedman, & Priscilla Wanjiru Kariuki 1990 "Women growing stronger with age : The effect of status in the United States and Kenya." *Psychology of Women Quarterly*, 14 : 567-577.

Vanyperen, Nico W., & Bram P., Buunk 1991 "Sex-role attitudes social comparison, and satisfaction with relationships." *Social Psychology Quarterly*, 54 : 169-180.

Weinstein, E.A.W.L. Devaughn & M.G. Wiley 1969 "Obligation and the flow of deference." *Sociometry*, 32 : 1-12.

Wylie, Philip 1942 *Generation of Vipers*. New York : Farrar & Rinehart.

Magdalena Villarreal

BATTLES OVER IMAGES : WOMEN'S STRUGGLE OVER SPACE AND IDENTITY IN A MEXICAN EJIDO

The 'ideology' and 'culture' of Mexican men, of the Mexican ruling party, of Mexican women, is said to be undergoing change. One would like to possess clear cut categories for describing these changes, for portraying the differences within neatly defined contexts, grasping crucial issues such as struggles for power, autonomy and independence. However, encountering the actual men and women in the field portrays a much more blurred picture. Ideology is not a fixed set of norms and ideas which determines behavior and can be detected within clearly defined boundaries. In the same way, culture cannot be merely described as an established context composed of traditions and shared understandings. Thus, our challenge is to be able to attain deeper insights into social change, to depict how 'collective' identities are recognized as such and, not only to describe how social groups perceive themselves as different from 'others', but how they struggle to impose or sell others their representations, the roles that are deemed suitable. The meanings attributed to traditions, the appropriate norms to determine behavior and ideas over adequate roles are the object of ongoing battles.

The case I am about to present highlights the difficulties in arriving at categorical conclusions, it shows the interweaving of trivial and crucial events, how shared and conflicting values coincide and cleave, and how multidimensional negotiations take place. I describe how the introduction of a government-initiated development project for women in Ayuquila, western Mexico, pulled the 'beneficiaries'—a group of beekeepers—into a confrontation between 'external' categorizations of themselves as women and their own diverse images and representations. This process discloses intricate situations whereby 'outsiders'—in this case Mexican bureaucrats—try to sell their definitions and models, while local actors attempt to broaden their margins for action, to create or maintain space for their own personal and collective projects, incorporating or adjusting the intervenor's projects to their own. In the whirl of events, issues concerning shared identities, struggles over meanings and discontinuities in terms of power come to the fore.

Crucial to these processes are the battles over images inherent to the interaction between the different actors' representations of the situation, of the roles ascribed to each other in an effort to 'win the struggles that take place over the attribution of specific social meanings to particular events, actions, and ideas' (see Long 1989:11). These battles involve disputes over social boundaries, negotiations over values and interpretation, manoeuvering of networks, and endeavours of enrolment as well as resistance.

My objective is to analyze these issues and the concrete mechanisms by which they occur in the everyday lives of the group of beekeepers. I hope to highlight the changes taking place in the images of themselves and the boundaries they set on their projects, as well as the battles they have to fight in the defense of their own space when interacting with 'outside' intervenors, but also with the 'ejidatarios'—whose institution, the ejido, is commonly recognized as a men's world in the village. In this endeavour, I examine what I consider critical social interface situations, where members of the group are exposed to encounters with people from 'the outside' and to their definitions, ideas, representations and interpretations.

The project from the point of view of planners and implementors : 'external' images.

Silvia Macias, a female lawyer from BANRURAL (National Rural Bank) was—at the time this study took place—head of the program of UAIMs in the state of Jalisco, Mexico. The UAIMs (Agrarian and Industrial Units for Peasant Women) were created under the guidelines of the New Law of Agrarian Reform, with the aim of incorporating peasant women into the country's 'development' by offering loans for group economic activities. We met Silvia in her office in Guadalajara to discuss this program. Before turning her attention to the interviewers, Silvia answered many telephone calls, giving the impression of a busy woman. Well dressed, her red tinted hair shinning, she pulls out a cigarette from a fancy box and explains with a smile :

> "The program is part of the women's struggle for their integration into the world of production, while at the same time recognizing them as apt to receive credit. It is a consequence of the struggle of peasant women, fruit of a social movement."

'Peasant Women's struggle for autonomy from the 'male' world'

The social movement Silvia is referring to is the Mexican Revolution which took place at the beginning of the century, after which the PRI—the ruling party to which she must adhere as a civil servant—took over. Her use of the term 'peasant women' apparently refers to the female inhabitants of rural villages, not only dismissing differentiations in terms of ethnicity, economic situations, occupation, age, status, personal experience, hobbies, interests, etc., but also assuming that they are homogeneously distant from access to financial services, that they all yearn for autonomy from male spheres and that their goal in to obtain an income independently from their spouses and families. This colors her understanding of the interests and goals of women. The program stresses that women should strengthen their economic roles and enhance their status in such a way that they constitute an active force in society. Furthermore, in her eyes, the 'world of production' is the world of progress, of development, of free enterprise which will provide a way out of poverty, and which of course is the domain of the 'experts', naturally from outside the rural scenario.

However, she is eager to portray an image of the bank as an institution sensitive to social problems and responsive to them, and depicts the programme as belonging to Mexicans, a voice for people who struggled to acquire this right, for women who yearn to incorporate themselves into what has been known as the 'men's world'. Silvia continues :

> "We have a multidisciplinary team in the bank, from geologists to sociologists and social workers. We want to develop the women as entrepreneurs, and for that, we have to assure ourselves that they will be able to make it. We always tell the people that we want to benefit them, not harm them with a programme that does not work out."

Collective entrepreneurship for liberation

Silvia believes that women are motivated to participate in these programmes, mainly because they are now recognized as apt for credit, as entrepreneurs, claiming that they have always laboured in the fields, but without remuneration. Her image of the programme, of its constraints and possibilities is also framed by her own self image, and by her notion of rural women, of their problems and potential. She describes herself as an entrepreneur, but more than that, a women with experience concerning the needs and difficulties of the rural poor, and with possibilities of offering options to them. However, the alternative model she proposes for rural women differs from her personal model in many ways : for one, entrepreneurship must be collective. Rural women are expected to work in groups, where private interests can hinder group development. Their personal aspirations must be channeled into group endeavours, where organization is a key word.

> "We can find real leaders in the groups, women who struggle to be recognized, but also many limitations, and those who are willing to organize themselves with other people in similar conditions are the ones that hold a chance of liberation".

In contrast to the model of individual entrepreneurial organization, she herself might follow in her private life, here it is important to keep the group as democratic as possible, and decisions must be taken within a transparent atmosphere, without affecting—of course—other public interests in their villages. She trusts that there is a possibility of arriving at 'collective' control of this organization with the advice and proper training from the programme's extension workers.

The women should acquire a 'strategic conception of their own development'

The 'revolutionary' model relies heavily on the notion of participation, although participation in only conceived within the boundaries of this largely per-defined project, not in terms of what the women themselves might have considered their own projects. Moreover, the women should acquire a "strategic conception" of their own development as peasant women, that is, they should see themselves as an important social force, they should disregard small, trivial interests which hinder their progress. This implies a "societal perspective" on the use of their resources and profits, and will only be possible if they consolidate a set of practices that allow them to make the appropriate collective decisions. From her point of view, this in not easy, and some obstacles have to be sorted out:

> "There is *'atavismo'* (ties to old, backward ideas), and *'machismo'* as well as inferiority complexes in the women, and they come out with things like 'my husband doest's allow me', 'my brother does not want me to join the group'.
>
> "The problem is the different interests that exist between them, the different conceptions of life and development which do not allow people to see further. We are facing social atavisms and it is a matter of fighting them with appropriate education. If you manage to get two or three women together, you sing victory, because they can become smal poles of development."

Silvia's interpretation of the programme and its prospects is more or less shared by other government officials who, in one way or another, have influence on the women's groups. Her words are not uncommon in Mexican politics, as the PRI campaigns under the slogan : 'The party of the Mexican Revolution'. Furthermore, it in no coincidence that Silvia and other civil servants express themselves in this way about women's struggles and aim to convert them into entrepreneurs, as this has also constituted an important part of government rhetoric and slogans in the past years, although the implementation of these ideas is of course entangled within all sorts of political practices. While government discourse concerning women's programmes stressed the need for radical change, the creation of UAIMs did not directly threaten authority, or land tenure patterns, neither was the intention to change the terms of gender organization in the household or in the fields. The amount of money allotted to the project and the legislation which stipulated that the *ejido* institution function as a convenient mediator between the women and the government, limited the potential of the project to start with.

Changing Boundaries and Identities[2]

From the point of view of the women 'beneficiaries' of the UAIMS, on the other hand, one could find different interpretations of the scope and possibilities of such a project. The beekeepers focus of our study conceived its prospects within the boundaries of what they considered their roles and oriented their activities to suit their own aspirations and immediate needs.

However, these boundaries, shaped by the individual or shared identities and self-images of the members of the group, should not be considered as fixed : the women presented themselves differently according to the audience and circumstance, and their self-images changed in the course of events. In the actual implementation of the project, the notions of *peasant women, women entrepreneurs,* and *'strategic development', reached the* beekeepers in different ways, incarnated within intricate social situations and transformed and crossed by different social processes. The new ideas generated were, of course, internalized or resisted, or rather recreated within shared contexts to conform to their needs. One can identify changes in the boundaries the women set on their projects within key interface situations where power flows cannot be overlooked. Direct and indirect information, passed on through discursive and non-discursive communication, leaked into the group, not as 'pure' data, but reinterpreted and recreated differently by each 'receiver' as well as by each 'sender'. This 'joint creation of knowledge' (see Long, 1989) constitutes an ongoing, dynamic activity which shapes interface situations in many ways, while at the same time being shaped by these encounters.

Initiation of the project

In 1980 a social worker from the Mexican Ministry of Agrarian Reform presented herself to the head of the *ejido* of Ayuquila[3], the *comisariado* ejidal, hoping to organize an Agrarian and Industrial Unit for peasant woman (UAIM).

A number of women attended the meeting that the *comisariado* arranged on behalf of the social worker. The names and signatures of the women who were interested were listed; and in this way they became recognized as a group that could receive aid under the government scheme. In accordance with the law, the ejido was compelled to give up a piece of land for the new UAIM initiative, with the government matching this with credit for the enterprise.

Two years passed (during which time the women never met as a group) until another social worker, now from the Government Rural Bank (BANRURAL), came to offer them credit to raise goats, pigs, chickens, or whatever economic activity they wanted, as long as it fitted into the formal requirements. The group now had 22 members. In the intervening period, some had married and were not permitted by their husbands to continue, and others had gone out to work or study. The group finally choose bee-keeping, as it did not involve a daily commitment. They now laugh at this decision, saying that they picked the worst activity, because they are constantly being stung by the bees.

In 1984 the project was formally initiated with a loan of 775,000 Mexican pesos (approximately 1550 U.S. dollars) from BANRURAL for the purchase of the beehives, bees and basic equipment. They started with 50 hives, which they bought in a nearby village with the aid of a social worker, who helped them buy the new equipment and explained how they should keep their account and minute books. In addition, they receives some formal training, although the women say it was not enough, for it was too theoretical. Once they began working, they encountered major problems which they solved by contacting some bee-keepers in the vicinity, who gave them other more practical courses and much advice.

Adopting strategic labels

In October 1986 the group was extracting honey. The yields were very good. Petra—who was then Vice-President but later became President of the group-comments that it was like a dream to see so much honey. They gave away pieces of honeycomb and jars of honey to friends, neighbours, relatives, and to public officers they interacted with. After that it was even better. As soon as they had finished extracting the first yield, the combs were full again. Although their actual profits were meager, they harvested again in November, then in December, and once again in January.

For many people of the village the success of the beekeepers was a surprise. Many say they had not believed that the women could really do it. There had also been conflicts because some of the *ejidatarios* did not agree to their being given land, arguing that they were women who did not do the things they should, they neglected their duties (*'desquehaceradas'* with no household obligations) and would not know how to manage the enterprise.

Even the beekeepers described themselves many *times as 'mujeres pata rajada'* (with cracked feet). *Pata rajada* is commonly used in this region to describe a hard working "Indian", a tough person who can work in the fields barefoot, thereby getting cracked soles. Fissures on the soles are the result of walking barefoot on the hot earth, or wearing typical *huaraches* (cheap sandals), but it is something local people refer to as a trait characteristic of a lower category of people, in contrast to *'la gente refinada'* (refined people), who wear shoes and therefore do not suffer from cracked soles. Sometimes, however, the word was used by the beekepers with a mocking connotation, a way of 'putting themselves down' strategically, while obviously not really believing it themselves to its full implications. The beekeepers had sown their plot in the hillside themselves—'with their fingernails" as they say, commenting that only "primitive" people will do it in this way, but their resources were too scarce to do otherwise.

Nevertheless, their self-conceptions and the commitments to a certain type of project, although largely influenced by project planners, were embedded in the acceptance or negotiation of shared values and practices in the village. More striking, however, was the way their identity was shaped by the practical actions they undertook, by 'playing the game' of the project, by acting out roles in the village to avoid social problems, by attending meetings, by interacting with government officers, and by committing themselves to beekeeping activities.

Identity as an unintended consequence of action

There is a shortage of land in Ayuquila, with many *ejidatarios* having less than one hectare of arable land. These are given plots on the nearby hillside, which they use either for grazing cattle, if they have some, or for producing pasture for sale. The women's group, which had been donated hillside land by the *ejido,* adopted the same strategy of selling pasture. With the money they earned, as well as from that received from the sale of their honey, they decided to build a small store. It was a big sacrifice for them not to receive a share out of their small earnings, as each one had many ideas on what she would do with her share. But it was a real problem to store all their tools, the bulky extractor, the big 200-liter can, and the growing number of wooden boxes and frames for the wax in their houses. When they were extracting, it was an even greater inconvenience, not only because the sticky honey and wax got all over the place, but because the house immediately filled up with hungry bees.

The decision to construct a store was unanimous, given the need for a physical space in which to work, to store their things and to hold meetings. An ejidatario sold them a small piece of his urban plot and they contracted a local bricklayer. Although the store was small, it satisfied the requirements of their enterprise. They only needed sufficient space for the extractor and the decanter, a space for capping the combs, and a place to keep the boxes and frames. The space was also big enough for the 16 members to meet. Benita, one of the beekeepers, caressed the walls fondly : "This"-she said-"this is ours".

The construction of the store had implications in terms of the women's conception of themselves as part of a project. It sealed an unwritten pact to proceed as a group, and revealed ambitions to continue the enterprise, however small. The beekeepers would carry on despite criticisms from some of their neighbours, who had scornfully labelled them *'abejeras'* (instead of *'apicultoras'* which is the technical word used for beekeepers)[4]. However, they took it lightheartedly, and half mockingly assumed the term themselves, giving it a different connotation altogether. *'Abejeras'*, pronounced by the members of the group, implied a *'pata rajada'* who worked under the sun, covered from head to foot with dirty, smelly clothes (they explained that bees do not like the smell of perfume and attack more readily when they use this or certain soaps) but at the same time it denoted progressive women who defied criticisms and dared shoulder a responsibility such as the beekeeping enterprise.

The image of 'respectable woman'

However, the women delimited what they considered could be the scope of their project according to the boundaries they placed on their own roles and aspirations, accommodating them to conflicting and common interests. For example, *'ama de casa'* (housewife) was a term often used to address themselves. None claimed explicitly to be a model housewife, but Petra, the President of the group, often boasted about here skill in cooking and was proud of the way she had reared her children, in spite of the problems she had with her husband, who did not agree with her religious activities and wanted her to spend more time in the house. Sara (another beekeeper) spoke with satisfaction about how good her sons were, the way they went to church on Sundays, but also about her kind and faithful husband, and how she walked kilometers across the fields to take him a hot lunch and then stayed a bit to help out with his chores. She proudly showed her sewing and embroidery to her visitors. Socorro (one of the eldest of the group) bragged quietly about how she cooked for her family, which was now only composed of boys, since the girls had married out.

Presenting themselves as good housewives meant conforming to what was considered a 'good', ' respectable' role for women in the social circles in which they interacted. Although the actual implications of the notion varied for different people within different scenarios, it was certain these would include the role of mother, housekeeper and wife. It was thus convenient to present themselves as women whose priorities were in the household, women who shared, who gave and suffered[5]. The price was high, as it included, among other things, a degree of confinement to the household and a degree of subordination to 'male authority', but open failure to conform carried with it unwanted penalties. It was not uncommon to find the beekeepers emphasizing their housewife activities to present themselves as 'respectable'. However, the women did not always comply to these expectations and found ways of justifying their conduct, many times using the very image of 'respectable woman'.

Internalizing and negotiating self-images

One could observe, however, that the beekeepers self-images underwent certain changes. The label of "*mujer campesina*" (peasant women) would be used once in a while. It was not a category the women placed themselves in before the start of the projects, as it implied a view of wider horizon, i. e. a contrast with working women of the cities, or with industrial women. Many of the beekeepers have visited other places, where they have worked for some periods, doing different types of odd jobs, from cooking in a restaurant, making tortillas or feeding working squads in the agricultural fields, to sewing in garget factories. Their work has never been restricted only to agriculture, and their description of themselves does not make a clear cut differentiation depending on type of work. They consider themselves basically as the same women, and their roles and responsibilities towards their households have not changed drastically.

It was not until they experienced the project, until they faced the possibility of acquiring credit when belonging to such a category, until some of the discourse had been internalized, that they addressed themselves as 'peasant women'. The category 'peasant' obviously contains a strong agricultural flavour and would probably not therefore encompass fully the livelihoods of these women, who have strong links to their sons and relatives working in urban areas, and some are themselves much involved in non-farm work. Petra, as I once observed in a maize field, could not tell the difference between a ripe ear of corn and a tender one, and Socorro confesses she only goes to the fields with the beekeepers. However, they have quickly learned to apply the term 'peasant women' to themselves, which they perceive as something worthy of dignity, using it especially when presenting themselves to outsiders since it allows them to receive attention from the public sphere.

On the whole, the label *'mujeres empresarias'* (women entrepreneurs) was seldom used in serious conversation to refer to themselves, although the notion was sometimes implied. While it was clear that some toyed the idea, for others to use it was to move too far. Nevertheless, when having fun, they would use it often, satirizing it, and expressing it as something remote and impossible. Instead, the women liked to think that they were now becoming "relevant to our village and our country." It appeared that there had to be a 'do-gooder' justification for their project, not just crude business. They would provide jobs, they would bring fame to the village (thus conforming to the image of 'respectable woman' and avoiding a direct war with male **ejidatarios** and other skeptical people in the village). Petra—a Jehovah's Witness—rationalized the idea of a women's enterprise drawing upon her religious conviction, which encourages images of 'development' and modernization. Thus, the idea of a new enterprise was imbued with a certain religious understanding, producing a different meaning of the notion.

The group's margins of action, however, were defined and changed in the interaction, interwoven as they were with common understandings, cultural frames and power relations.

The Mechanics of Change : social and organizational struggles

The women did not—as was implied by project planners and other 'outsiders'—lack strategic conceptions of themselves, of their own development. Their strategies frequently differed from those expected by observers simply because the 'battles' they were fighting were different: they had different enemies, different timing, different goals and anticipated different 'spoils'. However, both the beekeepers and the intervenors changed positions, strategies and objectives in a short period of time. This came about within a process of social and organizational struggle whereby the women changed the boundaries they set on their project, negotiating what they considered they were capable of achieving.

The process was not simple, and they did not accept the changes passively. The situation was never experienced exactly in the same way by all of the women, and each dealt, manipulated, and recreated her own distinctive dynamics of conditions and meanings. One could identify points of consensus but also of conflict, both within the group as between it and the *ejidatarios* as well as with other local officials. All of the parties involved used—individually and as groups—mechanisms of resistance, of accommodation and strategic compliance in their efforts to win over defintions of the project and of their roles and capacities.

Other 'strategic conceptions of women's developments': at the interface

Local government officials from the Ministry of Water Resources (SARH) previously outside of the scenario—detected the group and perceived other potentials for it. They had different ideas of the possibilities of the beekeeping enterprise, and not only that, but they conceived ways in which the group itself could fit in different 'development' programmes, providing them with a large donation, plus a loan, to create a 'real' agro-industry, with a larger storehouse and a good marketing programme. This adjusted nicely with personal interests within the officers' political careers and their possibilities of attracting financial resources to their own programmes.Thus they envisaged 'gender roles' for the beekeepers with regard to their undertaking as 'entrepreneurs', but also within their households with implication to their different networks in the village, and with respect to the country, as it was stressed that they would become a model for other peasant women (here again making claims to the image of 'respectable' or 'good' woman) and even for other men who were reluctant to organize and 'develop' themselves further. As a male officer put it, the women should :

> "... develop and integrate themselves, so that they do not see their actions as merely subsistence and hobby,but with a managerial mentality; it is important that they (the women) understand that they can grow with the products they have. The group can export their products, and become a source of development for all the bee-keepers on the region. Of course, they would first need an intensive technical training, in order that they are more prepared".

To enrol the women

Involving the group in this process was not easy, as it implied willingness on the part of the beekeepers to change, it involved breaking through resistances, building upon points of consensus and an internalization of different objectives and interpretations of their roles and capabilities. Enrolment, as Callon (1986) explains it,

> 'designates the device by which a set of interrelated roles is defined and attributed to actors who accept them. Interessement achieves enrolment if it is successful. To describe enrolment is thus to describe the group of multilateral negotiations, trials of strength and tricks that accompany the **interessements** and enable them to succeed.'

It was vital that the women accept the new store immediately, because if not, that part of the budget would have to be returned to the central office and allocated to another zone. There is a certain amount of prestige for the field worker and for the departments involved with this type of work, especially if it is a women's group, since the present government discourse emphasizes the importance of the development of peasant women *(mujeres campesinas)*.

These ideas found echo in Petra, the President of the beekeeping group, who was quite enthusiastic about the promise of a new, big store. She saw her dreams of a productive and efficient enterprise reflected in this project. It was no problem for her to put her household chores to one side. On several occasions she commented that all her time was at the disposal of the project. For her it meant the possibility of growing, even if they had to sacrifice a little for the moment. Being a Jehovah's Witness, and loving commercial activities, it fitted in nicely with her personal projects. Petra was supported to a degree by a network of close ties. centered around the current office-holders and women in her kin grouping, although they had some reservations.

And overcome resistance

However, the new proposal posed a problem for the group and led to some resistance, for the convenience of having a new store was not clear to all of them. Having to spend their earnings on labour was only part of the problem, though it was an important part, for as one of the oldest of the group, Eugenia, put it :

> "I would rather have my share, even if it is only enough to buy myself tennis shoes, for it will not be long before I die, and I want to see the profits of my work, If I die, my daughter will not take over and risk being stung by the bess !"

Eugenia is 67, and often jokes symbolically about her desire for a pair of 'tennis shoes'. She loves to watch TV soap operas. She is said to have enjoyed *'la vida alegre'* (i. e. the 'good life', implying having had many lovers) before she married. She has a sympathetic husband who helps with the bees and has an adopted adult daughter.

Another part of the problem was that they feared they would run out of money half way through the project and not be able to fulfil their commitments. Some, especially Sara, a peasant woman who had spent all her life helping raise cattle and cultivate the family plots, and who is 'finely in tune with nature', felt that the present store was enough for their needs, that it was near and convenient for everyone. Dora—one of the young beekeepers—for example, could leave her new born baby with her mother who lived close, and could then easily go to meetings and still be within calling distance. Another member, Benita, has quite severe problems with varicose veins, and when she cannot work because of this, she can at least get to the meetings. These individual problems had collective underpinnings: the perception of themselves as housewives more than as entrepreneurs led them to desire a small, centrally located meeting place, which could facilitate a combination of beekeeping with home responsibilities.

Furthermore, the idea of a new store implied looking for a new plot, which was unlikely to be located close by. They wanted a centrally situated place where they could be observed by neighbours and kin, in order to avoid gossip. The new plot would also involve more problems with the *ejidatarios*, who were in fact short of land and had been quite reluctant to allot them the first one. An additional problem was that they would require a new loan from the bank. They were relieved that they had almost finished paying the original loan, uninterested as they were in a large enterprise, and thus were reluctant to take out a new one.

The display of resistance might not have been very open, and is difficult to pinpoint in retrospect, since one tends to highlight only the 'relevant' events. Yet, as Scott (1985) describes in the case of Malaysia, it manifested itself strongly in everyday, routinary interaction. Constant mumbling, gossip and personal attacks to Petra—who represented the ambitious idea of expanding—as well as a degree of absenteeism to meetings, *tortuguismo* (working slow, 'as turtles') and a reluctance to learn new things about the bees were a few examples. Although it might have been difficult to discern open, explicit actions of resistance, one could fell the unmistakable atmosphere of tension that manifested itself when the issue was brought up.

Most of the members agreed that it was an opportunity they could not easily turn down,but they did not conceive of their project as a large enterprise that required such a big and costly building. The thought of expanding had not been one of their dreams, and it implied more time away from their household tasks and their families, as well as the fear of not being able in the long run to fulfil the commitment to the enterprise. Finally the group decided to tell the extension worker that they did not want the store.

Clear evidence of the scope of the beekeepers' resistance might be best 'measured' by focusing on its impact : The beekeepers rebuff was discussed in a municipal committee meeting, where all the relevant authorities of the district met every month to concert actions. The heads of the different *ejidos* were present, as well as the Mayor of the municipal capital, El Grullo, and officers from the local directories of the different ministries. It was agreed that the mayor himself would pay them a visit, which he did, urging the women to accept the challenge and offering to give them a hand when they required it.

Building upon points of consensus

An imposing visit from an important local authority helped to 'tip the scale', but also cultural frames, interwoven as they are within issues of power and prestige, served as points of consensus to trigger a change in their decision. The women's personal projects within their village networks were at stake, especially when the head of the village, whose support was crucial for their spouses' and family undertakings, had his own interests in the new enterprise. He had put a lot of effort into getting the funding through. He had told them that they had to accept. If not, he threatened to claim it for himself, making them lose their opportunity. He is a respected person in the village and has helped them on many occasions, which made it more difficult to refuse.

This became a strong point of consensus, where shared values were recognized by the group. It was important for the women to identify themselves as members of kin and other networks, and their loyalties were not to be disregarded. In this way, consensus was not a fixed set of norms and ideas, but was circumstantially negotiated within local power processes.

The beekeepers thus conformed to this authority and played the 'game' which implied recognizing certain social rules. Legitimizing themselves as women in close relation to an institution such as the ejido, with all its commitments, carried with it social costs : they should listen to the authorities, understand that what they said was best for them.

Burawoy describes this issue nicely, although he refers it to the emerging relations within a factory :

> "...consent rests upon—is constructed through—playing the game. The game does not reflect an underlying harmony of interests; on the contrary, it is responsible for and generates that harmony. The source of the game itself lies not in a preordained value consensus but in historically specific struggles to adapt to the deprivation inherent in work and in struggles with management to define the rules" (1979 :82).

Defining their position towards the new store also implied defining their identity as 'peasant women', 'respectable' women and *'abejeras.* These images also served as points of consensus to influence their decision.

The women accepted the store, deciding not to share out the profits from that year's harvest and thus save as much as possible until they knew how much the labor was going to cost. They also decided that if they had no other alternative, they would sell their small store, but that would only be as a last resort because they had become fond of this small building. After all, it was the product of their own work and adequate to their current needs. Nevertheless, they did not want to let the authorities down by not agreeing, and they preferred to have some cash in hand, since they constantly explained : "What if the people from the ministry come and we have nothing?"

In the end, the agreement was that the store would be constructed, and that the bank would provide credit for the necessary implements, plus—and here lay an important problem—the purchase of at least 400 more hives. The officers alleged that the investment was too large for the 100 hives that the women already had. They had to think big, to think of a real enterprise. The women wondered how they would be able to manage, since coping with 100 hives was already a big issue. Some of them were still reluctant to neglect their household tasks, as well as other small enterprises—such as selling shoes or perfumes—from which they obtained extra income.

It would be too simplistic to describe the women as completely powerless, as victims of external and male influence, although it is obviously difficult to label them as 'winners', since their conception of the project seemed to be losing ground. However, it was surprising to find that very soon the beekeepers did describe themselves as winners, as being privileged with a new store, and even denied the fact that there had been some resistance. To a degree, they had internalized identities such as 'peasant women' and 'women entrepreneurs' and adapted to the roles that were expected of them in the project; they had changed positions and goals. This cannot be explained as them having 'lost' the battle, since, during the process, the beekeepers themselves influenced the path of the project, undermining, for example, its strong 'economic-efficiency' focus and negotiating conditions such as not having to pay the labor for the construction of the store. However, many of their actions, while having been oriented to defend other spaces within the village and their households, also had the effect of favoring an escalation of the 'entrepreneurial' project. As a consequence the beekeepers now needed an urban plot for the group. This plot should be a flat accessible piece of land, not far from the urban area. Thus, an extra-ordinary *ejido* assembly was called to discuss the issue with the *ejidatarios*.

Interlocking Projects and Collective Identities

Margins for action

The law concerning UAIMS stipulated that the *ejido* function as a mediator between the government and the women's groups. The aims were twofold : on the one hand, it would force the village to support such a group and to allot them a piece of land, 'enhancing' a process of integrated community development *(Desarrollo Rural Integral)*. On the other hand, the group could be encouraged, but also controlled and endorsed by the 'male organization'. If economic or political problems arose, the *ejido* was expected to respond.

This allowed space for the *ejidatarios* (members of the *ejido*, most of whom are men) to insist that if the group of beekeepers were to receive help, then this would have to be through the *ejido*. Also, women had to accomodate themselves to the decisions of a predominantly 'male' organization that controlled the distribution of *ejido* land, and follow the established procedure for exploring other possibilities. This included who can be consulted and how, and what words should be used, *etc.* The beekeepers had to measure their steps carefully and make sure they did not transgress any social norms. For example, before making a decision with respect to which plot of *ejido* land they would request from the authorities for their beekeeping enterprise, the different beekeepers consulted prominent male members of their kin networks. This brought into the group some of the power struggles going on between family groupings within the village, since the request could affect the personal interests of whoever claimed to control the plot or hoped to use it in the future. Hence the women had to manoeuvre to sustain an acceptable image as 'the wife of' or the 'niece of' particular persons and thereby connected to certain families.

Male enterprises and claims to the image of 'respectable woman'

This struggle over symbolic space and images also involved negotiation over territorial frontiers,i.e. the *ejido* land. While it was not uncommon to find women laboring in the fields or helping their husbands, female ownership of *ejido* plots was not easily accepted. Even widows or women heads of households would have to make use of strong networks in order to hold on to inherited land[6] since it was commonly argued that they could soon remarry and the land would be left in the hands of who-knows-which male.[7] Many *ejidatarios* considered the beekeepers should not have been given the first plot, much less be allotted a second one. Personal fictions, kin loyalties, as well as the defense of particular economic interests were involved in the discussion, each party recurring to taken-for-granted rules concerning what is male and what is female, concerning women's roles in the household, in small village-located commercial enterprises, or in the fields. Conflict over representations of space[8] was intrinsic to the debate, where images of what comprised a 'respectable woman' were battled in order to win arguments.

Certainly we cannot speak of *'the men'* just like that. It was obvious that their positions varied. Don Jose, head of the *ejido*, proudly defended the beekeeping project. If they won, which he was sure they would, he would have one more positive action to add to his curriculum as head of the village. His stand towards the SARH (Ministry of Agriculture and Water Resources) would be improved, and his authority within the village probably enhanced. On the day of the meeting with the people from the Ministry he had given his word that he would help, and he considered himself a solid person *('gente maciza").*He made it known that he was a man who kept his word, and his townsmen respected him for it. Don Jose also prided himself in possessing more information that other comrades about the workings of the official institutions and in having direct links to these information sources, which he used to strengthen his status in the village. In this way he gained legitimacy and credibility, useful to influence local people's evaluation of such institutions, controlling to a degree the interpretation of information flows and thus the access of these institutions to the *ejido* itself. Thus he was 'manipulating claims to knowledge which underpin claims to power'.[9] (Fardon, 1985 : 147) At the time of the assembly, he held the post of local representative for the municipal council.

Federico, husband of one of the beekeeper, saw no challenge to his position as head of his household in the women's project, since his wife made it a point to 'give him his place', and followed closely his advice with respect to the group. Besides, she was always careful to be home when he came to take his meals, etc. In fact, he once confided it was better for him that she occupied herself in this type of group. He agrued that they had never gained anything as an enterprise and never would, but it took her mind off other family worries. (He mentioned her high blood pressure and the fact that her daughter was away, but there was also the fact that he was a real *'don Juan'* and could be seen all over the place within different women, which, although his wife herself never mentioned it explicitly, was described by relatives and friends as a big problem for the whole family.)

On the other hand, for Pancho, Petra's husband, the fact that Petra found herself a relevant project and gained influence was up to a point dangerous. He had complained often about her never being at home to look after him and the children, and Petra was becoming more independent, especially in the use of her time. Their marriage had, several times, been hanging by a thread. Furthermore he claimed that the group had never earned a significant amount of money to make the project worthwhile. However, at the moment he was engaged in a fierce battle with Alejo—another *ejidatario*—over the use of a tractor they were partners in. Alejo headed the opposition towards the women. He was owner of a large number of cattle and felt the women were mismanaging the land which was previously used for pastures in benefit of the *ejidatarios*. Pancho was becoming quite irritated by Alejo's manner and what he called apparently logical but purely selfish points of view.

Both Federico and Pancho, while not really interested in the beekeeping enterprise in itself, found no harm in the possibility of the women acquiring land, and considered that those who did not want to donate it to them were scheming up other businesses for themselves. As Federico explained later, some people were already thinking of running for comisariado the next term. An ejido plot was a juicy source of money, whether they sold it or decided to construct a communal building there[10].

Collective identities and reciprocally-structuring processes

In this way, the personal projects of the different parties involved mingled with each other, enrolled and changed one another—not in smooth, harmonious patterns, but engaged in battles where issues of power, prestige and loyalty cannot be overlooked. The projects thus interlocked in dynamic processes building upon, but also shaping what came to be recognized as 'collective' identities. The emerging elements both constrained and enabled the margins for action of the different parties, constituting a dynamic backbone, not only for the 'shared' project, but also in many ways for their individual and personal projects. These set of parameters served at given moments to organize the discourse, the social relations and struggles taking place in other arenas of village life, constituting emergent and provisionally shared notions and experiences. Long and Van der Ploeg highlight this process when desribing the concept of structure :

> "...Structure can be characterized as an extremely fluid set of emergent properties, which, on the one hand, results from the interlocking, and/or distantiation of various actors' projects, whilst, on the other hand, it functions as an important point of reference for the further elaboration, negotiation and confrontation of actors' projects" (1991:22).

It is thus that one cannot explain the path followed by the project and the women's processes by recurring to 'external forces','dominant ideology' or the subordination of one sector of the population by the other. A composite project was forged and structured through circumstantially shared parameters and overlapping views of the world.

Strategic use of social meanings and interpretations

The beekeepers had different ways of enrolling others in their own projects, or selling their own self-images and trying to impose them on others.[11] This formed part of a process of negotiation in which they attempted to change some components of their conditions while at the same time striving to maintain certain other element as they were.

To enroll the ejidatarios...and themselves

An assembly was called in the village to discuss the issue of a new plot for the women. Don Jose, head of the *ejido,* was planning to ask for consent to assign the women a piece which was perfect for their plants but was affected by certain complications, not the least of which was the 'intrusion' of women within 'men's' boundaries : the ejido land. According to the Agrarian Law, the assembly of *ejidatarios* is the maximum authority of the ejido, and as such, is entitled to decide on the allotment of land. It was commonly held that the men knew more about cultivation and the efficient use of the land, which was, formally 'their' space, while women should restrict themselves to the household. There were many exceptions, however, since some of the *ejidatarios* were in fact women who managed their land efficiently, although most of them appealed to male sons or close relatives when certain decisions were at stake.

Privately, the members of the women's group were all pessimistic about the possibility of gaining support from the *ejidatarios*, remembering that only a few weeks ago they had been called *huevonas y desquehaceradas* (idle and irresponsible towards their household obligations) by some of them.

The beekeepers, many of whom had rejected the idea of a big enterprise a few days before, were placed in a position to defend just that project. They now needed the new plot and were obliged to convince the *ejidatarios* that they could become entrepreneurs, that their project could be successful and they could have different roles as women.

Going through the motions of subordination

Juana, the previous President of the group, spoke out during the assembly, reassuring the men that they would not be left out. She used images previously used by SARH officers to propel her own, and her voice was no longer hesitant :

> "They (meaning people from the SARH) have many plans for us; *that it will not only be for our benefit* since we will soon be old. With time it can become a big industry. Our grandchildren...it will not only be for women, there will also be work for men,

> because...well, we were taken to see a honey plant, it was well furnished by the ministry, and there we learned what it is to work big... For many reasons we have not made more and more, but there are many jobs for men in that place".

Backstage, she was delineating her project. She was portraying the boundaries she sets on the group of women with respect to this particular audience and was defining their identity. Only a few days before the meeting, she had been skeptical about the new big enterprise they were urged to push forward. Now circumstances had driven her, not only to embrace the idea, but to sell it to the *ejidatarios*, knowing perfectly well that to succeed the beekeeping group would have to go through the motions of subordination and give their fellow countrymen their due quota of power. She was probably aware of the force of their own petition, endorsed as is was by the officers that had visited them, as well as their profit as a group in terms of prestige, but she had to reassure the audience that she had no intentions of running against the interests of men, nor challenging the role of women per se, which, in fact, she had not.

Juana had been a 'fatherless' child. Although she adored her mother while she lived, she speaks sadly of their situation and is happy to offer her children the chance of living with a father. To achieve this, she has to comply to unwritten norms, tolerating situations which she does not totally agree with. When—for example—she arrived very late but very tired one stormy day after retrieving the hives from the flooded banks of the river, she found that the door of her house had been locked by her husband. To avoid a quarrel, she placed the blame on herself, excusing her husband for locking her out with the justification that he doesn't like anyone arriving after 10 o'clock.

The price for maintaining her family united is to give her husband his 'quota of power', subordinating her activities in some ways to his likes and dislikes. In village social life, she will be seen as a good woman because she accords her man "his place". She thus conforms to social norms and behavior, but she also reproduces and legitimates these norms and behavior, Furthermore, Juana is forging specific roles for her man, who must be a respected father and husband. She creates space for him according to her interests, as he now will have more possibilities of being esteemed in the village because he is obeyed and respected at home. In this way, she is not only passively obeying social norms, but is finding her way through them to convey a specific image of her man as father and husband, and thus fulfill her own goals.

Downplaying their potential as women and enrolling more 'knowledgeable' outsiders in their legimitation as a group.

However, without probably seeking it consciously, Juana was trying to sell others her new image of peasant woman. If the *ejidatarios* accepted that women could do more than stay at home and take care of children, it was more likely that they accept to give them a new plot of land. Her own process required defining the previous ideas of women's roles and possibilities as backward and obsolete, pushing forward the notion of enterprising peasant woman she had previously rejected. However, she had to be very careful and not let the men feel threatened.Thus, the new images had to be implanted but declared nonexistent. Everything is o-k, she was implying; it will not be forever a women's project. We know that it is the men that need good jobs in Ayuquila. We will not threaten their position. Now she was really drilling a space for herself and for their project as a group, although they would have to accommodate to those roles where the control apparently lay in the hands of the men.

Petra also admitted strategically that they were small and inefficient, but used the image portrayed by the more 'important' people to defend her point, thus enrolling the ministry in their defense :

> "For the government, for the Ministry it is convenient because in this way all our work can be exported and also benefit our country. That is why they support us."

Although Petra was careful not to contradict certain "sacred" ideas that the ejidatarios might hold, she was clear about her position and the changing role of women. Unlike Juana, she wanted them to understand that as women they can get a boost out of the project.

It was essential for her to get across the image of an enterprising peasant woman. In Petra's view, the ejidatarios lack the knowledge, the experience of having listened to these people, and understanding, not only of the implications of the project, but of what 'peasant women' should be. She was looking for endorsement from the ejidatarios for what should now be the identity of the group, invoking the definition that had been put across by the SARH, who, by opening the possibility of credit and access to entrepreneurship for the women, gives legitimacy to this image. Her aim is to extend the SARH's definition of women to the audience, first by touching on their personal interests : "Look, it's in your own interest" she was saying implicitly, "may be your wife or daughter can also enjoy the benefits," but also by pointing out their value as women using the 'accepted' image of 'respectable women' : "we are relevant to our village and our country".

She is prepared to accept that as beekeepers the group might not be very capable, if that is the criticism made by the men, but they would take special courses. "It is in the hands of the ejidatarios", she is now saying—to a degree it will depend on their will if this good project grows. Thus, the future of their enterprise depends on whether they give them the plot or not.

Her message concerns the importance of the group, an importance which she might only just be beginning to recognize fully. Indeed we might ask; to what extent was the failure of recognition from the ejidatarios forcing her to bring these thoughts to her own consciousness ?

Acknowledging male 'paternity'

The *ejidatarios* finally agreed to give them the plot, but the epilogue of the discussion showed another underlying argument concerning the *ejido's* authority and legitimation. An *ejidatario* complained that a close friend had overheard the women saying that they needed the ejido for nothing *('para madres')*, that what they had, they had earned themselves. He stressed that he did not like such gossip. In this way he evoked an unwritten law stipulating that the women should recognize that if they have a group, possess land and are given financial aid, it is because of the *ejido*, because of the organization of the men, without whose support the group would not even exist. Strategically, the women showed surprise, and Petra conceded in an apologetic tone that maybe it could have slipped out from one of the members, that maybe one of them could have said something jokingly, but that, as a group, they did not hold to these ideas, and they thanked the ejidatarios for their support.

Power and Room for Manoeuvre

Power, negotiation, enrolment, obedience, consent: how can we identify the mechanisms by which these processes take place ? One cannot escape the dynamics of demarcation that are implied, the constant changes that the confines of peoples' actions and ideas undergo, the attachment to or detachment from others' wills. Our case points to the ways in which the different women conceived and changed their projects, but also how they worked up space within their social arenas to achieve their goals, to resist unwanted conditions or to endure inevitable burdens.

This implies the creation of room for manoeuvre (see Long, 1984) which involves a degree of consent, a degree of negotiation and a degree of power--not necessarily power stored in a given economic or political position, but the possibility of control, of prerogative, of a degree of authority and ability, be it front or backstage, for flickering moments or for long periods. Power has frequently been conceptualized as a heavy weight that oppresses and penetrates to the roots of the lower classes. The discussion has mainly focused on who possesses power and how it is exercised. Some analysis focuses strongly on determining constraints, on access to resources on rigid hierarchical categories and hegemonic ideologies that oppress passive victims. However, we have found power as fluid and difficult to measure—almost unnecessary to measure—but imperative to describe more precisely. As Foucault puts it.'

> But in thinking of the mechanisms of power, I am thinking rather of its capillary form of existence, the point where power reaches into the very grain of individuals, touches their bodies and inserts itself into their actions and attitudes, their discourses, learning processes and everyday lives' (in Gordon 1989 : 39).

It is not only the *amount* of power that makes a difference, but the possibility of gaining edge and pressing it home. The scope of power, commonly defined[12] as the capacity of an individual to impose his/ her own will upon others, must be unpacked to allow for an understanding that includes the probability of achieving only part on one's own project, of accepting compromises, but then pressing home one's moderate gains in an attempt to dominate as big a part of a situation as possible so that one can consider one's aspirations consummated. Thus, when looking for power, we see struggle, negotiation and compromise. Those labelled as 'powerless' or 'oppressed' within specific circumstances are not utterly passive victims and may be involved in active resistance. Conversely, the 'powerful' are not in complete control of the stage, and the degree to which they are also themselves forged by the 'powerless' is not to be disregarded.[13] Furthermore, reifying the power of domination leads to a paralysing attitude : 'nothing can be done except by changing the complete system'. As our case shows, the issue of power is much more complex. It also involves personal abilities and the perspicacity to perceive 'edges' and 'social interstices' that can be taken advantage of. This brings us back to the notion of life-worlds, to the constraining and enabling elements encountered in specific social processes, to the cultural and normative repertoires embedded within these processes and to the concept of agency, that is, to the ways in which people deal with and manipulate these constraining and enabling elements. Social networks are key elements in these processes[14]. Interpersonal networks mould to a degree the aims and definitions of their members, while containing within them power processes, and at the same time constituting relevant power instruments that can be used by the individual members. The 'strands' of the network will be used in later (as in previous) evaluations of situations, thus helping to form opinions, impose images, and consolidate social commitments.

While we found no strong, visible manifestations of power in the interactions of the beekeepers with 'others', we could detect small, flashes of command that peeked out from behind the screens. More than solid, rigid blocks of control that are possessed or dispossessed, power presented itself as of a fluid nature that fills up spaces, sometimes for only flickering moments, taking different forms and consistencies, which made it very difficult to measure, but conspicuous enough to describe.

Space, identity, power and battles over images in the forging of a project

The different interface situations involving the government officers, the women beekepers and the villagers, have opened up windows that reveal their complexities : we have seen how intervention is continuously being modified by the negotiations and strategies that take place between the various parties involved, and how the project—initially planned within the Ministry—took different concrete forms and representations.

As a group, the beekeedpers, often regarde by other actors as of lower status—as 'marginalized'—were offered a paternalistic deal, both by government agencies and by the head of the ejido, who described the group as powerless, as 'people in need of help'. This labelling was instrumental in the attempt to maintain the status quo, since it made institutions appear in tune with 'progressive' government discourse which claimed as a central objective 'the incorporation of peasant women into society'. The interest of the village authorities was motivated then by the desire to 'show off' the project, through taking pictures of the group and bringing important authorities to visit the women, in an effort to win the approval of central government.

The economic rationality of the project, of primary importance in its initial design, was negotiated in practice to stress other types of factors, becoming more than an aim for the women to reach, a justification in favour of a certain image of women. While the women were arguing that they were capable of running the enterprise, they were reluctant to acquire more hives which an efficient cost-benefit rationality would require. Their goals, enmeshed within everyday interests and motivations, within loyalties and roles as houswives and mothers, could not be circumscribed as a desire for financial autonomy or a strengthening of their economic role.

In this way, the notion of development programmes as providers of 'sustainable' options that can be applied uniformly in different groups and regions crumbles to pieces when one as much as glances into the actual practice on intervention. 'External' notions of 'collective control' and 'community participation' prove to be hopelessly simplistic and one-sided. I hope to have provided evidence to ground a critical view on such processes, a view that includes the interaction of project implementors and 'clients' as part of the object of analysis. As I have described, the actions, ideas and values of the intervenors played an important role in the process, but their effects can only be understood when studying them in their interrelation with the actions, ideas and values of the other parties, when focusing on the mutual permeation and joint transformation taking place. Thus, the project is forged in practice through everyday negotiations of space for manoeuvre: through establishing and trading identities; through coalitions of interests and interlocking of projects, aspirations and expectations; and through processes of enrolment and resistance.

The battles over images did not only take place within the formal arena of the project itself, but were catalysts for the creation, exchange and contest over images in the different spheres of the life-worlds of the actors. The 'strategic' conception of women as an active force in society, for example, which the planners were so eager to convey, clashed in many ways with the beekeepers' own strategies: the women adopted identities—such as peasant woman when it involved certain benefits, *'pata rajada'* when it was necessary to put themselves down strategically, or 'enterprising women' when they wanted to sell their project to the ejidatarios—while creating their own space, while recognizing their own broadened boundaries. They also used convenient identities of the other parties, as was the case when stressing the knowledgability of the extension officers and their images of their potential as a group to convince the men of the value of their enterprise. Thus, multiple identities were defined and managed according to the situation : indeed, one might even argue that many of the women beekeepers learnt the language of 'subordination' in order to extract benefits from it, while at the same time to some degree subverting this very ideology.

The women internalized the rights depicted in the law and legitimized by the officials and head of the ejido, and used these 'new' interpretations to push forward their own projects. The case highlights, not only how Petra's 'hobby' as a beekeeper influenced her life-world, but how she used it—consciously or unconsciously—to achieve more space within her household. It provides insight into how, the impact of Juana's conduct when accepting the rules of her husband, has the effect of portraying a harmless conventional image of herself, which she finds necessary in order to create space for her other projects. Sara apparently subordinated her projects to those of her husband and takes a hot meal for him to the field everyday, where she helps out with small tasks, from cutting weeds to taking the cows home. But in the end, this is an effective way of her influencing his activities, of putting pressure on him to clearly establish what is 'proper' work, and of opening up crucial decision-making moments where she can get her points across. Thus, the women accept roles for themselves in order to win arguments useful for battles elsewhere.

It was interesting to observe this situation in the *ejido* assembly, for example. In response to outright opposition on the part of some of the men present, to dubious silence from others, and even to some support from a few husbands and authorities, the beekeepers were obviously downplaying their potential as a group, their power as women and their capacity as beekeepers: Petra was prepared to accept that, as women beekeepers, they were not so capable and thus needed training from government experts. At one point, when one of the members of the beekeeping group remarked that they did not need the *ejido* for anything, she immediately reacted against this, arguing that she was the first to recognize that everything they had was in fact due to the men's organization. Likewise, Juana tried desperately to make male ejidatarios see that the benefits from the beekeeping project would not be for women, and that they had no intention or runing counter to the interests of men or of challenging traditional female roles.

Thus women are not passive victims of an external gender situation. Barbara Roger's discussion (1980) on how women are discriminated into 'domestic' spheres by development projects, while valid in many ways, appears somewhat simplistic in that she does not consider the complex interweaving of relations and the multifaceted changes that take place within these processes. Though we should not blind ourselves to the ways in which women are constrained and moulded by circumstances and conditions—some of which they themselves recreate and forge—we must acknowledge that they have the capacity to manipulate these limitations, using what we have called 'women's weapons' in order not only, as it were, to survive in deep water, but to use the current whenever possible to bring the boat in their direction.

I have argued for the importance of looking into the efforts of these women in the creation, appropriation and conservation of space for themselves (see Long, 1984). The beekeepers' situation as well is a clear example of how women manipulate and rework their constraints in their struggle for this space. In the reconstruction of their social worlds, however, making room for manoeuvre involves a degree of independence in certain spheres and a degree of 'dependence' in others. It implies enrolment of other people in one's projects, which in itself has a lot to do, not only with a 'trade' of images, but with a 'war' of imposing upon others those images which are useful for one's own purposes.

While male and female images, roles and attributions are the object of conflict, these are interwined with other values, kin loyalties and personal ambitions. Women do present battles as a group, and many times support each other in defense of a certain identity, of space for their project. This, however, cannot be analyzed unmistakenly as an interpretation of women's projects as against men's. The whole process is enmeshed in power struggles, where, as I have stressed, power is not held in a fixed way by any of the parties, but is constantly negotiated.

Thus, collective identities come to be recognized as such through processes of enrolment and consensus. Consensus, as I implied before, does not possess a passive existence. Consensus is sought, it is negotiated and fought for. The war to 'impose' consensus is a difficult one, since it implies willingness on the part of the opponent, it involves resistance and power. This underlines the relevance of battles over images, of imposing certain identities which might stress distinctive traditions and overlook or suppress others and which carry with them specific roles, norms and commitments. In this way, 'collective identities' are multifaceted and circumstantial.

Notes

1. The ejido is a socio-legal entity concerned with the administration of land and other collective properties. Ejidos were established under the 1920's land reform law that followed the Mexican Revolution. The term ejidatario is used for those who possess land rights to specific plots and who are listed formally as members of the ejido. The utilization of ejido land is, however, complicated by the existence of different kinds of renting and lending arrangements both among ejidatarios and between them and non-ejidatarios.
2. Part of the field data included in this analysis was collected by Gabriel Torres and Norman Long. Both contributed to an earlier unpublished paper which deals with these themes, and the latter was co-author with me of a paper entitled "The Changing Life Worlds of Women in a Mexican Ejido : The Case of the Bee-keepers of Ayuquila and the Issue of Intervention, "which was published in 1989 in "Encounters at the Interface, A perspective on social discontinuities in rural development" edited by Norman Long.
3. Ayuquila, a settlement of 174 households, is located along the main road linking the Municipal capital of E1 Gruuo to the State capital of Guadalajara, in Jalisco, Western Mexico. The ejido of Ayuquila consists of individual household plots, one third of which are irrigated, divided among ejidatarios and a commual grazing area on the hillsides. A total of 17 mothers in Ayuquilal combine household work with other family based economic activities, such as the running of small shops, selling of milk, or making and selling of tortillas (a Mexican staple),

and a further seven regularly assist their husbands with agricultural tasks. Of the other most active economically a majority of whom are members of the beekeeping group—six sell clothes, shoes, perfumery, and prepared foods, and six are dress makers. Eight more work as teachers or secretaries outside the village and at least eight others work as day laborers for the tomato companies.

4. One can make a parallel between this labelling and the commonly used "zapatero remendon" (instead of the normal zapatero), which literally differentiates actual shoemakers from shoe 'patchers' but is used to stress the difference between 'experts' and laymen within this trade.
5. Joke Schrijvers (pers. com.) points out that the image of 'respectful women' is forged by the rulers, by the dominant male forces in society. Melhuis (1990) suggests that suffering is considered an essentially female virtue in the Mexican village she studied, and that it is related to prevailing ideologies of 'machismo' and 'marianismo', characteristic of dominant moral codes in Mexican culture. Exploring these issues would reveal the multifold way in which these notions do favour certain sectors of the population, how they in fact facilitate women's subordination. One could also explore the way other institutions such as the Catholic Church, propel them further in certain directions. However, I wish to distance myself from approaches that adjudicate authorship to specific categories of people or individuals. The point I want to make is how the women themselves—in interaction with others where issues of power and domination cannot be overlooked—assume, recreate or reject these notions, and struggle to impose on others the meanings they consider appropriate.
6. See also Brunt (1989), for a description of the situation of women working their way through ejido organization—i.e. through male authorities and through their networks—within a different village in the same region.
7. However, some women do manage to negotiate favourable conditions for themselves, and there are two cases of widows in Ayuquila who have not only kept their land, but increased it. Both have held posts in the ejido administration committee. There is another woman who, after fierce struggle, was allotted her migrating son's plot, although her husband already possessed land as member from a neighbouring ejido. On the other hand,

there have been several cases of widows in the village who have been dispossessed of land as soon their husband dies.

8. See Moore : Space, Text and Gender (1986) for a further discussion on this issue.
9. See Richard Fardon 1985. "Power and Knowledge. Anthropological and Sociolgical Approachess".p. 147.
10. If they sold it, the comisariado or treasurer could manage things in such a way as to sell it cheap to himself or a relative, or keep part of the income from it. On the other hand, building public works normally involved dealing with cement and other materials whose formal and informal prices could be negotiated under the table, or quantities modified for crooked businesses.
11. In their article on 'Demythologizing Planned Intervention, Long and van der Ploeg (1989 : 231) suggest that in intervention situations a 'trade of immages' takes place.
12. A much used theoretical definition of power is Weber's who describes it as 'the probability that one actor within a social relationship will be in a position to carry out his own will despite resistance, regardless of the basis on which this probability rests' (Weber, 1957: 152). This point of view tends towards a voluntaristic, interactionist model, dichotomising with a model of power as residing in structured relations.
13. James Scot (1985) describes these issues beautifully in *Weapons of the Weak*. I disagree, however, with the way he assimilates them into pre-fabricated class categories, the way he makes the pieces of the puzzle fit predefined models.
14. Net works, of course, are emergent social forms always being reshaped. Long discusses this issue more fully in 'Knowledge' Networks and Power : Discontinuities and Accommodations at the Inter facet.' Paper presented to the European Seminar on Knowledge Systems and Information Technology, Wageningen, November 23-24, 1989.

References

Brodkin Sacks, Karen 1989 Toward a Unified Theory of Class, Race and Gender, in *American Ethnologist* vol. 16, nr.3 p. 534-550.

Brunt, D. 1989 'Social Networks, Symbolic Boundaries and Social Identities : Women and Access to Land in a Mexican Ejido'. Paper presented to the advanced research seminar. Wageningen Agricultural University. Department of Rural Sociology.The Netherlands.

Burawoy, M. 1979 Manufacturing Consent : Changes in the Labour Process under Capitalism. Chicago : Universitiy of Chicago Press.

Callon, M. 1986 "Some elements of a sociology of translation :domestication of the scallops and the fishermen of St. Brieuc Bay in J. Law (ed) *Power, Action and Belief : A New Sociology of Knowledge ?* London, Boston and Henley : Routledge and Kegan Paul.

Cohen, A.P. 1985 *The Symbolic Construction of Community*, New York : Tavistock.

Fardon, R. 1985 *Power and Knowledge, Anthropological and Sociological Approaches.* Edinburgh : Scottish Academic Press.

Fielding, Nigel 1988 *Actions and Structure : Research Methods and Social Theory*, London : Sage.

Genovese, E.D. 1974 *Roll, Jordan Roll : The World The Slaves Made.* New York : Pantheon.

Gordon, C. (ed) 1980 *Power/Knowledge : Selected Interviews and Other Writing 1972-1977 by Michel Foucault* United States : Pantheon Harvester Press.

Knorr-Cetina, K. 1981 *The Manufacture of Knowledge : Towards a constructivist and contextual theory of science.* Oxford : Pergamon Press.

Knorr-Cetina, K. 1988 The Micro-Social order: towards a Reconception in Fielding ed. 20-54.

Latour B. 1986 "The Powers of Association" in J. Law (ed) *Power, Action and Belief : A New Sociology of Knowledge ?* London, Boston and Honley : Routledge and Kegan Paul.

Long, N. 1984 Creating Space for Change : A perspective on the sociology of Development, Wageningen Agricultural University, The Netherlands.

Long, N. 1989 *Encounters at the interface : A perspective on social discontinuities in rural development,* Wageningen studies in Sociology 27, Wageningen : the agricultural University.

Long, N. and Villarreal, M. 1989 The Changing Life Worlds of Women in A Mexican Ejido : The case of the Bee keepers of Ayuquila and the Issue of Intervention', in N. Long (ed). *Encounters at the Interface, A perspective on Social discontinuities in rural development*,Wageningen Studies in Sociology 27, Wageningen Agricultural University : p. 103-144.

Long,N. and Van Der Ploeg, J. D. 1989 Demythologizing Planned Intervention : An Actor Perspective, *Socilogia Ruralis*, XXIX 3/4, 226-249.

Long, N. 1989 Knowledge, Networks and Power : Discontinuities and Accommodations at the Interface, European Seminar on Knowledge Management and Information Technology, Wageningen.

Melhuus, M. 1990 'A Shame to Honour—A Shame to Suffer'. Ethnos. Stockholm, No. 1-2 (p. 5-25).

Mohanty, C. 1988 'Under Western Eyes : Feminist Scholarship and Colonial Discourses;, *Feminist Review* No. 30, Autumn 1988.

Moore, H. I., 1986 *Space, Text and Gender : an Anthropological Study of Manakwet of Kenya*, Great Britain :Cambridge University Press.

Moore, H. L. 1988 *Feminism and Anthropology* Cambridge : Polity Press.

Risseeuw, C. 1988 *The Fish Don't Talk about The Water. Gender Transformation, Power and Resistance among women in Sri Lanka*. P.H.D. Thesis : University of Nijmegen.

Rogers, B. 1980 *The Domestication of Women : Discrimination in Developing Societies* London : Kogan Page Limited.

Schrijvers, J. 1985 *Mothers for life. Motherhood and Marginalization in the North Central Province of Sri Lanka*, Leiden : Research and Documentation Centre Women and Autonomy.

Schrijvers, J. 1988 Poor Women, Partiality and Power; Problems of a dialogical Approach. *Working paper* no. 81, University of Leiden : Institute of Cultural and Social Studies.

Schutz, A. and Luckmann T. 1973 *The Structures of the life world*. Evanston, Illinois : North Western University Press.

Scott, J. C. 1985 *Weapons of the Weak : Everyday Forms of Peasant Resistance*, New Haven and London : Yale University Press.

Villarreal M. 1990 "A Struggle over Images : Issues on power, gender and intervention in a Mexican Village. " Wageningen Agricultural

University. M. Sc. Thesis.

Villarreal, M. 1991 'Systems Actors Power and Change : Two perspectives'. Paper presented to society of Latin American Studies. Glasgow.

Villarreal M. 1992 *'The Poverty of Practice : Power, Gender and Intervention from an Actor Oriented perspective* . in Long, Norman & Long, A. (eds). (1992) *Battlefields of Knowledge : The Interlocking of Theory and Practice in Social Research and Development.* Routledge, London.

Villarreal M. 1992 *"Yo no Soy Nada" ; in their struggle for space, rural Mexican women face subordination in different ways,* Cultural Survival Quaterly. Winter 1992, vol. 16. Number 4. pp. 31-33.

Weber, M. 1957 *The Theory of Social and Economic Organization,* Glencoe, Illinois : Free Press.

Rishikeshab Regmi

STATUS OF WOMEN IN NEPAL

Introduction

Nepal is one of the poorest country in the world situated in between the two big neighboring countries, India and China in south and north respectively. Except for a few professionals and businessmen, and some big farmers, everyone in Nepal is poor. The population of Nepal is 18,642,081 out of which female population consist of 9,241,167 (1991 census). The infant mortality rate is 107 out of 1000 and under five mortality rate is 165 out of 1000 live births, sixty five per cent of the adult population is illiterate, with 82 per cent female illiteracy. The maternal mortality rate is 850, out of 100,000, one of the highest in the world. Seventy one per cent of the total population live in absolute poverty. Nepal's GNP per capita income in only $ 202 (Nepal Planning Commission, 1994, June).

People work very hard but seventy per cent of the production is of a subsistence nature and does not go through the cash economy. In this labor intensive subsistence environment, children in the ten to fourteen years group works about five hours a day. Women spend much more time than men on subsistence activities and domestic work. Sixteen per cent of all human labor is devoted to fuel and fodder collection alone, not counting carrying water. These chores are done by women and children in addition to farming and grazing. Most women in Nepal are either pregnant or nursing for much of the short lives. Although the law sets the minimum age of marriage a sixteen, studies suggest that twenty two percent of girls are married by the age thirteen and fifty per cent by age sixteen years (UNFPA, 1990). Nepal is one of only three countries in the world where the life expectancy for women is lower than that of men.

In general, women have less access to income, wealth and modern avenues of employment, education and health facilities than men. They suffer from higher rate or malnutrition and morbidity than men, and have fewer legal rights than men, especially in property and family matters. In the hill communities women enjoy greater freedom in marriage and mobility and have greater decision making roles within the household but suffer from over work and poorer physical and social infrastructures.

Cultural Background

There are several dozens of ethnic groups residing in Nepal since time immemorial. No serious studies on various aspects of these communities have been done either by private researcher or by any agency on the overall topic of women community of Nepal.

The literature on women in Nepal potrays the Nepali women of different ethnic groups as highly varied, their rituals vary, their position within their own respective societies vary according to the larger social framework distinctive of their own ethnic society. However, the main population of Nepal is composed of Aryan and Mongoloid stock in particular, their social position to some extent has similarities especially in their roles as wife and mother. In Nepal women's role and position symbolically and socially is defined according to the patrilineal concept and values of the Hindu society to a large extent. The Hindu perception of women in higher castes society is evidenced in the social, mythical and ritual structure. The study like that of Lynn Benett (1986) on women of higher Caste Brahman, The Chhetry of Kathmandu valley, illustrates that women in the day to day activities interpret and manipulate social, ritual and mythic perceptions of themselves in order to achieve real life goals. The analysis was based on the notion of purity and pollution which is so common in the Hindu culture of Nepal. In the higher caste society of Nepal, daughters and sisters are placed with different realms according to the notion of purity and pollution. The Hindu world view plays important role in shaping the status and actions of women in all society of Nepal in general. Women in their natal homes are viewed as both pure and auspicious. As daughters and sisters, these women do not subject their natal male relatives to their dangerous and polluting sexuality. Thus the position of women in this situation is a positive, warm and living one and the rituals of Hindu households aid in the protection of the male relatives.

The Family and the Women

In Nepal, by the time a man passes the age of fifty, he becomes an authority figure. He has access to the managerial tasks of the land and the agrarian resources of the family. He controls over the subsistence of tenants and laborers and has the authority of a father and grand father. He is able to take in charge of the economic and emotional needs of the problems including those of the established practice of the household, the preconditions of which was to have enough agricultural lands to support several generations.

The wife gains prestige and recognition with her husband, although her social mobility is restricted according to her community postition. In all the functions of her lineage and related lineage she holds a highly respectable position, which gradually increases in her age. She is an authority figure especially to her daughters and grand daughters, whose needs are met through her direct or indirect intermediary role with husband. She also manages the servants who work inside the home and meet the reasonable obligation towards them. Such obligation include offerings of food during family function of both master and the servant and help rendered to the servent's family during life cycle ceremonies. Women in Nepal receive especial devotion from their male children, whatever may be their personal and social position. This devotion reaches the point of worship, as if towards a deity, alongwith the old women's increase of age, and when the women becomes bedridden and later dies. Ill treatment of old woman by her husband is irreligious. The woman shows enormous tolerance to her husband's misdeeds, including his extramarital adventures. Usually in the higher castes and prestigious people divorce is never thought of by either partner. A significant outcome of the triangular relationship among husband, wife and children is that they mutually reinforce the attachment for each other economically and emotionally. In the Nepali society the girls are disciplined to care for the old because when they get married and are observed in their husband's households one duty that they have to take care is about the needs of the old father-in-law and mother-in-law. If a woman shows any disrespect to her father-in-law and mother-in-law, husband and other members of his household, even neighbors will not excuse her such behavior. The elderly women in Nepal play the most active part in the socialization of children. A good part of the socialization is done through story telling, of which their own life stories and those of ancestors become dominant. A as result the children are integrated into the family and society by developing associated cognitive structure in them. This provides an opportunity for tolerance and solidarity.

The Conditions of the Poverty Stricken Women

Research and documentation of women's activities in Nepal started only during 1970s. The women's movement and the UN decade for women gave an inputs to women's studies. At present lot of documents regarding the productive role of women has been noticed. For a long time, women have been considered peripheral to the process of development. In Nepal, women play an important socio-cultural and economic roles within household sphere but very little outside the home primarily because they are heavily burdened with domestic and farming chores. A life confined to the house and the farm provides few opportunities for women to become engaged in market sector activities. But most women are culturally restricted in their contacts with strangers especially men and their behavior in general follows culturally prescribed rules.

Women Chores of Activities

There are four main chores of activities of women at present in Nepal. They are :

(i) Household chores

(ii) Agricultural activities

(iii) Local market economy

(iv) Outside the village economy i.e. employment through short term migration.

The women domestic and farm activities are quite immense. Eighty six per cent of domestic work and fifty seven percent in subsistence agricultural activities are predominately done by women (source MPHBS, special tabulation, in Acharya, 1994). The income generated by the Nepalese women amounts to fifty eight percent as opposed to forty four per cent of men.

Women's participation in the market economy has increased their status and this is more conspicuous among Tibeto-Burman language speaking communities, while women from the more orthodox Hindu communities are mostly confined to non-market domestic and subsistence production and have little role in major household decision making process. The returns from subsistence farming are very low. Women are paid less than men as agricultural or other laborer.

Women have started working since few years in carpet

weaving, and wool-spinning is mostly done at cottage industry level. Working conditions in these industries are poor and unhealthy. At higher level of jobs, women are less represented.

Women in poor households have less security as they are poor economically than men. They lack individual ownership of assets (especially land). They are denied tenancy of lands and are discriminated against in the allotments of settlement plots. Their labor force participation is more tenons. They work twenty five per cent more than men, their calories requirements are insufficiently met due to socio-cultural discrimination, they are less likely to get medical care when sick, and they are left behind to fend for themselves and their children in the off-farm seasons. They have less access to education and new skills and are therefore concentrated in low skill jobs.

A women has no inheritance rights to parental property and enjoys only limited inheritance and disposal rights in her husband's property. Women own little property. Women have also to get permission from men in the household to undertake any activity, particularly economic activities. Banks also usually demand a parental guarantee of repayment for safeguarding bank loans if their clients are unmarried women, because when girls get married they leave the natal household. There is a dilemma here. It is this young generation of women who can be educated and mobilized quickly for accepting new ideas and ventures, but it is they who are most strictly controlled in terms of their mobility.

Many plans and programs to involve women in development and training are in process. Most of the training and activities planned and implemented for women are still stereotyped and relate mainly to home management, family nutrition and health.

Women's Participation in Power and Politics

Women's participation in the regular political process and access to positions of power had been in general low. Very few women reached positions of power prior to 1990. Women's access to positions of power in executive bodies such as the cabinet and bureaucracy and the courts have also been limited.

According to Acharya and Bennet two major tenets of the South-Asian (Indo-Aryan) culture, namely the ideology of virginity leading to various forms of female seclusion and restrictions on her mobility, and the patrilineal inheritance system, placing service limits on women's access to resources, generally limits on women's political engagement in Nepal.

At the present time, constitution of Nepal guarantees gender equality without any discrimination on the grounds of religion, race, sex, caste and tribe in the application of law. It also provides for the right of freedom, right of the property. The article on election requires political parties to file at least five per cent women candidates in the elections for the House of Representatives. Such kind of provision did not existed before. In the May 1991 elections, seven women candidates were elected to the 205 member House of representatives, and three women have been selected for Upper House which is composed of 60 members.

Traditional Problems

Physical violence against women (acceptance of beating by the spouse and the other male household members) as socially legitimate, physical abuse by landlords, and sale of women into prostitution is another serious problems for women in poor households of Nepal. These problems can only be tackled slowly, but they cannot be ignored in any programe of economic progress for poor women.

Institutions Dealing with Women

Not many new institutions concerned with women have been added in the government or non-government sector since 1987, but :

(i) Women's organization allied to various political parties have recently emerged.

(ii) The women's Development Division in the Ministry of Education, Culture and Social Welfare has been strengthened.

(iii) The women's development Division in the Ministry of Local Development has been strengthened and upgraded from its earlier section level.

(iv) A number of new research and action groups have been established as the NGOs in the private sector.

Most of the efforts directed at institution building during the 1980, however have been top down, Kathmandu based and unable to reach the village level. Women's cells in various ministries are still very weak, and lack adequate staffs and budget to function properly. With the restoration of democracy in April 1990, some of the women's organizations have registered themselves and a number of new ones have been added. Each political party now has a women's organization. Nevertheless, a few distinguishing features of the current women's movement are already apparent. Although almost all of the women's organizations are informally aligned with one or other political party, all of them have emphasized the need for creating conditions of economic equality for women. All of them have submitted recommendations demanding equality for women in all spheres of life. The issues these organizations raise are those of equal property rights, quotas in education and job, and a voice in the political parties and the government.

Conclusion

In the overall social structure, women enjoy lower social status than men because of the traditional patriarchal values. This is more so among the higher caste Hindus such as the Brahmins and the Chetries. Among the Mongoloid communities like the Rai, Limbu, Magar, Dhimal, Gurung, Tamang, and the Sherpa women traditionally enjoy relatively more freedom. Because of the modernization and westernization, the young educated women are demanding more freedom and right at present but their age old insecurity problem and traditional values have not yet left them free for future. If women are to be emancipated and encouraged it is male chauvinism and their attitude that has to be changed. Unless men and women work together with mutual respect and understanding, there is less chance in Nepal to raise their status even if strong laws and rules are enacted merely by the government.

References

Acharya, Meena	1994	*The Statistical Profile on Nepalese Women,* IIS, Kathmandu.
Bennett, L.	1986	*Dangerous Wives and Sacred Sister ; Social and Symbolic roles of High Caste Women in Nepal* Colombia University Press, New York.
Jones, Rex L. & Jones S. K.	1976	*The Himalayan Women,* Palo alto Mayfield Press, U.S.A.
UNICEF	1992	*Children and Women of Nepal : A Situational Analysis,* His Majesty's Government of Nepal and UNICEF Kathmandu.
UNFPA	1990	Inventory of Population Project in Developing countries Around the World, NewYork.

Muhanna Haddad

HOUSING AND SOCIAL STRATIFICATION IN JORDAN

Introduction

Housing has always formed an obstacle in the course of development in Jordan whether this was educational, economic, social or others. Housing was destined for the extended family if not the Khamash (five generation). Social classification in the country was found cross-cut the tribal boundaries, characteristic of the socio-cultural structures in the three types of habitation : nomadism, rural (ism) and urbanism.

The rapid change in the country since the 1950's brought with itself two processes leading to viro-and neolocality of marriage instead of patrilocality, or to the nuclear family pattern. This neant the break off of the extended family and thereby also to the need for more houses. The one is urbanisation and the other is the expansion of both the administration and the education. As a consequence the agrarian nomadic, rural or urban cooperative group began to loose its function for the survival of the individual. Individualisation, though restricted to certain aspects of life, became a rapid process and the need for more houses became bigger while social mobility became easier.

In fact the society underwent a process of restructuring. Strata differences became more obvious. The new structure was more manifest in cities which grew at the expense of the rural areas. The question is :

How far the new societal structure (the new stratification) helped promoting or agravating the housing problem ?

Yet the more important development despite some international reputation the country got of executing regional and national development plans, has been the shift to democracy. It seemed to have promoted the housing problem to a crisis, urging the search for a solution if it had to be sustained and sofisticated. Democracy is a socio-political system the prerequisites of which are given socialisation and enculturation processes which the individual has to undergo at home, in the house. Democracy is the system of freedom, independence and privacy. Housing in this respect has the task of making possible the new socialisation required to preserve the new system. The question is :

> How far the Jordanian society is equiped with an adequate housing to be able to maintain democracy?

To answer these questions, I reconsidered the literature and statistical data with the eye fixed on the less privileged in the society : the poor people.

1. Origins and Development

The state of Jordan emerged as an Emirate in 1921 and was promoted to Kingdom by its independence in 1946 under the name : The Hashemite Kingdom of Jordan. Until the 1970's very little attention was given to the housing problem which remained in the private sector.

Analogical to population distribution there were three types of dwellings in Jordan as everywhere in the Arab East : Urban, Rural and Nomadic. But the social structure was the same, tribal in all the three.

a) Nomadic housing consisted of hair-tents, each of which could, at any time, be split into male and female parts. Despite the rule of sex segregation, interaction between the sexes was tolerated. The rate of occupation density of the tent was very high due to the extended-family pattern, and a high birth rate. Yet some clear distinction could be made between the tents of the chiefs and those of followers. Such distinction was found across the nomadic tribes, so that one could speak of two classes : Sheikhs (leaders or elite) and commoners. Though slow, social mobility was possible. But the distinction was based on criteria as possession, descent, political power, recognition and other socio-psychological factors (Jaussin, 1948).

b) Village or rural housing differed only in kind : instead of tents people lived in houses built either of mud bricks or mud and stone. The greater majority of houses consisted of one single but large room used in the dry months by humans, and in the rain months by both man and animal. The house consisted of two levels : a lower level for animals and an elevated one for humans. Sex segregation in the family was not possible. The same house was used for food storage. Occupation density was even high if not higher for the same reasons. So also, distinction could be made between houses of elites (Sheikhs) and commoners due to the same social structure. The Sheikhs' house consisted of more than one room one of which is the *madafa* (guest room). But in the village diversification of houses, and thereby also social mobility were more possible. The smith, the merchant, the carpenter or other professionals had more opportunities to imitate the elite and cooperate with them. The distinction between the two classes, Sheikh and professionals Vs commoners was more visible (H. Horani, 1975; R. Antoun, 1973).

This visibility was also due to another factor inherent in the composition of village inhabitants. Some villages were inhabited by more than one tribal group, and even by more than one religious group. The more the inhabitants were diversified, the clearer were the two classes of houses.

(c) Houses in the city, in fact, formed a more diversified example of the village, due to its agrarian economic nature. The Jordanian city remained rural in nature until the seventies and many of them as Irbid, Mafraq, Jarash, Karak a. o. are, to a certain degree, still so. The establishment of the state brought with itself a movement of employment leading to a clear distinction among people and manifested itself in housing, education and income (Gubser, 1973).

2. Housing and Social Stratification

The theory held for social stratification, or classification of individuals into social classes, based on criteria like education, income, housing and other psycho-social criteria had proved inapplicable to the situation not only in Jordan but in the Arab World in general. C.A.O Van Nieuwenhuyzen (1965) made that very clear in his treatise on the subject. This need not mean that the matter is to be left without reconsideration, for the situation urges the discovery of a suitable analytical device to reach an understanding of the emerging social structure in these societies. The absence of such a device leaves us to mercy of either the political leaders who explain it in the way desired to consolidate their power, or to Western scholars emprisoned by their stereotypes of tribalism.

The social structure outlined by the former scholars (Patai, 1958; Berger, 1964; and others) was applied in times when basic needs could only be satisfied through collective cooperation. Since the 1960's, communal cooperation in the (so-called) extended family structure began to loose its function and became gradually replaced by the nuclear family; a shift which, in cases, reached extreme forms, despite the fact that the extended family and tribal cohesion continued but was restricted to crisis situation. Housing was the most clear proof of this shift (M.D.Khairy, 1984; A. Zaghal, 1989).

The literature on housing distinguishes three types of income groups : high, middle and low or limited income groups. The basis for this classification is the income of the nuclear family unit. In terms of money this is per year 800 J.D. and higher, between 400 and 1000 J. D.and up to 400 J.D. respectively. (The Housing Foundation, Laws and Regulations, 1980).

The latter category does not meet the criteria to benefit from the Public Housing Foundation. The size of this category is estimated at 20% of the Jordan population. The middle limited income at 30% and the higher limited income at 25%. The limited income group is thereby 75%. Housing, indeed, became the manifestation of membership in a given social class.

Such manifestation is clearer in cities than in villages, and in some cities more than in others (Amman, Irbid and Zerka as compared to Mafraq, Jarash, Ajlun and Karak). The development of housing in the state of Jordan at present show three categories of houses : aristocratic, middle range and popular. If we apply the sub-classification of the class theory as did W. L. Warner (1965) each of the categories mentioned will show similar sub-classification into high, middle and low. The criteria to be held in this case are the total costs, type of material of construction, number of rooms and saloons, type of furniture, the price of the land on which the house is built, and the location (Al-Fandi, 1980). The three classes of houses emerged as the result of many factors among which the following are important.

(a) The development of the state itself brought with itself periodically various and successive distinctions of social groups : first Sheiks versus commoners, then, professionals and Sheiks, versus commoners, to be followed by a period in which privileged groups emerged to be added as laymen and Sheiks as distinguished from commoners. The first groups formed a core of a class of capital holders who were, more than others, perceptive to future developments and planned for future wealth since the forties and the fifties. Further bureaucratisation led to the emergence of the limited income-groups who became dependent on the investors in the housing section to get a house. The increase of this group led capital holders to invest more in house construction. Up to 1975 house construction costs were low and enabled the owners to rent their houses against low prices. After 1975, not only the construction costs went higher but also land prices. This period produced a small group of brokers who, in few years time, made enormous wealths adding themselves to the group of capital holders. There were either engineers who founded construction companies or simple brokers.

The development of the state since 1948 witnessed two Arab-Israeli Wars (1948 and 1976), the result of which was the addition of a new housing genere to Jordan housing variety, namely the Refugee Camps. On the long run, this became a prominent feature among the housing aspects of Jordan. Other refugees enlarged the three existing residential groups. Before 1967,the aristocracy ambified villas in the West Bank, mainly in Jerusalem and Ramallah,but after that most wealthy people went to Amman which came to contain more than one third of Jordan's population. Irbid, the second city shelters more than one third of the governorate population.

(b) The development of land ownership and prices. In the Ottoman period the land was owned by the state. This situation remained until the formal distribution and registration of land between 1930-1940, in the period of the emirate (1921-1946). Due to this distribution many remote areas were owned by people who used to exploit them. Therefore many areas which became parts of the big cities were owned by people from the neighbouring villages. Due to immigration into the big cities, increased demand on housing, many areas were included in the planning of the central municipalities to become areas of house construction. This planning raised the prices of land enormously so that its owners were able to gather great sums of money and became very wealthy.

The distribution of the housing construction areas in the cities, therefore, was self regulating; those who had much money bought land in expensive areas whereas others bought their pieces of land in areas where the prices were either middle or low.

Since 1975 land prices mounted sharply and differences in price of land in various areas made the distinction of residence areas very clear. People with limited income became unable to buy land in given areas of the cities, and even if they were able to do so they were economically incompetent to meet other socio-economic requirements. Given parts of the Jordanian cities, mainly Amman and Irbid, were postulated as aristocratic.

People of limited income, as employees, army officers, middle size and small merchants, manual professionals and the like occupied other less expensive areas whereas other areas in cities were inhabited by groups of middle limited income groups. Low limited income groups lived in the outskirts of the cities.

(c) The economic and political developments in the region in general and in Jordan in particular gave the emerging housing classification an extra push forward. Jordan, in fact, lacks rich natural resources and is economically dependent on three sources : inter-dependence of the Arab States, international support and basically on revenues of its labour forces working abroad. The last factor is significant in the development of housing. The external labour market for Jordanians started with Europe and the USA in the fifties and sixties. After the 1970's the markets of the Gulf States absorbed the Jordanian labor forces. These emigrants used to come back to Jordan where housing became a major investment section. Labor migration, in fact, enlarged the two higher classes of house owners. This meant also more competition on acquisition of land destined for construction, continuously higher developing prices and costs of houses (Housing Foundation, Proceeding of the 4th Conference of Jordanian Emigrants, 1988).

The foregoing does not mean that labor migration only reduced the limited income-groups but it also increased it with a sub-stratum of foreign workers who were introduced to fill the gap caused by emigrating labor forces. This new sub-proletariat (mainly from Egypt and Syria) used to live on the margin for the individual earnings, did not reach half the sum of poverty line. Housing of this group was extremely difficult and many house-owners were willing to exploit the situation. There were at least some 100,000 living primitively in groups between 5-8 persons in one single room built of concrete blocks or in a neglected old-fashioned houses (A. Daher, 1985, pp. 109-119).

3. Factors Influencing the Housing Crisis in Jordan

Real attention to the problem of housing in the Kindom did not start until the 1970s, after the civil war, when the government chose for applying development plans, first the three years and since 1976 the five years plans. Al-Khouri contends that the housing crisis led the average Jordanian in the cities to spend some 30% of his income on housing (1974 : 11). This percentage was no more than 20% in the industrialised countries, whereas the wages in Jordan were very low. Specifying the factors leading to the crisis of housing, Ahmad Al-Fandi (1980) related them to the housing market in its both supply and demand. The factors considered as leading to decrease of supply were :

- Low income and high costs of houses;
- increasing rise of land prices;
- higher developing prices of construction materials;
- inadequacy of laws and regulations;
- the high costs of architectural and technical institutions;
- the lack of skilled workers in the construction; and
- shortage of subsidising channels for house construction.

On the demand side, the factors leading to its increment Al-Fandi mentions :

- the rise of natural increase of Jordan population;
- unregulated migration from rural areas to urban centers;
- compulsary migration caused by the wars of 1948 and 1967;
- loosening of the extended family and splitting of the nuclear family;
- the movement of people to new houses instead of the older traditional ones; and

— sedentarisation of nomadic groups.

These factors are general, but there are other factors relating specifically to the housing sector. Among these are the availability of a comprehensive programme which takes into account the regional distribution of population, of the economic activities, and of the presence of basic services as electricity, sewage, water etc., financial means; prices of construction materials; the living standards; kind of buildings, goals of housing projects etc.

Most tragic in this matter as Al-Fandi (1980) projects it, is that the individual opportunity to own a house goes at the expense of other basic needs as food and clothes of the family, education, health communication, and dependence on housing financial institutions.

Relating these issues to social stratification and to information provided by the different housing institutions such as the Housing Bank-Jordan, the Department of Urban Development a. o., it can be noted that the poor in Jordan can have no access to respectful housing particularly when considering the rising living standards and immobility of wages.

4. Acquiring a House in Jordan

Acquiring a house in Jordan occurs through one of the following ways :

(a) Inheritance.

(b) Building a house with own financial means and self-supervision.

(c) Building an own house with financial loans from one of the Banks or institutional sources.

(d) Buying a house from private housing associations on loan to be extracted from the own salary. So we have in Jordan particular housing associations for the army, educationists, physicians, engineers, university teachers and employees, etc.

(e) House cooperatives.

(f) Renting a house.

5. Some Characteristics of the Population in Jordan

A look at the statistical characteristics of the Jordanian population will show that the majority of people in fact live within the poverty line.

Table 1. Estimated Population by Governorate and Sex at the end of 1989

Governorate	Male	Female	Total
Amman	680300	616800	1297100
Zarqa	235500	214400	449900
Irbid	388300	365100	753400
Mafraq	56380	52620	109000
Balqa	111950	102750	214700
Karak	69600	63200	132800
Tafiela	23540	22260	45800
Ma'an	61430	46870	108300
Total	1627000	1484000	3111000

Table 2. Estimates of Urban* and Rural Population by Governorate for 1988 and 1989

Governorate	1988			1989		
	Rural	Urban	Total	Rural	Urban	Total
Amman	185750	1062830	1248580	192015	1105085	1297100
Zarqa	41475	392525	434000	42805	407095	449900
Irbid	328450	399750	728200	342570	410830	753400
Mafraq	75350	30100	105450	77790	31210	109000
Balqa	92355	115145	207500	95465	119235	214700
Karak	102830	25620	128450	106255	26545	132800
Taiela	26915	17355	44270	27810	17990	45800
Ma'an	48460	56090	104550	50030	58270	108300
Total	901585	2099415	3001000	934740	2176260	3111000

Source : *"Urban" includes localities of (5000) Population or more as were defined in 1979.

Table 3 :* Percentage Distribution of House Type

Type of House	%
Dar (traditional house)	72.8
Appartment	24.9
Villa	1.0
Barraks	1.0
Other	0.3

Table 4 : Percentage Distribution of Type of House Units by Number of Rooms

Type of House	Number of Rooms				
Units	1	2	3	4-5	6-8
Dar	7.4	22.3	34.9	22.7	2.7
Appartment	7.8	28.0	33.4	21.7	2.8
Villa	4.4	26.5	40.5	25.8	2.7
Barraks	37.3	40.3	20.0	—	—

70.9% of this sample were found in the cities and 21.1 in the rural areas. The distribution is as follows :

Table 5. Percentage Distribution of Type of House Units by Urban Rural

Type of House Units	*Urban*	*Rural*
Dar	63.9	94.6
Apartment	33.5	4.1
Villa	1.3	.2
Barraks	1.3	.5

*This and the following tables are abstracted from :

Source : Dept. of General Statistics, A study of Repatriating and Internal Migration and Human Forces, Amman, 1986.

Important in this classification are different aspects among which is the type of building material. Houses of cut stone and concrete are considered higher in kind than concrete cement. About 10% of the houses are of cut stones whereas 20.3% are of concrete cement and 64.5% are of cement bricks; 3.8% are built of stone and mud.

These variations do not mean that owners of similar houses have similar income or belong to the same similar income groups. In the capital, or more specific in given parts of the city, the situation may be so, but in many others they may differ widely in income. It is perhaps the groups income (family income) which plays a role in this distribution. This same situation affected even the choice of marriage partner : men, nowadays, prefer to marry a working partner. The living standard urges them to do so. The average Jordanian does his atmost best, and in many cases at the expense of food, clothes, education and other needs to have his own house as shown in the following table.

Table 6. Percentage Distribution of Housing Units by Type of Tenure, Building Material and Urban Rural

	Mud Bricks Mud & Stone	*Cement Bricks*	*Cut Stone*	*Concrete Cement*	
Total	5.-	64.50	10.25	20.3	100%
Owned	5.2	65.48	8.58	20.65	74.-
Rented	3.2	62.10	15.4	19.28	23.1
For work	10.5	61.00	10.5	19.79	0.6
Others	12.8	53.67	8.36	17.98	2.3
Urban					70.9/100
Owned	4.1	65.7	13.3	16.92	67.2
Rented	4.4	67.3	12.-	16.3	29.9
For work	2.5	62.7	16.4	18.4	0.5
Other	13.1	60.7	9.7	16.5	2.4
Rural					29.1/100
Owned	7.3	61.6	2.5	28.5	90.6
Rented	6.9	62.2	2.4	28.5	6.4
For work	19.-	59.5	4.8	16.7	0.9
Other	11.96	54.3	4.3	29.3	2.1

Clearer in the distribution of house units by the number of rooms. Most of the houses do not contain more than three rooms of which one is a living room, one kitchen and one bedroom. This distribution says, de facto, something about the extent to which the Jordanian child has the opportunity to develop and independent personality, to learn what is privacy, and to develop to individualism. The opposite development is more probable.

Table 7. Percentage Distribution of Housing Units by Type of Tenure, Number of Rooms and Urban Rural

	Number of Rooms					
	1-7	*4-5*	*3*	*2*	*1*	*Total*
Type of Tenure						
Total	3.1	22.7	34.8	32.0	7.4	100
Owned	3.8	25.5	35.7	29.5	5.6	74
Rented	1.2	14.9	33.0	40.0	11.0	23.1
For work	2.1	12.6	25.3	25.3	34.7	0.6
Other	1.7	14.2	25.4	36.2	22.3	2.3
Urban Total	3.0	22.6	36.1	31.0	7.3	70.9/100
Owned	4.0	26.2	37.8	27.0	5.2	76.2
Rented	1.1	15.1	33.0	40.0	10.8	29.9
For work	1.9	12.4	25.5	37.1	22.9	2.4
Other	1.9	22.6	30.2	22.6	24.5	0.5
Rural Total	3.0	22.9	31.9	34.4	7.6	29.1/100
Owned	3.2	24.1	32.1	34.1	6.5	90.6
Rented	0.3	12.8	32.8	40.4	13.8	6.4
Forwork	2.3	2.4	19.1	28.6	47.6	0.9
Other	1.1	19.6	25.0	33.7	20.7	2.1

The distribution of families by have and have no kitchen and bathroom may tell more about poverty and housing as in the table below.

Table 8. Percentage Distribution of Households by Availability of Bath and Kitchen and Urban-Rural.

	Kitchen Not Available	*Toilet Not Available*
Total	8.03	14.05
Urban	4.8	8.92
Rural	14.75	26.57
Amman	4.5	6.9
Urban	3.8	5.0
Rural	15.5	21.5
Zarka	4.1	10.5
Urban	3.6	8.4
Rural	8.55	26.8
Mafraq	17.4	28.05
Urban	2.0	6.0
Rural	23.6	37.0
Balqa	9.9	21.9
Urban	7.2	16.6
Rural	15.0	32.0
Irbid	13.05	19.7
Urban	9.2	15.9
Rural	17.2	24.0
Karak	12.05	26.4
Urban	15.4	26.2
Rural	11.2	26.4
Tafilah	14.4	28.4
Urban	6.9	17.2
Rural	21.7	39.2
Ma'an	13.8	21.0
Urban	3.4	11.2
Rural	25.2	32.0

It is important to know that 64% of the families in Jordan consist of more than five persons whereas 36% consist of 5 persons and less. The distribution of families by the number of rooms makes clear that 74.2% have between one and 3 rooms.

Table 9. Percentage Distribution of Families by Size of Household, and Urban-Rural

	Size of Household	
	2-5	*6-more*
Total	36.-	64.-
Urban	37.9	60.1
Rural	31.4	68.6

Table 10*. Percentage Distribution of Family Income Per Month by Urban-Rural

	Total	*Urban*	*Rural*	
>50	5.0	4.3	6.7	
				30
50-99	19.0	16.9	24.0	
100-149	27.7	24.4	30.5	
150-199	18.0	18.6	16.9	
200-299	17.4	18.9	13.7	
300-499	10.0	12.0	6.6	
<500	3.9	4.9	1.6	
	100.0%	100.0%	100.0%	

*Abstracted from Survey of Health and Nutrition; Dept. of General Statistics, Amman 1987 : 417.

A study of Khalid Shuraydah and others 1988 showed that poverty line was 100 J. D. per month. Since then, the living standard arose some 300% regardless currency devaluation (from 3 USA Dollar to 1.5 per J. D.), absence of any form of wages increase to adapt to the situation and without considering the effects of the Gulf Crisis and the rise of unemployment. Additionally the re-immigration caused a crisis in the housing market : Demand became very high while supply retreated due to the situation.

Housing Foundations

It was around the end of sixties that the government began to think seriously of the housing problem. There are two major Housing Foundations : The Department of Urban Development, and the Housing Bank. Despite the services they render to Jordanians, most services are destined for the better off.

A. The Public Housing Foundation (PHF) was set up in 1968 with the aim of solving the crisis of housing in the Kingdom through :

1. owning the land, putting construction designs, building houses according to fixed programs, selling or renting the houses to employees and people with limited income; 2. giving loans for the purpose of building houses to amorph institutions, housing cooperative associations and individuals (Law and Regulations of the Housing Foundation, 1980, p.6 article 4 (1 and 2).

Art. 4 of the loan regulations (p.11) gives priority to governmental employees, public institution and then to people with limited income. To get the loan the applicant had to own the land on which the house would built, be married and had served a longer time span in the state service (art. 5, a-d). The total sum of the loan may not exceed the 4x monthly salary. (art. 8). Loans are given to those who have a family. The family is defined to consist of a man, wife and their unmarried children who live with them (art. 2. of Regulations no. 26 (1970). The family annual incomes is the sum total of the incomes of the family members, seen against the income classification of the limited income families (i.e. Annual income of not more than 1500 J. D.).

Presenting the social factors influencing the housing problem in Jordan Al-Nabusi, H. (1986 : 27) mentions that Jordan has the peculiarity of a technical demographic structure in which the financial responsibility is very high. This has the consequence that 55% of the working people have an income below 100 J. D. It was made clear that 20% of the Jordanians were not able to benefit from the housing projects run by the government.

Yet there is another bigger problem in this all. An average high limited income per month means 130 J. D. 4x this some is about 520 J. D. This is not enough to buy the cement for a house. One sac of cement weighing 50 kg. costed at that time 1.8 J. D. to build a house of 100m^2 needs at least 400 sacs, the costs of which were 720.—J. D. If this information is taken into consideration compared to the information given on income, it can be concluded that 35% of the families in Jordan have no access to governmental housing.

Recruitment for housing occupation forms another factor. Needless to say that a number of the mentioned projects were destined to universities' employees, high ranking officers, teachers, physicians etc. Except for school teachers, the others, are considered as a very high income group.

Employees below a monthly salary of 150 J. D. are considered as now/at this time, of low wages, particularly after the devaluation of the valuta and the increase in living standard, despite that the government maintains the old wage ratio as criterion. This makes a lot of confusion to the receiver of information, so not to say bias.

B. The Housing Bank : The Housing Bank was established in 1973 as a governmental institution with the aim of securing the necessary capital to contribute solving the housing problem, support and stimulate the construction development in the country. Its capital grew from 1/2 million in 1973 to 607.2 millions in 1990 (Annual Report 1990).

The Bank supplies various loans to individuals, institutions and associations. The loans to individuals are of three types : loans to individuals having low and middle income, i.e. income not exceeding 300 J. D. per month. The value of the loan was decided in maximal at 27x the monthly salary to be returned in a period of 20 years. The discount was decided at 8.5%, 1% of which was life insurance for the client. Loans to individuals with high income up to 20.000-J.D. to be paid back in a period of 10 years. Other loans are given to various housing institutions and associations. Until 1985, the Bank extended 23.308 of such loans to the first group and 419 to the second group. This total reached 81808 loans which means the number of household heads. Yet the Bank has, on the long run, become commercial as any other Bank.

Both the Housing Foundation and Housing Bank are the basic financial pillars of all the housing associations in the country. Each of the public employment sections in the government founded such an association.

Conclusions

Over aginst the slight diversification in the past, present day Jordan has a great variety of housings from the hair tent to the palace. Though housing has changed to virilocal and at the same time neolocal residence assuring a great shift to the nuclear family pattern, it remained very precarious. Population increase, shism of the extended family, exchange of old fashioned houses and internal migration caused a crisis in the housing section. The rising living standard, the devaluation of the valuta, the stabilisation of income and rising of cost and land prices, led to a diverse housing climate, in which the poor became rather excluded. The proportion of the people to be classified as poor on the basis of monthly income, housing and rate of room occupation grows rapidly. The lack of natural resources, the limited financial aid to the country, and the lack of well equiped administrative apparatus make all efforts done for progress fail. The result is that the gap between rich and poor is becoming wider and wider. Poverty line at present is laid at about 64 of the families, particularly after the Gulf Crisis (Y. Al-Adwan 1991).

Housing in Jordan will pertinently work against consolidating democracy in the country for it does not help promote independence of the individual due to the high rate of room occupation, accommodation and lack of privacy, in addition to economic dependence.

References

Al-Adwan, Yasser	1991	*Economic and Social Realities of the Development Units in Both the Regions of Mafraq and the Northern Badia. (Irbid.)* Yarmouk University Press (in Arabic).
Al-Fandi, and A. Muhammad	1980	Present and Future Consequences of the *Housing Problem in Jordan.* Kuwait : Arab Institution for Planning.
Al-Nabusi, and Hand Allah	1986	*"Housing and Finance in Jordan"* In : *Proceedings of the Sumposium for Housing held in Amman.* Union of Arab Banks.
Antonn, Richard	1972	*Arab Village, Bloomington : Indiana* University Press.
Daher, Ahmad	1985	*Incoming Labor Forces in Jordan.* (Amman: Al-Manar Library (in Arabic).
Deptt. of Public *Statistics*	1986	*A Study Of Internal Migration. Repatriation and Human Forces.* (Amman).
	1987	Survey of Health, Nutrition, Human Forces and Poverty (Main Resuits).
	1989	Annual Statistical Publication.
	1979	Results of the General Census of Houses and Inhabitants.
Gubser, P.	1973	*Politics and Change in Al-Karak-Jordan.* (London : OUP).
Jaussin, A.	1948	*Les Countume Des Arabes Dans Les Pays de Moab* (Paris : Librarie d' Amerique et d' Oriento).
Khairy, Majdu-Din	1985	*Social Relation in Some Nuclear Families in Jordan.* (Amman : Jordan University)

		(in Arabic).
The Housing Bank Jordan	1973 1990	Annual Report Several Reports (Amman : Central Office). (in Arabic).
Housing Foundation	1980	*Jordan* : Laws and Regulations, Amman.
	1988	*Jordan* "Symposium of Reducing House Construction Costs." Amman.
Nieuwenhuijze, and *C.A.O. Van*	1965	*Social Stratification and the Middle East: An Interpretation.* London. E. J. Brill.
Zaghal, Ali	1989	*Change in the Structural Characteristics of the Family in North Jordan : An Empirical Study* Irbid : Yarmouk University Press.) (in Arabic).

Faisal Al-Matalka

JUVENILE DELINQUENCY IN JORDAN

The Hashemite Kingdom of Jordan is a developing Arab country which achieved independence on 25th May 1946. It has borders with Syria on the north, Iraq on the east, Saudi Arabia on the east and south, the Red Sea to the south and occupied Palestine on the west (Anonymous, 1986).

Topographically Jordan is a rocky country with deserts and mountains. Of the total area of Jordan, 80% of the land is desert, 18% under agriculture and 1 to 2% is forested (Govt. of Jordan, 1974).

The population of Jordan is about 4 million. Arabic is the official language and Amman is the capital of the kingdom.

Jordan has its strategic location since long. It has been the path-way of traders, caravans, armies and conquerers like the Roman, Nabatans, Byzantines and the Islam. It has its important roles as a transit route and a meeting point linking to Yeman, Hejaz, Syria, East Africa and Mediteranean countries (Harris, 1958).

Jordan, though an ancient land in the legacy of human civilization, in the modern sense in comparatively a young country. It is infested with various peculiar and distinct problems.

The present study is confined to male juvenile delinquency and carried out between the years 1992-1994. The sampling design in based on informations collected from both pronounced and the potentially delinquents of different cities of Jordan. The study has been specifically limited to the span of eleven years (1980-1990).

Crime in general is kept at low level in Jordan. Juvenile delinquency seems to get out of hand. There are some indications pointing to its substantial increase. The last few years registered the highest number of juvenile arrests in the country's history.

The following table (Annual Reports, 1980-1990) gives us a clear picture of the same.

Number of male delinquents cases since 1980-1990

Year	1980	1981	1982	1983	1984	1985	1986	1987	1988	1989	1990
No.	3671	3458	3453	3325	3279	3622	4235	4248	5136	6230	5896

The above table gives us a clear idea about the constant increase in the delinquent acts. The year 1989 has recorded the highest number of delinquent acts in the country's history.

Juvenile delinquency is one of the serious social problems confronted by most of the modern and complex societies of the world. It hampers the smooth functioning of the society quite a lot because it is the genesis of crime. Crime arises when individuals break the social norms and do not bother about the repurcussions the society will have to bear because of adjustment problems of the child in the family, school, peer group, and society at large.

A juvenile delinquent is a person who is not an adult but a child or an adolescent and has fallen prey to various difficult situations at home or outside which forced him to deviate from the normal standard of behavior and thereby commit an offence which may be intentional or non-intentional.

The treatise is dealt with the problems of juvenile delinquency in Jordan. Delinquency has existed in all cultures of all ethnic groups; and in all epochs of recorded history. It is observed that there is not a single contemporary society, in which misbehaviour of young people does not exist. Juvenile delinquency is a problem that has been causing great concern all over the world.

Even in the developed countries, inspite of a high standard of living, ensuring adequate necessities and many amenities of life, compulsory university education upto a fairly high age and ample opportunities for recreation, the number and percentage of juvenile delinquents are not only increasing, but the quality and complexity of the offences and a serious observations and perversities manifested there in, are intensifying and causing serious anxiety.

Delinquency means offences recorded by one or more of the public authorities directly concerned with criminal law enforcement and the administration of justice. According to Mowrer (1961) delinquency is the moral deficiency. He has taken into different culture. Lykken (1957) is of the same opinion and believes that it is due to underactivity of the central nervous system. However, delinquency is afterall concerned with some offences when it is considered inappropriate behavior in terms of social norms in the society (Quay, 1965).

In fact, it is agreed that the meaning of delinquency is related to activities concerned with misbehaviour along with some other offences which are also to be considered as illegal offences in question, since all misbehaviour may not be considered as delinquent,both the quality of behavior and the degree of social deviance are factors in considering as acts of delinquent. The term may be considered when there is question of morality to be involved in term of technical violation of laws for the welfare of one-self or others. According to Quay, (1965)

> "The delinquent, then would be a person whose misbehavior is a relatively serious legal offence, which is inappropriate to his level of development, is not committed as a result of extremely low intellect, or severe mental or metabolic dysfunction; and is alien to the culture in which he has been reared. Whether or not the individual is apprehended or legally adjudicated is not crucial."

The age limit of juvenile delinquents differs one society to another. The majority of countries throughout the world accept either seven or eight years as the lower age limit according to the Encyclopaedea Americana (1971). Moreover, in Jordan a juvenile delinquent is an individual who attains seven years of age and continues till he becomes eighteen years old (Juvenile Act, 1968).

In a study of juvenile delinquency be it social, economic or legal, the most interrelated problem is whom shall we call juvenile delinquents and of what stages : Often a child accused of a wrong is called juvenile delinquent. According to Kratcashi Couple,

> "broadly considered juvenile delinquency could mean any type of behavior by those socially defined as juvenile (non-adult) that violates the norms (standard of proper behavior) set by the controlling group."

In the narrower sense, on the other hand, it means,

> "any action by some one designated as a juvenile that would make such a young person subjected to action by the juvenile court' (Mitra, 1988). According to Sethna, (1952) "Juvenile delinquency involves

> wrong-doing by a child or by a young person who is under an age specified by the law of the place concerned."

The juvenile delinquent is a person who has been adjudicated as such by a judicial court though he may be no different from masses of children who are non-delinquent untill the time of the court contact and adjudication of any rate. Delinquency is defined by acts, the detection of which is thought to result in punishment of the person commiting them by agent of the larger society. The most widely quoted definition of deviant behaviour is probably of Chohen (1959), who states,

> "We define deviant behavior as behavior which violates institutionalized expectations, that is, expectations that are shared and recognized as ligitimate within a social system."

According to Cloward and Ohl in, (1969)

> "The delinquent act is behavior that violates basic norms of the society and when officially known, it evokes a judgement by agents of criminal justice that such norms have been violated."

From the foregoing, we observe that there is no unanimous and scientific definition of juvenile delinquency, but it is agreed and accepted by all that law breaking and anti-social activities upto certain age limit of the children is called juvenile delinquency. To us Juvenile delinquency may be defined as

> "A deviant act against the accepted norms, values and laws of the society committed by a child who is seven to seventeen years old, who has been a victim of faulty family socialization."

In Jordan today there is a wide belief that delinquent behaviour is a lower class phenomenon (Rbeihat, 1987). Children from a lower socio-economic status are believed to have a higher rate of delinquency than those who belong to more affluent social group. This notion has received wide support from official data. According to the official account of delinquency more than 60 per cent of juveniles who committed delinquent act, were school dropouts who were driven to the labour market at an early age by poverty and school failure.

The picture of a delinquency pointed by official account is found to be similar to the one pointed by earlier theories developed in the United States. Early theorizing about delinquent behavior saw it is a lower class phenomenon. Prior to 1960 many theories emphasizing poverty and membership in lower class as a cause of law-breaking behavior came into existence (Merton, 1957; Croward and Ohlin 1960; Shaw and McKay, 1942). These theories were based on data drawn from official sources. According to these theories delinquency is due to social inequality, lack of opportunity, a sense of frustration and identification with like-minded peers.

While several sources of data on the extent and seriousness of delinquent behavior are available in the west there is an urgent need for more and better information about the size and magnitude of the problem in Jordan due to the increase in numbers of juvenile cases in the country. It is felt that the available data about juvenile and their law-breaking behavior is very limited. Official data can tell us nothing about the vast number of unsolved offences or about the many cases in which/ delinquents are dealt with informally instead of being arrested or referred to court.

The causes of juvenile delinquency cannot be attributed to a particular factor, but is related to various factors. In this paper we will present the most important factors that cause delinquency in Jordan. These factors are the outcome of an intensive study carried out on the male juvenile delinquents in Jordan. Bad family environment is the most important factor among all other factors like, dropouts of school, bad campanionship and unhealthy delinquency area.

Family Environment

The family is the primary socializing group in society. Not only does it establish the child's basic personality, but it also introduces him to the mores and norms of the larger culture. Thus, in a variety of ways the family sets the direction for the individuals development in later life. It is his springboard into adulthood and the broader society.

The condition of the family and what goes on in the family life are of great importance to a growing child. The process of socialization and character of the person take their first and often permanent form under the umbrella of family life and culture heritage. The family is the first great training school in behavior and conduct, depending upon the nature and type of family life in which a child is reared. It is the chief socializing agent, but it may produce anti-social traits also. The child tends to acquire certain moral and social qualities as taught and examplified in the family.

The environment of the family can be appropriated for knowing the causes of delinquency. This section will discuss family environmental factors that can have impact on producing delinquents in the Jordanian society.

(a) Broken Homes

Broken homes have been regarded as one of the major factors that causes delinquency. In our study of the home structure of the respondents, we have found that 77.64 per cent of the delinquents and 100 per cent of the potentially delinquents have come from broken homes, whereas only 22.35 per cent of the delinquents have come from physically intact families.

Thus, the broken homes are found to be a great contributor to the increasing problem in the Jordanian society as these supply maximum number of delinquents.

(b) Disoriented Parental Relationship

The most important factor of family life is whether child's parents are alive and, if so, what is the nature of their relationship. Children not only need the love and care of parents, but also expect that parents love each other. Inspite of good social status and economic condition of the family, the life of a child may be full of anxiety, dejection, dissatisfaction or even anger on account of discard in the family.

This study shows that disoriented parental relationship is an important factor that contributes to the problem of juvenile delinquency in Jordan. It reveals that in case of 64.70 per cent of the delinquents and 66.66 per cent of the potentially delinquerits the relationship between their parents are unhealthy whereas only 12.35 per cent of the delinquents reveal that the relationship among their parents is healthy. Another 22.94 per cent of the delinquents and 33.33 per cent of the potentially have failed to reveal the type of relationship that their parents are having. Therefore, defective parental relationship has a direct effect on the child and help in developing deviant character.

(c) Defective Parent Child Relations

A functionally inadequate home is one which does not or cannot meet with the basic needs of the child. It is either incapable or too maladjusted to perform the function necessary for the development of healthy and well adjusted personality of the child. Wholesome food, shelter, clothing opportunities for education and recreation, medical aid and economic stability, in general, are certainly essential for the healthy growth of the child, but the parent-child relationship is far more important than any of those. Defective parent-child relationship is a great handicap for the growing child.

Our study of the parent-child relationship has revealed that 79.45 per cent of the delinquents and 100 per cent of the potentially delinquents, are having strained relationship with their fathers, whereas only 20.54 per cent of the delinquents are found to have pleasant relationship with their fathers. Whereas 64.51 per cent of the delinquents and 92.85 per cent of the potentially delinquents are having unpleasant relationship with their mother, only 35.48 per cent of the delinquents and 7.14 per cent of the potentially delinquents are seen to be maintaining a good relation with their mothers.

In short, we can say, that unloving, rejecting, absentee, inadequate and maladjusted parents, all in their varying ways and degrees, contribute to a poor quality of home life which is closely associated with child delinquency.

(d) Disoriented Parental Discipline (Control)

The destructive and disorganizing impact of delinquency is especially strong when family function has been deficient. A deficiency in familiar socialization may thus encourage delinquent conduct by failing to develope adequate socio-ethical personalities.

In the present study, we found defective parental discipline is dominant factor in delinquency. We have observed that more than 70 per cent of our respondents have been deprived of the direct and indirect parental discipline and control. Here the parents are so lax, overstrict or erratic in their discipline and control that very few of them are firm but kind in their discipline and control practices. Therefore, the defective parental discipline and control practices are the important factors that force the adolescents of involving in delinquent behavior.

(e) Large Family and Inadequate Housing Facilities

In our study of the size of the delinquents families we found that 41.17 per cent of their families consist of 9-11 members, followed by families with 12 and more members. Another 16.47 per cent have 6-8 members in their families and only 8.23 percent of them belong to families which consist of 3-5 persons.

We have also found houses of 45.29 per cent of the delinquents consist of one room, followed by those of 35.29 per cent having two rooms, another 11.76 per cent said their houses consist of three rooms, whereas only less than 8.00 per cent delinquents have revealed that their house consist of four or more rooms. One thing has become very clear that their houses are significantly overcrowed. They are found to have no privacy, and both sexes, elders and youngers. Parents and children sleep in the same room. And the slums and refuge/ camps where they stay are very much congested, poorly constructed, dirty and quite unhealthy place to live in.

Therefore over-crowding and inadequate housing facilities lead to unpleasant situation in families; in such a situation children there are found to be restless and wish to stay away from home very often. Thus, it is clear that overcrowding and inadequate facilities in the house deprive the respondents of home life and compel them to take refuge in the street and crowded trading markets which give them the chance to become delinquents.

(f) Low Family Income

Studies on the relationship between income and delinquency have shown that juvenile delinquency is highly correlated with all the indices of low income and with other social problems resulting from poverty.

The present study on the income of the delinquent families reveals that 47.05 per cent are having a very low monthly income i.e. 100 Jordanian Dinnar (JD), followed by 35.88 per cent families who get between 100-150 JD per month, another 12.94 per cent have disclosed their monthly income in between 150 and 200 JD, and the rest have more than 200 JD.

Therefore, many poverty stricken homes are almost drab places in which to live and to rear children in a proper way is mighty difficult. Inadequacy, frustration and emotional insecurity that often accompany families with low economic standard, play a real part in delinquency.

(g) Working Mother

Employment of especially the mother of small children had been regarded as an important factor in the slackening of family control and attachment, and consequently this often contributes to delinquency. The present study supports this notion. It is found that in case of 77.41 per cent of the delinquents their mothers are working, whereas only in 22.58 per cent cases they are housewive only.

The findings of this study show a strong relationship between working mother and juvenile delinquency in Jordan.

(h) Father-Absence

The study of the family background of the delinquents shows that in case of 84.24 per cent of the delinquents their fathers are not staying with their families, whereas only in 15.75 percent cases they are found to stay with their families.

The absence of the fathers and the family condition that is developed following his absence, have been important factors in allowing the child of taking step towards violating the law and norms of the society.

2. Truancy and Dropout of School

In Jordan the compulsory education is upto 9th standard. Some pupils virtually leaves school before they complete their compulsory education due to habitual, long-continued periods of truancy, or due to poor enconomic conditions or tension at home. Many early dropouts find it difficult to get hold jobs, especially jobs that will provide them with money to buy the clothing and afford them the amusement they want. And in the absence of more constructive activities, it is feared that they often turn to delinquency. As evidenced in truancy, revolt against the school itself can be first step toward crime. Delinquents generally are retarded in reading, writing, and arithmetic and find shool a continuing irritation and threat to their sense of worth.

The educational background of the delinquents in the present study clearly focuses that 60 per cent of the delinquents are dropouts of school, whereas only 40 per cent of them are school students. It is also found 85 per cent of the delinquents who are in school are habitual truants.

It should not be assumed that all dropouts are not delinquency prone or that they are a homogeneous group lacking aptitudes. However, the analysis of dropouts reveals the strong etiological similarity to delinquency.

3. Bad Companionship

Play group or companianship plays an important role in effecting the behaviour of the individual to a great extent. Friendship with delinquent effects the new friends in one way or another. In the beginning they involve a friend in deviant activities for the sake of fun, but soon he becomes a member of misbehavior. When a child is introduced with the delinquents, the later try to involve him in their deviant activities otherwise he will not be accepted as a member of their group. This is also clear that the main source of support for the delinquent to commit deviant acts is his friends.

It is found that 53.53 per cent of the delinquents are having delinquents friends whereas 46.47 per cent of the delinquents who do not have delinquent friends, themselves are friends to non-delinquent boys. Furthers 84.70 per cent of them say that they commit their deviant behavior with the support of other friends. Therefore, it many be concluded that bad companionship is an important factor that contributes to the increasing number of delinquents in the Jordanian society.

4. Delinquency Area

In Jordan 60 per cent of the population live in its two largest cities, Amman and Zarga (Rbeihat, 1987). We found that the urban areas in Jordan which are considered to be the main hideouts of delinquency, have accommodated 59.41 per cent of our respondents. Therefore, the delinquency rate increases with the growth of urbanization.

The second important contributor to the increase of delinquency in Jordan is the refugee camps and slum areas. According to the official data (Annual Reports, 1980-1990) there is a high association between slums and delinquent behavior. The present study shows that 24.11 per cent of the total delinquents are from refugee camps which are the second largest contributor to the total number of delinquency in Jordan. Therefore, it may be inferred that the refugee camp and slum in the urban centres and its neighbourhood are important contributors towards juvenile delinquency in the Jordanian society.

Conclusion

In the foregoing pages a discussion has been made on the delinquency in Jordan and factors responsible for this. From the above discussion the following propositions/hypothesis can be derived.

1. **The More the Defective Family Relationship, the Less the Child is likely to obey the Prevalents Norms and Laws of Society.**

The findings of the family background of the respondents reveal that majority of the respondents belong to broken homes, or to families with faulty parent-child relationship and maladjusted parents, with defective parental control and discipline.

As the atmosphere is defective and abnormal for the healthy development of a child, the respondents become a victim of this unhealthy atmosphere at home. The unhealthy and undesirable atmosphere at home definitely affects the normal growth of the children because of lack of affection and interests of the parents in taking positive part for upbringing of their children. Hence a feeling of fear and insecurity crops up in the mind of the child making him a rebellious in every way as is indicated in this study.

2. The Larger the Family Size the More the Child is Likely to Involve in Deviant Activities.

Majority of the respondents in the present study are found to have come from large size family and this size of the family has affected the behavior pattern of these children. Large size family denotes limited earning members with too many children to be fed. Due to overcrowding in such families children do not find enough space to bring friends and also for extra-curricular and creative activities. Since there are too many children to be looked after in the family the parents can hardly shower love, affection and proper guidance to every child. Hence there is a feeling of neglect, hatred and frustration in some of these children either towards their parents or towards siblings.

The lack of privacy, space, overcrowding and a feeling of insecurity at home induce the children to seek pleasure and comfort outside the house, particularly in the company of bad peers and all types of people far from home. While doing this, they get mixed up with other complexity of the outside world which gradually affects them in a negative way. Involving in group misbehavior is very common for them, and hence delinquency has become a way of life with them.

3. The Lower the Economic Standard the More the Children are Likely to Commit Delinquent Act.

The family with low economic standard is unable to provide all the necessary prerequisite of the child which developes in him a feeling of jealousy towards affluent families. This brings a change in the behavior of the respondents, many of whom take to stealing and similar types of acts which are contrary to the accepted norms and values of the society. Besides, there is a constant pressure on these children from the family members to suppliment income which forces them to leave the schools and accept different jobs according to their capacity.

These children due the materialistics dissatisfaction have taken to such acts like burglary, theft and begging to fulfill their desires by hook or by crook or undertake jobs. This snatches their innocence and childhood at a very early age which is rather shocking to them and a rebellious attitudes towards life is developing in them. Hence, they take to deviant acts.

4. The Lesser Time the Mother Spends with Her Children The More They are Likely to go Astray.

It is a well established fact that a mother is the first and the foremost teacher of the child and it is she who developes the child into a true social being. Majority of the mothers are found to be working to support the family. This absence of the mother from home without proper substitute to look afterthe children, gives the children many opportunities to behave as they wanted without any discipline. The children often feel neglected with no one to give them proper guidance whenever required, hence they are indulged in destructive activities and other deviant acts.

5. The Longer Duration of Father being away from Home, the more the Children are likely to Adopt bad Habits.

Majority of the respondents' fathers are not participating in the upbringing of their children because most of them are either separated/divorced and some have jobs out side the country due to which they are unable to look after their children.

The father figure have a very important place in the family because he is the one who exercises ultimate control and discipline over the children. He also supports the family financially and mentally during the time of crisis by having a thorough understanding of the attitude of the children capacities and the situation in which they are placed.

The absence of the father figure hampers the normal and healthy development of the respondents and lack of control by the father provided them with an outlet to behave in the way they want which usually lead them to undertake deviant acts.

6. Lesser the Educational Level of the Child, the More he is Likely to Commit Delinquent Act.

It is always the joint resposibility of the parents, teachers, classmates and other associates to promote a liking among children towards educating themselves and create for themselves a mental state of preparedness to behave in appropriate fashion during different conditions. This suggests that education brings maturity and a feeling of understanding among children which help them to take appropriate decision even in their later life.

In the present study, majority of the respondents are found to be school dropouts either due to poor economic condition, lack of adjustment with teachers or low grasping power and incapability to study hard.

Gradually these children start moving and mixing with the outside world and come in contact with different type of people. This affects their behaviour pattern in a negative way giving an expression to destructive activities.

7. **Less the Intimate Relationship Between the Child and His Teacher, The More He is Likely to Deviate From the Norms and Laws of the School.**

It has been found that majority of the respondents do not have close or definite relation with their teachers. These children are by no means favouring the ideas and teaching provided by teachers and have no respect for them. Teachers who are the backbone of a school provide all the necessary education and general know-how of the world to the children and shape the mind and personality of the child, cannot be taken lightly by a student. And when a child does just the opposite i.e. disobeys the teachers openly, insults or passes comments on them play fool behind their backs and intimacy between them is totally lacking, a child will remain far from following the framework of laws, regulations and discipline of the school. Our study reveals that most delinquents have failed to cooperate with teachers' instructions and do not take them seriously, and this has resulted that they have acted in unrully manner in class involve in group clashes and fighting in school, destroying school property and disobeying the discipline of the school. The way their relationship with the parents make or mar a child at home, in a similar way acts their relationship with the teacher. When proper communication is lacking and children in the study refuse to pay heed to teachers' remarks and warning, then it may be understood that there is a total flop relationship between them.

8. **Children with High Number of Delinquent Friends will Have High Delinquent Possibility.**

Children outside home meet their friends and indulge in various activities which may be beneficial or harmful to them. Our study shows that majority of the respondents who mix with delinquent children, suffer the worst. It is noticed that children innocently joining gangster activities, initially fail to guess the consequences. Later on they adopt bad habits of drinking, smoking, gambling, stealing, etc. and even commit major crimes. There are also delinquents who force upon such conditions because of lack of proper guidance and delinquents friends teach the respondents the bad habits. Bad company always affects adversely. Respondents who fall in the company of delinquents, commit more serious and major crime as compared to those who do not have delinquents as friend. Thus, from this study it was quite clear that delinquent friends and delinqency for the respondents are related terms.

9. **More the Rate of Growth of Industrialization and**

Urbanization More would be the Rate of Delinquency.

Life in the city is quite different from that of the simple orthodox and conventional villages and small towns. In the city, the children are found living in slums crowded and polluted areas, and some also work in industries/factories and small workshops as child labors. These children living in unhealthy and unhygenic atmosphere, become fond of smoking and intoxications.

Both industrialization and urbanization are factors of modern world which have introduced new educational, sports and recreational activities. All these activities do bring some sort of change in the entire social set-up thereby bringing about change in the fabric of family system, marriage pattern, socialization of children etc. Previously the family, school elders were exercising control and guiding children about everything. But these factors have brought alongwith them a tremendous change in thinking of the parents.

In the present study, the observations have shown that misuse of these activities leads to misbehavior in children, further making them delinquents. But if these games or recreational activities are made available with strict guidance in the control of some specialized persons, these children would be safe and getting benefit of it.

10. More the Child Leads His Life in Idleness, More He is Likely to Commit Misbehavior.

Any person, specially a child having idle mind is like keeping a reservior of knowledge, energy and hardwork packed up, wasted away. Children who due to reasons of poverty or bad circumstances are unable to attend school, loiter in the house premises or on the streets, disturb the members, disrupt the work of the neighbours, create unnecesssary tension and chaos and always think of way and means of offending others by pranks and games. Majority of the respondents in this study were idle, who make plans to disturb others in some way or the others. Their minds since not busy in constructive works, will lead them to stealing for fun and amusement, force them to fight with individuals or in groups for passing time and will gather will friends who spend time in un-conventional activities. Delinquents are not born, but made. Circumstances of course make them but also they play an important part in making themselves delinquents specially when they are not kept busy in academic, sports, cultural and educative/informative and amusement activities.

When these delinquents are kept away from ordinary lives of normal children involving school extra-curricular activities, children muddle up their lives and also of others around them.

11. The Greater the Effectiveness of the Reformative Agencies in Eliminating the Root Causes of Juvenile Delinquency the Lesser would be the Repetition of Delinquent.

So far as the question of reformative agencies are concerned, it can be said that they have been found to be a significant instrument of controlling the behavior of the respondents and bringing about change in their outlook towards life. Vocational training and guidance about major decisions in life and adjustment with family etc. are given to children. In a way, the reformative schools or agencies provide these neglected children opportunity to rise in life and behave like normal citizens. Finding of the study seem to support the proposition.

Suggestions

Suggestions are being proposed here to the concerned people which could be helpful in further research and to improve or enhance the knowledge in bringing about a state of normalcy in the society which is turn would be a boon for keeping a check on the increasing rate of juvenile delinquency in Jordan.

1. Bringing about Awareness in Parents about Their Role in Socialization of the Child.

Family is the child's first and far the most important school of learning where parents are found to equally influence and shape the character of the child. Hence it is necessary for the parents themselves to be well adjusted with life thereby bringing about a conducive atmosphere at home. Discipline by parents should be moderate which will certainly help in the formation of a well adjusted child.

Awareness among parents regarding their role as socializing agent of the child, can be brought about through mass media and communication sources like T. V., radio, news-paper, magazine, public meetings, propaganda, social work etc.

The awareness of parents should be in term of realization of the child's inclusion as an equally important family member with distinct identity. He should have a say in the discussions of significant family matters. Parents should be well conversant with the interest and activities of the child and should make it a point not to force the child for activities rather than his choice.

2. Enhancing or Improving the Relationship Between Family and School.

So far as this suggestion is concerned, emphasis is laid upon regular visits of the parents to the school, participation in parents-teachers meetings, encouraging children to participate actively in school activities such as social gathering, sports, study tours etc., having discussion with the teachers about the child's temparament, capabilities in studies and other activities. The parents should not object even if the teachers sometime punish the child. They should have faith that the punishment given by the teachers is for the good cause of the child, and that it would definitely lead to a positive change in the child. The teacher should maintain regular records of each student and inform the parents accordingly.

3. Use of an Expert in the School for Guidance.

To make available in every school a specialized person to observe and study the problematic cases of children and thereby try to solve them. The above mentioned professional will have to keep direct contact with the respective class teachers who will in turn report such problematic cases. The professional will have to keep a close eye on the behavior of the concerned child, try to locate the different causes of the problem and gradually take the child into confidence and have face to face discussion with the deviant child. It is the duty of the professional to visit the family of the child and discuss the prevalent problem of the child. In this visit he will be able to see the behavior of the siblings as well and will come to know the general background of the family. This will help him in the diagnosis and treatment of the child.

The professional can help the police in providing additional information about the delinquent child and then decide the possible corrective measures for the child.

4. Compulsory Education should be Strictly Implemented.

Though education has been made compulsory in Jordan for Children, it should be applied for all. In our study as well as through the offficial records it has been observed that there are quite a number of school dropouts who due to idleness and aimlessness fall in the company of anti-social activities, hence they become delinquents.

The significance of education had been recognized by people of all spheres. They feel that education not only helps the child in adjusting with new social environment besides his family but also builds up his moral character and furnishes him with a strong base for coping up with adjustments in later life and in taking proper decisions whenever required.

5. Abolition of Child Labour.

Children who are school dropouts, are generally found to be engaged in jobs where they hardly receive any return apart from hard work. In such jobs there is always mental, physical and financial exploitation of the child by the employer. Many a time these children take to the habits of smoking, drinking, stealing etc.

These children should get an opportunity to seek admission in technical school which are generally job oriented. This will help these children to specialize in a particular skill and avoid exploitation by the workshop owner.

The Government should strictly abolish child labor and should see that these children are given recruitment only after asserting that the concerned children have got certificate from the certified technical schools.

6. Fruitful Recreational Activities should be made Available for All.

One possible solution for checking the increasing number of juvenile delinquents is that every child must have a happy and loving childhood. Affection, love and control of parents are restricted at home only, but in the outside world attention can be denoted by educational institutions. The child should get the feeling of concern by being involved in many recreational courses. For example school can involve children in educational tours where the trip is educative; children learn to be together and manage things on their own. Tours to factory, mills, other Government and private sector organizations can impart knowledge and make them constructive. The public libraries particularly in the rural areas for children, would provide them with facilities of books and magazines which are informative, educative and knowledgeable. Group activities will help children to keep them busy, and thus they have less time for wasting away in fruitless activities.

Sports and games help development to body and mind. Participants learn discipline, leadership and participation from game which do not allow them qualities to forget the fitness. Children love games and so if they are involved in these type of activities, they can spend their time after studies in sports rather than spending time with idle companions.

7. Specialized Training for Officials.

In the remand homes, officials attending the children, look

into their needs and daily requirements. Officials performing their duties must by adequately qualified, having considerable experience and skill to cope with their strict and tough duties. It is in the remand homes where delinquents are brought in order to improve their future, they are provided some constructive knowledge and training, depending on the aptitude and interest of each child. For contributing and bringing out the best from each child, the staff officials should themselves be specialized to extract the best from juvenile delinquents.

So many juvenile delinquents living together, will surely come out with various problems among themselves. Unless the officials are not fit enough to solve these with patience, tact and skill, they will create chaos and unrully atmosphere in the system of the remand homes.

8. Bifurcation of the Delinquents.

Different kinds of junenile delinquents come in the remand home. Each has a different background, life style, crime committed and behavioral pattern. Unless the officials have knowledge about the hard core and the mild juvenile delinquents, there will be total tension and disorganized system in the remand homes. There must be a division between the hard core delinquents, such as, murderers, the milder lots of theives, molesters and snatchers, and the gentler ones like ones involve in mild fighting or petty thefts. This distinction will create a separate class of delinquents who by nature and crime being somewhat separate, and will not influence the other milder ones. Also the ones who have committed crimes and have spent lesser number of days in remand home, thus get more chances of improvement. But if they get mixed with the hardcore juvenile delinquents they have chances of learning further techniques of crime and unrully behavior.

The study has attempted to analyse the causes and nature of delinqency. The family, school, peer group and social mileu etc. are significant aspects which influence the young children. Appropriate paradigm in convenience with the reality of Jordanian society, ought to be build up for understanding, counselling and rehabilitation of these children.

References

Anonymous 1986 Jordan, Middle East Economic Handbook, 1st Ed., Euromonitor Publication Ltd. London.

Cohen, A. K.	1959	"The Study of Social Disorganization and Deviant Behavior", "Sociology Today" (ed.) R. K. Merton, NewYork, Basic Books.
Cloward, R.A. and L. E. Ohlin	1960	"Delinquency and Opportunity" NewYork, The Free Press.
Govt. of Jordan	1968	Juvenile Act No. 24, Ministry of Social Development, Govt. of Jordan, Amman.
Govt. of Jordan	1974	Land and People. Published by Ministry of Culture and Information, Govt. of Jordan, Amman.
Govt. of Jordan	1980 to 1990	Annual Reports, Directorate of Social Defence, Ministry of Social Development, Govt. of Jordan, Amman.
Harris, G. L.	1958	"Jordan :Its People, Its Society Its Culture," HRAF Press, New Haven.
Merton. R.	1957	"Social Theory and Social Structure," New York, Free Press.
Mitra, N. L.	1988	"Juvenile Delinquency and Indian Justice System," New Delhi, Deep and Deep.
Quay, H. C.	1965	"Juvenile Delinquency : Research And Theory," D. V. Nostrand Company INC, Princton, New Jersy.
Rbeihat Sabri A.	1987	"Explaining Male Delinquency In Jordan," unpublished Ph. D. Thesis. California University.
Shaw, C. R. and H. D. McKay	1942	"Juvenile Delinquency and Urban Area," Chicago : University of Chicago Press.
Sethna, M. J.	1952	"Society and The Criminal," Leader's Press Ltd., Bombay.
The Encyclopaedia American	1971	Vol. 16, P. 270.

Kenneth Maddock

FROM TERRA NULLIUS TO MABO

The title of my paper captures the story of Aboriginal rights—or lack of rights—to land in Australia. As I tell it, the story is one in which both legal and anthropological views can be discerned. But, until relatively recently, each perspective ran its own course, rather than engage in interplay with the other.

The importance of law in the definition of Aboriginal land rights should surprise no one, for the legal arena is a place where rights are asserted, denied and worked out. It is not, of course, the only such venue. The importance of anthropology may be less expected. In Australia it has come about through a number of factors, one of which is the absence of interest on the part of just about everyone except anthropologists in traditional Aboriginal culture. Another is the lateness with which a class of educated or professionally trained Aborigines has emerged, the members of which are able to contribute to the rights debate in the wider society.

Before going further, three points of clarification or information can usefully be made :

(1) My concern in this paper is with rights that Aborigines have—or are asserted to have—by virtue of their traditional culture, which is that of the indigenous population, modified in various ways since British settlement began in 1788. Rights of the kind the settler or incoming population may have, and which in many instances are held by Aborigines also, are outside my scope.

(2) Aborigines comprise perhaps 1.5 or 2 per cent of Australia's population of 17 million. Many of them are only part Aboriginal by descent, but mixed ancestry does not, as such, affect their rights.

(3) Australia has a federal system in which state and territory governments as well as the Commonwealth (or federal) government may legislate for Aborigines within their jurisdiction. Until 1967, however, the Commonwealth government had no power under the constitution to make laws for Aborigines; it was given the power by referendum that year.

Two significant events in my story are the Gove Case (decided in 1971) and the Mabo Case (decided in 1992).[1] Only twenty one years separate the judgements in the two cases. Astonishing as it may seem, however, the Gove Case was the first in which an Australian court adjudicated on an Aboriginal claim of rights in land. There can be few if any parts of the former British Empire in which fundamental questions about the relations to land of the pre-colonial population had to wait until the last third of the twentieth century before finding a judicial resolution. Indeed, there can be few parts in which this population was treated, politically and administratively, as having no rights to land arising from its pre-colonial presence.[2] The significance of the Gove Case is that it upheld the *terra nullius* doctrine; the significance of the Mabo Case is that it overturned this doctrine.

In the first part of my paper I shall consider how lawyers and anthropologists viewed Aboriginal rights to land up until the Gove Case. It will be seen that their positions were diametrically opposed. In the second part I shall look at the Gove Case, in order to show how these two strands of received opinion—the legal and the anthropological—fared at the hands of Justice Blackburn in the Supreme Court of the Northern Territory. In the third part I shall trace the aftermath of the Gove Case. It could be said that though the Aborigines lost the battle in court it was but one episode in a war which eventually they won. A very anthropological definition of rights to land was embodied in law as a result. In the fourth part I shall deal with the Mabo Case, in which the full High Court of Australia, by a 6-1 majority, carried out 'a judicial revolution', as the sub-title of a recent collection of essays puts it (Stephenson and Ratnapala, 1993). Finally I shall consider what lies ahead for Australia.

I. Legal and Anthropological Views Before Gove

The prevailing legal view before the Gove Case was that the indigenous population had no rights to land which survived the British acquisition of sovereignty. A rationale for this view can be found by referring back to William Blackstone. In 1765, some years before colonization of Australia began, he drew an important distinction :

> Plantations, or colonies in distant countries, are either such where the lands are claimed by right of occupancy only, by finding them desert and uncultivated, and peopling them from the mother country; or where, when already cultivated, they have been either gained by conquest, or ceded to us by treaties. And both these rights are founded upon the law of nature, or at least upon that of nations. (1765 : 104)

Blackstone left no doubt about the significance of this distinction :

> ......there is a difference between these two species of colonies, with respect to the laws with which they are bound. For it is held, that if an uninhabited country be discovered and planted by English subjects, all the English laws are there immediately in force. For as the law is the birthright of every subject, so wherever they go they carry their laws with them. But in conquered or ceded countries, that have already laws of their own, the king may indeed alter and change those laws; but, till he does actually change them, the ancient laws of the kingdom remain...(1965 : 104-5)

The sense of a word in legal language may differ from what it has inordinary speech. This is shown by the meaning which words like 'uninhabited' and 'uncultivated' came to bear in the law. According to one author, vacant land is 'conveniently taken to include territory possessed by "savage" tribes" (Nicolas, 1969 : 132). According to another, settled colonies were those 'in which British subjects were the first settlers with a developed system of laws' (O'Connell, and Riordan 1971 : 1). As for Australia more particularly, 'since the Australian aborigines were held incapable of intelligent transactions with respect to land Australia was treated as *terra nullius*' (O'Connell 1970 : 409). *Terra nullius*, that is to say land owned by or belonging to no one, could be appropriated by occupying it.

The outcome was that aborigines, whether conceived as savages or as having an undeveloped system of law or as lacking the capacity for transacting intelligently in land, were considered not to 'inhabit' (in a legally relevant sense) the country in and off which they lived.[3] Governments in Australia did set aside land for Aboriginal reserves, but it often happened that these portions were changed in size or even done away with altogether without regard for Aboriginal wishes (for an account of reserves and other allocations of land in favour of Aborigines, see Peterson 1981). Dwellers on reserves seem never to have been regarded as having proprietorial rights to them. In any event, the question of the rights Aborigines had to reserves or to land which they and their ancestors had occupied since pre-colonial times was not to be tested until the Gove Case, almost two centuries after the arrival of British settlers. The possibility was not seriously considered that, even if the settlers were governed by the English law they brought with them in relations among themselves, the laws and customs of the Aborigines might continue to apply to Aborigines.

A quite different view was taken by anthropologists. It must be remembered, of course, that they were proceeding in their own way and were not arguing about the legal consequences of British acquisition of sovereignty. Nonetheless it is impressive that they frequently asserted the ownership of land by Aborigines.

A.R. Radclifee-Brown, the first professor of anthropology in Australia (he held the foundation chair at Sydney from 1926 to 1931, but had begun his association with this country before World War I), stated emphatically in an early paper that land was owned by a group of a kind he called the 'horde' (1918 : 222). A horde :

> ......is a small group of persons owning a certain area of territory, the boundaries of which are known, and possessing in common proprietary rights over the land and its products—mineral, vegetable and animal. It is the primary land-owning or land-holding group. (1930 : 35)

On Radcliffe-Brown's view the membership of a horde is typically determined by patrilineal descent, with no provision for a person to change membership except by marriage in the case of females. Thus a typical horde consists of male agnates together with their unmarried female agnates plus the wives of the men. Later in his life he seems to have changed his mind as to the identity (and hence the composition) of the landowning group :

> The clan is corporate in the sense that its adult male members can and do engage in collective action, and that as a clan they have collective ownership and control of a certain territory with its food resources and its 'totem centres' with their

> associated rites and myths...A woman belongs to her father's clan but to her husband's horde. (1956 : 365)

In an important paper of his middle period (originally published in 1935, and reprinted 1952 : 32-48), Radcliffe-Brown had tried to elucidate the jural relation of a horde to its territory :

> The relation...does not correspond exactly to what we regard as 'ownership' in modern law. It has some of the qualities of corporate ownership, but also partakes of the nature of the relation of a modern state to its territory, which we may speak of as the exercise of 'dominion'. Rights of ownership over land and rights of dominion have seemingly both had their origin by development and differentiation from such a simple relation as that exemplified in the Australian horde. (1952 : 34)

Throughout his career, then, Radcliffe-Brown insisted on the ownership of land by Aborigines, though he was prepared to admit the cultural specificity of their relation to the land. The main difference which occured in his thinking had to do with the position of married women. On the view that hordes own land, a woman shares ownership with the other members of her horde, which is her father's until she marries but thereafter is her husband's. On Radcliffe-Brown's later view, however, it would seem that her ownership is not affected by marriage, for land is owned by the clan and she continues to belong to her father's clan.

Put another way, Radcliffe-Brown's earlier view was that land belongs to the group of people who live and forage together in a territory. He called this group the horde; other writers have used such terms as 'band', 'community' and 'local group'. It is constituted by co-residence and economic cooperation. His later view was that land belongs to a group of people who are patrilineally related to one another. He called this group the clan. It is constituted by descent in the male line. Because women marry out the clan is not a co-residential group; its members are necessarily dispersed between hordes.

It is unnecessary here to trace the opinions of other writers who speak of the ownership of land by Aborigines, let alone to try to resolve controversies over the nature and composition of groups (see, for discussion of these questions, Hiatt, 1989;

Maddock, 1980: 30-54, 1983 : 43-9; Peterson and Langton, 1983). Suffice it to say that the main division is between those who maintain that descent groups own land and those who attribute ownership to the people who live and forage together. R.M. Berndt, L.R. Hiatt and Nicolas Peterson could be named as taking the former view along with the later Radcliffe-Brown. N.W. Thomas, A.P. Elkin and M.J. Meggitt could be seen as taking the latter view in company with the early Radcliffe-Brown.

My description of anthropological views is over simplified—individuals are not always consistent, and additional details may enter their accounts to complicate the picture—but it will do for our purposes. The significant points are, first, that ownership is asserted, and second, that it is located in a group. There seems to have been much more interest in examining and debating the composition of groups than in elucidating what their ownership amounts to. By the 1960s, however, it was quite commonly accepted by anthropologists that there were two main types of relation to land, the ritual or religious and the economic. It was also quite commonly accepted that the relation of a clan to land was ritual. The horde, as Radcliffe-Brown used to call it, or the band, community or local group had an economic relation, since it was composed of people who lived and foraged together.

It follows from this distinction, when taken together with what I was arguing earlier,,that some writers see ownership primarily (if not solely) in ritual or religious terms, others in economic terms. We might, of course, wonder that the use of the word 'ownership' adds to anthropological accounts of groups and their relation to land. Ownership collapses, as a rule, into ritual or economics.

II. The Gove Case

In the 1960s the Commonwealth government leased part of the Gove Peninsula to Nabalco for mining bauxite. The land affected had been part of the large Arnhem Land Reserve in the north of the Northern Territory, that is, it was land reserved for 'the use and benefit' of Aborigines. But the local Aborigines were not consulted about the excision from their part of the reserve or about the mine and the town which would accompany it, though they would benefit from royalties.

The anthropologist R.M. Berndt who, with his wife C.H. Berndt, had long research experience in the area was active in publicizing the worries of local Aborigines, for example their fears of damage to places of ritual or totemic interest and their apprehension about the influx of large numbers of miners and others into what hitherto was a remote and isolated locality. Berndt became the main anthropological adviser to the lawyers who prepared the case, and he appeared in it as an expert witness.

The Aboriginal plaintiffs (or, more exactly, their lawyers on their behalf) asserted that the relation of their clans to the land was of immemorial age and of proprietary nature. They asserted further that this relation was protected by a doctrine of communal native title, which formed part of the general law of Australia. They denied, that is to say, that Aboriginal rights to land were cancelled (extinguished) when the Crown acquired sovereignty. The rights persisted until and unless the Crown extinguished them which, according to the plaintiffs, had never happened in their area.

Justice Blackburn of the Supreme Court of the Northern Territory ranged over many issues in his judgement, partly it seems because he wished to deal with all the arguments raised, though he obviously regarded the case as one which the plaintiffs lost on almost every point. I shall consider just two of them, which relate to the previous section of my paper.

His Honour found that 'the law relating to the application of English law to the overseas possessions of the Crown was, in principle, well settled by 1788', and that Blackstone's expression 'desert and uncultivated' had 'always been taken to include territory in which live uncivilized inhabitants in a primitive state of society' (judgement, p. 201). Whether a colony was settled, as distinct from conquered or ceded, is a matter of law, not of fact, and it cannot be re-opened by a fresh examination of anthropological or historical data (judgement, pp. 202-3).

Justice Blackburn cited as binding authority (judgment, p. 243) the decision of the Privy Council in the 19th century case of *Cooper* v. *Stuart* that the colony of New South Wales, of which the Gove Peninsula was then part, was settled or occupied, not conquered or ceded. According to the Privy Council :

> There was no land law or tenure existing in the colony at the time of its annexation to the Crown; and, in that condition of matters, the conclusion appears to their Lordships to be inevitable that, as soon as colonial land becomes the subject of

settlement and commerce, all transactions in relation to it were governed by English law.

Thus the Gove Peninsula, as part of a settled or occupied colony, was subject to English law from 1788 so far as it was applicable. English law, as applied in England, had no rule that communal native title must be respected. English law, as applied in the various colonies, had no doctrine of communal native title except under express statutory provisions, none of which were ever made in Australia, or except where it had been policy to accept such title, which had not happened in Australia either. Let us now turn to the question of ownership or proprietary right. Two aspects of Justice Blackburn's approach call for comment.

First, there was the use of legal concepts by anthropologists to describe the relation of groups to land. The defence objected that Berndt and W.E.H. Stanner, in giving evidence for the plaintiffs, tended to apply unwarranted conceptions of their own to Aboriginal behavior, even to the extent of anticipating the court's findings. For example, they spoke of 'rights' the Aborigines had to land. Justice Blackburn's response was that while it was acceptable for the anthropologists to express themselves in jurisprudential terms, there were two questions which were for the court alone to answer. On the one hand, a question of fact : was the expert's conclusion, whether or not stated in terms of 'rights', one to which the court should come ? Here the court had to guard against allowing its conclusions to be unjustifiably affected by the expert's use of words. On the other hand, a question of law : were the 'rights', as they were tentatively called, subsumable under categories that would enable them to be recognized by common law ? Were they, for example, properly characterizable as proprietorial ? In short, Justice Blackburn could accept Berndt's or Stanner's talk of 'land-owning' or 'land-possessing' groups without prejudicing his own task of deciding whether it was jurisprudentially correct to say that the groups 'owned' or 'possessed' land (judgment, pp. 164-5).

Second, there was the contention by counsel for the plaintiffs that the Aboriginal clans had property in the land. The defence argued against this that the question whether the rights were proprietary did not arise, because the Aborigines had nothing recognizable as law. Justice Blackburn rejected the argument. The evidence showed the Aborigines to have a system of law. However, he could not accept that their relation to land was proprietorial. For example, though the Aborigines might 'think and speak of the land as being theirs' as belonging to them', such a way of expressing oneself can carry many meanings and does not necessarily imply a property relation. The proposition could be restated more neutrally as : 'they think and speak of the land as being in a very close relationship to them'. Again, it was asserted that other Aborigines who went on the land of a clan acknowledged it to belong to that clan and that there were never any disputes over land. But such contentions took the matter no further. They only showed that the relation of a clan to land, whatever it might be, was not disputed by other clans (judgment, pp. 268-70).

Justice Blackburn also addressed himself to the substance of proprietary interests. He thought that in English and other major systems of law known to him property 'generally implies the right to use or enjoy, the right to exclude others, and the right to alienate.' Even allowing that these rights might be qualified in various ways and that they might not all need to be present, he could not see that the Aboriginal relation to land was proprietorial. Thus the plaintiffs expressly denied that land could be alienated. There was no evidence that a clan could rightfully exclude others from its land. And it made little sense to speak of a clan's right to use and enjoy land, for although its members could use and enjoy the land of their clan so, too, could members of a number of other clans and correspondingly its members could use and enjoy the land of those other clans (judgment, pp. 272-3).

If the relation of a clan to land is not proprietary, what is it ? Justice Blackburn used the neutral term 'attribution' to indicate that Aborigines thought of the land 'as consisting of a number of tracts of land each linked to a clan...though the boundaries between them are not precise in the sense...understood in our law' (judgment, pp. 179, 181).

The net effect of the Gove Case was therefore to uphold the received legal doctrine that Australia was *terra nullius* and to dismiss the common anthropological opinion that Aboriginal groups owned land. Law and anthropology had met for the first time, to the dicomfiture of the latter.

III. Aftermath of Defeat

The plaintiffs lost at Gove, but within a few years they—as part of the Aboriginal population of the Northern Territory—had won the war. Consider the chronology. Justice Blackburn handed down his judgment on 27 April 1971. In February

1973, following a change of federal government, a commission of inquiry into land rights was set up, headed by Justice Woodward who, as A.E. Woodward, Q.C. had been senior counsel for the Aborigines in the Gove Case. He issued a first report five months later and a final report after another nine months—the latter appeared in April 1974, three years to the month after the Gove judgment. By 1975 an Aboriginal Land Rights Bill was before the Commonwealth Parliament, substantially embodying his recommendations. There was a change of federal government before it could be enacted, but the new government introduced its own bill in 1976, which also followed Woodward closely, and which became law the same year as the *Aboriginal Land Rights (Northern Territory) Act* 1976. Less than six years lay between judgment at Gove and passage of land rights legislation.

A few points about the commision's terms of reference:

(1) They directed attention especially to the Northern Territory which, not being a full state, was subject to extensive Commonwealth legislative power. The Territory is a little more than 500,000 square miles in area.

(2) They assumed that rights would be granted. It was unnecessary, therefore, for Justice Woodward to argue in favour of rights; his job was to recommend where, to whom and in what form land should be granted.

(3) They referred neutrally and generally to 'traditional rights and interests' which were to be given legal force as property but which did not need to be shown as having been proprietorial in the past.

The 1976 Act, which applies only in the Northern Territory, provided for existing reserves to become Aboriginal land (they comprised about 18 per cent of the Territory). It also provided for 'traditional land claims' to vacant Crown land and to land held by or on behalf of Aborigines (another 30 per cent of the Territory has been or is in process of being claimed); however land in town areas may not be claimed. Claims are heard by an Aboriginal Land Commissioner, who is a judge, but he is not bound by the usual procedures and rules of evidence of a court. Having heard a claim he reports with recommendations to the Commonwealth government's Minister for Aboriginal Affairs. Land which is successfully claimed, like land which used to be part of a reserve, is transferred to an Aboriginal Land Trust, which holds it for the benefit of all Aborigines traditionally entitled to use or occupy that particular land.

In other words the 1976 Act creates a scheme for Aboriginal land rights. Though created by statute, it is intended to reflect tradition. An important concept introduced in the legislation is that of 'traditional Aboriginal owners', defined as :

> .....a local descent group of Aboriginals who...
> (a) have common spiritual affiliations to a site on the land, being affiliations that place the group under a primary spiritual responsibility for that site and for the land; and
> (b) are entitled by Aboriginal tradition to forage as of right over that land.

The significance of this concept is that a claim can succeed only if the Land Commissioner finds that there are Aborigines who satisfy the requirements of the definition for that particular land. Once land becomes Aboriginal no use of it or even entry upon it may be made without the consent of its traditional owners. For example, they have a power of veto over development proposals. Apart from a few exceptions, such as the police in the course of their duties, the only persons exempt from this control by traditional owners are Aborigines entitled by tradition to use or occupy the land, and even they are restricted to such forms of use and occupation as are in accordance with Aboriginal tradition. Some of these traditionally entitled people will be traditional owners of the land, but others will have a relation to it which falls short of traditional ownership as defined in the 1976 Act.

It may be noted in conclusion that the conception of Aboriginal ownership expressed in the Act is similar to the model of clan-land relations for which Woodward, Q.C. had argued in the Gove Case. That model, in turn, reflected the opinions of Berndt and Stanner, the two anthropologists on whom he relied for expert advice and evidence. There was no particular originality about their views, the essential elements of which can be found in Radcliffe-Brown's account of Aboriginal ownership.[4]

IV. The Mabo 'Revolution'

It may be helpful to begin this section by recapitulating the argument thus far. Before 1971 Australia was seen as *terra nullius* by the lawyers, but as subject to Aboriginal ownership by the anthropologists. The Gove Case, decided in 1971, confirmed the *terra nullius* view and rejected the argument that Australian law knew a doctrine of communal native title. The same case could be seen as a body blow to the anthropologists, in the sense that it showed how problematic was their talk of ownership. The 1976 Land Rights Act overcame these difficulties by creating a scheme of Aboriginal title and ownership. It did not reject *terra nullius* or affirm the native title doctrine or assert that Aborigines traditionally had property rights in land in any Western-law sense—the Act sidestepped the difficulties by creating its own reality.

The Mabo Case was decided in 1992. It begin in 1982, when a number of Torres Strait Islanders, including a man named Mabo, sought a declaration of their traditional rights. They claimed that the Murray Islands, which lie in the Torres Strait between Australia and Papua New Guinea, had been continuously inhabited and exclusively possessed by their people, who lived in permanent settled communities with their own social and political organization. They conceded that the Crown acquired sovereignty by its annexation of the Torres Strait Islands last century, but maintained that their rights to land continued until extinguished by the new sovereign. According to the claimants, these rights had never been validly extinguished by the Crown.[5]

For reasons which need not be gone into here, the case moved around between courts, which helps to explain why it took so long. The important part of the story is the decision of the full High Court, handed down on 3 June 1992. Six of the seven judges upheld the claim, though not always on quite the same basis. Moreover, they judged the case in a way which had clear implications for the Australian mainland and its Aboriginal inhabitants; they did not limit themselves to pronouncing on the rights of those Torres Strait Islanders who live on the Murray Islands. It seems to be generally accepted that the minimum statement of the High Court's position was made by Justice Brennan. His judgment included a nine-point summary (conveniently reprinted in Brennan 1993 : 43-4), which I have further reduced :

(1) The Crown's acquisition of sovereignty in Australia cannot be challenged in an Australian court.

(2) When the Crown acquired sovereignty, it also acquired a radical title to the land.

(3) There is a native title to land which survived the Crown's acquisition of sovereignty and radical title, but it is exposed to extinguishment.

(4) If the Crown grants an interest in land that is wholly or partially inconsistent with a continuing right to enjoy native

title, then native title is extinguished to the extent of that inconsistency.

(5) If the Crown appropriates land to itself and the appropriation is wholly or partially inconsistent with a continuing right to enjoy native title, then native title is extinguished to the extent of that inconsistency.

(6) Native title is ascertained according to the laws and customs of the indigenous people who, by those laws and customs, are connected with the land. It does not matter if the laws and customs have changed since the Crown acquired sovereignty as long as 'the general nature of the connection between the indigenous people and the land remains.'

(7) A group will lose its native title if it 'by ceasing to acknowledge those laws, and (so far as practicable) observe those customs, loses its connection with the land'; native title is also extinguished when the last member of the group dies.

(8) Native title to particular land can be surrendered to the Crown by those groups which, 'by the traditional laws and customs of the indigenous people, have a relevant connection with the land but the rights and privileges conferred by native title are otherwise inalienable to persons who are not members of the indigenous people to whom alienation is permitted by the traditional laws and customs.'

(9) The Crown becomes the absolute beneficial owner if native title to waste lands is extinguished.

The Mabo Case is revolutionary in the sense that it has overturned the previously existing law in Australi: the doctrine of *terra nullius* is rejected and the doctrine of native title affirmed. It may be said that the High Court has simply brought Australia into line with legal theory and practice in most of the former British Empire. But to do so more than 200 years after British sovereignty was first acquired and British (and other) settlers began to arrive is a complicating factor. If anything is clear, it is that much dust is waiting to settle. There is no general agreement on what the case means. At one extreme are those who say that property law and the security of land titles have been thrown into confusion. These consequences are denied by others, including ministers in the Commonwealth government. But the former position seems the better based : first, the Commonwealth government announced soon after the case was decided that it would found test cases to explore the extent and implications of the decision; and second, the government has now announced that it will legislate to confirm the validity of all titles issued since 1788.

In the meantime, a number of Mabo-type claims, as they are being called, have been launched. For example, a claim was lodged to the Central Business District of Brisbane, capital of the state of Queensland and third largest city in Australia. This claim has been withdrawn, but I do not know whether it was discontinued on legal grounds or out of political expediency. Claims have been lodged to very large areas of thinly populated but perhaps minerally rich land in Western Australia. There is also a claim to much of New South Wales, including farming country. One of the most interesting cases, however, has arisen from conflict between Aboriginal groups. Some Northern Territory Aborigines have asked the court to restrain the Minister for Aboriginal Affairs from issuing title to an Aboriginal Land Trust under the 1976 Land Rights Act. It appears that the Land Commissioner found that there were traditional owners, as defined in the Act, of land to which a traditional claim had been made under the Act. He recommended that a grant be made to a Land Trust. But some Aborigines (who may or may not overlap the traditional owners—I do not know) say that they have native title to the land. They fear that a grant to a Land Trust will extinguish their native title (see points 3 and 4 of Justice Brennan's summary outlined above).

Whatever the outcome of these impending claims, it is clear that they are just the tip of an iceberg. Some commentators fear that it will do for Australia what an earlier iceberg did for the *Titanic*. Others dismiss such concerns as madness and hysteria.

V. What Lies Ahead ?

My opinion is that at least ten or twenty years will be needed to work through the implications of the Mabo Case. There can be no quick solution to the many problems the High Court has raised. In the Northern Territory, for example, for which traditional owners and traditional claims were defined by statute in 1976, the claims process is still under way and there is continuing argument about ownership. Native title is far more complicated, and it touches on all of Australia. Only by a most remarkable effort could it be conclusively dealt with 2010, let alone 2001, the centenary of Australian federation. Let me end my paper by putting some of the questions which are waiting for answers.

(1) Has the Crown a fiduciary duty to the indigenous people of Australia ?

(2) Is compensation due for past actions of the Crown or will it be due for future actions of the Crown ?

(3) What relation is there between native title and the various forms of statutory title created for Aborigines over the last three decades (for example, in Victoria in 1970, South Australia in 1966 and 1981, Queensland in 1978, 1982 and 1991, the Northern Territory in 1976 and New South Wales in 1973 and 1983) ?

(4) Are the legal consequences of the Mabo Case limited to the law of real property, as some contend, or do they open the way for the recognition of pre-colonial rights in other areas of life such as crime (Mulqueeny, 1993) and intellectual property (Puri, 1993) ? It is instructive that Aborigines charged with a crime have, on several occasions, denied the court's jurisdiction on the ground that they and their forbears had never surrendered sovereignty. These pleas failed, but the cases were pre-Mabo, and it is likely that the same argument will be tried again.

(5) Will mainland Aborigines be able to establish native title ? Their forbears lived by hunting and gathering which, in the Australian environment, meant that human presence in a given locality was generally intermittent rather than continuous. Since 1788 they, or their forbears, have often moved or been moved from ancestral country. Points 6 and 7 of Justice Brennan's summary (outlined above) are richly ambiguous, and will allow anthropologists to come into their own. The Mabo claimants, by contrast, had slight evidentiary problems, for they occupied very small areas of land on which they built houses and cultivated gardens, and their *de facto* occupation of the diminutive Murray Islands had never been seriously disturbed. They lived where their forbears had lived.

(6) Will a political settlement be attempted, under which native title is extinguished through surrender all over Australia ? The Commonwealth government is obviously seeking Aborigines with whom it may deal, but its method seems to be to create organizations, such as the Land Councils in the Northern Territory or the Aboriginal and Torres Strait Islander Commision, to which it imputes a range of powers and provides finance. Point 8 of Justice Brennan's summary (outlined above) suggests that these bodies lack even the barest competence to deal in native title. This is a rock on which the government's attempts at what it calls 'reconciliation' are likely to founder. Oddly enough, we are thus brought back to the old doctrine of

terra nullius, which found part of its justification in the absence, among Aborigines, of persons who were entitled to enter into authoritative transactions with the outside world.

Acknowledgements

An earlier version of this paper was delivered to Faculty of Law seminars at the University of Cape Town and the University of the Witwatersrand in April and May 1993. I am grateful to the Human Sciences Research Council for facilitating my visit to South Africa and to Macquarie University for its support. As the Australian scene is changing rapidly, I should mention that the present version of my paper was completed in September 1993.

Notes

1. *Milirrpum* v. *Nabalco Pty. Ltd. and The Commonwealth of Australia* (1971) 17 Federal Law Reports 141; *Mabo* v. *The State of Queensland* (1922) 66 Australian Law Journal Reports 408. There is an extensive literature on these cases—see, for example, Bartlett (1993), Durack, Brunton and Rutherford (1992), Stephenson and Ratnapala (1993), all of which concern Mabo; and Hiatt (1984), Maddock (1980, 1983), Peterson and Langton (1983), all of which deal with Gove or its aftermath.

2. The Bushman (sometimes called 'San' , in recent English-language publications) of southern Africa have also found it difficult to have their rights to land accepted (in their case against Bantu pastroralists rather than European settlers)—see, for example, Gordon (1989), Hitchcock (1982), Wilmsen (1989a).

3. It is amusing that the rise of conservationism has led to the valuation of what is called 'wilderness'. What conservationists call 'wilderness' invites comparison with what Blackstone called 'desert and uncultivated'; what is meant in each case appears to be a tract of country which may or may not have had human inhabitants but which, metaphorically speaking, has remained 'untouched by the hand of man'.

4. For the process by which anthropological lead was transmuted into legal gold, see Maddock (1980 : chs 2 and 3, 1983 : chs 3 and 4), Peterson and Langton (1983 : various chapters).

5. According to McIntyre (1993 : 33), 'The *Mabo* case was conceived as a test case arising from a meeting of Barbara

Hocking (a Melbourne Barrister), Eddie Koikoi Mabo, Fr Dave Passi, Flo Kennedy (of Thursday Island), Noni Sharp (of La Trobe University) and the writer at a conference on Race Relations and Land Rights at James Cook University, Townsville in 1981.' Eddie Koikoi Mabo was the leading plaintiff in the Mabo Case; Thursday island is in the Torres Strait; and McIntyre was involved in the conduct of the Mabo Case. There can be little doubt that the case was conceived as a stepping stone to the mainland of Australia, the Murray Islands being seen by those who instigated or brought it as more favorable ground for a claim of native title than anywhere else. According to a recent newspaper column (Santamaria, 1993), the genesis of the case had much to do with Henry Reynolds, an historian at James Cook University. It was through Reynolds that Eddie Mabo learned that traditional rights to land were regarded as extinct under Australian law. The historian is quoted as writing that : 'From that time on he determined to seek redress in the courts. The chance to pursue the matter came...at a land rights conference in Townsville...After discussion with leading activists and lawyers, it was decided that Mabo and other islanders would take a land rights case to the High Court.' Work by Reynolds, and also by Hocking, was drawn upon by Justices Deane, Gaudron and Toohey of the High Court for their judgments in the Mabo Case. I do not know whether they were aware that Reynolds and Hocking had played a part in launching the case.

References

Bartlett, R.H. 1993 Ed., *Resource Development and Aboriginal Land Rights in Australia.* Nedlands, Western Australia.

Blackstone, W. 1765 *Commentaries on the Laws of England,* Book 1. Oxford.

Brennan, F. 1993 Mabo and its implications for Aborigines and Torres Strait Islanders. In Stephenson and Ratnapala (1993).

Durack, P., Brunton, R. and Rutherford, T. 1992 *Mabo and After.* Jolimont. Victoria.

Gordon, R. 1989 Can Namibian San stop dispossession of their land ? In Wilmsen (1989b).

Hiatt, L.R. 1989 Ed., *Aboriginal Landowners.* Sydney.

Hitchcock, R.K. 1982 Tradition, social justice and land reform in central Botswana. In Werbner (1982).

McIntyre, G. 1993 Mabo v State of Queensland : retreat from injustice. In Bartlett (1993).

Maddock, K. 1980 *Anthropology, Law and the Definition of Australian Aboriginal Rights to Land.* Nijmegen.

1983 *Your Land Is Our Land : Aboriginal Land Rights.* Ringwood, Victoria.

Mulqueeny, K.E. 1993 Folk-law or folklore : when a law is not a law. Or is it ? In Stephenson and Ratnapala (1993).

Nicolas, B. 1969 *An Introduction to Roman Law.* Oxford.

O'Connell, D.P. 1970 *International Law,* vol. 1. London.

O'Connell, D.P. and Riordan, A. 1971 *Opinions on Imperial Constitutional Law.* Melbourne.

Peterson, N. 1981 *Ed., Aboriginal Land Rights : A Handbook.* Canberra.

Peterson, N. and Longton, M. 1983 Eds., *Aborigines, Land and Land Rights.* Canberra.

Puri, K. 1993 Copyright protection for Australian Aborigines in the light of Mabo. In Stephenson and Ratnapala (1993).

Radcliffe-Brown, A.R. 1918 Notes on the social organization of Australian tribes. *Journal of the Royal Anthropological Institute* 48 : 222-53.

1930 The Social organization of Australian Tribes. *Oceania* 1 : 34-63.

Radcliffe-Brown, A.R. 1952 *Structure and Function in Primitive Society.* London.

1956 On Australian local organization. *American Anthropologist* 58 : 363-7.

Santamaria, B.A. 1993 Regarding Henry : a few home truths. *The Weekend Australian,* 18-19 September.

Stephenson, M.A. and Ratnapala, S. 1993 Eds., *Mabo : A judicial Revolution.* St. Lucia, Queensland.

Werbner, R.P. 1982 Ed., *Land Reform in the Making.* London.

Wilmsen, E.N. 1989a Those who have each other : San relations to land. In Wilmsen (1989b).

1989b *We Are Here : Politics of Aboriginal* Land Tenure. Berkeley, California.

Peter T. Suzuki

URBAN DESIGN AND APPLIED ANTHROPOLOGY IN WEST EUROPEAN CITIES

> "..(E) thnic approaches are needed because some cultural constraints may create hindrances to the acceptance of any change related to a particular group of people. If knowledge and practice go together then the objective of research must bring fruitful results which can be utilised while preparing or formulating the plans for the overall development of the people or the country" (Bhowmick, 1990 (1976): 29).

These insightful observations by Professor Bhowmick are the basis in this paper for examining some of the recent trends with reference to urban design considerations for cities in West Europe. They are indeed apposite for a subject which is left to professions other than anthropologists but one which can use anthropological insights. Accordingly, this paper is an attempt to apply certain concepts in an area rather untouched by anthropologists—urban design. In this connection, it tries to follow in a modest fashion what Professor Bhowmick has so eloquently done for various aspects of Indian society.

The emphasis of this paper will be on the significance of the new ethnic groups in North European cities and their potential impact on urban design and the role that anthropology might play in designing cities more suitable for all ethnic and nationality groups.

Many North European cities and those of the former East Bloc are at the threshold or redeveloping and redesigning their Central Business Districts (CBDs). In paying deference to the medieval legacy of these cities. strict fidelity to this past should lead planners and architects to the indisputable fact that medieval European cities accommodated many types of people, of various ages, cultural traditions, and lifestyles. In contrast, the decided trend of European planners to affect an international style of modernity and sleekness for their cities will vitiate some of the basic precepts and philosophies of urban life as spelled out in Medieval Europe. Therefore new immigrant/foreign-worker/refuge populations of their cities should be entered into the calculus of what could be sound urban design and planning.

One might mention some appropriate examples of attempts of revitalizing inner cities. Lille, a large metropolitan area of France's industrial north, has its four Operations Groupees, with their revitalized *ilots* (city blocks). They are combined with the Operations programmees, which, unlike a confiscatory policy found in some French cities undertaking urban renewal programs, emphasize voluntary action. The Operations Programmees, thus, place their emphasis not only upon the usual amenities—green spaces, traffic-free zones, parking lots, and the like—but also upon low-income housing as well.

The Marais District of Paris, on the other hand, epitomizes the worthy attempt to preserve and/or restore historic buildings and to rehabilitate housing in the entire area, but at the cost of having driven out the working class. The same may be stated for what took place in certain parts of Lyon, Nancy, and, to some extent, Nantes, from which can be concluded that French cities battled to prevent the "donut" from being formed as had developed in numerous American counterparts (Chatelain, 1967; Mauroy, 1992).

Ever since the de Gaulle administration, French urban policy has been to revitalize the older areas of cities and to combine revitalization with the preservation of historic buildings and districts.

Until the collapse of the Berlin Wall in November 1989, West Germany's policy had been much more *laissez faire* than France's, and one of the consequences has been to renovate rather willy-nilly based on the whims of the various city fathers. Some notable successful examples often cited in the literature are downtown Munich's Marienplatz, Cologne's many pedestrian zones around its famous cathedral, and, indeed, the wholesale introduction of pedestrian zones in countless cities (Hajdu, 1988; for the same phenomeon in France, see, Matalow, 1976).

Since reunification, and owing to the large number of refugees and asylum seekers from Eastern Europe and the Third World, there has been a situation analagous to America's "white flight" in Germany's cities. In America's cities, middle-class whites have been deserting the traditional inner cities by droves, while in like fashion, German cities, especially those in the west, have seen a major influx of foreigners and has resulted in some inner-city areas being given over to the new populations.

Holland has taken a somewhat different path. This nation has actively promoted and encouraged suburbanization as a practical solution to its overpopulation problem and as a means of satisfying the desire of a large majority of the Dutch to live in the Haarlem-Amsterdam-Utrecht-Rotterdam Randstad (conurbation). This is not to deny that a policy of preservation and restoration has been implemented; but, only after a disastrous policy of urban destruction through the renewal policy had been activated (Suzuki, 1982).

To a great extent, Belgium, Holland's neighbor to the south, mirrored what took place in the Netherlands as far as a destructive urban renewal program followed by a historic preservation and renovation policy (to redress the terrible program which had preceded it) for its cities (Suzuki, 1980). Here a study of the housing policies of Bruges, the quintessential Flemish city, can be cited with profit because of this city's pioneer efforts—for Belgium—for urban restoration. In essence, Bruges experienced wholesale destruction of many historic structures through a 'bulldozer renewal" policy until a group of concerned citizens banded together to fight it and to replace it with a more sensible restoration, preservation, and rehabilitation policy (Suzuki, 1988; also, cf. 1986).

In addition to urban revitalization, another commonality among the nations mentioned in the previous sections is that all of them continue to be hosts to increasing numbers of foreigners from the Mediterranean region, the Third world, and Eastern Europe. Because the inner cities are the places where these foreigners have been residing—and will continue to be the major residential areas for those coming to these and other nations of western Europe—designers and planners have a unique opportunity to accommodate the newcomers' cultural values, lifestyles, and perspectives. And it is here that the anthropologist can assist those officials engaged in designing their cities for cultural diversity because of anthropologists' unique knowledge and training.

Although not the 'total approach" suggested by the architect Amos Rapoport years ago in the standard work on urban design and culture (1977), designing and/or redesigning cores of cities where foreigners live or commonly use can be implemented to take into account what he identifies as an "open-ended design method" linked with designing for cultural pluralism (355-56). This kind of dynamic, empathetic, and ever-receptive approach to design will not violate the layout, structures and architectural features of the traditional old centers of many of these cities set in the matrix of the medieval tradition. The medieval city was, after all, highly tolerant of various social systems (Barel, 1977 : 299-438), and in such places as the markets, a diversity of patterns and lifestyles coalesced in a fortunate way to enrich and embellish the way of life of that era. Likewise, the structures, layouts and plans of the traditional hearts of these cities can be maintained—nay, enhanced—by taking into consideration some of the following dynamic features of urban and rural lifestyles which, for example, Mediterranean workers bring to North European cities.

If one were to focus on accommodating urban design for Mediterranean peoples in West European CBDs—since the 1950's they have comprised the largest foreigner populations in these urban places—the following specific features are worthy of attention.

1. Railroad Station

The main railroad station (*Hauptbahnhof, central station, gare,* in Germany, Holland, and France/Belgium, respectively) had come to be the place where many of these foreigners from the south congregate to promenade or to induldge in informal social interaction (Suzuki, 1976). Although there have been some strong reactions to their congregating at the stations, such places have become a surrogate plaza-piazza-pazar (pazar is bazaar in Turkish), where in the natal lands, promenades and almost ritualistic social interactions take place. Rather than attempting to discourage use of stations by these foreigners for loitering and other purposes—at Copenhagen's station, all benches were removed to discourage foreign workers from using it as a "hangout"—additions such as broad pedestrian zones and open areas would not only help reconcile the requirements of these people but could also even further enliven these usually dreary arenas of human traffic. The medieval city's counterpart certainly was the square fronting the church—over time it came to be the town square—where religious rites and plays, announcements, and festivals were held.

Mediterranean Color Schemes

Most Mediterranean cities exhibit a great variety of colors and forms in their official buildings and residences, have colored tiles inset in the sidewalks (Cartagena in southeastern Spain comes to mind), and, in general, show greater improvisation and informality in street use, small retail-shop arrangements, and recreation patterns in CBDs than are found in their northern European counterparts. As an example, the bright blues, greens, reds, yellows, oranges, and shades of these colors, so prevalently found in towns and cities of the Mediterranean-rim countries tend to "wash" into shades of cream, gray, and brown in northern European cities with their timbered buildings, and, if new, in the concrete grays of the sleek modern built environment. Here again, without going against the grain of the traditional colors found in the CBDs of host cities, the brighter, gayer colors employed in the Mediterranean cities could be incorporated unobtrusively.

It shoud be kept in mind that medieval cities—despite their fairly monochrome and monotonous color tones—were centers of gaitey, vibrance, exuberance, and color. The markets, with their dazzling flowers and herbs; striking clothes of jugglers, jesters, and jokers; and hues of bright colors of the goods preferred, all added zest and zip to the otherwise austere lives of the citizens of that period. Thus, to write of blending in the bright, sparkling, and audacious color schemes of Mediterranean cities is not to deny there is no tradition in the northern cities of such tones.

Pedestrian Activity and Behavior

That strolling, window shopping, and loitering in the downtown area are not solely physical acts goes without saying. Hence, the Mediterraneans, familiar as they are with the hustle and bustle of life in the cities of their natal metropolises, use CBDs in ways which are quite different from those of their hosts; and it is not just the physical layout of the inner cites which accounts for the differences.

Perceptions of the built environment, territoriality, spatial configurations, cognitive maps, form, and distance are some less-than-tangible aspects of urban life which are subject to cultural interpretation (Greene, 1992; Rotenberg and McDonoguh, 1993). Ice cream and ice cream shops—prosaic as they are—are a case in point. In the warmer Mediterranean countries, ice cream is a readily-availabe treat which can be purchased at an ice-cream parlor or from a peddler all year around. In the cities of northern Europe before the vast influx of foreign workers, one would have been hard put to buy an ice cream cone in a parlor, let alone from a push-cart peddler, during the non-summer months. In was not until the number of foreign workers—especially Italian—increased that the retail business structure of the CBDs changed, with a major increase in the number of year-round ice-cream parlors with their distinctive Italian decor (including decorations with the national colors of red, green, and white). (1) This phenomenon has also changed the gustatory and dietary habits of northern Europeans in that these northerners no longer think of ice cream as just a summer dish as they used to before the Mediterraneans arrived on their shores in great waves. Pizza, shashlik (a Turkish meat dish), kebab, raki (a Greek drink with anise) etc., are other well-known examples of the same order which have changed not only the tastes and values of the "natives" but also the physical, retail trade, and social structures of the cities where these new delights have rooted through shops, snack bars, and eateries.

Consequently, in revitalizing and redesigning CBDs, planners would do well to encourage citizen participation among these Mediterraneans in the planning process (Suzuki, 1989; Greene, 1992). Certain shops—boutique size—for ethnic wares and ethnic restaurants, to be nanned by migrants from the south, could be set aside when an urban renewal program is ready for operation. Along these lines, it would also make sense to incorporate Meditteranean design features for any new open-air market places or even shopping centers.

If the attention is now turned away from objects to people, the elderly among the Mediterraneans may not be numerous, yet they form a higher percentage of their population in their new homelands than do the native elderly of the northern countries and merit consideration in urban design. Owing to stronger family ties than their northern European compatriots, along with the economic factor, the guest workers and their dependents do things together more frequently as families. Furthermore, the newcomers are less likely to be institutionalized than their northern European counterparts can be seen doing many things their children—the original migrants—are also doing (Suzuki, 1977; 1991). These observations are consonant with what Greene has identified as the four "major principles of community design" (1992 : 180):

Function requires that the design work effectively to the convenience and comfort of all its users.

Order assures that users can become oriented to the environment and understand it.

Identity denotes a visual image of the environment that reflects special or unique qualities.

Appeal characterizes a design that gives pleasure to its users over time.

Specifically, the use of appealing movable street furniture, some reserved exclusively for the elderly (e.g., comfortable chairs, benches, stools, and other resting accoutrements) should be expanded both in number and locations for use by a wide variety of people—of different ethnic backgrounds, classes, occupations, ages, and physical states.

In the same vein, the traditional concept of CBD can be modified so that, as in many American cities where the elderly are found near the cores, multi-purpose social-service centers for the new ethnic groups and their elderly can be established. The ubiquitous Turkish cultural associations in Germany, to cite an example, could establish storefront centers whose decor and design would be such that they harmonize with the surrounding built environment. Similarly, the various comparable associations for the other ethnic groups would function in the same ways.

Placing these centers near the heart of the city follows sound principles of accessibility and mobility in urban design.

Conclusion

The thrust of this brief essay has been in conformity with Professor Bhowmick's lifelong quest for a meaningful application of anthropology, *viz.*, to further knowledge and to help improve the human condition. Special attention has been paid to a facet of urban life which has not received due attention by anthropologists; that is to say, urban design, in this case, with special reference to West European cities.

The rapid changes which West European cities are presently experiencing because of the unparalleled migration of peoples from the former East Bloc countries, the Third World, and the Mediterranean rim present a formidable challenge to policy makers and ordinary citizens of these cities. In some places, such as Berlin, the challenge is being met with new urban developments and plans (Frick, 1991), yet as regards urban design, they fail to take into account the new population groups entering its boundaries so that the kind of open-ended design suggested by Rapoport has fallen by Berlin's wayside and thus an opportunity for "designing for multiculturality" is being lost. Certain segments of Berlin's Hauptstrasse, for example, have numerous Turkish shops. There is even a storefront mosque. Yet this entire district has no specific markers—except for a few signs—which give it a Turkish flavor. Traditionally a working-class area, Hauptstrasse's staid old buildings, colors, and street furniture hardly belie a strong Turkish element.

It would be an exaggeration to aver that the kind of urban design suggested in this paper could have helped obviate some of the recent violent reactions to Turks and other foreigners in Germany (here the murder of six members of a Turkish family by a fire bomb in Sollingen in June 1993 as the most recent and brutal act against Germany's foreigners comes to mind). The purpose of urban design, rather, is to enhance the quality of life for city users of all backgrounds.

Professor Bhowmick's admirable study of street cleaners in Calcutta shows the innate curiousity and concern that this anthropologist has by virtue of his dedicated application of anthropological concepts, perspectives, and tenets to a group of urban workers who traditionally had been neglected by social scientist because of the social position of the subjects (Bhowmick, *op. cit.* (1967-68):125-133). Other anthropologists can now follow his lead in pursuing their profession in an urban setting, with reference to design features, which could improve the lot of city residents.

Note

1. In Leiden, Holland, its Stationsweg had an Italian ice-cream parlor since the 1950s, one which was open throughout the year. Its owner was thought to have been very daring because the Dutch simply were not accustomed to this kind of shop.

References

Barel, Yves 1977 La Ville Medieval. Grenoble : Presses Universitaires du Grenoble.

Bhowmick, P.K. 1990 1967-1968 "Living conditions and social disabilities of the sweepers : An example of West Bengal," *in* : *Action-*

		Applied-Development Anthropology by P. K. Bhowmick. Calcutta : Sri Dipak Guha, 1990 pp. 125-133.
	1990	1976 "Role of Social Scientist in Developmental Plan," *in : Action-Applied-Development Anthropology* by P. K. Bhowmick. Calcutt : Sri Dipak Guha, pp. 25-33.
Chatelain, Paul	1967	"Quartiers historiqes et centere ville : L' example du quartier du Marais,' *in*: Urban Core and Inner City, by W. F. Heinemeijer *et al.* (eds.). Leiden. E.J. Brill. pp. 340-355.
Frick, Dieter	1991	"City development and planning in the Berlin convrbation," *Town Planning Review* 62 : 37-49.
Greene, Sherwin	1992	"Cityshape, communicating and evaluating community design," *APA Jounal* 58 : 177-189.
Hajdu, J.G.	1988	"Pedesterian malls in West Germany : Perceptions of their role and stages in their development," *APA Journal* 54 : 325-336.
Matalow, B.	1976	La Marchee a Pied : Voisinage et accessibilities. Marseilles : Bureau Detude technique pour 1 'urbanisation et 1' equipment de la region Mediterraneenne.
Mauroy, Pierre	1992	"The Lille metropolis and city world," Ekistics 59 (No. 352-353) : 61-64.
Rotenberg, Robert and Gary McDonogh (eds.)	1993	*The Cultural Meaning of Urban Space.* Westport, CT : Greenwood.
Suzuki, Peter T.	1976	"Gemans and Turks at Germany's railroad stations : Interethnic tensions in the pursuit of walking and loitering," Urban Life : Journal of Ethnographic Research 4 : 387-441.
Suzuki, Peter T.	1977	"Social work, culture-specific mediators, delivering services to aged Turks in Germany and aged Chinese in Francisco," International Social Work 21 : 13-19.
	1980	"Le Parnasse : A new town in the heart of Brussels," *Urban Design International* 1 (4) : 34-35.
	1982	"Housing and urban planning policies in the Netherlands," *Habitat International* 6 :387-393.

1984 "The national urban freeway system of the Netherlands : Transportation policies an innovation in a small nation," *Transportation Quarterly* 38 : 551-558.

1986 "Current transportation policies in a medieval city (Bruges)," *Transportation Quarterly* 40 : 521-532.

1988 "Housing rehabilitation in Bruges," *Habitat International* :12 :89-101.

1989 "Citizen participation as an instrument of change : Transportation planning in the Netherlands," *Citizen Action* 1 (4) : 1-9.

1991 "The psychological effects of German reunification on Turkish guestworkers," *Mind and Human Interaction* 2:90-97.

J. B. Ganguly

ECONOMICS AND HUMAN VALUES

The economic theory that is being tought in the universities in the western and most of the third world countries is of the Neo-Classical orthodoxy. Economics as a discipline is considered a social science which is distinct from other social sciences like history, sociology, political science, anthropology, etc. Neo-Classical economics uses the abstract-deductive method of analysis which has facilitated the use of mathematical tools of analysis and has endowed it with an appearance of intellectual rigour. The establish its claim as a 'positive science' it has also been characterized as a value-free system. Its laws have been claimed to be objective and valid in all circumstances at least so far as its 'core' is concerned. Milton Friedman asserts : "Economics is a scientific discipline that has a core that is common to almost all professional economists" (1970 : 80). The core represents the following features of a free market exchange system:

The consumers purchase commodities in the market in accordance with their subjective preference ordering so as to reach the highest level of satisfaction which is attained when the relative prices of commodities equal their marginal rates of substitution.

The producers' decisions on what commodity mix to produce and how to produce are governed by their desire to maximize profits which is fulfilled when production is so arranged that the marginal rate of substitution between any two inputs of production is equal to the ratio of their prices and that the marginal rate of transformation between any two goods is equal to the ratio of their respective prices.

The number of buyers and sellers in the market is assumed to be so large that no individual buyer or seller can affect the price by his own purchase or sale respectively.

The theory of distribution, that is, the distribution of the output among the inputs production, is a special case of the theory of price. The supply and demand for inputs (just as the supply and demand for commodities) determine their prices and such prices of inputs equal their respective marginal productivities.

The basic axioms of the system are taken as valid without any argument. And from these premises by deductive mathematical reasoning it is proved that in such a system resources are most efficiently allocated and that goods are produced at their optimum levels. The test used for proving this point is that in the case of a competitive equilibrium situation none could be made better off without making someone worse off. Economics being a positive science would preclude any normative preference for any change involving the betterment of one person or a class of persons.

Such academic economics, says Joan Robinson, "has been concerned with propagating the ideology of *laissez faire* and of the benefical effects of the free play of market forces" and in doing so "it has done more harm to distract attention from the actual operations of the capitalist economy than to illuminate them". (1976 :167) The idealized Neo-Classical system is at variance with realities in some crucial respects. Externalities of production leading to the enjoyment of increasing returns to scale give rise to the growth of monopoly control over prices. Secondly, as Hunt has pointed out, " Some commodities are 'consumed socially' and their production and sale would never be profitable in a *laissez faire* capitalist economy even though they may be deemed highly desirable by most citizens within the economy' (e. g,, roads, schools, (armies, etc.) 1973 : 189). Thirdly, private costs and benefits of producing some commodities differ from social costs and benefits. The typical cases of such variations are the pollution of water and atmosphere and ecological damages caused by producers for the sake of earning profits. Finally, left to the free play of market forces the economy is prone to suffer from periodical depressions causing widespread miseries. Various forms of state interventions have been suggested by the liberal economists to free the capitalist system form such blemishes.

The so-called value-neutral perfectly competitive model is actually value-loaded. For it justifies the appropriation of the surplus produced in the economy in the form of profits the rate of which is determined through the operation of market forces. The argument runs like this. The capitalists contribute to production by supplying with the required quantity of capital. And just as labor earns wages the rate of which equals its marginal productivity so capital earns profit rate of which gets fixed according to its marginal productivity. The operation of the market forces bring this about. But economists led by Piero Sraffa have conclusively proved that the concept of a 'quantity of capital' has no meaning apart from the rate of profit" so that the economic theory of the rate of profit being equal to the marginal productivity of capital involves circular reasoning.

This development does not only demolish the Neo-Classical capital theory alone, it also means that we have to look to non-economic factors for an explanation of the existing pattern of distribution of the surplus as wages and profits. In other words, the institutional arrangement, such as, customs and conventions, social mores, traditions and even political power structure influence the determination of the sharing of the national cake (national income) by the wage-earners and profit-earners. Wage rate may be fixed by collective bargaining between labor and employer or by the government or some wage-fixation boards appointed by the government or even by social convention. Similarly we may think that the rate of profit depends on the 'level of money rates of interest' which in turn is influenced by social, political and legal status of lenders and the borrowers besides the pattern of distribution of assets in the society.

It is undeniable that prices of goods and inputs are rarely determined in conditions of perfect competition in the capitalist system. Therefore the claims about objectivity, positivism and value-neutrality are untenable. In fact such assertions have sought to preclude ethical considerations informing human behavior in respect of production, consumption, distribution, etc. But, as Dmitri Likhachev has said, " No economic laws operate where there is not a minimum of morality". (Bashkin, 1990 : 19). That economics as a social science must be concerned with human values has become imperative on account of the fact that the humans cannot continuously go on enjoying more and more consumptions of goods and services without any limit. For there is an absolute limit to the availability of energy in usable form as the laws of thermodynamics envisage. But the economists in developing growth models utterly neglected this eventuality.

In extending the tools of analysing the economic relations in a static frame to explaining the economics of growth, Neo-

Classical economists have assigned the crucial role to the process of accumulation of capital in increasing output and income. Capitalists contribute to growth by saving out of their income and investing that for increased production of goods and services. This calls for analysing the distribution of growing income among the capitalists and workers. Assuming that the capitalists' propensity to save is high while that of the workers is very low, if at all, and that the basic problem is that of generating effective demand to match the increases production of goods and services (as it is the case in a developed economy at or near full employment level), it is shown that it would be possible to achieve growth of income steadily as the capitalists earn what they spend and workers spend what they earn.

In the production of goods and services the various factors of production are used. In a simplified model, the number of factor or inputs are taken as two, namely, capital and labor. It is presumed that the factors of production are substitutable for one another without any limit. And the scarce resource is substituted by the abundant one depending on their relative prices. As a resource becomes relatively scarce its relative price rises. Therefore the tendency will be to employ more of the abundant resource price of which is relatively low. This will lead to a change in the capital-labor ratio in production which will entail a change in the technology of production. Growth of labor supply depends on the growth of population and productivity of labour depends on technical progress. It has, therefore, been explained that growth of population and technical progress ultimately determine the longrun rate of economic growth.

Based on such premises the economists have worked out several versions of 'golden age' of growth by which is meant a state of dynamic equilibrium which can be continuously maintained by achieving the desired rate of accumulation of capital given the growth of population and output per labor (which depends on the rate of technical progress). This ushers in the so-called 'golden age' because starting from a state of full or near full employment 'and a composition of the stock of plant appropriate to the desired rate of accumulation', as explained by Joan Robinson, output and income go on growing continuously while maintaining the state of full or near full employment in the country. That is, there is no ups and downs in economic activities and no cyclical unemployment and misery. Also in such a state per capita consumption grows at the maximum rate which is the equilibrium rate. And this situation has been equated with maximum social welfare which the people enjoy ever after.

The basic premise of such constructions of static and dynamic equilibria is that human welfare depends on material wealth and that welfare grows as the acquisition of material wealth grows. And there is no limit to growth of production of goods and services as there is absolute scarcity of resources required for production though there may be relative scarcity. But a relatively scarce resource can always be substituted by a relatively abundant one. The competitive market mechanism brings about the optimum allocation of resources for production of different goods and servies and also the distribution of the output or income among the different factors or production according to their respective contributions to the total output.

This mechanism is morally neutral. It does not bother about the inequality of distribution of income and sufferings of the poor and the needy. "It is", says Paul Johnson, "materialist, impersonal and non-human" (1990 : 18). But this kind of approach cannot sustain a system for long as it cannot ensure development of human potential to the fullest possible. And human potential is to be recknoed in terms of both material and spiritual dimensions. This has been the message that India from the ancient times, has been conveying to the west. Rabindranath. Vivekananda, Gandhi and other sages have repeatedly pronounced that material urges must be moderated with spiritual aspirations, otherwise peace and happiness will elude humankind. Such thinking is also attributable to seers in other countries. The Russian philosopher Vladimir Solovyov, in his study *The Justification of Good*, wrote:

> "The recognition of material wealth as the goal of economic activity might be called the original sin of political economy...The aim of work in relation to physical nature- is not its utilisation for the acquisition of things and money, but its own improvement—the reviving in it of the dead, the spiritualisation of the material." (Bashkin, 1990 : 19). And so Bashkin asserts : "We need moral investment in the economy no less than we require financial inputs."

According to the laws of thermodynamics, energy can be neither created nor destroyed and heat cannot flow from one source to another at a higher temperature without the application of energy from an outside source. Therefore, 'throughout the universe energy tends to be disssipated in such a way that the total available energy becomes more disorganized and more difficult to trap and use.' And it follows that ultimately a day will come when same temperature will prevail in every part of the universe, entropy will be zero, that is, no further disorganization of energy will be possible and so it will not be possible to use energy. This eventuality is referred to as the 'Heat Death of the Universe' (Isaacs : 136-37). If the laws of thermodynamics are valid and if the universe is actually a closed system, it will have a finite end. Taking the cue from these laws and noting the realities of "the fixed solar flux, the intricately coevolved interdependences of the ecosystem, and the pattern of geologic concentrations of minerals in the earths' crust' Herman e. Daly (1979 :38) has formulated an impossibility theorem by which it is established that an everincreasing consumption standard for an ever-increasing world population is an impossibility.

The problems of unequal distribution of income, unemployment and poverty have been brushed aside by many countries thinking that growth of output and income will take care of these problems. And the economists have constructed models is of continuously increasing output and income without any limit thanks to the assumption of substitutability of the scarce resource by the abundant one infinitely. But the impossibility theorem contradicts these formulations. Therefore, it follows that growth cannot be a substitute for redistribution. The human must cultivate the values of sharing and moderation.

The basic cause of the predicament needs to be understood. A symposium on Science and Culture for the 21st Century : Agenda for Survival was held at Vancouver, Canada from 10 to 15 September 1989. It was organized by the Canadian Commission for UNESCO under the auspices of the UNESCO. The famous Vancouver Declaration on Survival in the 21st Century emanated from that symposium. The declaration has highlighted the fact that certain scientific developments 'gave to human beings a power over nature that has, until recently, produced an ever-increasing, and seemingly boundless, supply of material commodities. Swept up in the exploitation of this power, humankind has tended to shift its values to those promoting the maximal realization of the material possibilities that this new power provides. Suppressed, correspondingly, were the values associated with dimensions of the human potential that had been the foundations of earlier cultures.

"In contemporary science, the older mechanical picture of the universe is replaced by concepts that permit a universe that is formed by a continual creative input that is not rigidly constrained by any mechanical law. Man himself becomes an aspect of this creative impulse...."

"The human species has reached limits in its use of the external world and also limits in its capacity to live in a changing social and cultural environment...The present critical situation in mankind's occupancy of the planet requires new visions..."

"Such visions change the conception of man in nature and call for a radical transformation of models of development; the elimination of poverty, ignorance and misery; the end of the arms race; introduction of new learning processes, educational systems and mental attitudes; implementation of better forms of redistribution to ensure social equity; a new design for living based on a reduction of waste; respect for bio-diversity, socio-economic diversity, and cultural diversity that transcends outmoded concepts of sovereignty".

Appropriately, the perception of development has changed in the recent years. Earlier the emphasis was on 'economic' development now it is on 'human' development. The United Nations Development programme has been publishing annually since 1990 reports on human development. The 1990 Report highlighted the fact that people must be at the centre of all development. Therefore it is not only the income level that is significant 'but how well that income has been translated into human lives.' And, therefore, the goal of human development is ' to increase people's choices.' This to be a reality, people 'must enjoy freedom—cultural, social, economic and political.' All this is stressed for creating ' a conducive environment for pepole, individually, and collectively, to develop their full potential and to have a reasonable chance of leading productive and creative lives in accord with their needs and interests".

Development of the human potential is being measured in terms of longevity knowledge and decent living standards all of which can be quantified. The 1991 Human Development Reports has underscored the importance of human freedom though it is extremely difficult to measure it. These Reports have undoubtedly focused our attention on the human face of development or the material and social goals of development. Realization of these goals in all countries, particularly the developing third world countries, will call for global dialogue aan cooperation. Dr Mahbub ul Haq, an Economist from

Pakistan who is the chief architect of these Reports, has recently spelled out the vision of a new human order in which no single human being "is ever condemned by the sheer accident of birth, but has equitable access to the entire range of national and global opportunities to develop his or her full human potential. This alone will translate the notion of one planet into one humanity. This alone will create a new human order". (The Sentinel, Guwahati, 5 May 1992).

But there must be the required moral basis for such a world order. Humankind needs to aspire for not only material and social progress but also that of spiritual upliftment and pursuance of moral values.

References

Bashkin, Victor	1990	Economics and Morality, *Soviet Land*, New Delhi, No. 12.
Daly, Herman E.	1979	Ethical Implications of Limits to Development, published in, *The Morality of Scarcity*, Edited by Finnin, Willam M. Louisiana State University Press, Baton Rouge and London.
Friedman, M.	1970	'Oh Paul Samuelson, *Newsweek*, 9 November.
Hunt, E. K.	1973	Economic Scholasticism and Capitalist Ideology, published in, *A Critique of Economic Theory*, edited by Hunt, E. K. and Schwartz. J.G., Penguin.
Haq, Mahbub ul	1992	Human Development in a Changing World, *The Sentinel*, 5 May, Guwahati.
Isaacs, Alan	1963	*Introducing Science*, Penguin Books.
Paul, Johnson	1990	Capitalism as a Moral Force, *Span*, New Delhi, October.
Robinson, J.	1976	*Selected Economic Writings*, Oxford University Press.
Solovyov, Vladimir	1990	The Justification of Good, quoted by Bashkin in *Economics and Morality*, United Nations Development Programme, Human Development Report for 1990, 1991, 1992.
UNESCO	1989	*Vancouver Declaration on Survival in the 21st Century*.

N.K. BEHURA

STRUCTURALISM OF LEVI-STRAUSS : NATURE, PROBLEMS AND PROSPECTS

Structuralism is an intellectually complex, historically evolving an academically popular movement. In anthropology it goes with the name of Levi-Strauss. His work is ideal-typical of structural anthropology as a whole. There is no unanimity about the intellectual-historical background of structural anthropology. However, some authors have attempted to reconstruct an intellectual-historical background on the textual bases provided by Levi-Strauss.

Levi-Strauss considers Rousseau as the prophetic founder of cultural anthropology (1963 a : 11). Rousseau probably was the first thinker to have paid attention to history's most important ontological problems, that is, man's passage from animality to humanity, from instinct to intellect and from nature to culture. This is based on "the emergence of a logic operating by means of binary oppositions and coinciding with the first manifestations of symbolism" (1963 b : 101). Levi-Strauss has followed similar argument in Totemism (1963 b), primitive logic (*The Savage Mind*, 1962), mythology and social organization (1970). Scholte says that each of these intellectual creations and their attendant social institutions must be understood as more or less successful cognitive means and organizational efforts to mediate the multiplex and fundamental passage from the naturally given to the culturally created (1973 : 639). Levi-Strauss has used this transition in his analysis of socio-cultural facts to promote structuralism which produced scientific explanation overcoming this philosophical impasse. Among many crucial causes an important psychic quality, which Rousseau called "pity" was involved in this significant transition from nature to culture. Pity has been defined as man's capacity to identify himself with his fellow human beings and with all living creatures (Scholte, 1973 : 639). This identification and understanding of both man and other animals have contributed to the systematic comprehension of the similarities and differences between them as in totemic systems (1963 b : 77 f).

"Pity" is the fundamental condition for intersubjective and ethnographic understanding, "Pity or empathy entails a desire for identification with others, and a total refusal of identification with oneself. There is no doubt that such capacities are circumscribed by the ethnographer's own personal circumstances. Yet he can learn to use himself as his own instrument of observation (Scholte, 1973 : 639). He can learn to know himself objectively by treating himself as another person. Levi-Strauss draws the conclusion from Rousseau that the ethnographer must identify with his essential humanity the humble third person "he" within himself (1963 a:11). Rousseau's formula proclaims the emergence of "unconditional objectivity" and the resolution of the epistemological schism between the self and the other, and between the outside observer and native participant (1973 : 640). This is the root of self-objectification.

Levi-Strauss again turns to Rousseau for another conclusion that human condition neither predates nor transcends social organization; and one should build an ideal model of man's culture and therein discover what is original to man and what is artificial (cf. 1973 : 640). In order to find out the "natural man" one should discover the "society of nature". But such a pristine society may never have existed. One may infer some of its ideal-typical characteristics from Levi-Strauss's praise of primitive societies. For him primitive societies are demogratic and harmonious and generally resist temporal change. However, he is quite aware of the ever present contingencies of historical change and temporal vicissitudes. His concept of scientific anthropology is to preserve primitive societies from the "cannibal instincts of the historical process" (Levi-Strauss, 1969 : 101-19).

Emile Durkheim and Marcel Mauss, like Rousseau, have profoundly influenced Levi-Strauss's concept of structural anthropology. Levi-Strauss is in agreement with Durkheim that "the principal objective" of the social sciences "lies in the discovery of general relations between phenomena" (Durkheim, 1962 : XXXIV). But as regards the logical genesis of these general relations Levi-Strauss significantly differs from Durkheim. Sometimes Durkheim "affirms the primacy of the social over the intellect", but elsewhere he also admits that social life "presupposes an intellectual activity in man of which the formal properties, consequently, cannot be a reflection of the concrete organization of society" (Levi-Strauss, 1963 b : 96-7). Durkheim's main problem was insufficiency of concrete data.

Levi-Strauss is heavily buckled to the French sociological school for many of his anthropological assumptions. "*Structural Anthropology* (1958) is still dedicated to Durkheim, since, he, more than anyone else, incarnates the essence of France's contribution to social anthropology" (Scholte, 1973 : 642). He too has imbided a lot of insight from the works of Marcel Mauss. While praising the works of Rivers he writes that his contemporaries and successors have chiefly acknowledged his historical and geographical interpretations, while psychological and logical aspects of his theory were quietly assimilated by Mauss, Radcliffe-Brown, and Malinowski, who developed them further with great brilliance" (1969 : 163 f). Here he is referring to Mauss's "notion of total social fact and the principle of exchange", which have gained their concrete and universal significance. Social facts are concrete and systematic, that is, "they are lived by men, and subjective consciousness is as much a form of their reality as their objective characteristics" (Levi-Strauss, 1967 : 14). A comprehensive understanding of social facts as total phenomena requires both emic and etic perspectives. Phenomenological (or empirical) interpretations can be made scientific if the observer develops systematic awareness above the objective determinants of social facts. Sometimes, the existential or lived in experience may consist of "the nationalized interpretations of the native who often makes himself into an observer and even a theoretician of his own society" (Levi-Strauss, 1967 : 12). Commenting on this Scholte says that "such conscious beliefs may also be fictitious and ideological. To assess their scientific validity and ethnological importance, the anthropologist must determine their dialectical relation to the systematic and the collective" (1973 : 645). The collective, says Levi-Strauss "is not governed by the singular, subjective, and phenomenally given, but by a universal, collective, and hidden reality that underlies and generates all appearances : the unconscious brain" (1946 a : 528).

The importance attributed to the mental substructure of reciprocity is intelligible better in the context of the writings of Durkheim and Mauss. They have delineated a method which aims at unraveling mental common denominators or collective archetypes. In the writings of Levi-Strauss there is a progressively more intense commitment to the discovery of mental substraction of which social life is the raw material. French tradition reveals a lingering influence of Cartesian rationalism. The relevant components of this approach are the structures of thought. For Levi-Strauss there is a basic propensity of human mind to build logical categories by means of binary contrasts. For him human cognition is the social fact.

Binary oppositions suggest the dilectical process as formulated by Hegel and refined by Marx. Levi-Strauss meticulously pursues a dialectic mode of presentation : first the superficial facts, then the hidden negation, and finally the dazzling insight into a new and more fundamental reality (1969 : 31-8). The concept of "unconscious", the most important premise of structural anthropology, reduces phenomenal realities to a common infrastructure. Whether this scientific reduction is placed "in the context of the epistemological passage from culture to nature or in the specific domain of the substantive explanation of social relations by their intellectual genesis, the unconscious and universal human brain invariably sustains and always accounts for observed ethnographic data and inferred ethnological realities (Scholte, 1973 : 645). This also applies to Rousseau's formula of "the me is another", and only the unconscious can mediate the opposition between self and another, subjectivity and objectivity (Levis-Strauss, 1950 : XXVII).

Scholte (1973) maintains that Levi-Strauss derives the nature of the unconscious reality from Mauss's (1954) concept of reciprocal exchange. Mauss stated that the exchange of gifts, a total social fact is a synthetic, relational, and systematic process. For Levi-Strauss this process reflects the structure of the unconscious, which consists of three principles, namely, (i) the exigency of the rule of reciprocity as a rule, (ii) the notion of reciprocity regarded as the most immediate form of integrating the opposition between the self and the others, and (iii) the synthetic nature of gift, which means that the agreed transfer of a valuable from one individual to another makes these individuals into partners.

These principles of the 'unconscious' are the *a priori* assumptions of Levi-Straussian structuralism. They are latent in the social facts and every social fact is explainable in terms of these principles. Levi-Strauss's popular examples are linguistic, economic and kinship phenomena (1969 : 296).

Nature of Structural Anthropology

There are intimate ties between anthropology and linguistics in the French tradition of social sciences. Durkheim's sociological contribution provided a poignant intellectual stimulus to Ferdinand de Saussure's linguistics. The distinction between *la parole* and *la langue* is very crucial in the understanding of the French social science tradition. Durkheim and Levi-Strauss view language as a "counter-sign of thought" (Firth, 1964: 94). For Bloomfied and Malinowski language is a "mode of action". This difference entails methodological consequences, because for structuralism semantics is a part of structural linguistics. Influence of structural linguistics (the Prague school) over the French sociological tradition has flourished and culminated in the works of Levi-Strauss. He "explicitly seeks to mirror the methodological principles and substantive aims of cultural anthropology after those of structural linguistics" (Scholte, 1973 : 658). Levi-Strauss is of the opinion that structural linguistics can play a renovating role in respect of the social sciences. He outlines Troubetzkoy's structural methods which are reduced to four basic operations. First, structural linguistics shifts from the study of *conscious* linguistic phenomena to the study of their unconscious infrastructure; second, it does not treat *terms* as independent entities, taking instead as its basis of analysis the *relations* between terms; third, it introduces the concept of system...finally, structural linguistics aims at discovering *general laws*, either by induction, or...by logical deduction, which would give them an absolute character (1969 : 33).

The relevance of these points to structural anthropology is the importance of the unconscious factor. Language is a social phenomenon, and it manifests two fundamental characteristics which make it susceptible of scientific study; first, much of linguistic behavior lies on the level of unconscious thought. A speaker is not conscious of the syntactic and morphological laws of his language while speaking; and second, he is not normally conscious of the phonemes which he employs to convey different meanings. And further, he is rarely conscious of the phonological oppositions which reduce each phoneme to a bundle of distinctive features". Thus language as a social phenomenon manifests both independence of the observer and statistical runs. In structural linguistics researches" have reached beyond the superficial conscious and historical expression of linguistic phenomena to attain fundamental and objective realities consisting of systems of relations which are the products of unconscious thought process" (Levi-Strauss, 1969 : 58). Now the question is whether it is possible to bring about a similar reduction in the analysis of other forms of social phenomena ? Levi-Strauss concludes that various other social phenomena such as kinship, totemism and myth are equally the products of "identical unconscious structures" (1969 : 62). And thus one can reach a truly fundamental and identical formulation in respect of these phenomena.

By drawing our attention to the methods of linguistics, Levi-Strauss does not reduce "culture to language nor anthropology to linguistics". "He does seek to formulate relations between conscious cultural givens and their unconscious mental infrastructures. To do so, he adopts a linguistic model, among others to elucidate these universal structures of the human brain" (Scholte, 1973: 660).

Structural linguistics deals not with terms but with the relations between them. Similarly anthropology can become a theory of social relationships, and "then it will be possible to analyse societies in terms of the differential features characteristic of the systems of relationships which define them" (Levi-Strauss, 1969 : 95-96).

Levi-Strauss is aware of the fact that structuralism invokes cybernatic and mathematical models in addition to related methods in linguistics. And thus he cautions that "a too literal adherence to linguistic method actually betrays its very essence" (1969 : 36). Kinship terms have a sociological existence, and at the same time are elements of speech. "A kinship system comprises two quite different orders of reality (i) system of terminology, and (ii) system of attitudes". Thus as in linguistics, atomism in the analysis of kinship system must be eschewed.

Ferdinand de Saussure's contribution was the concept of language as a system, while the term 'structure' was introduced by the Prague Circle (Scholte, 1973 : 660), Levi-Strauss has used the concepts of "structure" and "system" with similar connotation. Therefore, the question is whether 'social structure' is systematic like language? If so, socio-cultural systems can be studied as more or less integrated symbolic structures of language itself, that is marriage rules, economic relations, and artistic, scientific and religious systems (Scholte, 1973 : 660). Thus once again the human brain comes into focus as the source of symbolic function and as the ontological basis for structuralism in anthropology.

For Levi-Strauss structural anthropology, like linguistics, seeks to establish general laws. He seems to be rejecting de

Saussure's dichotomy between the diachronic and the synchronic, and favoring Jacobson's synchronic explanation, which is mechanical, morphological, topological and telcological (see Jacobson in Tax 1953 : 310-11). He avers that "it is solely (or almost solely) diachronic analysis which must account for synchronic phenomena" (1969 : 34). This means that one can analyze changes in terms of a synchronic pattern. In respect of ethnological phenomena an unconscious logic exhibits a morphological determinism while their conscious representations are only the results of 'a sort of dialectical average among a multiplicity of unconscious systems".

For Levi-Strauss both the linguistic sign and the ethnographic element are arbitrary *a priori*, but cease to be so a *posteriori*. The moment they are placed in their proper contexts, systematic and deterministic conceptions of their respective nature and function appear. Thus linguistics and anthropology formulate the methodological strategy for structural study of the appropriate determinants of socio-cultural phenomena.

Elementary Structures

Levi-Strauss's work, *The Elementary Structures of Kinship (Les Structures elementaries de la parente)* is a remarkable feat of analysis in anthropology. For Levi-Strauss himself it is an introduction to a general theory of kinship system (1970 : XXIV). It is an erudite 'effort to produce a sort of inventory of mental constraints, an attempt to reduce the arbitary to an order' and 'to discover a necessity immanent in an illusion of liberty'. He chose kinship because it was a domain which might seem to be characterized by 'its incoherent and contingent character', but it was possible to reduce this domain to a 'very small number of significant propositions'.

For Levi-Strauss, "elementary structures of kinship are those systems in which the nomenclature permits the immediate determination of the circle of kin and that of affines, that is, those systems which prescribe marriage with a certain type of relative, or alternatively, those which, while defining all members of the society as relatives, divide them into two categories, viz., possible spouses and prohibited spouses" (1970 : XXIII). Thus kinship "relations offer immediately to the mind a framework of logical classification; this framework, once it is conceived, is used in order to situate, by reference to these pre-established categories, individuals with whom anyone happens to be, or not to be, empirically related" (See Korn, 1973 : 2).

Levi-Strauss seems to be against classification of kinship systems on the basis of terminological types, such as 'classificatory' and 'descriptive'. For him, every kinship system is at the same time descriptive and classificatory (See Korn, 1973 : 2). Following Durkheim, he draws a distinction between consanguinity and kinship *(parente)*. Consanguinity is only the sufficient condition of kinship and the latter is essentially a series of juridical and moral obligations, and these obligations are neither classified nor regulated as consanguineal relationships (Korn, 1973 : 3). Levi-Strauss is in agreement with Kroeber as regards the fallacious differentiation between 'classificatory' and 'descriptive' terms (1909). He attempts to establish the criteria upon which relationship terminologies are built. From his discussion it is evident that relationship terms denote social categories and not 'degrees' of kinship. The status position which a set of relationship terms denotes, is specific to the society in which it occurs. "The comparability of a set of relationship terms with another can only be seen by reference to the classificatory principles involved in them" (Korn 1973: 3).

This position leads him to think to relationship terms as social categories. Korn (1973 : 3) points out, and it is a fact, that Levi-Strauss in his book, *The Elementary Structures of Kinship*, uses 'prohibited degrees' while referring to the category of people that a person cannot marry (1970 : 99, 107, 122).

Levi-Strauss's central idea about kinship systems is that they always manifest some sort of exchange between groups, no matter whether they are composed of 'degrees' or 'categories' which signify different types of rules of marriage. For him, even though incest prohibition has its roots in nature, it can be fully grasped as a social rule. He says that "prohibition is less concerned with true consanguinity...than with the purely social phenomenon by which two unrelated individuals are classed as 'brothers' or 'sisters', 'parents' or 'children'. The prohibition and the rule of exogamy are therefore, merged (1970 : 29). Sometimes both the institutions exist side by side. Logically 'exogamy' by itself is not enough to prevent the marriage of a mother with her son in a patrilineal system, nor of a father with his daughter in a marilineal system. But in many cases it is the rule of exogamy or the kinship system itself, which is decisive, without taking real relationships, apart from those of the first degree, into account. Thus prohibition is not always expressed in terms of degrees of real kinship but refers to individuals who use certain terms in addressing one another.

In the preface to the second edition of *The Elementary Structures of Kinship*, Levi-Strauss writes that "many new facts and the development of my own thought mean that now-a-days I would no longer express myself in the same way. He believes "that the prohibition of incest is to be explained entirely in terms of sociological causes" (1970 : XXVIII). Although he says so, he does not provide an alternative solution to his earlier appraisal of incest taboo. He continues to consider 'incest prohibitions' as the theoretical counterpart of his definition of 'elementary structures'. For him 'incest prohibitions' comprise the ultimate reason for the very existence of elementary structures'. He avers that his proposal is to 'trace the line of demarcation between the two orders guided by the presence or absence of articulated speech" (1970 : XXIX). But in fact, says Korn, "that he traces the line of demarcation by the presence/absence of the incest prohibitions themselves" (1973 : 9). The concepts of 'nature' and 'culture' are related to Levi-Strauss's own definition of 'incest prohibitions'. This raises the question, as to what is the logic of relationship between these concepts and incest prohibitions.

He criticises Westermarck (1891), Durkheim (1898) and Frazer (1919) who have dealt with this problem, and have explained it either by reference to natural causes or to cultural phenomena. And alternatively when taking into account the double character-natural and cultural-of the phenomenon, they proposed an extrinsic connection between them (Korn, 1973 : 9). But for Levi-Strauss, 'incest prohibition' is neither purely cultural nor purely natural in origin; it belongs to both domains and functions as a bridge. Being the bridge between nature and culture it is at the same time universal and governed by rules. He says that "no empirical analysis can determine the point of transition between natural and cultural facts, nor how they are connected. It can only be understood either by the presence or absence of rules in patterns of behavior removed from instinctual determinism" (1970 : 8). Thus 'incest taboo' marks the introduction of 'culture' into human life. This obviously leads us to examine the characteristics of 'nature', 'culture' and 'prohibition' of incest' as envisaged by Levi-Strauss. For him 'nature' is universal, spontaneous, non-normative, repetitive and represents biological heredity. 'Culture' on the other hand, is particular, non-spontaneous, normative, accumulative and expresses the cultural fact of alliance (1970 : 8-30). He argues that 'everything universal in man relates to the natural order', and avers that the prohibition of incest is universal, and again, prohibition of incest is a rule. Therefore, it belongs to both domains, and inseparably combines, two characteristics which recognize the conflicting features of two mutually exclusive orders (1970 : 8).

The defining characteristics of 'nature' and 'culture' constitute pairs of opposites. There are some problems concerning the demarcation of the sets defining the domains of 'nature' and 'culture' in the context of the phenomenon of the 'prohibition of incest'. Nature is universal, so also the prohibition of incest and culture is governed by rules, so also the prohibition of incest. Thus incest taboo is a bridge between these two distinct domains.

'Incest Prohibition' constitutes a rule, and as such, it is an institutionalized deviation from random sexual behavior among certain social categories. For Levi-Strauss 'incest taboo' has an important functional value. It "asserts that natural distribution should not be the basis of social practice regarding women; and "the first logical end of the incest prohibition is to freeze women within the family, so that their distribution, or the competition for them, is within the group, and under group and not private control" (1970 : 44-45).

Incest prohibitions constitute some sort of organizations under which each man receives the daughter or sister of another man as his wife". "In point of fact, marriage rules do not always merely prohibit a kinship circle, but occasionally also fix one within which marriage must necessarily take place, under pain of the same scandal as would result if the prohibition itself were violated" (Levi-Strauss, 1970 : 45).

The prohibition of incest is not merely a prohibition because while prohibiting it also orders. "Like exogamy, which is its widened social application, the prohibition of incest is a rule of reciprocity. The woman whom one does not take, is, for that very reason, offered up" (Levi-Strauss, 1970 : 51). Sometimes she is offered to an institutionally defined group, and sometimes to an indeterminate collectivity.

Prohibition of incest and endogamy 'constitute the basis for the distribution of women in marriage, and they in certain social systems connote a principle of reciprocity, which is 'expressed in kinship terminology and the corresponding set of marriage rules'. According to Levi-Strauss reciprocity is a feature of 'those kinship systems that can be defined as an elementary', in which all the possible spouses are classified into two categories: prohibited and prescribed. Elementary contain a distinction between parallel cousins and cross-cousins...for maintaining an indefinite extensible balance of matrimonial exchanges between consanguineal groups' (See Korn, 1973 : 15). "This distinction", says Korn, "is nothing else than the positive aspect of a rule of which the prohibition of incest...represents only the negative aspect" (1973 : 15).

Prescription of a certain social category in some kinship systems operates as the reverse rule of incest prohibitions. And prescriptive systems or elementary structures "exist because there is a basic principle of reciprocity underlying the incest prohibitions" (Korn, 1973 : 15). Korn maintains that one cannot prove that the existence of the principle of reciprocity contributes to the existence of the prescriptive system in isolation of the prohibition of incest (1973 : 15). Prohibition of incest is universal, whereas prescriptive system is found in less number of societies. If "every prohibition is at the same time...a prescription", then, prohibition of incest should invariably follow a prescriptive rule of marriage (Korn, 1973 : 15). This correlation is not empirically valid.

Prescription and Preference

Levi-Strauss's concept of 'elementary structures' is considered in structural parlance as a useful analytical scheme for the study of kinship systems.

It is incumbent here to recall Levi-Strauss's definition of 'elementary' and 'complex structures'. He says that "elementary structures of kinship are those systems...which prescribe marriage with a certain type of relative" and "the term complex structures is reserved for systems which...leave the determination of the spouse to other mechanisms" (1970 : XXIII).

Although Levi-Strauss's own definition of elementary structure goes alongwith prescription, he himself disagrees with Needham's interpretation of 'elementary structures' as prescriptive systems. He seems to be arguing that his use of the terms 'prescriptive' and 'preferential' freely is not random rather purposive. The notions of prescription and preference are relative for him. He avers that "a preferential is prescriptive when envisaged at the model level; a prescriptive system must be preferential when envisaged on the level of reality" (1970 : XXXIII).

Needham states that in Levi-Strauss's work "there is no operational definition of preference" (1971 : 125). In reply to this Levi-Strauss asserts that he has employed the notions of preference and obligation indifferently; however, "they do not connote different social realities, but rather correspond to slightly differing ways in which man envisages the same reality (1970 : XXXI-XXXII). Further he says that "a fundamental misunderstanding is bound to arise if the opposition between 'elementary structure' and 'complex structures' becomes assimilated to that between 'prescriptive marriage' and 'preferential marriage, and if one is then substituted for the other" (1970 : XXXIII). What he means is that an 'elementary structure' is equally prescriptive or preferential, and has to do with a theoretical issue. Levi-Strauss's definition of 'elementary structure' implies the existence of a positive rule concerning marriage between certain category of persons.

According to Levi-Strauss "all systems of kinship and marriage contain an 'elementary' core which manifests itself in the incest prohibition (See Korn, 1973 : 37). Thus prohibition or prescription of marriage with a person of a particular social category constitutes the 'elementary' core of a kinship system. In other words 'elementary' structure goes along with the rules of prescription or prohibition affecting marriage. On the other hand 'complex structures' are concerned with choice

Therefore : Prohibition = elementary (1)
Choice = complex (2)

As regards models he states that 'societies which...have a mechanical model to determine prohibited marriages and rely on a statistical model for those which are permissible" (1969 : 284). And that being the case the typology of prohibited and permissible marriages implies the following code :

Prohibition = mechanical model (3)
Choice = statistical model (4)

Logically from (1) and (3), says Korn that "we can deduce that an ideal 'elementary structure' is to be represented by a 'mechanical model', and from (2) and (4) that an ideal 'complex structure' is to be represented by a 'statistical model'.

In this endeavour to illustrate the difference between mechanical and statistical models with the help of the rules of marriage Levi-Strauss writes that in primitive societies "these laws can be expressed in models calling for actual grouping of the individuals according to kin or clan, these are mechanical models. No such distribution exists in our own society, where types of marriage are determined by the size of the primary and secondary groups to which prospective mates belong, social fluidity, amount of information and the like...it would be a statistical model" (1969 : 283-84). From this it is evident that Levi-Strauss classifies his own society as a 'complex structure', and hence we find that :

Elementary Structure	=	mechanical model	(5)
Complex Structure	=	Statistical model	(6)

Dealing with the criteria of prescription and preference Levi-Strauss writes that "the sole difference between prescriptive marriage and preferential marriage is at the level of model. It corresponds to the difference which I have since proposed between what I call a 'mechanical model' and a 'statistical model'..." (1970 : XXXV). From this one can deduce that :

Prescription	=	mechanical	(7)
Preferential	=	statistical	(8)

From (5) and (7) and from (6) and (8) Korn (1973 : 38) deduces the following :

Elementary	=	prescriptive	(9)
Complex	=	preferential	(10)

Korn (1937-38) quotes Levi-Strauss who states "that an elementary structure can be equally preferential or prescriptive" (1970 : XXXIII). And in support of this Korn (1973 : 38) draws the following logical conclusions :

Prescription	=	preference
Elementary	=	complex

However, Levi-Strauss has made it clear that "neither prescription nor preference is the test of an elementary structure" (1970 : XXXIII-IV).

Models : Prospects and Problems

Construction and casting of scientific models are part of the general aims of a structuralist enterprise. Scientific procedure of structuralism involves observation of phenomena, their description, analysis and classification as well as formulation of laws which govern the relationship between phenomena. The important aim of structuralism is the discovery of 'invariants beyond the empirical diversity of human societies'. Structural models help to reduce the multiplicity of empirical observations to a small number of manageable variables. Theoretically they make the observed ethnographic data intelligible and manageable, "and also allow for the delineation of structures and for the logical experimentation with, or deductive manipulation of scientific facts" (Scholte, 1973 : 669). Structures as models make scientific explanation of phenomena possible. They serve the ultimate aim of cultural anthropology, i.e., the discovery of relations between phenomena. The delineation of structure in systematic terms permits classification of social morphologies or types, which is an important analytical step, since, "a morphological study is the basis of all scientific investigation" (See Scholte, 1973 : 669). Social life is a system in which all elements are 'origanically related' to constitute a "total social phenomenon or pattern". the socio-cultural components are all part of a whole. In Levi-Strauss's opinion "there is a close relationship between the concept of transformation and the concept of structure" (1960a : 30). Structure does not imply haphazard arrangement of elements, but it must meet the requirement of a system, that is demonstrating internal cohesiveness, which is inaccessible to observation in an isolated system, be revealed in the study of transformations, through which the similar properties in apparently different systems are brought to light (Levi-Strauss, 1967 : 31). The notion of holism is indeed appealing, but it is not quite amenable to description.

The other characteristics of Levi-Strauss's structural model, namely, predictive value and exhaustiveness of the models demand rigorous scientific activity, that is, the transempirical epistemology. The third requirement involves experimentation, that is, a "set of procedures aiming at ascertaining how a given model will react when subjected to change and at comparing models of the same or different types" (Levi-Strauss, 1969 : 280). Experimentation leads to the delineation of the final characteristic of models. They make immediately intelligible by exhaustively accounting for the observed facts. But Levi-Strauss has been criticized for having drawn a categorical distinction between the levels of observation and experimentation which leads him "to deny the empirical reality of the positional models built in order to explain a body of social phenomena" (Nutini 1965 : 277). Nutini avers that Levi-Strauss has not provided any analytical argument in support of the usefulness of this distinction, which would have clarified the substantive and epistemological distinction of such a stand. He alleges that Levi-Strauss does not explain the meaning of the terms "real" or "reality", as he uses them in expressing the epistemological status of the models vis-a-vis empirical phenomena (1965 : 278).

Structural models and their empirical correlates may be

defined in terms of their proximity to or distance from the unconscious structure of human brain, and this has correspondence to Levi-Strauss's distinction between a culture's "homemade" models and the models constructed by the anthropologist. He maintains that though we should never underscore the ethnographic importance of indigenous models, we should remember that "conscious models, which are usually known as 'norms', are by definition very poor ones, since they are not intended to explain he phenomena but to perpetuate them" (1969 : 281). Therefore, he maintains that the "native conscious representations, important as they are, may be just as remote from unconscious reality as any other" (1969 : 282). In view of this, the ethnographer should seek to reduce conscious models to the unconscious basis that is said to underlie them and which determines their manifest reality (see Scholte 1973: 671).

"The relation of mechanical and statistical models to infrastructural reality is somewhat more difficult to determine than that of unconscious and conscious models" (Scholte, 1973 : 671). Mechanical and Statistical models are distinguished in terms of the "relation between the scale of the model and that of the phenomena" (Levi-Strauss, 1969 : 283). Thus they are characterized by their epistemological function; whereas unconscious and conscious models are defined in ontological terms. The scientific purpose of both mechanical and statistical models is epistemological, that is, to recognize and isolate levels of reality from a strategic point of view (Levi-Strauss, 1969 : 284).

Structuralism is criticized for its "relational logic of the synchronic, universal and unconscious mind" which generate "the empirical givens of historical, particular and conscious circumstances". Scholte says that "we can document the underlying and syntactical operations of this generative and transformational logic by means of inductive, descriptive or empirical procedures, and by means of deductive, manipulative, or experimental methods" (1973 : 688). This paradigm rests on scientific rationalism. The empiricist paradigm criticizes structuralism because it is unempirical and its procedures are abstract and circular.

This apart, there is also phenomenological or dialectical criticism against structuralism. This criticism involves crucial insights into the limitations of structuralism. There is a debate currently going on between structural anthropology and phenomenological or dialectical philosophy. It revolves around two sets of related issues : "the nature of history and the use of diachronic explanations on the one hand and the definition of meaning and the applicability of linguistic methods on the other" (Scholte, 1973 : 689). Each of these entails certain objectives, such as, 'irreducible objectivity or socio-cultural mediation of scientific activity'. However, notwithstanding the opposition from phenomenology and dialectical philosophy structuralism will continue to grow in strength. It would succeed in its effort towards 'self-objectification' and 'making the most intimate subjectivity into a means of objective demonstration. Phenomenology postulates a continuity between 'experience and reality'; and the resultant illusions of subjectivity" are incommensurable with a truely scientific mission : to understand. Being in relation to itself, and not in relation to oneself" (see Scholte, 1973 : 690). Structuralism's premise rests on 'reflection, discourse, and historicity' which are 'reducible to a universal infrastructure that is objective, systematic and synchronic'. Structural enthropology seeks to complement comparative objectivity with existential reality. It mediates the relation between objective necessities and subjective plans (see Scholte, 1973 : 692). It throws new light on social structure, comparative religion and scientific methods.

References

Durkheim, Emile,	1962	RULES OF SOCIOLOGICAL METHOD, New York : Free Press.
Firth, J.R.	1964	Ethnographic Analysis and Language with reference to Malinowski's views IN MAN AND CULTURE : An evaluation of the work of Bronislaw Malinowski, ed. R. Firth, pp. 93-118, New York : Harper and Row.
Leach, Edmund, R.	1970	LEVI-STRAUSS. London : Collins.
Levi-Strauss, C.	1946	French Sociology. In TWENTIETH CENTURY SOCIOLOGY, ed. Georges Gurvitch and W.E. Moore, pp. 503-37. New York Philosophical Library.
Levi-Strauss, C.	1950	INTRODUCTION a l'oeuvre de Marcel Mauss. In Marcel Mauss, *Sociologic anthropologie*, pp. IX-III. Paris : Presses Universitaires de France.
	1962	THE SAVAGE MIND : London : Weidenfeld and Nicolson.
	1963	ROUSSEAU : The Father of Anthropology

UNESCO : Courier 16.

1963 b TOTEMISM, Boston : Beacon Press.

1967 THE SCOPE OF ANTHROPOLOGY, London : Cape.

Levi-Strauss, C. 1969 a Structural Analysis in Linguistics and in Anthropology. In STRUCTURAL ANTHROPOLOGY, PP. 31-54, New York: Basic Books.

1969 b Language and the Analysis of Social Laws, In STRUCTURAL ANTHROPOLOGY, PP. 55-66. New York: Basic Books.

1969 c The Concept of Archaism in Anthropology. In STRUCTURAL ANTHROPOLOGY, PP. 101-119. New York: Basic Books.

1969 d Do Dual Organizations Exist ? In STRUCTURAL ANTHROPOLOGY, PP. 132-163. New York : Basic Books.

1969 e The Structural Study of Myth. IN STRUCTURAL ANTHROPOLOGY, PP. 206-231. New York : Basic Books.

1969 f Structure and Dialectis. In STRUCTURAL ANTHROPOLOGY, PP. 232-241, New York : Basic Books.

1969 g Social Structure. In STRUCTURAL ANTHROPOLOGY, PP. 277-323, New York : Basic Books.

1970 THE ELEMENTARY STRUCTURES OF KINSHIP, London : Eyre and Spottiswoode.

Mauss, Marcel 1954 THE GIFT. Trans. I. Cunnison, Illinois: Glencoe.

Needham, Rodney 1971 RETHINKING KINSHIP AND MARRIAGE. London : Tavistock.

Nutini, Hugo G 1965 Some considerations on the Nature of Social Structure and Model Building: A Critique of Claude Levi-Strauss and Edmund Leach. AMERICAN ANTHROPOLOGIST 67 : 707-31.

Scholte, Bob 1973 The Structural Anthropology of Claude Levi-Strauss. In HAND BOOK OF SOCIAL AND CULTURAL ANTHROPOLOGY. ed. J.J. Honigmann PP. 637-716, Chicago : Rand McNally.

Tax, Sol, ed. 1953 *An Appraisal of Anthropology Today.* Chicago : University of Chicago Press.

Part—II

Edward J. Jay

LEVELS OF SOCIOCULTURAL INTEGRATION IN INDIAN SOCIETY : A PRELIMINARY STATEMENT

INTRODUCTION : DIVERSITY IN INDIAN SOCIETY

The extreme diversity of Indian society is so well known that hardly a book, article or paper can be written without acknowledging at least some aspect of this diversity or providing a disclaimer indicating that the conclusions may not pertain to *every* group, religion, region or other dimension of the sociocultural whole. Most frequently identified diverse segments are : (1) region and/or ethnicity; (2) language; (3) religion; (4) caste; (5) social class: and (6) demographic characteristics such as age or gender. Obviously there are others, such as occupation or education, though they may be incorporated into the above categories or cut across them in various ways. Indeed, many aspects of social diversity, including some of the above, are found in any complex society and are not unique to India. However, in my teaching and in discussions with people who are unfamiliar with Indian society and culture, what seems to be most surprising to students and others is the *extent* and *extreme expression* of some of these differences. For example, except for caste (at least in its specifically Hindu form), the above elements of diversity exist in the United States as well. But regional, ethnic and linguistic differences within India are elaborated to a point where communication becomes difficult across these boundaries and customary behaviour within many institutional systems (marriage, kinship, inheritance, religion, etc.) is so varied that we seem to be dealing with Indian cultures rather than a single unified culture. Moreover, the socio-political consequences of many of these differences are considerable, often leading to competition and conflict. Neophytes and experienced India hands alike frequently express surprise that such heterogeneity can be accommodated in a single society.

In addition to these often mentioned aspects of diversity, another significant dimension of variation which characterizes Indian society as a whole is what I refer to here as "levels of sociocultural integration," borrowing the term from Steward (1955) but adapting it for specific application to Indian society. Steward (1955 : 47) introduced this concept to facilitate the analysis of "national cultures," which he said are "divisible into two general kinds of features : first, those that function and must be studied on a national level; second, those that pertain to sociocultural segments or subgroups of the population." He (1955 : 47-48) felt that "the methods of direct observation used by ethnology" would be appropriate for the study of subcultural groups but "not to national institutions." He (1955 : 51) maintained that "the distinctions between the different aspects of national culture clearly imply that a great many different methods must be used to study any national culture in its totality." In his formulation of the term "level of sociocultural integration," a national "culture" as a whole becomes such a level, and although he implies that a nation-state may include several such levels, he does not distinguish clearly among them (1955 : 51-52) :

> In the growth continuum of any culture, there is a succession of organizational types which are not only increasingly complex but which represent new emergent forms. The concept is fairly similar to that of organizational levels in biology. In culture, simple forms, such as those represented by the family or band, do not wholly disappear when a more complex state of development is reached, nor do they merely survive fossil-like, as the concepts of folkways and mores formerly assumed. They gradually become modified as specialized, dependent parts of new kinds of total configurations. The many-faceted national culture previously delineated represents a very high developmental level.

Part of the difficulty in applying Steward's formulation may be the exclusive emphasis on "culture" without including aspects of social structure which might apply to the concept of levels operating within a single system. My intention, however, is not to critique Steward's work, but to utilize certain aspects of it in conceptualizing the structure of a civilization as a whole, which, of course is larger and more complex even than the concept of a national state.

Clearly one of the defining characteristics of civilization as a type of society is the contrast between rural and urban dimensions. It is this distinction which led to Redfield's (1947) formulation of the "folk society" and the notion of the "folk-urban continuum." But modern complex societies, particularly those such as India, which have developed from a base of traditional agrarian civilization, cannot be characterized in terms of a simple dichotomous rural-urban dimension. If we look at levels of sociocultural integration in modern India it is possible to discern diversity in lifestyles, political and economic relations, religious activity and many other variables ranged along a continuum from very simple, relatively isolated rural communities to the most complex, technologically advanced and highly modernized urban centers.

Yet this continuum is divided or marked by social units which have sociocultural reality and are not just arbitrarily chosen points. The easiest way to think about these units is in bounded, coresidential terms, but this is to some extent an oversimplification, and they have significance in other ways as well. In operational terms these units are used here to identify four distinct "levels of sociocultural integration" : (1) tribal village; (2) peasant village; (3) town; and (4) city. In this paper I attempt, in a preliminary way, to refine these labels and explore their significance in relation to diversity in Indian society. Although the existence of these social units certainly is well known, and the characteristics of specific places have been described in detail by social scientists, I believe that the significance of these four points along the folk-urban continuum in India, as dimensions of diversity or variation *as such*, has not received much attention.

Ethnographically we have looked at village after village, town after town, but have not formulated explicitly a conception of how village life *in general* differs from town life *in general*. I feel that these levels of sociocultural integration cut across ethnic and linguistic regions in India and are helpful in understanding both similarities and differences within the total Indian sociocultural system. Those familiar with Redfield's work will no doubt recognize his inspiration here. In *The Folk Culture of Yucatan* (1941), he presented a comparison of four communities existing contemporaneously on the Yucatan peninsula of Mexico. These were : Tusik, a tribal community; Chan Kom, a peasant village; Dzitas, a town; and Merida, a city.

Obviously, although the culture of Yucatan is vastly different from that of India, there are structural-functional similarities among the four communities and comparable ones in India. Moreover, what I particularly want to stress is that the *interrelationships* among these four types of community are roughly parallel in the two civilizations.

Although the concept of "level of sociocultural integration" is Steward's and not Redfield's, I believe it is an apt designation for the kind of phenomena dealt with here. Redfield's study in Yucatan was a *synchronic* rather than a *diachronic* comparison of four communities, so employing a term such as "stages" to refer to them would be misleading, although the study, and his later formulation of the folk-urban continuum in his paper "The Folk Society" (1947) do have implications for evolutionary theory. This aspect of the formulation, however, is not the primary objective of this paper. The concept of "level," as I use it, refers to certain sociocultural characteristics of community life which exist contemporaneously within the same complex society or civilization.

A term which *has* been borrowed from Redfield is "folk." I deplore the continued use of alternatives such as "primitive", "simple", "small scale", and even worse "savage" (as in the writings of Levi-Strauss) in contemporary anthropological literature. Not only are these terms derogatory, they are inaccurate in their implications. "Primitive" implies that people so designated are comparable in their characteristics to our prehistoric ancestors; such comparability must be demonstrated, not assumed, and the chances are that it is wildly inaccurate. Societies referred to as "simple" may be simple in technology compared with modern industrialized societies, but in kinship structure, sociopolitical conceptions and behaviour, ideology and other aspects of social life may be every bit as "complex" as modern societies or even more so. The alternative "small scale", used by a number of researchers, is vague and somehow fails to capture the essence of the contrast being sought in comparative discussions of types of society. How "small" must a society be to be considered "small scale ?" As wholes, China and India are enormous societies, yet contain within them sub-units of a different and smaller scale. Moreoever, why should size alone be used as the diagnostic criterion in comparisons ?

The term "savage" implies the absence of social controls, rules of ethics and etiquette, elaborate philosophical systems and perhaps esthetics (art and music), despite the observations of generations of ethnographers that so-called "savage" or "primitive" peoples do not conform in the slightest measure to any of these stereotypes. "Savage" is often contrasted unfavourably with a "civilized" lifestyle despite the irony of large-scale warfare, genocide, slavery, colonial exploitation, sociopolitical disorganization, environmental destruction, drug and alcohol abuse, excessive crime, mental illness and high suicide rates, etc., associated with so-called "civilized" societies ! Anthropologists, of all people, should know better than to employ terms which are inaccurate as well as derogatory when referring to types of human society. Worse, such terms and characterizations are stereotypes and have no place in scientific discourse.[1]

The term "folk" suggested by Redfield may have its own ambiguities, but it is clearly less derogatory and has the advantage of being understood as a dimension of life in complex societies as well, as in the terms "folklore" and "folksong." Therefore "...it suggests the inclusion in our comparisons of peasant and rustic people who are not wholly independent of cities..." Redfield (1947 : 293). As employed by Redfield, the concepts of "folk" and "urban" are not dichotomous, bounded classes, but *ideal polar types* constructed by using a number of variables such as relative isolation, types of social relationships (communal or associational), relative presence or absence of social classes, ethnic diversity and subgroups, degree of secularization, etc. Although there seemed to be much misunderstanding of the point at the time he wrote "The Folk Society" (1947),[2] empirically real or *actual* human societies were to be placed along a conceptual continuum between these polar types; few if any known societies would be at or even close to either end of the continuum.

In this formulation, a society is not just "primitive" as opposed to "complex" or "civilized," but it is *more or less* "folklike," and to some extent every society has its "folk" dimensions. As an example, in India, so-called "tribal" peoples are the most "folklike;" urbanites are the least "folklike," but not totally devoid of all "folk" characteristics. Although my purpose here is not to revive old controversies regarding the folk-urban continuum and its usefulness,[3] I feel that some introductory discussion of the terms used in the paper will be helpful in the discussion of social heterogeneity that follows.

With these preliminary observations and definitions out of the way we can turn to a discussion of the four levels of sociocultural integration in Indian society which are the main subject of this paper.

Levels of Sociocultural Integration in India

General comments

The formulation of levels of sociocultural integration presented here results from a lifelong project of social anthropological research in India begun in 1958-60 with fieldwork among the Hill Maria Gonds of Bastar, as the basis of a Ph.D. dissertation presented to the University of Chicago.[4] This research focused on a single tribal village known as Orcha, with a population of 200, and its ties to a wider area. Although I do not take this village or this tribal area to be "typical" of all tribal peoples in India, for me it formed the basis of a concept of "tribal" which does have wider application in the Indian context. I hope to make this clear in the discussion below.

The second, or peasant level in my research is represented by the Chhattisgarhi village for which I use the pseudonym Devagaon, located about twenty-five miles southeast of the city of Raipur in Madhya Pradesh, studied initially for eight months in 1967-68 and revisited for shorter periods of time in 1970 and 1977-78.[5] At the time, the population of Devagaon was about 1,000, and although the village is only about 150 miles north of Orcha, certain structural features of the community as well as the general culture of the area differ markedly from that of Orcha. A general description of the two little communities has been published as "A Comparison of Tribal and Peasant Villages in India" in the Journal of the Indian Anthropological Society (Jay 1974). Some of the conclusions of that paper will be summarized below.

The third, or town level is represented by a 1977-78 study of Devagaon's neighbours,[6] the twin towns of Rajim and Navapara Rajim, with a collective population of about 20,000. To date I have not compared systematically the characteristics of these towns with the village of Devagaon, but hope to soon in a book in preparation titled *Village and Town in Central India*. Some remarks relevant to such a comparison, however, are included in the present paper. In my view town life in India constitutes a distinct level of sociocultural integration intermediate between the village and the city.

Since Chhattisgarh is an area defined by distinctive linguistic, cultural and geographical characteristics (Babb 1975), after completion of the Rajim/Navapara Rajim study, my intention was to conduct research in the largest community of the region, the city of Raipur, as representative of the fourth or "urban" level of sociocultural integration. During my previous research in Chhattisgarh I had already observed extensive connections between people of the countryside and the city of Raipur. Many villagers and townspeople had relatives in Raipur; some wealthier families sent their children there for higher education; people sought employment there; and frequent interaction with institutional structures such as administrative offices, courts and hospitals was evident. Therefore Raipur would have been the most appropriate focus of urban study, holding the culture of Chhattisgarh constant while looking at structural differences between city and surrounding contryside. Moreover, with its population of approximately 340,000, Raipur seemed to be a manageable entity for my purposes. Accordingly, I applied for and received a Senior Fellowship from the American Institute of Indian Studies to conduct the research in 1989-90, but unfortunately government clearance for anthropological research in Chhattisgarh was not forthcoming, forcing me to consider various alternative urban locations for study. After considerable thought and consultations with knowledgeable Indian administrator acquaintances, personal friends and social science colleagues concerning the characteristics of urban centers in other cultural regions of Madhya Pradesh, I finally decided on the state capital of Bhopal as the place of research. Although outside the Chhattisgarhi culture area, the experience in Bhopal has given me a sense of urban life and its contrasting patterns with rural India. This experience in part constitutes the basis of the observations on the urban level of sociocultural integration which follow. Bhopal's population, according to the 1981 Census of India, is about 671,000, which makes it unfortunately a less manageable entity than Raipur for study by a single researcher. However, by focusing on just one middle class *mohalla*, I was able to conduct research on tradition and modernity in an urban environment which I believe to be sufficient for conclusions concerning urban life in contrast to tribal, peasant and town life.

It may be possible, in the Indian context, to concep-tualize a still more urban, complex, heterogenous level of sociocultural integration, that of the super-city or "megalopolis." In various trips to India I have spent a considerable amount of time in Delhi and have visited at least briefly a number of other large cities, such as Bombay, Madras, Calcutta and Ahmedabad, although I have conducted no formal research in any of these urban centers. However, in an impressionistic way I sense in them features of social life distinctly different from those in relatively small cities like Bhopal. Moreover, studies of various aspects of life in large cities abound. [Singer's (1958, 1968, and 1972) research in Madras is especially relevant and significant]. Some general comments concerning this possible fifth level, therefore, are included in this paper, though the issue is not explored in depth.

Although the conception of "levels of sociocultural integration" presented here could be constructed solely on the basis of the published literature, I believe that my personal experiences living and working in communities at all four levels have resulted in a set of vivid impressions which could not have been acquired through reading alone. These impressions have served to inspire and guide me in the general propositions offered here. To some extent I have also incorporated perceptions gained from various theoretical or ethnographic publications to support or reinforce my position, but this paper is not intended to be a general or comprehensive review of the relevant literature.

The tribal level of sociocultural integration

The term "tribe" has been used extensively in the Indian context by anthropologists, administrators, politi-cians and laymen, but without a standard definition and without, in my view, much accuracy in application. Rather than review the various definitions that have been proposed (an excessive time and space exercise without much purpose), I would like to suggest that as a *type of society* the term has very little meaning with respect to India. As I argued in my paper comparing tribal and peasant villages in India (Jay 1974 : 40-41), today :

> ...the word 'tribe' applied to most *adivasi* peoples in India is a misnomer...The literal meaning of the word *adivasi* is, of course, autochthone or aborigine, implying that these people are the original, non-Aryan inhabitants of the land. If taken in its literal sense, then, *adivasi* would have to be applied to the people of the Harappan civilization, as well as to the many inhabitants of contemporary India's hills and jungles to whom it is ordinarily applied. Moreover, the Dravidian peoples of southern India should in the same historical sense be referred to as *adivasi*, regardless of their level of cultural development.

Needless to say, such characterizations would not please many Indians today, and indeed, serve only to highlight the state of confusion that exists regarding the question : "what is meant by 'tribal' ?"

In his *Profiles in Ethnology* (1978), Elman R. Service distinguishes five "societal levels" : the band, the tribe, the chiefdom, the primitive state and modern folk societies, i.e., peasants. This classification may serve his purposes, but if one seeks to distinguish among societal levels *within* a single civilization, the scheme I have proposed (tribe, peasant, town and city) appears to be more accurate and more useful. Nevertheless, in contrasting bands and tribes he emphasizes certain features of tribal society absent in bands, such as the existence of *pantribal* associations like clans, "age grades, kindreds, secret societies and clubs for such single special purposes as the curing of illness or the performing of particular ceremonies" (Service 1978 : 5). On the other hand, "tribes, like bands, are *segmental*—the corporate residential units are alike, largely economically self-sufficient, generally equivalent in organization, and therefore capable of considerable autonomy" (1978 : 6). Obviously bands are smaller units than tribes and ecologically usually are associated with hunter/gatherers or nomadic pastoralists. In ecological adaptation tribes are more frequently associated with horticulture or agriculture, though in many cases hunting and collecting or pastoralism are carried on as supplements to cultivation and sometimes there is a transhumant pattern, with semi-sedentary villages established during the growing season but breaking down into bands, kindreds or families during the rest of the year. Interestingly, many of the features which Service proposes as distinctive of "tribes" are characteristic of both "tribal" and "peasant" peoples within Indian society.

In the paper cited above (1974 : 39) I stated that "the word 'tribe' to me implies a homogeneous ethnic group with a specific sense of identity based on common language and culture, large enough to be a viable entity, but small enough to be mobilized for common action." I go on to observe that most so-called "tribal" people in India really are peasants, that is, "part-societies with part-cultures," to borrow Kroeber's (1948 : 284) well-known phrase. In general India's "tribals" are ethnic groups which occupy certain well-defined territories, sometimes to the exclusion or near exclusion of other ethnic groups, but which are not organized for common action (except sometimes politically in the modern nation state of India) and which, depending on the degree of isolation from the wider society, maintain a language and culture relatively distinct from the surrounding communities. Orans (1965 : xi) observes that the Santal tribe of Bihar, numbering over three million people at the time of his study, "has never been politically unified so far as historical records indicate," but he employs the term "encysted society" in referring to these people because they constitute a kind of society within a society (1965 : 126). This term is useful in conceptualizing the tribal level of sociocultural integration in India, because tribals in general manifest a certain level of social solidarity but at the same time are so intimately involved with the society and culture of the wider society that rarely can they be considered independent entities. Indeed the Santal, due to what Orans (1965 : 123) calls the "rank concession syndrome" and its resultant pattern of emulation of the dominant society and culture, occupy an ambivalent position in which emulation means loss of identity but failure to emulate concedes power and privilege to those around them, i.e., non-tribals or "Hindus." He refers to this as the "emulation-solidarity conflict" (1965 : 55-56) :

> The very orientation and practices which served so well to separate the Santal from the Hindu are simultaneously the attributes of low status in the prevailing system of caste ranking. To maintain these practices...is to forego the opportunities of rank improvement through emulation of high Hindu practices. The ambivalence which this situation arouses, and which continually manifests itself in the course of Santal-Hindu relations, shall be referred to as the "emulation-solidarity conflict."

The situation among the Santal is further complicated by the fact that many of them now live and work in an industrial setting in the steel town of Jamshedpur, though the majority continue to be employed in agriculture and related occupations. This has led to much stronger acculturation pressures and involvement in regional and even national politics. Clearly, compared with the Hill Maria Gonds of Bastar (described below), the Santal are much further along the folk-urban continuum, constituting a more fully-developed peasantry and a partial urban proletariat.

Tribal peoples in remote border areas such as Assam, Manipur and Nagaland maintain especially distinct cultures because they never have been incorporated fully into Indian civilization. But the groups on the Indian peninsula have been in continuous first-hand contact with wider structures in the civilization for centuries or even millenia, and their contemporary distinctiveness is largely relative to the degree of isolation. What then defines the "tribal" level of sociocultural integration as the term is used here ? How can groups as disparate as the Hill Maria Gonds and the Santals both be characterized as "tribal" ? In my view the key to understanding this dilemma or paradox is in the word "relative." Some rural communities in India are smaller and more isolated than others with respect to economic, political, religious and other institutional systems of the wider society. Historically, *some* of these communities are *relatively* homogeneous in culture, casteless and classless in organization, possessing of certain now archaic institutions such as the adolescent dormitory, and in extreme cases, relying on a typical, pre-agricultural forms of subsistence, such as swidden horticulture, hunting and collecting.

A good example of a "tribal" society in this sense was the Hill Maria Gond ethnic group when I studied one of their villages in 1958-60. At that time these people lived in the hilly, jungle-covered area of west-central Bastar, M.P., known as the "Abujhmar" or "unknown place." During the period of research there were about 10,000 people classified traditionally as Hill Maria Gonds, or as they called themselves, Koitur.[7] The major ethnographic characteristics of the Hill Maria Gonds, as represented at Orcha, and a detailed analysis of their ties to the wider society, have been covered in previous publications (Jay 1961, 1965a, 1965b, 1966, 1967, 1968, 1971, 1974). Here I wish to emphasize only certain salient features of their sociocultural organization which make them representative of the most basic, or "tribal" level of sociocultural integration in Indian society.

In comparing the tribal village of Orcha with the peasant village of Devagaon I observe (Jay 1974 : 63) :

> Beginning with the principal coresidental group, the village, we note that Orcha is more homogeneous in the sense that the village consists primarily of one caste, the Hill Maria Gonds....This cultural, economic and political homogeneity, plus the small size of the community, contribute to a stronger sense of social solidarity and unanimity of action than we find at Devagaon. The complexity of the latter village, consisting of more people, more castes, and certain significant sub-cultural and economic differences among the various castes and even families within the castes, results in a weakening of overall solidarity and unanimity of action.

Although caste exists as a cultural concept among the Hill Maria Gonds, their villages are not divided into sets of hierarchically arranged, endogamous units, i.e. caste segments. This absence of caste differentiation places an emphasis on "mechanical" as opposed to "organic" solidarity in Durkheim's terms. The peasant village of Devagaon, on the other hand, is divided into 20 or more caste segments at any one time, resulting in greater emphasis on organic solidarity and less on mechanical, since the various castes have different identities and often conflicting interests, but at the same time are interdependent. In general, caste identities and caste interests are significant features of the peasant level of sociocultural integration, while at the tirbal level they are embryonic :

> The concept of caste exists in both places, but the behavioural expression of caste is far more elaborate and pervasive in Devagaon. The existence of *jati sabhas*, and the sub-cultural variations from one *jati* to another provide Chhattisgarhi castes with a sense of individual distinctiveness. Moreover, caste organization, centering on the *sabha*, constitutes an organizing principle which can mobilize the caste, or a significant segment of it, for action. These horizontal ties of caste, to borrow Srinivas's (1952 : 31-32) terminology, act as a counterpoise to the vertical ties of the village. The situation is far less complex in the Abujhmar, where villages are occupied basically by a single caste and this caste dominates a wide region....A paradox posed by the term "tribe," is that for the Hill Marias at least, there is no governing body, leader, or integrating principle to bring the group as a whole together. On the other hand, many Chhattisgarhi castes do possess mechanisms contributing to the integration of the group as a whole, or at least a significant portion of it, and in this sense at least, are more "tribal" than the Marias (1974 : 63-64).

Another distinctive difference between Orcha and Devagaon is the absence of social class in Orcha, and its conspicuous presence in Devagaon. Indeed, as shifting cultivators, in the 1958-60 period the Hill Maria Gonds made no permanent claims to the land. Land use rights were based on *usufruct*—whoever uses a piece of land has rights to the crops it yields—but swidden land can be cultivated productively for only about four years. The cultivator then moves on to other available land; the vacated land will not fully regain its fertility for at least 20 years, and by then may be occupied by a new cultivator who has come along.

Under this system, wealth in the form of land cannot be

accumulated, and there is no other sufficient basis for class differentiation.[8] In fact during the research I made detailed lists of possessions, earnings and expenditures of all 35 families in Orcha and found no significant differences in wealth.

This kinship systems of the two societies are very similar. Both are strongly patrilineal, virilocal, patripotestal, and generally male-oriented and male dominated. Kinship units such as the joint family and patriclan are common to both societies. On the other hand, greater sexual permissiveness, love marriages, and a preference for cross-cousin marriage, are more characteristic of Orcha than of Devagaon. Some differences between Gond and Chhattisgarhi kinship may be related more to the fact that the Gonds are Dravidians and the Chhattisgarhis Indo-Aryan. That is, the Gond terminological system (Iroquois-Dakota) and other formal features of kinship closely parallel Dravidian peasant systems of the south. But the main point is that the overall importance of the kinship principle in regulating behaviour, particularly with respect to the strong emphasis on intra-familial bonds, is equally significant in both communities, or very nearly so. Kinship, therefore, is not a principle that can be used easily in distinguishing between the tribal and peasant levels.

On the other hand, the Hill Maria Gonds and many other tribal peoples in India include in their institutional system an adolescent dormitory, which is absent at the peasant level. Among the Hill Maria Gonds it is called the *gotul* and is limited to male participation. Among other groups, such as the Muria Gonds of northern Bastar, both males and females participate in dormitory life (Elwin 1947). This institution has absolutely no counterpart in Devagaon. Youth activities, therefore, are integrated more fully into the life of the joint family, and not divided, as at Orcha, between two different institutions.

In my previous discussion of similarities and differences between Orcha and Devagaon I observed that (1974 : 65) :

> The religious systems of Orcha and Devagaon possess certain underlying similarities, despite many surface differences. Both systems are polytheistic and concerned with crops and disease. Similar conceptions exist relative to the nature of deities and the importance of propitiating them. Absent from the Chhattisgarhi ceremonial structure is shamanism, though random possession occurs during periods of religious excitation at ceremonies....[9]
>
> Perhaps the most striking difference between the two systems is the closer connection with great tradition

> Hinduism observable at Devagaon. Readings from the Ramayana, pilgrimage to outside religious centers, the use of Brahman pandits in ceremonies, and the relatively close conformity of ceremonies to the ritual requirements of Sanskritic texts, are ways in which this connection is manifested. The Hill Maria system has no such direct connection, unless attendance at outside *melas* is so interpreted. But *melas* generally stress parochial elements in the religion, rather than universal, or at least Brahmanic ones. With respect to *melas*, Chhattisgarhi and Maria behaviour is similar, as the *mela* is an important institution in both areas.
>
> When we focus on the more local aspects of Devagaon's religious system, we note that ceremonies are not performed by Brahmans or guided by Sanskritic texts. Low-caste priests minister to the twenty-one village deities, including the smallpox goddess. Worship of the smallpox goddess, in fact, is a very similar feature of both systems. Though I do not have the space here to detail them, I could show that many specific features of ritual, not only in relation to the worship of Mata, but with respect to all forms of Maria worship, closely parallel those of Devagaon. Maria deities, as well, resemble in attributed powers and other characteristics, the "high gods" of Hinduism, especially in the local forms manifested in Devagaon. On the other hand, key features of Devagaon ritual, such as *hom jag*, worship through the sacrificial fire, are included even in these non-Brahmanic village ceremonies as well as in the Sutra-based ceremonies performed by *pandits*, but the use of fire is not a part of any Maria ceremony.

This discussion could be extended, but enough has been said to demonstrate that religious beliefs and practices in the two communities fall roughly within the same cultural sphere. In the previous article I suggested that it is "...quite proper to apply the term 'Hinduism' to both religious systems" (Jay 1974 : 66). However, relatively speaking the Maria system is a more extreme example of "little tradition" or localized Hinduism :

> Parochialism also characterizes the religion of Devagaon, but at the same time pervasive ties to the great tradition render this parochialism less extreme, and introduce or at least reinforce certain all-India religious conceptions and practices. What we find at Orcha has parallels at Devagaon. But there are many aspects of the religious system

> encountered at Devagaon which have no such parallels at Orcha. Because of Devagaon's greater richness and complexity we cannot characterize the two systems as identical (1974 : 66).

To what extent are we justified in extrapolating from the Hill Maria Gond data to a wider conception of a "tribal" level of sociocultural integration in India ? Obviously there are many variations in culture, social structure, integration into the wider society and other factors among the various peoples who have been called "tribal" in India. As long ago as 1957 Sinha attempted to define "tribals" and "peasants" in India as "two kinds of cultural systems" (1957 : 102). By comparing habitat, economy, social structure and ideological system, he concluded (1957 : 117) that :

> If we leave aside the problem of *specific historicity* for the time being and try to look upon the total social field of India touched by the Great Tradition, the tribal cultures fall within this field in terms of structural comparison. We have also seen that within this field they represent a distinctive level (relatively the lowest) of complexity. In order to make this distinction clear, it seems best to describe the tribal cultures as a special dimension, namely, the *primitive or folk* dimension of the little traditions of India. At least, on a formal level of abstraction, the folk (or tribal), peasant and urban dimensions of Indian tradition and culture-community represent a series of increasingly complex levels of socio-cultural integration with evidence of continuity in core pattern.

In a subsequent paper he compared my data from the Hill Maria Gonds with his own from the Bhumij of Barabhum and observed (1965 : 77) that :

> As we move our focus from the Abujhmarh Hill Marias to the Bhumij of Barabhum, it indeed involves a rather sharp swing from near the ideal 'tribe' pole to near the 'peasant' and 'caste' pole....Here we find a systematic and yet sharp progression toward lessening of ecological isolation and increase in ethnic heterogeneity in regional demographic pattern and in social interaction, social stratification and emergence of indigenous elite class and enlargement and diversification of the network of spatially defined social relationship with civilizational centres....The final contours of the two polarities are guided by the degree of ethnic heterogeneity and the degree of the

> complexity and hierarchy in the pattern of interaction between and within the ethnic groups of a region. The above factors, in their turn, are directly dependent on the nature of territorial isolation of the group under consideration....The kind of regularity in progression revealed by comparing two societies so obviously apart in their possible position in our ideally conceived continuum may [however] mislead us to imagine that it may be a simple task to evaluate the relative position of more nearly related societies on the proposed continuum. It is quite likely that within the proximal range, all the criteria used in defining the continua will not move at the same rate.

The point I wish to stress, following Sinha, is that not all "tribal" societies in India are alike or at exactly the same point on the continuum between "tribal" and "peasant". On the contrary, precisely because our conceptual mode is that of a continuum, it is likely that we will encounter a great range of variation among tribal peoples with respect to any of the variables used to define levels of sociocultural integration. Some groups will be far more integrated into the wider social system, hence less "folklike" than others. Indeed, there is no precise point at which tribal and peasant levels merge; the best we can do is to look at the range of variables and conceptualize communities in *relative* terms. Returning to our earlier question of how it is possible to conceptualize groups as widely disparate as the Santal and the Hill Maria Gonds as belonging to the "tribal" level of sociocultural integration, the answer is that both appear to be more "folklike" and to occupy, as a consequence, a position closer to the "folk" end of the folk-urban continuum than the Chhattisgarhi village of Devagaon (or other, similar peasant villages). However, when comparing the Santals and the Hill Maria Gonds, the Santals definitely are closer to the "peasant" level of sociocultural integration in most particulars. Because virtually all rural peoples in India are integrated into the wider society to some extent, and share with the wider society a basic corpus of cultural and structural features, in my view virtually all groups are in fact peasants. The constitutional designation of "scheduled tribes" as contrasted with "scheduled castes" is based on certain traditional and arbitrary criteria. For sociopolitical purposes the distinction may have merit, but sociologically speaking it cannot be made so sharply.

Similar points were made by Bailey in a number of works back in the fifties and sixties (1957, 1960, 1961, 1963), though contrasting "tribe" and "caste" rather than "tribe" and "peasant," in my view he complicated the conceptualization by placing emphasis on just a particular set of variables, such as clan territory ("tribal") versus village ("caste"), and by referring to tribes and castes as "societies" (rather than parts or dimensions of a single, wider society). Yet in many particulars I am in complete agreement with him, and no doubt he highlighted the *relativity* of the distinction (1961 : 15) :

> Why is it more useful to place actual tribes and caste societies on a continuum, rather than to see then as exclusive exemplifications of delimited categories ? If we persist in trying to find criteria—cultural, geographical, historical, or even sociological—which enable us to see particular societies disjunctively as *either* tribes *or* castes, but not both, then we get into difficulties. No acceptable list of definitive criteria has been produced. Even if it were produced, such a classification *of particular societies,* disjunctively into opposites, would make it difficult to understand the process by which a tribe becomes absorbed into the caste system, or holds out against it. While it might be necessary for the Administration, in the process of distributing benefits and privileges, to consider particular societies as *either* tribes *or* elements in a caste system, there is no reason why we, as sociologists, should do this.

The general proposition of conceptualizing tribal society along a continuum was also accepted (rather reluctantly) by Dumont (1962), but he too fails to dispense with the awkward comparison of *tribes* and *castes* rather than tribal and peasant communities. We shall consider the matter again in the summary and conclusions section of this paper.

The peasant level of sociocultural integration

The general characteristics of this level are, of course, at least implicit in the discussion of the tribal level, above. There now exist countless ethnographies of peasant communities in nearly all regions of India. The village of Devagaon, located on the bank of the Mahanadi in Raipur District of Madhya Pradesh is used here to represent the "peasant" level because it is the community with which I have first-hand familiarity, but not because it is "typical" or an ideal example of the type. Indeed, as suggested earlier, there is so much sociocultural variation among India's rural communities that no particular village could be characterized as "typical." In what follows I shall not try to summarize all the features of Devagaon that contrast with Orcha. That would be beyond the scope of this paper and not really necessary for our current purposes. The reader is again referred to my previous paper (Jay 1974) for a more systematic comparison of the two communities. Rather, here I will suggest only a few salient features of similarity and difference.

At the time of my initial study (1967-68) Devagaon was approximately five times as large as Orcha, with a population of about 1,000 (200 families). At Devagaon, as throughout most of Chhattisgarh, rice is the staple crop, and the majority of the community's inhabitants made their living either directly or indirectly from agriculture. In contrast to Orcha, swidden cultivation, hunting and forest-collecting were absent. The nearby town of Navapara Rajim provided easy marketing facilities for Devagaon's peasant farmers. In the 1960's there were about fifteen rice mills in town, and a grain market or *ganj* where grain provided by farmers and jobbers was sold at auction to the mill owners.

As in peasant communities all over India, the village was divided into numerous caste (*jati*) segments which displayed both vertical and horizontal relationships, to borrow Srinivas's (1952) terminology. That is, the village displayed considerable heterogeneity internally, with traditional patterns of stratified interaction governing the relationships among castes, and the families or households which represent each caste segment maintaining ties of kinship and marriage to segments in other villages. Each caste in the region was associated with a traditional occupation, though of course as elsewhere in modern India, the traditional occupation was no longer always followed, at least not by all members of the caste. In Devagaon the principal landowning caste was the Brahman, and seven of the eight Brahman households constituted a kind of "elite" of the community. The village *sarpanch*, or headman, at that time was the former feudal lord (*malguzar*) of the area, who enjoyed considerable prestige though stripped of his formal powers by the Malguzari Abolition legislation of the 1950s. When I returned to the village in 1970 the Brahman ex-*malguzar* was being challenged by a wealthy member of the Sutaha Kosta (weaver) caste for political dominance of the village.[10]

There were two castes with weaving as their traditional occupation. Besides the Sutaha Kostas (literally "cotton weavers") there were several households of Kosaha Kostas ("silk weavers"). Members of these castes did not intermarry, but both did precisely the same kind of cotton weaving only. (Silk weaving had long since been discontinued). Other occupations actively carried out by the castes traditionally associated with them were fishing (by the Kevats), herding and water-carrying (by Ravats), bamboo weaving and basket-making (by the Kararas) and leather-working (by the Chamars and the Kanojia Mehars). Through a system of contract labor called *paune pasari* the village *panchayat* hired a barber (the Nau) and blacksmith-cum-carpenter (the Karigir).

In addition to these traditional occupations, all the families of the village except those of the Brahman and Gond Thakur castes rolled *biris* (Indian leaf cigarettes) for supplementary income. Landless or nearly landless people worked for the landowners, especially the Brahman families, as field laborers or worked in town as porters, clerks and other kinds of general laborers.

Almost all the castes of Chhattisgarh at the time of the study had caste councils (*jati sabhas*), each headed by a hereditary leader referred to as *sarpanch, mukhia* or *maharaja*. These councils regulated intra-caste matters, including marriage disputes, divorce, occupational policies, caste customs and the maintenance of caste temples. Powers and policies varied by caste, but in some cases strong sanctions, including fines, ostracism, and outcasting could be brought to bear on individuals or families as a means of social control. Most councils levied dues on caste members by means of which a treasury was maintained. Funds were used mostly to make loans to individual members in need and to maintain the caste temple. Such horizontal organization was important in the context of multi-caste social structure but was absent in the Hill Maria Gond uni-caste tribal area where it could serve no useful purpose.

Other institutional comparisons could be made, such as the kinship system, but, as already noted, the general pattern and significance of kinship is not diagnostic of differences in sociocultural level, at least not for the communities here compared. Such differences as do exist appear to be related more to the Dravidian-Indo-Aryan cultural split. There are also contrasts in technology, building construction, transportation and other aspects of life which relate to the very different techno-environmental and ecological systems in the two areas. The basic point is that Devagaon exists in a complex milieu with an elaborate division of labor, caste and class distinctions, and extensive connections to wider marketing networks which contrast sharply with Orcha's relatively self-contained techno-environmental system. This general characterization will not be pursued further for lack of space, but of course the ecological and economic setting of the two communities within the wider society contrasts sharply.

The only other institutional system which I will mention here because of its interesting set of similarities and contrasts in the two areas is religion. As already indicated, Hill Maria Gond religion is characterized by the centrality of shamanism and the absence of Brahman specialists. Moreover, not only in Chhattisgarh, but everywhere in peasant India people are active participants in pilgrimage to holy sites and have access to nearby temples which are foci for more orthodox, great tradition ritual practices. On the other hand, at Devagaon worship of 21 village deities is conducted or supervised by a Chamar village priest (*pujari*) and his Kevat "disciple" (*cela*). The purity-pollution syndrome, with its emphasis on the polluting nature of bodily fluids and consequent isolation of menstruating females, avoidance of after-birth substances, excreta, semen and blood generally, and of course nume-rous ritual avoidances such as those surrounding death and the corpse are present in both communities, though not expressed always with the same observances and certainly not with the same purifying rituals.

The two communities represent deities both anthropomorphically and non-anthropomorphically, and seem to view the human-superhuman relationship in similar ways. Basic elements of ceremonies, such as invocations and sacrifice are parallel in the two systems, though of course at Devagaon, especially among Brahmans and other castes served by Brahman *pandits, sastric* and other great tradition elements elaborate and embellish ceremonial observances in a way that is entirely absent at Orcha. As for mythology, the great Hindu epics, the Ramayana and the Mahabharata are also absent from Hill Maria culture.

I should also mention one other way in which religion differs in the two areas. Whereas the Hill Maria Gonds participate in a system which is completely homogeneous, Chhattisgarh includes considerable variation in religious traditions by caste, and of course several completely different religions are present in the region, such as Jainism, Islam, Sikhism and Christianity (though none of these faiths were represented in Devagaon at the time of the study). Although the Marias did encounter people of diverse religious traditions in marginal ways at markets and fairs, there was little if any interaction of religious relevance. In Chhattisgarhi villages, including Devagaon, ceremonial specialization by caste existed at the village level, and some knowledge of other religions was evident, even if stereotypic in nature.

Just as the tribal level of sociocultural integration cannot be characterized as homogeneous throughout, but must include peoples of diverse culture, language, regional styles and patterns of interaction with the wider society, so the peasant level exhibits great diversity of features throughout the Indian subcontinent. In this paper the tribal and peasant communities which have been compared have been chosen fortuitously, only because they are the two examples with which I have first-hand familiarity. The specific similarities and dissimilarities between tribal and peasant might be very different if groups in other parts of India had been compared. Nevertheless, certain features emerge which can be used to contrast the levels *as levels*, irrespective of their geographical locations and specific cultural patterns. We shall return to this issue in the conclusion, below.

The town level of sociocultural integration

The town used as the prototype for this paper is Rajim, or more accurately, the twin towns of Rajim and Navapara Rajim, located about 25 miles southeast of the city of Raipur in Chhattisgarh, just a mile from Devagaon. Rajim, with a population of approximately 5,400 during the period of study (1977-78), is located on the eastern bank of the Mahanadi, which flows from south to north at this point. Navapara Rajim occupies the western bank, and at that time had a population of about 12,500. A concrete bridge, completed in 1972, links the two town areas. Previous to that only a temporary earthen causeway was erected, which was swept away annually by the turgid waters of the Mahanadi during the monsoon season. After the rains, before the causeway could be rebuilt, the only way to cross the river was in rowboats provided commercially by local operators for a small fee. Since the erection of the permanent bridge the two towns have become better integrated economically and socially, despite the fact that they are located in different tahsils of Raipur District.

My initial research interest was to study Rajim proper as a well-known temple center in southern Chhattisgarh. The major foci of religious activity there are the seventy century A.D. temple of Rajiv Lochan (the "lotus-eyed one," an *avatar* of Vishnu) and the twelfth or thirteenth century Shiva temple known as Kuleshvar Mahadev Mandir. The construction of these temples and their subsequent eminence in the region no doubt was related to their propitious location at the confluence (*sangam*) of the Mahanadi, a lesser stream called the Pairi, and a mythological one known as the Sonru. Rajiv Lochan originally was built right on the river bank, but changes in the river's course have resulted in the present location about 300 feet from the river's edge. Kuleshvar, on the other hand, occupies an island right in the middle of the river about a quarter of a mile from the actual juncture of the Mahanadi and Pairi. These temples (plus eleven others of lesser importance) are the site of several significant religious fairs, or *melas* on the Hindu calendar. The most famous of these are Mahashivratri and Magh Purnima, both in the month of Magh (January-February). The latter is said to be the birthday of Rajiv Lochan, and is attended by from 100,000 to 150,000 pilgrims annually. Rajiv Lochan and Kuleshvar also constitute the nucleus of an important local pilgrimage circuit known as *panc kosi yatra* (Jay 1990). Navapara Rajim (known locally simply as "Navapara"), is primarily a commercial center which developed around the turn of the century and the first World War, originally out of the need for products from nearby forests, which were extensive at the time. An important grain market, 15 rice mills, four oil-pressing plants, a lumber yard, petrol station, daily and weekly vegetable, fish and livestock markets, a major agricultural cooperative, some small-scale handicraft manufacturing, and several hundred retail establishments were located here during the period of the study. (On subsequent brief re-visits I noted considerable growth in the town's boundaries and expansion of economic activity). A narrow-gauge railroad, running from Raipur also terminated here, and the town was well-connected by bus routes in all directions.

The disclaimer previously applied to Devagaon as "representative" of the "peasant" level of sociocultural integration applies also to the "town" level. I do not claim that Rajim/ Navapara Rajim are in any way "typical" of small towns in India, but clearly we can see in this community[11] a considerably more complex level serving specialized commercial and religious functions and representing social and economic diversity far more pronounced than that of peasant villages. One obvious difference between a town and a village is size. The Census of India (1981b : 2) defines towns as "all places with a municipal corporation, municipal board, cantonment board or notified area, etc..." and "all other places which satisfy the following criteria : (i) a minimum population of 5,000; (ii) at least 75% of the male working population engaged in non-agricultural (and allied) activity; and (iii) a density of population of at least 400 per Sq. Km. (1,000 per Sq. mile)..." Because both Rajim and

Navapara Rajim have municipal boards or corporations, they meet these criteria. More importantly, they satisfy the conditions of population, population density and male occupation.[12] However, for our purposes, the social and economic complexity of these twin towns is the principal diagnostic feature.

According to the local *patvari's* list, some 29 different caste segments were present in Rajim at the time of the study. However, this list probably was not complete, and in some cases combined several different *jatis* of the same ethnic group. For instance, "Maratha" was listed as a *jati* but in fact included families belonging to different Maharashtrian *jatis*. Similarly, "Panjabi" was given as a single category though it is an ethnic division, not a caste identity.

I could obtain no "official" list of the various caste, ethnic and religious communities in Navapara, but clearly there were perhaps twice as many groups as in Rajim. In fact the considerable diversity in Navapara was striking for such a small town. And close scrutiny of each group revealed complexities that only enhanced this perception of diversity. For instance there were two *jatis* of bronze or brass metalworkers, the Kaser and the Tamprakar. But the Kaser originally were immigrants from Orissa and continued to be bilingual in Oriya and Chhattisgarhi Hindi. There were about 200 houses of Kaser (500 people), who practised their traditional ocupation of manufacturing rugged bronze *(kansa)* utensils by smelting and hand-hammering. By contrast, there were only a few families of Tamprakar, who are Chhattisgarhi craftsmen specializing in the production of fine, highly polished brass *(pital) lotas* using lathes and polishing machines. But the interesting point is that the two kinds of metalsmiths were separated not only by *jati* membership and details of occupation, but by ethnicity as well. In addition, many of Navapara's castes were further subdivided into exogamous subcastes *(upjatis)*. And religious groups were also subdivided. For example, there were about 50 households each of the Digambara and Svetambara Jains. Each group had its own temple, but the Svetambaras were further subdivided into *murti pujak* (idol worshippers), *gair murthi pujak* and *terha pant*. The last two groups do not worship idols, hence do not participate in temple rites, but do join in Jain public processions. The Muslim community was similarly split into five separate sub-divisions : the Sunnis (about 26 households), the Shias (about a dozen households, mostly in Rajim proper), two large joint families of the Bohras (who maintain a tradition of

Yemeni origins), a family of the Khaujas (followers of the Agha Khan), and two families of the Maihman Muslims from Kutch, in Western India. Moreover, there were separations among the Muslims by occupation as well, and these divisions were significant in the marriage system. For example, those Muslims with a traditional occupation of bangle-selling (Manehars) would allow their women to marry into other groups, such as the oil-pressers the Telis), but would not allow their men to marry women from Other groups. There were 17 Christian households, 9 in Rajim and 8 in Navapara Rajim. All belong to the United Church of North India, but one family identifies itself as Methodist, while the others are "Evangelicals".

Besides the various immigrant ethnic groups already mentioned, there were households of the Gujeratis, Sindhis, and the Rajputs. Also, many castes had traditions of immigration into the area from different places in Uttar Pradesh many generations ago. Enough has been said to illustrate the point that the town is far more ethnically and religiously diverse, and includes a vast array of castes, occupations, industries and activities lacking in the surrounding villages. At least no *one* village would exhibit this much heterogeneity, though collectively some of this diversity was present among them.

It would be far beyond the scope of this paper to describe the various religious, political and social mechanism which serve to unify or at least coordinate action within the twin towns. But it is clear that despite such broad organizational features, the town is not a unity in the same sense as the village. It is far too large, complex and impersonal. Though most people look familiar to their neighbors, intimate association for the most part is limited to members of one's family, caste, workplace or neighborhood. In Weberian terms, associative relationships predominate over communal ones in the public arena of interaction, and Durkheim's mechanical solidarity for the community as a whole is much weaker than in the peasant village.

I have already alluded to the main functions of Rajim (temple and pilgrimage center) and Navapara (commercial and marketing center), respectively. I should also mention that a large number of householders in both communities continued to work the land surrounding the towns as farmers and landless laborers, though I am not sure what percentage were thus engaged. But the direct relationship of these twin towns to agriculture was obvious in terms of the grain market *(ganj)* and rice mills in Navapara and the general dependency of all enterprises, including retail marketing at Navapara and the religious activities of Rajim, on the surrounding peasant villages. At these centers farmers sold their produce and shopped for tools and supplies, attended religious fairs and temple *pujas*. The size, complexity and specialized functions of these twin towns I believe to be characteristic of the "town" level of sociocultural integration generally. Furthermore, the very nature of towns means, of course, that there will be fewer of them relative to peasant villages.

Other studies in the literature, I believe, tend to confirm my contention that the town in India represents a distinct level of sociocultural integration, qualified by the point stressed repeatedly in this paper that the differences among the various levels are *relative* and arranged along a continuum. Corwin (1977) describes the cultural traditions of the small town of Mahishadal in Midnapore District of West Bengal. Although it has a population of only 7,000, she conceptualizes it as a "minimal urban centre":

> Such a centre is the smallest rural settlement above village level, possessing both urban functions and an urban-oriented population. Residents of such minimal urban centres are drawn from both large cities and small agricultural villages. The lifestyle of much of the population of a small rural town differs significantly from that of nearby villagers : it is modelled on that of distant urban centres.
>
> The small rural town as minimal urban centre is the smallest and lowest in a hierarchy of urban centres of increasing size and complexity. These towns and cities are centres in the networks that ultimately link each peasant village with the wider society of which it is a part. As minimal urban centres, then, rural towns are extremely important settlements in terms of the social and cultural integration of complex societies.

Although I might quibble with applying the term "urban" to the community she describes, Mahishadal shares with Navapara Rajim many important features, including market functions and social diversity of several varieties. Her study and many others which would be beyond the scope of this paper to cite, reinforce the notion of a level of sociocultural integration represented by the town, which is midway conceptually between the peasant village and the city. The general features of towns are extended still further in the Indian city, to which we turn next.

The urban level of sociocultural integration

"For sociological purposes", asserted Louis Worth in 1938 (Wirth 1975 : 31), "a city may be defined as a relatively large, dense, and permanent settlement of socially heterogeneous individuals". Though somewhat vague (how large ? how dense?), this may serve as a concise and minimum definition of cities in general. It may or may not serve as an adequate definition in all civilizations, with their different cultures and located in different times and places. It also seems to me that the city cannot be conceptualized adequately without contrasting it with smaller, more rural communities, that is, to non-cities. Urban centers can have no meaning, indeed, cannot exist except in relation to rural hinterlands. In a sense "rural" becomes part of the definition of "urban."

As stated earlier in this paper, my original intention was to study aspects of society and culture in the Chhattisgarhi city of Raipur, with a population of 338,000 (Census 1981 b : 363). Specifically I had hoped to look at urban immigrants from the surrounding communities in a manner analogous to Vatuk's (1972) study of migrants in Meerut, to assess the degree and types of change in lifestyles as rural people adjusted to their new urban experience. Since this was not possible for reasons beyond my control, I turned my attention to the Madhya Pradesh capital of Bhopal, with a population of 671,000 (Census 1981b : 89). This city is important not only as the capital of India's largest state, but as a major industrial center. It became infamous in 1984 as the site of the world's largest industrial disaster, the Union Carbide gas explosion in which 3,828 people were killed outright, 19,000 permanently disabled, and up to 150,000 others injured. Before independence, Bhopal was not only a city, but a small central Indian state governed by a succession of Muslim rulers beginning in the eighteenth century. Bhopal's lakes, known as "upper" and "lower" respectively provide a central focus around which the city is built. Bhopal is also known for its beautiful parks, the range of green hills which overlooks it, and its quaint "old city", which continues to be largely Muslim in population and character.

Like any city, Bhopal is divided into many neighborhoods with distinctive characteristics. Because it was not feasible to study the city as a whole, I chose one of these neighborhoods, or *mohallas* for intensive study. Since the main focus of the research was on traditional and modernity, a middle-class neighborhood seemed most appropriate, and accordingly I settled into the *mohalla* of Shaktinagar in the Bharat Heavy Electricals (BHEL) area on the southeastern outskirts of the city. The BHEL plant, which now employs some 18,500 workers, was established as a public sector enterprise in 1961 by the Government of India with the goal of producing much-needed heavy electrical equipment such as hydrolectric dynamos, high voltage transformers, generators, electirc engines for rail transit, and so forth. Because of the scale of the enterprise, a large tract of land was set aside for a planned community surrounding the plant. This community is nearly a small town of its own, with housing, schools, medical facilities, markets, places of worship, parks, a sports complex, and recreational centers. In 1981 the population of the BHEL area as a whole was about 86,000 (Ali 1987 : 5-6).

Shaktinagar was populated mostly by managerial and technical personnel and their families. I lived with a host family within the *mohalla* and was accompanied by my wife during part of the period of research, August 1989—May 1990. In addition to "participant-observation," I supervised the conduct of 325 basic data interviews, assisted by three sociology graduate students from Barkatullah University, and carried out 66 follow-up, indepth interviews from among families of the original survey. I also travelled to other parts of the city, attended functions at Bharat Bhavan, the city's new center for display and performance of art, music and dance, and was introduced to university faculty, government officials, artists, writers and others living in various parts of Bhopal.[12] On the whole I believe that I got a good feeling for life in a relatively small, yet important city of central India.

Shaktinagar consists of 68-acre parcel of land with 476 house plots, 438 of which were occupied by dwellings in the 1989-90 period. Plans for the *mohalla* were drawn up by the BHEL Employees Co-op Housing Society in the 1960's, with the land provided by the BHEL administration specifically for a subsidized residential colony of managerial and supervisory personnel. The lots are of four sizes, 100'x 60',80'x 50', 60' x 40', and 50'x 30', and the houses built on them proportionate to the occupational status, and therefore the income, of the residents. In some cases these are two-storey buildings, one storey occupied by the owner and another by tenants. Many of the houses are elaborate and "modernistic" with front porches or patios overlooking lawns and gardens. There is a great variety of architectural styles and floor plans. All have modern plumbing, bathrooms and kitchens. Virtually all kitchens are equipped with gas stoves, refrigerators, blenders, toasters and other appliances. TV sets are universal and VCR's very common in these homes. The homes of higher paid employees inevitably have an automobile parked in the driveway and sometimes one or more motor scooters as well.

The basic data interviews revealed an extremely diverse, well-educated population in the *mohalla*. There were 273 Hindu, 16 Jain, 15 Muslim, 14 Sikh and 7 Christian households in the sample. Among Hindus, the castes *(jatis)* were numerous and diverse; when grouped under their *varnas* (four-fold division of Hindu society), there were 109 Brahman households, 72 Kshatriya, 66 Vaisha, 7 Shudra and 20 unknown or uncertain (due to omissions in the data collection). The residents were also ethnically diverse, coming from virtually every region in northern India and several in the south. The total number of persons was 1,506 or an average of 4.6 per household. The residents of 234 of the households, or about 72% lived in nuclear families; the other 91 household, or 28% consisted of extended or enhanced families. I have not completed analysis of the raw data, but the following preliminary findings are noteworthy : an average of 3 out of the 4.6 household members either held an advanced degree (above matriculation) or were studying for one. BHEL has its own elementary and high schools, but some residents were sending their children to private schools outside the BHEL area. Of significance is the fact that of 906 offspring produced in the 325 households of the sample, 687 or 76% were going or previously went to English-medium schools, while only 63 or 9.7% of the parents of these offspring attended English-medium schools. This is an interesting example of educational improvement and upward mobility among these middle class families.

Most of the BHEL employees in the sample were engineers, though some were physicians, technicians, accountants, and administrators. All employees were grouped into three basic salary grades by employment position : workmen, supervisors and executives, with salaries ranging from Rs. 800 to Rs. 5,000 per month. (During the 1989-90 period there were about 18 rupees to the dollar). In Shaktinagar, nearly all the household heads in the houses occupying the 37 largest plots were in executive ranks, although a few were physicians, who have a different but also very lucrative salary scale. In addition to the basic salary, employees received a monthly "dearness allowance" linked to the cost of living index as revised quarterly. This may be anywhere from Rs. 200 to Rs. 1107, depending on the base salary. There were additional perks, such as paid leaves with a transportation allowance, low-cost loans, medical and retirement benefits, etc. It would seem, therefore, that both by income and lifestyle my informants in this community were "middle class" urban dwellers.

A major goal of the research was to determine the extent to which these middle class families adhered to "traditional" lifestyles and to what extent their lifestyles had been "modernized." Without getting involved here in an elaborate discussion of what constitutes "tradition" vs. "modernity" in the contemporary Indian context, for the purposes of this paper let it suffice to think of traditional norms and behavior in terms of those patterns prescribed in religious scriptures, those revealed in the ethnographic literature of the last 40 years, particularly for rural areas, and those understood from my own observations in the village and town studies described above. The term "modern" is widely used in India to refer to a set of values which is more permissive, liberal and individualistic than that which is rooted in traditional Indian life. A typical example would be tolerance for inter-caste marriage. Another might be acceptance of "love" marriage rather than arranged marriage. Attitudes toward religion, caste customs, womens' roles, kinship relations and many other aspects of Indian life seem to be changing, i. e., modernizing, and although difficult to quantify, it appears that this process is progressing more rapidly among urban, middle-class Indians than among other segments of the population.[14] Let us see what my data show.

In my interviews, I probed for information on adherence to traditional religious beliefs and participation in religious activities, the persistence and importance of kinship ties, the nature of family organization and division of labor, attitudes toward women, health, medicine, industrialization and science, and leisure activities. These interviews were as open-ended as possible, lasted about an hour on average and generally were conducted with male heads of household, often with other family members present.

Briefly summarized, the following preliminary observations about tradition and modernity were made :

(1) Kinship and marriage : It is obvious that most

families have liberalized their attitudes and practices relative to marriage. Although parents remained responsible for finding potential spouses for their children, and for making the wedding arrangements, young people enjoyed more freedom in expressing their approval or disapproval of life partners. No longer did potential mates wait until the wedding to see each other. At the very least they met before marriage, and this practice was becoming so common it was regarded as customary. Most male informants said they would not object to their children choosing their own mates, but often qualified this by adding that they would want to check on the background and families of the bride or groom to be. Older women in these families were less tolerant of so-called love marriages. Although nearly all male informants maintained that they would not object to intercaste marriage, when pressed they admitted that marriage into the same "community" is preferred and upper caste informants rigidly drew the line on marriage to low caste or untouchable people. In this respect, if it is typical, urban middle class behavior has not changed much since the 1960's when Gould (1974 : 285) noted for business and professional families in Lucknow and Kanpur that "...elite families adhered in general terms to the rule of caste endogamy regardless of how 'advanced' they seemed or alleged themselves to be in other respects." But generally speaking most informants in my study were more concerned about social class considerations, such as occupation, wealth and education than about traditional caste and kinship criteria.

Although I have not yet compiled the data, another point of interest relating to marriage is the obvious fact that young people were postponing marriage to a later age than was true traditionally. Again, this is consistent with urban patterns elsewhere, especially for business and professional elites. (See for example Gould 1970 : 67).

I have already noted that about 28% of the households in the total sample of 375 consisted of extended or enhanced families. Most commonly one found a household head's elderly parent or parents living in the home, but siblings living elsewhere. However, there were also cases of two or three brothers and their wives, children and elderly parents occupying a household in the traditional manner. But whether or not there was residential unity, virtually everyone maintained close ties with lineal and various types of collateral relatives, wherever they may be. Many BHEL families came from rural or small town communities elsewhere in India where they still had an ancestral home. If their parents or other relatives continued to live there, frequent visits were made and many people spoke of plans to retire there. Many additional examples could be cited to demonstrate the continued importance of traditional kinship ties.

(2) Household routines and the division of labor : Most of the households remained traditional in the sense that the male head went off to work and his spouse stayed home to do housework, prepare food and raise children. However, there were also many households in which a son and his wife both worked and the grandparents or an *aivah* (nursemaid) took care of the children. Virtually all of the well-to-do households, and many with quite modest incomes hired women from the nearby *jhugees* (shanty towns occupied by poor rural immigrants) to clean house, do dishes and help with the laundry, as a minimum.

(3) Caste behavior: Among these middle class families, traditional restrictions on interdining were largely ignored. Social gatherings at public functions such as weddings or parties at the "club" included people from many castes and all religions. At private homes as well, the guest list was likely to be very diverse, organized in terms of one's workmates, neighbors, acquaintances, etc., without regard to caste or religion.

Caste identity came into play in relation to marriage, as mentioned above, and also in relation to certain social and political activities. In the BHEL community there were a number of regional and/or caste organizations, or *samaj*, which brought together people of the same community in an attempt to maintain selected aspects of their culture, such as performances of folk music, folk dramas, mythological recitations and the like. In some instances apparently such organizations also served as mutual aid groups and tried to advance the interests of the group with reference to social and political issues. The traditional complex caste hierarchy and its structured integration so characteristic of village life was absent here, but all vestiges of caste identity had *not* been eliminated.

(4) Occupation, education and the position of women : As we have seen, most of the male occupations involved engineering and technical fields of various kinds. Accordingly, most of the senior males in the sample had university or other higher education degrees, such as engineering certificates from technical

institutes. Most had a good command of English as well as one or more Indian languages, since English is required for most of the supervisory and managerial positions at BHEL. Virtually all offspring of college age, both male and female, were indeed attending a college or university. One finding that surprised me was that many of the young *women* were going into engineering fields. One reason for this was the BHEL policy of hiring automatically, in positions for which they were qualified, the male *and* female offspring of BHEL employees. Other fields popular with the younger generation were medicine, law, and business. Clearly, as the next generation matures fewer women will remain housewives exclusively. It is likely that, just as in Europe and the U.S., both spouses will work and increasingly household help will be hired to deal with the menial chores at home.

(5) Religion : Religion appeared to remain the most traditional sphere of activity for these middle class people Although purity-pollution considerations relative to caste interaction were greatly relaxed, in other ways religious beliefs and practices remained strong and traditional. The Hindus, Muslims, Sikhs and the Christians continued to perform their respective household rituals (or prayers) and life-cycle rites, observe religious holidays, visit places of worship, go on pilgrimage and generally participate fully in religious activities. Moreover, though a few informants expressed some mild skepticism about metaphysical concepts, most seemed to accept the core of beliefs associated with their religion. Again, this seemed to be in general accord with Gould's (1974 : 289) findings among urbanites in Lucknow and Kanpur nearly three decades earlier, though he does stress changes in the belief system a bit more : "While still strongly identified with the need to have elaborate and expensive ceremonies performed at the most important *rites de passage,* especially marriages and funerals,...in the domain of religious philosophy, very considerable departures from the orthodox norms were frequently discernible."

(6) Recreation and entertainmet : Because BHEL is such a self-contained community, most of the people of Shaktinagar were able to stay within the area for most kinds of recreation and entertainment. Those who qualified for membership went to the Senior Officers' Club where they attended periodic functions such as dramas, musical shows, "lotto" games, weekly movies, and other events in the club's amphitheater. During the hot season the club's swimming pool is open and in the fall the tennis season begins, with a relatively small but devoted group

of male tennis players participating daily in spirited doubles play. The club also offered billiards, cards, and a reading room with some periodicals and books available. Other classes of workers in BHEL had their own clubs, but they were smaller and less pretentious.

Some of the wives of senior managers in Shaktinagar participated in a "kitty club." This group met once a month and contributed a sum of money to the "kitty." A drawing was held and the winner took the money in the kitty but then also became obligated to host the next meeting. This meant opening one's home as the meeting place and providing tea or coffee and refreshments. The main activities were card playing, discussions of issues on the day and of course gossiping about local events. In a more traditional vein, some women also met every Thursday for the singing of *bhajans* (religious hymns).

Family picnics were popular on Sundays, and during vacations people often travelled by car or train to various places of interest outside Bhopal, frequently combining religious pilgrimage and tourism.

Finally, the most universal form of entertainment in the colony seemed to be television. Though limited to just three channels at the time of the study, TV carried a variety of programming with wide appeal. And many people had VCR's, so that renting movies was becoming a major alternative to going out to the cinema.

General comment : Judging by this study of middle-class families in an urban environment, contemporary patterns of sociocultural change may be observed at two levels : those on the surface, such as the relaxation of rules regarding arranged marriages, and those deeper, infrastructural features, such as industrialization and the modernization of production. These deeper aspects of change have resulted in a shift from rural sources of wealth. i.e. landlordism, to urban sources of wealth, i. e. professional and technical pursuits as well as business and commerce. At the same time, certain persistent features of traditional life, such as advantages accorded higher castes, influence access to the new urban roles and lifestyles. The most substantial changes seem to be in areas such as consumer technology (TV, automobiles, refrigerators) and entertainment/ recreation. On the other hand, religious belief and behavior and the general importance of kinship seem to have changed only superficially if at all.

It is also striking that among the middle-class families of this study at least, women are attaining access to education and therefore non-traditional occupations, including the professions, in a way which was unthinkable a generation ago. We have also observed that there is a great relaxation of rules governing intercaste behavior, and indeed caste in the traditional sense has lost much of its meaning here. Still, there is a persistent objection to intercaste marriage. Such a combination of modern and traditional attitudes with regard to the same institution apppears to be the predominant feature of urban middle-class values that I have observed.

When the urban level of sociocultural integration is compared, as a whole, with the other three levels already considered, it is clear that the city is a coresidential unit much larger than village or town, even more heterogeneous in ethnic makeup, occupations, castes, social classes, religions and functions. The concept of "neighborhood," though certainly not absent in villages and towns, takes on new significance in the city : there are old and new neighborhoods, lower, middle and upper class neighborhoods, slums and shanty towns and of course all the specialized neighborhoods such as shopping areas, financial districts and factory zones.

Furthermore, because of their size and functions, of course there are fewer cities than villages or towns; the process of urbanization means increasing population and "urban sprawl," but not necessarily an increase in the number of cities. And because cities are in the forefront of commercialization, industrialization and the communication revolution, modernization progresses more rapidly within them, and especially within the middle class, a prominent component of contemporary urban life. Modernization does not mean only advances in technology; it means also changes in values and attitudes. Although such change is also evident at the town and village levels to some extent, in general it has progressed further and more deeply at the urban level.

Redfield and Singer (1962 : 332) have distinguished two important roles of cities, the "orthogenetic" and the "heterogenetic." The former consists of "the *carrying forward into systematic and reflective dimensions an old culture*" and the latter the "*creating of original modes of thought that have authority beyond or in conflict with old cultures and civilizations.*" [Italics original.] Judging by the lifestyle, values and attitudes of my middle class Bhopal informants, the heterogenetic functions of urban life appear to be foremost, but if one were to observe the city as a whole, including the old city and other areas outside of BHEL, the orthogenetic function would also be apparent. Urban areas, such as Bhopal, which have grown rapidly in India since independence appear to display predominantly heterogenetic characteristics, however. This would be consistent with Redfield and Singer's (1962 : 335) obervation that :

> We...see in every city its double urban characteristics: we may identify the institutions and mental habits there prevailing with the one or the other of the two lines of transformation of folk life which the city bring about. The heterogenetic transformations have grown with the course of history, and the developments of peoples and especially those incident to the expansion of the West, have increased and accelerated this aspect of urbanization. The later cities are predominantly cities of the technical order.

One of the most important factors in heterogenetic transformations no doubt is industrialization (Gould 1960; 1970 : 53-56; Saberwal 1977 : 8-10; Steward 1967 : 10), but a thorough consideration of this process is far beyond the scope of this paper.

At the outset it was suggested that still another level may be discernible in contemporary India represented by the supercity or "megalopolis." Although I have spent some time in Delhi, which undoubtedly qualifies for megalopolis status, it is not clear to me whether this level is *qualitatively* different from what has been indentified here as the urban level, or whether it is just *quantitatively* larger in area and population. There is no doubt that India's four largest cities—Bombay, Calcutta, Delhi and Madras—differ from one another in distinct ways, partly because of somewhat different functions, but I am not sure whether they represent collectively some "super-urban" level which is clearly distinct in terms of the variables used to identify the other levels, namely, complexity of structure, heterogeneity of populations and diversity of functions. A related complication in urban studies is the observation made by Fox (1975 : 51) that "... different city types are associated with different kinds of hinterlands...." That is, just as coresidential units of the other three levels of sociocultural integration defined here are not identical in structure and function with other units of the same level, so much variation in urban centers exists (1975 : 51) :

> To understand the full extent of urban variation, the anthropologist cannot be content with gross typological distinctions between, for example, preindustrial and industrial cities. He must also study the dynamics of secondary urban variability, the directions which this variability takes, and the sociocultural factors which lie behind the specific adaptive paths of individual cities.

Space limitations preclude further exploration of these issues, which must be left to a future publication.

Summary and Conclusion

The general idea of "levels of sociocultural integration" presented here is not entirely new. Cohn and Marriott in their paper "Networks and Centres in the Integration of Indian Civilisation" (1958 : 1) Observe that : "The integrative functionings and centres in traditional India might be examined in areas of greater or lesser scale for social and cultural diversity is met at a multiplicity of levels." They go on to discuss sociocultural diversity at each of four levels : "all-India," The "region." the "sub-region," and the "local level." They perceive the greatest diversity and therefore greatest problems of integration at the highest level (1958 : 1-2) :

> here...Indian civilisation as a whole confronts sharp breaks among at least ten of the fifteen regions which are defined by the major literary languages. Each major linguistic region has its unique hierarchy of castes, and is thus separated from adjacent regional hierarchies not only by difference of language, but also by lack of marriage...and by the absence of those defined, ritualized relations of rank which are essential to Indian community life.
>
> Next, subregions, especially the areas of the principal spoken languages or dialects, generally show some cultural distinctiveness and shifts in particular castes. Finally, beneath subregional diversity there are further differences and cleavages among the basic territorial units. These basic territorial units are in some subregions coextensive with villages, in other subregions coextensive with larger entities such as petty kingdoms or the territories dominated by branches of certain clans.

Citing Barnes (1954) and Redfield (1956) they distinguish between supralocal rural "networks" of social relationships in general and those denser concatenations of relationships which may be called "centres" (1958 : 3). The networks which they delineate are defined by economics, marriage and kinship, politics, and religion, and serve to integrate rather than divide the society. Centres serve to connect various points in the networks and (1958 : 4-5) :

> If a multiplicity of levels of integration may be distinguished in examining regional diversity, so (a) multiplicity of centres may be distinguished at many levels of greater and lesser scope. Excepting temporarily neat structuring in the political and administrative field, one does not generally find clear territorial segmentation and subordination among civilisational centres. In other words, one finds little of what is generally understood by the term 'centralization' in Europe. Instead there are conflicting jurisdictions both among centres of the same type and level (as) among centres of different type and level...Even if a single city comprises markets, shrines, and a seat of government, the chances are that the area served by each will differ widely....
>
> > Centres perform specialised functions and are typically the abodes of specialists. Following a marriage network, for example, one finds in the town centre the marriage broker, the most learned astrologer who can determine the suitability and the time of marriage, sometimes the genelogist, and certain higher types of sacramental priests, musicians, and entertainers for the wedding. Commercial networks have their nexes in markets and fairs and in the shops of wholesale traders and bankers. Centres in the network of pilgrimages naturally display many orders of shrine priests, teachers and other religious experts of all sorts (Redfield and Singer 1954; Singer 1955; Vidyarthi 1958).

Because of their diverse functions, the specialists in rural centres "typically face two ways in their functioning. On the one hand, they look toward smaller centres and to the rural networks; and on the other hand, they look toward larger and more complex centres" (1958 : 5). Moreover, "both the diversity of their rural clientele and the demands of their specialisation in the Indian caste context promote social heterogeneity among the specialists. And citizens of civilisational centres are in fact more heterogeneous in caste and occupation than are people of the next lower level" (1958 : 6).

In Cohn and Marriott we perceive some rationale for the existence of different "levels" in the civilization, though they do not go very far in defining them. Clearly, the central and most cogent reason for the existence of distinct levels of sociocultural integration is the specialized functions of certain institutions such as marketing, manufacturing, administration or "great tradition" religious institutions. Because of their scale, specialized knowledge, resource requirements, position in a communication network or other factors these institutions cannot exist in small-scale tribal or peasant villages. Centers such as towns and cities provide these institutional functions and thereby integrate the society as a whole in both horizontal and vertical dimensions. Looked at within a region, a town links together villages and other towns in a horizontal network; but at the same time vertically it links together units of simpler and more complex organization. It is a "center" intermediate between the villages below it and the cities above it. The image that comes to mind is one of a pyramid, with tribal and peasant villages at the bottom, towns in the middle and cities at the top. Perhaps the four megalopolises of Bombay, Calcutta, Delhi and Madras should be placed at the very apex of the pyramid. The increasingly complex functions of centers as one looks from bottom to top assures that the centres will be larger in size and that there will be fewer of them.[15]

And because higher level units provide more functions than lower level ones, they are more complex in organization and therefore more heterogeneous and diverse in their populations from almost any standpoint : occupation, caste, social class, ethnicity, language, etc. This diversity in turn leads to different lifestyles; towns people have a different outlook on life than villagers. They are more amenable to change and less traditional even though still rooted in basically rural folkways. City people are still more modern and less trditional, though my emphasis continues to be on the *relativity* of these concepts. As we have seen, the middle class sample from Bhopal shows some changes in attitudes toward caste interaction, the position of women and marriage arrangements, yet traditional norms have not vanished entirely. Though many people in the Bhopal study expressed a certain nostalgic admiration for village life, few, especially those of the younger generation, would trade their present circumstances to return to the village. I have stressed this point because I believe that differences in sociocultural levels are not just differences in complexity of organization. It is not simply that there are more occupations and castes in towns than in villages and still more in cities than in towns. That is true, but in addition there are profound *cultural* differences among the levels and these differences are not just those of region, language, religion or any of the other factors normally cited as expressing cultural variation. They are also differences based on the *general level of sociocultural integration regardless of regional differences*, which of course are not denied. My hypothesis is that people who live in peasant villages throughout India have certain characteristics in common regardless of cultural region. And people living in cities have a great deal in common regardless of region. Urbanites in Delhi, Bombay, Calcutta and Madras may have more in common in terms of lifestyle and behavior than any of them have with the rural populations of those in the immediate hinterland.

Related observations have been made by others. Saberwal (1977 : 16), in providing "a sociohistorical perspective" on Indian urbanism, has chosen "to focus on the inter-urban spread, and not on particular urban centres,...on the premise that a particular urban centre has very much less of the 'sociological reality' than what Dumont and Pocock (1957) would grant even an Indian village to have had." He gives "analytic primacy" to the process of industrialization in establishing commonalities across various urban centres. At the urban level caste stratification gives way to stratification by social class (1977 : 16) :

> ...the supralocal caste group continues to be important for many urbanites; but we have noticed that the processes of dispersion and decompression have tended to pull caste groups generally out of shape. These are often crosscut, furthermore, by other sorts of identity, other frames of reference, which invite consideration in their own right.
>
> In any large urban centre, a great many channels of authority, power, and influence—and symbols to match—lie entwined : a change of government in Calcutta affects the steel plant of Durgapur...as well as the laboratory in Calcutta...; and the mix varies greatly from one centre to another.

Rowe (1973) has stressed sociohistorical factors in the founding of cities in India, and compares patterns of urban immigration in Bombay and Bangalore. Clearly immigration, whether of the "temporary", "recurrent" or "permanent" type, appears to be an important element in the diversity of Indian cities, but at the same time maintains strong connections between urban and rural levels in the society. Rowe makes an interesting point in suggesting, at least for northeastern India, that "...urban migrants have extended the resources of the village to include the city" (1973 : 242). Migration becomes a strategy for utilizing urban resources through maintaining economic relations with the migrants' families and kin back home. The significance for culture change needs further exploration, but surely this phenomenon has important implications for values and lifestyles at both urban and rural levels of sociocultural integration, and demonstrates still another way in which the two levels are functionally interrelated.

The point is further reinforced by Hardgrave (1970 : 39), who points out that urban migrants do not merely bring the country to the city, but rather are confronted with new situations, new institutions and patterns of behavior to which they must adapt if they are to operate effectively. But :

> At the same time, these institutions are changing, in part because of migration itself. The village, however, is not unaffected, for the ties between the migrant and the countryside provide a channel of linkage for influence and change.

Berreman (1972 : 580-581) has summarized a major contrast in the social experience of urbanites and villagers:

> The village comprises people whose statuses are largely a function of their membership in corporate groups (families, sibs, castes). They tend to remain in their "home territory"—the familiar setting of the village and its region. Religious diversity is often absent, and where this is not the case, it is handled in traditional fashion, very often on the model of caste differences. Villagers interact in terms of their total identities on a personal basis with others who know them well....As a consequence...there is relatively rarely a novel interactional situation to be figured out, rarely status incongruity to be coped with, rarely important interaction with strangers. In the city, on the other hand, ethnic diversity is great. A large proportion of one's interatction is outside the "home territory" of one's neighborhood, and is with strangers or casual acquaintances. Even those who are not strangers often know little about one another and see one another in limited, stereotyped situations.

He qualifies this observation, however, with the point that "urban residential neighborhoods are often relatively homogeneous ethnically, and stable over time, so that interaction approximates that in the village" (1972 : 581). Therefore, his characterization of urban interaction as stereotyped and impersonal applies mainly to the workplace and more public contexts; "It is less applicable to interaction within residential neighborhoods and relatively "private" settings" (1972 : 581). Berreman thus expresses clearly another dimension of the complexity of urban life : the need to behave differently in different contexts. Moreover, the "public" context is replete with difficulties for the newcomer, the urban immigrant. He or she must learn to respond appropriately in new situations not found in the village, and to develop some knowledge, however stereotyped, of unfamiliar ethnic, religious, caste and occupational identities and statuses. At the same time, within the residential neighborhood, where one's neighbors and acquaintances may be from the same rural area and often even from the same village, the migrant must maintain more traditional patterns of interaction. Then again, in special circumstances such as Shaktinagar in Bhopal, the neighborhood itself is diverse and is defined largely as a "public" setting. This situation, of course, is more likely to occur in planned communities such as BHEL, where neighborhoods are organized in terms of professional statuses and/or income levels.

Gould (1970 : 51) has credited Redfield with being "the first anthropologist to study what today are called 'developing societies,' and admits (1970 : 52) that "Redfield and those who followed him persistently asserted that peasantries are in reality components of large-scale, complex, and highly diversified societies that are economically, culturally, and politically dominated by elites situated primarily in cities and towns," but he (1970 : 52) is critical of the actual village studies undertaken, which stressed the inward-looking, or "centripetal" qualities of these little communities:

> That is, one talked about the "self-sufficient subsistence economy," the self-contained networks of social interaction, the parochilized system of religious beliefs and practices,... etc... The problem, one realizes in retrospect, was that Redfield and the first generation of field workers who concentrated on peasantries mistakenly treated the peasant communities they studied as *separate societies* in spite of the fact that theories like the folk-urban continuum indicated that by definition they were not.

If space permitted, I believe I could demonstrate that this is something of a distortion of the history of peasant studies that Redfield inspired. Omitted are the observations of Redfield, Singer, Marriott, Cohn and others concerning great and little traditions and their interrelationships, such as Marriott's (1955 :197-203) processes of "parochialization" and "universalization" as linking concepts. Moreover, although some village ethnographies may have focused primarily on what Gould calls "centripetal" tendencies, in other works, such as the Cohn and Marriott (1958) paper on "Networks and Centres in the Integration of Indian Civilisation" cited earlier, and Redfield and Singer's (1954) "The Cultural Role of Cities" not to mention Singer's 1955, 1958, 1960, 1968, 1972) studies in Madras, etc., more recent ethnographic studies were employed specifically *to refute* the notion of villages as "little republics, having nearly everything they want within themselves" (Sir Charles Metcalfe 1832 quoted in Srinivas !955 : 21), as so often depicted by early administrators and missionaries. Rather, peasant communities have been viewed as tied to one another and to towns and cities by a myriad of complex relationships.

Gould (1970 : 53) also reduces peasantries to occupational categories within a more encompassing, complex society. Although they clearly comprise the rural, mostly agricultural dimension of a state society, peasantries must be defined by more than occupational status. As I have tried to show above, there are characteristics and functions which relate the peasant level of socio-cultural integration to the town and urban levels in many ways. I agree with Kroeber (1948 : 284) that :

> Peasants are definitely rural—yet live in relation to market towns; they form a class segment of a larger population which usually contains also urban centers, sometimes metropolitan capitals. They constitute part-societies with part-cultures.

If Gould's formulation were broadened to include more than just occupational categories, certainly I would agree with his (1970 : 56) conclusions that :

> to a certain extent, many of the new occupational roles associated with modern state systems have grown out of the introduction of industrial technology. Yet many old occupational roles remain and, moreover, remain implanted in the fabric of kinship structures where they retain their ascriptive quality.

> This situation provides exciting opportunities to examine our proposition that peasantries are one of a number of occupational categories found in pre-industrial state systems which, like all such categories, manifest certain features of social organization as a consequence of their structural relationship to the whole society and not because they comprise a society in themelves.

Obviously cities are not new on the Indian subcontinent. The Indus Valley cities of Mohenjo-daro and Harappa developed their roots some four and a half millenia ago, and major cities which are more direct historical antecedents of today's cities existed in the Gangetic Valley, the Panjab and other areas perhaps as early as 800 B. C. But these cities of a Pre-industrial age no doubt owed their growth primarily to orthogenetic development and one assumes that the urban level of sociocultural integration was not differentiated from the town and village levels quite as sharply as it is today.

In this paper I have stressed the heterogeneity and functional distinctiveness of each of four levels of sociocultural integration as aspects of diversity in Indian civilization every bit as striking as other types of diversity, such as language, ethnicity, caste and religion. But just as there are cultural continuities across these categories of diversity, so there are continuities from one sociocultural level to another. Also, unlike these other categories, the four sociocultural levels are integrated both horizontally and vertically in a mutually functional way, and are universal throughout the entire society. Although the idea of levels of sociocultural integration is not new, I have endeavored here to define these levels with additional precision, to suggest some salient features of their vertical interrelationships, and finally to emphasize their singular importance in understanding the structure of Indian civilization as a whole.

Notes

[1]Still other terms, such as "preliterate" or "nonliterate" have been proposed, but these emphasize only one particular characteristic, and that is not necessarily a diagnostic one. Why emphasize only literacy as the single element distinguishing between types of society ? And a society may not have a system of writing of its own, but through acculturation may have adopted a system from another society and yet maintain many other characteristics typical of more extreme folk societies. The term "preliterate" is particularly inappropriate because it implies a

stage in an old-fashioned evolutionary scheme. Similar problems arise with terms such as "pre-industrial" or "nonindustrial." Steward (1955 : 43-44) uses the words "primitive" and "tribal" synonymously, and attempts to define this type of society in terms of a distinctive form of "culture." In my view this formulation muddies the waters still further, especially since the features he employs in his definition are partly cultural, partly structural, though he refers to them collectively as "tribal culture."

[2]Redfield (1962 : 294-302) attempted to clarify some of the misunderstandings that arose following publication of his earlier work, but unfortunately these misunderstandings tend to persist even to the present day. However, a consideration of the controversy is somewhat tangential here and beyond the scope of this paper.

[3]For some reason, use of the "folk-urban continuum" concept always tends to evoke controversy or at least comment of some sort. Rowe (1973 : 212) mentions it in connection with his comparison of urban life in two cities of modern India, but deliberately avoids "an explicit discussion" of it, though he admits that "it is not a totally moribund concept" and complains that "in some recent Indian demographic studies of cities the authors force the rather obviously unwilling data into the mold of the classical Chicago school." It is interesting that the concept has now been labelled in terms of "the classical Chicago school," as though there were some party line to be followed by those of us who (sometimes) draw inspiration from Redfield and his associates !

[4]And later published as *A Tribal Village of Middle India* by the Anthropological survey of India (Memoir No. 21, 1968).... The research was supported by a Ford Foundation Foreign Area Training Fellowship.

[5]This research was supported by a grant from the American Institute of Indian Studies in 1967-68 and a paid sabbatical leave of absence form California State University, Hayward, combined with an AIIS travel grant in 1970-71.

[6]This research was supported by a paid sabbatical leave of absence from California State University, Hayward, combined with personal funds. During my earlier study of Devagaon I frequently visited the twin towns of Rajim/Navapara Rajim so had considerable informal familiarity with them and their residents before beginning the 1977-78 study. A number of people were particularly helpful in making housing arrangements for my

wife and myself and aiding the research in numerous ways. Among them I am especially indebted to Talib Mumtaz, a local writer, poet and teacher whose valuable assistance and warm friendship continue to this day.

[7]In fact all Gonds refer to themselves as Koitur, without distinction. But to avoid confusion the term Hill Maria Gond (used by Elwin, Grigson and many other early ethnographers) is retained here. Other Gond populations include the Muria Gonds, Dandaria Maria Gonds, Raj Gonds, Koya, etc. Altogether there are at least four million Gonds and closely related peoples (such as the Koya), but the last Census which provided figures on tribal populations was 1961, and surely the population has increased considerably over the last 30 years. [See Banerjee and Bhatia (1988) and Furer-Haimendorf (1982 :14-21) for discussions of Gond populations and their distribution.]

[8]A minor exception to this situation existed at Orcha, where a few acres of settled rice land were cultivated along the river's edge. Significantly, according to Hill Maria tradition this land was "owned" outright by the families which cultivated it, and was inherited in the paternal line. However, the plots were few and small and the system of cultivation inefficient. "Ownership" of this land did not constitute a significant variable in producing differences of wealth. See Jay (1961) for a discussion of swidden versus rice cultivation at Orcha.

[9]Shamanism certainly exists in other peasant areas. It has been reported for northern India by Berreman (1964 :133-136; 1964) and by Harper (1957) and others for the south; it may not be a universal phenomenon in peasant India, but apparently is quite widespread, and certainly "possession" phenomena of some sort are indeed a universal aspect of Hinduism.

[10]This factional dispute has been described and analyzed in a previous paper (Jay 1978).

[11]The reader is asked to excuse a certain ambiguity in referring to Rajim-Navapara Rajim sometimes in the singular, sometimes in the plural. This ambiguity reflects a problem in conceptualization, since in one sense they constitute a single community, joined by geographical proximity and elaborately remifying social and economic ties, and in another sense are two separate communities with different identities and specialized functions.

[12]Curiously, however, both places have been left out of the

1981 Census, though they are present in the 1971 Census.

[13] I should mention that this was not my first trip to Bhopal. On previous occasions in India I had visited my lifelong friend, the Hindi writer Shanni and his family who resided in the city for many years before relocating to Delhi, where Shanni became Hindi editor at the Sahitya Akademi until his recent retirement from that position. I am much indebted to him in all kinds of ways, but in the present context for introducing me to many officials and intellectuals in Bhopal, many of whom were quite helpful to me during my 1989-90 research there.

[14] Singer (1972) has provided some very thorough and very stimulating observations on the notions of "modernity" and "tradition" which I would like to incorporate into this paper, but space considerations simply will not allow it.

[15] An additional point that could be made about towns and cities is that often they contain within them some of the functions of villages. Rajim/Navapara Rajim is a case in point : a significant number of the residents continue to cultivate fields surrounding the town, and of course many, indeed probably most, of the same castes found in the neighboring villages have households in town. But the reverse is less true, because many of the specialized functions of the town simply cannot, and do not exist in villages. Moreover, those socioeconomic and religious traditions and behaviors shared by villagers and townspeople alike are not really identical. Their presence in the relatively more urban (or less folklike) environment of the town converts them into variants which differ in many ways from their village expressions. This point could be demonstrated with additional data, but would require still more space in an already overly-long paper.

References

All, Syed Ashfaq — 1984 — *Bhopal—Past and Present.* Bhopal : Jai Bharat Publishing House.

Babb, Lawrence A. — 1975 — *The Divine Hierarchy : Popular Hinduism Central India.* New York : Columbia University.

Bailey, F. G. — 1957 — *Caste and the Economic Frontier.* Manchester : Manchester University Press.

— 1960 — *Tribe, Caste and Nation.* Manchester : Manchester University Press.

	1961	"Tribe" and "Caste" in India. *Contributions to Indian Sociology.* No. 5 : 7-19.
	1963	*Politics and Social Change. Orissa in 1959.* Berkeley : University of California Press.
Banerjee, B. G. and Kiran Bhatia	1988	*Tribal Demography of Gonds.* Delhi : Gian Publishing House.
Barnes, J. A.	1954	Class and Committees in a Norwegian Island Parish. *Human Relations* 7 : 39-58.
Berreman, Gerald D.	1964	Brahmins and Shamans in Pahari Religion. In *Religion in South Asia.* Edward B. Harper, ed. pp. 53-70. Seattle : University of Washington Press.
	1972	Social Categories and Social Interaction in Urban India. *American Anthropologist* 74 (3) : 576-568.
Census of India	1981 (a)	*Standard Urban Areas.* New Delhi : Registrar General.
	1981 (b)	*Town Directory.* New Delhi : Registrar General.
Cohn, Bernard S. and McKim Marriott	1958	Networks and Centres in the Integration of Indian Civilisation. *Journal of Social Research* (Bihar) 1 (1) : 1-9.
Corwin, Lauren Anita	1977	Great Tradition, Little Tradition : The Cultural Traditions of a Bengal Town. *Contributions to Indian Sociology* (NS) 11 (1) : 22-44.
Dumont, Louis	1962	"Tribe" and "Caste" in India. *Contributions to Indian Sociology* 6 : 120-122.
Dumont, Louis and D. Pocock	1957	Village Studies. *Contributions to Indian Sociology* 1 : 23-41.
Elwin, Verrier	1947	*The Muria and Their Ghotul.* London : Oxford University Press.
Fox, Richard G.	1975	Rationale and Romance in Urban Anthropology. *In City Ways.* John Friedl and Noel J. Chrisman, eds. pp. 46-70. New York : Thomas Y. Crowell Company.
Furer-Haimendorf,	1982	*Tribes of India : The Struggle*

Christophe von — *For Survival.* Berkeley : The University of California Press.

Gould, Harold 1960 Some Preliminary Obsevations Concerning the Anthropology of Industrialization. *The Eastern Anthropologist* XI (1) : 30-47.

1970 Occupational Categories and Stratification in the Achievement of Urban Society. In *Urban India : Society Space and Image.* Richard G. Fox, ed. pp. 51-76. Duke University Program in Comparative Studies on Southern Asia. Monograph Number 10.

1974 Cities on the North Indian Plain : Contrasting Lucknow and Kanpur. In *South Asia : Seven Community Profiles.* Clarence Maloney, ed. pp. 258-293. New York : Holt, Rinehart & Winston.

Hardgrave, Robert L. Jr. 1970 Urbanization and the Structure of Caste. In *Urban India : Society, Space and Image.* Richard G. Fox, ed. pp. 39-50 Duke University Program in Comparative Studies on Southern Asia. Monograph 10.

Harper, Edward B. 1957 Shamanism in South India. *Southwestern Journal of Anthropology* 13 (3) : 267-287.

Jay, Edward J. 1961 Social Values and Economic Change. *Economic Weekly* of Bombay 14 : 1369-1372.

1965 (a) A Case of the Absence of Conflict : The Hill Maria Gonds of Bastar. *Man in India* 45 (4) : 275-282.

1965 (b) Structural Obstacles to Tribal Acculturation : The Case of Regional Ceremonial Integration in Bastar. *The Eastern Anthropologist* 18 (3) : 159-164.

1966 Religious and Convivial Uses of Alcohol, in a Gond Village of Middle India. Quarterly *Journal of Studies on Alcohol* 27 (1) : 88-96.

1967 Leadership and External Relations in a Tribal Community of Middle India. In *Leadership in India.* L. P. Vidyarthi, ed. pp. 185-199. Bombay and New York : Asia Publishing House.

1968 *A Tribal Village of Middle India.* Calcutta : Anthropological Survey of India. Memoir No. 21.

1971 Some Aspects of Change in a Hill Maria Gond Village. *Indian Anthropologist* 1 (1) : 65-79.

1973 Bridging the Gap Between Castes : Ceremonial Friendship in Chhattisgarh. *Contributions to Indian Sociology* (NS) 7 : 144-158.

1974 A Comparison of Tribal and Peasant Villages in India. *Journal of the Indian Anthropological Society* 9 : 39-69.

1978 Authority Structure, Factions and Social Change in a Chhattisgarhi Village. *In Main Currents in Indian Sociology. Volume III : Cohesion and Conflict in Modern India.* Giri Raj Gupta, ed. pp. 199-223.

Jay, Edward J. 1990 Panc Kosi Yatra : A Sub-Regional Pilgrimage of Southern Chhattisgarh, India. In *the Social Anthropology of Pilgrimage.* Makhan Jha, ed. pp. 99-117. New Delhi : Inter-India Publications.

Klass, Morton 1972 Community Structure in West Bengal. *American Anthropologist* 74 (3) : 601-610.

Kroeber, Alfred L. 1948 Anthropology, New York : Harcourt, Brace and Company.

Marriott, McKim 1955 Little Communities in an Indigenous Civilization. In *Village India.* Chicago : University of Chicago Press.

Orans, Martin 1965 *The Santal : A Tribe in Search of a Great Tradition.* Detroit : Wayne State University Press.

Pocock, David F. 1960 Sociologies : Urban and Rural. *Contributions to Indian Sociology* 4 : 63-81.

Redfield, Robert 1941 *The Folk Culture of Yucatan.* Chicago : The University of Chicago Press.

1947 The Folk Society. *American Journal of Sociology* 52 (4) : 293-308.

1956 *Peasant Society and Culture.* Chicago : University of Chicago Press.

1962 The Natural History of the Folk Society.

In *Human Nature and the Study of Society*. Margaret Park Redfield, ed. pp. 294-302. Chicago : University of Chicago Press. [Originally Published in Social Forces XXXI (3), March 1953].

Redfield Robert, and Milton Singer 1954 The Cultural Role of Cities. In *Human Nature and the Study of Society*. Margaret Park Redfield, ed. pp. 326-350. Chicago : University of Chicago Press. (Originally published in Economic Development and Social Change III (1) : 53-73 (1954) (Research Center in Economic Development and Cultural Change, University of Chicago).

Rowe, William L. 1973 Caste, Kinship and Association in Urban India. In *Urban Anthropology*. Aidan Southall, ed. pp. 211-249. New York : Oxford University Press.

Saberwal, Satish 1977 Indian Urbanism : A Sociohistorical Perspective. *Contributions to India Sociology* (NS) 11 (1) : 1-19.

Service, Elman R. 1978 *Profiles in Ethnology*. Third Revised Edition. New York : Harper and Row.

Singer, Milton 1955 The Cultural Pattern of Indian Civilisation. *Far Eastern Quarterly* XV (1) : 23-36.

1958 The Great Tradition in a Metropolitan Centre : Madras. In *Traditional India : Structure and Change*. Milton Singer, ed. pp. 337-388 (Special Issue of the Journal of American Folklore 71 (281)

1960 The Expansion of Society and Its Cultural Implications. In *City Invincible*. Carl H. Kraeling and Robert M. Adams, eds. pp. 249-267. Chicago : University of Chicago Press.

1968 The Indian Joint Family in Modern Industry. In *Structure and Change in Indian Society*. Milton Singer and Bernard S. Cohn, eds. pp. 423-452.

1972 *When a Great Tradition Modernizes : An Anthropological Approach to Indian Civilization*. New York : Praeger.

Sinha, Surajit 1957 Tribal Cultures of Peninsular India as a Dimension of Little Tradition In the Study of Indian Civilization : A

Preliminary Statement. *Man in India* 37 (2) : 94-118.

1965 Tribe-Caste and Tribe-Peasant Continua In Central India. *Man in India* 45 (1) : 58-83.

Srinivas, M. N. 1952 Religion and Society Among the Coorgs of South India. London : Oxford University Press.

1955 Introduction to India's Villages A Collection of Articles Originally Published in the Economic Weekly of Bombay. pp. 1-18 Cal. Development Dept. W. B.

Steward, Julian H. 1955 *Theory of Culture Change.* Urbana : University of Illinois Press.

1967 Perspectives on Modernization : Introduction to the Studies. In *Contemporary Change in Traditional Societies.* Julian H. Steward, ed. pp. 1-55 Urbana : University of Illinois Press.

Vatuk, Sylvia 1972 *Kinship and Urbanization : White Collar Migrants in North India.* Berkeley : University of California Press.

Vidyarthi. L. P. 1961 *The Sacred Complex in Hindu Gaya.* New York : Asia Publishing House.

Wirth, Louis 1975 Urbanism As a Way of Life. In *City Ways.* John Friedl and Noel J. Chrisman, eds. pp. 26-45. New York : Thomas Y. Crowell Company. (Originally Published in American Journal of Sociology 44 (1) : 1-24 (1938).

Brian Morris

THE HINDU CONCEPTION OF THE SELF

Hinduism is a religion, a way of life, a philosophy, as well as a social system, and these are intrinsically connected. It is thus very difficult in the Indian context to separate out religion and philosophy, and even more problematic to delineate a Hindu "psychology". In his important study of Indian culture A.L. Basham (1954) has discussions on astronomy, mathematics, physics and chemistry, physiology and medicine, and on logic and epistemology : but he has no section at all on psychology or sociology. And yet as Agehananda Bharati points out all Hindu systems of thought have been centrally concerned with issues of the "self". Indeed it has been seen as *the* central theme in Hindu thinking, for the quest for enlightenment, for the prefection of the human person, has been viewed as the "essence" of Hinduism. But importantly the self in the Hindu context is essentially a religious or metaphysical concept and writers in the Hindu tradition have little interest in the empirical self. As Bharati writes :

"All Hindu traditions talk about the self either in order to reject its ontological status (as in Advaita Vedanta and in Buddhism), or to assimilate it to a theological and metaphysical construct which is a self with a capital 'S'. When any of the Hindu traditions speak about what might look like the individual, like an empirical self, it is not to analyze it but to denigrate it...the self as the basis of such important human achievements as scholarship, artistic skill, technological invention, etc. is totally ignored in the Indian philosophical texts" (1985 : 89).

It is evident that in the Indian context, metaphysical concepts drawn from an elite Brahmanic tradition penetrate the wider culture. Concepts such as moksha (salvation), dharma, karma, and Brahman, are not simply abstruse intellectual ideas of relevance only to a Brahmanic elite, but constitute what the psychoanalytic writer Sudhir Kakar has called the "Hindu world image" a consistent cultural template or world-view that permeates the everyday life of ordinary people, giving it structure and meaning. Whether consciously acknowledged or codified in rituals, this "world-image" has deeply influenced the way Hindus think and act. It is, Kakar suggests, so much in a Hindu's bones, that a person may not be aware of its influence (1981 : 15).

Nevertheless in acknowledging the influence of Hindu religious metaphysics, there is a danger of going to the other extreme, and, equating Advaita Vedanta with Hindu culture, to propagate the "fiction" which holds that the basis of Indian thought and culture is fundamentally "spiritual". The clearest proponent of this view is the Indian philosopher Sarvepalli Radhakrishnan, himself a high-caste Brahmin. His voluminous writings on Indian religion, philosophy and culture are well-known. A typical quotation from his writings will cogently express this standpoint. He writes:

"Philosophy in India is essentially spiritual. It is the intense spirituality of India, and not any great political structure or social organization that it had developed, that had enabled it to resist the ravages of time and the accidents of history. The spiritual motive dominated life in India...the dominant character of the Indian mind which has coloured all its culture and moulded all its thought is the spiritual tendency. Spiritual experience is the foundation of India's rich cultural history".

He even suggests that such spirituality is in essence a "mysticism" that leads to the realization of the spiritual (1933 : 1/24-25, 41). This extract is from his treatise on "Indian Philosophy". In his "An Idealist View of Life", a study which expresses very well his conservatism, he writes in a similar fashion, contrasting the rationalistic logic of the west with the "mystic contemplation" inherent in the Hindu system of philosophy. This "myth of Indian Spirituality" has been questioned by scholars such as M.N. Roy and Debiprasad Chattopadhyaya. The propagation of the 'myth' was certainly influenced by the German romantic movement of the early nineteenth century, which, in its necessary critique of the mechanistic tendencies of the Enlightenment, took an especial interest not only in the European folk tradition, but also in Indian culture and religion. Max Muller, the famous Sanskrit Scholar, inherited this perspective. What the myth does in essence is to equate one school of philosophy, the Vedanta, with Indian thought generally. The Vedanta tradition, systematized by the idealist philosopher

Sankara in the eight century, and popularized and propagated not only by Muller, but by such luminaries as Vivekananda and Aurobindo, is in fact less of a philosophy than a theology.

What Roy and Chattopadhyaya conclusively demonstrated was that the religions and idealist perspective in early Indian philosophy, rather than being the dominant tendency was in fact a minority one. They showed that the major schools of Indian philosophy—Samkhya, Nyaya and Vaisesika—were all essentially materialist philosophies as well as expressing, like early Buddhism, an atheistic viewpoint. Thus they stressed that these philosophical writings, together with those associated with Carvaka or Lokayata ("the philosophy of the people") were, in their critique of religious conceptions and ritual, and in their defence of the reality of the material world, essentially characterized by Secularism, a rationalistic logic and Science (Roy, 1940 : 76-112; Chattopadhyaya, 1959; 1969; 1976).

We shall turn to both Samkhya and Vedanta philosophy in a moment, but one needs therefore to be aware that although Brahmanic concepts drawn from the Vedanta literature are indeed pervasive in Indian culture, it is misleading to equate Hindu thought with mystical idealism. When Vivekananda wrote that "the Indian mind is first religious" he was expressing the Vedantic view-point, and conflating Hinduism with the Vedanta doctrine—a tendency widespread among many Indian scholars. Swami Nirvedananda's well-known text "Hinduism at a Glance" (1944) is a typical example.

Although Hinduism is not a philosophy in the western sense, it is generally recognized that there are six orthodox systems of Indian philosophy, and these are traditionally divided into three groups of two, namely Nyaya—Vaiseshika, Samkhya-Yoga, and Vedanta-Mimamsa. These schools of philosophy (Darshanas) are generally associated with six sages, respectively, Gautama, Kanata, Kapila, Patanjali, Badarayana and Jaimini, where aphoristic writings (Sutras) appeared somewhere between the seventh and second century B.C.

Nyaya was a form of analytical philosophy largely concerned with logic and inference, while the Vaiseka system was more interested in cosmology. It posited an atomic theory of matter, and suggested that the world was made of nine basic substances (Dravya), four material substances (air, water, fire and earth), and five inferential substances (ether, time, space, mind and self). It accepted the notion of god, not as a creator-spirit, but as an agency giving order to the universe. Each self has a characteristic individuality marked by its particular status or condition, and in the empirical state (Samsara) is connected with the body and mind (Manas). The Nyaya-Vaiseka thus postulated a dualism of matter and self (soul), and salvation comes when one has true knowledge of reality, and thus the eternal and separate nature of the self is recognized.

Samkhya is also a dualistic philosophy, since it recognizes two basic categories in the Universe—the Purusa and the Prakriti. Although often seen as secondary to the Vedanta system by contemporary religiously-inclined scholars like Radhakrishnan, in many ways Samkhya forms the underlying basis of Hindu culture. As Stephen Tyler writes : When we look for the underlying cognitive categories of Indian culture we will find that it is the Samkhya system that comprises the fundamental structure of Indian thought. It certainly forms the basis of Ayurvedic medicine (1973 : 73).

The Samkhya system, as M.N. Roy (1940) has argued, is essentially an atheistic and materialistic philosophy which developed a rational and naturalistic system of metaphysics. It is one of the earliest of the six schools of philosophy and is reputed to have been founded by the sage Kapila. Oddly enough, in spite of his atheism, great reverence is attached to his name, and like the Buddha, he is considered an incarnation of Vishnu. He is reported to have lived as a recluse in the seventh or eight century BC. The term Samkhya means number, calculation or reason, and it is an appropriate one, for Samkhya is a thorough-going, rational philosophy. Knowledge, it holds, is derived from three sources only; sense perception; inference through the faculty of reason; and valid testimony. Thus Kapila came to reject the notion of a supreme being, whether in terms of a personal god or an impersonal absolute, and was equally opposed to the vedic scriptures and rituals. Through reason we gain knowledge of primordial matter (prakriti or pradhana) which is eternal, unproduced, and conceived as containing the potentials of everything in the universe—it is, in its undeveloped or unmanifested state (Avyakata), the primary cause. Through its three modes—Sattva (sentience, goodness), Rajas (passion, energy) and Tamas (inertia, enveloping), nature "acts" and develops itself. From nature (Prakriti) thus emerges intellect (Buddhi or Mahat), from intellect ego-consciousness (Ahamkara), and from this evolves the mind (Manas), the five sense organs (hearing, touch, sight, taste, smell), the active senses (speech, holding, walking, evacuation and procreation), the five subtle elements (sound, touch, colour, taste and smell), and the gross elements Mahabhuta-Akasa (ether), Vayu (wind), Agni (fire), Jala (water), and Prthvi (earth). This makes a total of twenty four categories, a scheme that is adopted by Charaka in his treatise on medicine. It is clear that Kapila not only viewed nature as having ontological primacy, but he followed tantrism in viewing prakriti as embodying the female principle. Although the above concepts and schemes are not easily understood, the Samkhya system, in essence, postulates a cosmic evolution and views the body and all forms of consciousness in material terms. But as a philosophy, Samkhya is often called Dvaita, or dualism, because Kapila also postulated the existence of a twenty-fifth category, the purusa or soul. Interestingly, Chattopadhyaya suggests that the literal meaning of this term is "male person". But in the Samkhya system the soul is "isolated, neutral, perceptive and inactive by nature" (Samkhya Karika 19). It exists apart from the creative and ever-changing matter, and as an early translator put it : "It dwells apart in a lofty but barren isolation" (Davies, 1894 : 100).

Having nothing whatever to do with the basic theme of the Samkhya system, the cosmic evolution of nature, the role of the Purusa, as many writers have noted, is somewhat "anomalous" and "superfluous". It is possible that later followers of Samkhya, like Iswara Krishna [who wrote the Samkhya Karika (Exposition of the Samkhya] around the second or third century AD] were heavily influenced by the salvation ethic of the Vedantists, and thus came to identify the purusa (soul) with the ultimate reality, or at least to assume that the whole process of the evolution of prakriti was teleological : designed for the ultimate liberation of the soul. But then the soul is always detached and isolated according to Kapila. However, the internal contradictions of the Samkhya system were quickly seized upon by the Buddhists and by Sankara, who in his commentary on the 'Brahma Sutra' clearly perceived that the Samkhya system, with its stress on "unconscious primeval matter...as the world cause" was the main opposition to his own Vedanta doctrine, and he spent many pages outlining the Samkhya system, and attempting to refute it.

The Samkhya system of philosophy was, of course, taken up by Patanjali in his treatise Yoga Sutra, compiled around 200 BC. The 'Yoga system' of philosophy, however, is something of a misnomer, for yoga, as we shall see, is essentially a method for the discipline of the body and mind leading to a higher form of contemplation (Samadhi); it is not a school of philosophy. Patanjali simply grafted the theistic notion of god on to the Samkhya system.

Yet although Samkhya philosophy was essentially an atheistic doctrine, it was, like Buddhism, a philosophy of salvation. Both Samkhya and Yoga affirms that there are as many purusa (souls) as there are human beings, and thus each of these souls is, in a sense, a 'monad'. But essentially, though pluralistic, the purusa is a transcendent and autonomous principle completely independent of nature (prakriti). Thus importantly, as Mircea Eliade emphasized, psychomental states (mental cognition, perception, consciousness, intellect) belong to a different ontological order than that of the purusa (spirit, soul, self,—however it is translated into western concepts); "they belong to two different modes of being : (1958; 15). Prakriti is as real and as eternal as purusa; but unlike the soul it is dynamic and creative. The individual person (Jiva) consists of both prakriti and purusa, and the soul is seen as enmeshed, held in "bondage", by the material world. Ignorance (Avidya), according to Samkhya doctrine "consists in confusing the motionless and eternal Purusa with the flux of psychomental life. To say "I suffer", "I want", "I hate", "I know" and to think that this "I" refers to spirit, is to live in illusion not prolong it; for all our acts and intentions, by the simple fact that they are dependent upon prakriti, upon "matter", are conditioned and governed by Karma" (*op cit*, 27). Thus the natural world is devoid of spirit (soul) and salvation consists of the knowledge (in the sense of gnosis) the realization that the purusa is distinct from matter, from psychomental life. Purusa, the self, is pure, eternal and free when detached from the world. This knowledge is quite different from normal intellectual activity. But importantly the world is real for Samkhya and Yoga, not illusory as it is in Vedanta philosophy. The classical Yoga system of Patanjali develops the salvation aspect of Samkhya suggesting that gnosis only prepares the ground for the realization of freedom (Mukti); true emancipation can come about only through ascetic techniques and contemplation. These we shall discuss later in the essay.

The Mimamsa system, whose primary source is the Sutra of Jaimini (circa 300 BC) is the most orthodox of the systems of philosophy. It takes the Vedas to be infallible and authoritative, and it is not so much a school of salvation as an exposition and interpretation of the sacred texts. But perhaps the most influential of the Hindu darshanas, is the Uttara ("last") Mimamsa, or Vedanta ("the end of the Vedas"). The Basic text of the Vedanta system is the Brahma Sutra, attributed to Badarayana, who probably lived in the early part of the Christian era. Vedanta is essentially concerned with developing some of the religious and philosophical speculations of Upanishads, and the Brahma Sutra, together with Bhagavad-Gita, form the foundation texts of the system. But classical Vedanta is intrinsically associated with the South Indian philosopher Sankara, and it was largely due to his writings that Hinduism, in its modern form, arose.

Buddhism was not, as is often supposed, driven from India by Brahmanic persecution, but rather its disappearance was the natural result of the gradual and peaceful assimilation of Buddhist ideas and rituals by the Brahmin caste. At the level of popular worship temples and pilgrim centres were promoted—though temples were unknown before the Buddhist revolution. Image-worship became the established form of ritual and, influenced by Buddhist ethics, with its stress on non-violence, the vedic sacrificial rites were abandoned. To support and promote this popular Hinduism, the Kings and landed aristocracy built temples and supported the Brahmin caste. The Brahmins in turn produced the Puranas, popular accounts of the Epics, which recorded the heroic exploits of various deified rulers like Krsna and Rama. At the level of philosophical discourse there was likewise an essential continuity between Mahayana Buddhism and the new emergent religion. The key figure in this transformation was Sankara. He not only favoured monastic orders throughout India and wrote devotional songs, but his many commentaries on the scriptures fully established the Vedanta system. Although Sankara was engaged in an intellectual battle on two fronts, against Buddhism and against the Samkhya doctrines, the similarity between his own ideas and those of Mahayana Buddhists can be gleamed from the fact that he was often accused of being a "crypto-Buddhist". As Ramesh Dutt put it; the notion of a "universal soul" first mooted in the Upanishads, then modified by the various doctrines of the Mahayana Buddhists, was eventually accepted back again as the cardinal principle of Sankara's Vedanta philosophy. Sankara, of course, was quite happy to support popular devotional cults and image-worship for the masses, but reading the Vedas and salvation seems to have been restricted to the twice-born, the ruling elite of warriors, priests and merchants. In a very real sense, then, modern Hinduism begins with Sankara : an esoteric mysticism for the elite and popular cults of various spirits for the working people.

Sankara is credited with the systematization of the Upanishad writings, and as having a function similar to that of Thomas Aquinas with respect to medieval Christianity. Sankara's basic ideas, as Bharati suggests, are intellectually quite simple, for he suggests a form of absolute idealism known as Advaita (Non-dualistic) Vedanta. Sankara thus postulates that there is one and only one being in existence—the absolute (Brahman), an impersonal 'spirit' or soul that is fundamentally the only reality, the individual soul *(Atman)* being simply an individuated aspect of this reality. Brahman and Atman are in essence identical. Brahman is without form, and both immanent and transcendent to the empirical world : "everything within nature has its existence in and through Brahman. God has not created the world out of nothing. He has projected it out of Himself. He is both the efficient and material cause of the universe"—So writes a modern Vedanta Scholar in very anthropomorphic terms. (Nirvedananda, 1944 : 142). The "ground" of the universe, the only reality is thus spirit, and the individual soul *(Atman)* is identical with it. This reality is often described in Sanskrit by the term Saccidananda—meaning absolute being *(Sat)*, absolute consciousness *(Cit)* and absolute bliss *(Ananda)*. In relation to this external, unchanging reality, Brahman, the phenomenal world is seen as essentially unreal, as appearance. The world is an illusion—Maya. "Sankara explains the appearance of the world with an analogy. A person may mistake a rope for a serpent. The Serpent is not there, but it is not entirely an illusion, for there is the rope. The appearance of the serpent lasts until the rope is closely examined. The world can be compared with the Serpent and Brahman with the rope" (Sen 1961; 83).

The world is thus neither real or unreal; it is an appearance based on the reality of the ultimate spirit, Brahman. This impersonal deity is often equated with the Buddhist void *(Sunya)*, but it has to be recognized that Brahman is an objective reality, a "something" not nothingness. Salvation is achieved in Vedanta through the practical realization (not merely the theoretical awareness) of the identity, the oneness, of the self *(atman)* with the absolute (Brahman).

Samkhya, as the earliest school of philosophy, accepted the reality of both the phenomenal world and of spirit *(Purusa)*, but nonetheless suggested detachment of the soul from the empirical world, Buddhism denied the reality of the "soul-spirit", understood as an irreducible spiritual unity, and replaced it by "States of consciousness". Vedanta went to the other extreme, accepted the reality of absolute Spirit, and, seeking to avoid the difficulties in specifying the relationship between spirit (soul) and the universe, denied the reality of the universe, regarding it as Maya, illusion (Murti, 1955 : 10; Eliade 1959 : 32). But what all these three philosophies had in common was the implication that salvation *(Moksha)* involved the detachment of the individual from the phenomenal world. This was particularly pronounced in Vedanta.

Sankara, following Samkhya and other schools of Hindu philosophy, viewed the self on several levels. It is related to the physical body, and to the internal organ *(Antah-Karana)*, the material, thinking, perceiving mind. It is also related to inner consciousness and the ego. And finally it is related to what Menon calls the "inner self" or soul *(Jiva)*—although this self is not a separate entity, not an individual soul, for this self is at one with Brahman. Now while Buddha denied the reality of an inner self or *atman*, Sankara, in a manner similar to Descartes, appeals to the sense of certainty one has regarding the existence of oneself. "A man", it has been said, "may doubt of many things, of anythings *else;* but he can never doubt of his own being", for that very act of doubting would affirm its existence. It is thus eventually through something in ourselves that, according to Sankara, "we are able to judge of reality and unreality" (Hiriyanna, 1949 : 162; Menon, 1976 : 20-21).

But identifying one's true self with spirit (Brahman) implied a dualism similar to that of the Samkhya system, a dualism not between body and mind, but between spirit and the phenomenal world. Vedanta is non-dualistic *(Advaita)* only in the sense of identifying Brahman with *atman*, and in denying the reality of the world, as *Maya*.

One has to realize that in the Vedanta system, as with the Samkhya doctrine, spirit *(atman, purusa)* and psychomental states belong to two different orders of being. The soul *(atman)* is seen as the substantive part of a living being and is quite distinct from the physical body, the sense organs, perception, and the mind. The soul is seen as being "encased" in three bodies, the physical body, the subtle body of the Tanmatras (sound, touch, colour, taste, smell) and the subtle *Bhutas*, which consist of the mind *(Manas)*, intellect *(Buddhi)* the five Pranas (vital energy) and the finer counterparts of the sense organs. Thus all Hindu notions about the mind, cognition, the entire psychological aspects of life are seen in philosophical terms as material conceptions, as part of the phenomenal world of change and karma. And these are seen as distinct from the inner self. The self, in Vedanta, is not the body, the ego, nor is it a series of mental states or a logical postulate. Neither can it be grasped or understood by rational thought. It is only revealed by intuition, by revelation, when it is understood to be at one with the universal spirit (Brahman), (Menon, 1976 : 24). As Bharati describes the relationship between the self and material existence in Hindu thought:

"From the canonical manifestations of mind (*Buddhi*, "intellect"), via *Manas*, "the thinking organ", conative energizer, to the body of flesh, all these are conceived of as matter, albeit of different degrees of subtlety and density—the body is the crudest, thickest of these material entities, *Buddhi* the subtlest. These are visualized as layers superposed on one another, literally called "sheaths" *(Kosa)* in Hindu philosophical thinking. In the canonical Upanisads, the self is successively defined as the gross body, then the senses, the mind, intellection, and finally the *atman* which equals brahman, the ubiquitous absolute which has no form and no matter. The underlying notion seems to be that short of the full, intuitive identification with non-material Brahman, we—i.e. our bodies, senses, and minds—are material selves" (1985 : 193).

In a sense two selves are recognized in Hindu thought—a material or phenomenal self, and an "inner self"—the latter, identified with spirit, being formless, immutable and absolute. In her study of the "mind" in Indian philosophy Sarasvati Chennakesavan stresses that both Samkhya and Vedanta philosophical schools make a clear distinct between mind *(Manas)* which belongs to the physical order of things—as "subtle matter"—and the "self", Brahman, the "Cosmic self", "pure consciousness"—the "eternally existing real" (1960 : 35).

In a later period the Vedanta doctrine was modified by such religious scholars as Ramauji and Madhava, who developed more dualistic *(Dvaita)* doctrine, denying the Upanisadic identity of spirit and the human Soul *(atman)*. Madhava stressed the distinction between three separate realities, the physical world, God (Vishnu) and individual souls *(Jiva)*. In salvation, obtained through devotion *(Bhakti)*, the soul is united but not identified with the deity.

In Hindu thought the realization of the "true" self—whether or not identified with spirit—essentially implies a detachment from the phenomenal world of becoming, not only from desires and material attachments, but from the flux of psychic life itself. We shall later explore the four main paths to salvation (*Jnana, Bhakti, Karma* and *Yoga)* that have been stressed in the Indian context.

In Hindu tradition three secular goals of life are regarded as legitimate—*Kama, artha* and *dharma. Kama* means desire or pleasure, and the hedonistic aspect of life is seen as important in Hindu culture, particularly in aesthetics and heterosexual love. The erotic preoccupations of ancient India are well known, and evident in art and in literature of all kinds—both religious and secular. But the pursuit of pleasure, as a legitimate goal in life tends to be down-played by many contemporary Hindus; indeed the puritanism of many religious writers is almost pathological, leading them to deny the erotic quality of much religious symbolism.

The second goal, *artha* refers essentially to the wealth and possessions one gains from honest means. It designates the instruments for success in the worldly life, and includes the pursuit of social and political goals, as well as material things. The pursuit of prosperity, security, political power and social well-being are all included under the heading of *artha*. Kautilya's famous political text is entitled Arthasastra.

The third of life's goals in Hinduism is the quest for *Dharma*, living one's life according to the sacred or moral law. *Dharma* is a central concept in the epics and *sastras* (scriptures) and has been variously translated; duty, sacred order, the essential nature of a thing, right conduct. It is derived from the Sanskrit root *shri* (to uphold or sustain) and in a narrow sense it means custom and law. It encompasses the first two aims of life, and has an essentially social content. It has been described as the "social cement", and the "principle of social restraint" that checks the unbridled pursuit of pleasure and power. It is instrinsically connected with the concept of *Karma* and with the vision of an organic society in which each person has a specific role, and a clearly defined set of duties, obligations and privileges. As it is expressed in the Mahabharata "Neither the state nor the King...governs the people; it is only by Dharma that people secure mutual protection" and it was the King's job to protect and uphold the Dharma. In the Indian context Dharma essentially refers to the caste system, which is a hierarchical social system that proclaims the fundamental inequality of humans. In the classical literature four castes (*Varna*, meaning colour) are outlined and given divine sanction, and each has a different distribution of *guna* and *karma*. As the Bhagavad Gita puts it :

> "Severity, self-restraint, austerity, purity, forgiveness, and also uprightness, knowledge, realization, belief in a hereafter—these are the duties of the Brahmans...
>
> Heroism, vigor, firmness, resourcefulness, not flying from battle, generosity, and lordliness are the duties of the Kshatriyas.
>
> Agriculture, cattle-rearing and trade are the duties of the Vaisyas, born of their own nature; and action consisting of service is the duty of the Sutras born of their own nature." (Chidbhavananda, 1984 : 909-913).

And the text goes on to suggest that :

> "Devoted each to his own duty, man attains the highest perfection...Better is one's own dharma, though imperfect, than the dharma of another well performed. He who does the duty ordained by his own nature incurs no sin" (*op cit* 917-920).

The Dharma thus postulates a divinely—sanctioned social order, similar to that of Plato's Republic. Plato saw his three "castes"—Guardians, military auxiliaries and artisans—as corresponding respectively to three aspects of the individual psyche—reason, will and appetite.

Likewise, as Arthur Danto has suggested, the four castes are associated not only with body-parts (head, heart, loins and feet) but with the four goals in life, *moksha* (the supreme aim), *dharma, artha* and *kama*, in a corresponding hierarchy of values (1973; 40). Thus the Brahmins are concerned with *moksha*, the Kshatriya's with upholding the *dharma*, and the Vaisyas with wealth and together they form the twice-born castes. The later refers to their two births, once as a natural birth, and again at their initiation, when they were invested with the sacred thread and received into the Aryan i.e. aristocratic society. Normally the initiation was confined to boys. Only the twice born castes had access to the Vedic scriptures.

The division of Hindu society into four castes was an ideal model : in reality the caste-system was far more complex and consisted of a diverse number of caste-groups *(Jati)*. Caste membership was hereditary, each caste was to a degree occupationally specialized and endogemous, and the system was further bolstered by strict rules of purity and pollution. But it has to be noted that historically not all Hindus have been supporters of the caste system and that the Vedanta doctrine of Brahman implies the fundamental equality of all humans, whose self is identical with the Cosmic Soul.

The caste system is intrinsically linked, as said, to the theory of *karma*, a term that literally means action or deed. It is a theory of moral causation and implies that every human action has consequences for good or ill. All events thus have antecedents and what a person is determined by past actions. According to Hindu doctrine therefore a person is not born a "tabula rasa" but is endowed with certain fundamental characteristics, that were largely determined by actions in a previous life. As the Chandogya Upanisad puts it :

> "Those whose conduct here has been good will quickly attain a good birth, the birth of a Brahmin, the birth of Kshatriya, or the birth of Vaisya. But those whose conduct has been evil, will quickly attain an evil birth, the birth of a dog, the birth of a hog, the birth of a (low caste) Chandala" (4.10.7).

Thus a theory of transmigration, the continued existence of the soul *(Jiva)* in a succession of rebirths, is a necessary corollary to the doctrine of *karma*. This leads us on to the fourth, and the highest in value of life's aims, that of *moksha*, the liberation or release from the cycle of rebirths. This is also the fourth stage in the Hindu four life stages *(asramas)*.

Just as society was divided into four castes, so, theoretically, a persons life was, in classical Hinduism, divided into four stages. The scheme clearly applied only to males belonging to the twice-born Aryan castes. The first stage, after the person had been invested with the sacred thread, is that of the Brahmacharya, the individual taking on the life of a student. He receives instruction in the vedas, leads a celibate life, and under the guidance of a *guru* (teacher) learns meditative exercises, the performance of rituals, and various forms of knowledge. The second stage is that of the householder *(Grhastha)*, begun after marriage and lasting until late middle age. Having established a family and achieved worldly success, a man was towards the end of his life then expected to withdraw from the world, and become a forest dweller *(Vanaprastha)*. Finally a man enters the final life stage, that of a *sannyasin*. He completely abandons the things of this world, devoting his life to religious penance and meditation, and enters a world beyond *dharma*. As a wandering ascetic he is concerned only with liberation *(moksha)*, freedom from the cycle of rebirths, by concentrating his mind wholly on Brahman. A man's life therefore is said ideally to have two stages, one devoted to the things of this world *(pravrtti)*, the goals of *karma, artha* and *dharma;* the other devoted to attaining a release from the things of this world *(nivrtti)*. Swami Nirvedananda refers to them as the path of desire and the path of renunciation.

Moksha (or Mukti), like the Buddhist concept of *nirvana*, essentially refers to the primary goal of life, release, liberation from the world of *karma*, the continual cycle of rebirths *(samsara)*. It signifies not only retirement from worldly activity but a rejection of the world. It constitutes, in Hindu culture, the ultimate aim of existence. Nirvedananda describes it as follows :

> "This state of liberation from *samsara* is called *Mukti*. The liberated man *(Mukta Purusa)* realizes the essence of his being as none other than God, and, therefore, becomes divine in all his bearings. External peace reigns in his heart. He has no want, no misery, no fear. Love and compassion for all move him..." (1944 : 42).

The Hindu tradition recognizes four basic paths *(marga)* that lead to the realization of salvation *(moksha)—jnana, karma, bhakti* and *yoga*. We may consider each of these in turn.

1. *Jnana Marga* (or *jnana yoga*) is the way of knowledge. In Hindu culture, it has been said, that a knowledge of reality is the key to self-realization. Knowledge and learning have always been given high priority, and both Samkhya and Vedanta scholars see jnana (knowledge) as the way to liberation. As the Bhagavad Gita put it : "Even if you be the most sinful of all sinners, yet shall you cross over all sin by the raft of knowledge" (4; 36). But such knowledge was centred on the human subject, and subordinated to the desire for liberation. Sankara puts an important emphasis on liberation through knowledge, although he accepted religious worship and devotion. He suggested four stages in the development of liberation—an emphasis on *sattva* living, constantly associating with *isvara* (god) through ritual acts, the consciousness of identity with god, and the absolution of all difference between the self and *isvara*. By such practices Sankara contented "knowledge purifies the embodied soul stained by ignorance, and then itself disappears". A person's identity with Brahman *(isvara)* is realized; not through ritual or

ascetic exercises, but through spiritual practice *(sadhana)* (Organ, 1970 : 204).

One of the most well-known advocates of Jnana Yoga is Ramana Maharshi, who follows the Advaita-Vedanta teachings of Sankara. And the teachings of this modern mystic echo those of Sankara in making it clear that the self is in no way related to the body, but is identified with an impersonal deity, Brahman. Ramana Maharshi's method of "self enquiry" has been described as follows :

> "The plenary experience of the non-dual self is the goal; enquiring into the nature of the self is the means. When the mind identified the self with the non-self (the body, etc.), there is bondage; when this wrong identification is removed through the enquiry "Who am I ?" there is release...Self-enquiry is not the mind's inspection of its own contents, but tracing its first mode, the "I"—thought, to its source which is the Self." The 'self' that is realized is not the empirical self, but the supreme self *(atman)*, the only reality. The distinction between "God" and "Soul" is not real (Mahadevan, 1977 : 82- 83).

It has to be stressed however that knowledge in this context is not empirical knowledge of the world and of human existence but religious knowledge or gnosis. As Jonathan Parry has written of the Brahmanical tradition, "real knowledge is knowledge of a metaphysical truth which liberates the soul from the endless cycle of existence—a knowledge which is revealed in the texts but which is generally thought to be obtained only by years of submission to a rigourous ascetic discipline" (1985 : 206). The 'self', therefore, in the Hindu tradition is essentially a metaphysical self.

2. *Karma Marga* is the way of action. This path of liberation stresses the importance of social duty and the performance of selfless actions. It is given its classic expression in the Bhagavad Gita, and is a path clearly associated with the Kshatriya caste. The epic Bhagavad Gita (the Song of the Lord) records the moral dilema of one of the Pandava brothers, Arjuna who on the battlefield of Kurukshetra, faces many of his own kinsmen in battle. He is moved and disturbed at the thought of killing his own kindred, and turns to his charioteer, Krishna, for advice. The charioteer reveals himself as an incarnation of the god Vishnu, and what ensures in the dialogue is that Krishna

convinces Arjuna that it is his duty to fight, and thus to kill his own kith and kin. It symbolizes the dominance of the state or territorial principle, over the kinship ethics of tribal society (Sardesai and Bose, 1982 : 23). The message of the Gita is that one should follows the *dharma*, and so through selfless action *(karma)* achieve salvation. As Krishna suggests :

> "Whatever obligatory work is done, O Arjuna, merely because it ought to be done, abandoning attachment and also fruit, that abandonment is deemed to be *sattvika*...The relinquisher imbued with *sattva* and a steady understanding and with his doubts dispelled, hates not disaggreeable work nor is he attached to agreeable one...An action which is ordained, which is free from attachment, which is done without love or batred by one not desirous of the fruit, that action is declared to be sattvika" (18 : 9-10, 23).

Thus Arjuna is instructed to follow the obligations of his caste—to perform without attachment or thought of reward, his function as a warrior. Yet although the *karma marga* stresses the importance of activity in the world, and action, its aim is to transcend *dharma*. "The notion of agency must be given up. The act is to be disinterested" (Organ, 1970 : 247). The notion of an empirical self is thus transcended. As Krishna suggests to Arjuna :

> "Conquer the enemies and enjoy the unrivalled kingdom. By me have they been verily slain already, you be merely an outward cause" (11 : 33) Spirit is the only reality, and cause.

3. *Bhakti Marga*—The way of devotion.

The Bhagavad Gita discusses not only *jnana* and *karma* yoga, but introduces a third path, that of *bhakti*. The terms comes from the root *bhaj*, meaning to be attached to, to be devoted to, and essentially means the unconditional surrender to the deity, with profound feelings of love and devotion. It represents the theistic tendency in Hinduism, and was given its fullest expression in the hymns of the early Tamil devotees of South India. *Bhakti* cults flourished during the medieval period, and were particularly associated with those religious scholars who accepted a qualified form of Vedanta—like Madava and Ramanuja. These cults focussed around two deities--Krishna (an incarnation of the god Vishnu—hence called Vaishnavism) and Siva (the Saiva cults). The *bhakti* path implied no lengthy meditation, no penance, no intellectual insights into the mysteries of Brahman/*atman*—simply loving devotion directed towards the deity. Its advocates stressed its superiority to the other paths : "*Bhakti* is indeed greater than action, knowledge and *yoga*...Love is its own reward", sang Narada, Nirvedananda suggests that *bhakti-yoga*, the "path of love", "rests on the simple truth that one can realize God by loving Him. Nothing else is required—neither abstract thinking nor any mechanical exercise of body and mind" (1944 : 86). The Bhagavad Gita clearly implies that this path is the one most suited to those of "inferior birth"—the Vaisyas, Sudras and Women (9.32), and Krishna suggests that "I am the same to all beings...those who worship Me with devotion, they are in Me and I also am in them" (9.29). But whatever form of yoga—*dhyana* (meditation), *jnana*, *karma* or *bhakti*—the sacred text insists on a hierarchy of values and indicates that true selfhood is only achieved in the union of the individual's soul with God. Thus

"The senses are said to be superior to the body; the mind is superior to the senses; the intellect is superior to the mind; and what is superior to the intellect is Atman". (3.42).

Bhakti, as with the other paths, is a form of salvation that involves then a detachment from the empirical world. This is particularly evident in a contemporary devotional cult, the Hare Krishna movement (International Society for Krishna Consciousness) founded by Bhaktivedanta Swami Prabhupada in New York in 1966. For this Movement stresses a fundamental dualism between the body and the self. "I am not this body" is the title of a chapter in Francine Daner's study of the cult. The devotees of the cult believe that identifying with one's material body is one of the greatest pitfalls in human life, for the body is seen as a "disease", a "lump of ignorance" and a prison. Controlling one's senses and bodily desires is, therefore an aid to "Self realization" (1976 : 72). In one of his lectures Prabhupada states :

> "We are not meant to undergo suffering, but we are suffering because we are trapped in the material world and identifying with material bodies...Real happiness can be found in the spiritual world where there is pure unallayed bliss with no trace of suffering, but as long as we are attached to the temporary pleasures of the material body we are in a prison. We should be working towards getting

free and entering into the real life that awaits us outside the prison boundaries" (*op cit*, 75).

Swami Prabhupada made it clear that "real life" meant following the Bhakti tradition, devotion to Krishna (God). None of the followers of *jnana, joga* and *karma* can know god, he argued—only the *Bhakta* (devotee). He quotes from the Gita "only through the process of *Bhakti* can one understand god" (18 : 55; 197 : 13). Such understanding and devotion implied the "Severance" of the roots that bind us to material existence, and "to renounce everything related to the material conception of life" (*op, cit*, 8). Through devotion to Krsna we came to realize that "we are part and parcel of god" and this realization involves an evolution—"back to godhead". And he continues : "We consider that we are born and that we die. Such thinking is called *maya*, or illusion, and as soon as we get out of this illusion of identifying the soul with the body, we attain the stage of *Brahma-bhuta*. When one realizes "I am not this body; I am spirit-soul, part and parcel of the Supreme Brahman" he attains what is called Brahman realization" (1977 : 237).

Prabhupada conflates god, soul, life and self, but clearly sees deity as a "Supreme Self", of which the individual 'soul' is but a part. But he insists that god is 'personal' and considered Sankara's theory of an impersonal spirit (Brahman) to be a form of atheism though a necessary doctrine to counter the void of Buddhism. Unlike the early Bhakti movements which were against caste restrictions, and supported largely by the low castes, Prabhupada, in accepting the Vedas as of divine origin, supports the caste-system and sees his devotees as a new elite group of Brahmins (see my article on the Hare Krishna cult [1979] for a discussion of its politics).

4. *Yoga Marga*. Besides being one of the six systems of philosophy, *Yoga* also constitutes a system of discipline that leads to salvation, and thus represents one of the four paths *(marga)*. The term *yoga* is derived from the Sanskrit root *yuj* which means to join, to bind, to yoke together. It thus implies the union of the individual soul with the universal spirit. This is possible, as Mircea Eliade suggests, only if the "bonds" that unite the spirit to the world are detached. This implies a preliminary detachment from matter. (1958; 7). The term *yoga* is therefore often applied to the three Hindu paths to salvation, *karma yoga, bhakti yoga* and *jnana yoga*. But the classical system of *yoga*, known as Raja Yoga, was that described by Patanjali in

his Yoga Sutras. There is some debate as to who this person was, but it is generally felt that he was a grammarian who lived in the second century BC. Patanjali, as we have noted, followed the Samkhya system, but accepted the existence of a supreme spirit *(isvara)*. He stresses too that salvation is not attained through metaphysical knowledge, but through various techniques of body control and meditation.

In his *yoga sutras*, Patanjali defined *yoga* as the control of thought processes in the mind, and following Samkhya doctrine the mind *(chitta)* is made up of several functions, *manas* (mind as a sensing organ), *buddhi* (intelligence or intellect) and *ahamkara* (ego, or self-consciousness). (Chennakesavan, 1960 : 17-34). Such thought processes take into account perception, knowledge, delusions, dreams, sleep, memory. Through non-attachment one achieves freedom, freedom from desire for what is seen or heard. The aim of *yoga*, as with the other three paths, is to achieve salvation, defined as non-attachment to the empirical world.

"When, through knowledge of the *atman*, one ceases to desire any manifestation of nature, then that is the highest kind of non-attachment" (1, 16). Patanjali also notes that concentration may be attained also through devotion to god *(isvara)*. But Patanjali's scheme of salvation is less concerned with knowledge and devotion than with outlining a course of graded mental concentration or spiritual discipline in order to obtain "union" *(yoga)*. As with Buddhism, Patanjali accepts that the empirical world is one of suffering—all experiences are painful. "For even the enjoyment of the present pleasure is painful, since we already fear its loss. Past pleasure is painful because renewed cravings arise from the impressions it has left upon the mind" (2, 15). Patanjali defines *atman* as the "pure consciousness" of the subject which is "unchangeable", and stresses the reality of the empirical world of experience to someone who has not reached the "state of liberation". As with Vedanta, mind and *atman* are distinct.

"To identify consciousness with that which merely reflects consciousness—this is egoism" (2, 6).

Patanjali suggests that a person can obtain "knowledge of *atman*" (salvation, or non-attachment) through a series of seven stages, leading to the highest state, that of *samadhi*, complete absorption, the experience and realization that the self is nothing but divinity. The stages are.

1. *Yama*—Self-restraint, the "abstention from harming others,

from falsehood, from theft, from sexual activity, and from greed" (2.30). This stage incorporates the principle of *ahimsa* (not to kill) which runs completely counter to the *karma-yoga* advocated in the Bhagavad Gita.

2. *Niyama*—the observances, a series of disciplines designed to further spiritual progress. Cleanliness, serenity, ascetism *(tapas)*, the study of Yoga metaphysics and devotion to god *(isvara)* are all specified (2, 32).

3. *Asana*—posture. Patanjali advocates the adoption of certain bodily postures "to be seated in a position which is firm but relaxed". The most famous position is the so-called Lotus-posture *(padmasana)* in which the feet are placed on opposite thighs. In the texts of *hatha-yoga* and tantrism many other postures are detailed.

4. *Pranayama*—refers to various techniques of breathing that may be adopted in order to enhance physical and spiritual discipline. Patanjali defines *pranayama* (*prana* essentially means vital energy) as the "arrest of the movements of inhalation and exhalation". He only devotes three *sutras* to the disciplining of respiration, but this subject is dealt with at more length by the *hatha-yoga* treatises.

5. *Pratyahara*—restraint; refers to the withdrawal of sensory activity from the external world. It is the final stage of psychophysiological ascesis, the detachment of the sense-organs from the world. As Patanjali defines it, "When the mind is withdrawn from sense-objects, the sense organs also withdraw themselves from their respective objects and thus are said to imitate the mind" (2, 54).

6. *Dharana*—concentration, is

"holding the mind within a center of spiritual consciousness in the body, or fixing it on some divine object" (3, 1). It involves the fixation of thought on a single point or object.

7. *Dhayana*—meditation, is the "unbroken flow of thought toward the object of concentration". It is not meditation in the normal sense of the term, i.e. to think discursively around a subject, but rather implies an act of "penetration" into the essence of an object, the mind then ceasing to have any function.

Finally this leads to the state of *samadhi*, an "enstatic" (as Eliate describes it) experiential state, where there is no differentiation between subject and object. When, in meditation, writes Patanjali, "the true nature of the object shines forth, not distorted by the mind of the perceiver, that is absorption *(samadhi)*" (3, 3). Together, concentration, meditation and absorption, constitutes *samyama*. The achievement of *samadhi* is the final result of the ascetics' spiritual exercise, and the difference between mind *(citta)* and Spirit *(purusa* or *atman)* collapses in the trance experience. The final stage comes when the yogi shifts his meditation to this (or her) own mind, and realizes that the very core of his being is nothing but god (Nirvedananda, 1944 : 72). Mircea Eliade sums up the Yogic path as follows :

> "it is by stages that the Yogin dissociates himself from life. He begins by suppressing the least essential habits of living—comforts, distractions, waste of time, dispersion of his mental forces etc. He then attempts to *unify* the most important functions of life—respiration, consciousness. To discipline his breathing, make it rhythmical, reduce it to a single modality...to fix the flux of consciousness, to realize an unbroken psychic continuum, to "unify" thought...all these exercises pursue the same goal, which is to abolish multiplicity and fragmentation, to re-integrate, to unify" (1958 : 97).

But such integration and unity is spiritual, enstatic, one of identify not dialectical. For Eliade however the Yogic state is a form of trans— or super-consciousness, quite different from that of ecstatic trance, and certainly not be equated with the primordial undifferentiated state associated with infancy. The yogic experience, he affirms, is not a regression to childhood. (*op cit* 99, see Kakar, 1978 : 26-27).

For Patanjali *atman* was pure consciousness, unchangeable, and it was separate from prakriti—the world, the body, and the mind in all its manifestations. When "*Atman* shines froth in its own pristine nature, as pure consciousness" (4, 39) that is liberation, freedom.

Patanjali's "Yoga Sutras" is not an original text. Its philosophy is largely derived from Samkhya doctrine, and its advocacy of yogic techniques derives from a long tradition in Indian culture. References to yoga practices are to be found in the earlier Vedic scriptures, particularly the Upanisads, as well as in Buddhist texts. Patanjali merely codified an approach to salvation that had its origins in historic times. In a later period other forms of Yoga developed. Two are worth mentioning here. One is *hatha yoga*, the "*Yoga* of Force". The term *hatha* is composed of the words *ha* (sun) and *tha* (moon), and this form of *yoga* is an elaboration and development of the first four stages of Patanjali's *raja-yoga*. *Hatha yoga* is almost exclusively physical, focussing on the body—its purification through various cleansing practices and its mastery through breathing techniques *(pranayama)* and elaborate body postures *(asana)*. The second is tantric *yoga*, which has been seen as a synthesis of the *yoga* and *bhakti* traditions.

Tantrism is an important religious tradition in India, though little known and universally condemned by Orthodox Hindus. Its philosophy is largely derived from Samkhya; Siva is seen as the guiding "male" *purusa*, while *prakriti* is spiritualized as shakti, the mother goddess, conceptualized as divine energy or force. The rites of tantric cults are highly unorthodox, and focus around five sacraments—the eating of meat, the eating of fish, the drinking of wine, the taking of aphrodisiac grain *(mudra)*, and sexual intercourse. The latter is a ritual act by the devotees, which symbolizes the integration of male and female divine principles; the emphasis is therefore on control through yoga rather than on sexual pleasure or release. (Preston 1980; 15).

Central to both *hatha* and Tantric *yoga* is a theory of "subtle physiology" which suggests that a reserve of sexual/spiritual energy resides at the base of the spine known as *kundalini* it is conceptualized as a snake (*kundalini* means "coiled one") or as the Goddess Shakti, or as a kind of cosmic energy. The human body itself—seen as a microcosm of the universe—is seen as having within it six *chakras*, (literally wheels or discs, but usually translated as "centres"), located at various points along the spinal cord.

Each *chakra* is symbolically associated with an animal, a colour, a specific number of lotus petals, an element, two deities and body functions. The six *chakras* are indicated in the figure below. The body is also made up of a certain number of *nadis* (literally, canals, arteries but also nerves), and the chief of these, known as *susumna*, runs through the spinal cord connecting the *chakras*. Simplifying it could be said that vital energy, in the form of "breath" circulates through the *nadis* in the body, and that cosmic energy exists in a latent state in the *chakras*, particularly in the *muladhara* (literally "root support") *chakra*. The essence of Tantric *yoga* therefore is to open and cleanse the principal *nadis*, by yogic practices (*asana*, *pranayama* etc.) and to "awaken" the *kundalini*, the Serpent power coiled at the base of the spine, so that it will ascend through the *susumna* to the top of the head. This is termed the *sahasrara*, the "lotus of the thousand petals", and it is here that the final union of Siva and Shakti, the final goal of tantric *sadhana* is realized. The *sahasrara* is seen as beyond all the six *chakras*. The Yogic experience fixes on a "single point", stills, immobilizes, makes static (hence Eliades appropriate term for this experience "enstasis") three aspects of the human being, breath, thought and semen—the yogic texts essentially referring to a male adept. Audrey Cantlie has written perceptively on the way that ascetic practice *(tapas)* is inherently related in the Indian context to heat, sexuality and the source of spiritual power. The belief that ascetic power and spirituality derives from the retention of semen is, she writes, "rooted deep in Hindu tradition and literature" (1977 : 248). Thus in tantric yoga *bindu* (semen) is seen as moving upwards to the brain, conceptualized by the raising of the coiled Serpent *kundalini*, which normally resides in the *muladhara*. Yogic techniques are thus designed to generate internal heat, to awaken the *kundalini* and induce the spiritual energy (Shakti) to rise up through the spinal cord *(susumna)*. Ritual intercourse is intended therefore to arouse this energy source, but should not involve the emission of semen. And the object of yoga path is not "eternal life" or life after death (for in Hinduism both life and death—like good and evil—are both aspects of the *karmic* world) but rather the "escape" from life (and death). In the Yogic experience, she concludes, "Life is arrested by the immobilisation of breath, thought and semen. These three are equated" (*op cit*, 257). Thus the extinction of life (as we ordinarily understand it) is positively evaluated in Hinduism as the highest goal of spiritual effort and mystical achievement. This is the state of liberation *(moksha)*. It is the complete detachment from the empirical world. As one of the yogic texts put it :

"The Yogi, engaged in *samadhi*, feels neither smell, taste, colour, touch, sound, nor is conscious of his own self. He, whose mind is neither sleeping, working, remembering, destitute of memory, disappearing or appearing, is liberated" (Hatha Yoga Pradipika, 4 : 108-9). Cantlie interprets the Yogic experience as a disguised expression of the death instinct, an urge, as Freud described it, inherent in organic life "to restore an earlier state of things" (1955 : 36). But as conceptualized in the Hindu tradition, the path to salvation moves in the opposite direction, in detachment from the world, and the progressive move of the self towards spirit—via the body, senses perception, and the various cognitive faculties, namely, *manas* (the thinking organ), *ahamkara* (ego consciousness) and *buddhi* (intellect). *Moksha* means liberation from this empirical world of rebirth, and perfection comes when the "mind", as Patanjali writes, "becomes as pure as the *atman* itself"—unchangeable, eternal. This is conceptualized in Yoga not as a void, but as the realization, as the experience, that the "true self" is at one with Spirit (Brahman/*atman*). The distinction between the mind and *atman* is crucial to Yoga (as it is with the other paths to salvation). Bharati has stressed, importantly I think, the crucial difference between the Buddhist concept of no-self *(anatta)* and *sunyata* and the Hindu conception of Brahman—the crucial difference being that the Buddhist *nirvana* has no ontological status (1965 : 26-27). *Samadhi* and *nirvana* both involve non-attachment to the empirical world : but the former mode of enlightenment entails the idea that the self is a spiritual reality. The notion that all forms of yoga have a common aim, namely "self-improvement" and "self-realization" (McCartney, 1969 : 9) is quite misleading if the "self" in this context means the empirical self, and hardly more meaningful if it is used as referring to the *atman*. And to suggest that the central idea of Indian thought, *moksha*, implies "the identification of the ego with the universe" (Lannoy, 1971 : 355) is equally meaningful only if by "universe" the writer means spirit (Brahman). The central idea of Hinduism, the "perfection of man", is the quest for *moksha* (liberation), which means non-attachment to the empirical universe not "identification" with it. The self does not embrace the world : it is in essence spirit (Brahman)—immutable and unchanging. *Yoga* is not the "key to life" : it is, as Cantlie writes, the denial, the renunciation of it.

In his well-known study "Homo Hierarchians" Louis Dumont suggests that there are fundamentally two different kinds of society, modern capitalist society, and precapitalist or "traditional" society, each characterized by a specific conception of the human subject. It is worth quoting some relevant extracts from his writings to indicate his theory : he distinguishes between two conceptions of the individual :

> "(1) The empirical agent, present in every society, in virtue of which he is the main raw material for any sociology. (2) The rational being and normative subject of institutions : this is peculiar to us (modern society) as is shown by the values of equality and liberty."

> As opposed to modern society, traditional societies which know nothing of equality and liberty as values, which know nothing, in short of the individual, have basically a collective idea of man" (1970 : 9).

Dumont's analysis refers specifically to India but he generalizes his conception of holism to all pre-capitalist societies. I have elsewhere (1978) discussed the problems with Dumont's analysis, pointing out specifically to the existence of many forest communities in South India—the Paliyan, Yandi, Hill Pandaram—which have been characterized by their ethnographers as indicating an important emphasis on "individualism" and on egalitarian relationships. But Dumont's analysis is also limited in relation to the caste system itself for he fails to emphasize that in caste ideology the individual is not a part of society in a sociological sense, but of a cosmic order that extends beyond the world we experience. As in medieval Europe, with its conception of universitas, to be a member of a specific caste is to be a member of a universal order. The "collective idea of man" which Dumont describes as characteristic of Indian culture, refers not to "Society" (a concept bound up with the "abstract individual") but to a dharma-like order. It is precisely this point which is stressed by Khare (1975) for he rightly accuses Dumont of ignoring the implications of certain key religious concepts that imply a spiritual totality.

Dumont therefore goes on to suggest that to be an individual in India is to be a "world-renouncer". Individual identity is achieved by repudiating all ties which bind a person to the caste-system and the world. According to Dumont (1960) a person only realises his individuality paradoxically by renouncing it. The only way to be an individual in a theoretic system is, so to speak, to detach oneself from it—to achieve *moksha* or liberation. There is thus a distinction between the this-worldly (Brahman) and the other—worldly ascetic *(sannyasin)*, but both importantly are striving for liberation *(moksha)*. Thus "self-realization" in the Hindu context means essentially the loss of "individuality", in that the "self" is equated with spirit (Brahman). The Hindu self is a "metaphysical self".

In ordinary every day contexts the Indian person tends to see his or her self identity largely in terms of kin relations and caste membership, and as Bharati puts it, the "empirical ego" comes last in the formulation of identity. But outside the ritual context interpersonal identity tends to be social rather than metaphysical (1985 : 211). Yet fundamentally in the Hindu context the "self" is identified not with the body nor the social but with a spiritual realm. In contrast with Western thought the empirical self in Hinduism is seen as weak, ephemeral and essentially material, but the real self is spiritual. For Hindus the "I" is neither an empirical self, the object of "I", nor an ego, as an inner agency of the psyche, but rather it is "pure consciousness", the *atman* of Vedantic thought. The very term of health in Hindi, as Kakar points out—*svastha* from the root "*swa*" (I) and *'astha'* (stable)—implies something which is present and stable in the "I", not in the body, not in the mind, but in the underlying *'atman'*. (1981 : 33). Bharati thus concludes that the empirical self, the "self-in-the world", is not in Hinduism a firm, homogeneous entity, as it is in the Judae-Christian traditions, and it is "systematically marginalized in the Indian tradition so as to exalt the "true" i.e. the non-empirical self, often identified with the cosmic absolute pure and simple" (1984 : 226). Thus, as many have observed, whereas mysticism in the Western religious tradition (Judaism, Christainity and Islam) is marginalized and considered heterodox, in Hinduism mysticism, *moksha*, is the basic and specific form of Hindu religiosity.

In his psychoanalytic study of Indian culture Sudhir Kakar (1981), like Dumont and many other scholars, stress the importance of the religious ideology and the caste hierarchy in Hindu conceptions of the subject. Personal identity and individual autonomy, he suggests, is generally subordinated to caste and family interests, and personhood is largely conceptualized within a "Hindu world image" which gives Vedantic concepts—Moksha, Karma, dharma—primacy. Personal identity is thus "fused" with group affiliation and, at a higher level, with Brahman. Family, caste, spirit is thus seen by Kakar as all encompassing in definitions of the self-giving little room for individualism and personal autonomy. The maintenance of ego boundaries—between inside and outside, between the self and others, and the sensory experiences and social relations based on these separations—which form the very essence of Western thought—are systematically downplayed, he suggests, in Hinduism (1981 : 20). But Kakar goes on to suggest that there is a tension inherent in the theme of "fusion"—with the group of Brahman—for the individual fears a loss of identity and the "death" or obliteration of the self. Kakar therefore postulates that an essential psychological theme of Hindu culture is the polarity between fusion and separation, which at extremes leads to the obliteration of individual autonomy on the one hand, and unimaginable loneliness and emptiness on the other. He concludes that the Hindu norm rejects a dynamic balance between separation and fusion, in postulating that the goal of human life is Moksha, the "disintegration of individuality in the state of fusion" (1981 : 34-36).

Quite a different conception of the person is outlined by Mckim Marriott and his associates. Marriott, like both Dumont and Kakar, stresses a lack of "individualism" in Indian culture, but his approach is transactional and transformational—stressing another indigenous logic—rather than holistic. He writes :

> "Persons—simple actors—are not thought in South Asia to be "individual", that is, indivisible, bounded units, as they are in much of Western social and psychological theory as well as in common sense. Instead, it appears that persons are generally thought by South Asians to be "dividual" or divisible. To exist, dividual persons absorb heterogeneous material influences" (1976 : 111).

As with Dumont the "individual" in India is seen as non-existent, not because the self form part of a social collectivity or is fused with spirit, but rather the person is thought to be a composite of material substances—essences, residues and other active influences—that together form the "dividual" self. Such substances are transferable, and play an important role in marriage transactions and in the maintenance of caste heirarchies (Barnett, 1976 : Nicholas and Inden, 1977).

Recent anthropological studies have questioned the undue emphasis placed on holism, and on the heirarchical collectivist view of the Indian person. For this emphasis on religious ideology and the caste hierarchy has tended to imply that there is little scope for the empirical self or for individual autonomy in Indian society. But studies of Indian life-histories have shown that the perception of self-interest and control over decisions affecting one's life (autonomy) play a crucial role in the lives of many Indian subjects. Achieving a degree of personal autonomy is an important theme of adult life and this is often associated with rebellions against the caste hierarchy (Mines, 1988). One therefore must be cautious in overstressing the mystical dimension to Hindu thought, even though, in ideological terms, this is all-encompassing. But the suggestion that the Hindu view of the person is "sociocentric organic" (in contrast to the "egocentric

CHAKRA	*BODY LOCATION*	*LOTUS FLOWER OF*	*NUMBER PETALS*	*SENSE SYMBOLS*	*ELEMENTS*	*DIETIES*
1. ÄJANÄ (Command) White Triangle)	Between eyebrow	white	2	willing	cognitive forms (*Budhi/Manas/ Ahamkara*	Paramasiva/Kakini
2. VISUDDHA (purity)	at throat	purple	16	having commcaha	Ether/break blue circle	Sadashiva/Shakini
3. ANÄHATA (mystical sound)	At Heart	golden	12	touch emotions	air/blood blackhexagon	Ishav/Kakini
4. MANIPURA (city of jewels)	at Naure	blue	10	sight	fire/body red triangle	Rudra/Lakini
5. SVÄDHISTHANÄ	At genitals/ pelvis	Vermilion	6	taste	water/vital being white crescent	Vishu/Rakini
6. MULADHÄRA (Root support)	At Base of Spine	Red	4	Smell	Earth/Matter yellow square	Brahma/Dakini

(after ELIADE 1958; 241-43, WOOD 1959; 149-156).

contractual" self of western culture) (Shweder and Bourne, 1984) is highly 'Eurocentric', in that it ignores completely the religious dimension to Hindu thought.

Reference

Barnett, S. 1976 Coconuts and Gold : Relational Identity in a South Indian Caste. *Contrib. Indian Social.* 10; 133-156.

Basham, A.L. 1954 *The Wonder that was India 1967* ed. Calcutta, Fontana.

Bharati, A. 1965 *The Tantric Tradition.* Bombay BI Publications.

1985 The Self in Hindu Thought and Action in A.J. Marsella Ed. *Culture and Self Asian and Western Perspectives,* London, Tavistock.

Cantlie, A. 1977 Aspects of Hindu Asceticism in I.M. Lewis ed *Symbols and Sentiments.* London Academic Press.

Chattopadhyaya, D. 1959 *Lokayata : A Study in Ancient Indian Materialism.* New Delhi, People's Publication House.

1969 *Indian Atheism : A Marxist Analysis.* New Delhi, People's Publication House.

1976 *What is Living and What is Dead in Indian Philosophy.* New Delhi, People's Publication House.

Chennakesavan, S. 1960 *Concept of Mind in Indian Philosophy.* Delhi, Motilal Banarsidass.

Chidbhavananda, S. 1984 *The Bhagavad Gita.* Elanor, Ramakrishna Tapovanum.

Daner, F.J. 1976 *The American Children of Krsna.* New York, Holt, Rinehart.

Danto, A.C. 1972 *Mysticism and Morality.* Harmondsworth, Penguin Books.

Davies, J. 1894 *Hindu Philosophy : Exposition of the System of Kapila.* New Delhi, Cosmo Publication.

Dumont, L. 1960 World Renunciation in Indian Religions. *Contrib. To Indian School.* 4; 33-62.

1970 *Homo Hierarchians : The Caste System*

		and its implications. London, Weidenfeld and Nicolson.
Eliade, M.	1958	*Yoga; Immortality and Freedom*. London, Arkana.
Freud, S.	1955	*Beyond the Pleasure Principle*. London, Hogarth.
Hiriyanna, M.	1949	*The Essentials of Indian Philosophy*. London, Allen and Unwin.
Kakar, S.	1981	*The Inner World*. Delhi, Oxford University Press.
Khare, R.S.	1975	Hindu Social Inequality and some Ideological Entailments *in* B.N. Nair Ed. *Culture and Society*, Delhi, Thomson.
Lannoy, R.	1971	*The Speaking Tree*. Oxford University Press.
McCartney, J.	1969	*Yoga : The Key of Life*. Bombay, Taico Publication House.
Mahadevan, T.M.P.	1977	*Ramana Maharshi, The Sage of Arunacala*. London, Allen and Unwin.
Marriot, M.K.	1976	Hindu Transactions : Diversity Without Dualism *in* B. Kapferer Ed. *Transaction and Meaning*, Philadelphia, Inst. Study of Human Issues.
Menon, Y.K.	1976	*The Mind of Adi Shankara*. Bombay, Jaico Publication.
Mines, M.	1988	Conceptualizing the Person : Hierarchical Society and Individual Autonomy in India *Amer. Anth*. 90; 568-79.
Morris, B.	1978	Are there any Individuals in India. *Eastern Anihr*. 31; 365-77.
	1979	The Hare Krishna Cult, *New Humanist* 95; 73-75.
Murti, T.R.V.	1955	*The Central Philosophy of Buddhism*. London, Unwin.
Nicholas, R. and R.B. Inden	1977	*Kinship in Bengali Culture*. University Chicago Press.
Nirvedananda, S.	1944	*Hinduism at a Glance*, Calcutta, Ramakrishna Mission.
Organ, T.W.	1970	*The Hindu Quest for the Perfection of Man*. Athens, Ohio University.
Parry, J.	1985	The Brahmanical Tradition and the Technology of the Intellect *in* J. Overing Ed. *Reason and Morality*. London,

		Tavistock.
Prabhavanada, S.	1953	*The Yoga Aphorisms of Patanjali,* Mylapore, Ramakrishna Math.
Prabhupada, A.C.B.	1977	*The Science of Self Realization.* London.,Bhaktivedanta Trust.
Preston, J.J.	1980	*Cult of the Goddess.* New Delhi, Vikas Publication House.
Radhakrishnan, S.	1933	*Indian Philosophy,* Vol. 1. London.
Roy, M.N.	1940	*Materialism.* Delhi, Ajanta.
Sardesai, S.G. and D. Bose	1982	*Marxism and the Bhagavad Geeta.* New Delhi, People's Publication House.
Sen, K.M.	1961	*Hinduism.* Harmondsworth, Penguin Books.
Shweder R.A. and E.J. Bourne	1984	Does the Concept of the Person vary cross culturally *in* R.A. Shweder and R.A. Levine (Ed) *Culture Theory* Cambridge Univ. Press.
Tyler, S.A.	1973	*India : An Anthropological Perspective.* California, Good Year.
Wood, E.	1959	*Yoga.* Harmondsworth, Penguin Books.

S. K. Chatterjee

EMERGENCE OF THE SCHEDULED CASTES IN THE INDIAN POLITY

The term 'Scheduled Castes' was first used in the Government of India Act, 1935 to mean "such castes, races or tribes or parts of or groups within castes, races or tribes, being castes, reces, tribes, parts or groups which appear to His Majesty in Council to correspond to the classes of persons formerly known as 'the depressed classes', as His Majesty in Council may specify". In essence, they were those who appeared to His Majesty in Council to correspond to the erstwhile Depressed Classes. Even the term "Depressed Classes' was of recent origin. It became a part of the official vocabulary from the middle of the second decade of this century, 1916 to be precise, to denote the 'Untouchables', that is, the lowest section of the Hindu caste system, also variously known as 'Panchamas', 'Antyaj', 'Exterior castes', and even as 'Harijan', a term coined by Gandhiji. It lacked any official definition because of the difficulty in giving a definition to the Depressed Classes which should apply to all provinces (Indian Statutory Commission, 1930 : II : 66-67). The Government of India—

> "have consistently avoided themselves making any precise classification of the groups forming what are called the depressed classes if only on the ground that owing to the social disabilities to which members of the depressed classes are exposed it would be in the highest degree underdesirable that any official authorization might appear to extend to such classification. The fluidity of social distinctions and the efforts of the classes lowest in the scale, aided by social reformers, to

> improve their status make it the more desirable that Government should abstain from doing any thing which would tend to give rigidity to these distinctions" (Indian Statutory Commission, 1930 : V: 1941).

In the absence of an official definition the term 'Depressed Classes' was used by the officers of Government and the different official bodies for about two decades to mean that section of people, who, according to their own perception of the criteria, degree and manifestation of untouchability, which necessarily did vary widely, were untouchables, till the substitution by the wider term of 'Scheduled Castes.' The transformation of the undefined 'Depressed Classes' to the defined 'Scheduled Castes' within a span of twenty years was the culmination of the British efforts pursued since the Rising of 1857 of dividing the Hindus by successfully playing the caste card. It was part of a wider policy of dividing the Indians on the basis of religion, region, language, caste, community and the like in order to perpetuate its rule in India.

(I)

The British brought with them a casteless culture and a literature full of thoughts on individual liberty. As prudent foreigners wishing to consolidate their power over a strange land and people they decided to leave the peculiar institution of caste entirely alone except when it egregiously violated their cherished ideas of government. They recognised the integrity of caste organization and held that social privileges of the membership of a caste were to be wholly within the jurisdiction of the caste. This was more or less their avowed policy till the first war of independence in 1857. The Rising opened the eyes of the administrators of the country as well as the students of British Indian history to the potentialities of caste. It was almost the unanimous opinion of persons connected with the Government of India that the deep causes of the Rising were to be found in the fact that the Bengal Army was composed largely of the higher castes, viz., the Brahmans and the Rajputs. The lesson of the Rising, viz., that the safety of the British domination in India was very closely connected with keeping the Indian people divided on the lines of caste, was driven home to the British rulers. The maxim of 'divide and rule' began to be preached by historians and journalists alike (Ghurye, 1990 : 285). Because the Rising was largely the work of soliders of the high castes of the Brahmans and the

Rajputs, there was a clamour in England that the high-caste sepoys should be removed. Suspicion on the high castes, therefore, dates from the Rising. The valuable lesson so dearly acquired was not going to be lost. It being repeated in the form of the general principle of 'divide and rule', could not have failed to influence the policy and conduct of later officials. It is perhaps no coincidence that in the post-Rising period a large number of British intellectuals, most of them being members of the Indian Civil Service, conducted studies of the various caste groups in different parts of the country. But for these studies, which provided a wealth of data on the life, custom, manners and religious beliefs of different castes, our knowledge about them would not have been complete. It is, however, a matter of debate whether these intellectuals were solely inspired by their intellectual curiosity or were guided by their administrative zeal to tighten the grip of the British rule in India. It has also been pointed out that—

> "the valuable ethnographical data available through the curiosity of British officials, the gazetteers, the reports on castes and tribes, the settlements reports, the learned journals, and the decennial censuses etc., only provided to increase fissiparous tendencies in Indian society on the basis of caste." (Sinha, 1986 : 30).

Since then, the Britishers pursued a dual policy—the policy of disintegration of the traditional Hindu caste system so that the institution of caste which had always been an important factor in the country's economic life and structure, trade, commerce and industry could not be a centre of power in the changed government set up, and the policy of consolidation of caste system, that too in the way they wished. This apparent contradictory approach was the outcome of a very well-conceived policy. Thus, their policy of non-interference in caste matters changed in the second half of the nineteenth century, specially after the Rising, to a policy of active interference in caste matters so that the traditional organization of caste became almost irrelevant. This policy was given a new orientation in the twentieth century, when the demand for independence gained momentum, to widening the existing cleavage, and chasms and fostering separatism and new alignments in the hierarchy so that they could perpetuate their rule by dividing and sub-dividing the Hindus on the basis of caste as well. Thus, there was disintegration as well as crystallization of the caste system, displacement of caste as a unit of administration of justice as well as livening up of the caste spirit, loosening of caste bondage and hardening of caste solidarity, upward mobility of caste as well as downward mobility of caste and above all, groupings of certain castes at the dictation of government. Like the earlier Hindu kings, they assumed the 'power to raise and lower castes' (Census, 1931 : I : Pt. I :443) and also took upon themselves the responsibility of upholding the institution with the help of their civil power, and became the ardent champion of the very system which they deplored earlier, simply because it suited their very objective of prolongation of their rule by following the 'Divide and Rule' policy. Like any other predatory conquests where the ruling class was different from the people it ruled, the British rulers had to ensure that they were not outmanoevered by any force inimical to their rule like the institution of caste which had always sprang into action in times of unstable political condition. They not only neutralised the caste as a potent weapon in power struggle but on the other hand, nursed it as a powerful instrument of fission by creating new alignments and new loyalties and by opening new areas of conflict

Thus, whatever measures they initiated in their 200 years rule, specially after the 1957 Rising, in administrative, legislative, economic, educational and above all, the political fields, were aimed at achieving those obejectives. The British Government assiduoulsy 'nursed rather than ignored the spirit of caste' (Ghurye, 1990 : 283) in their actions and policies enunciated during this period.

(II)

The Census operations carries on regularly every ten years covering every human life became, in course of time, a potent weapon in the hands of the British Amdinistrators in divinding and subdividing the people on the basis of castes and in creating new alignments and new loyalties. Plowden, as Census Commissioner of 1881, recommended that lists of castes and occupations should be prepared for each district. Since then Census was tied to the apron-strings of castes and tribes. From 1891 onwards Census Superintendents adoptd the easier method of utilizing the decennial census for collecting and presenting information and indulging in the theorise of the origin of caste (Ghurye, 1990 : 278). This procedure reached its culmination in the Census of 1901 under the guidance of Sir Herbert Risley. With a view to helping—

> "us towards presenting an intelligibel picture of the social grouping of that large proportion of the people of India which is organized, admittedly or tacitly on the basis of caste"

the clasification was changed into one based on—

> "social procedence as recognized by the native public opinion at the present day and manifesting itself in the facts that particular caste are supposed to be the modern of representative one or other of the castes of the therotical Hindu system" (Census, 190, I : 537-38).

Risley distinguished the castes into seven groups upon an elaborate classifacation. the first group contained Brahmans only as the acknowledged superiors of all other classes. In the second group were placed castes whose respectability was never in question and who were either twice-born or were held to be superior to all other Sudra castes. The third group consisted of the so called Navasakh or nine branches all characterised to offer water the drinking of which would not pollute the higher classes. The fourth group contained clean castes with degraded Brahmans. The fifth contained castes lower than group four whose water was not usually accepted. The sixth comprised of low castes abstaining from beef, pork and fowls and the seventh enbranching castes by whom forbidden fodds were eaten and who pursued the most degreded occupations as scavengers, etc. Risley's attempt to draw up a list of castes according to their rank in society sowed the dragon's teeth of 'depressed' and 'scheduled' tribes and castes and left a most troublesome legacy and a vast field of political and social manoeuvring, and so Hutton remarked—

> "all the subsequent census of ficers in India have cursed the day when it occurred to Sir Herbert Risley to make the attempt" (Census, 1951, Castes and Tribes of West Bengal : 1).

Risley became, as Ashok Mitra, the Census Superintendent of West Bengal in 1951, puts it, "Our modern Ballala Sen" *(Idib)*.

Various ambitious castes quickly perceived the chance of raising their status. They invited conferences of their members, and formed councils to take steps to see that their status was recorded in the way they thought was honourable to them. Other castes that could not but resent this 'stealthy' procedure to advance, equally eagerly to controvert their claims. Thus a campaign of mutual recrimination was set on foot.

> "The leaders of all but the highest castes frankly looked upon the Census as an opportunity for pressing and perhaps obtaining some recognition of social claims which were denied by persons of castes higher than their own". (Census, 1911 : 5 : 440).

It provided and oportunity to castes to assert their claims for upward position in traditional hierarchy. This turned out to be, as Srinivas puts it,

> "the equivalent of the traditional copper-plate grants of Indian kings declaring the ststus, rank and privileges of a particular caste or castes." (1966 : 96)

The tendencey on the part of castes to claim to be recorded in the census as a high caste increased as the years went by, and more and more people became aware of the existence of a new and government-sponsored channel of caste mobility. O' Malley has recorded that at the time of the 1911 census operations.

> "there was a general idea in Bengal that the object of the census is not to show the number of persons belonging to each caste, but to fix the relative position of different castes and to deal with questions of social superiority. The feeling on the subject is largely the result of castes having been classified in the last census report in order of social precedence. This warrant of precedence gave rise to a considerable agitation when the census operations were instituted in 1911. Hundreds of petitions were received from different castes—their weight alone amounts to one and a half mounds—requesting that they might be known by a new name, be placed higher up in the order of precedence, be recognized as Kshatriya and Vaishya, etc., Many castes were aggrieved at the position assigned to them, and complained that it lowered them in public estimation." (Census, 1911 : 5 : 440).

Caste statistics became a nightmare to census officials more so because the return of caste, tribe or race, excited the only interest by the census in the general public. The attempt to use the census to freeze the rank of castes had the opposite effect of stimulating mobility, and also increased intercaste rivalry. It is small wonder then, that nationalist Indians began to regard the recording of caste at the census as yet another manifestation of a sinister design of the part of the Imperialist British to keep alive if not to exacerbate the numerous divisions already present in Indian society. Their suspicions were further strengthened by the attempt to distinguish Untouchables from other Hindus in the 1911 Census operations. Moreover, while the earlier census reports recorded caste divisions not only among the Hindus but also among the Muslims and the Christians as Well, the later reports recorded only the former; this confirmend the nationalists in their worst suspicion. (Natarajan, 1959 : 118).

In 1911 the Census Superintendents were instructed that instead of raising the question whether the members of particular castes should be regarded as genuine Hindus or not, a list should be prepared of the castes and tribes contributing more that 1 per mile to the total population and returned and classed as Hindus, which *qua* castes did not conform to certain standards or were subject to certain disabilites, viz.

(1) denied the supremacy of the Brahmans;

(2) did not receive the *mantra* from a Brahman or other recognized Hindu Guru;

(3) denied the authority of the Vedas;

(4) did not worship the great Hindu Gods;

(5) were not served by good Brahmans;

(6) had no Brahman priests at all;

(7) had no access to the interior of the ordinary Hindu Temples;

(8) caused pollution (a) by touch, (b) within a certain distance;

(9) buried their dead; and

(10) ate beef and did not reverence the cow (Census, 1911 : I Pt. I : 117).

The separation of the untouchables from the Hindus was insisted upon by the Muslims in a memorial to the Government dated Jaunury 27, 1910 in which they claimed that their representation in the political bodies of the country should be in proportion to the population of Touchable Hindus and not Hindus as a whole because they contended that the untouchables were not Hindus. Therefore, this attempt of the Census Commissioner of grouping together castes on the basis of these tests was perceived by the Hindus as aiming at separating the Depressed Classes from the Hindus and thereby reducing the strength of the Hindu community and its importance. It was even said that this attempt of the Census Commissioner was the result of a conspiracy between the British Government and some other non-Hindu community to divide and weaken the Hindu community. It was alleged that what was behind this move was not a genuine desire to know the population of the untouchables but the desire to break up the solidarity of the Hindu community by separating the untouchables from the touchables. Many protest meetings were held all over the country by the Hindus and this plan of the Census Commissioner was condemned in the strongest term. (Ambedkar, 1989 : 5: 232).

Two Powerful movements now became articulate—

(a) Hindus were quick to detect the seeds of disintegration in these inquiries and, determined to keep themselves united, set afoot the movement that no Hindu henceforth should return his caste; and (b) while closing their ranks, realising that strength lay also in recruitment, they employed their energies in claiming all borderline and aboriginal people into the Hindu fold. While response to the first was lukewarm, the second movement caught on, owing to the age-old glamour that Brahminism held over the people.

The list of 'Depressed Classes' was sought to be prepared for the first time in the 1921 Census but the Census Commissioner refrained from giving any guideline to the Provincial Superintendents but asked them—

> "to let me have an estimate based on census figures of the approximate strength of castes who were *usually* included in the category of depressed." (Census, 1921 : I, Pt. I : 225).

There being no criterion by which one can objectively determine a particular caste to be depressed, the lists prepared by different official bodies during the period 1916-1930, differed from one another. In the most elaborate attempt to specify criteria by which to identify untouchable groups, Hutton, the

1931 Census Commissioner, proposed a series of tests which revolved around the incidence of disabilities :

1. Whether the caste or class in question can be served by Brahmins or not.
2. Whether the caste or class in question can be served by the barbers, water-carriers, tailors, etc., who serve the caste Hindus.
3. Whether the caste in question pollutes a high-caste Hindu by contact or proximity.
4. Whether the caste or class in question is one from whose hands a caste Hindu can take water.
5. Whether the caste or class in question is debarred from using public conveniences, such as roads, ferries, wells or schools.
6. Whether the caste or class in question is debarred from use of Hindu temples.
7. Whether in ordinary social intercourse a well-educated member of the caste or class in question will be treated as an equal by the high-caste men of the same educational qualifications.
8. Whether the caste or class in question is merely depressed on account of its, own ignorance, illiteracy, or poverty and but for that, would be subject to no social disability.
9. Whether it is depressed on account of the occupation followed, and whether but for that occupation it would be subject to no social disability. (Hutton, 1946 : 194).

The castes to be included in this category were finally listed, i.e., scheduled by the Government of India in the Government of India (Scheduled Castes) Order, 1936 and since the 1941 Census they are being counted and tabulated separately.

The utility of caste tabulations has been questioned. Sinister motives have been attributed and it has been criticised for society. Ghurye finds it difficult to see any valid public reason for this elaborate treatment of caste in the Census Reports. The conclusion is unavoidable that the intellectual curiosity of some of the early officials is mostly responsible for the treatment of caste given to it in the Census, which has become progressively elaborate in each successive Census since 1872. The total result has been a livening of the caste-spirit (Ghurye, *op. cit.* :

279).

The Census provided more than sufficient incentive for the consolidation of the caste-group. Middleton, one of the two Superintendents of Census Operation in Punjab in 1921, observed thus :

> "I had intended pointing out that there is a very wide revolt against the classification of occupational castes; that these castes have been largely manufactured and almost entirely preserved as separate castes by the British Government.
>
> Our land records and official documents have added iron bonds to the old rigidity of caste. Caste in itself was rigid among higher castes, but malleable amongst the lower. We pigeon-holed every one by caste, and if we could not find a true caste for them, labelled them with the name of an hereditary occupation. We deplore the caste-system and its effects on social and economic problems, but we are largely responsible for the system which we deplore. Left to themselves such castes as the Sonar and the Lohar would rapidly disappear and no one would suffer...Government's passion for labels and pigeon-holes has led to a crystallization of the caste system, which except amongst the aristocratic castes, was really very fluid under indigenous rule....If the Government would ignore caste it would gradually be replaced by something very different amongst the lower castes. (Census, 1921 : XV, Pt. I : 433-34).

What a penetrating and correct evaluation it was : The process of pigeon-holing and thus stereotyping the castes set in motion by caste tabulation has, in effect, kept the caste-solidarity quite intact. Though Hutton repudiates the suggestion that recording of caste at the Censuses tends to stabilise the existence of the system, it cannot be denied that the mere recording of caste is an important factor in keeping the castes, specially those in the lower rungs of the ladder, more self-conscious.

The political uses to which caste tabulation has been put, have been many and caste has always been, in the distant as well as in recent past, a powerful weapon of political and social country by force and guile, to rule by dividing the people. In the hands of such a Government there can be few weapons as powerful and lethal as caste.

The first decade of the twentieth century is marked as the trend-setter of the future course of event of Indian history. It legitimised the birth of two powerful forces—communalism and casteism—, all in pursuance of the 'divide and rule' policy, which in course of time changed the entire complexion of Indian polity. As nationalism grew and the movement towards greater Indian participation in the governance gathered momentum in the late nineteenth century, the British Government was forced to revaluate its policy of giving more representation to the Indians in the Administration. Lord Minto, the Viceroy, took a new approach to give representation to the Indian people in legislature. He hit upon a novel idea which introduced communalism for the first time in the polity of the Indian state after the advent of the British rule and adopted a clever ploy of exacerbating of the open rivalry between the two dominant religious communities—the Hindus and the Muslims. A deputation called the All-India Mohammedan Deputation, met the Viceroy on October 1, 1960 in Shimla. This deputation made the demand for separate electorates for the Muslims in any scheme of political reform and said that the representation of the Muslims should be more than what was warranted by their numerical strength in the country. They further demanded that only Muslims should be allowed to choose the Muslim members of the council, and also a due share in the gazetted and the subordinate administerial services. Lord Minto assured them that in all electoral organizations, whether it affected a municipality, a district boared or a legislative council, the Mohammedan community should be represented as a community.

Lord Minto's assurance was reflected in the Minto-Morley Reforms of 1909 which introduced for the first time a separate communal electorate with weightage to the Muslims, that became a permanent feature of Indian political system since then. Commenting on this provision for separate electorate Eleanor Zelliot observes—

> The granting of an electorate for Muslims in which they alone would vote brought the idea of communal electorate for minorities to the forefront in the minds of all communities which feared their submersion in a government run by the dominant caste Hindu community. The granting of special electorates to the Muslim community also made numbers

> important. Whether the vast number of untouchables were truly Hindu and to be counted as such, or not, became an important question for the first time (Galanter, 1984 : 26).

At the same time the policy of enumerating Depressed Classes as a separate group from the Hindus in the Indian Census for 1911 accentuated concern about Hindu majority. The Muslim leaders quickly seized this opportunity and demanded that properly speaking, the outcastes were beyond the pale of Hinduism, and, therefore their strength should not go to swell the numerical strength of the Hindus.

'Untouchability' was thus propelled into a prominent place on the Indian political stage, which it was to occupy until after Independence.

After the end of the First World War the British Government declared its policy of 'increasing association of Indians in every branch of the administration' and enacted the Government of India Act, 1919 to give effect to some constitutional change as suggested by the Montegu-Chelmsford Report. The 'Mont-Ford Report' said that with regard to the Depressed Classes—

> "we intend to make the best arrangements that we can for their representation, in order that they too may ultimately learn the lesson of self-protection of Indian Constitutional Reforms" (1918 : para 155).

But when details of the constitution were framed, they were granted representation by nomination.

The grant of representation to the Depressed Classes, even it by nomination marked the beginning of a new era in Indian politics. It accorded legitimacy to the claim of the Depressed Classes for separate representation in the Legislature, a claim which became a bone of contention in later years. The 1909 Act legitimised communal politics, which in course of time engulfed the country so much that it resulted in the vivisection of the country within a span of 40 years. The Mohammedans indeed pressed for and obtained from Lord Minto a promise that they should elect their own members in separate Mohammedan constituencies. Now it was the turn of the Depressed Classes. Once representation was offered to a section of population on the basis of their hierarchical position in the Hindu society, they could channelise their activities in building up enough pressure on the government to accede to their claim to representation on the basis of their number. As very aptly summed up by Dr. Ambedkar—

> Thus the right of the Depressed Classes to special representation in the Legislature had become a principle which was not only accepted but adopted in the Constitution (of 1919). So well was this principle recognised that it had been extended to District Local Boards, School Boards and Municipalities. A claim which had been given legal recognition in 1919 and which had thereby become a right and which had become perfected by user, the representatives of the Depressed Classes felt, could not be deputed by any body. (1989 : 5 : 312).

The next step was consolidation of the gain and increasing the quota in future constitutions. The period from 1920 onwards till the enactment of the 1935 Act witnessed heightened activities on the part of the leaders of the Depressed Classes for more and more political power on the basis of their hierarchical position in the Hindu society.

The formation of the Statutory Commission presided over by the celebrated constitutional Lawyer Sir John Simon for the purpose of inquiring into the working of the system of government set up under the 1919 Act and reporting on the constitutional changes which might be considered desirable was announced on November 27, 1927. The announcement in India—long advocated and anxiously awaited—of the appointment of the Statutory Commission aroused a storm of indignation and protest. The reaction of the Depressed Classes to the Simon Commission's tour to India was far different from that of other political parties and organisations. Eighteen Depressed Classes associations testified willingly to the Commission, sixteen of them making for separate electorates for untouchables. While Ambedkar's students walked out of his class of Government Law College in protest Ambedkar told the Commission that the untouchables were relieved of anxiety because the Simon Commission did not include an Indian, since such a nominee could not be truly representative of all groups. He urged that the depressed classes should be treated as a distinct minority. As there was really not much of link between the depressed classes and the Hindu community, they must be regarded as a distinct and independent minority. He claimed for greater political protection than any other community in India because of the educational backwardness and economic and social barriers. As a matter of demand for political protection, representation on the same basis as the Mohammedan community was asked for. Reserved seats if accompanied by adult franchise or separate electorate in the absence of adult franchise and certain safeguards either in the constitution or else in the way of advice in the instrument to the Governor regarding the education of depressed classes and the entry into public services were claimed by him. 22 seats reserved out of 140 seats, in case of adult suffrage, and the same number of seats through separate electorates in the Bombay Council if adult suffrage was not granted, he informed the Commission, would satisfy him and the organisation he spoke for the Bahiskrit Hitakarini Sabha (Society for the uplift of the Depressed) (Indian Statutory Commission, 1930 : XVI : 27-37), which he founded in 1924 to work for social and economic betterment of the Depressed Classes.

After two years of consistent work the Commission prepared and published its report in May, 1930. But even before the submission of the Simon Commission Report, the labour Government of Great Britain, which came into office following the general election in May, 1929, announced its intention of giving the Dominion Status to India and also of convening a Round Table Conference to which it invited delegates from all parties and prominent groups to discuss the future system of government for India. The Indian National Congress boycotted the Conference.

Dr. Ambedkar and Dewan Bahadur R. Srinivassan of Madras represented the Depressed Classes. They presented a joint memorandum which may, without exaggeration, be described as a charter of the 'untouchables' demands. These were set forth in the memorandum in legal language with penalities provided for their violation. It suggested that the untouchables should elect their representatives on the basis of adult franchise through separate electorates for the first ten years. Afterwards they might be elected by joint electorate with reserved seats. At the same time joint electorates should not be forced on the untouchables against their will. It also made it clear that no community should be granted weightage at the cost of the untouchables and that the depressed classes would never agree to any community getting representation on better terms than themselves. The Charter of safeguards included the basic demand for equal citizenship and equal opportunity for the untouchables. To ensure this there should be equality before the law for them. Provisions for the free enjoyment of equal rights were also suggested. Social boycott, which seriously affected the Depressed Classes, should be banned, condign punishment being provided for anybody who practised it. Along with adequate representation in the legislatures, the memorandum pressed for adequate representation of the Depressed Classes in the Services because it was necessary for their political and social development. It also asked for adequate provision for their education and for sanitation in the places where they lived. Creation of special department in charge of a Minister for the purpose of watching the interests of the Depressed Classes and promoting their welfare as well and representation of the Depressed Classes in the Cabinet were also demanded (Round Table Conference, III : 168-174). When Ambedkar drafted this Memorandum for consideration of the Round Table Conference he had not even the faintest idea that it would develve on him, as chairman of the Drafting Committee, to give constitutional recognition to his own demands in the Constitution of free India.

Though the First Round Table Conference was adjourned without any decision, the representatives of the Depressed Classes did succeed in convincing the Conference that they were entitled to recognition as a separate entity for political and constitutional purposes. Mahatma Gandhi, as the sole representative of the Congress, attended the Second Round Table Conference held between September 7 and December 1, 1931. As the delegates were unable to reach an agreed solution on the question of representation in the legislatures, the British Prime Minister adjourned the Conference *sine die* with a suggestion to the delegates to put in a signed requisition authorizing the Prime Minister to arbitrate and give his decision on the communal issue (2nd Round Table Conference, III : 1386).

Ramsay Macdonald, the British Prime Minister, announced his decision known as Communal Award on August 4, 1932. This Communal Award Conceded separate electorates to the Muslims, Sikhs, Indian Christians, Anglo-Indians and Europeans. Labour, commerce, industry, mining and planting, land-holders and universities were also given separate constituencies and fixed seats. It also suggested the formation of general constituencies in which all persons other than Muslims, Sikhs, Christians, Anglo-Indians or Europeans were entitled to vote. For the first time the Depressed Classes were. Were recognised as a separate community be awarding them separate electorates. Separate seats were allotted to them out of general seats. They were given right to exercise two votes each, one in the general constituency and the other in special constituencies. On the question of separate electorates for the Depressed Classes, Mahatma Gandhi undertook his 'fast unto death' which resulted in the signing of the Poona Pact. Ambedkar proved to be a hard bargainer and could extract a higher compensation for the Depressed Classes in place of the separate electorates given to them by the British Government. Poona Pact gave them 148 seats while the Award had given them only 71. The term of the Poona Pact was given effect to by the British Government by embodying them in the Government of India Act, 1935 when the number of 148 seats was raised to 151 in making adjustments of seats for Bihar and Orissa.

Now that a substantial number of seats, about 19% of the general seats were earmarked for representation of the Depressed Classes by election, the necessity of 'Scheduling of Castes' for the purpose of electoral arrangements brooked no delay. The provincial Governments were asked to send their recommendations on the listing of castes in the Schedule to the Government of India. The Government of India, in turn, forwarded the provincial Governments' lists to His Majesty's Government in Great Britain.

His Majesty in Council then issued the Order known as the Government of India (Scheduled Castes) Order, 1936 listing about 450 castes which later came to be known as 'Scheduled Castes' in relation to the nine Indian Provinces.

(IV)

Though the term 'Depressed Classes' was used by different official bodies and the Government as an euphemism for the term 'Untouchables', it lacked any official definition because of the difficulty in giving a proper definition to such an ill-defined group as the 'Depressed Classes' of the community. This difficulty in giving a proper definition to the term, however, did not deter the official bodies from identifying the Depressed Classes and estimating their number. While preparing the list of Depressed Classes, they generally included the 'untouchables' in the list of 'depressed classes', according to their own concept of 'untouchablity'.

The 1911 Census, without directly mentioning the Untouchables or the Depressed Classes, sought to find out the castes which were subject to certain social and religious disabilities, according to the 10-point test evolved by the Census Commissioner. Along with the identification of those castes, their numbers were also extracted in each of the British Provinces, except Madras and U. P. In Madras the Census Superintendent did not identify the depressed classes because he thought that the disabilities mentioned in the Census Commissioner's instructions were experienced by all sections of Hindus irrespective of their position in the social scale. In U. P. very few were found who did not fulfil any of the prescribed tests. The number of castes which fell under any one of the 10 categories in the 1911 Census was 187 and their population was 42.5 millions in India excluding the United Provinces and Madras.

Later, in 1932, the Lothian Committee considered only those coming under categories 7 and 8 i.e., those who had not access to the interior of the ordinary Hindu temples and who caused pollution (a) by touch, (b) within a certain distance, to be depressed. Of these 187 castes, only 87 fell under categories 7 and 8 and their population in British territories was only 17.8 millions.

The question of depressed classes came into prominence in 1916 when in pursuance of a resolution in the Imperial Legislative Council the Government of India addressed local Governments to ascertain their views on the subject of the amelioration of the condition of the depressed classes. In the course of their letter they stated that some definition was required of the term "depressed classes". Apart from incidental references to the humbler sections of the community whose condition was largely due to poverty the tenor of the discussion in the Imperial Council was to include in this expression :

(1) crimianl and wandering tribes,

(2) aboriginal tribes, and

(3) untouchables.

The Government of India asked that the heads to be adopted by local Governments should be—

(a) depressed classes (i. e., 'untouchables')

(b) aboriginal and Hill tribes, and

(c) criminal tribes,.

and that the actual casts or tribes in each group should be enumerated.

In pursuance of this directive the provincial Governments (expect Assam and Punjab) furnished the lists along with an estimate of their population. These lists accounted for 104 castes with a population of 27.4 millions (Indian Statutory Commission, 1930 : V : 1341-47). The number of castes under the depressed classes increased marginally in the hand of the Provincial Governments, compared to that of the 1911 Census. It, however, did not mean that all the 87 castes falling under categories 7 and 8 in the 1911 Census were considered depressed, i.e., untouchables by the Provincial Governments. As many as 40 out of these 87 castes were not listed as depressed by the provincial Governments.

The next important reference is to be found in the Seventh quinquennial Review of the Progress of Education in India for the years 1912-17. This Review prepared by Sir Henry Sharp, who was at the time Educational Commissioner under the Government of India. In the Report the depressed classes were specifically dealt with from the point of view of educational assistance and progress. In that Review statistics were given separately of

(a) aboriginal or hill tribes,

(b) depressed classes, and

(c) criminal tribes.

A list of castes and tribes constituting the depressed classes was given. His estimates of the depressed classes population in British India of 31.5 millions were apparently based on the Census Report of Press of Education in India (1912-17 : 1 : 204-206). There was not much difference between Sharp's lists and the Government lists except in the case of Madras. Sharp, however, furnished lists of depressed classes for Assam and Punjab as well.

The next reference to this question is found in the Report of the Franchise Committee (Southborough Committee), 1918-19. This Committee, established to advise on the Franchise under the 1919 reforms, gave population figures in respect of each Governor's provinces and divided the Hindus into.

(1) Brahmins

(2) Non-Brahmins, and

(3) Others.

The Committee, however, did not specifically mention the castes included in the group 'Others' but quoted the Census Reports on which these estimates were based. It furnished a figure of 42.2 millions with Province-wise break-up (Franchise Committee, 1919 : I :19-80). By back calculation the castes could be identified in some provinces but in others it could not be arrived at. In absence of the particulars of the castes taken into consideration by this Committee it is difficult to say which castes were actually considered depressed by it. In any case, their total number would be more than 127.

In the 1921 Census, the Census Commissioner tried to obtain some statistical estimate of the number of that section of the community being referred to as the 'Depressed Classes'. Many Census Superintendents did not indicate in their reports who were the depressed classes. Only the Census Superintendents of Madras, the Central Provinces, and Berar, Bengal, and Bihar and Orissa did specify the castes considered depressed/ untouchables and their population. But the Census Commissioner did not accept their lists and modified the estimates on the basis of figures of Sharp's lists and of information from the 1911 Census reports and tables. Of the 52/1/2 millions for which the Census Commissioner gave actual figures less than 43/1/2 millions were to be found in British India (Census, 1921 : I, Pt. I : 225). He, however, refrained from mentioning the castes which accounted for this population and the area from which those were extracted.

The Reforms Enquiry Committee of 1924, popularly known as the Muddiman Committee, relied on the Census figures of 1921 in its report (Reforms Enquiry Committee, 1924 : 56).

The Moral and Material Progress Report on India for the year 1925-26 reported that there "are said to be no fewer than 60 millions" of depressed classes in India (Moral and Material Progress Report, 1925-26 : 237).

This wide variation in the figures of the Depressed Classes population estimated by different official agencies—approximately 30 millions by Sharp in 1912-17, 55-60 millions for the whole of India by the Census Commissioner in 1921 and 60 millions in the Moral and Material Progress Report for 1925-

26—was pointed out by Lala Lajpat Rai in the Legislative Assembly on February 16, 1928. Later, while participating in a debate in the Legislative Assembly on February 23, 1928, G. S. Bajpai, the then Secretary to the Government in the Department of Education, Health and Lands, stated that he wished to correct the figure of 60 millions quoted by Lala Lajpat Rai in his speech. He stated that he had calculations made in the light of available materials and that according to his calculation, the so-called depressed or untouchable classes (and he was careful to explain that he did not include the backward classes generally) in the Governor's provinces, excluding Burma and Assam, numbered 28 1/2 millions. Bajpai's calculations had been compiled in the Department of Education, Health and Lands after references to the annual and quinquennial reports of the Directors of Public Instruction of the various provinces, to the Census figures, and the special reports of provincial Governments sent in 1917-18 (Legislative Assembly Debates, 1928 : I : 721).

The next reference to the number of Depressed Classes population was made in the House of Commons on March 26, 1928, by Wellock when he asked the Under Secretary of State for India what was the most recent estimate of the number of depressed classes in British India. The Government asked for time and on April 23, 1928 Earl Winterton in his reply stated that—

> "the Government of India inform me that the latest Census figures indicate 43 millions as the number of members of the so-called depressed classes, and that from information provided in provincial educational reports they estimate that of these some 29 millions are 'untouchables'. Neither term is capable of very precise definition, consequently these figures are somewhat indefinite (Parliamentary Debates, Vol. 216 : Cols. 601-602).

In reply to another question the Home Member to the Government of India informed the Legislative Assembly on September 4, 1928 that

> "the classes generally considered as depressed beside or in addition to the untouchables are hill tribes, aboriginals and criminal tribes"

and a list of castes which were generally, according to local usage and custom, regarded as untouchables was laid on the table of the Legislative Assembly (Legislative Assembly Debates, III : 2-3).

It may be noted that there was no material difference between the two Government lists of 1917 and of 1928. In 1917, the Provincial Governments identified 104 castes as depressed. In 1928 this figure went up to 106. Chuckler in the Madras list of 1917 was omitted from the 1928 list and the new additions were the Bhangi in the Bihar list and the Chamar and Chuhra in the Punjab list. It may be remembered that the Punjab Government did not furnish any list in 1917 as the "idea of population by mere touch was rapidly dying out." Like the 1917 list, the 1928 lists also did not speak of any untouchable caste in Assam.

The Depressed Classes and its population continued to dominate the political scene of the late 20s. The Simon Commission, constituted in 1927 to report on the constitutional changes, was confronted with the question of reservation of seats for the Depressed Classes. The Commission in its report submitted in May, 1930 recommended reservation of seats for the Depressed Classes. While rejecting the proposal for a separate electorate for the Depressed Classes, it pointed out that a separate electorate for the depressed classes meant, as a preliminary a precise definition of all who were covered by the term, and the boundary would be in some cases difficult to draw. While admitting the difficulty of giving a definition of the Depressed Classes which should apply to all provinces, it recommended the appointment of a Franchise Committee one of whose tasks was 'to frame for each province a definition of Depressed Classes (which may well vary, sometimes even between parts of the same province) and to determine their numbers so defined.' (ISC 1930, II : 67). The Commission, however, adopted the definition "cause pollution by touch or by the approach within a certain distance" and "after studying various figures and analysing the evidence put before it, made 'the next estimate' that total population of the 'untouchables' in British India was 43.6 millions, with a stipulation that there was a wide margin of possible error in the case of Bengal, the United Provinces and Bihar and Orissa (*Ibid*, I : 40-41). Since the Commission was not sure of its own estimation, it recommended that "when the definitions are settled and the correct totals ascertained the number of seats to be reserved for depressed classes should be settled." (*Ibid*, II : 67).

Before the submission of the Simon Commission Report, two other Commitees identified the number of Depressed Classes in 1929. The Hartog Committee accepted the Government list of 1928 and after making a calculation of its own gave a figure of 29.76 millions (Hartog Committee, 1929 : 217-218). The Indian Central Committee, however, accepted the figures of 44.5 millions supplied by the Governments (Indian Central Committee, 1929 : 44).

Hutton, as Census Commissioner of 1931, formulated a 9-point test and instructed the Provincial Census Superintendents not to include non-Hinduised, hill and forest tribes as well as criminal tribes in the depressed classes. The total of depressed classes reported by the Provincial Census Superintendents was 407 with a population of 40.8 millions but the Census Commissioner did not concut with the Provincial Census Superintendents in all cases. He identified 351 of them as depressed classes (exterior castes) having a population of 39.1 millions in British India and another 11.1 millions in the States and Agencies—making a total of 50.2 millions (Hutton, 1946 : 199).

None, however, bothered about the exact population of the Depressed Classes and none questioned the accuracy of the Census figures of the Depressed Classes till the discussions in the Round Table Conference, convened in London in 1930-32, crystallised towards making adequate provision for the representation of the Depressed Classes, if necessary through separate electorates, mainly at the instance of Dr. Ambedkar. In consequence of the recommendations made by the Franchise Sub-Committee of the Round Table Conference as well as by the Simon Commission the Indian Franchise Committee, popularly known as the Lothian Committee, was appointed after the close of the second session of the Round Table Conference in December, 1931. One of the terms of the Committee was to come to some conclusion on the total population of the Untouchables in British India for making adequate provision for the representation of the Depressed Classes in the legislature.

Now that the 'depressed classes' were to be recognised as a distinct element of population for political purposes, the Lothian Committee felt it necessary to have a more precise classification of them. It, therefore, considered that

"the term depressed classes should not include

> primitive or aboriginal tribes, nor should it include those Hindus who are only economically poor and in other ways backward but are not regarded as Untouchables" (Indian Franchise Committee, 1932 : I : 109).

The Committee was "of opinion that the term should be applied only to those who are untouchables." that is, those satisfying the tests of untouchability, mentioned under heads 7 and 8 of the 10 tests of disabilities categorised during the 1911 Census operation, which was found by the Committee to be the generally accepted tests of untouchability, namely,

"(7) are denied access to the interior of ordinary Hindu temples,

(8) cause pollution,

(a) by touch,

(b) within a certain distance".

The Committee made it clear that its "proposals in regard to the 'depressed classes' should extend only to those castes who are included in these categories." *(Ibid).*

The Lothian Committee received conflicting estimates from a number of quarters. The Provincial Governments supplied figures which varied between 37.44 millions and 30.22 millions, the Provincial Franchise Committee produced figures that ranged between 18.67 millions and 17.37 millions. The dissenting members of the Franchise Committee minimised the number even further to 14.42 millions. The Franchise Committee itself was unable to arrive at a firm figure.

It is better to remember that the Franchise Committee on its own, did not make any estimate of the Depressed Classes population. It depended entirely on the information and reports received from the Provincial Governments and the Provincial Franchise Committees. After considering the reports from these agencies as also the replies to its questionnaire, it accepted the figures as 'substantially correct', where there was general agreement betweent the provincial committees and local governments, as happened in the case of Madras, Bombay, the Central Provinces and Assam. In this context the Lothian Committee observed :

> In the three provinces, Madras, Bombay and the Central Provinces, the distinction between the

> depressed and other classes of the Hindu community is clearly defined, and there is general agreement between the provincial committees and local governments in regard to the numbers and castes to be included. We are also satisfied from the replies which we received to our questionnaire and from the statements of witnesses who appeared before us that the numbers for these three provinces are not disputed by other communities in these provinces. The Census estimates of 1931 closely correspond to the numbers given to us by the committee. In the view of this unanimity we are ourselves prepared to accept the figures given to us as substantially correct, and believe that they are not likely to be open to serious criticism (*Ibid* : 111-112).

But unanimity in view did not mean that the figures of Depressed Classes population was extracted only for that segment of population which came within the definition settled by the Indian Franchise Committee. But, as pointed out, the Committee did not bother to check up whether the figures furnished by the Governments of Bombay and Madras confirmed to its own definition of the term 'depressed' (*Ibid* : 217).

The estimates of the Bombay Government were based on the investigations of a Committee of officials and non-officials appointed by that Government in 1930 to report on various economic and social problems affecting the depressed classes in that Presidency. This Committee was appointed long before the definition of the term "depressed classes" was settled by the Lothian Committee, but the figures furnished by the Bombay Government had not been examined in the light of the Lothian Committee's definition of the term.

The Madras Government had for purposes of their own, defined the term 'Adi-Dravida' in the Madras Local Boards and the Madras District Municipalities Acts, 1920 and the provincial Government as well as the provincial Committee viewed that this definition of 'Adi-Dravida' would be suitable for the definition of 'depressed classes' as well. Nine communities were included within the term of "Adi-Dravida" under these Acts. Again by a notification issued under G.C. No. 1541 - L & M dated May 7, 1931, i.e., after the publication of the Simon Commission Report and before the constitution of the Lothian Committee, a supplementary list of another 21 communities was included in this category. The population of these 31 castes, even if it was accepted that they all belonged to the depressed classes, was much less than the population projected by these bodies, which meant that some more castes were considered as depressed by them as well.

In Bihar and Orissa there was practical agreement in regard to the castes which should be included in the term 'depressed classes', Incidentally, this is the solidary case where the Committee gave a definite opinion both in regard to the Depressed Classes population as well as the castes which should be included in that category.

In regard to Bengal, Uttar Pradesh and Punjab, there was no general agreement between the local Government and the Provincial Franchise Committee in regard to the number who should be classed as depressed, and the Indian Franchise Committee, therefore, failed to give any estimation of the number and castes to be included as depressed classes in these three provinces. It, therefore, recommended that the local Governments should examine the varying figures and arrive at a final estimate of the number after completing the enquiries in regard to the castes which should either continue on or be taken off the 1911 list in accordance with their social position at that time (*Ibid*, I : 117-118).

As we have seen, a number of agencies estimated the Depressed Classes population during the period 1911-36. All these agencies, however, attempted at estimating the Depressed Classes population according to their own criteria of untouchability. The total population classed as depressed, therefore, varied primarily because of lack of uniformity in identifying the criteria of untouchability and in following any general principle in this regard. The variation in the figures arose largely from a difference in the meaning and application given to what was at all times a rather vague term. Though there was no difference of opinion in the inclusion of only the Untouchables in this category, the difference of opinion was manifest in the degree of untouchability and consequently who should be treated as Untouchables. What was more important than the estimates of the depressed population was the identification of the castes which accounted for this population. Table - 1 will indicate that many of these bodies including the Census had refrained from mentioning the castes whom they considered depressed. The number of population may vary for different reasons and in any case, all these agencies depended on the Census reports for the population figures. But what about the castes considered depressed by them? Curiously enough even the Lothian Committee failed to specify the castes considered depressed by it even in those provinces whose population was accepted by it without any reservation.

Tablel - 1

Period	Name	No. of population	No of caste
1911	Census all categories 1 to 10	42.57 million	187
1911	Census categories 7 & 8	17.81 "	87
1917	Government list	27.40 "	104
1917	Sir Henry Sharp	31.49 "	106+163 for Assam
1919	Franchise Committee (Southborough Committee)	42.21 "	127+
1921	Census Superintendent (only of four provinces)	29.35 "	85
1921	Census Commissioner	43.36 "	not mentioned
1924	Reforms Enquiry Committee	43.36 "	"
1928	Government list		106
1929	Hartog Committee	29.76 "	106
1929	Indian Central Committee	44.50 "	106
1930	Indian Statutory Commission	43.60 "	not mentioned
1931	Census Superintendents	40.76 "	407
1931	Census Commissioner	38.87 "	351
1932	Provincial Governments	37.44 - 30.22 mills	49-161
1932	Provincial Franchise Committee	18.67 - 17.37 "	95 - 86+
1932	Dissenting members of the Indian Franchise Committee	14.42 millions	66 +

In 1911, the Census authority could identify 87 castes in the Indian provinces except Madras and U.P., which satisfied the twin criteria of untouchability accepted by the Lothian Committee in 1932. The number of untouchable castes/depressed classes increased to 104/106 in 1917 and to at least 127 in

1919. The number again came down to 106 in 1928 but showed a four-fold increase at the hands of the Census Superintendents in 1931 which was reduced to 351 by the Census Commissioner. Their number ranged between 161 and 66 in 1932 when the Lothian Committee was called upon to define and estimate their number. It, however, did not mean that all these castes were common in all the estimates. A caste treated as untouchable/depressed by one body was not considered as such by another body, which included the Census authority as well. This trend was seen in almost all the provinces.

(V)

Having failed to come to any decision on the depressed classes population in the three provinces of Bengal, U.P. and Punjab, the Lothian Committee recommended that the provincial Governments of these provinces should estimate the depressed classes population of these provinces on the basis of the depressed classes lists to be prepared after taking into consideration the 1911 list. But immediately after the submission of the Committee's report and before the actual number of depressed classes population in these three provinces could be estimated, the British Prime Minister announced on August 4, 1932 the Communal Award assigning a number of seats for the depressed classes which was raised to 151 on the signing of the Poona Pact. It may be remembered that the Simon Commission had specifically recommended that once the correct totals of Depressed Classes had been ascertained according to settled definitions, the number of seats should be settled (ISC, 1930 : II : 67). Contrary to the Simon Commission's recommendation, the seats were fixed without ascertaining the numbers. Since the seats had been fixed it devolved on the provincial Governments to find out who would be entitled to be returned from these constituencies. The strength of the Depressed Classes should not be allowed to suffer any diminution, because the seats in the legislatures must have some bearing on population ratio as well. It must be commensurate to the seat allotted. Whereas the proper course should have been to define the depressed classes and then enumerate them and only after that allot a quota, if it has to be given, according to the population figures, as very rightly suggested by the Simon Commission, This process was, however, reversed in the case of the Depressed Classes. First allot seats and then find out the population according to some definition. If the definition stands in the way, modify it in such a manner that it does not stand in the way of enumeration of such a class. This is precisely what the British Government did. The wording of the Communal Award also supports this view. Para 9 of the Communal Award states :

> The precise definition in each Province of those who will be entitled to vote in the special Depressed Classes constituencies has not yet been finally determined. It will be based as a rule on the general principles advocated in the Franchise Committee's Report. Modification may, however, be found necessary in some Provinces in Nothern India where the application of the general criteria of untouchability might result in a definition unsuitable in some respects to the special conditions of the Province.

Trouble started over this modification of the Lothian Committee's twin criteria of Depressed Classes. In accordance with the discretion given to them by the British Government, the Provincial Governments were asked to prepare a "Schedule of Castes" for electoral purposes. If the Provincial Governments had strictly adhered to the Lothian Committee's twin criteria of untouchability, the number of castes considered depressed would have been much less and consequently their population. But the Communal Award, as modified by the Poona Pact, had already fixed the number of seats for the Depressed Classes in the Legislatures. So far electoral purposes the provincial Governments started modifying the lists of Depressed Classes, thereby including in the lists even those castes, which were not depressed according to the definition of the Lothian Committee. In preparing the "Schedule of Castes" the Provincial Governments not only did not follow the recommendations of the Lothian Committee but went beyond the discretion allowed to them by the Communal Award. The Communal Award envisaged that the modification to the general principles advocated in the Lothian Committee's report would be necessary in some provinces in Northern India only. But the Provincial Governments not only of the Northern India but also of other regions as well including Bombay and Madras Presidencies and the Central Provinces, where, as was generally believed, 'there was little dispute about who were the untouchables,' took liberty in adding to this Schedule such castes which were not enumerated as depressed in the Census reports or even mentioned by any other official bodies earlier."

A study indicates that of the 450 castes scheduled in 1936 as many as 258, i.e., 58% came into this category only from 1931 onwards, and 126, i.e., about 50% of the new comers were from the South which was acclaimed to be a place where the line of demarcation between 'touchables' and 'untouchables' was clearly drawn for a long time. Incidentally, in the South these 126 castes constituted more than 72% of the castes included in the 1936 list. This is a pointer to the fact that as the stigma of untouchability started petering out due to various factors—social, religious, economic, administrative and political--it was matched with a corresponding effort to rope in more and more castes within the ambit of 'untouchables'. As the rigidity of untouchability became less pronounced, as the lower castes' claimed higher status for them in the society and stepped up their attempt to obtain quality with the 'higher castes', which were more marked in the 20s and early 30s, there was an effort to segregate a sizable section of Indians from others, to raise a barrier around them, *albiet* in the name of their social, economic, educational and political development, so that they can never integrate themselves with the other sections of people. Ruling party saw in them a potential weapon to keep the Hindus divided, the communal forces used them to perpetuate the communal divide on the basis of caste, the elites among the so-called 'untouchables' utilised them as a stepping stone for garnering more power -- political, social and economic -- and a new power centre emerged which rivetted round the forces of casteism. The cumulative effect of all these factors and forces was the inclusion of a large number of castes as 'untouchables' and later in the 'schedule' in the mid-30.

It may be remembered that the 'Schedule of Castes' prepared in 1936 did not reflect that will of the people belonging to a particular caste. A number of castes in Bengal, Bihar, C.P., U.P. and Punjab and in many other provinces claimed higher status during the Census operations and even asked to be allowed to be returned in new names. Some of them also demanded of the provincial Government not to include their names in the list of Depressed Classes and consequently in the list of Scheduled Castes. But their representations were not honoured because the Government officials found them "socially, politically, economically and educationally, backward and that was the reason for their inclusion. So it was not the untouchability but the "social, political, economic and educational" backwardness, as perceived by the Government officers, which merited their inclusion in the list. This list strictly speaking was, therefore, not a list of "Depressed Classes" in the sense in which that term was used by the Indian Franchise Committee in 1932 or was viewed by the political leaders or the social reformers, and no caste was excluded from the list of 'Schedule of Castes' merely because it failed to satisfy the Franchise Committee's twin criteria of untouchability. This list is not a list of 'Untouchables' but a list of castes whose 'social, political, economic and political' development was considered by the Government of the day to be such as to warrant their inclusion in the list. A number of seats in the legislatures having been provided for in the 1935 Act for a section of undefined people, known as depressed classes, the Government was duty bound to find out the persons who should be clubbed together for this purpose. 'Scheduled Castes', writes D.R. Prentice, Member of the Executive Council of the Governor of Bengal, were 'a new political creation' for the purpose of special electoral arrangements contemplated by the Communal Award, and the Government of the day did everything possible to honour that commitment.

Earlier the prevailing idea had been that inclusion in the list of Depressed Classes might affect the social prestige of the castes. The scheduling of castes on the basis of social, political, economic and educational level of development removed that stigma so much so that there is a clamour for inclusion of castes in the list of Scheduled Castes in independent India. The higher mobility within the caste witnessed in the first four decades of this century was aimed at elevating the social position of the caste by the sanskritization process. This mobility, which was vertical in nature and socio-religious in character, has not only been stalled but has been completely reversed. A study shows that the castes which had persistently claimed higher status in the Census operations but whose claims were not conceded either by the Census authority or the provincial Governments and therefore, were ultimately included in the lists of Scheduled Castes, have since witnessed substantial increase in their population in the Censuses during the period 1931-1981. In Bengal (now West Bengal) the population of this group of castes registered a sharp fall in the 1941 Census compared to that of the 1931 Census. Even in the 1951 Census, their total population was less than that of the 1901 Census. In the 1951 Census they accounted for 61.16% of the State's total Scheduled Caste population which increased to 70.02% in the 1981 Census. In U.P. this group of castes accounted for 61.58% of the total Scheduled Caste population according to the 1931 Census which increased to 67.66% in the 1981 Census. This increasing trend in their population explains the fact that the splinter groups which sought higher mobility by assuming new names and thus kept some distance from their parent community so long, have started coming back to their original fold. Having understood the futility of maintain their separate identity, they are no longer keen to do so.

Another trend which needs mention is that even those castes which pressed for the achieved higher status in the social scale due to their efforts or were not included in the list of Scheduled Castes' due to their own representations, have now staked their claim for being listed as a Scheduled Caste and, if it is not at all possible to be enlisted as such, then to be classified, at least as a member of the Other Backward Classes. This process has been set in motion after the commencement of the constitutional of India mainly for enjoying the political, economic and educational benefits and privileges enshrined in the Constitution. This is no doubt a mobility towards achieving political and economic power and is basically horizontal in character. It is to be seen whether the substitution of the socio-religious mobility by the politico-economic mobility helps in starting the process of secularisation of the caste system or whether this mobility, being dependant on the caste system for its very survival, meets with the same fate as that of the westernisation process.

References

Reports

Census of India	1901	India, Vol. I, Pt. I.
Census of India	1911	India, Vol. I, Pt. I.
Census of India	1921	India, Vol. I, Pt. I.
Census of India	1931	India, Vol. I, Pt. I.
Census of India	1911	Bengal, Bihar, Orissa and Sikkim Vol. 5, Pt. I.
Census of India	1921	Punjab, Vol. XV, Pt. I.
Census of India	1951	West Bengal, The Tribes and Castes of West Bengal.
Franchise Committee and the Committee on Division of Functions	1919	(Lord South Borough, Chairman)
India Central Committee	1929	(Sankaran Nair, Chairman)
Indian Constitutional Reforms	1918	(Mont-ford Report)

Indian Franchise Committee	1932	Vol. I to III (Marquess of Lothian, Chairman)
Indian Statutory Commission	1930	Vol. I to V (Lord Simon, Chairman)
Interim Report of the Indian Statutory Commission	1929	(Hartog Committee)
Proceedings of Sub-Committee	1930 to 1931	Indian Round Table Conference, Vol I—VIII 12th November—19th January, 1931.
Proceedings of Federal Structure and Minorities Committees	1931	Indian Round Table Conference (Second Session), 7th September, 1931 to 1st December, 1931, Vol. I to III.
Progress of Education in India	1912 to 1917	
Moral and Material Progress Report	1925-1926	
Reforms Enquiry Committee	1925	(Chairman, A.P. Muddiman)
Legislative Assembly Debates	1928	Vol. I and Vol. III

Books & Journals

Ambedkar, B.	1989	*Writings and Speeches*, Government of Maharashtra, Vol. 5, Untouchables or the Children of India's Ghetto.
Galanter, Marc	1984	*Competing Equalities*, Oxford University Press.
Ghurye, G.S.	1990	*Caste and Race in India*, Popular Prakashan, Bombay, fifth edition.
Hutton, J.H.	1946	*Caste in India*, Oxford University Press.
Sinha, R.K.	1986	*Alienation Among Scheduled Castes*, Manas Publications, Delhi.
Srinivas, M.N.	1966	*Social Change in Modern India*, Allied Publishers.
Natarajan, S.	1959	*Century of Social Reforms in India*, New Delhi, Asia Publishing House.

Horst F Rolly

ON BELONGING TOGETHER AND BEING DIFFERENT

This year in summer, my wife and I were strolling down the main street of Heidelberg, which is a small, old university town in Southwest Germany. Heidelberg's main street is a very long, straight pedestrian lane leading through the old parts of the town with plenty of fashionable shops, pubs and little theatres. Suddenly a familiar sound struck my ear and slowly it increased in volume and yes, here they were, quite outstanding from the rest of shopping crowd, with their saffron robes, shaved heads, dancing up the street making a joyful noise with their cymbals and drums chanting, "Hare Krishna, Hare Krishna, Hare Rama, Hare Rama". My wife and I were certainly happy with the freedom of expression displayed. Somehow these disciples of the International Society for Krishna Consciousness did not really fit into this Western establishment, but we would certainly safeguard with all our means, that they be allowed to express themselves as they wish, and operate as they want, likely on the basis of the same conditions as outlined in Article 25.1 of the Indian Constitution..."subject to public order, morality and health".

Still, when reflecting about the event and about the phenomenon of religious movements of this nature one is tempted to apply certain stereotypes, about the group as such, its mode of operation and its doctrines. Possibly one will grant the movement a purpose, function and service that it might render society by providing an alternative environment to assemble frustrated drop-outs and channel their protest and cultural pessimism in a relatively harmless subculture. The emphasis is on the group and the observed data of the group in relation to a wider sociological context and not on the experience of the individual shaped by a lifehistory and his/her personal concept of truth. Even as cultural identities tend to stick to associations and follow certain prescriptions as a group in terms of behaviour, thought and action, the existential perception of the group should not supersede the individual member of the group leading to categorical assumptions which do not give justice even to the group itself, as it is the individual who constitutes the group and not the group, the individual.

In a pluralistic society like India, collective identities constituted through religion, language, ethnicity or any other type of belongingness, are not only forming segregated communities, but also exist in a more or less dissolved relationship as singularised next-door neighbours. Secular policies of liberal democratic statecraft claim to have the solution for the harmonious coexistence of diverse cultural identities. The basic tenet of equality along with the constitutionally safeguarded freedom of conscience seem to even out discrimination and fragmentation between minorities and majorities and one will not find anything wrong in being a neighbour to someone owning up to a religious or any other given identity different of one's own. It is acclaimed that social and cultural diversity is productive for the advancement of a civilization and its peaceful sociability may even serve as an indicator for the quality of a functioning democracy.

The historical argument that ethnic, linguistic and religious identities were socially more isolated and fragmented before the industrial revolution and the political establishment of secular democracy is not shared by everybody (Nandy, 1990). The questions as to what really constitutes a cultural identity and what are the existential options still prevail. Is there any need to exhibit to the neighbourhood what we are and where we belong ? Or is an identity construct a straightjacket confined by Aristotelian two-value logic, to narrow too allow complex personality types to evolve ? What are the external conditions providing the structure, categories and coordinates to locate an identity ?

From a historical point-of-view, we agree that these conditions have been changing over time. Traditional India is said to have been more open with reference to religion and culture in the sense of give-and-take relationships of different existential orders. In these relationships adjustment and change were fluent and they allowed a manifold of sects and subcultures to evolve. On the other hand the systematic conceptualizations of accidental Aristotelian logic do not favour this kind of fluency and the consistent attempt to delimit the One from the Other found its way in structural manifestations of society (Korzybski, 1973). But sticking to a cultural identity should as such be no indication of an existential disharmony of differing identities. Identity diffusion, identity delimitation and, if one wishes, to change one's cultural identity should be acceptable and respectable in an open reference.

Apart from these structural manifestations of epistemological parameters in tradition and culture, there is some factual evidence in India and elsewhere that the total impact of modernization on people, especially the increasing complexity of the division of labour was instrumental in overcoming geographical isolation and ethnic clustering, and thus identity diffusion took place. The restrictions of hereditary vocations and traditional gilds gradually declined, resulting in social differentiation and change, even when this process was a painful one. Along with the ongoing trend to maintain the individualistic lifestyle of an open-ended society, the power of group pressures and the loyalty to narrowly constructed identities seem to have lost momentum. One has existential options and one has reason and justification to follow one's self-determination out of a freedom of conscience, expecting tolerance and respect, with the readiness to render the same to others. Everything should be well in this pluralistic society. Even as the propagation of religion is a constitutional right, a neutral observer, not inclined or fixed to any tradition would hope that a healthy competition of lived faiths and religious denominations would promote a sharpening of profiles, refinement and reformation for the advancement of the nation, a growing civilization and a better world.

Yet, the ideal of a secular and liberal-democratic value system safeguarded by basic human and civil rights is marred by the present dramatic recollection and revitalization of communal alliances not only in India, but also in other parts of the world leading to communal strife, secessionist movements and war. Before we loose ourselves in polemic arguments about historical causes and responsibilities, it is submitted, that it is mainly the focus on the group superseding the individual member of the group, particularly the quantitative increase of a group as a political majority factor, which has been responsible for the forging of narrow loyalties through indoctrination, discrimination and the alienation of differing groups from each other. It is apparent that the vested interests and forces responsible for this are external to the common man who has become a victim of power games and political propaganda.

Let us examine in this context the existential options at hand which have been described as open ended for the individual decision making process and which may not be as open as they are acclaimed. For this purpose we will focus on the concept of universalism which should be able to give some explanation in this regard.

Ethnic, cultural and religious identities generally have the connotation of the particular referring to their distinctiveness in a diverse social environment. The fear that social and cultural diversity could disintegrate and end up in social unrest and civil strive has led to constant and consistent efforts to assimilate ethnic particularities into more universal designs. Justifications, which have been called into play for this vary : a common civil code, a generally binding value system, a political approach to social justice, or paradigms of social science. These justifications may claim contextual validity, yet quite often they have been projected to exercise dominion of one group of people over the other. The structural demands towards assimilation which weaker ethnic collectives are confronted with, evoke frequent resistance and assertion of especially those features which are to be given up and changed. Even when concessions of ethnic groups have been made and assimilation has taken place it may only be a superficial one. Underneath the adjustments towards a homogeneous surface structure, ethnicity may live on sub-or unconsciously—and if repressed may recollect itself as a stronger force to reckon with (Fischer, 1990 : 196).

Factually, the diffusion of traditional identities caused by modernization, when not properly rationalized by an eclectic or any other philosophy of life, may result in general disorientation which is likely to be compensated by displaying loyalty and assertion to a stabilizing collective identity. This may especially happen when group pressure prevails and economic interest and advantages are in the bargain.

The promotion of universal values with the intention to homogenize society and culture has thus succeeded only partially in reducing civil unrest and strive of a communal nature. Universalism is obviously not a neutral concept but is linked to theoretical presuppositions. The structure-functionalist school tends to associate universal norms and values with the paradigm of social evolution of which the advanced western industrialized nations form the peak and to which other less developed countries and cultures have to assimilate for survival or face extinction through natural selection (Parsons, 1966). When existential options are limited within a questionable evolutionary framework enforced by socioeconomic constraints, diverse cultural and ethnic identities have to locate themselves in relation to these external parameters and categories and the result will be paradoxically an increased rate of social and cultural polarization and even segregation on the basis of a created significance of being universal or being outside the realm of universality[1].

Of concern should be the common man like you and me, who finds himself or herself in these complex internal and external forces constructing identities. As life styles are not to be imposed either by an obsolete tradition nor by an artificially designed universalism, one will have difficulties in defining one's identity especiall with reference to the complex nature of socialization, education, spiritual values, science, etc. one is exposed to and the maze of categories involved. The sociocultural demand to display one's cultural identity may incorporate a number of pressure groups playing variable tunes of narcissism to comfortably project an identity into a value system. One may end up with a number of identities, one which a person secretly believes in, another one which is generally obliging and acceptable within a socioeconomic and cultural setting and a third one which is the economically most profitable in the context[2]. After all tracking down in the maze of existential categories often leaves a person stuck in a contradicting range of possible identifications : As a religious person can I still fully believe in science ? What about the degree of demythologization I am or I am not to adhere to as a rational being and my acceptable contribution as a religious scientist to a progressing society ?

It is even more difficult for the anthropologist and social and behavioural scientist to find a truthful place in the maze of possible identity constructs than it is for the common man as they have to verify their existential options with falsifiable academic parameters. Again, some conceptual compulsions may restrict a scientist from reflecting a complex state of affairs, even when the factual evidence is given. One is caught in a trap to prove or to disprove and interdisplinary relevances with consequent modifications of the whole theorem are avoided for the sake of simplifications and readymade explanations. Modernization, secularism, universalism and imperialism are framed into one picture while traditionalism, communalism, cultural relativism and underdevelopment into another without a realistic interaction and interrelation of concepts between the two pictures corresponding to the complexity of our lifeworld. It seems that many intellectuals have been trapped by this transfixed Aristotelian either/or encapsulation. In these teleological and normative settings, minorities and cultural identities are framed as objects to be assimilated, integrated or diffused, to fulfill a function, to play an externally designed role (Srinivasan, 1989 : 20ff) and in the case of so called criminal tribes, to be isolated.

The cultural and ethnic identities themselves contribute to their objectivization by claiming apriori metaphysics, preset histories and an ontological status of their own. At least this is what they believe in or what they are made to believe by an institutionalized order. Indications are given to people that their adherence to a given belief, order or philosophical school would make them very special human beings qualified and distinguished by the consolidated ideals they are confined to. They would possibly allow the Other, simply by not belonging to the same order to existence, to be categorized as being not special, not truthful to the extent that the Other may not retain the status of a fellow human being with similar needs and feelings but acquire the status of an alien, infidel, or enemy.

This is not to claim that loyalty to an identity construct is wrong as such, but to remind ourselves that so called objective reality including metaphysics and the objective sciences are founded in the lifeworld of human beings, they are an expression of human activity, they are generated by subjectivity and cannot claim apriori status for the sake of it (Berger 1990 : 13ff). For this reason it seems to be futile to add any other paradigm to the maze of existing ones to reconcile cultural and ethnic minorities and majorities by referring them to abstract formula of objectivity, universality, and modern system theory, as if these were isolated from their subjective constitution. Rather than stressing on the "What"—on the end result of human activity to come to conclusion about reality as a group or as an objectivized doctrine projected on the group, a change of orientation is required to the "How" these results are being constituted, i.e. to an innovative epistemological approach as a sociology of knowledge. The way out from the outlined structural confines will be the return to the pretheoretical reality of everyday life and interaction. For the value of a human being is not determined by its belonging to a certain religion, caste or scientific community but by one's free constituting subjectivity and very personal values and character.

Human beings with their existential experience in this life; their intersubjective exchange of ideas, norms and values; their negotiated affirmation and negation and eventual habitualization and sedimentation shape a tradition and culture. New generations are socialized in these traditions and will reinterpret internalized values in a geographical and historical context adding modifications and change. As any institutionalized order of religion, culture and ethnicity cannot be separated from its human constitution, any sense and meaning of life have to be relativized to the human activity which have generated it (Berger, 1980 : 78).

The philosophical school which comes closest to the realization of the constitutive value of subjectivity in terms of knowledge generation and its reflection in shaping a lifeworld is phenomenology. It is not the purpose of this paper to give a detailed outline of phenomenology as a school of thought or as a science. For this purpose the reader may refer to Husserl 1969, Schutz 1967, Natason 1973, Psathas 1973, Luckmann 1978). Rather it is intended to point out the existential consequences of following phenomenology and its basic tenets for social life and the lifeworld in general.

By referring to subjectivity as the origin of the production of knowledge systems, all scientific and metaphysical apriori claims are at the disposal of the investigating subject, i.e. not only can they be taken for granted or rationalized within given parameters but as another option, they can be exposed to healthy epistemological doubt as a means to arrive at a higher transparence of thought and action. The latter will help to escape from and to avoid mental encapsulations and commonplaces in the first instance by liberating oneself from any presuppositions, preconceptions, loyalty to given groups and bias and prejudice against others and enable oneself to start one's investigation from a radically neutral and epistemologically honest position. One's commitment to radical doubt and consistent analysis, clarifications and refinements of one's intentions and ontic encounters with the outer reality has the potential of eventually asserting common sense, reason, transparence and true knowledge in the investigating subject. The phenomenological innovations, which open to the intentional field of consciousness flexible alternatives of cognitive competence realize themselves in the continuous flux of time. Existentially lived time is shared with others by interaction, communication, socialization and responsible assertion of what is found to be true, eventually constituting genetic intersubjectivity.

In the same way others can only be fully comprehended by a direct reference to the subjective experience of these individuals who constitute the reality to be comprehended and not by given formalised criteria of a group consciousness and categories of existence. It is not possible therefore to learn about a religion by reading its holy scriptures alone. A full understanding is only achieved when the religion in question is actually experienced as a participant in a spiritual community, where religious meaningful phenomena and intuitions are empathized, lived and intersubjectively asserted with reference to practical issues of every day life. An anthropological survey to describe the lifeworld of ethnic and cultural groups from a distance is not permissible.

To get to know the reality of a given people, Husserl developed an elaborate method of empathy of which a short outline is given in the following : As stated above, the physical presence of the researcher in the lifeworld of the community to be comprehended is a necessary precondition. The researcher starting from a refined neutral point of reference cannot directly experience the social reality of the other, as one would think or feel with the mind or with the body of the other. Any empathized phenomenon has to go through the experiencing filter of the researcher as if the experience and the feelings of the Other would be one's own. The researcher's body is actually organically responding to the body movements of the Other by being kinaesthetically evoked in a simultaneous fashion : certain actions, non-verbal clues, feelings are thus mediated through physiological reflexes providing intuitive support for the mental reconstruction of verbal utterances. Husserl does not encourage analogies, inferences and inductive reasoning as a means to grasp the ontic reality of the Other as here again formalized criteria of reasoning gain control over empathy which will lead to jumping to conclusions and superficial understanding. The psychophysical characteristics of the Other are appercepted by identification and associative pairing of the Other's with one's own content of experience which defines the common intentions to the world. Yet, phenomenological empathy is not confined to psychological phenomena and not to be interpreted as such. As human subjectivity is generally orientated towards the outer world with its objective manifestation in space and time, the participating researcher empathizes how individuals are referring to the world around constituting the same with their particular meaning and sense (Husserl, 1973 : 447ff).

Understanding of the Other includes changes of one's own perception of the world, otherwise no knowledge would have been attained. Yet, the researcher does not give up one's reflective distance to the Other or else identities are fused and neutral analysis and description become impossible. It is only in the dontext of genetic intersubjectivity in which experienced and lived reason, truth and common sense remain the guiding factors of individual competence shared with others and in which existential options are shaped accordingly, that an open-ended learning experience consisting of personal exchange of knowledge, ideas and values will take place. The willingness to share, to take and to give, to engage in ideal interpretations and to assume consequences for the incorporation of genetic implications, free from any encapsulation and imposition will constitute this open-ended learning experience.

The reflections outlined above do not favour any metaphysics, but that metaphysics as such exist even with an apriori nature, was claimed by Husserl himself in the conclusions of his Cartesian Meditations (Husserl 1960). Only these metaphysics, which he calls the answer to "the highest and final questions" are to be constituted by an authentic subjectivity and genetic intersubjectivity based on existential verification of the truth aiming at a true universality. Finally, as a philanthropic reference it is not the reality of life which in a continuous fashion is reconstructed and constituted, but the ideality of a better life.

NOTE

1. Compare the falsification of the structure-functionalist approach with reference to the Indian social and cultural development by Ishwaran (1975). His study consolidates not only the insight that the revitalization of traditions is often linked to the resistance of so called universalism but also, that different concepts of what is considered to be universal exist.

2. Compare the issue of Non-Hindu Scheduled Castes and Tribes claiming Hindu status to remain eligible for the government scheme of "compensatory discrimination" (Galanter 1991 : 305ff).

Bibliography

Fischer, M.M.J. 1980 Ethnicity and the Post-Modern Arts of Memory, in : Clifford Jand Marcus G.E..., (ed.) *Writing Culture : The Poetics and Politics of Ethnography*, Delhi/Bombay.

Galanter, Marc 1984 *Competing Equalities*, Delhi/Bombay.

Husserl, E. 1960 *Cartesian Meditations*, The Hague.

1969 *Ideas : General Introduction to Pure Phenomenology*, London.

1973 *Zür Phaenomenologie der Intersubjektivitatet*, The Hague.

Ishwaran, K. 1983 *Religion and Society Among the Lingayats of South India*, New Delhi.

Korzybsky, A. 1973 *Science and Sanity*, Clinton.

Luckmann, T. (ed.) 1978 *Phenomenology and Sociology*, Harmondsworth.

Parson, T. 1966 *Societies : Evolutionary and Comparative Perspectives*, New Jersey.

Psathas, G. (ed.) 1973 *Phenomenological Sociology*, New York.

Schutz, A. 1967 *The Phenomenology of the Social World*, New York.

Srinivasan, N. 1989 *Prisoners of Faith*, New Delhi/Newbury Park/London.

Dipali G. Danda

WOMEN OF INDIA : CERTAIN DISTURBING ISSUES

We the city-bred educated section of women in India feel proud when we come across such news that so and so girl stood first in the University examination in engineering, medicine or any other discipline, or has been awarded coveted foreign scholarship. By such news, self image of women gets boosted up and the social workers may think that women in India today are storming all bastions of males which were once considered as their exclusive preserve and proving themselves to be equally good, if not superior in many walks of life. Indian women generally do not lag behind. It is very much expected that being provided with equal opportunity they may prove their worth in every field from mountaineering to military service. In fact, women police or police officers are rated better than their male counterparts so far as their professional performance is concerned. It is also expected that women would turn relatively less corrupt in certain departments which are known for such undesirable practices. As women are newcomers in many fields, they are to prove their worth in the male dominated set-up by establishing the good reputation of being uncorrupt and efficient. Besides, to an Indian women, home still remains very important. She will, therefore, devote less time and energy in extra-curricular activities in order to save time and energy for the home front.

Ordinarily it is believed that women have physical limitations when compared with men, hence less laborious jobs are assigned to them. In reality, however, their forebearance is more and biologically they are superior to man (Montague, 1953).

Nature provides women with immense capacity for tolerance in order to preserve the species. It is, nevertheless, not that significant since the same is true for other animals too. Physical social strength as such turns to activity when it is added with one's will power to work. Recently we had an interesting exposure in Chhattisgarh when we visited that area in connection with the project 'Women Poverty and Rural Development'. There we found women do most of the laborious works relating to cultivation. We came across such women there who plough agricultural fields even at the rate of payment. In certain cases women were preferred as labourers because they never indulge in idle gossip or smoking. They are by and large found eager to work and return home. This suggests that women are as capable as any man in handling matters, even involving physical labour. We came across a woman who had to manage the family by herself as she became a widow at a very young age. She was found specifically disinterested in village politics. When we enquired for the reason why she was not taking interest in the affairs of village council when she could do any work like a man, she replied, "Where is the time for a woman to indulge in such idle work ? Man have lot of leisure at their disposal, as they can spend time in such activities. After cultivation work we the women, are eager to came back home to take care of children as well as the home. Men are free, almost do nothing in the domestic sphere unless compelled by circumstances."

When we worked out the ratio of work done by men and women in the field of agriculture it became evident that the major share, was borne by women. Man's involvement in this regard is rather peripheral. Perhaps this is true for all other parts of the Indian subcontinent. Men in general appear to work less but enjoy more leisure and privilege. Perhaps in general appear to work less but enjoy more leisure and privilege. Perhaps this is true for all other parts of Indian subcontinent.

Men in general appear to work less but enjoy more leisure and privilege. Perhaps this is true for all other parts of Indian subcontinent.

The recent ILO report (*The Hitavada*, Nagpur, Sept. 9, 1992) also corroborates the same fact. From this fact it can be said that the women are being exploited and not given their due share. The women who work as wage labourers are found to give the entire amount of earnings to their husband.

On the other hand, men spend more money on narcotics or other articles of addiction. The same situation is believed to prevail in the slum area of the cities.

Here it can be said that the trend of exploitation in all likelihood, started with the wake of civilization. The more the society has advanced technologically, the more the women have become overburdened with the domestic responsibilities. Although some amount of domestic work is required to be done in all societies, various jobs relating to maintenance of household appear to be considered inferior and assigned to women. The above referred ILO report also remarked that the world over men are reluctant to perform household activities. Thus the bulk of women are denied the privilege of having exposures beyond their domestic limits. Their world has been confined primarily around home and children. By and large they have not been allowed to share responsibilities of life equally with men. The statement may appear somewhat hypothetical though is not much different from reality. I have some exposure to a very primitive group like the Onge of Andaman Island and I have closely observed the transformation of the Onge women from the status of food-gatherer to housewife though the process is yet to be completed. As they are now a days supplied with free cereal food by the Andaman and Nicobar administration, the women need not go for collection of root-food which was once the source of their carbohydrate. Protein food is not supplied through free ration hence men still go for hunting. In earlier times there was no such dictum that only women have to cook. In fact there was no sharp division of labour in this matter. Since men also participated in cooking and attended to other domestic chores, the Onge women in those days used to get more time for leisure. Now that situation is changing very fast. Women have to cook, clean the utensils, and do other related jobs besides looking after children.

Consumption of cereal as food is not the only item that has been introduced to the Onge, the entire food-complex of alien people is being thrusted upon them. As a result, the Onge women have to sacrifice their freedom, leisure and enjoyment for the so-called development. This is not altogether a new phenomenon. Even in the industrial set up we find that when a machine is introduced, women workers are the first to make way for the same as if they are incompatible with machine. With adequate training, both men and women could be equally competent to handle the same. Still it is the women who are to suffer.

This is still very much a fact that where women directly take part in the productive process, they enjoy relatively better freedom (Danda, 1978) but necessarily better social status. Studies conducted by various scholars in North India and by Mencher (1978) in South India corroborate the statement.

II

When we examine issues related to status of women, we by and large become very much scripture conscious. India is one among the oldest living civilizations with great traditional load. But such tradition often reflects a double standard, specifically when the position of woman is the basic issue. In Hindu traditions, women are endowed with exalted positions. If we glean through various scriptural documents, we find that such positions are generally attributed to mothers only i.e. whatever status or prestige a women enjoys, it comes to her at the last quarter of her life. In reality, however, even a mother enjoys power and prestige in a family only when she becomes a mother-in-law. Until then, being daughter or daughter-in-law she is assigned with no significant role either in the family or society. As a result, when she becomes important, very little interest is left with her to enjoy the life of her desires. Further, the power or status endowed with her by and large can have expression only while dealing with her fellow species who are available as daughter-in-laws. Nevertheless, such power and status often manifest themselves in the extant of ragging the alternate generation. Power and status to women thus, in real sense, remain ever elusive. In view of the over-all position, women scarcely have free will to decide matter for themselves. Either, the father, husband, or son, depending on the life situation, mostly decides matters for her.

It is often repeated that women's status was relatively high during the early Vedic period. Since there are references about some women scholars during that period, there is a tendency to accept the same as a sure reflection of their superior status. It has to be understood that presence of few female scholars does not prove anything definitive in this respect, neither does it indicate equal opportunity across sex. Presence of even a woman Prime Minister or a Legislator does not mean much or suggest that most of women in India are either very enlightened or progressive. Exceptional talents have always been applauded but they hardly-recommend the overall patterns. What one can safely conjecture is that there was no anti-woman prescription during that period, which was so common during the period of Dharmasastra. Let me hasten to add here that the emphasis of the given reference is not necessarily on wifedom or any other role of women. But somehow the association between women and motherhood seems inherent.

The following verse from Grhyasutra will make the point clear. 'O Indra, make this wife mother of good sons and fortunate. Give her ten sons, make her husband the eleventh : (Quoted from Evolution of Hindu Marriage by Nilakshi Sengupta). It directly suggest that women are primarily required as an instrument for producing particularly male children. The role of companionship of a woman with respective husband received very scarce attention. However, till then women were not considered as property of liability. We do not find any reference to *Kanya Sampradana* or gift of girl by the father to the bridegroom in the early Vedic period. As mentioned by Sengupta,

> "It is very strange that this *Kanyadana* which is considered to be one of the essential ceremonies of the later period, is not mentioned by most of the Grhyasutras. The Vedic references...show that it was believed that the bridegroom received the bride as a gift from the gods and not from the father" (1965 : 49).

There is no reference of child marriage or dowry either in that period. With the passage of time, however, the society changed considerably and in the period of *Dharmasastra*, transference of girl as gift as well as payment of dowry have come into practice which signifies sufficient loss of status of women in the society. Even in Srimad Bhagvad Gita, the women were treated at par with the Sudra and extra emphasis has been paid on female chastity, particularly in the context of war.

In the hands of Manu, the ancient law giver, the status of wife in the family declined to that of a maid servant. According to his prescription a husband must always be worshipped, even if being a drunk or debauch or devoid of any virtue. It is believed by many scholars that lower status of women is a matter of later incorporation as there are many contradictory remarks noticeable in *Manusamhita* regarding position of women. However, during this period child marriage, polygamy and such other practices became very popular. Unfortunately such situation continued for centuries together. Even in the writings of Bankim Chandra Chattopadhyaya, who admired women power, a husband has been referred to as the only god to a woman, and her prime duty, as prescribed, was to serve her husband.

Has the situation changed after so many years of Bankim Chandra ? We do not have any evidence in favour of that. There is no denial of the fact that the social reformers of the 19th century started major movements for emancipation of women. During the post-Independence period, such movement gained further momentum. During recent decades, women's year, women's decade, or women's day are being formally observed. Year of the girl child has also been popularised. Various mechanisms are also being adopted for generating awareness among people so that girl children are not discriminated against. In this respect the role, particularly played by the electronic media is very important. Whenever we switch on the radio or television we are exposed to a presentation discouraging differences between a male and a female child or propagating affection to daughter. All such programmes through electronic media or posters virtually have no effect on the society. Still we seem women far behind in terms of literacy from their male counterparts. In 1991 the number of male illiterates in India was 12 crores, for women it was 19 crores. Out of every 100 girls from primary standard, only one girl reaches upto 12th standard (Radio report). This is certainly not an encouraging picture.

The reason behind this situation is not difficult to explain. The girls in general are still not that welcome in the Indian society. A girl child was perhaps never wanted by the Hindu. Nowhere in Vedic literatures find any reference welcoming a girl child. The discrimination between a female child and the male child in all probability started from that age. There are innumerable verses which express the desire for sons and offer prayers for the same. The verse makers were alert enough to reflect the choices and moods of any society. It is, therefore, only natural that they offered prayers for sons and fortunes.

It may be mentioned here that in ancient India a male child was preferred to a female child since as per prescription of the tradition only the sons could salvage their ancestors from their sufferings in the hell. Though women at that period were relatively statusless, they were not considered burden to or curse of the society and were certainly spared of the cruelty of female infanticide. Now a days religious consideration is not the main criterion for preference of male children. With the development of science and technology, the people do not depend on the mercy of gods for male progeny. They themselves assume the traditional role of gods by exterminating, on the plea of practical considerations, the second or third born girl child immediately after birth. Even at foetal stage a female progeny is discriminated against with the help of aminocentesis.

The people want to be less burdened with girl children not necessarily because of having no affection for them. In fact, often girl children are also found to enjoy as much affection of their parents as their male siblings. Harsh realities of the existing social system makes the difference. As a result, often we come across such news that 'Girls in Salem are born to die' (*The Times of India*, Bombay, August 23, 1992). From here and there news pour in that female children are being killed or female foetus is being destroyed. "Pre-natal sex determination tests cashing in on age-old prejudices against the female sex, result in an estimated 3,500 female foetecides every year in Jaipur city alone, a study of the Department of Anatomy of S.M.S. Medical College" (Female foeticide on the rise. Jaipur, Jan 30 (UNI) The Hitavada, Jan 31, 1990).

Such news invite our attention not only because they are discriminating against female children. Killing of any children or foetus is bound to disturb the conscience of any enlightened mind. Such news emit shock waves when a 30 year old mother declares, 'For the sake of my family I will continue to kill all female babies till I get a boy. She justifies her action by saying, 'I felt sad, but I had to think of her future which would have been bleak since we could not afford another dowry' (The Times of India, Aug, 1992).

It is certainly not just a stray case. A recent survey has disclosed that 'female infanticide is rampant in Tamil Nadu'. In that part of the country it is an age-old practice and still continuing. Strangely enough, nobody seems to consider it as something sinful or a criminal activity.

Whether illiterate or educated, rich or poor, everybody has

his own reason for justifying such behaviour and indulging in unlawful activities. Even the lady doctors of the area seem to be sympathetic to such activities since they do not consider it a crime and directly discourage this practice. One of them observed, 'I support the policy of female infanticide and refuse to admit that it is a sin'. The parents would certainly prefer to kill their female children in infancy instead of seeing them being killed after nurturing them to young girls. Lady doctors further say, "...They have to kill because society is against women. Their mothers have suffered so much that they do not want the pattern repeating in their daughter's lives. They are not committing murder". They try to say that this sort of killing is not murder. It means protecting the dignity of female children. Thus not only women support female infanticide, men too bear more or less the same opinion. Seeing ill-treatment of their daughters in the hands of in-laws they feel helpless to the extent of advocating female infanticide.

Extraordinarily high rate of dowry prevalent in this area is perhaps the major killer in this region. Among the affluent section of the society, payment of dowry may not be that important a reason. Still for keeping the family property intact and within the family circle people prefer to have male children. *The Times of India* News Service reports that this practice of female infanticide is being adopted by other people also from states like Bihar and Orissa who have settled down in this part of the country. As it seems, creation of awareness about the problem through media could not make any dent in the age-old practice of the area or arouse the conscience for any positive action in this respect yet.

III

The question again and again disturbs us is why the state of affairs perpetuates over centuries. Is there no impact of preachings and sacrifices of so many great sons and daughters of the country who fought for equality of gender ? All of them stressed on emancipation of women through education that would help in awakening of their self.

It has already been mentioned that human beings are born equal and in pre-class or pre-agricultural social structures the gender bias was not that conspicuous. The societies were basically egalitarian. Inequality of any sort appears to be the product of civilization. Man to man differences on the bias of class, religion, and gender have become acute with the growth of civilization.

From the facts of history it is learnt that women were victims of gender bias and had to suffer from subjugation the world over. The cause of this, however, is rooted in traditions, values, social structure, and the social system as a whole. Everywhere in the world there were movements for removal of depredation suffered by women. But we are yet to come across any solution to this nagging problem.

The initial efforts to emancipate women were primarily based on the idea of liberalism, which aimed at equality of gender. There is no gain saying of the fact that everywhere the males provided the leading roles in such movements, though the root cause of primary social division is perhaps the male domination in the society. Later on, with enlightenment of women another kind of movement, initiated particularly by the women in the west grew. This may be considered as seperatist in character since they are extra-vocal regarding male domination. The rationale and scope of such movements may be a matter of debate and in India, in particular such movements are yet to gain momentum-particularly in rural and tribal areas.

Most of the movements in India, whether they are organised by women or neutral body, aim at assuring social justice to women and awakening of their self-consciousness. India being exposed to various reform movements from pre-independence days, the government adopted deliberate means to improve status of women through various legislations. The earliest of these are pertaining to abolition of *Sati*, widow remarriage, age at marriage of a female child etc. After independence, in particular many more legislations have been enacted. Above all, special constitutional safeguards have been provided for women. In fact, the principle of equality of status is one of the specific objectives of the Preamble, Fundamental Rights, Directive Principles of State Policy and such others. The Constitution of India provides that the State shall in particular direct towards securing the citizen, men and women equally have the rights to an adequate means of livelihood and equal pay for equal work for both men and women. Subsequently, considering the gravity of the problem various enactments have come into effect among whom mention may be made of a few here : Special Marriage Act (1954), Succession Act (1954), Dowry Prohibition Act (1961), Indecent Representation of Women

(Prohibition) Act (1956), the Commission of Sati Prohibition Act, (1989), Suppression of Immoral Traffic Act or SITA (1956) etc.

All these enactments are directed toward betterment of women's position and concomitant social change. But social phenomena as such are very complex and do not necessarily follow the underlying directives of the Constitution. Social phenomena in general do not demonstrate any concern for the relevant legislations. Hence ageold practices related to female infanticide, child marriage, dowry etc. still go unchecked in the country. Somehow progress in the field of education, industrialization and wider opportunities for participation in the social processes could not lead to unified results. There are instances when they have accentuated inequalities in some cases and reduced them in certain other.

It is generally believed that education and better employment opportunity for women will prove more effective in strengthening the women's position. With the development of self-consciousness they will be in a position to resist discrimination. This hypothesis needs testing in actual social situation. It is expected that higher education and suitable employment would put the women in a better position to fight against social evils. Somehow this has not happened so in all situations. It appears rather puzzling when we observe that with the increase of education the rate of dowry also shows an increasing trend in the society. While discussing women's problem with a number of educated persons belonging to both the sexes I was rather baffled to see that they do not consider dowry necessarily as one of the social evils. A number of women support this system. In this connection I may refer to our experience in a village near Nagpur. Before launching a reaserch project on women we visited the village for pre-testing our schedules. There we discovered that dowry was not the custom among the earlier generations. It has now become a practice to demand dowry at the time of marriage only of the younger generation. The parents whose marriages were contracted about 30 to 40 years back neither paid nor received dowries. They however, demand dowry for their children, as if expenses on education have to be compensated through realisation of dowry. No one objected to the dowry system. Rather higher was the rate of dowry, higher was his/her status in the society. Thus dowry has become a status symbol. How we would explain this phenomenon ? With progress in education and technology is the society moving back to mediavalism ? It would involve a deep probe to find out an answer to this question. It can, however, be safely suggested that all social changes do not necessarily culminate to any progressive development of the society. With the socalled development, human beings have often been devalued to commodity, salable in the market. Greater human values are evaniscing. We, therefore, are unashamed to declare the rate or price of medical or engineering graduate or civil servants in the marriage market. As an educated lady remarked, "in this part of Maharashtra the highest rate of dowry is bid for a doctor. There are differential market rates for boys belonging to different cadres."

In the rural areas though women actively participate in the productive process, and contribute relatively more, still they have accepted their ageold inferior position in relation to men. Their contribution to family economy could not bring about any qualitative change in their life. At best we can say that in the city area educated middle class women are now aware of their rights as well as privileges and can raise their voice individually or collectively against any discrimination. There are at least a few success stories as reflected by the determination of service rights of the Air Hostesses, of the attempt to given recognition of prostitutes' children in public life. Still women have not achieved the right of adoption and guardianship of children in the event of divorce.

Despite the criticism, whatever has been achieved so far in India is not that insignificant. But a good deal more needs to be done and we have to think in relatively more practical terms. Constitutional safeguards and the legal provisions notwithstanding, women in general are neglected when it comes to the question of better food, health and nutrition facilities. The major burden of family planning too, is borne by women. Still there is no definitive programme to improve their physical condition. A recent study of Jodi L. Jacobson, who worked in India, indicates that the single most important and leading cause of poverty and population growth in India and in other third world countries is the discrimination against women. As she observes,

> "this discrimination exacerbates poverty by preventing hundreds of millions of women from obtaining the credit, education, training, health services, child-care and legal status needed to improve their prospects despite the fact that women in India work

> longer hours and devote larger share of their earnings in supporting families than men do."

She further comments,

> "successive governments in India...have spent more to curtail women's fertility than to improve their health and productivity. As a result of this women find themselves in a 'population trap'. Over the last decade the status of women has declined....The increased workload ensures that birth rates stay high since women depend on 'children' to lend them a hand in all their chores like fuel-gathering, fieldwork as well as drawing water." (Report study by the World Watch Institute, The Hitavada, Nagpur, September 15, 1992)."

Gender bias is noticed in every sphere of the society. Women worked more, but never receive their due share. As an individual, she has equal right but the society bears a double standard for her. So far women are concerned, any right extended to them in general indicates as if some concession is being made to them. In needs a thorough attitudinal change to curb the wrongs. It is certainly not a matter of concession, rather a matter of right as follow human beings. Women should not be considered as competitors of men, they are the better half of the society. As commonly said, man and woman are two wings of a bird. When one is weaker than the other, development suffers. To overcome this weakness, men's education in this respect is equally important. Only this can perhaps brings about structural change in the society. In the earlier referred report Jacobson further remarked, "a complete reorientation of development strategies with more emphasis on improving women's status and less on her reproductive capacity is also needed to reduce population growth and relieve environment." Almost hundred years ago (1901) Swami Vivekananda remarked that with the aid of Smriti codes women of this country had been turned to 'manufacturing machine'. A nation or a country cannot progress unless the women over there are not honoured or given their due share. Humiliation of women is one of the major reasons of the downfall of this country, he observed.

Hence for the greater interest of the country important changes are needed in our views regarding women's problems. The issues should not be kept restricted only to the gender related problems—rather a thorough over-hauling of developmental strategies for the society as a whole has become an imminent necessity. Study of women or their problem cannot merely be the concern of women alone. Since they are related to structure and overall system of the society, a comprehensive approach, involving both men and women seems at this stage essential, if not imperative.

References

Bhargava, Dupali 1987 *Manu Smriti*, Rawat Publications, Jaipur.

The Constitution of India 1992 Nineth edition, Eastern Book Co. Lucknow.

Danda, Dipali G. 1978 Differential Status of women in Rural India', *Down the Memory Lane*, Indian Women Scientists Association, Bombay.

1993 'Transformation of Onge Women through Development', paper presented at the Seminer, 'Concept of Age and Sex in Tribal Societies.' Delhi University.

I C S S R 1975 *Status of Women in India : A Synopsis of the Report of the National Committee on the Status of Women*, (1971-74). Allied Pub. Pvt. Ltd., Bombay.

Leonard, Kaver 1976 Indian Women in Family and Society : Caste, Class and Regional Variations, Paper presented at the conference on Women and Development, Wellesby, Mass.

Mazumdar, R.C. 1953 Ideal and Position of Indian Women in Domestic Life, in *Great Women of India*, (ed) Swami Madhavananda and R.C. Mazumdar, Almora, Advaita Ashram.

Mencher, Joan P. 1978 'Agrarian Relations in two Rice Regions of Kerala', *Economic and Political Weekly*, Annual No., February.

Montagu Ashley 1953 *The Natural Superiority of Women*, the Macmillan Company, New York.

Ragharan, C.G., S.L. Rai and S.L. Deshpande. 1991 'Human Rights, Accountability and Judicial Process', Paper presented at

		the National Seminer on *Sociological Jurisprudence-Perspectives, Issues and Indian Legal System*, Nagpur University, Nagpur.
Reiter, Rayna R. (ed.)	1975	*Toward an Anthropology of Women*, Monthly Review Press, New York.
Sengupta, Nilakshi	1965	*Evolution of Hindu Marriage*, Popular Prakashan, Bombay.
Srimad Bhagavad-Gita	1985	Translation by Swami Vireshwarananda, Sri Ram Krishna Math, Madras.
Swami Vivekananda	1991	Messeges and Essays (Compilation in Bengali) 3rd edition, Udbodhan Karyalaya, Calcutta.
The Hitavada	1992	September, 9.
	1994	September 15, 1992 and January 31, 1994, Nagpur.
The Times and India	1992	August 23, 1992 and December 8, 1992 Bombay.

D.K. Behera

STRATEGIES OF DEVELOPMENT AND INTEGRATION OF SLUM IN URBAN COMMUNITY IN INDIA

The phenomenon of slum has come to be regarded as one of the major problems of urbanization. While no Indian city is free from slums, the problems appear to be more acute in metropolitan cities. Slums are known by different terms in different regions of India—*katras, gallis, juggijhopdi* (in Delhi); *chawls* (in Bombay); *ahatas* (in Kanpur); *bustees* (in Calcutta); *cheris* (in Madras); *keris* (in Bangalore) and *petas* (in Andhra Pradesh).

It is very difficult to define the term 'slum' precisely, because slums are the product of the socio-economic conditions of a particular area. They vary from region to region and from nation to nation. However, scholars have been trying to define the concept from a socio-cultural perspective.

Ford (1936) defines slum as "a residential area in which the housing is so deteriorated, so sub-standard, or so unwholesome as to be a menace to the health, safety, morality or welfare of the occupants."

Similar ideas have been expressed regarding slums by other writers. According to a UNESCO document, a slum is a buildings, a group of buildings or area characterised by overcrowding, deterioration, unsanitary conditions or absence of facilities or amenities which, because of these conditions or any of them, endanger, the health, safety or morals.

Bergel (1945) defines slum as an "area of substandard housing condition within a city. A slum is always an area. A single, neglected building even in the worst stage of deterioration does not make a slum."

Having examined the meaning of the term 'slum' it is now pertinent to discuss the factors responsible for rapid growth of slums in urban India. Shah (1983) considers the following eleven factors as significant in this regard.

(1) The first and the most important factor is poverty. Despite the industry, commerce, trade and the ever expanding 'informal sector' and despite the visible show of wealth, a large portion of urban population is still very poor, earning less than what is needed to buy two square meals, adequate shelter over the head and minimum education and health care for the family. Whatever they do and wherever they go, until their poverty remains they will be in slums.

(2) An increasing number of poor from rural areas are migrating to the urban areas in search of jobs as the rural economy is not able to sustain them (the push factor).

(3) Ever expanding job opportunities in urban areas are attracting people from the villages (the pull factor).

(4) Relatively easily available social services—education, health, entertainment—also attract some people.

(5) The overall response to the problem of slum is *inadequate* (small, fragmented measures in the face of massive growth and wide spread deterioration of slum), *improper* (biased definition and a monofactoral approach highlighted by an excessive emphasis on expensive housing at the cost of other basic needs), and *unimaginative* ('people are seen as a burden rather than a resource').

(6) In planning, the regional perspective is missing. Development action is largely confined to the city boundary and is adhoc, arbitrary and short-sighted.

(7) The market mechanism dominated by speculative forces severely restricts the small man's access to buildable land.

(8) The existing institutional structure is either hostile or indifferent to the less privileged—the corporation fails to provide or maintain services; credit facilities are not available or not usable, if available, building bye-laws render their efforts illegal and unauthorised.

(9) The housing supply, both in the private and the public sector is woefully inadequate compared to the massive backlog and the increasing need.

(10) The new houses built by the formal housing agencies

are beyond the reach of the poor as they are expensive.

(11) The projects offering a low cost and affordable solutions—such as sites and service, environmental improvement, etc., are not taken up on a large enough scale and with any degree of conviction to make a significant difference.

We shall now observe some of the efforts and strategies adopted in Indian society to achieve integration of slums into the community. It seems that there is near unanimity between men in power and social thinkers over the three ways contemplated in achieving integration and development of slums in urban community in India. Those are :

1. Physical improvement of the slums.
2. Establishment of welfare service centres.
3. Providing economic opportunities to the slum dwellers.

Physical improvement of the slums involves the provision of house to the slum dwellers and improvement of the slum environment by way of providing better roads, underground drainage, public bath rooms, drinking water facilities, etc. Provision of new houses to every slum-dweller is very costly affair. Hence various programmes aiming at rehousing the slum-dwellers have not been successful in terms of achieving their targets. The following illustration highlights this point.

The new slum redevelopment scheme for Dharavi as put forth by the Maharashtra Government (1991) consists of granting 180 square feet carpet area built-up tenement to the slum dwellers for Rs. 15,000/-. The proposal sounds very attractive as a poor slum dweller has to make a down payment of Rs. 5,000/- and the remaining amount will be made available as loan to be repaid over a period of about 15 to 20 years. But critics point out that the scheme will result in a virtual take-over of the easily accessible slum sites by the affluent section of the society. Even if the slum dwellers get a tenement, they will have an incentive to sell these. This will be more so in the face of increasing economic compulsions.

Says A. Jockin, President, National Slum Dweller Federation, "The scheme is nothing but a conspiracy to drive out the poor from their slums. Only the builders and the affluent people will benefit from the project". To support his argument, Jockin points out the plight of slum dwellers covered under *Dharavi* Redevelopment Scheme, which is part of the Prime Minister's Grant Project. "Over 50 per cent of the slum dwellers who has moved into their "dream houses" have already sold them and returned to slums. The chief promoter of a housing society in Dharavi, for instance, has purchased 16 tenements at a price of Rs. 25,000 to Rs. 30,000 each." (Sunday Mail August 23-29, 1992). The woefully inadequate financial support fails to have any visible impact in the housing problem of the ever-growing cities. The result : increasing congestion, plummeting life standards and denial of even drinking water to thousands of people who help sustain the life of the metropolis.

The second way of taking up slum improvement is by establishing social welfare centres in the slums. The social welfare centre is the first agency to go into slum areas to undertake welfare activities. Such welfare agencies appear to be useful in bringing about desired changes in the slum areas, but it has been discovered by social scientists that those agencies have failed to enlist the active participation of the residents of slums. Those have never succeeded in bringing about real change in the life of slum dwellers, as they fail to understand the aspiration, needs, and values of the slum-dwellers. The free services provided by the centres, sometimes, lead to continued dependence of slums on welfare centres.

The third approach suggested to improve the slums is by providing economic opportunities to the slum dwellers. They are provided with better economic opportunities than mere services provided by the social-welfare agencies. But the problems of slums cannot be solved adequately only through providing economic opportunities. A community development approach is followed to solve the problems of the slum dwellers in some of the Indian cities.

In the pre-independence period, slum improvements, if any, were left to the discretion of the slum landlords or hut-owning middlemen; however, with the strengthening of municipal institutions, some attention began to be focused on slums in the first Five Year Plan (1951-56) and the earliest response to the issue of low income urban settlements after independence was through the subsidised slum clearance and improvement scheme introduced in 1956. During the Second Plan (1956-61) and Third Plan (1961-66) periods, the scheme was in the central sector and during this time the sanction of projects under the scheme and the release of funds were made by the Central Government, while actual execution of the scheme was entrusted to the State Governments. The scheme was transferred to the state sector from April 1969 when the State Governments were given the responsibility not only of execution of the projects but also for their budget provision and sanction (Ribeiro 1983).

However it was gradually realised that improvement of slum at site would be preferable to a policy of relocation of slum dwellers and construction of tenements and in April 1972, the Government of India introduced the central scheme for Environmental Improvement in Slum Areas and financial assistance was given to the State Governments to undertake slum improvement programmes in Calcutta, Bombay, Delhi, Madras and other metropolitan areas. The scheme was transferred to state sector in the Fifth Five Year Plan (1974-79) to be financed as part of the Minimum Need Programme and the coverage of the scheme increased to all cities with a population of 3 lakhs and above.

Nehru Rozgar Yojana (NRY)

In order to deal with the problems of urban poverty, the Nehru Rozgar Yojana was introduced by the Ministry of Urban Development in October 1989. It was recast in March 1990 and accordingly the guidelines were suitably revised. The yojana consists of two major schemes : (i) The Scheme of Micro Enterprises and (ii) The Scheme of Housing and Shelter Upgradation.

The Scheme of Urban Micro Enterprises (SUME)

SUME assists the urban poor to upgrade their skills and to set-up self employment ventures. At present, the criterion of urban poverty is an annual household income of less than Rs. 7200/-. A subsidy is provided towards setting up the micro enterprise upto 25 per cent of the project cost with a ceiling of Rs 5000/- for SC/ST and women beneficiaries and Rs. 4000/- for general category beneficiaries. The remaining amount of the project cost is available from banks as a loan upto a maximum of Rs. 15,000/- for SC/ST and women beneficiaries and Rs. 12,000/- for general beneficiaries. This scheme is applicable to all urban settlements. The expenditure on the subsidy element of the scheme is to be shared between the central and the state governments/urban local bodies on 50 : 50 basis. More than 15,000 beneficiaries have been trained under SUME so far.

The Scheme of Housing and Shelter Upgradation (SHSU)

The Scheme of Housing and Shelter Upgradation seeks to provide assistance for housing and shelter upgradation to the economically weaker sections of the urban population as well as to provide opportunities for wage employment and upgradation of construction skills. A loan upto a limit of Rs, 3,000/- at 6.25 per cent rate of interest and a subsidy upto a ceiling of Rs. 1,000/- is provided under this scheme to entitled beneficiaries for housing/shelter upgradation. The loan amount of Rs. 3,000/ can be further enhanced by an additional amount of about Rs. 11,000/- under EWS Scheme of HUDCO. This scheme is applicable to urban settlements having a population between one lakh and twenty lakhs. Urban settlements in new industrial townships, Union Territories and in hilly districts having population below one lakh are also covered. The subsidy grants under the scheme are shared between the central and state governments/local bodies on a 80 : 20 basis.

Self Employment Programme for Urban Poor (SEPUP)

Started in 1986, the major objective of this programme is to expand employment opportunities and to help the poor to start a venture in the urban areas which has got relatively growing demand. The scheme is restricted to all the cities and towns having a population of 10,000 or more and which are not covered by IRDP. The scheme is presently being implemented by the Department of Banking, Ministry of Finance. Under this scheme the credit is being given to poor urban enterpreneurs whose incomes do not exceed Rs. 600 per month. The maximum credit available is Rs. 5000/-. The list of economic activities, for which loans are available, contains 35 items covering small scale ventures like hawking, handcart, laundering, welding, cycle rickshaw operation, shoe making and hairdressing, etc.

Urban Basic Services Programme (UBS)

UBS was introduced as a centrally sponsored programme in 1986 for provision of basic social services and physical amenities in urban slums. Functioning of the UBS is the joint responsibility of the Government of India, UNICEF and participating States as well as Union Territories, each of these agencies having financial responsibility of the total outlay to be shared in the ratio of 20, 40 and 40 respectively. The scheme envisages assisting the development of the urban poor through the provision of basic services and amenities like water supply, low cost sanitation, environmental improvement, education and programmes to improve the awareness and to motivate collective community organisations to promote cooperative group action. The main objective of the scheme is to enhance the survival and development of children and women of the urban low income families in selected least developed districts. Under this scheme the district has been identified as the planning unit for operation. The criteria for selecting the districts have been (i) where the growth of urban population has been disturbingly high, (ii) where the basic services are not available to a majority of the slum population, and (iii) where it would be possible to implement the programme alongwith other government sponsored programmes such as EIUS.

The programme emphasises community based development through neighbourhood committees of urban poor themselves. During 1990-91, the programmes was revised and enlarged and came to be known as Urban Basic Services for the Poor (UBSP). This programme seeks to bring about a functional integration between the provision of social services under UBSP and the provision of physical amenities under the state sector scheme of EIUS. Like old UBS during the VII Five Year Plan period, the revised scheme seeks to enable the urban poor to have access to basic services through convergence of the activities of specialist government departments. The revised programme has enlarged the shelf of social services to be provided to the urban poor by including special inputs tailored for street children, handicapped, aged and destitute on the one hand and for solving socio-economic problems characterising slums like juvenile delinquency, communalism, gambling and alcoholism on the other hand. The onus of choosing from competing social inputs has been given to the neighbourhood committees of the slum dwellers. Community or the beneficiary's participation is the markable characteristic of this scheme.

Environmental Improvement of Urban Slums (EIUS)

Although a programme of Slum Clearance and Improvement (SCI) was launched during the Second Five Year Plan with an aim to provide alternate shelter to slum dwellers, due to alarming increase in their proportion there were practical difficulties in slum clearance and therefore, this programme was given up. Subsequently Environmental Improvement of Urban Slums (EIUS) has been included as one of the significant goals in the strategies of urban and regional planning in the country during fifth, sixth and seventh Five Year Plan. Started in 1972 under the Central government programme of special welfare shcemes with 100 per cent central assistance at the rate of Rs. 120 per dweller, the thrust of the scheme is on ameliorating the living conditions of the slum dwellers and urban poor who are leading a sub-standard life in slum areas.

Presently, EIUS is a major programme of the Central Government designed solely for physical improvement of slums through the provisions of basic facilities. Basically, the following six services are provided to the slum dwellers as per the norms given below :

(i) One water tap for 15 people.

(ii) Open drains for outflow of waste water.

(iii) Storm water drains for quick draining out of rain water.

(iv) One community bath for 20 to 50 people.

(v) One lavatory seat (in community latrines) for 20 to 50 people.

(vi) Widening and paving the existing lanes and

(vii) Poles, 30 metres apart, for street lighting.

The improvements are meant for notified slums which are not earmarked for clearance within a limited period of 10 to 15 years time. Guiding norms or standards have also been worked out in respect of each of the aforesaid facilities which the state governments are expected to adhere to depending upon the local conditions.

The scheme got momentum when it was included under point 15 of the Prime Minister's 20-point programme in 1986. A considerable emphasis was put on the scheme during the Sixth Five Year Plan where after observing the slow progress of the scheme during the first three years of sixth plan, the central government had introduced a scheme of Central Incentives Grants to give a further impetus to the scheme.

For the integration of slums in the community, we have to follow a multi-dimensional approach. Following strategies may be adopted to improve and to integrate the slums into the community.

Strategies for Improvement of the Slums

Any move of integration of the slums in community or to establish relations between slums and community should be mediated in such a way that the distinctive internal properties and the boundaries of the system and entity remain unaffected. The differences among the members are neither suppressed nor compromised, but instead, they are organised, or synthesized, and are transmuted into a group idea, or group policy. In planning, the regional perspective should be given due weightage. We must think in terms of orthogenetic development in place of the heterogenetic model. The former neither destabilize the social system nor radically alter the normative system. With the advent of an exotic external system the social fabrics becomes weak and get destabilized.

In order to bring about planned change and development in the slums, community development projects are to be started on the model of Delhi or of Ahmedabad. The objectives of these projects should take into account the needs, values and aspiration of the slum dwellers. The projects should solicit the participation of slum-dwellers in decision making, problem solving and resource-mobilization. Human factors such as awareness, perception and motivation should be taken into account at the level of implementation of development projects. The development projects should assist in providing primary services like health, education and welfare to the slums to provide a base for human development. The main object should be to increase the productive abilities and earning potentialities of the people concerned. Our new approach should be development with the slum-dwellers in place of the earlier approach of development of the slum-dwellers.

We have to place special emphasis on increasing economic opportunities of the slum-dwellers. The slum-dwellers would appreciate better employment opportunities, where effective employment becomes so meaningful in their lives. The areas of interdependence between slum-dwellers and the community should be increased. The slum conditions to work and to have income sufficient to support at least modest aspirations for better living. It is the urgent need of every slum dwellers to seek job opportunities for their grown-up children, otherwise, they are likely to become deviants and criminals in society. Therefore high priority should be given to develop employment opportunities for younger generation. Training and re-training of young would go a long way in improving their socio-economic conditions. By that, we can make them more self-dependent. This will enable us to adopt a new self-help approach in place of the traditional welfare approach in relation to slum dwellers.

We have seen that slums are known for their low level of education. The schools help to improve the life chances of slum children. Efforts should be made to establish Balwadies and

Primary Schools, High Schools, and vocational training centres with all the necessary equipments in each slum area, and to enroll the maximum number of children from the school-going age groups. Medium of instruction should be the mother tongue.

Provision of new houses to every slum-dweller is very costly and an almost impossible task. It is worthwhile that further construction of dwellings in the existing slums is discouraged, and any new construction coming up in the old slums may have to be demolished. All new comers to the cities, and specially people from weaker sections, may have to seek the housing facilities to stop the further growth of the existing slum areas. Such a stop would be helpful in improving slum environment, and at the same time, prevent the growth of slum sub-culture.

The basic needs of the urban poor and their order of priority vary among communities but a general pattern in new slums and squatter settlements has of late surfaced in our cities. Thus in most cities whether the residents hold some form of legal tenancy to the land or not, the demand for public water supply, electricity, health services and basic education has high priority after food and employment opportunities. Other social needs include better education, development of skills, day-care centres, better public transportation and police protection. Finally and only after these needs have been specified, the most highly developed of the low income urban settlements begin to be concentrated with environmental pollution, refuse collection, the lack of parks and other recreational facilities and postal services. Surveys indicate that built houses are often in the lowest order of needs for low income urban settlements as by and large they prefer to undertake this themselves, given proper access to materials and loans. Slum beneficiaries should be granted security of tenure with needed safeguards to prevent speculation and trafficking in land. Services in notified slums, squatter areas and new resettlement/settlement areas must be adequate and above all must be properly maintained.

Meeting the challenge head-on requires much more a strong political will, an unwavering commitment, a capacity to take hard decisions, vision and a long term perspective of the city and its surrounding region. More importantly, it requires some fundamental changes in our ways of thinking and methods of working. To achieve results it is absolutely necessary to change our attitudes, both towards the people and the task to restructure and reorient our institutions and organisations;

to redefine our strategies, and, accordingly, to recast our policies, plans, programmes and projects (Shah, 1983).

The change in attitude towards the task will be easier if it is understood that the slums are people, not places and that the slum is more a reflection on attitudes towards life than on physical or environmental conditions. The slum is not simply a housing problem, but a complex socio-economic, cultural and political one. And therefore, to deal with it effectively, not merely housing projects, but an overall development programme is needed.

The change in attitude towards the people should start with a recognition that they, even if poor, are an asset not a liability and that they are a creative and productive resources and not social parasites. Most slum clearance/improvement projects do not respect people's strengths. It needs to be emphasised that the people have the skills to build and improve. What they need is support, facilities and incentives.

The fact that slums grow twice as fast as cities, indicates that people are indeed capable of building houses on their own. Whether or not we like the project—which is limited mainly by the quality, type and availability of materials and resources—slums are eloquent testimonies to poor people's motivation, resourcefulness, design ability and building skills. In short, it is helpful to recognise that slums are not so much a problem as solution to a problem. They signify a potential and represent a resource which must be tapped if the problem is to be solved.

If we are earnest in our desire to improve the situation, our style of working must also change which means that the institutions and agencies presently engaged in tackling the slum problem should change their present role from doing, to facilitating. Instead of investing their energies in construction of houses for the poor they should aid, promote and accelerate people's own housing actions. The present approach of delivering the finished product should be kept in abeyance, at least for the time being, in preference to a less dominant and supportive role which the poor usually build their houses and improve their environment. The central theme of this concept is to improve poor access to housing components—land, building materials, credit facilities and environmental services.

It will do us all a lot of good to know that solutions to the slum problem do exist; that the problem is indeed solvable. We also know that the resources required to tackle the problem exist with the government and with the target population. What is needed are political will, a vision for future, compassion, and people's unbending resolve and creative imagination. Various non-government organisations may be invited to play an active role in the search for such a solution. Arrangements should be made for them to function effectively. They may be involved in conducting studies, evolving strategies and planning and implementing specific projects for the development of slums and its integration into the urban community in India.

References

Bergel, E.E. 1965 *Urban Sociology*, McGraw Hill Inc. New York.

Ford, J. 1936 *Slums and Housing*. Harward University Press, Cambridge.

Riberio, E.F.N. 1983 "Planning for the Urban Poor : Basic Needs and Priorities," In Alferd de Souza (ed.) *Urban Growth and Urban Planning*. Indian Social Institute, New Delhi.

Shah, K. 1983 "Ahmedabad Slums : Redefining Strategies for Action," In Alferd de Souza (ed.) *Urban Growth and Urban Planning*. Indian Social Institute, New Delhi.

Jaan Valsiner

DEVADASI TEMPLE DANCERS AND CULTURAL CONSTRUCTION OF PERSONS-IN-SOCIETY

How is human personality culturally constituted, and how do personal actions participate in social change? This fundamental question has been asked by social sciences for at least a century, but to no avail. Basic assumptions of the existing social sciences (Valsiner, 1987)—borrowed from the European cultural traditions—may have complicated the search for adequate answers to these questions. In this chapter, I will show how personal lives and culturally organized vocational roles are intricately interdependent. This task entails two equally relevant parts. First, on the development of a theoretical system that affords making sense of that interdependence is on the agenda. Secondly, real-life cultural-psychological phenomena are to be found and analyzed for manifestations of the person-culture interdependence. The first part of the task is accomplished by a culture-inclusive theory of human development which is formulated in abstract generic terms. It is aimed at conceptualizing general lawfulness of cultural organization of human psychology, even in cases where the empirical phenomena are unique to specific persons within their life contexts. In order to carry out the second part of the task, a very unique form of human life course—that of Hindu temple dancers—is selected for in-depth analysis of the person-culture interdependence.

Persons within societies : understanding the dynamics of relationships

The phenomenon of interest in this chapter is human personality in its cultural-historical interdependence. Instead of the two usual directions in the theoretical explication of that interdependence (i.e., the "upward" reductionism—of personality to social entities; or "downward" reductionism of personality to the biological bases of human species), a third way is being used here. It entails elaboration of systemic relationships between person and the social world in the course of human development within real-life, culturally organized, life environments.

The general developmental perspective entails recognition of irreversibility of time in human development, and highly redundant control over the cultural canalization processes. Different active participants (persons, social institutions, etc.) set up heterogeneous contexts for human development, which are filled with polyphony of semiotically encoded messages (or "voices" : Smolka, 1994; Wertsch, 1991). This heterogeneity is hierarchically (but dynamically) organized in non-strict ways. Both persons (in their social roles), and "voices" within the collective discourse, are at times dominant over their counterparts, yet at other times such dominance dissipates. As the hierarchical (non-strict) organization emerges and vanishes in the course of real-life personal lives, it is the mutual relationships between the differentiated components of the whole (see Raheja, 1990 for an analysis of mutualities in Indian caste system) that guarantee the functioning of the psychological and social systems. In human development, hierarchies emerge with the ready propensity to disappear, and from the non-hierarchical (or undifferentiated) states in development new hierarchies of temporary nature are about to emerge.

Human beings develop within an inherently heterogeneous and episodically inconsistent socio-cultural world. They are surrounded with a variety of cultural texts (myths, narratives) and social suggestions which attempt to direct the developing person towards future life course in accordance with the goals of the active "social others" who create or re-narrate these social messages (see Ramanujan, 1991, on heterogeneity of women's tales in South India). Developing persons construct their own social roles in the middle of heterogeneous directionality of available social suggestions, and in ways that may range from extreme acceptance of some of those to equally extreme opposition to others. Such actively co-constructive role of persons guarantees maintenance of their common cultural-historical heritage in all of its heterogeneity, by way of constructing their personally unique life courses.

Theoretical basis : development via cultural constraining

The theoretical framework of the present cultural-historical perspective is outlined elsewhere (Valsiner, 1987, 1994a, 1994b). The central aim of co-constructivist developmental psychology is to explain the processes which are involved in the construction of *personal culture* under the canalizing directions of the *collective culture* (Valsiner, 1989 : 47-48). The collective culture entails communally shared meanings, social norms, and everyday life practices. Individual persons construct their personally idiosyncratic semiotic system of symbols, practices, and personal objects, all of which constitute the personal culture. Personal cultures emerge on the basis of the collective culture, yet their function is to organize the intra-and interpersonal worlds of the person in ways that provide personal sense to the encounters with those worlds. Previous linkages of that theoretical system had been made with the phenomena of personal development within orthodox religious community (see Lawrence, Benedikt, and Valsiner, 1992) and with Nepali women's ritual song construction (Skinner, Valsiner and Basnet, 1993).

The main mechanism that organizes constructive inter-change between collective and personal cultures is that of *internalization* and *externalization* (Lawrence and Valsiner, 1993), both of which are conceptualized as coordinated novelty-constructive processes. Human beings are active subjects who relate to their surrounding world by way of constant construction of semiotically mediated intra-psychological (i.e., personal-cultural "stream of consciousness" a la William James) and extra-psychological (external forms of conduct and manufactured objects) psychological devices. The externalization process is constantly being culturally organized by the social expectations per sons encounter in the sequence of varied activity settings that is part and parcel of their everyday lives. Collective-cultural constraints are set up for specific activity settings at two levels—those of action constraints (see Valsiner, 1987, for analysis of mealtimes), and of corresponding collective-cultural meanings. All human activity is semiotically mediated (Boesch, 1993, Cole, 1990), and directed by collective or social representations (Moscovici, 1982; 1988).

Human development within collective-cultural contexts proceeds through *feed-forward type constraining* (Valsiner, 1987; 1992) that delimits the range of immediately possible novel forms of action or intrapsychological semiotically organized affect and thought. Such delimiting at any particular time guarantees that human development is simultaneously continuous and discontinuous (or : conservative and opportunistic), structured (by way of constraints) and fluid (as the constraints allow for a range of possibilities, only one of which will become actualized (since real life proceeds in irreversible time). Personal cultures always are expected to transcend the expectations inherent in the collective culture (by way of constructive externalization), and provide the basis for introduction of person-initiated novelties into the collective culture.

The focus in the present chapter is in the cultural co-construction of the field of human feelings. This field entails a huge range of poorly definable feeling phenomena, ranging from sexuality and general sensuality to devotion and attachment. The whole field of human feelings is the ultimately personal subjective phenomenon, which is not directly accessible to extrospective analyses. However, already within persons' subjective intrapsychological world the field of feelings is constantly being differentiated by the use of semiotic mediation (Hochschild, 1983; Holland and Eisenhart, 1990; Lutz, 1988; Wikan, 1990). The flow of sentiments within the intrapersonal feelings field becomes reorganized by collective-culturally provided emotion terms, which become connected with different areas of the feelings field and provide it with temporary hierarchical structure.

Double regulation of the feelings field. The semiotically structured feelings field constitutes the semantic field of the personal sense at the given moment, and may become externalized by the person in a communicative effort. That effort is regulated by the person's self-reflection on the one hand, and by social norms of discourse, on the other. On the side of personal subjectivity, the feelings field is intimately based upon the physiological processes, upon which internalized personal sense constructs act as hierarchically superior organizers of the intrapersonal world. In the realm of extrapersonal regulators, one can easily point to the relevance of societal control of the person's social roles within kinship network (e.g., wife, daughter-in-law, husband, mother-in-law, etc.), vocational roles (e.g., nun, courtesan, or nurse), and situation-appropriate conduct rules. This amounts to double cultural canalization of human development : human conduct is redundantly organized by cultural meanings and corresponding activity constraints.

An analysis of time-bound intertwining of the intra-and extra-personal regulation of sensuality in everyday life contexts would provide a specific answer to the general question of person <—> society relations as forms of mutually constituting one another (see Cole, 1990). Likewise, personal subjective worlds are developmentally united with cultural worlds (Shweder, 1990 : 25).

The case of the historically interesting vocational role of Hindu temple dancers has all the necessary features to illuminate our theoretical understanding of collective-cultural double constraining of human personal feelings fields. First, the social role of the temple dancers has venerable history at the intersection of religious and political institutions on the one hand, and personal-cultural life-course organization, on the other. Secondly, the temple dancers' personal feelings fields are canalized in ways that would enhance the externalization of their sensuality in collective-culturally prescribed forms—in service of the highly specific ritual functions in the temple context. Finally, exactly through being highly constrained in their professional lives, the temple dancers were entitled to explore a considerable range of free movement in the sphere of education, devotional aspirations, and heterosexual relationships. Their life courses constitute an example of dependent independence (Winegar, Renninger, and Valsiner, 1989).

The cultural worlds of temple dancers

The case of Hindu temple dancers is a domain of socio-cultural and psychological phenomena that could provide contemporary cultural-historical psychology evidence about the constructive processes between collective and personal cultures. These women—Devadasis—were a relevant cultural-institutional profession all through the cultural history of Hindu temple contexts (Chatterjee, 1945). They were (and—wherever the tradition survives—continue to be) agents of promotion of the unity of personal-cultural and collective-cultural worlds, which is the main role carried by the temples in society (Beck, 1976; Desai and Ma son, 1993; Schnepel, 1993). The temple is an architectural construction that semiotically mediates interpersonal relations (Appadurai, 1985; Dayalan, 1992), and the socially prescribed roles within the temple create contexts for the visitors to the temple to undergo relevant psychological work upon their personal cultures (Obeyesekere, 1981; 1990), unique cultural life courses for persons involved in the temple service.

The term (*devadasi*) literally means the "servant to the God", or in other terms the temple dancers were referred to as "heavenly courtesans" (*swargabesya or apsaras*—Marglin, 1985 : 91). The latter designation links the temple dancers with the socially highly relevant roles of courtesans in history, including that of the complex social world of India (Hasan, 1983; Oldenburg, 1984, 1990). The dancers' main role was to perform specific ritual dances at ceremonies, as well as be involved in other duties in and around the temple. Hence the Devadasis were of critical relevance in the world of devotion to deities—not only did they become highly skilled ritual specialists themselves, but their role entailed social guidance of the visitors to the temple towards higher forms of religious devotion. The history of the special social role of Devadasis in Hindu temples is closely linked with the development of *bhakti* (devotional) religious movements in Southern India (Hardy, 1983).

However, as we know, history of human societies is rich in acts of colonization and stigmatization. Socio-moral dominance over the devotion and loyalty of persons go hand in hand with political control in societies. Hence after the British colonization of India, most of the reflections upon the Devadasi system have been under the influence of the European modern tendencies of viewing the world through the lens of economic commoditization (see Kopytoff, 1986). The social role of the Devadasis who united their personal sensuality with devotional religion made them an ambiguous target for Westerners' description and evaluation. Numerous non-Indian external observers as well as many representatives of different social movements in India (Heggade, 1983; Raghuramaiah, 1991; Ranjana, 1983) have labelled the Devadasis "temple prostitutes", in line with the unclear (but negative in connotation) meaning that the term "prostitute" has acquired in the social discourse in the Western world (see Davis, 1937). Within that social discourse, the Christianity-based repressive conceptualization of female sexuality has flavored most of the understanding of women in their many social roles (see Foucault, 1980, 1986). Thus it has been easy—from the power position of modern colonial powers—to stigmatize the widespread traditions of women's sensuality-linked participation in religious institutions all over the ancient world of pre-Christian times (e.g., Lerner, 1986). Social stigmatization through collective-cultural meanings of immediately emotiogenic connotations is a widely used semiotic vehicle for goal-oriented canalization of personal interpretations and knowledge in socially desired directions. For the social sciences aimed at reaching general knowledge, such stigmatization constitutes a phenomenon to be explained, rather than a starting point for any knowledge construction.

The historical background of the Devadasi custom

Although primarily known in Southern Indian contexts, the practice of young women's dedication to temple service was spread widely across the cultural diversity of India (see Patil, 1975; Shankar, 1990). The earliest record of the Devadasi custom dates back to 2nd Century B.C. and has been discovered at Jogimara cave in Ramgarh Hill in Central India (Desai, 1985 : 107). The institution of Devadasis started to gain prominence around 7th-8th centuries (Dayalan, 1992), reached its most advanced state by 11th-12th centuries (Prasad, 1990), and has continued even under socio-legal attacks upon the tradition up to the present time (Tarachand, 1991).

The conditions for the emergence of the Devadasi profession were economic as well as religious. The socio-historical role of Hindu temples as places for social regulation of dramas of power or devotion, as well as of economic interchanges (Appadurai, 1981). The accumulation of wealth generated by the feudal economic system led to the wave of temple construction in Southern India by the 7th-8th Centuries. The temples emerged as symbolic places within which unity of the powers of religious deities of various functions and kinds, the local kings (viewed as both rulers and servants of the deities—Appadurai and Breckenridge, 1976; Schnepel, 1993), and people of various castes and psychological needs, was maintained and renegotiated semiotically (Pandian, 1983).

However, needs of the local social system were linked with the differentiation of specific ritual functions to be performed by specifically, designated personnel of the temple. Dance in the context of a Hindu temple is a form of prayer, as it brings into motion relevant religious myths. Thus dance and recital of those texts requires specifically designated well-prepared specialists, who were deserving of their special status in the temple context. A dancing girl at South-Indian temples was expected to

> ...know all aspects of dance and must be young and beautiful. She should never be lazy but must constantly be practising her art. (*Natya-sastra of Bharata—4-5th Century A.D., cited via Dayalan, 1992 : 177)*

Devadasis became one category of the religious functionaries attached to medieval Hindu temples—others of the kind being priests, dancing masters, drummers, pipers, etc. By specific accounts, the number of dancing girls in the mediaeval Hindu temples was by far the highest, making up at times 2/3rd of the whole servant group (Prasad, 1990 : 29-30). They underwent extensive training in dance and education in the knowledge of religious texts, and—due to their special flexible status in the generally hierarchical social world—*de facto* belonged to the class of most educationally sophisticated women in mediaevel India.

Their advanced role was both produced and protected by their circumscribed social role in the temple context.

The social context of the proliferation of the Devadasis changed under the British colonial rule. In accordance with the European intolerance of the Hindu traditions of linking religious and sensual worlds of human existence (see Mitter, 1977), the Devadasi traditions became stigmatized as a "vice" to be eradicated. Hence a number of legislative actions since late 1800s have led to the legal downturn in the Devadasi system. Both British colonizers and Indian moralists joined their efforts in the "anti-nauch campaigns" ("nautch"=anglicized version of words for dance—see Marglin, 1985 : 6-7) in Madras in 1890s, which spread over all of India. Between 1910 and 1955, the Devadasi custom was legally outlawed in a number of states (Henriques, 1963 : 194-195). Nevertheless the practice is deeply related with the socio-economic texture of the society, and becomes transformed under change in economic conditions (Marglin, 1985), and continues within rural contexts (Tarachand, 1991). Changes in the social meaning of the dance forms are related with the changes in institutional roles of the local kings in the control over the temples. Moving the dance traditions out of the temple context in an art form has been socially guided effort to secularize the classical Indian dance, which nevertheless is continuous with the narrative tradition of the collective culture (Khokar, 1979; Kothari & Pasricha, 1990).

The predominance of the Devadasis in a temple context was no surprise the number of specific functions they were to perform during ceremonies was manifold. These women performed a multitude of social roles within the activity context of the temple, where the highest levels of the hierarchy occupied the rank next to the priests within the temple. This related to their special status—being married to the God and serving him in the temple—the main role of the Devadasis was religious servitude which made their social role highly unique (Marglin, 1985). That servitude entailed relevant unity of personal-sensual and collective-ritualistic worlds in the lives of the Devadasis.

Sensuality, sexuality, and cultural canalization

Human sexuality has always been an object of projection of social concerns by way of discourse (Foucault, 1980, 1986), as well as a vehicle for organizing and re-organizing social life in society. The functions of sexual conduct have been closely interwined with religious belief systems in history. This was a rather usual state of affairs both in Indian (Siegel, 1978) as well as

Western (e.g., Flandrin, 1985) contexts. Undoubtedly the specific forms of linkage between sexual and religious domains were different, covering the wide range from exclusion of sensual bodily functions from the realm of religion and their intra-psychological repression, to their explicit and collective-culturally meaningful inclusion in the public contexts of religious events. The former has been the case in the Christianity-dominated Eurocentric world, where such repression developed slowly over fourteen centuries, to reach its culmination in the 18th and 19th Centuries. It is exactly at the culmination period of that cultural-historical process that psychology as a discipline separated from philosophy, and a medical doctor in Vienna built a system of psychodynamic theorizing upon the culturally formed but deeply personal psychological problems of his patients.

The opposite direction was maintained in the cultural history of the role of the Devadasis. Their ritual functions in the temple were making explicit use of their sensuality—in full accordance with the religious texts their dances represented. The sensuality in Hindu context is culturally emphasized by the numerous versions of Radha and Krishna stories that circulate within the collective culture (Kakar, 1986; 1989). Hence there was nothing particularly exotic in the unity of sensuality, sexuality, and temple services in the case of the Devadasis. It merely continued (in highly ritualized, temple context) the indigenous beliefs in the magical fertility-bringing role of female sexuality in regulating human relations with the world at large (Desai, 1985, chapter 6). That world entailed the crucial role of local kings who (while being local rulers) were simultaneously servants (*cevarti*) of the deities (Appadurai & Breckenridge, 1976). In order to serve the deities of the temple, the kings were dependent upon the female symbolically constructed powers of the Devadasis—particularly in the public symbolism of granting fertility of the area (by evoking rain). While being the servants of the deity, and the "representative" of the deity in the form of the king, the Devadasis were nevertheless uncontrollable autonomous agents in their devotional use of their female powers in service of the common social good.

Much of South Indian temple history is linked with the tantric traditions in religion. That tradition within Hinduism built its social power on the unification of sensual and devotional experiences of women (Allen, 1982). The emergence and proliferation of the Devadasi system can be seen as a case of collective-cultural guidance of such beliefs to a highly sophisticated socio-religious practice, and employment of such practices for the purposes of social regulation of roles in a complex feudal state.

The Devadasis in temples

Devadasis' roles in the temple context were multiple and complex, including maintenance of the ceremonial environments. Many jobs were to be accomplished by the Devadasis—aside from dancing and singing, they were active in sweeping and cleaning the temple floors, putting oil in sacred lamps, fanning the deity figure during worship, carrying sacred lamp during processions, etc. (Patil, 1975). As responsible for culturally crucial ritual duties, the Devadasis were also the only women in mediaeval India who could become literate (Dubois, 1905 : 337), in contrast with the confinement of regularly married women to secluded lifestyles and illiteracy.

There exists substantial heterogeneity within the context of Indian history of the specific semiotic and activity-organization of the roles of Devadasis (Bradford, 1983; Patil, 1975). This heterogeneity stems from the highly heterogeneous nature of the set of traditions in Indian religious practices that have traditionally subsumed under the label of "Hindu religion", yet constitutes a myriad of very different (even if overlapping, and interdependent) collective-cultural meanings and practices (Kolenda, 1983; Preston, 1983). The emergence of the term "Hinduism" in the social sciences has its own peculiar history (Frykenberg, 1989). Contrary to the desires of Eurocentric scientists who are used to operating with homogeneous classes, the label is best treated as a depiction of a heterogeneous class (Beteille, 1965; Von Stietencron, 1989). It is in the context of conceptual recognition of heterogeneity that psychological phenomena can be adequately conceptualized (Valsiner, 1987).

Actual description of the Devadasi custom reflect a similar heterogeneity. In different regions they are named differently (e.g., *maharis* in Kerala; *jogatis* or *basavis* in Karnataka; *natis* in Assam; *bogams* in Andhra Pradesh; *muralis* in Maharashtra, *padiyilar* and *devaradiyar* in Tamil Nadu; etc.—Ismail, 1984; Patil, 1975; Shankar, 1990). Devadasis could be encountered in different kinds of temples—in rural or urban areas, and the rules that delimit their possibility to take on a marital status vary from strictly unmarriable with human males (since they were married to the deity), to married (Tarachand, 1991). They could be of highly varied caste backgrounds, and may have entered the religious service via a number of routes (Bradford, 1983)—intergenerational transfer of the dancer's role, adoption by a Devadasi as a child, dedication by parents to the temple as gratitude for deity's good deeds, or for need of money. Once within the temple service, the young girls were to remain on their life course as Devadasis all of their lives (even if the actual dancing roles may have ended in their middle age). The temple provided the Devadasis with basic means of subsistence (land, salary), to which gifts from visitors to the temples added further resources for life. The Devadasis were economically well- established ritual specialists in temple service, whose role was recognized as a positive, honorable, and necessary in the social world.

The Devadasis in the Jagannatha Temple

Most of the following analysis is based on the evidence reported from the Jagannatha temple contexts in Puri, Orissa (Marglin, 1982a; 1982b; 1985; 1990; Seigel, 1978). That context is described in greater detail than others (Geib, 1975), as Puri is one of the most famous locations for religious pilgrimages. The historical background of the Jagannatha temple (built in the 12th century—Kulke & Rothermund, 1986 : 137; Tripathy & Tripathy, 1992) blends the religious and secular history of power, making use of the collective-cultural constructions of local tribes. Jagannatha ("Lord of the World") was made the state deity (identified with Vishnu) by the king of Orissa in the 13th century, with the social function of blending king's secular and deity's sacral power roles. The Orissa empire declined in power as was conquered—first by the Muslims in 1568, and later (in 1803) by the British (Marglin, 1990 : 214). In terms of local life organization, however, relatively little changed. The local Hindu king remained the head of the Jagannatha temple (until 1960s, when the state government of Orissa took over the administrative control), and retains ritual role in the temple context to the present.

In terms of its complex of meanings, the Jagannath religious tradition is a result of historical combination of different aspects. Thus, it has absorbed tribal, Buddhist, Tantric, Saivite and Vaisnavite moments into its complex structure (Preston, 1983). It reflects the high syneretism of religious belief systems that proliferate within Orissa. Undoubtedly the religious-devotional functions of the town—its around 70,000 regular inhabitants encounter about 3-4 times as many pilgrims who visit the holy town, especially during major rituals of the chariot (*rathayatra*) and candan (*candanyatra*)—creates a highly specific social context different from other towns.

Devadasis as special servants : powers and limitations

The important aspect is the ritualistic status of the

Devadasis—they are not fitted into any special caste in the Indian tradition, as they are honored in specific ritual. The Devadasis (like the musicians—*bajantari*—see Marglin, 1982b, p. 159) are the only temple servants who are also considered servants in the king's palace. In the temple context, the Devadasis are considered to be the "walking goddesses" (in parallel with the king as being "walking Vishnu"). Thus,

> The *devadasis* embodying the female aspect of divine sovereignty are considered in most contexts to be living embodiments of the goddess *Lakshmi*, the consort of Lord Jagannatha. As such, the *devadasis* can have sexual relations with all the men who share in the sovereignty of their divine husband, the ultimate sovereign...The active sexuality of the devadasis ensures the fertility of the land through timely and sufficient rain; therefore, it ensures the prosperity of the kingdom. The king's function of bringing good rains and good harvests depends on a specifically female life force concretely materialized in female sexual fluid. This life force can be conceptualized as the female aspect of sovereignty, and the *devadasis* represent it in this world. Among normal married women, this life force is carefully channeled toward the continuity of their husband's lineage as well as to the welfare and well-being of the entire family including the ancestors; thus, married women are enjoined to be faithful to their husbands. By renouncing family ties, the *devadasis* make their life force available for the welfare and well-being of the whole kingdom. (Marglin, 1990 : 216).

The collective-cultural linking of female sexual functions with mythological belief in (and production of) fertility—beyond the direct aspect of producing offspring—is a widespread tradition in human cultural history (Desai, 1985). In fact, the Devadasis could perform their social role in the temple because they were of the female gender. In cases where their dance has become performed by boys who dress themselves as females and dance (*gotipuas*—see Kothari & Pasricha, 1990 : 44-48). The social role of Devadasis (maharis) is based on the feminine powerful meanings that have been maintained all though the history of Hindu mythology, and which entail unity of creative and destructive roles (Kolenda, 1981).

There existed many ways how a girl entered the social role of the Devadasi. That role could be inherited through affinal kinship, parents' decisions to dedicate one of their daughters to the deity, by young woman's wish to serve the deity, etc. (Bradford, 1983, Marglin, 1985, Tarachand, 1991). The central meaning of such dedication was the attainment of the married status (with the deity—an example of theogamy), and establishment of sensual but nonpermanent relations with persons representing the deity (e.g., local king, temple priests, etc.).

The ceremony of dedication of temple servants—male or female—is the same : "sari tying". From that day on, the Devadasis consider themselves married to Jagannatha. For the Devadasis dedicated before their menarche, a puberty ceremony at the first menstruation ("seeing menstrual blood for the first time"—*pratama raja darsana*) is performed, which entails her defloration by either the king or a person of comparable ritualistic roles (which could include a temple servant, by king's permission). After that the Devadasi could accept more or less temporary male partners from among the categories allowed (i.e., temple servants, local higher-caste persons, but no outsiders, e.g. pilgrims to Puri).

Rituals in the temple

In the context of the Jagannatha temple, the Devadasis participated in two daily rituals. They danced at the mid-day rituals (the *Sakal Dhupa*) which takes place during the morning/mid-day meal, and carries the meaning of royal offering of food to the deity (Kothari & Pasricha, 1990 : 42). At the evening ritual involving putting the deity to sleep—*Bada Singar*—the Devadasis (maharis) performed a similarly important but symbolically slightly different role. A more detailed account of those two rituals is necessory to outline the semiotic functions of the Devadasi role in the sacred and profane world of human relations with the cultural world of the deities.

The morning/mid-day ritual. The general specifics of the mid-day ritual are described elsewhere (Marglin, 1982b : 157-158; 1990 : 216-225) as "royal offering" of food to the deity. The important aspect of the Devadasi social role in this context is that (1) they *do not* actually participate in the food offering to the deity (which is performed by priests in the inner sanctum of the temple to where Devadasis have no right of access on this occasion), and (2) the ritual dance is *oriented outside*—towards pilgrims and visitors. It is supervised by the high official—*rajaguru*—who is a high-class Brahman and the representative of the king in the course of the mid-day ceremony (he does not participate in the evening ceremony—Marglin, 1982b : 158).

While observing the Devadasi dancing, the pilgrims and visitors can simultaneously face Jagannatha and the dancing girls. At the end of the dance some pilgrims were reported taking the dust from the Devadasi's feet, or rolling their entire body on the area where she had danced, to collect on their whole body the dust of her feet (Marglin, 1985 : 109). That dust becomes by semiotic construction to "contain" special "sacralizing" powers, attainable only through female powers for bringing good luck in the generalized sense of fertility.

The special dance of the Devadasis (*nritta*—a family tradition of the Devadasis) relates food, dust, *srngara rasa* (complex of erotic feelings that entails sensual experiencing of specific settings of interpersonal closeness—Marglin, 1990 : 212, 219; also : Siegel, 1978 : 200) into one devotional experience. In an explanation provided to Marglin, the *rajaguru* insisted that

> ...the sole purpose of the dance is the production by the dancer's movements of female sexual fluid (*raja*) which falls on the ground. According to his interpretation when the devotees roll themselves on the dancing floor they pick up dust and *raja*. Another meaning of the word *raja* is dust (or dirt), and this reinforces the link between the dust of the dancer's feet and her sexual fluid. (Marglin, 1990 : 218).

The sacralized functions of the female sexual fluid that is assumed to be emitted during the Devadasi dance (and also secreted during regular sexual intercourse) are central in the context of the mid-day ritual. The Devadasi here represents the fertile power embodied in her sexual functions, and the visitors and pilgrims recognize her superior status in this context (e.g., taking the dust from a person's feet, or washing the person's feet and sipping such water express the superiority of the person).

The pilgrims and visitors receive a food offering after the Devadasi dance ritual. Hence the divine food offering and Devadasi's dust-production are ritually integrated within the same thought complex :

> The act of picking up the leftovers of *Sakti* [=female life force, and tantric god] is the spectators' partaking in the goddess's *srngara rasa;* a physical-emotional-cognitive experience. The transformation, spoken of in Hindu India as an experience of tasting (*rasana, asvada, bhoga*) an essence or a juice (*rasa*), is rooted in the physical experience of food and eating...

> The source of tasting of an emotional essence is the divinized dancer. The *bhava* [=a separably manifest part of the dance; postural and gestural gestalt in dance] of erotic love (*srngara*) dominated the mid-day dance ritual, which is erotic love in action; it is a way of relating and communicating with another person, an activity at once physical, emotional, *and* cognitive. The mobile goddess is married to the god, and in their cosmic intercourse they produce a sexual leftover that fertilizes the land and produces well-being in the people. The dance is a divine sexual intercourse...The *bhava* of the dancer arouses in the spectators traces of their own erotic sensations that are constituted emotionally as *srngara rasa.* Should a spectator directly lust for the dancer, the performative efficacy of the ritual would have failed, and the erotic sensation would not be experienced as *srngara rasa* but simply as lust. (Marglin, 1990 : 224).

The social function of *srngara rasa* in the temple ritual complex is to grant symbolic empowerment for the persons participating, and rain for the region, which is an important task of the king. Much of the Puri ritual activity is related to water as life-sustaining resource (Geib, 1975; Marglin, 1985).

The evening ritual. The evening ritual in the Jagannatha temple (Marglin, 1982, 1985, 1990) takes place just before the deities "go to sleep" for the night and the temple is closed. A Devadasi stands on the threshold of the inner sanctum and sings verses from *Gitagovinda.* The song here is addressing not Jagannatha but Siva, who is represented by a metal figure taken out particularly for the ritual. The figure is carried (by Brahmin temple servants) through relevant places within the temple, accompanied by the singing of the Devadasis (who, in the evening ritual, are spatially separated from the onlookers—in relevant contrast with the mid-day ritual). The songs carry the theme of love between Krishna and Radha (from *Gitagovinda*) and are accompanied by gestural/non-verbal signification of the actions depicted in the text. Finally, the lights of the temple are extinguished, and the ceremony ends.

The evening ritual brings the deity close to the audience—a transition that is possible through the Devadasi's singing :

> The deity comes close to his devotees; in other words, he responds to their devotion as expressed by the *devadasi*, the ideal devotee. Through her dance and

> song as well as her nonattached social status she is able to extract the essence of devotion, total absorption in Krishna and single-minded centering of emotion, thought, and physical love for him. The essence of her devotion is *srngara rasa* which is aroused in her audience who, unlike that of the mid-day ritual, is the deity, not the visitors. The deity in this temple is conceived to be a real person with authority, ownership of lands, needs, and desires...
>
> As for the audience of visitors to the temple, the outward manifestation of an inward transformation is their taking of the leftovers of the deity : flower and flame. If, as for the mid-day ritual, one takes these as tangible signs of an inward emotional-mental transformation, one must conclude that the source of this transformation is the divinity, not the *devadasi*. The *devadasi* as the embodiment of refined and single-minded devotion is instrumental in bringing the deity closer to the devotees...By coming close to them the deity arouses in his devotees renewed and intensified love and devotion. (Marglin, 1990 : 230).

The emphasis on unity of the male and female is a major theme in the songs at the evening ritual. The Devadasis are not expected to enter into sexual relations within the times of their ritual performance in the temple, i.e., from morning until evening.

Semiotic direction by collective-cultural meaning complexes

Any historically pervasive socio-cultural practice is built upon semiotic bases that the persons have constructed and constantly reconstructed over generations. The Indian context is perhaps one of the best examples in the World where folklore texts organize personal lives (Kakar, 1981; 1985, 1989; Roland, 1988). It is in the process of intergenerational transfer of folklore texts that both the collective-cultural knowledge base is maintained (with modifications), and personal-cultural understandings of the world channeled in their general directions.

Role of folkloric texts in collective culture

Folklore texts entail meaning complexes that weave together general and concrete knowhow, marked specifically by connotational implications. The inclusion of moments foreign to everyday life experiences (e.g., transformations of persons into animals, monsters, and vice versa) allows for high flexibility to bring collective-culturally relevant focal meanings. The texture of folkloric complexes guides the persons towards collective-culturally fitting interpretations of their relations with the world. Such semiotic constraining performs the function of *symbolic empowerment* of the person—in the activity of construction of personal culture, the person can use folkloristic "anchor ideas" to assemble one's personal understanding with high flexibility in symbolic construction (Obeyesekere, 1981, 1990). Folklore does not merely reflect collective culture, it participates in the development of persons within it. The heterogeneity of *genres* in folklore texts allows for collective-cultural acceptance of multiplicity of personally constructed cultural solutions to human cognitive and affective tasks (Ramanujan, 1991). The multitude of versions of Krishna-stories in India that have proliferated over centuries have guided personal cultures towards synthesizing different facets of human experiences.

Jayadeva's *Gitagovinda*

Jayadeva was a professional court poet, whose *Gitagovinda* (composed around 1200 A.D.) is a major cultural text that by way of retelling the Krishna/Radha legend, guides patterns of internalization/externalization processes in respect to devotion and sensuality (Siegel, 1978). The legend itself takes many forms in Indian folklore (Kakar, 1986). Jayadeva's version carries traces from a variety of folkloric traditions in Orissa of the previous centuries (Hindu tantrism, *Bhagavata purana*—Hardy, 1983). It takes to poetic perfection the unification of sensual and devotional-religious experiences :

> The sexual experience was equated with the yogic experience in the attainment of the state of non-ego, vacuity, the suspension of thought-process and self-consciousness. The internal physiological process by which the state of vacuity was achieved was analogous to the union of the man and the woman and symbolized by the thunder entering the lotus. (Siegel, 1978 : 40).

Importantly, Jayadeva's version of the Krishna-legend became institutionalized in the Jagannatha temple as obligatory text on which all ritual dancing and singing activities of the Devadasis were to be based from the 16th century onwards, when the singing of songs exclusively from *Gitagovinda* was decreed in the Jagannatha temple (Siegel, 1978 : 229) onwards. In accordance with the collective-cultural regulation of women's relations with their bodily functions, the dedicated Devadasi would be expected to live according to the sensual patterns of loving the deity, culturally encoded in *Gitagovinda*. Within the text of the epic, the well-known encounter of Krishna with cowherdesses (*gopis*) is important from the standpoint of collective-cultural canalization of sensuality.

The *gopis* and their symbolic relevance

The *gopis* were important female characters in the myriad of legends involving Krishna and Radha, and numerous encounters of Krishna with the *gopis* (e.g., Krishna stealing the *gopis'* clothes; Krishna's dance and amorous play with the *gopis*, etc.) have been re-told in various versions all over India (Archer, 1957; Hardy, 1983; Singer, 1966). In Jayadeva's *Gitagovinda* the *gopis* appear in the context of sensual role presentation for Krishna, whose sensuality is imbued with the liberation from phenomenal existence (2nd song, stanza 21—Siegel, 1978 : 244). Krishna's "eye is a spotless lotus petal", he is both lover (of Janaka's daughter Sita), and destroyer of enemies in battle. He is both a person and a god. The active role of the *gopis* in the sensual play is reflected, in conjunction with highly symbolic descriptions of the trees, birds, and springtime. The following excerpt from the Fourth Song illustrates the rhetoric presentation in *Gitagovinda :*

39. [He has] a forest garland and a yellow garment on his sandal-smeared, blue body and laughter on his cheeks which are adorned with jewelled ear-rings shaking in play; here Hari plays in the coquettish and playful flock of artless [*mugdha :* lovely, beautiful, innocent] women.

40. Passionately embracing Hari with the massive weight of her swallen breasts a certain herdsman's wife sings a resounded fifth note [*pancama-raga :* a love cry made during or before coition to signify pleasure]; here Hari plays....

41. Another artless woman continually contemplates the lotus-face of the Killer-of-Madhu, [the face-lotus] produced love on account of the quivering of his eyes rolling about seductively [*vilasa :* in a love-play with amorous gesture]; here Hari plays....

42. Another [woman] with beautiful buttocks, came-up to say something into his ear and sweetly kissed the beloved on the surface of his cheek which was obliging [*anukula :* obliging by showing his pleasure—an ironic element here] with bristling-hairs; here Hari plays....

43. And another, with eagerness for the arts of love-play, on the bank of the Yamuna's waters, with her hand on his robe, pulled him who was in the beautiful cane grove; here Hari plays....

44. While his sweet-toned flute is sounded, rows of bracelets shake on their clapping hands; in the enjoyment of the *rasa* [pastoral circular dance] a deer-like young-girl, intent on dancing with him, praised him; here Hari plays....

45. He embraces one, kisses one, sexually-pleases some sexually-pleasing one, he sees yet another beauty more charming still on account of her smiles and he chases her; here Hari plays....

46. May this song of Sri Jayadeva, the secret of marvellous Kesava's love-play, lovely and famous in the Vrndavana forest, spread-abroad prosperities ! here Hari plays.... (Siegel, 1978 : 248-249)

Much of the Gitagovinda is dedicated to expression of feelings of Radha's jealousy and love at distance, and women's desire for sensual relation with Krishna. The complexity of Krishna's feelings about his leaving of Radha and longing for her are likewise narrated (7th song, Siegel, 1978 : 254-256). All through *Gitagovinda*, Jayadeva highlights the process of sensual experiencing, either in the Krishna's encounter with the *gopis*, or in his feelings about Radha. However, all of that experiencing is related with the devotional sentiment, which is generated by ambiguities of the feelings. The women are depicted as devotedly active with explicit recognition of their erotic (*srngara*) feelings. It is clear that in the Hindu *bhakti* context empowers women in religiously context-bound ways (see Ramanujan, 1982 : 316). In general, the belief that Indian women "are passive" may amount to no more than a Westerner's superficial reflection upon some particularly exotic rituals practiced in Hindu collective culture, rather than adequately capture the always context-bound reality (Ramanujam, 1992 : 48). The role of *Gitagovinda* in the cultural canalization in the context of the Hindu life is to provide meaning bases for personal-cultural reconstruction of the self's senual sphere.

Basic meanings : collective-cultural differentiations

The conceptual complexes that guide the organization of human development are undoubtedly difficult to translate directly from one semiotic code to another (see Wierzbicka, 1992).

Furthermore, the basic organizational schemes of concepts show how collective-cultural differentiation patterns guide our reasoning. Furthermore, it is not only the cognitive domain that is semiotically mediated. The domain of human feelings is likewise under collective-cultural guidance. In the context of India, the contrast with most assumptions taken by psychology is perhaps the greatest :

> In the Western cultural formulation emotion is conceived as an inherently irrational aspect of life and talked about in metaphors that center on ideas of chaos. In contrast, Hindu metaphors for emotion center on food and semantic similarities between emotion as an experience and the bodily experiences of eating and nurturing. (Toomey, 1990 : 174)

The personal-cultural worlds of the Devadasis provide an example where our usual concepts are inadequate. A major conceptual opposition that proves to be an obstacle for our understanding of the Devadasis is the Western social sciences' culturally constructed *exclusive separation* (Valsiner, 1987, 1989) of the opposites of "sacred" and "profane" domains of human existence. This classical-logical disjunction (either S or P) can at times be artificially dimensionalized—by invention of a "continuum" (or any ordered sequence of "states" or "stages") between the posited polar opposites (e.g., a "scale" ranging from "S" to "P"). Such constructions by social scientists constitute a priori projections of the investigators' views of the world upon complex reality. It has been repeatedly pointed out that the use of binary oppositions in case of making sense of Indian cultural complexity brings social science to an impasse (Das, 1976, 1992; Kakar, 1981, 1989; Siegel, 1978).

In contrast, the same ("sacred" and "profane", or any other) opposites can be viewed as separated but linked (by way of *inclusive separation* see Valsiner 7 Cairns, 1992), in which case different forms of the linkage between them are potentially open for investigation. This perspective allows for coverage on interdependencies between the distinguished opposites, and formulation of different multiple (rather than binary) interdependent oppositions between cultural meanings.

In the domain of making sense of the Devadasis' role, inclusive separation is necessary for viewing the difference and unity of two distinct Hindu concepts—*auspiciousness* (mangal or subha or kalyan) and *inauspiciousness* (*amangal* or *asubha* or *akalyan*). While being opposite terms, these concepts are linked together in ways that allow for a particular event or act (under some conditions) to move from one state to another in time (Samantha 1992). The *magal/amangal* complex is not equivalent to the widely used pure/impure contrast (Madan, 1991 ; Raheja, 1988, chapter 2).

Most of Hindu social life organization is based on the reading of good "signs" of the *mangal*, and avoidance of the bad omens of *amangal*. *Mangal* assumes a special "well-being" relationship between devotees and feminine powers. The Devadasis are clearly semiotically marked by belonging to the world of *mangal* (Marglin, 1985 : 98). Their auspicious nature creates their special status, both by setting up constraints (against undermining their auspiciousness by inauspicious conduct), and by promotion of their freedoms of action (in their auspiciousness they are close to the king). Furthermore, their auspicious status guides their semiotic organization of sensuality.

Conceptualizing desire : relations of *kama* and *prema*

The concept of *kama*—desire (includes both sensual desire and desire for any object) belongs to the core of Hindu central organizing concepts, together with *dharma* (religious duty), *artha* (wealth, and *moksa* (renunciation). These four constituents of the true purpose of existence can be viewed in different mutual relations (Das, 1982a). Of the four, *kama*, *artha* and *dharma* belong together under the term *bhoga*, which

> ...is derived from the verbal root bhuj which means enjoy, use, possess, eat, consume, exhaust, use up, have sexual intercourse with... All three of these goals were subsumed under the single notion of enjoyment...(Inden, 1982 : 100).

The meaning complex of enjoyment thus sets up the stage for making sense of *kama*. *Kama* is the procreative power which is claimed to "magnify the ego", yet be paradoxical and transcendable (Siegel, 1978 : 64-67). Pursuit of *kama* has been sanctified since the Upanishads as the foundation of human existence, as it unites in itself two different (yet interdependent) domains of sexuality—for procreation and pleasure on the one hand, and for mystical and magical power, on the other (Jha, 1979 : 7). However, in its wider meaning, *Kama* entails *any* kind of desire (Malamoud, 1982)

Kama exists between husband and wife, involves relinguishing seed and leads to childbearing. In contrast, *Prema* (devotional love) involves sensual-emotional love relation that is continuous, free of hierorchical social relations (e.g., those between Krishna and the *gopis*) and hence an integrated emotion complex :

> ...*prema* cannot be classified as either ascetic or erotic but seems to partake of both sides of the opposition...the absence of *kama* does not mean chaste, platonic love. Krishna and the *gopis* fondle, caress, embrace each other with abandon and show all the signs of sensual pleasure. What the absence of *kama* specifically refers to is the fact that in his love-making Krishna does not spill his seed. (Marglin, 1982 : 306).

The possibility for conceptualizing *prema* is thus based on the historical-cultural constraint by the meanings of semen loss, which is widespread in Indian folk theories (Bottero, 1991; Kakar, 1989 : 118-120). Sensual experiences paired with the avoidance of semen loss in non-procreative contexts might allow the meaning of *prema* to emerge on the foundation of *kama*. In the devotional religious contexts, cultural guidance for the personal construction of distinctive, elaborate and formalized attitude of devotion by sharing of the emotions of *prema* (as divine love) combined with joy (*ananda*) can lead to a generalized new feeling (Bennett, 1990).

The experiencing of the positive emotionality in sensuality is enabled by the meaning of *prema*, while *kama* dominates in specific (husband<—>wife) role relationships. It is viewed as selfish (and hence at times presented as an opponent to be overcome), and through its inherent oppositionality, can become *prema*. In the transition to *prema* the sensual focus of *kama* is not lost but becomes integrated into a new whole and subsumed within the dominant scheme of *prema*. Both *kama* and *prema* involve a sensual component, but are distinguishable on the basis of every-day-life (procreational) and mystical-sensual functions. Yet where there is "true love", *kama* is involved (Pandey, 1965).

***Prema* in the lives of Devadasis.** The highly specific collective-cultural role of the Devadasi leads to the construction of one's personal-cultural system in ways that may defy the usual Western models of understanding. The Devadasi case provides us with a sophisticated picture of cultural organization of personal life courses. The crucial personal-cultural construction starts from seeing one's self in terms of *prema* :

> The *devadasi* is not married and therefore lacks a married woman's feeling of possession toward a husband. As Haripriya, a *devadasi*, said to me, "A

> wife says I have a 'husband,' a statement that bespeaks ego feelings *(ahankara)*. When Haripriya spoke to me of her own life, she told me about an important liaison she had in which there was no feeling of attachment...On a different occasion, Sasi, another devadasi, told me : "We don't marry. We don't have children; we don't have a household; devotion is the one important thing for us." Haripriya herself explained to me at great length the nature of the erotic and passionate love of the *gopi-devadasi* for Krishna while all the time contrasting it to the attached eroticism of the married woman. Conjugal eroticism is never separated from procreative considerations, whereas the erotic love between the *gopis* and Krishna is completely separated from procreation. (Marglin, 1990 : 227)

By way of the highly symbolic social role, a woman creates for herself a personal life-world mediated by the general meaning of devotion to deity, which entails (as a meaning-complex) *prema* and allows to construct her marital self-definition in terms different from those of usual wives (who, in the Hindu context, bear children within a hierarchical dominance network within joint family).

The set of collective cultural meanings that were used to organize the Devadasis' personal worlds constitute a flexible and non-strict hierarchy. The status of being symbolically married to the deity constrains the Devadasis both in their actions (within their role performance in the temple; and in personal lives with men who in some sense are linked to the deity). This constraining by the meaning also makes the Devadasis to be of special status in otherwise status-conscious social world. Their particular internalized reconstructions of their marital status provide a variety of forms (Marglin, 1985, chaper 1), all of which led the Devadasis to not entering the role of a traditional Hindu wife.

Furthermore, the meaning of *prema* (and the Devadasis' perceived similarity with the *gopis*) make it possible to develop personal-emotional realationship with the world that transcends the usual role-relations of the wider society. The special status of the Devadasis enables them to organize their feelings field along the lines of *prema>>>kama*, while limiting their entrance into spheres of activities (e. g., childbearing) that are expected from women who proceed along the ordinary womanly life-course (and become wives of ordinary mortals).

Implications for theory : cultural process as basis for personality

The case of Devadasis leads to a number of serious questions about psychology's time-honored assumptions about the role of sexuality in human personality. Sexuality has undoubtedly been the favorite topic of psychologists since Freud. Although psychoanalytic uses of sexuality have been widely criticized (as well as defended) in psychological discourse, new basic assumptions need to be made about the ways in which sexual, sensual, and higher mental-affective functions are related within the human self. As is emphasized by Kakar,

> As a "depth psychology", psychoanalysis dives deep, but in the same waters in which the cultural river too flows. Preeminently operating from within the heart of the Western myth...—from myths of ancient Greece to the "illusions" of the Enlightenment—psychoanalysis has had little opportunity to observe from within, and with empathy, the deeper import of other cultures' myths in the working of the self. (Kakar, 1989 : 139)

Myths can be seen as collective-cultural constraining devices than channel personal cultures towards reconstruction of not only the knowledge transferred via those, but also of the affective marking. By way of acting about myths (as recipients, re-tellers, etc.), persons bring their personal cultures to bear upon modification of the collective culture. Collective-cultural narrated texts allow both disjunctive and conjunctive constructions to emerge in human subjective worlds. For example, *both* the separation (disjunction) and unification (conjunction) of the worlds of religious devotionalism and physio affective sensuality are granted by the *same* internalization/externalization processes (see also Das, 1982a; Gandhi, 1982), and can co-exist in diametrically opposite personal forms within the same society at the same time.

Collective-cultural texts are both the starting datum and product of the internalization/externalization process. The texts lead to subjectification of the personal lived-through experiences (Obeyesekere, 1981 : 137). The person uses the collective-cultural meanings to produce and justify innovative acts, which become objectified and conventionalized in social communication. The latter may lead to an ontological misattribution in the social sciences—a semiotically encoded feature that is created in conjunction with a goal of the encoder, may be made into a characteristic of the reality. Thus, various efforts to present the Devadasi custom as a case of prostitution may have reflected the investigators' socio-institutional goals and/or discomfort with the collective-culturally sanctioned unity of religiosity and sensuality in the Indian context (see Devereux, 1967, on researchers' psychological projections).

It becomes clear that psychology cannot posit the existence of basic motivating substances (such as libido) that has emerged as a result of collective-cultural synthesis in some areas of the World, as the universal basis for psychological functioning. The intrasubjective field of persons in any society includes domains of sexuality, sensuality, etc., yet none of these domains is to be viewed *a priori* as the basis for building a personality theory. Rather, the universal human process of semiotic mediation can create a number of different substance-like fictions of subjective kind, and interpersonal communication using such fictions is treacherously simple. It is nevertheless misleading, as it substitutes the fundamental process by its specific outcomes. The foundation for psychology's conceptualization of personality (or self) can be set up in that process—sign construction, reconstruction, and meaning-making are the core of human personality. Semiotic mediation *process* is the most fundamental mechanism of human functioning and development, it generates a variety of forms of meanings that are but specific outcomes of the process. The cross-societal universal of human psychology is the generative mechanism that allows for the construction of any variety of Krishna, Oedipus, or any other kind of myths—and which makes it possible to modify these myth families as particular conditions of living—through experiences trigger such novel constructs. In an analogy with modern genetics—it is not "the genes" that cause the synthesis of specific proteins, but the *process of translation* of the information encoded in the genes into the actual construction of proteins.

General Conclusions : Cultural guidance of human subjectivity

Human development entails personal construction of subjectivity under specific collective-cultural constraining processes. These processes are dynamic, take place in irreversible time and within structured contexts of real life. These contexts are meaningful, as their structure is organized semiotically. Since subjectivity primarily entails constant stream of operations upon the intrapersonal feelings field, the semiotic constraining operates both at the levels of emotional connotations and mental constructions.

This theoretical view on human development leads to the necessity for multi-sided consideration of lived-through experiences and their cultural organization. The case of temple dancers—even if distant from the scope of coverage of psychology by historical, cultural, and disciplinary boundaries—provides a glimpse into a realm of psychological reality where human sensuality becomes semiotically canalized in the direction of socially relevant goals. This is accomplished by a system of higher-order cultural organizer terms (like auspiciousness, *kama*, *prema*, etc.), specific narrated myths (Krishna's social interaction with the *gopis*), and conduct constraints for specific settings in the everyday lives of the Devadasis in the temple, and outside.

The present analysis of the leads to a new way to conceptualize affectivity of persons in their collective-cultural activity settings. These activity settings are organized on the basis of scripts from historical legends that have been preserved by re-narration over centuries. An analysis of the domains of promoted semiotic mediation in those texts (and their narration process—in dance or song) can explain the set of collective-cultural "input messages" that have been available for persons within these activity contexts. Thus, a content analysis of *Gitagovinda* in the 20th Century, together with the analysis of Odissi dance scripts, can provide us a reconstruction of what cultural psychological messages were available to the pilgrims visiting Jagannatha temple in Puri a number of centuries ago, Of course, the specific personal internalization results will not become available from such analysis (see also Lightfoot and Valsiner 1992).

A fundamental culturally canalized outcome is discernible in the two thousand years of the existence of Hindu temple dancers: the specific form of relating sensuality and religious devotion. Social stigmatization of their roles for any socio-moral discourse purposes cannot overshadow their psychological achievements. Devadasis were unique women not only in their role in their society, but in the form of synthesis of their selves in that role. Perhaps by taking a closer view upon temple dancers, our investigations can move towards deeper understanding of the vast complexity of viable psychological forms created by humankind in our contemporary tumultuous World.

ACKNOWLEDGEMENTS. Critical comments upon an earlier draft of this paper by Sumedha Gupta, Agnes Dodds, Gorjana Litvinovic, Angela Branco and Eleonora Magomedova are gratefully acknowledged helpful in bringing this paper to its final form.

Reference

Allen, M. 1982 The Hindu view of women in M. Allen & S.N. Mukherjee (Eds.) *Women in India and Nepal* (pp. 1-20). Australian National University Monographs on South Asia, No. 8. Canberra : ANU Press.

Appadurai, A. 1981 *Worship and conflict under colonial rule : A South Indian case.* Cambridge : Cambridge University Press.

Appadurai, A. 1985 Gratitude as a social mode in South India. *Ethos,* 13,3, 236-245.

Appadurai, A. & Breckenridge, C. A. 1976 The South Indian temple : authority, honor, and redistribution, *Contribution to Indian Sociology,* 10,2, 187-211.

Archer, W. G. 1957 *The loves of Krishna.* London : George Allen & Unlwin.

Beck, B. E. F. 1976 The symbolic merger of body, space and cosmos in Hindu Tamil Nadu. *Contributions to Indian Sociology,* 10, 2, 213-243.

Bennett. P. 1990 In Nanda Bana's house : The devotional experience in Pushti Marg temples. In O. M. Lynch (Ed.), *Divine passions : The social construction of emotion in India* (pp. 182-211). University of California Press.

Beteille, A. 1965 Social organization of temples in a Tanjore village. *History of Religions,* 5, 1, 74-92.

Boesch, E. E. 1993 The sound of the violin. *Schweizerische Zeitschrift fur psychologic.* 52, 2, 70-81.

Bottero, A. 1991 Consumption by semen loss in India and elsewhere. *Culture, Medicine and Psychiatry,* 15, 303-320.

Bradford, N. J. 1983 Transgenderism and the cult of Yellamma : heat, sex and sickness in South Indian ritual. *Journal of Anthropological Research,* 39, 3, 307-322.

Chatterjee, S. 1945 *Devadasi (temple dancer).* Calcutta : The Book House.

Cole M. 1990 Cultural psychology : A once and future discipline ? In J. Berman (Ed.) *Nebraska Symposium on Motivation.* Vol. 37 (pp. 279-336). Lincoln : University of Nebraska Press.

Das, V. 1976 Thc Uses of liminality : Society and cosmos in Hinduism. *Contributions of Indian Sociology*, 10,2, 245-263.

Das, V. 1982 (a) Kama in the scheme of purusarthas : the story of Rama. In T. N. Madan (Ed.), *Way of life : King, householder, renouncer* (pp. 183-203) New Delhi : Vikas.

Das, V. 1982 (b) *Structure and congition : Aspects of Hindu Caste and Ritual*. Delhi : Oxford University Press.

Das, V. 1992 Reflections on the social construction of adulthood. In S. Kakar (Ed.), *Identity and Adulthood* (pp. 89-104). Delhi : Oxford University Press.

Davis, K. 1937 The Sociology of Frostitution. *American Sociological Review*, 2, 744-755.

Dayalan, D. 1992 *Early temples of Tamilnadu*. New Delhi : Harman.

Desai, D. 1985 *Erotic sculpture of India : A sociocultural study*. New Delhi : Munshiram Manaharlal Publishers.

Desai, V. N., & Mason, D. (Eds.) 1993 *Gods, Guardians, and Lovers : Temple sculptures from North India A.D. 700-1200*. Middletown. N. J. : Grantha Corporation.

Devereux, G. 1967 *From Anxiety to method in the Behavioural Sciences*. The Hague : Mouton.

Dubois, J. A. 1905 *Hindu manners, Customs and Ceremonies*. 3rd edition. Oxford : Clarendon Press.

Flandrin, J. L. 1985 Sex in married life in the early Middle Ages: the Church's teaching and behavioural reality in P. Aries and A. Benjin (Eds.). *Western sexuality* (pp. 144-129). Oxford : Basil Blackwell.

Foucault, M. 1980 *The History of Sexuality*. Vol. 1. Introduction. New York : Vintage Books.

Foucault, M. 1986 *The History of Sexuality*. Vol. 3. The care of the self. New York : Random House.

Frykenberg, R. E. 1989 The Emergence of modern 'Hinduism' as a concent and as an institution : A reappraisal with a special reference to South India. In G.D. Sontheimer & H. Kulke (Eds.), *Hinduism Reconsidered* (pp. 29-49). New Delhi : Manohar.

Gandhi, R. 1982 Bhamacharya. In T. N. Madan (Ed.), *Way of Life : King, Householder, Renouncer* (pp.

205-221). New Delhi : Vikas.

Geib, R. 1975 *Indradyumna-Legende : Ein Beitrag zür Geschichte des Jagannatha-Kultes.* Wiesbaden : Otto Harrassowitz.

Hardy, F. 1983 *Viraha-bhakti : The early history of Krisna devotion in South India,* Delhi : Oxford University Press.

Haras, A. 1983 *Palace Culture of Lucknow.* Delhi : B. R. Publishing Corporation.

Heggade, O.D. 1983 A Socio-economic strategy for Rehabilitating Devadasis. *Social Welfare,* 39. 10, 26-28.

Henriques, F. 1963 *Prostitution and Society.* New York : Citadel Press.

Hochschild, A. R. 1983 *The Managed Heart : Commercialization of human feeling.* Berkeley : University of California Press.

Holland, D. C. & Eisenhart, M. A. 1990 *Educated in Romance : Women, Achievement and college culture.* Chicago : University of Chicago Press.

Inden, R. 1982 Hierarchies of kings in early medieval India. In T. N. Madan (Ed.), *Way of life : King householder, renouncer* (pp. 99-125). New Delhi : Vikas.

Ismail, K. 1984 *Karnataka Temples : Their role in socio-economic life,* Delhi : Sundeep Prakashan.

Jha, A. 1979 *Sexual Designs in Indian Culture.* New Delhi : Vikas.

Kakar, S. 1981 *The Inner World.* 2nd ed. Delhi : Oxford University Press.

Kakar, S. 1986 Erotic fantasy : The secret passion of Radha and Krishna. In V. Das (Ed.), *The Word and the World : Fantasy, symbol and record* (pp. 75-94). New Delhi : Sage.

Kakar, S. 1989 *Intimate relations : Exploring Indian sexuality.* New Delhi : Penguin.

Khokar, M. 1979 *Traditions of Indian Classical Dance.* London : Peter Owen.

Kolenda, P. M. 1981 Pox and the terror of childlessness : Images and Ideas of the Smallpox Goddess in a North Indian village. In P. Kolenda, *Caste, Cult and Hierarchy* (pp. 198-221). Meerut : Folklore Institute.

1983 The mother-goddess complex among North Indian sweepers. In G. R. Gupta (Ed.), *Re-*

		ligion in Modern India (pp. 215-288). New Delhi : Vikas.
Kopytoft, I.	1986	The Cultural Biography of things : Commoditization as process. In A. Appadurai (Ed.), *The Social life of Things* (pp. 64-91). Cambridge : Cambridge University Press.
Kothari, S., & Pasricha, A.	1990	*Odissi-Indian classical dance art.* Bombay : Marg Publications.
Kulke, H., & Rothermund, D.	1986	*A History of India.* London : Croom Helm.
Lawrence. J. A & Valsiner, J.	1993	Conceptual roots of internatization from transmission to transformation. *Human Development,* 36, 150-167.
Lawrence, J.A. Benedikt, R. & Valsiner, J.	1992	Homeless in the mind : A case history of personal life in and out a close orthodox community. *Journal of Social Distress and the Homeless,* 1, 2, 157-176.
Lerner, G.	1986	The origin of prostitution in Ancient Mesopotamia. *Journal of Women in Culture and Society,* 11, 2, 236-254.
Lightfoot, C. & Valsiner, J.	1992	Parental belief systems under influence : Social guidance of the construction of personal cultures. In I. Siegel, J. Goodnow, & A. McGillicuddy Delisi (Eds.), *Parental Belief system* 2nd Ed. (pp. 393-424). Hillsdale, NJ : Erlbaum.
Lutz, C. A.	1988	*Unnatural Emotions : Everyday sentiments on a Micronesian atoll & their challenge to Western theory.* Chicago : University of Chicago Press.
Madan, T. N.	1991	Auspiciousness and Purity : Some reconsiderations in *Contributions to Indian Sociology,* 25, 2, 287-294.
Malamoud, C.	1982	On the rhetoric and semantics of purusartha. In T. N. Madan (Ed.), *Way of life : King, Householder, Renouncer* (pp. 33-54). New Delhi : Vikas.
Marglin, F. A.	1982 (a)	Types of sexual union and their implicit meanings. In J. S. Hawley & D. M. Wulff (Eds.), *The Divine Consort : Radha and the goddesses of India* (pp. 298-315). Berkeley : Berkeley Religious Studies.
	1982 (b)	Kings and Wives : The separation of status and royal power. In T. N. Madan (Ed.), *Way of life : King, Householder Renouncer* (pp. 155-181). New Delhi :

Vikas.

1985 *Wives of the god-king : The Rituals of the Devadasis of Puri.* Delhi : Oxford University Press.

1990 Refining the body : Transformative emotion in ritual dance. In O. M. Lynch (Ed.), *Divine passions : The social construction of emotion in India* (pp. 212-236). Berkeley : University of California Press.

Mitter, P. 1977 *Much Maligned Monsters : History of European reactions to Indian art,* Oxford : Clarendon Press.

Moscovici, S. 1982 The Coming era of Representations. In J. P. Codol & J. P. Leyens (Eds.) *Cognitive analysis of Social Behaviour* (pp. 115-150). The Hague: Martinus Nijhoff.

Moscovici, S. 1988 Crisis of communication and crisis of explanation. In W. Schonpflug (Ed.), *Bericht uber der 36. Kengress der Deustchen Gesellschaft fur Psychologie in Berlin.* Vol. 2 (pp. 94-109). Gottingen : Hogrefe.

Obeysekere, G 1981 *Medusa's hair,* Chicago : University of Chicago Press.

1990 *The Work of culture.* Chicago : University of Chicago Press.

Oldenburg, V.T. 1984 *The Making of colonial Lucknow 1856-1877.* Princeton : Princeton University Press.

Oldenburg, V.T. 1990 *Lifestyle as Resistance : The case of the courtesans of Lucknow,* India. Feminist Studies, 16, 2, 259-287.

Pandey, S.M. 1965 Mirabai and her contributions to the Bhakti movement. *History of Religions,* 5, 1, 54-73.

Pandian, J. 1983 The sacred symbol of the mother goddess in a Tamil village : a parochial model of Hinduism. In G.R. Gupta (Ed.), *Religion in Modern India* (pp. 198-214). New Delhi : Vikas.

Patil, B. R. 1975 The Devadasis, *Indian Journal of Social Work,* 35, 4, 377-389.

Prasad, A. K. 1990 *Devadasi system in Ancient India.* Delhi : H. K. Publishers.

Preston, J. J. 1983 Goddess temples in Orissa : An anthropological survey. In G.R. Gupta (Ed.), *Religion in Modern India* (pp. 229-247). New Delhi : Vikas.

Raghuramiah, K. L. 1991 *Night birds : Indian prostitutes from Devadasis to call girls.* Delhi : Chanakya Publications.

Raheja, G.G. 1988 *The Poison in the gift.* Chicago : University of Chicago Press.

Raheja, G.G. 1990 Centrality, mutuality and hierarchy : shifting aspects of inter-caste relationships in north India. In M. Marriott (Ed.), *India through Hindu categories* (pp. 79-101), New Delhi : Sage.

Ramanujan, A. K. 1982 On women saints. In J.S. Hawley & D. M. Wulff (Eds.), *The Divine consort : Radha and the goddesses of India* (pp. 316-324). Berkeley : Berkeley Religious Series.

1991 Toward a counter-system : women's tales. In A. Appadurai, F. J. Korom, and M. A. Mills (Eds.), *Gender, genre, and power in South Asian expressive traditions* (pp. 33-55). Philadelphia : University of Pennsylvania Press.

Ramanujam, B. K. 1992 Toward maturity : Problems of identity seen in the Indian clinical setting. In S. Kakar (Ed.) , *Identity and Adulthood* (pp. 37-55). Delhi : Oxford University Press.

Ranjana 1983 Devadasis : The girls dedicated to temples. *Social Welfare,* 39, 10, 24-25.

Roland, A. 1988 *In search of self in Indians and Japan.* Princeton : Princeton University Press.

Samantha, S. 1992 Mangalmayima, sumangali, mangal: Bengali percentions of the divine feminine, motherhood, and 'auspiciousness.' *Contributions to Indian Sociology,* 26, 1, 51-75.

Schnepel, B. 1993 Die Schutzgottinnen : Tribale Gottheiten in Sudorissa (Indien) and ihre Patronage durch hinduistische Kleinkonige. *Anthropos,* 88, 337-350.

Shankar, J. 1990 *Devadasi cult : A sociological analysis.* New Delhi : Ashish Publishing House.

Shweder, R. 1990 Cultural psychology—what is it ? In J. W. Stigler, R.A. Shweder and G. Herdt (Eds.), *Cultural Psychology* (pp. 1-43). Cambridge : Cambridge University Press.

Siegel, L. 1978 *Sacred and profane dimensions of love*

in *Indian traditions as exemplified in the Gitagovinda of Jayadeva.* Delhi : Oxford University Press.

Singer, M. (Ed.) 1966 *Krishna : Myths, rites, and attitudes.* Honolulu : East-West Center Press.

Skinner, D., J. & Valsiner B. Basnet, 1993 Singing one's life : an orchestration of personal experiences and cultural forms. *Journal of South Asian Literature,* 26, 1 & 2, 15-43.

Smolka, A. L. B. 1994 Discourse practices and the issue of internalization. In A. Rosa & J. Valsiner (Eds.), *Historical and Theoretical Discourse in Social-Cultural Studies.* Madrid : Fundacion Infancia y Aprendizaje.

Tarachand, K. C. 1991 *Devadasi custom : Rural social structure and flesh markets.* New Delhi : Reliance Publishing House.

Tommey, P. M. 1990 Krishna's consuming passions : Food as metaphor and metonym for emotion at Mount Govardhan. In O. M. Lynch (Ed.), *Divine Passions : The social construction of emotion in India* (pp. 157-181). Berkeley : University of California Press.

Tripathy, G. M. & Tripathy, B. 1992 *Sir Jagannath Puri.* Bhubaneswar : Banita Publications.

Valsiner, J. 1987 *Culture and the Development of Children's Action.* Chichester : Wiley.

Valsiner, J. 1989 *Human Development and Culture.* Lexington, MA : D.C. Heath & Co.

1992 Interest : A metatheoretical perspective. In K. A. Renninger, S. Hidi, & A. Krapp (Eds.), *The Role of Interest in Learning and Development* (pp. 27-41). Hillsdale, NJ : Erlbaum.

1994(a) Culture and Human development : a co-constructionist perspective. In P. Van Geert & L. Mos (Eds.), *Annals of Theoretical Psychology.* Vol. 10. New York : Plenum.

1994 (B) Co-constructivism : What is (and in not) in a name ? In P. Van Geert & L. Mos (Eds.), *Annals of Theoretical Psychology.* Vol. 10. New York : Plenum.

Valsiner, J. & Cairns, R. B. 1992 Theoretical perspectives on conflict and development. In C. U. Shantz & W. W. Hartup (Eds.), *Conflict in Child and Ado-*

lescent Development (pp. 15-35). Cambridge : Cambridge University Press.

Von Stietencron, H. 1989 Hinduism : On the proper use of a deceptive term. In G. D. Sontheimer & H. Kulke (Eds.), *Hinduism Reconsidered* (pp. 11-27). New Delhi : Manohar.

Wertsch, J. V. 1991 *Voices in the mind.* Cambridge, Ma : Harvard University Press.

Wierzbricka, A. 1992 *Semantics, Culture and Congnition.* New York : Oxford University Press.

Wikan, U. 1990 *Managing Turbulent Hearts : A Balinese formula for living.* Chicago : University of Chicago Press.

Winegar, L. T., Renninger, K. A. & Valsiner, J. 1989 Dependent Independence in adult-child Relationships. In D. A. Kramer & M. J. Bopp. (Eds.), *Movement through form : Transformation in Clinical and Developmental Psychology* (pp. 157-168). New York : Springer.

Ajit K. Danda

LAND REFORMS AND THE RURAL POOR : CASE STUDIES FROM SOUTH INDIA

I

Nearly 80 per cent of India's total population being rural, by and large engage themselves in land-based economic pursuits. For very obvious reasons, therefore, land has became the most critical element for planning as well as development of the country.

Despite India's vast land resources, independent India discovered herself in rather an unenviable situation since the productivity rate of agricultural outputs was neither incommensurate with the quality of land, nor with the rate of growth of the country's population. As a result, India was becoming increasingly dependent on import of foodgrains which was neither without strings, nor stigma. Nearly 65 percent of India's population at that point of time being located below the poverty line, further added to the complexity of the problem. In view of the exigency of the situation, land reform initiatives were considered imperative on at least two major counts : (i) Planning for enhancement of agricultural products necessitated land reforms as a major pre-requisite; (ii) Even for reducing the level of disparity between those below and above the poverty line, particularly in rural areas, as well as for initiating measures towards redressal of the sense of deprination of the 'have nots', land reform was considered a basic instrument for bringing about change. Accordingly, relevant measures were initiated on an urgent basis. But the same being the state subject, enormous variations were observed in the land reform laws enacted by different State Governments. Since the role of Government of India in this respect was hardly beyond coordinating and supporting the measures in terms of ideas, schemes, and funds, the acts mostly reflected local considerations. It is, therefore, not only difficult but nearly impossible to project any all-India picture in this respect. Besides the constraints of the Acts as such, which due to local specificities made any comparison across States rather futile, because of the ideological commitments of the parties in power in various State, major differences were observed in the implementation of the programme, Comparison of concerned Acts, therefore, will reflect mere pious wish and not necessarily what has been achieved in this context. Due to such limitations and also because of the in-build constraint of space and time, the present account will concentrate only on South India, particularly Karnataka, Kerala and Tamil Nadu.

II

The research project of which the present account is the by-product was an all-India survey undertaken by the Anthropological Survey of India around mid-seventies of the century on 'Socio-economic Change among the Weaker Sections of the Indian Population since Independent'. The author had the privilege of designing, coordinating and supervising the said project when he was a member of that organisation.

Among the specific issues that could be responsible either to cause weakness to a particular section of the society, perpetuate the same, or to being about change; distribution and management of land was considered important. As the project dealt only with rural India where the bulk of the population subject on activities related to land, for assessment of any measure of transformation, same attention to land reforms was important. Since it was the objective of the exercise to understand the basic processes involved in the operation in lien of a quick survey based on strict statistical sampling procedure, it was decided to go for intensive village studies, even if it is at the cost of forgoing the benefits of having a perspective. Accordingly, intensive village studies were undertaken, at least one to represent each State of India. Thus, each of the four States of South India was represented by a village study each for that project. But due to inadequacy of information regarding the land reforms in the account of Andhra Pradesh, we are excluding that state from the purview of this discussion. The three villages that will respectively represent Karnataka, Kerala and Tamil Nadu have, for the purpose of this exercise, been named Vithva, Moorthy, and Palayasima. Vithva was studied at the field level for a period of about six months, by Dr. S.G. Morab. More or less the same period of time was spent at Moorthy by Dr. P.R.G. Mathur, Palayasima was studied by Dr. Smt. Rajlakshmi Misra. As already indicated, the present author coordinated and supervised the whole project. The responsibility of any emissions and errors, therefore, is exclusively of the present author.

III

Vithva

Vithva is situated 22 kms, away from Humnabad, a Taluk headquarters of Bidar District in Karnataka. It is slightly off the national highway connecting Sholpur with Hyderabad. It is a multi-ethnic village having 14 Hindu Castes, a fairly large Muslim population and some subscribing to Christianity.

The social layout of Vithva speaks of the existence of sharp boundaries for certain castes/communities. For instance, the Moleya and Moderu, both Hindu and Christians have their respective exclusive space called Molegeri and Madergeri. The Wadder also have their exclusive area in the village known as Waddergeri. As per prescription of the tradition, members belonging to these caste/communities are supposed to live outside the boundary of the village. Since the pressure on land did not actually permit so, the exclusiveness of their quarters symbolise this arrangement. Although in terms of physical proximity the distance between the village proper and these exclusive pockets is very little the social distance between these two sets is considerable. The members of the service castes occupy a space in between the two sets.

Agriculture provides the basic subsistence to the villagers. Besides agricultural and jobs performed by members of the service castes, other main economic pursuits in Vithva are blanket weaving, stone-cutting, masonary works, and such others.

In Bidar District, a three-fore classification of land owners is made for the purpose of granting development loans by the Small Farmers Development Agency, Co-operative Banks, and Co-operative Societies. Those who own land below 2.5 acres are designated as marginal farmers. Small farmers own between 2.5 acres and 10 acres of agricultural land. Farmers owning more than10 acres of land are consisdered big farmers. Accordingly, the Brahman, Jangam (Lingayat), Kabbaliga and Kudu Vokkaliga are big farmers who mostly engage themselves in the supervision of land. The actual agricultural operation involving manual labour is mostly done by the members belonging to Harijan castes.

There are three types of agricultural labourers at Vithva. When such labourers are engaged on annual basis, this is known as *chakri* or *noukri*. Those who work on daily wage basis are *dinaguli* or *bidiguli*. When jobs are assigned on pre-rata basis such labourers are *guttige*.

At Vithva marginal farmers usually lease out their lands to share-croppers on *charane* (1/4), *athane* (1/2), or *baroane* (3/4) basis. Small farmers usually take land for share-cropping. Sometimes land is also leased out on fixed annual contract irrespective of the actual production. Such a contract is known as *Keulu*.

The Mysore Land Reforms Act has been passed in 1974 with a view to putting ceiling on land holdings and redistribute excess lands if any, to the Scheduled Castes/Tribes, landless and other categories. According to the categories of land classification, the ceiling on dry areas having no assured sources of water from any government tanks and canals, lift irrigation system, etc. as specified in the Act has been 54 acres. According to the provision, it is possible to allot a few acres to any additional members in a family. There are four such cases at Vithva where the amount of land possessed exceded the limit of ceiling. But no land has actually been realised by the Govt. according to the provision of ceiling for redistribution or otherwise.

With the abolition of Zamindary system, land at Vithva has virtually come under the control of those belonging to the so-called high castes and several Lingayat and Kurubagend are presently in possession of most of the village lands. The Harijan and service castes like Panchal (carpenter), Kumbar (potter), and Varik (barbar) get *inam* lands for rendering services to the villagers but the measure of such lands are very small. Fragmentation of land holdings due to breaking up of joint family system has made the landholdings of service castes economically non-viable, indirectly forcing them to lease out the lands.

There are some people at Vithva who are economically, politically, and socially dominant. Despite the fact that the small farmers actually cultivate lands of big farmers as well as of marginal farmers, various land reform measures were no match to the manipulating capability of the dominants. As a result, the land reform measures could hardly change the hierarchical structure of the village society. Even the Agricultural Cooperative Society at Vithva, which was formed particularly to protect benefits of the small and marginal farmers, due primarily to influence of some dominant individuals, has now gone defunct. This has done away even with the expectation of bringing about any change in this respect.

Moorthy

Moorthy is located in Palghat District of Kerala. It is a multi-ethnic village situated 30 kms South West of Palghat. The settlement of the village is spread over a large area. Houses of people belonging to the so-called low and untouchable castes are located in certain pockets away from the houses of the higher castes. In early days, the Irava, Cheruman and other low castes were not allowed to use tile or timber for construction of their houses. After independence of India such restriction have gradually been withdrawn. .

The village is divided into three *tara*, each having its own caste council. Different castes living in each of the three *tara* had prescribed functions to discharge at the time of annual temple festival managed by the Nair.

Women belonging to Irava, Cheruman, Kammala and other lower castes, as per traditional practice, were not permitted to cover their breasts. Since independence this situation has also undergone change.

The analysis of relationship between different castes of Moorthy needs to begin with a description of the principles of the land tenures. During the past few decades, the nature of relationship has experienced major change. In olden times, execution of eviction decrease was the major instrument by which many Irava families in Moorthy were alienated from their lands. Even after passing of the Malabar Tenancy Act of 1929, eviction remained a powerful weapon to exert more *pattam*, reducing the Irava peasantry to paupers. Eviction were also directed against a number of intermediary tenants. Since 1952, though several laws were enacted to protect the interest of tenants, there existed several intermediary rights yet to be abolished. Due to the emergence of strong organised peasant movements it was possible to alter the situation through Kerala Land Reforms (Tenancy) Rules, 1969. All rights, title, and interests of the landowners and intermediaries in respect of land held by cultivating tenants entitled to fixity of tenure, atleast theoritically, have been vested with Government on January 1, 1970 under the provisions of the Kerala Land Reforms (Amendment) Act, 1969. In practice, however, at Moorthy the right of ownership is yet to be conferred on the tenants.

At Moorthy, the Nair chieftains and the temple trusts are the absentee landlords, whose position became progressively weak since 1952. In 1970, the imposition of a ceiling of 6 to 20 acres of land gave a severe blow to the big landowners. At the village, however, not many were directly affected by this law since all estates in the village had already been partitioned among the adult members of a family. Sometimes the title deeds were registered in the names of distant kin living elsewhere. In fact, at Moorthy the holdings of several individuals are managed and administered by a single person who does not have land beyond the limit of ceiling in his personal name. Such strategies have in effect defeated the provision of ceiling in the Land Reforms Act, 1969. Ceiling, however, had a profound effect in the attitude of investment among the land owners. It has been observed at Moorthy that no surplus land is available for distribution among the landless poor because of the implementation of provision of ceiling. As a result, the relationship between the rentiers and farmers has been virtually snapped, making the farmers already difficult existence precarious. As a result, a fairly large number of the Cheruman. who used to live on agricultural labour, became bonded labourers. There were however, organized movements against such practice and Karshaks Thozhilali Union led by the CPI (M) and Desiya Karshak Thozhilali led by the Indian National Congress are important among them. Despite the fight put up by them, at the time of research investigation at Moorthy, as many as 20 per cent of the Cheruman labourers were still bonded. Formerly, a Cheruman used to receive a pittance of paddy for his hard day's labour of ploughing, harvesting, and such other activities. Agrarian movements and consequent initiative of the State Government could, however, ensure a better wage for them. The State Government also passed the Kerala Karshaka Thozhilali Rules in 1974. This legistation has made provisions for security of employment, provident fund, higher wage etc.

Despite the fact that the over-all hierarchical arrangement has remained by and large as it was, certain conspicuous changes have already taken place at Moorthy. Although in proportion to the requirements, this appears utterly inadequate, the same is certainly not insignificant. Nevertheless, it would need a deep probe in order to assess to what extent they are due to land reform measures or otherwise.

Palayasima

Palayasima is a multi-caste village in Chingleput District of Tamil Nadu. Members of 15 Hindu castes live in this village among whom the Harijan constitute the majority (about 60 per cent). Ritually and socially, the Brahman and Kanakku Pillai occupy high positions. In economic terms the Kanakku Pillai and Mudaliar are better off than the rest of the castes. In case of people belonging to the so-called low castes, assignment of no such distinction is possible to the collectivity. Individually some command respect, due primarily to their accumulated wealth.

From the point of view of income, landholding, and education, the Harijan are the weakest. In the caste hiarchy also, they are placed at the lowest, suggesting their weakness as rather absolute. The style of address of the people in the village reflects their respective socio-ritual positions. Even the degree of refinement of langauge depends upon the rank of the castes spoken to.

Making an accurate assessment of distribution of land at Palayasima was difficult. The village land records with the Karnam was inaccurate on multiple counts. There was cases of partition of land holdings without due entry into official records. There were also cases of land mortgage, locally called *suddhabegyam* with special right to the creditor of cultivating the land till complete repayment of the loan, which found no mention in the village land record. A similar tendency is observed with reference to lease arrangements. The settlement pattern of the village as such provides interesting leads toward understanding the nature of social stratification existing in the village. The Brahman of Palayasima occupy the centre, the Harijan being placed at the outskirt. Numerical strength and economic status do not seem to have brought any change in the socio-ritual hierarchy in the village. Some individuals belonging to so-called lower castes could improve their economic condition. As a result, they enjoy only this much leeway now that the overall social situation is not as harsh on them as on their impoverished caste fellows.

The Tamil Nadu Land Reforms (fixation ceiling on land) Act 1962 (Act 58/61) has fixed the ceiling limit from 30 to 60 standard acres depending on the number of members in the family and certain factors. In continuation of this, the Tamil Nadu Land Reforms (Reduction of ceiling on land) Act 1970 (Act 17/70) was added in 1970 limiting the ceiling from 30 to 15 standard acres. There were also other acts such as the Tamil Nadu Occupants of Kudiyiruppu (Conferment of ownership) Act (1971) and the Tamil Nadu Cultivating Tenants Protection Act, 1955 which were in favour of the tenants and labourers. Though no one has been directly affected by these acts in this village, they have made the land lords alert and hence no land lord wishes to give his lands on long term lease. He keeps on changing his tenants every year. This has created a feeling of insecurity among tenants. This and the increase of man per acre of land has made people rush for land. As a result, land rents have enormously increased. The amount of rent has increased fourfold between 1971 and 1973. This leaves scope only for marginal profit of tenants. As most of the village lands depend on rain water, the tenant not only lose marginal gain but become indebted in case of any drought. Agriculture is still the main source of livelihood at Palayasima. Villagers having enough capital adopt agricultural innovations such as improved variety of seeds, chemical fertilisers, pesticides, and irrigation facilities. A few Brahman land owners some Muduliar, Kanakku Pillai, and a few Naickers have adopted these new practices. People having control over enough resources if falls short of money, they can obtain loans from banks and other agencies. The small land owners are unable to take advantage of modern innovations because they lack supporting funds or any control over resources.

Though the Harijan are numerically dominant in the village, due to intra-group as well as inter-group conflicts, they failed to derive any benefits.

The entire framework of Palayasima, as it appears, is still based on caste principles, as was in the past with the only difference that the Brahman who were earlier dominant in all spheres of activities are not in the same commanding position any more. In fact, since independence, there has been a steady decline in the strength of the Brahman population of the village due to emigration of cities. Those who are still at Palayasima, have developed rather a resigned attitude toward village affairs. For Tamil Nadu as a whole, consolidation of non-Brahman forces and rise of middle range castes led to the decline of authority of the Brahman. This shift, however, did not result in any structural change of the society, except in the political domain. At Palayasima, instead of the Brahman, Kanakku Pillai or Mudaliar dominate the scene. The Naickers and Harijans, however, continue to be at the bottom as before.

IV

Modern laws provide three different kinds of rights over land. They are : (i) right of use and occupancy, (ii) right of inheritance, and (iii) right of transfer. Basic heteregeneity of population composition in India, regional specificities, influence of personal and customary laws have considerably added to the complexity of the situation. Various kinds of tenancies assigning descrete terms of contract as well as rights, obligatory and semi-obligatory nature of relationships between land-owner and tenants, and influence of other spheres of activities on the land management system make any comprehension of the overall situation extremely challenging, if not difficult. In fact, nature of relationships in Indian villagers speak of different sets of multiplex where nature of interaction in one sphere of life is influenced by several simulteneously or adseriatim. Under the circumstance isolating the pattern on a single sphere or any attempt to pin point specific influence of one aspect on others appears nearly impossible.

The case studies of Vithva, Moorthy, and Palayasima indicate such complexity in specific situation of Karnataka, Kerala and Tamil Nadu respectively. Differences in terms of socio-cultural contexts of the three situations are apparent though, conspicuous similarities are observed in terms of their nature of complexities.

Measures initiated by State Government concern, toward land reforms vary. For obvious reasons, therefore, results too, differ. But it will certainly be an over-statement if it is claimed that the variations in results are primarily due to the dissimilarities of the programmes as such. In fact, in social phenomena it is not considered very judicious to endeavour for establishing any one to one relationship or direct casualty. Neither it seems possible. As the case studies under reference indicate; Tamil Nadu, despite its somewhat abbreviated programme of land reforms, has experienced change which is very close to structural transformation. In comparison, Kerala appears to have quite an elaborate land reform measures to its credit. Still the Cheruman remain where they were. In Tamil Nadu, again, the Harijan even being the majority continue to occupy the bottom-most slot but the middle range castes have been able to dislodge the Brahman from their positions of eminence. Whether the land reform measures initiated by that government had at all any influence in this respect is, however, not definitely known. In Kerala the Irava, Cheruman and other low castes after independence of the country could shade away same of the indignities they had been subjected to through ages. Again whether this phenomenon has at all any relationship with the land reform measures cannot be said with any appreciable degree of certainty. Vithva, in comparison, remains mostly disturbed in this respect and its traditional polarisation between the 'haves' and 'have nots' persists more or less as it was before initiating any such programme.

Despite apparent disappointments, the picture is certainly not that grim. Particularly, the case study of Kerala suggests certain development which, along with others are likely, due to exposures to land reform programmes. Emergence of various movements in support of implementation of the programmes establishes the state government's seriousness about the commitments and peoples' involvement therein. Although Tamil Nadu also experienced certain movements, they were not necessarily in accordance with the commitment of the state government. In Karnataka, any such major development is yet to be perceptible. On the whole, thus, despite indifferent results, it is distinctly clear that a beginning has been made and blissfully in the right direction.

P.K. Samal, R.V. Ramarao* and R.C. Prasad

WHAT IS WRONG WITH INDIA'S TRIBAL DEVELOPMENT PLANNING? AN ANALYSIS AND APPROACHUAL FRAMEWORK TO STRATEGY

Part I

The tribal tracts constitute a very significant part of backward areas of the country. They comprise about 18.7 per cent of the total geographical area, and 8.13 percent of the total population of the country numbering to 51 millions as per the 1981 Census are tribals (Planning Commission, 1981). In Indian context, a tribe is defined as a group with traditional territory, specific name, common language, a strong kin relations, association with clan structure, tribal authority and rigid inclinations to religion and belief (Majumdar and Madan, 1970). Functional independence, homogeneity, primitive means of exploiting resources, economic backwardness, rich culture and tradition and least desire to change are some of the other characteristics, dominated among tribes (Hasnain, 1990).

Despite their habitation in different zones there prevails a few common features in the economic and social life of all the tribal communities. Agriculture forms the basic livelihood being supplemented by cattle keeping, foraging, and other allied activities. In some parts of North-East and Central-Southern regions, some tribal communities mostly subsist on shifting agriculture. The tribal communities have a qualitative symbiotic relationship with the forests, which they have established through experiences of difficult survival. Low acreage in land holding, indebtedness and malnutrition in economic life; low literacy rate particularly among fairer sex, stringent adherence to religion, rich cultural heritage and democratic socio-political institutions in social life are few common traits found among all tribes with minor variations necessitated to maintain a harmonious coordination between resource availability and the population structure. The socio-cultural life of tribal communities is woven with the economic life and, their resource management practices are expressions of inherent cultural traits (Samal, 1992). The tribal ecosystem is perpetuated through culture totally in balance with the production system and social heritage. Besides, the traditional productive social economy of the tribal communities is a characteristic manifestation of their interactions through various institutions with nature (Das, 1990). These institutions evolve strategies that make effective use of resources through adoptation. In this process of adoptation the tribal communities have resorted to eco-cultural adjustments for a harmonious articulation between technologies of the communities and the institutions (Cohen, 1968).

Since the tribal communities suffer from socio-economic handicaps that push them to a disadvantageous position, supplementary programs for their development were being considered under Backward Class Sector, in addition to the General Development Programs. During the various plan periods beginning from First Plan itself separate financial outlays have been earmarked for development of tribal populace. The distinguished provision spelt out by Plan-Periods for development of tribal communities are adoption of sub-plan strategey during Fifth Plan period with creation of Integrated Tribal Development Project (ITDP) : devolution of funds through special component plans and special central assistance during Sixth Plan period : and importance to special mechanisms to create awareness among the tribals against non-tribal exploitation in addition to alleviation of poverty during Seventh Plan period. Time and again, various committees, commissions and study groups have been constituted to study, review and suggest strategies to develop the tribal communities. The Indian constitution envisages special provisions for the protection and reservations for tribal communities in addition to provisions for special development programs and financial assistances.

Considering the complex agro-climatic and inhospitable terrain zones the tribals inhabit, the strategy for their development has been based on a two-pronged approach-areas of tribal concentration and dispersed tribal population. Area development approach for the former and family oriented programs for the later have been recommended (Planning Commission, 1981), taking into consideration the resource availability and ownership pattern, as in the areas of tribal concentration the tribes will have full command over the local resources, while in case of the dispersed tribals, their physical command over resources is extremely limited (Planning Commission, 1981). The ideology behind these exercises was to ensure social justice to the long neglected tribal people and to bring them in par with the main stream of Indian people.

However, experience of development planning during the last four and half decades has underlined the fact that despite the efforts made by the government to ameliorate the well being of the tribal people the programs failed to rise as befitting substitutes to the tradition and value oriented life style of tribals. This apprehension was being reflected by Planning Commission itself when it stated that a majority of the tribal people remained isolated and backward; alienation of land had continued and about 2 lakhs of tribal families did not possess any right to the land; and the development programs had adverse impacts on the tribes (Planning Commission, 1981).

Part II

An attempt is made in this part to establish the realities in the apprehensions relating to tribal development programs and consequential achievements through a micro level case study. The tribal tract of Visakhapatnam district in Andhra Pradesh forming an intrinsic part of the Eastern Ghats physiographic region was selected as the case study. The tract consists of 11 tribal development mandals, synonymous with block, with an area of around 6293 sq. kms. About 3.54 lakhs of tribal people (Census of India, 1881) from 25 tribal communities inhabit the tract. The dominant tribal communities are the Bagatha, the Valmiki, the Kondadora, the Kammara, the Gadaba, the Kotiya, the Paroja, the Kondakapu and the Samantha.

Eco-Culture

Contrasting physiography is observed in the tract. The relief ranges from175 mts. to 1615 mts. above MSL. The physiography is dominated by widened hilly nallas, which are extensively cultivated to deep gorges, erosional valleys and denuded hilly slopes. The climate varies according to the elevation the mean maximum temperature is about 40 Celsius while the mean minimum temperature is around 12 Celsius in a year.

The forests constitute 60.5 per cent of the total area of the tract. Barren and uncultivable land constituted nearly 21.0 per cent. The net area sown is only 11.5 per cent of the total area.

Both settled and shifting cultivation is practised in the tract. Settled cultivation, including both dry and wet crops, is practised in the valleys and terraced fields. Shifting cultivation is categorised into Kondapodu, when practised at hill tops and Chilkapodu when practised at foot hills. Rice dominates the cropping pattern, occupying around 20.0 percent of the total cropped area. While 95.0 per cent of the cropped area is under food crops, only 5.0 percent is under non-food crops. The livestock essentially comprises of cattle (2.2 lakhs), buffaloes (29.374), sheep (32.426) and goats (86,940).

Workers comprise 43.8 per cent of the total population, of which 92.81 percent are associated with agriculture. Percentage of family holding land is highest among the Bagatha (77.16), followed by the Kotia (76.56), the Kondakapu (75.00) and the Paroia (64.06). The lowest was found among the Kondhs (14.00), a primitive tirbal community.

Development Interventions and Change

A number of developmental programs on soil conservation, control of shifting cultivation, introduction of high yielding varieties of crops, social forestry, coffee plantation, distribution of milch animals and construction of housing colony etc. are being undertaken by the Integrated Tribal Development Agency (ITDA). The financial allocations for various sectors were Rs. 1392.2 lakhs for the Sixth Plan period and Rs. 744.0 lakhs for the 4 years of Seventh Plan period (Table-1).

Among the Scheduled Tribes, the literacy is only 6.0 per cent, while particularly among females it is as low as 1.3 percent (1981 Census). The roads give a coverage of 4.35 kms. to every one thousand population and 24.0 kms. for every 100 sq. kms. The availability of doctors and hospital beds accounts for one doctor serving 9635 persons and one bed serving 4618 persons, against the ideal ratio of one doctor serving 3500 people and one bed serving 1000 persons, as stipulated under Minimum Needs Program. Around 50.0 percent of total population remains 5.0 kms, away from the nearest road and medical infrastructure.

As Assessment

Since the Integrated Tribal Development Agency (ITDA) came into existence in the district from 1978, evaluation of the development activities was restricted for 6th and 7th Plans Periods only.

A survey covering 1200 households from all major tribal communities was conducted to evaluate the efficacy and viability of these development programs, targeted towards betterment of the tribals. In general, it was observed that 51.00 percent of the households were aware of the various ongoing developmental programs, while 38.00 percent were beneficiaries of one or the other program, 48.00 percent have opted for schemes related to agriculture and 38.00 percent opted for animal husbandry related schemes, while 21.0 percent did not know exactly to opt for which program. Soil conservation program was not upto the level of expectation, as area brought under this program constituted only 16.0 percent of the area that had to be conserved. The factor for failure, as assessed, was uncritical identification of the locations. The locations where the soil conservation programs had been undertaken were not the most critical and priority areas, where the measures were to be undertaken to obtain the necessary impact.

A two pronged approach—horticulture species on barren land and coffee plantation on optimal conditions was adopted to control shifting cultivation. In addition, attempts were made to convert shifting cultivators to settled cultivators by providing housing colonies with appreciable amenities for education, electricity, drinking water and irrigation facilities. However, shifting cultivation still persists and the programs have hardly any impact. The horticulture and social forestry programs failed mostly as they lacked the concerns for the immediate survival of the tribal people. The factors those attributed to the failure of these two programs could be classified into 3 categories :

Technical : Plantation of market oriented trees, species selection and spacing, faulty policy planning and defective forest policy.

Administrative : Program conceptualization and Implementation.

Economic and social conditioning : Lack of cultural perspectives in the program.

Food insecurity and lack of secured income for survival kept the tribal pre-occupied with activities to meet the requirements for immediate survival than participating in social forestry program where they could gain after lapse of considerable period. Besides, two major species cultivated under social forestry program were mango and cashewnuts. The persistence of these two varieties might lead the tribals to a major economic disaster, since the depth of the top soil in this area did hardly exceed 50 cms., necessiating a longer gestation period for the plants. Secondly, improved varieties of mango were not capable of resisting high velocity winds and hailstorms, which were common between April to July (Reddy, 1983).

However, coffee plantation had been appreciably accepted by the tribes, as it was a perennial crop that provided employment to the tribals round the year. Besides, it was traditionally grown by the tribals. Coffee plantation had the other positive impact as an effective ground cover for soil protection. The housing colony did not have the appreciation of the tribals since it lacked both cultural and environmental ethics. The houses were too small and lacked provision for sheltering livestock. The tiled roof and cemented floor provided no protection against the extreme coldness of the area.

In agriculture, the adoption of modern agricultural practices—high yielding varieties, pesticide and fertilizer was lesser than 10.0 percent to the total agriculturists. Again adoption and putting to actual practice were two different things. Among the adopters, 45.0 percent consumed the seed, 21.0 percent sold the seed in the market, 24.0 percent got no or least profit while only a marginal 10.0 percent received the expected output. The failure was attributed to the lack of cultural and ecological perceptions of the area by the introductors. Besides, optimal advantage was taken by the dominant tribal communities.

Though, the objectives of distribution of milch animals among the tribals of the tract was a laudable effort, in reality it was an unsuccessful exercise. As Reddy (1983) argued "The milch cattle distributed in the area were purchased in the plains. Because of the collusion between the government agents and the plain seller, invariably substandard cattle were purchased". The difference in feeding the cattle and climatic conditions worsened the exercise as the previously stall fed animals became weaker because of climbing and descending the hills for grazing. The cattle suffered high casualties in winter, being unable to withstand the heavy chilly weather (Reddy, 1983). Dr. Reddy's arguments were found quite justified. In addition, the modalities of loans given, were found to be unconducive for successful implementation of the program, as animals were never purchased in many a cases.

The survery too revealed the inefficiency and non-efficacy of the developmental programs, as 49.64 percent of the total household surveyed turned out to be indebted, of which 52.87 percent have borrowed keeping land as security. Interestingly, tribal communities, comparatively more dependent on agriculture were found more indebted in percent since maximum indebtedness was observed among the Kotiya (59.32 percent of the households surveyed), followed by the Kondakapu (55.96%), and the Bagatha (54.59). Despite the concerted efforts made to increase the rate of literacy it raised from 6.3 percent in 1961 to 8.1 percent in 1981 for the tract. The in-equality between sexes continued and tribal women had remained vulnerable to non-tribal sexual exploitation (Samal, 1919 : Mandal and Sahoo, 1992). Taking road as a parameter of development, the number of villages located 5.0 kms from the main road reduced from 63.0 percent in 1975-76 to 53.0 percent in 1987-88.

Part III

The evaluation of the development programs establishes the fact that the programs failed to rise as befitting substitutes to the tradition and value oriented life style of the tribals and were devoid of ecosystem perspectives. The strategies adopted were too simplistic in process characterised by elitist and urban bias, and undertaken in isolation for individual sectors without being interlinked with each other. Lack of coordination between various departments of ITDA itself and other organizations, departments and institutions, either governmental or otherwise operating in the tract was as major cause for the failures. The departments work in isolation, sometimes with identical objectives through separate strategies which have resulted confusion in the minds of the tribal folk.

Though, the interlinks between community resources socio-economics, culture and environmental needs have been recognized, they have not been articulated in terms of clear policies and programs. The traditional tribal cultures—political, organizational and societal—and their intricacies in the process of resource management and the tribal perception towards development have been ignored by attempting to achieve development drawing replications from external reasonings. The development targeted interventions were self imposition of allien attitudes on tribal people that have eliminated or suppressed indigenous systems, which were instrumental in sustaining the people. Further, the resource available to the tribal people of the tract were very limited and appropriate technological interventions for sustainable use of these resources were either not existing or limited.

It, further, became apparent that the projected strategy disregarded the basis tenet that the tribal culture is an integrated whole and the system necessiates an assessment of the felt-needs of the tribal people from the eco-cultural perspectives. What is needed is an integrated approach to development which takes into account all the factors—ecological, economic, social, cultural and governmental—involved in the functioning of man-environment systems in the tribal ecosystem (UNESCO, 1988).

The Approach to Strategy

The envisaged approach to strategy is based on the hypothesis that unsustainable trends of development are well known but the answers on how could they be replaced (Saxena and Rao, 1991) are little known. Planning and development strategies which could avoid adverse effects on an ecosystem operation without compromising the social and economic well being of tribal communities are well conceptualized but not available in acceptable and replicable form (Radcliftt, 1987). The need is to identify markers of development, which are sustainable and in conformity with socio-political, ecological and cultural dynamics of tribal communities. Sustainable development of tribal communities should aim at judicious utilization of land, water and biological resources based on ecological principle of conservation and recycling (Anonymous, 1987).

The main concerns of the envisaged strategy are man and the environment. The man and his environment are to be studied in totality in the mandal (block) or watershed incorporating all the associated factors. The mechanism to implement the model are the following :

1. Accurate precision and predictability in association with social perceptivity should constitute the core of the development strategy. It necessiates a marriage like alliance between natural and social scientists based on tolerance and mutual respect (UNESCO, 1988). A holistic approach to an understanding of tribal ecosystem assumes significant than studying specific components such as agriculture, animal husbandry, and forestry and suggesting non-coordinated strategy to specific component (Spedding, 1975; Chandra et al, 1976; Reddy, 1981; Maikhuri and Ramakrishnan, 1991). Delineation of interlinks between community resources, socio-economics, culture and environmental needs could only be possible by a coordinated efforts of both natural and social scientists. Failure of introduction of high yielding varieties of crops and cross breeds of animals and non-appreciation of housing colonies among the tribes of the present study area could be attributed to lack of coordi-

nation between persons engaged in the process of development from both natural and social sciences.

2. Evaluation of the natural resource endowment through new technologies makes the role of natural scientists very significant. Study of watershed characteristics like morphometric analyses; identification of degraded land using remote sensing technology; terrain evaluation comprising slopes, reliefs and soil characteristics; meteorological parameters and biodiversity by natural scientists will help assessing the level of ecoconservation prevailing in an area.
3. Data on socio-economic and cultural diversity need to be made the basement for any development planning. Traditional environmental knowledge, conservation practices and technologies and resource management practices are pragmatic in nature (Purohit, 1991; Maikhuri and Ramakrishan, 1990). These inherent knowledge need to be sought and considered before contemplating any planning for development and protection of tribal communities. The appreciation of the complexities of the traditional knowledge system and its systematic documentation incorporatin significant variations between tribal groups within an area are equally important (Purohit, 1991; Samal and Sharma, 1992). Many a legislations, policies and administrative arrangements designed to develop and protect tribal communities and culture, though have embraced to traditional knowledge systems are based on half truths and distortions (Baines, 1989; Purohit, 1993). The proper identification of social unit on which primary rights are based should constitute focal component of the tribal development (Baines, 1989).
4. Coordination between scientists, planners and the tribal people is the most important facet of the development planning. Active participation of the locals, particularly of women is an inevitable component, since it has now been convincingly established that tribals cannot be developed, rather can develop themselves through their own action (Anonymous, 1992).
5. Computation of indicators would help in identifying the levels of development and disparities within regions and groups. Development is not uniformed throughout within an area and the disparities in it are generally attributed

to the co-existence of cultural pluralism, ethnic diversity and economic dynamics. A detailed knowledge of stage and potentialities of development at the regions verified as much as possible by quantitative data and analysis of causal connections to disparities would help in formulating concrete strategies (Bronger, 1986) to attain equilibrium within regions. The indicators, selected should be precise and pertinent, particularly from economic, natural resources and socio-cultural arena. The indicators must have to be opted keeping in view the ecology, economy and cultural dynamics. The ranking of the regions and communities (cultural groups) in terms of natural resources and socio-cultural indices would help in understanding the relative response of each community and thus identify 'target region' (Thelen, 1972) and 'target groups' (Samal, 1991).

6. Computation of carrying capacity of the area on demand and deficit of food, fuel, fodder and water is prerequisite.
7. The infrastructure development needs to be optimal totally in conformity with tribal culture, ecology and economics. Efforts to reduce poverty are unlikely to succeed unless social services are made an integral component of the strategy to development (World Bank, 1990).
8. An optimal mix of modern and traditional technologies is the focal point to any development planning. An ideal example is the wisdom of the Lahaulis and Spitis of the Western Himalaya. The Lahaulis and Spitis cross the Holstein and Jersy cows with their local yaks and produce a species called *Churus* which can withstand the climatic hazards at subzero temperatures and can meet the milk demand of the populace. The *Churus* give less milk than high-breeds but more than the yaks.
9. Any development effort must envisage developing sustainability rather than sustaining development which could be feasible when markers of sustainability of a tribal ecosystem are precisely identified.
10. The role of culture, though need not be romanticised, can be ignored as well. Any development effort should invariably take the integral nature of the tribal culture into consideration before contemplating an idea of development.

Conclusion

The model probably, does not advocate any thing new on strategies to be followed for developing the tribals and their area. However, the theme suggested is approach to strategy, that will have a positive effect in developing the tribes and their area. The tribal areas with associated remoteness, truly embrace to many a specificities such as inaccessibility, fragility, marginality, diversity, niche and human adoptations (Jodha, 1992). The resource management practices in tribal communities are regulated by the above specificities in addition to other factors like interlinks between common property resources and private property resources, annual and perennial production, intensive and extensive land use etc. Besides, though the role of culture on resource management cannot be romanticized it cannot be ignored either (Samal, 1993). In a dynamic ecosystem like that of tribal area, enhancement or even protection of sustainability options depend upon the system linkages with other systems both for input acquisition and output disposal, (Jodha, 1992.) Sectorial approaches in formulating tribal development policies with over emphasis on increase production of one resource in isolation from other has to be discarded (Saxena, Rao and Kothyari, 1990) and holistic approach based on integrated efforts of both natural and social scientists in association with planners and local tribals should constitute the core of tribal development planning. As such, the tribe and its ecosystem need to be perceived from an integral percaption on culture and ecology rather than either from cultural or ecological angles. From this integral perception, a tribe could best be reckoned as a group that is Traditional, Resourceful Indigeneously but Backward and Endangered (TRIBE).

Note : The article was presented in the Anthropology and Archaeological Section of 80th Session of Indian Science Congress Association, 3-8, Jan. 1993 at Goa. The third author is a new addition who has immensely contributed to the theme of the article when it was modified recently.

Table-1 Financial Allocations for 6th and 7th Plan Periods.
(Rs. in Lakhs)

Sector	VIth plan	VIIth plan			
	1980-85	1985-86	1986-87	1987-88	1988-89
Agriculture	446.7	9.9	38.0	49.4	85.6
Horticulture	115.9	5.8	0.4	0.0	0.0
Sericulture	20.0	8.5	13.3	35.9	22.6
Animal Husbandry	160.8	2.1	3.8	8.6	18.2
Minor Irrigation	88.7	36.9	8.9	29.9	83.4
Pisciculture	0.0	0.4	0.6	6.0	9.0
Industries, services and business sector	56.0	7.8	6.0	51.7	38.8
Infrastructure	503.9	11.7	7.4	16.0	24.5
Administration	0.0	43.9	19.1	15.1	16.0
Total	1392.2	127.0	97.5	212.3	307.1

Source : Chief Planning Officer, Visakhapatnam District (1987-88).

References

Anonymous 1987 Our Common Fouture. The World Commission on Environment and Development. Oxford University Press, Oxford.

Anonymous 1991 Builiding a Sustainable Society in Caring for the Earth : A Strategy for Sustainable Living. IUGN. UNEP and WWF. Gland. Switzerland.

Anonymous 1992 Education as a resource. Economic and Political Weekly, Vol XXVII, 41 pp. 2226-27.

Baines, G.B.K. 1991 Traditional resource management in the Malanesian South Pacific : a development dilemma. In : Berkes Fikret (ed.) Common Properly Resources. International Book Distributors, Dehradun, India. pp. 273-295.

Bronger, Dirk 1986 Regional Disparities as a problem of spatial development in countries of the third word-case of India with reference to Andhra Pradesh. Annals, Vol. VI, pp. 14-37.

Chandra, S., J. P. Everson and A.J. Deboer 1976 Incorporating energetic measures in an analysis of crop production practices in Sigto Ka valley, Figi, Agricultural System, Vol. 1, pp. 301-11.

Chief Planning Officer 1987-1988 Statistical Abstract : Visakhapatnam District. Chief Planning Officer, Visakhapatnam.

Cohen, Y.C. 1968 Man in Adaption : The Cultural Present (Ed.) Aldine Publishing House, Chicago.

Das, J. C. 1990 Socio-economic and cultural profile of the Himalaya. *In* : Biswas, S. K. (Ed.), Strategy of Development in the Himalaya. Institute of Social Research and Applied Anthropology, Calcutta, pp. 35-69.

Hasnain Nadeem 1990 Tribal India Today. Harnam Publications, New Delhi.

Jodha, N.S. 1992 Sustainable issues in mountain context; emerging scenario. *In* : Proceedings of the Workshop on Approaches to Sustainable Development of the Indian Himalaya. Manali, Himachal Pradesh.

Maikhuri, R.K. and Ramakrishnan, P.S. 1990 Ecological analysis of cluster of villages emphasizing land use of different tribes in Meghalaya in North-East India. Agriculture, Ecosystems and Environment. Vol.

31, pp. 17-37.

1991 Comparative analysis of the village eco-system function of different tribes living in the same area in Arunachal Pradesh in North-East India. Agricultural Systems, Vol. 35, pp. 337-99.

Majumdar, D.N. and Madan, T.N. 1970 An Introduction to Social Anthropology. Asia Publishing House, Bombay. India.

Mandal, B. B. and Sahoo, K.R. 1992 Status of women in tribal Bihar. Man in India, Vol. 72, 3. pp. 281-92.

Purohit, A.N. 1991 Biological production, resource management and development in the Himalaya. In : G.B. Pant Institute of Himalayan Environment and Development (Ed.), Himalayan Environment and Development : Problems and Perspectives. Gyanodaya Prakashan. Nainital, India. pp. 107-23.

1993 Himalayan eco-system and some universal eco-hotspots. In : Proceedings of the National Academy of Sciences, India 63 (B) 1, pp. 37-45.

Planning Commission 1981 Report on Development of Tribal Areas. National Committee on the Development of Backward Areas, Planning Commission, New Delhi.

Redcliftt, M. 1987 Sustainable Development : Exploring the Contradictions. Methuen, London.

Reddy, A.K.N. 1981 An Indian village agricutural ecosystem : Case study of Ungra village. Part 11 : Discussion, Biomass, Vol. 1, pp. 77-88.

Reddy, G. P. 1983 Environmental and ecological dimesions of economic development among the tribes of Eastern Ghats in Andhra Pradesh. In : Mitra, S. N. and Singh, Bhupinder (Eds.) Tribal Area Development. Society for the Study of Regional Disparities, New Delhi. pp. 151-163.

Samal, P.K. 1991 Strategy and Methodology for Planning and Development of Tribal Areas : Doctoral Thesis. Andhra University, Visakhapatnam, India.

1992 Ecodevelopment in the Himalaya : a cultural interpretation. CHEA Bulletin. Vol. 11, pp. 26-36.

Samal, P.K. and 1992 Institution building at community level :

Sharma, S.		understanding the constraints in it from a micro-analysis. In : Proceedings of the Seminar on Sustainable and Replicable Ecodevelopment in Uttaranchal, Vol. 11, pp. 1-17.
Samal, P.K.	1993	The status of women in Central Himalaya : a cultural interpretation. Man in India, Vol. 73 (1), pp. 87-95.
Saxena, K.G. and Rao, K.S.	1991	Sustainable development in the Himalaya : a nebulous goal. Occasional paper. G. B. Pant Institute of Himalayan Environment and Development, Almora, India.
Saxena, K.G. K. S. Rao and B.P. Kothyari	1990	Social forestry in a broad perspective of integrated resource management and sustained production. International Journal of Ecology and Environmental Sciences. Vol. 16, pp. 15-16.
Spedding, C.R.W.	1979	An Introduction to Agricultural Systems. Applied Science Publishers. London.
UNESCO	1988	Man Belongs to this Earth. UNESCO, Paris.
World Bank	1990	Poverty : World Development Report—1990. Oxford University Press, 200 Madison Avenue, New York.

Amal Kumar Das

THE CHANGING LEPCHA SOCIETY : AN OVERVIEW

The Lepcha have attracted the attention since long, of persons who have come in contact with them because of their simple, amiable, cheerful, helpful, cooperative nature and character. They lack in spirit of conflict. The original habitat of the Lepchas, described as *Mayel Lyang* and considered by them as their sacred heritage, is now covered by Sikkim, parts of Eastern Nepal (Ilam), the Darjeeling district of West Bengal and a section of Bhutan. Among the Mongoloid tribal groups and Indo-Aryan people who have settled in narrow fertile valleys and the arable hill sides of the Himalayas, the Lepchas constitute historically, culturally and linguistically an important ethnic group. They are recognised as a small tribe with 23,409 souls in West Bengal (more than 90 percent of them reside in three hill subdivisions of the district of Darjeeling—Kalimpsong, Kurseong and Sadar) as per 1981 Census. In Sikkim, their total population in 1931 was 13,060 (estimated population in 1981 was 35,000). There are also a large number of them living in Ilam (East Nepal) since the beginning of Nineteenth Century (Subba, 1989 : 118).

Two rivers, the Rangit and the Tista, met at Peshoke near Darjeeling District creating three divisions, one known as Rinjong or Dandjung (this area falls on the other side of the Tista river in Sikkim), another known as Tamsang or Damsang (this area falls in Sikkim, Darjeeling and Bhutan), and the last one known as Ilam (Ilam district of Nepal). In the past inhabitants of each of these divisions used their surnames after these groupings but now-a-days these divisions are non-existent (Das, 1978 : 96).

In the past the Lepchas were known as the *Rong*, meaning thereby the dwellers of rocky land. The term *Rong* has been derived from word *Rinjong* meaning rocky and full of respectable people. Even today some of them refer to themselves in their own language as *Mutanchi Rong*, 'the beloved children of God' and calling their country *Nye Myel Renjyong*, *Lyang*, 'the land of the holy and of external purity' (*ibid*, 241).

The term Lepcha is in common use since long. It may be the anglicised form of the word *Lapche* which means 'vile speakers' in Nepali. Subba, however, stated that this is not true. This word makes no sense in Nepali. Lapche by all indications, according to him, appears to be a Kirata contribution to one of its groups but how the morphological reversal from Lapche to Lepcha took place is not explained linguistically by any scholar till date (Subba, *op. cit.* : 117).

About the original homeland of the Lepchas, there exists a good deal of controversy. Some believe that they have been living in Sikkim from long past and are the autochthones of the region. Some legends point that they migrated to Sikkim from southern Tibet. Another legend indicates that at first they used to live in a valley called *Mael* in the neighbourhood of Kanchenjunga. In other legends other places in the neighbourhood of Kanchenjunga are indicated as their original habitation. With the increase in number they slowly spread over the whole area. The Lepcha sib names (Agit/Ptso) support this and point towards legendary relations with various mountains in shose neighbourhood they have settled and often worship the said mountains. It became customary that each *Agit* had to perform an annual sacrifice to the spirits of a particular mountain (Das, op. cit : 106). The term 'children of Kanchenjunga' is very much associated with the Lepcha. There are some other views also about their original habitat and migration.

Risley, however stated that the tribe has its origin in two waves of immigrants of Mongoloid race, the last one coming in the middle of the seventeenth century (1891 :7). Hermanns has drawn a line of difference between the hunters and the farmers, two typical groups among the Lepchas. The hunters are tall Rong type and characterised by the larger physical build, the long small face, the open eye and the long small high nose. The farmers, on the other hand constitute the second group with shorter physique, broad face, broad nose, Mongoloid eye fold and permanent cheek bones. Hermanns believes that the hunting component of the Rong (Lepcha) are the primitive indigenous inhabitants of the forests of Sikkim. The farmers came from the east and have connections with the people alike the Naga, Lolo and Miau (Hermanns, 1954 : 106). Christop von Furer-Haimendorf has mentioned that the Lepchas were originally shifting cultivators inhabiting the foot hills and middle ranges of Eastern Himalayas closely related to the

Nishi, Adi, Miri and others, and they would still be part of the ancient population if they had not been forcibly subjected to the influences of the Tibetans, Nepalese and the Bhutanese and had not been partly converted to Christianity (Foning, 1987 : xiii).

The Lepcha mythologies point to some 'Panoos" (kings) of their own. King "Turve Panoo' is mentioned in a large number of tales. The first batch of the Lepchas came to Sikkim under his leadership (Mainwaring, 1876 : 146). After the death of Turve Panoo his three sons succeeded to the throne one after another. After the death of 'Tur-ayek Panoo' his vacant throne was seized by a Tibetan, Phuntsog Nam-gyal.

Although the Lepchas settled in Sikkim sometimes between ninth and thirteenth century it became a political entity in the fifth decade of the seventeenth century, when the Lama of Lhasa, with the aid of two other Lamas, converted the people of Sikkim into the Buddhist faith and appointed Phuntsog Namgyal to be the first king. Since then a number of kings came into power in Sikkim. In 1835 the King of Sikkim 'presented' the hills of Darjeeling 'out of friendship' to the East India Company. By the treaty of 1961, Sikkim became British India's protectorate. In 1947, after Independence, India inherited the responsibilities of Sikkim from the British. Sikkim became the twenty second State of India since 1975.

Thus the Lepchas passed through different phases of history. At the beginning, they lead a life under the control and guidance of their own chieftains' kings. They were the original and sole inhabitants of Sikkim practically faced no invasion from outside till the fifth decade of the seventeenth century when their life and culture were marked by the first major contact with the Tibetans. During this phase there were frequent attacks by the Bhutanese and the Gurkhas on the kingdom's eastern and western frontiers. Thereafter, next phase of the Lepchas life and culture started after their contact with the British from the third decade of the nineteenth century. With the advent of the British Rules perceptible changes took place in the socio-economic sphere of life and activities and the infrastructural development of the area also progressed. Vigorous Missionary activities started in this part of the country and a section of the Lepchas was converted to Christianity. After Independence of India, more particularly after 1975 when it became the twenty second State of India new phase of the Lepcha life started. This phase through which the Lepchas are still continuing is the phase of development of their socio-economic and cultural life in the post-Independence era. The impact of all these external and internal forces is clearly reflected in their material, technological, bio-social, cultural, economic, political spheres including their psychology, directly or indirectly.

II

The writings of the nineteenth century authors give us an idea about the life of the Lepchas of that time. Though these writings are not based strictly on scientific investigations still the observations made by them throw some light on the Lepchas, their life and activities. Observations of some of these authors are given below for providing a Lepcha profile in a nut-shell.

The Lepchas were amiable, intelligent and of inquiring turn of mind. They were poor agriculturists, nomadic in their habits forming no permanent villages and cultivating barely sufficient for their subsistence. When they ran short of foodgrains, they subsisted on wild roots, mountain spincah, fern tops, fungi etc., seldom remaining more than three years in one spot. They had no ploughs, and just used to scrape and softened the earth for reception of seeds. They used to eat all kinds of animal food, and were fond of spirituous and fermented liquors. They could not marry young mostly due to delay in procuring sufficient bride price which sometimes forced them to adopt marriage by service. They were Buddhists in religion and used to bury their dead (Campbell : 1840). Death was regarded with horror, the dead body was burnt or buried. Omens which were practised are now gradually disappearing (Hooker : 1855). Their priests were also medicine men and exorcists and directors of feasts, ceremonies and sacrifices in honour of evil spirits; but not withstanding all these Lepchas were as good Buddhists as the Nepalese (Latham : 1859).

Lepcha language once the language of the whole country of Sikkim and was also spoken by the Tibetans, Bhutias or others who entered the country. Under the rule of Colonel Lloyd, business was carried out, justice in the English courts administered and documents were written and recorded in this language and recorded (Mainwaring : 1876).

According to Risley (1881) the Lepchas were divided into two branches—Rong and Khamba. The former claimed to be the original inhabitants of Sikkim. Polyandry though comparatively rare, was not entirely unknown among the Lepchas. Owing to the difficulty of getting the bride-price men used to marry late. It was considered proper for a widow to marry her late husband's younger brother. Most of the Lepchas were Buddhists but it was clear, however, that once their sole belief was on shamanistic animisn. Conspicuous traces of this faith still survive among them, imperfectly hidden by their veil of Buddhistic usage (Risley: 1891).

They are extremely interesting not only for their many charming traits, but also chiefly because they represent the states of primitive men when they subsisted by fishing, hunting and gathering wild fruits and digging roots; and they are now a vanishing race, fast disappearing before the tide of emigrants from the more active and civilized communities who have lately swept in a large number of waves into their country. A pure Lepcha can easily be distinguished from other groups as well as Sikkimese Bhotias due to his distinguishing physique, features, dress, speech, manners, customs and character. They are losing their identity by the extensive absorption of their women into the Bhotia and Limboo Tribes, with whom they freely inter-marry (Waddell : 1899).

The Lepchas are deeply versed in knowledge of the edible value or otherwise of every root, herb and berry that grows in their country. Their ancient patriarchal customs are dying out. Their literature was almost entirely destroyed and their traditions are being rapidly forgotten. Once free and independent they are now the poorest people in this mountainous country (Donaldson : 1900).

In addition to the above W. W. Hunter (1868), E. T. Dalton (1872), B. H. Hodgson (1847) and others also wrote about Lepchas and their land.

All these personnel on different occasions with different purposes visited or stayed in this part of the country and got interested on the Lepchas and through their writings tried to focus those aspects of Lepcha life, which attracted them most.

The twentieth century writings may be divided into two parts—those written upto the first half of the century i.e., till the end of the British Raj and those written thereafter i.e., after the independence of India, more particularly those studies which were carried out after Sikkim becoming the twenty second State of India.

White (1909) who served as Political Officer in Sikkim for over twenty years, has evaluated the rulers of Sikkim.

In his study Stocks (1925) discussed the mythology and religious beliefs of the Lepchas as reflected in their folk tales while Schermann (1926) has presented an introductory note on Sikkim and its people with particular emphasis on the Lepchas.

Grierson (1927) has narrated about Lepcha (Rong) dialect spoken in Sikkim and presented a brief grammatical outline of the language including lists of standard words and phrases.

Macfarlane (1939) on the basis of her field work in 1937 in Kalimpong furnishes information on blood types of the Nepalese, Lepchas and Tibetans.

John Morris', *'Living with Lepchas : A Book about the Sikkim* Himalayas' (1938) and Geoffrey Gorer's book *'Himalayan Village : An Account of the Lepchas of Sikkim'* (1938) deserve special mention as they collected and presented data from anthropological point of view. They selected the village 'Lingthem' the private Lepcha Reserve for their study. In 1937, they stayed in Linghthem for three months from March to May. Lingthem, the village with 33 households and 176 persons (179 persons according to Morris) has since been known throughout the world. Most of our knowledge about the economy, social organization, sexual behaviour, socialisation etc. of the Lepchas are largely based on the information culled from this tiny village (Gowloog : 1991). This village is situated in Talung valley of Dzongu reservation in Sikkim. It is not known exactly when Dzongu was created as a Lepcha reserve though it is quite probable that this was created towards the end of nineteenth century or beginning of twentieth century when it was clear that unless given special protection the Lepchas would completely wither away. Dzongu is a name given by Bhutias meaning a place with 'nine districts'. It falls in the north district of Sikkim. The total area covered by this Reserve is 15,845 hectares. The total population according to the 1981 Census is 7745 including 3414 seasonal labourers from Nepal. Lingthem village is located in the upper Dzongu (Gowloog, op. cit). Morris (1938) while describing about the Talung valley, states in his book,

> "It was the only purely Lepcha place still in existence. In all other parts of Sikkim the people had intermarried with the Tibetans and Nepalis, to such an extent that they had lost all traces of tribal consciousness. Not so, however, in the Talung; for this valley formed the part of the Maharaja's personal estate and none but Lepchas were permitted to own land or to settle in it."

Morris quoted in his book a personal communication of Dr. J.A Graham who worked among the Lepchas for fifty years. In Graham's own words,

> 'The fact that they lived an isolated life among the forests of Himalayas before the Nepalese migrated to their sanctuary made them interdependent. They were not good farmers and their agricultural implements

> were primitive. Their dependence upon forest roots and fruits which were got free by the labour of their lands, encouraged the gospel of sharing; and they share everything. The Lepchas, however, have learned much from the Nepalese as to the village of land, and many of them are now quite as good farmers as their instructors."

Dr. Graham pin points sacrifice of cattle and fowls on the advice of their priests in times of illness as one of the causes of poverty of Lepchas.

Gorer (1938) states that with its unique conglomeration of attitudes, the Lepchas are certainly disappearing for their culture presupposes a homogeneous interlocking community, and this, as well as their complete suppression of competition and aggression, causes and inevitable breakdown of their culture in any mixed community. He further states that it is only in Dzongu and in one or two small villages outside the reserve that there is a homogeneous Lepcha society, practically undisturbed by alien influence. Gorer employed various methods of different disciplines, anthropological and psychological, functional, freudian in his study.

Gorer and Morris over emphasized the indulgence of the Lepchas in too much sexual activities which has been attributed as one of factors along with heavy drinking habit to be the cause of sterility. However, the Lepcha scholars like Tamsang and Foning did not agree to this and think it to be a hasty conclusion tarnishing the image of the Lepchas as a civilised community.

These two books are still considered as important all embracing ethnographic document on the Lepchas in spite of having several drawbacks. In this connection Gowloog states,

> "From 1950 onwards they have been extensively quoted, corroborated, and also criticized severely by many scholars including the Lepchas. Yet no later scholar has been able to bring out equally rich ethnographic treatise on the Lepchas".

From 1951 onward, Nebesky—Wojkowitz, Rene von has written a number of articles in different Journals on different aspects of the Lepcha life and activities. His observations are based mainly on investigations in Sikkim during 1950-53 and 1956-57. He made discussions on the beliefs about the death and funeral practices of the Lepchas in Sikkim; presented text of wedding songs of the Lepchas with discussions as to their significance in the life of the

Lepchas of Sikkim; described the religions practices relating to and significance of drum divinations among the Lepchas; hunting and fishing among the Lepchas etc. etc.

Rock's writing (1953) presents excerpts from the History of Sikkim which was written by Sir Thutob Namgyal and Maharani Yeshay Dolma (1908). This also includes ethnographical notes.

The Lepcha myths connected with the creation of the world, creation of man, deluge, the land of the Gods and spirits, soul, concept of God, Mun & Bongthing etc. and tries to trace out the parallels to the myths and the rituals are some of the important aspects of the Lepcha culture covered by Hermanns (1954). Then he touches upon the social classes, economic life etc., of the Lepchas, closes the chapter on the Lepchas with a discussion on the anthropological classification of the people.

Though according to Siiger, the earliest European reference to Sikkim is that of Ippolito Desideri, who has referred to the existence of Bree-me-jong (or Sikkim), but it was only after J. D. Herbert published *"Particulars of a visit to the Siccim Hills"* in 1830 that the world came to know about Sikkim and its inhabitants (Gowloog, op. cit). Siiger as a member of the Third Danish Expedition to Central Asia in 1949 spent several months among the Lepchas of Sikkim (Tingvoong) and his preliminary report (1956) touches upon Lepcha history, material culture, social structure etc. and makes a somewhat detailed discussion about the Lepchas religion—its origin, similarity with others etc. In his own words "The knowledge of Lepcha ritual and prayer is very fragmentary..and that it might throw much light on Lepcha religion, I decided to devote my main attention to Lepcha religion and culture (Siiger, 1967).

Nakane's analysis (1966) of the plural society of Sikkim throw light on the greater flexibility of Tibetan Buddhist societies as compared with the rigidity of a close Hindu society. Discussing the relations between the indigenous, originally 'pagan' Lepchas and the Bhotia representatives of the Tibetan Buddhist civilization, Nakane shows that the Bhotias did not form an exclusive group but enabled Lepchas to acquire religious learning and joint monastic communities on equal terms. The Bhotias and the Lepchas intermarry, though not on a large scale, and in so far as the upper strata of society are concerned there is no feeling of status distinction between the Bhotias and the Lepchas. The Hindu immigrants from Nepal on the other hand, have remained outside the framework of the local Lepcha—Bhotia societies. Not only the cultural gap between the politically dominant Buddhist population and the economically forward and rapidly increasing Nepali settlers is too great to allow of easy assimilation, but the Hindu immigrants also resist the absorption into a non-Hindu society. Although many of them stem from tribal communities which had originally no strong sense of caste—status, they have all been influenced by high caste ideas of purity and exclusiveness.

The first major work by an Indian Anthropologist on the Lepchas is by Das (1962) with the assistance of Banerjee. Since 1963 onwards Das made quite a number of field trips till 1969 in different parts of Darjeeling District of West Bengal and his findings published in 1978 under the title "The Lepchas of West Bengal" present an overall profile of all the facets of life and activities and the culture pattern and also changes therein of the present day Lepchas.

Neethivanan (1961) studied Lepcha language in Darjeeling District as also of Gangtok area of Sikkim and the findings of the study help in understanding the affinity and position of Lepcha language and morphology thereof.

The only local but a non-Lepcha scholar who has written on the Lepchas is Subba. Subba carried out his studies both in North Sikkim.

Thakur (1988) has discussed about the socio-cultural aspects of the Lepchas of Darjeeling, Kalimpong, Kurseong and Sikkim.

Foning in his book "Lepchas : My Vanishing Tribe" (1987) presents an inside view and recounts his personal experience and give vivid descriptions of events and ceremonies in which he was involved as a participant.

Bhasin's study among the Lepcha and Bhotia of North Sikkim (1989) discusses about the relationship between man & nature, and the mechanism and areas of interconnection between eco-system and socio-cultural system.

Besides Foning, some of the Lepcha scholars have also contributed to the Literature on Lepchas. Some of them like G. Tshering and La Tshering Lepcha have written in the Nepali language while others like Sonam Wangdi Lepcha, K.P. Tamsang, and A.R. Foning have written in English. Sonam Wangdi, is probably the first Lepcha to have done a doctorate on the Lepchas *(ibid).*

Ghosal carried out a study among the Lepchas of Kalimpong Sub-Division of Darjeeling District and Lingdong in the Lepchas reserve of Dzongu in Sikkim) in different ecological situations and tried to ascertain the socio-economic changes and adaptations taken place among the Lepchas during this Century.

Gowloog, a Lepcha scholar, conducted a diachronic (among the Lepcha in Lingthem village, situated in upper Dzongu of North Sikkim in 1987-89 who were also studied by Moris and Gorer in 1937. Side by side, she restudied the village Tingvoong situated about 13 km. away from Lingthem but very much within Dzongu, once studied by Siiger in 1949. Gowloog discussed about the changes that have taken place in these villages located in Reserved area along with the Lepcha society as a whole.

Thus we find that the Lepchas have drawn attention of many scholars since Ninteenth Century onwards who visited Darjeeling or Sikkim. These writings provide outsider's as well as insider's views thus presenting a wholastic picture of the society and culture. During recent past, some important studies have been conducted by the trained anthropologists analysing the changes that have taken place in Lepcha life and culture.

III

In the foregoing pages comments and observations of Nineteenth and Twentieth Century authors have been placed to present an overall profile of the Lepchas in brief so that the changes that have taken place through decades become quite clear. Now, in the forthcoming pages, some findings of studies carried out rather recently in Sikkim (Lingthem, Lingdong, Tingvoong in Lepcha reserve Dzongu) as well as in Darjeeling (Nassey, Pagang, Tanek, Purbong etc. in Kalimpong Sub-Division) mainly showing nature and extent of changes in the Lepcha society and culture over time and space, are placed. This section of the paper is based mainly on studies conducted after 1975 when Sikkim became twenty-second state of India. These studies are current additions to the existing literature on Lepchas and are the outcome of the intensive as well as extensive investigations by the trained anthropologists. Findings of Subba (1989), Ghosal (1990), Gowloog (1991) and Foning (1987) have been utilized profusely in this section of the paper. In addition, observations of Das (1978), Siiger (1967), and Bhasin (1989) have been incorporated as and when needed. These studies were conducted by both Lepcha as well as non-Lepcha scholars thus providing insiders as well as outsiders views and observations.

Ghosal has observed tremendous amount of change in the subsistence sphere of the Lepcha life. Within a span of only hundred years or so, they have transformed their subsistence economy from hunting—food gathering to settled plough cultivation in permanent terraces with intermediate stage of shifting cultivation (Ghosal, 1990).

Subba also observed same type of changes among the Lepchas (1989 : 119).

Gowloog (1991) noticed transformation of agriculture from shifting to settled and terraced cultivation for which credit should be given to the immigrant Nepalese. There is a shifting from consumption oriented crop to cash crop (cardamom, ginger etc.).

With the low level of technology at the beginning of it was not difficult for the Lepcha to maintain a small population with whatever natural resources available to them. But with the increase in population shifting cultivation was adopted gradually. The immigrant Nepali population created pressure on land, and the Lepchas were compelled to take up terraced cultivation with better implements, thus began the era of better use of natural resources with improved technology. But the Lepchas could not compete with the Bhotia and Nepali population who had higher level of technology. The Lepchas subsisted on poorer and scanty resources whereas the Nepalese and Bhotias had the control of better economic persuits. In Sikkim, outside Dzongu reserve the Lepchas possessed very little land and in Darjeeling except a few villages in Kalimpong Sub-Division their control over the natural resources are being minimised by the Nepalese (Ghosal, *op.cit.)*. In this connection Subba (1989) observes that the immigrant Bhutias and Tibetans were small in number and basically engaged in trade, herdsmanship or administration; they brought no change whatsoever in the prevailing technology of cultivation. The immigrant Nepali population were brought by the British to work as labourers as they would not require to adopt to the climate of this region and thus to incur health hazards. Majority of the early settlers from Nepal were absorbed in the tea gardens while the remaining population was either engaged in road construction or agriculture. These Nepalese introduced settled cultivation to the Lepchas. The Lepchas would not have taken up terracing so easily if there were no restriction imposed by the British Government on the utilization of forest resources (Subba, *op.cit.* : 119-120).

The Bhotias on the other hand, were fewer in number and instead of going for land they exerted influence over the political sphere of the region, more particularly of Sikkim. In the economic sphere they preferred to work more in trans-Himalayan trade than to till the soil. Tremendous amount of immigration in the hills of Darjeeling had badly afffected the ethnic composition, ethnic balance and power structure of the region. Objectively, one can see that the Lepcha have lost ground in almost all spheres of life to the Bhotia and Nepalese (Ghosal, *op.cit.)*.

It was a common belief that the land owned by the Lepcha was passed into the hands of Nepalese in spite of restrictions. The Nepalese purchase the land in the names of their Lepcha wives whom they intermarry. Ghosal found twelve cases of Nepali-Lepcha marriage in two villages studied in Kalimpong. Alienation of owned by the Lepcha continued even after they fully adopted settled cultivation. Even before the large scale Nepali immigration began, the Lepchas were pushed to lower altitudes by the immigrant Bhutias from the north. Though alienation of the lands owned the Lepcha after India's independence was strictly stopped but the Bhutias could buy the land from the Lepcha even after that and has indeed continued even today. It was a fact that land owned by the Lepcha passed on to many Nepalese but this process worked effectively between 1850 and 1949 only. After that the Nepalese count not buy much land from them (Subba *op.cit.* : 120-121).

The agrarian character has changed in Lingthem due to the emergence of new land tenure system—the Lepchas have emerged as landlords and the immigrant Nepalese as the tenants. There are cases of alienation of land owned by the Lepchas by Nepalese and Bhutias outside Dzongu but for reserved status this had been averted in Dzongu (Gowloog, *op.cit.*).

In Tingvoong cardamom cultivation quite limited in the past, was very extensive in 1989 being the most important crop of the village. Use of high yielding variety seeds, pesticides, fertilisers are in the increase. A trend in the increase of migrant Nepali labourers has been noticed since recent past. The process got accelerated since 1975 and the dependence of the villagers on the migrant labourers from Nepal gradually increased. It was as high as 57 per cent of the total population of the village. The abundance of such labourers from Nepal has both good and bad affects—good in the sense that this has saved the Lepchas from the health hazards in cultivating cardamom and provided them with the opportunity for their children to go to school and even to take higher studies whereas, the bad effect of the situation is that they are growing more and more dependent on migrant labourers. On the whole, it has affected their life style, language and culture *(ibid)*. Ghosal found that the additional cash money earned from cardamom cultivation is used by the Lepchas of Dzongu in different rituals. They also use a portion of it to modernise their dwelling houses by replacing the traditional thatch roof with galvanised iron sheet though in the matter of dresses and other social aspects they still follow the traditional way of life. The Lepchas of Kalimpong, though have less income from cash crops, bear indications of social changes whereas in Dzongu modernisation is hurdled as the income from cash crop of cardamom is spent in religious ceremonies. Therefore, cash cropping may not always bring social change. The Lepchas of Dzongu lag behind their brethren in Kalimpong in agricultural techniques, gross production of crops and use of fertilisers etc. Occupational mobility is also more among the Lepchas of Kalimpong (Ghosal, *op. cit.*).

In Lingthem the animals are no longer objects of sacrifice, these are also important source of income. In non-agriculture sector business (shop-keeping) and service are growing in popularity. In animal husbandry hybrid variety with better sheds are increase in Tingvoong (Gowloog, *op. cit.*).

Gowloog also mentions about significant changes in the material life of the Lepchas. Due to improvement in communication system Lingthem is no more an isolated place disassociated with outside world. The Passidanga hamlet has emerged as a semi-urban place with rows of shops, schools, primary health centre, Panchayat Office, Post Office etc. In 1937, there were only 33 households and 176 persons (179 according to Morris) in Lingthem whereas in 1987, the total number of the Lepcha households in the village was 117 with total population of 732, males numbering 356 and female 376, Settlement pattern has changed. Some of the houses fellow traditional line as observed by Gorer and Morris but others have changed or are in the process of change. Materials of construction including household furniture have changed. At present electrification and tap water are the characteristics of the village. Dress of the Lepchas in 1937 was highly Tibetanized but at present it is considerably westernised. Most important change occurred in the field of education. When there was no school in 1937, there were two high schools and three schools under ICDS within the village in 1987. The Lepcha children now attend schools in large numbers. As has already been mentioned this has become possible due to the coming of the seasonal labourers from Nepal, who have taken up the work which would otherwise have to be done by the Lepcha children also. With the inception of statutory Gram Panchayat in 1965 the changes are taking place more rapidly in the village. The growth of population was considerably hampered in the past due to widespread sterility caused by veneral disease *(tanji)* etc. In 1959, a medical team camped in the village to treat all men and women in the village Lingthem. It was only after that the sterility is reported to be completely removed and the villagers gradually started bearing children. This is responsible for the low population of the village even after fifty years. The world view of the Lepchas has widened. They are more conscious about their surroundings than that of the earlier days. Radio and wrist watches are common. Gowloog mentions about the presence of two television sets in 1987.

Gowloog states that the total number of households in Tingvoong was approximately 40 with 190 persons in 1949. A socioeconomic survey conducted in 1981-82 (by the Planning and Development, Deptt. of the Govt. of Sikkim) in Dzongu among the Lepchas revealed that there were 98 households with 557 population in that year. It was also noticed the infiltration of the Nepali population in the Reserved Area. The Lepcha houses in 19th Century were entirely made of bamboo. Siiger in 1949 found bamboo houses as on exception and reported about wide spread use of timber and thatch roofs. Forty years after, in 1989, a lot of changes were noticed.The thatched roofs were replaced by corrugated and galvanized iron sheets. Cement became popular and in almost every house a separate living room existed which in 1949 was only a part of the hearth room.

There was not a single school in Tingvoong in 1949 but at present there are as many as 286 students reading in Tingvoong school. In 1989, this school had 26 graduate teachers representing various Sikkimese and non-Sikkimese communities.

Das states that the proportion of the Lepcha population to the general population in Darjeeling District is gradually decreasing. This gives an idea of heavy migration of other community people into this district. Immigrants exerted tremendous influence on the material, economic, socio-cultural and political life of the Lepchas, directly or indirectly (Das, *op.cit.* 35-36). He has also found the following five categories of occupations among them—cultivator, agricultural labourer, daily labourer, service holder, craftsman. He states that being mainly agriculturists the income of the Lepchas is mostly in kind. Earning from limited cultivation of the cash crop is also meagre. The income from livestock is also meagre as they themselves consume a good proportion. Due to the existence of middle men they suffer a lot of every economic transaction. Apart from low income the people have become spend-thift in nature. Whenever they get money they spend that lavishly. The drinking of *chi* is a curse to them. Their socio-religious functions also compel them to spend a lot. The most characteristic feature of the Lepchas is that they are cooperative minded. But lack of proper management capacity and funds often make their condition pitiable. But the economic cooperation between the members of the family help them in facing the crisis. This is a relieving feature in the economic condition of the Lepchas (*op.cit.* : 75-77).

But due to the impact of modern forces a trend is developing among them to be individualistic. This is confined among some of the urban Lepchas at present. In the past they were very honest, amiable and very pleasant companions. But now a few dishonest and selfcentered people can be easily found among them. Their food habit is gradually changing. They are now consuming vegetables more than before, and taking more cooked food than before. The Lepchas were never business minded in the past but now a few of them have taken to business and adopted business terms, tactics, manners etc. The Lepchas are gradually becoming conscious about modern medical treatment and knowledge and modern training facilities in different technological aspects. Traditional arts and crafts which used to play a dominant roll in the past, are gradually dying out. Folk songs are gradually loosing hold on the Lepcha life and dwindling away day by day. Their dresses and ornaments are also going through changes and developments of modernised ideas are taking place (*op. cit* : 260-261).

Lepcha language had a respectable position till the end of Nineteenth Century. At present most of the Lepchas have forgotten their language totally and accepted Nepali as their language for all practical purposes. Excepting Lingthem village nowhere Subba found two Lepchas speaking in their own language for a long time. There has been some revival of the Lepcha language after Sikkim became one of the States of India in 1975. Provisions are made to teach this language upto secondary level of education in more than a dozen schools in Sikkim. However, there is no such provision yet for the Lepchas of Darjeeling District (Subba *op. cit* : 124-125).

To Subba's comments of overall dominance of Nepali language over Lepcha language, Gowloog remarks that the situation in Dzongu is not so bad but if the immigrant labourers from Nepal remain there for another couple of decades. Dzongu may not be much different from Darjeeling in this respect.

About the changes in social sphere of the Lepcha life Ghosal observed that despite changes in economic and religious spheres their social structure has remained static and quite unchanged which has perhaps caused the lack of adaptive capability to changing circumstances. This is evident from little occupational mobility among them. Due to this lack of adaptive capability, the Lepchas could not compete with the Nepalese who are more versatile in this respect. Their deep attachment to land also prevented them from accepting new types of occupation.

Traditionally the Lepcha families were joint or extended type consisted of large number of members. This pattern was followed from the security point of view (fear of aggression of the Bhutias from the east and north and the Gorkhas from west) and management of cultivation and household activities (monkhood, tending of animals, bringing water and fire wood and guarding crops from monkeys and other animals). It is reported that emergencc of nuclear familes was notable particularly after '50s because of the availability of the Nepali labourers for looking after their agricultural and cardamom fields (Subba, *op. cit* : 123-124). Gowloog found in Lingthem that joint familes were disappearing in forms but not in spirits. Families were much more autonomous than that fifty years ago. In Tingvoong families remained same as found by Siiger in 1949 i. e., an admixture of nuclear, extended and the joint (Gowloog, *op. cit.*). Das found majority of the Lepcha families in Darjeeling to be of nuclear type; next in order was stem family i.e., minimal extended family. The next major type of family was extended which consisted of full-fledged family of orientation and family of procreation. The Lepcha families move on cyclic order from nuclear to vertical, lateral or vertico-lateral extended types having the starting point of nuclear one. The cause of this circulation are internal and external. A rise in size of the family leads to mismanagement of both internal and external affairs of the household resulting into smaller family units and the comparative economic independence and cash money have played a definite role in causing such changes. Alternation in the circumstantial behaviour has loosened the kinship tie. Majority of the Lepcha families are small and medium sized. Very big sized families are less in occurrence. The residential patterns are patrilocal neolocal, and in some cases matri-patrilocal (Das, *op. cit.*, 101-102).

Many old Lepchas reported to Subba about their traditional 'double descent' where the sons trace their descent through their fathers and the daughters from their mothers. But at present they have strong patrilineal descent called *ptsho* (Subba, *op. cit.* : 123).

After family the next social unit based on blood is the *agit* (may be termed as clan/sib following the definitions of the authorities who are in favour of using this type of nomenclature) among the Lepchas of Darjeeling District. Das has found in most of the Lepcha areas of Darjeeling District, the members of an *agit* acknowledge a traditional bond of common descent in the paternal line. Here the sons and daughters are both associated with father's *agit* i.e., *agit* name descends from father to sons and daughters.

But in some interior villages of Kurseeng on the other hand, a daughter gets her mother's *agit* and a son his father's. In other words it may be stated that the descent of *agit* here is unilineal in nature but sex linked in character. Now-a-days sex-linked character of *agit* is generally diminishing. This is mainly due to the influence of neighbouring communities like Nepali Hindus as also Christians who give absolute prominence to father's line only. This is further added by the impact of urban influence (Das, *op. cit* : 103-104).

The Lepcha kinship terms are overwhelmingly of classificatory nature, though a few denotative terms are also used. Subba has very rightly pointed out,

> 'since the organization of group is related to the need for the exploitation of nature for food these terms indicate the necessity of kin organization necessity to work in groups for hunting, roaming in dense forests for collecting food' (Subba, *op. cit.* : 123).

After analysing the Lepcha kin terms that are in use in the areas of Darjeeling District Das found that the kinship terms of the Lepcha are not large in number, rather these are very limited in each generation. Different types of kinsmen are grouped under a few broad kin terms (Das, *op. cit* : 115). Gowloog states that kinship structure has not changed much in Lingthem of Dzongu in North Sikkim.

The Lepchas are in endogamous community but deviations occurred in many cases. There were large number of cases of the Bhutia males marrying the Lepcha females. That mainly took place during the Tibetan rule in this region. But very few Lepcha boys have been found to marry the Bhutia girls. Many Lepchas girls, especially from Darjeeling, were also married with the Bengalees and the Anglo-Indians but none from these communities is reported to have married into the Lepcha society. Looks, family and socio-economic background play an important role in choosing a partner but it is religion which decides their preference to day (Subba, *op.cit.* : 121-122).

The Lepchas are monogamous though polygamy is allowed. In Lingdong and other villages of Dzongu, especially upper Dzongu, the frequency of polygamy is more. Inheritance of either brother's widow and sharing of elder brother's wife by younger brothers without being married to her is present in Dzongu but absolutely absent in Kalimpong and other areas of Darjeeling District. It is mainly due to the fact that surplus land is available in plenty in Dzongu (Ghosal, *op. cit*).

However, Subba states that the traditional form of Lepcha marriage is considered by many to be polygamy but earlier authors have noted the practice of monogamy also among them...He further, comments

> "Marrying father's younger brother's wife and elder brother's wife, whether their husband being deceased or not is socially acceptable. But only two such instances were reported from Lingthem (Sikkim) in October 1987 while none from Tanek and Purbong (Darjeeling) in 1980. There are some resident son-in-laws even today in Lingthem but in Tanek and Purbong there is none" (Subba, *op. cit* : 122).

In Lingthem, where Gorer studied fifty years ago, the practice of early marriage is still prevalent to a large extent but in Tanek and Purbong villages of Kalimpong it is never to be seen except very occasionally (*op. cit* : 121). Gowloog also finds early marriage still in practice in Lingthem though late marriage (after 25 years) are becoming popular. She also finds polygamy is in decline giving way to monogamy; Levirate and sororate still practised, majority of the marriages are of negotiated elopement type i.e., elopement takes place after obtaining consent of the parents. Inter-community marriages are still rare in Dzongu though incidences of such marriages are found outside the area. While narrating situation in Tingvoong Gowloog states that presence of polygamy and polyandry was reported by Siiger but at present polygamy is found but not polyandry. Here age at marriage is at present determined not by tradition but by situation in the family.

The female's right of inheritance of landed property was still very rare in 1949, females inherit only the movable property of the family.

In the Lepcha society, elderly persons are generally choosen as members of the Panchayat.They respect an uneducated old man more than an educated young man and hence the panchayat is largely composed of old men. Formerly in each village, there was village council of their own but now-a-days in many villages, their very existence cannot be found; wherever they are found they occur in vestigeal form (Das, *op. cit* : 125). In Kalimpong the Lepchas have more or less accepted the statutory village panchayat but in Dzongu the influence of *Mondals* are still much more than that of the statutory panchayats (Ghosal, *op. cit*).

The life cycle and the rituals associated therewith of the Lepchas show the existence of traditional beliefs and practices side by side with the Buddhistic ideas, somewhere instead of total replacement there exists a blending of ideas and practices. The balanced role of *Mun Bongthing* and the Lama in different ritualistic performances of the Lepchas further strengthens this blending of two cultural values in a unified manner thereby strengthening integration in cultural as well as psychological level (Das, *op.cit* : 183).

Hermanns states that the earliest religion of the Lepchas may be termed as *animism* or *shamanism* in which the *Mun* or priestess and *Bongthing* or the priest held the centre position (Hermanns, 1954 : 46-54). Subba states,

> 'It is believed that Buddhism was first introduced in Sikkim around 1641. But it is not known exactly when the Lepchas began to accept this religion. It may only be guessed that such a process could not have begun before 1697 when the first over monastory *(Sanga)* was established in Sikkim. By the turn of eighteenth century, the horizontal spread of Buddhism among the Lepchas was complete in the sense that there was not one Lepcha who did not call himself a Buddhist by then. But the vertical spread was partial which is best indicated by the fact that it was the Buddhist Lepchas who accepted Christianity in large numbers. About 30 per cent of the Lepchas in Darjeeling and 8 per cent of them in Sikkim are Chistians today. They are in almost every sect but the Roman Catholics preponderate over others. Such Lepchas are generally more educated and urbanized than their Buddhist counterparts. The clevage between those two religious groups, is almost turning into a major crisis of their society. Such a development has, instead of making them a strong ethnic group, weakened them considerably' (Subba, *op. cit* : 126-127).

Ghosal states that the conversion of the Lepchas in Buddhism was not very deep rooted that was why it was easy to convert a Lepcha from Buddhism to Christianity. The high expenses of Buddhist rituals and Bongthings performances in the form of animal sacrifices accelerated the conversion of Darjeeling Lepchas into Christianity. The indigenous cult centred on spirits and local deities has been over laid with Tibetan Buddhism and this in turn has been challenged by Nepali Hinduism and Christianity (Ghosal, *op. cit*).

Gowloog states that ancestor worship among the Lingthem

Lepchas has been affected several due to change of crops as well as cultivators. *Mun Bongthism* has been wiped out from the realm of their religion. This is mainly due to the spread of Lamaism under the Royal patronage of the Namgyals till 1974.

But most important feature is that the form of Lamaism introduced among them was almost identical with *Mun-Bongthism* and hence easily accepted by them. Individualism and sense of sin in Lamaism have not been accepted by the Lepchas. Gowloog further states that in 1985, Subba found widening clevage between the Buddhist and Christian Lepchas but to her this clevage is yet to merge in Dzongu due to the virtual absence of the Christian Lepchas. Subba's finding of spread of Lamaism more horizontal than vertical seems to be true of Dzongu also. Had the vertical spread been significant the Lepchas would not probably embrace Christianity so easily outside Dzongu.

About the Lepchas of Tingvoong Gowloog states that *Bondism* was widely practised in 1949. Influence of Lamaism was insignificant (findings of Siiger). The period between 1949 to 1989 is very important about religious changes of the Lepchas. This period seems to have witnessed considerably disappearance of the traditional Lepcha religious figures like *Mun* and *Bongthing* and spread of Lamaism among them. In Lingthem there was only one *Bongthing* in 1989, Tingvoong still had one *Mun* and couple of *Bongthings*. It is interesting to note that in Lingthem there was renewed respect for the *Muns* and Bongthings among the youths but no such attitude was noticed in Tingvoong (Gowloog, *op. cit*).

Foning, though critical of some of the methods of Christian missionaries, gives them credit for the printing of books in the Lepcha language, and the special script developed under 1987 : XII) the sponsorship of the kings of Sikkim.

About the characteristics of the Lepcha religious beliefs and practices Das states that these present a balanced mingling of their traditional indigenous beliefs and practices as also the Lamaism, the newly adopted religion. This balanced integration i. e., the existence of these two different forces of beliefs and practices side by side with the balanced blending and smooth functioning is possible due to the nature and character of the Lepchas and their society, which is non-aggressive in nature and tolerant in character and this can be observed in different spheres of life and activities of the Lepchas. Religion of the Lepchas is no exception to that rather here the integration is more profoundly visible than in other spheres of their life (Das, *op.cit* : 215).

Ghosal observed some revivalistic movements among the

Lepcha of Sikkim as well as Darjeeling, especially current among the younger generation. Under the leadership of the Darjeeling Lepcha Association the people of Nassey village have already partially stopped the sacrifice of animals. In Pagang village too it is going to be stopped soon. As organisation named as *Mayel Nyam* in Dzongu of Sikkim has been advocating that all Lepchas should send their children to schools *(op. cit).*

Foning visited the Lingthem village in the summer of 1946 and found the Lepchas there of the same mental make-up, of the same intellectual and physical standards and following the same sets of tribal maxims as their other kinsmen outside the reserve (1987 : 254). He of course ignored the external changes taking place outside Dzongu due to westernization and education (Gowloog : *op. cit*). Siiger who conducted study in 1949 also found the similarities between the culture of the Dzongu (Tingvoong) and that of the Lepchas of Kalimpong more conspicuous than the differences (1967 : 35). Das also draws no difference between the Lepcha of Darjeeling and those of Sikkim except that the Lepchas of Darjeeling are unware of any sort of chronic sterility leading to decaying population among them (1978 : 104). Bhasin has observed some difference in ecology of the Lepcha settlements within and outside Dzongu but socially and culturally the differences were hard to point out (1989). Gowloog points out that the three major geographical distribution of the Lepchas -Kalimpong (Darjeeling). Sikkim and Ilam (Nepal) should be borne in mind. For various reasons the Lepchas of three regions have received different influences. For instance, the Lepchas of Kalimpong have considerably Christianised and westernized while those of Sikkim have greatly been Tibetanized; but those in Nepal Hinduized or Nepalized. These influences have been noted in terms of language, dress and costumes. Therefore, the detribalization of the Lepchas is multilinear due to the differences in the socio-cultural and political environments of those three major concentrations of the Lepchas.

The changes started taking place in the Lepcha life and culture since they came in contact with the Tibetans in the seventeenth century. But major changes took place after their contact with the British in the nineteenth century. As a result we saw settled cultivation, land alienation, obliteration of early marriage, religious endogamy, patriliny, spread of Nepali language, cleavage between the Buddhist and Christian Lepchas, and so forth. Almost every change in their society can be traced from the historical development that occurred after seventeenth century and particularly after nineteenth century. The forest dwelling Lepchas have considerably been changed today. The constitutional safeguards with protective and ameliorative measures and different developmental activities have helped them to improve their socio-economic and educational standards. Today many of them are placed at the highest echelons of our bureaucratic set up. A fairly good number of them prospered after migrating to many foreign countries like Nepal, Bhutan, Malayasia, Singapore, Brunei etc. In spite of this a vast section of them still remains illiterate (Subba, *op. cit* : 127-129).

The acquisition and cultural penetration of this habitat was effected partly by military conquest, partly by the amalgamation of the Lepchas with such population as the Tibetans, Nepalese and the Bhutanese. While Foning recongnizes the cultural benefits derived by the Lepchas with their contacts with Tibetan Buddhism, he emphasizes the disastrous results of the Nepalese immigration, and particularly the destruction of forests by the newly settled cultivators (*op. cit* : xii).

The Lepchas of today should not be viewed as a tribal group living in isolation but they should be considered as a reacting community within the broader framework of Indian civilization. Ghosal has observed recently of some efforts on their part to maintain their ethnic and cultural distinctiveness but this will be difficult to achieve until and unless the land, the core element of their economy is allowed to be retained by them. Modernization of their agriculture to give them a better sustenance and proper land management may perhaps help them to regain their ethnic pride and confidence *(op.cit)*.

The discussions in the foregoing pages, provide an overall profile of the Lepchas, a scheduled tribe of the lower Himalayan region, in time and space perspective, possessing some unique characteristics of their own. They are the glaring example of change and continuity of a culture.

References

Bhasin, Veena 1989 *Ecology, Culture and Change : Tribals of Sikkim Himalayas.* New Delhi : Inter India Publications.

Campbell, Archibald 1840 "Note on the Lepchas of Sikkim with a vocabulary of their language," *Journal of the Asiatic Society of Bengal,* IX Part 1,

Dalton, Edward Tuite 1872 *A Descriptive Ethnology of Bengal.* Calcutta : Office of the Superintendent of Government Printing.

Das, A. K. and S. K. Banerjee 1962 *The Lepchas of Darjeeling District.* Calcutta Tribal Welfare Department, Govt. of West Bengal.

Das, A. K. 1978 *The Lepchas of West Bengal.* Calcutta : Editions Indian.

Donaldson, Florence 1900 *Lepcha Land or Six Week in the Sikkim Himalayas.* London : Sampson, Low, Marston.

Foning, A. R. 1987 *Lepcha : My Vanishing Tribe* New Delhi : Sterling.

Ghosal, Sumit 1990 The Lepchas of Darjeeling and Sikkim, a study in cultural ecology and social change (an unpublished Thesis).

Gorer Geoffrey 1938 *Himalayan Village : an Account of the Lepchas of Sikkim.* London : Joseph. (reprinted 1967).

Gowloog, Roshina 1991 Lingthem After Fifty Years (A Diachronic Study of a Lepcha Village in Dzongu, North-Sikkim), an unpublished Thesis.

Grierson, George 1927 *Linguistic Survey of India,* Vol. III. Tibeto-Burman Family.

Hermanns, Matthias Fr. 1954 *The Indo-Tibetans : The Indo-Tibetan and Mongoloid Problem in the Southern Himalaya and North-East India* : Bombay K. L. Fernandes.

Hodgson, Brian H. 1847 On the Aborigines of the Sub-Himalayas. *Journal of the Asiatic Society of Bengal.* Vol. XVI.

Hooker, Joseph Dalton 1855 *Himalayan Journals : Note of a Naturalist in Bengal, the Sikkim and Nepal Himalayas, the Khasia Mountains etc.* London : Murray, 2 Vols.

Hunder, William Watson 1968 *A Comparative Dictionary of the Languages of India and High Asia : with a Dissertation based on the Hodgsonlists, Official Records and Mass.* London : Trubner.

Karan, Pradyumna P. & Jenkins, William M. 1963 *The Himalayan Kingdom : Bhutan, Sikkim and Nepal.* Princeton Van Nostrand.

Latham, Robert Gordon 1859 *Descripive Ethnology. Vol. J. Eastern and Northern Asia-Europe/London* : Van Voorst.

Macfarlane, Elden W. Erlanson 1937 Eastern Himalayan Blood Groups. *Man.* XXXVII.

Mainwaring, George 1876 *A Grammar of the Rong (Lepcha) Language*

Byers *as it exists in the Darjeeling and Sikkim Hill.* Calcutta : Baptist Mission Press.

Morris, John 1938 *Living with Lepchas : a Book about the Sikkim Himalayas,* London Heinemann.

Nakane, Chie 1966 *A Plural Society in Sikkim Caste and Kin in Nepal, India and Ceylon,* ed. Christoph Von Furer Haimendorf. Bombay : Asia Publishing House.

Namgyal Thutoband 1908 History of Sikkim. Jr. Lama Dawa

Jeshay Dolma Kazisamdup (unpublished-in Press).

Nebesky Wojkowitch, 1951 Ancient Funeral ceremonies of the Lepchas

Rene Von *The Eastern Anthropologist,* Vo. I, No. 1.

1953 Hunting and Fishing Among the Lepchas, *Ethnos,* XVIII, Nos. 1-2.

1954 A report on Ethnographical Research with Sikkim Himalayas, 1950-1953, *Wiener Volkekundilche Mitteolungen* II No. 1.

Nebesky-Wejkowitch, 1951 The Use of Thread Crosses in Lepcha Lam-

Revevon, and Gorer, G. aist Ceremonies, *The Eastern Anthropologist.* IV, No. 2.

Neethivanan, J. 1967 A Note on Investigations among the Lepchas ed. Datta Gupta J. *Census of India 1961, Vol. XVI (West Bengal and Sikkim)* Part V-A Govt. of India Press.

Risley, Herbert Hope 1891 *The Tribes and Castes of Bengal : Ethnographic glossary.* Bengal Secretariat Pressl. Vols. 2.

1896 History of Sikkim, Appendix II of the *Journal of the Buddhist Text Society of India,* IV.

Rock Joseph F. 1953 Excerpts from a History of Sikkim, *Anthropos.* XLVIII.

Schermann, L. 1926 Ethnographisches aus Sikkim *Der Eraball.* F.

Siiger, Halfdan, 1967 *The Lepchas : Culture and Religion of a Himalayan People.* Part I and II National Museum Ethnographic Srs., Vol. II, Pt., I, Copenhagen.

Stock, C. de Beauvoir	1925	Folklore and Customs of the Lepchas of Sikkim, *Journal and proceedings of the Asiatic Society, of Bengal,* (New series) XXI, No. 4.
Subba, T. B.	1985	The Lepchas : From Legends to the Present Day, *Religion and Society,* 32 (2).
	1989	Dynamics of Hill Society : A case study of the Lepchas. *Journal of Social and Economic Studies,* New series, First Issue.
Thakur R. N.	1988	*Himalayan Lepchas,* New Delhi : Archaives Publishers.
Thakur, R. N. and S. W. Lepcha	1981	Who are the Lepchas. *The Eastern Anthropologists* 34 (3).
Tshering, G	1971	*Lapche Jatiko Sankhipta Parichay,* (In Nepali) Darjeeling : Shyam Brothers.
Waddell, Lawrence Austine	1899	*Among the Himalayas,* London : Constable.
White, J. Claude	1909	*Sikkim and Bhutan : 21 Years on the North East Frontier, 1887-1908,* New York : Longmans, Green.

R.M. Sarkar

UNDERSTANDING MAN OF THE HEART A LOOK INTO THE CULTURAL TRADITIONS OF THE BAULS

I

Man is the Unique creation in the world. Efforts have been made by the man himself to focus discernible light, at different times, on the nature and extent of man. He tried his level best to explore the integrated perspective of human achievements. Sometimes he became successful, at other times he failed to explain the very mysteries encircling man. Thus total understanding of man by man has become problematic and the understandable man has been left to himself. But man does never remain uncared for; his thought—pattern and activity—oriented life has been deeply analysed and categorically explained by some devoted groups of people whose life and activities are processed through a particular sentiment that is highly influenced by inartificial love for humanity. This particular community is known by the term Bauls. The Bauls represent a particular community which highlight the specific portrait of the rich cultural heritage of the traditional land and people of Bengal. They are specially recognized as the community of singers which move about in the vast open areas of the Nature and sing melodiously in the praise of man. It is their speciality and at this point the Bauls differ from all other human communities of the world which have got traditional perspectives characterized by artful activities.

The Bauls represent the folk tradition of Bengal. The subject matters of their thinking and specific nature of their behaviour—patterns are all influenced by the air and water of Bengal. The soil of Bengal gives them the requisite impetus to devote their body and mind at the feet of that man who is at the top of everything. It is very difficult to reach him because of the fact that this man could only be approached if there develops an inartificial searching mentality, a deep-based devotion towards the man in question. The Bauls are the traditional searcher of this particular man. They believe that this man lives in the hearts of every individual and here the man concerned is seen in the highest esteem. The Bauls are the worshippers of that particular man who resides in the hearts. Baul philosophy is specifically oriented centering round the Man of the Heart[1]—he is the Soul's Companion or *maner manus*. Through his various experience the Baul believes that this Man of the Heart can be understood by means of subjective understanding. It is very difficult to come in line with this very understanding. In order to reach this state of perfection it is necessary to pass through a number of ordeals both in spiritual as well as in material levels. The Baul in always busy all through his life and work in the eternal quest for the Ultimate Reality. This Ultimate Reality is known as the Supreme Beloved. When a Baul can reach this state of perfection to acquire a practical knowledge about the Supreme Beloved, he can gather the adequate knowledge for understanding the Man of the Heart. The attempts for realization of the Ultimate Being is in other words the self-realization. From the long time past the Baul has been in the deep search of himself. The particular comprehensive pattern of human self gives vent to the realization of the Divine Self. When these two spheres meet a unique perspective is brought to light in which is seen a broad-based reflection of the total man. It is the Man for whose quest the Bauls have stated their long-term journey through the ages.

The Bauls present the subject matter of tremendous surprise. From the remote past they have been attracting the attention of many people belonging to various spheres of life. The Bauls are the products of the rural society of Bengal. All of them have come from the peasant society and for this reason they share the very philosophy of peasant community of the particular landmass. The Bauls are always alert to keep themselves aloof from the society within which they move about and perform various activities. But, it is to be mentioned that, they are not detached completely from the society—they love the land and show profound respect to the people as the Baul philosophy is rooted to the inartificial love for the mankind as a whole.

The Baul Cult, which is centralised on love and respect for humanity, has been developed through the interactions of diversified thoughts and ideas. These traditional worshippers of man behave in such a way which runs unparallel to any existing thinking pattern of the world and here lies the essence of the Baul thinking and understanding. Love is given the supreme position in the Baul cult which attains the highest order of the society and culture. This feeling of love has been originated from the core of the heart and which tries to embrace all the human beings of the world. Love for mankind signifies the basic background of the Baul line of thinking. Love is regarded as eternal—it is divine. Without this love human life in the world cannot be flourished properly. When love vanishes, human society becomes disorganised. Thus the Bauls move through the hills and dales, forests and open fields, and through the village paths in search of this love. And when they find it necessary to implant this love in the inner recess of man they do it with full devotion. It is to be noted that the social and religious life of the Bauls are not guided by any conventional social customs and religions rituals. The religion of the Bauls does not aim at the collective observance of rituals worship of images and the like or individual performance of religious procedure where god is conceived to be inside the human body. The Baul philosophy is based on the idea that god resides in each human being. On this ground the total emphasis is given on the individual human being. It is anticipated that the individual human being should dedicated himself at the feet of the Ultimate Reality through deep-based effort for making himself fit to prepare his body and mind for the purpose of self-realization.

Liberation of the soul is regarded as the most important concept in the Baul Cult. They are the staunch believers in the line that until and unless the knowledge of Truth is procured through the God's grace liberation of the soul is not effected. The precious moment of mystic union of the self with the Supreme Being brings the divine level of enjoyment and the world becomes pulsated with heavenly delight. It is a rare event but it must be done for the welfare of the human communities with all these sentiments the Bauls have devoted themselves for the cause of the humanity. They think for man, work for man and live for man.

II

The very word 'Baul' means mad. The Sanskritic derivation of the term Baul is 'vatula' which indicates madness. The Hindi variant of this term is 'Baura' or the person having incoherent behaviour. This particular term is seen to be extensively used in the western part of rural Bengal in the day to day conversation. As the Bauls possess this particular type of incoherent behaviour and behave differently from the people of rural societies, they have been termed as 'Baura'. It is more probable that the word Baul has come from Baura i. e. the group of people who have developed out and out indifference to the worldly affairs. The Baul is characterized by great antiquity. In the ancient literatures and religious texts this word i. e. Baul has been largely used. In the *Krishnavijay* written by Sri Maladhar Basu the word Baul was used, first of all, to indicate the behaviour—pattern of a particular person. Sri Krishna Das Kaviraj in his *Chaitannya Charitamrita* profusely used the word Baul to highlight the nature of the devotees for the grace of the Lord. He mentioned Sri Gouranga as an eminent Baul. In some other ancient books also the term Baul has been indiscriminately used to signify the craziness or madness of the persons.

The Bauls follows well-organised patterns of *sadhana* or meditation in order the understand the self. This self is above the human self, which is regarded as the finite menifestations of divine self. The spiritual realization of the Bauls is attained only when the human self annihilates and the body remains above the physical sensation. This leads to the melting away of the human self into the divine self. The *sadhana*[2] of the Bauls is specifically characterized by sexo-Yogic practices which are not only complicated but also unique in the sphere of meditational activities. The Baul accepts the female consort as the *sadhika*.[3] Both of them must be purified by ritualistic procedures and the body should be the ideal one for the endurance of the austere practices. The mind must be completely controlled so that any base passion does not work. The *sadhana* is centred round the successful attempt of making complete control over the body and sense organs and total control over the breathing system. In order reach the total success, there must be a long term practice. The Baul *sadhaka*[4] acquires full command over the sexual practices through a continuous process of painstaking procedure; it is through this he can withdraw the semen at the extreme moment of sexual intercourse and thereby throws it back in the upward direction. It is a very secret act and each and every Baul must develop it as an honourable act. Then there is the special cult known as ritual of 'Four moons'. At the particular stage of *sadhana* this ritual must be performed by the Bauls, otherwise it will be difficult for them to enter into the domain of the traditional Baul cult. This very ritual is meant for purifying the body and mind to fit these with the deep sense of meditation. The 'four moons' signify the four essential elements of human body; these are semen, menstrual flow, stool and urine. On the specific day during long term meditation the ceremony of the "piercing of the four moons", popularly known as *Charichan draved*[5] is held. During this the *sadhaka* and the *sadhika* exchange these four elements between each other in such a way that one cuts across the other. This indicates the acquirement of perfect body and mind to win over all the worldly affairs relating to body and mentality. On performing this particular performance the *sadhaka* and the *sadhika* reach at the level where sexual desire vanishes, and they develop a particular pattern where there grows out a perfect sort of purified love of divine nature. At the last stage of the ritual of *Charichandaved* the *sadhaka* and the *sadhika* understand the basic nature of purified love and through the help of which they can reach the metaphysical state of tranquillity.

The Baul *sadhana* is Guru[6] oriented. The Guru or the Preceptor is the person who can lead the individual Baul to the realm of *sadhana*. In Baul philosophy Guru is held in the highest position. The Guru acts as the mediator between the man and the Absolute. The Bauls conduct the most hazardous journey to the Absolute and here the Guru works as the path-finder because of the fact that the Guru has got the ability to show the correct way to reach the realm of Man. In Indian society Guru is always held in high esteem, so also the Bauls. But the Bauls look at the Guru in a somewhat diffferent way.

The Guru in not God or a part of God; he is Spiritual guide to deal in clearing the darkness of ignorance and imperfect feeling that develop in the mind of man. The essence of the Baul philosophy pin-points the idea that cloud of ignorance covers up the sense organs which resist in doing perfect acts and thus the persons are distracted. This situation is unfortunate and it can be overcomed through the direct assistance of Guru. The individual Baul depends upon his own capacity and ability for the conduct of his *sadhana* but he cannot deny the fact that his actual success for acquiring the perfectness in *sadhana* lies on the help and active cooperation of the Guru. Whithout blessings from the Guru the Baul cannot proceed forward. The Baul life and *sadhana* are dedicated to the feet of man. The propitiation of man is the essence of the Baul philosophy. The Bauls attach highest value to the human body, which is conceived by them as the macrocosm of the universe. The Bauls draw analogy between the human body and the Universe. They think that the human body is the abode of all sense and truth. It is the sacred seat of Ultimate Reality. The body is inevitable for *sadhana* and this body is the abode of God. The basic elements constituting the body are thought to be the sky, earth, water, fire and water. In Baul understanding the body is viewed from two different angles and these are material and physiological. The body is composed of materials of diverse nature, and most of the time this materialistic body is compared with cage, boat, building and similar phenomena. This material body is subject to destruction at any moment and, therefore, it is advised to try to achieve the ultimate realization without delay. The physiological concept of the body is centred round the complicated idea on the rearrangement and functions of the plexuses with the special references to the main three vital nerves—*Ida*[7], *Pingala*[8] and *Susumna*.[9]

Like the body, the mind is also given prime importance. The Bauls believe that all spiritual life is rooted to the mind. The mind is regarded by them as the instrument of action in the full sense of the term. The sun-moon theory or the Surya-*soma talttwa* is the basic conceptual theory which is extensively followed by the Bauls. This particular theory indicates the following principles. The sun represents *prana* which may be individual or cosmic. It represents the vital force of the cosmic energy. *Soma* stands for moon. It indicates mind or *Ida* of the human body. Sun is the essential factor for energy, activity and vitality, whereas moon is meant for sustenance. The full control of the mind is an essential part of *sadhana* for which the Bauls move forward. In order to arrive at the climax of metaphysical attainment it is required the mind must be well trained to throw away the worldly pleasures, The *Rupa* and *Swarupa* concept is based on a significant principle in the way of life and philosophy of the Bauls. *Rupa* indicate the physical form and beauty of men and women, whereas the *Swarupa* signifies the spiritual form and sublime activities. The spiritual nature is dwelt in the physical form and former is always existent in an unrealized state. The attempt of understanding of the spiritual nature through physical existence forms the core of the Baul *sadhana*. The divine self is manifested in the human self, and in order to understand the true nature of divine self the *sadhana* must proceed through the human self. *Swarupa* is manifested in *Rupa* and *Swarupa* can properly be understood only through the keen analysis of *Rupa*. *Rupa* stand for gross existence and *Swarupa* signifies the divine existence. *Rupa* relates to the finite manifestation of the infinite *Swarupa*. This *Rupa-Swarupa* concept helps the Bauls to transform gross love into divine love. Ultimately it is seen that the *Rupa*, in the long run, fuses with the *Swarupa* and there remains no basic difference between the two.

In Baul *sadhana* the worldly love between men and women as well as six passions have been attached considerable importance. It is accepted that the purified and divine love is raised from the gross love. The gross love is a passion when the human beings desire for complete union with the lover and in this activity the hunger for sex union dominates. In this domain of love, the frantic passion leads to the sexual activities based on the bodily union of the male and female and from which worldly pleasure in drawn. In Baul philosophy this pattern of sexual union is accepted, and they cannot deny that there is an eternal pleasure in this type of union. At this particular sphere of thinking the Bauls run in line with the Freudian concept that sex activities are the basic phenomena of human life. Freud tried to establish the fact that the desire for sexual activities gives shapes to marry human social and cultural thinking patterns. The Bauls do not deny it, but they differ from the Freudian physiology when they think of the sexual desires beyond the worldly affairs. The Baul philosophy surpasses the activities of bodily enjoyment through sexual activities and ultimately react the domain of divine love.

III

The Bauls as a whole can be distinguished into two types—the Ascetic Bauls[10] and the Domestic Bauls.[11] The Ascetic Bauls are very keen in observing the rules and regulations of the Baul way of life in a rigid pattern. They are specifically devoted to maintain the particular philosophical perspectives assigned to the Bauls. But the Domestic Bauls do not follow the rules rigidly as are done by their counterparts in the Ashrama. But mention should be made that many of them try their level best to follow it, at least the basic instructions of the Baul traditions and any sort of failure in following the regulations is regarded as their utter inability conditioned by their life with so many obligations.

The Ascetic Bauls take initiation in the line of *sannyasa* and lead the life of ascetic mendicancy. An Ascetic Baul is to stay in any *ashram*[12] either established by himself or in the *ashram* by others. These *ashrams* are found to be sprung up in the rural setting. At a solitary place, just at the outskirt of the village and surrounded by green vegetation the *ashram* depicts an ideal picture of devotional life and activities. In this *ashram* the Bauls and other ashramites are to maintain their living through *madhukari*[13] or celebrated begging. The *ashrams* are represented by mud-built and strawthatched houses which are constructed following the traditional patterns of the rural Bengal villages. A visitor to these *ashrams* will be highly impressed by the silence and sanctity of the whole surroundings and also by multicoloured flowers in the carefully grown flower garden in the vicinity of the *ashrama*. The ashramites must follow a disciplinary way of life all through the time. In the *ashram* there are regular observances of ceremonies relating to the pattern of thinking and path of adoration. Besides these annual festivals are also observed to celebrate the foundation day of the *ashram*, the birth day of the founder and the like. The people belonging to all castes, classes and religious groups are free to attend these ceremonies and have a look to the different items of festivals. These cermonies are known by the term *mahotsab* or great festival. At this time all are cordially invited to take *prasad*[14] which is to be taken by sitting in a row without maintaining any restriction of caste and creed. The ashramites collect contributions mostly in kinds from the villagers. Some *ashrams* have got rent-free agricultural lands from the income of which the *mahotsabs*[15] are arranged.

In these *ashrams* an air of sacred discussions, sometimes of high philosophical levels, love and respect for mankind always prevail. During leisure hours the villagers, mostly agriculturists, come to there *ashrams* habitually and have free exchange of talks with the ashramites. The villagers possess a reverential attitude towards these *ashrams* and there is a custom in many localities to offer the first *arhi*[16] full of paddy to the village *ashram* at the time of measuring the harvest in the barn. In addition to this, the villagers are under the obligation to contribute their mite to the *ashram* authorities during the marriage ceremony and other allied social customs performed in their houses. The ashramites, in their turn, look into the occasional devotional performances that are held in the individual houses. These are the occasions when the villagers seek direct help from the ashramites in solving many of their problems, especially related to the spiritual affairs. In this way a close link exists between the Baul *ashram* and the villages and through mutual understanding there develops an amicable background which helps in flourishing the spiritual life on the village in the strict sense of the term.

On the other side of the picture, it is seen that the Domestic Bauls do not necessarily live in the *ashrams*. It may be the fact that during their long tour for *madhukari* or attending any kind of socio-ritual festivals they may take shelter in the *ashrams* but they strictly follow the familial life. They live in the full-fledged family of procreation. Very often these familes are called as *grihastha ashrams* i. e. the family hermitage. Almost all of them are to look after the family and, therefore, regular income is essential for them. They are to haunt for money and other allied materials for the maintenance of their families.

The Baul community is the outcome of the close integration of diversified religious thoughts. They are neither the Hindus nor the Muslims. It is to be noted that the people belonging to different castes, classes and communities have come under the influence of the Baul life. From a close set survey of the phenomenon it is seen that the heterogeneous groups of people have come together through the clarion call of a particular philosophy of love and mutual understanding. The trend of activities of the Bauls indicates a close resemblance of this community with the Buddhist *Tantra*, Hindu *Tantra* and the Vaishnavas. Sometimes their very mode of thinking dates back to the Pre-vedic period. The Bauls have got specific resemblances with the Sufis. The life and thought of the Sufis are against all religious formalities. They are of opinion that the ritualistic performances work as the barriers between man and god. The God is to be realized as the Absolute and He can be understood only through love. It is the true love which brings man nearer the God. The ultimate realization of the Absolute is known as the *Fana* state of life when total annihilation of the individual existence results. It corresponds to the idea of *jyante-mara*[17] or death in the living state as conceived by the Bauls. According to the sufistic idea, the God is the real Truth in the Universe. He is not only marked by eternal *Truth* but also by endless *Love*. It is the ultimate aim of everybody to have this divine love. The purpose of propitiation of God is to be one with Him and to feel the impulse of extreme delight that come out of the celebrated union. This is the main principle of Sufistic idea and the Bauls corroborate this particular thinking pattern.

The Baul sentiment is largely dominated by the Indian folk tradition, rather than any religious perspective. It is rooted to the very ancient folk culture characterised by a particular philosophy based on the love for humanity. This folk tradition might have originated in the hoary past and assimilated many thoughts and ideas of various socio-religious sentiments during its journey through time.

IV

The Baul tradition is specifically expressive through large number of songs sung by them. In these songs there is total reflection of the Baul sentiment and philosophical standpoint. These songs are said to be the mirrors through which the overall reflections of the Baul life are to be seen clearly. The Baul life and thinking are highly characterized by the expression of various ideas on the total behaviour-patterns of the Bauls are based. But most of the time these expressions are made through indirect perspective. The songs bear double meaning—one is external and the other is internal. The songs not only give shelter to diverse philosophical understanding but also act as the store house of various evidences of social interactions that have been taking place through the ages. The Baul songs have got distinctive speciality. These songs are not only characterised by the presence of vast amount of materials relating to the complicated way of thinking of the Bauls, but also melodious turing and ideal presentation of these songs brings the listeners to the highest level of performance. The Baul songs play the essential role in bridging up the gap between them and the public. The popularity of this particular community lies principally on their melodious songs. The impact of these songs on the mind of the public is conspicuous. These songs emphatically nourish and bear the rich—cultural heritage of this part of the country. Therefore, the life of the Bauls cannot be properly evaluated without putting due importance to these songs.

These songs are presented through the playing of a number of specially made musical instruments which are indigenous in nature. The most common form of instruments are *ektara, dotara, dugi, anadalahari* or *gabgubi* and *sarinda*. These are very often used by the singers during their performance. The instruments are indigenously prepared and are always constituted by the local raw materials. These are made and repaired by themselves. There are of course, some indigenous experts who look into the technical side of the instruments. The instruments are considered by them as the life force of their *sadhana*, the principal part of which is centralised on the presentation of songs i.e. honour of the Man of the Heart. The offerings of songs, they think, must be made from the very core of the heart by sincere appeal, and the instruments through which the songs get animation should be provided with due sacredness and genuineness. It is due to this fact the Bauls take all possible care to maintain the sanctity of the instrument used during the song recital. The Baul song has two different points of view—one is the special tuning and the peculiar mode of presentation and the other one signifies its literary value and lyricism. The Baul songs have got a common central theme and most of the time these are devotional in character. If one analyses the general theme of these, one will see that it is of three types—(a) there are indication of reaching the particular goal (b) these specify the diverse difficulties that are to be faced by the followers of this spiritual path, and (c) these show the ways to overcome the difficulties. Besides these there is a clear covering of ritualistic and humanistic feature of thinking. Most of the time these songs have got high literary value and provided with multiple meaning. Moreover various patterns or interactions of various religious faiths and traditions are seen to be reflected in these songs.

The Baul songs have got specialities of their own. These songs are so neatly composed and so beautifully presented that these leave a prominent impression in the inner recess of the hearts of the people. The long drawn struggle among the three sects of the Hindu—the Sakta, Vaishnava and Saiva—has been washed away by the Baul philosophy. There are a large number of songs in which the Bauls communicate their earliest desire to ward off the artificial barriers that have been developed on meaningless ground. At times the Bauls to against it through their songs—the heavily conflicting attitudes that are seen amongst the various religious faiths like Hinduism, Islamism and Christianity. Social stratifications as have been developed through castes and classes go against the Baul line of thinking. The Bauls learn to adore the Man of the Heart through the presentation of songs. This Man of the Heart is unique in himself. He is far away from differentiation—he cannot be brought under any sort of artificial barrier created by man. All the people are tied together in a close unit of divine relationship. It is to be felt and thereby honoured. Thus the Bauls always inspire, especially through their songs, the people to establish brotherly feeling in their minds at the time of dealing with any human being. Universal brotherhood is the motto of the Bauls and some of their songs directly reflect their particular line of thought.

The dance is regarded as the integral part of the Baul song. The body of the Baul is subject to various movements during the presentation of songs. The movement is conditioned by rhythmic circulation of the different bodily parts and the whole process is characterized by a particular idealistic procedure which is entirely personal to the Bauls. Through these rhythmic movements the Baul singer finds its easy to place his cordial appeal at the feet of the Man of the Heart. An individual Baul is expert in the joint presentation of song and dance with the playing of musical instruments by taking no help from anybody. The dance is conducted through rigid procedures and everything is based on technical perspective.

In these features the Bauls no doubt represent the typical features in rural Bengal. They are conspicuous not only in the manner of living but also bear speciality in their dress and other related make up of the body.

The Bauls have special reverence for their songs and dances. These are regarded by them as blossoms of the forests. The general devotees belonging to the different classes and communities pluck these flowers and thereby pay homage to the deities—the Baul songs are dedicated to the feet of the Ultimate

Being with sincerity and devotion. The main aim of singing and dancing is to submit oneself in the propitiation of the Ultimate Being though they outwardly engage these in asking alms from the general public. Baul songs are so delicately composed that these focus dual meaning. The internal theme of these songs is deep-rooted where a high psycho-philosophical horizon is categorically opened, but this becomes out of reach of the common people. They enjoy only the outward general meaning of the songs that are sung so elegantly to the accompaniment of rhythmic *anandalahari* and sometimes *ektara* which change the whole atmosphere of the surroundings. The flow of sound that emits from the especially designed *anandalahari* really oscillates the mind of the general people and when it is accompanied by the highly specialized tone of the Bauls, characterized by sudden ups and downs, the audience are held spell-bound.

V

India is well-known to the world as a land of diversities, and it is their contrariety which gave her a conpicuous position to the global perspective. The life-ways and thought-ways of the people of India are specifically conditioned by compromise and tolerance, and there is always a sense of accommodation and mutual understanding. India is characterised as a country of variegated religion and in this regard this country proves itself unparallel in the world. But it has become a very delicate issue in the socio-political life of the country. In the recent past, religious feuds had taken place which stirred the length and breadth of the country. In reality it was the direct effect of some sorts of misunderstandings amongst the various religious groups. Of late, it has been felt by the scholars, administrators and politicians that an integrated pattern of religious sentiments is to be implanted in this country for smooth running of the societies with diversified though patterns and philosophy of life.

It is to be noted that the Baul community in Bengal is the living embodiment of religious integration. The philosophy of these people is specifically influenced by love for humanity where there is no difference between various human groups. The Bauls are regarded as the representatives of a particular community which has been found through the direct and indirect interactions of ritualistic and cultural traditions through the ages. It has been observed in the different scholarly studies that the Bauls are nothing but the products of diverse religious interactions which reached its culmination during the Buddhist influence through the length and breadth of the then Bengal. The Buddhist beliefs and ideas that have permeated the life-ways and thought-ways of the emerging community, known as the Bauls, faced certain new modes of behaviour when the Vaishnavite rulers became the dominating figures in the country. The phenomenon in question resulted in the deep rooted interactions between two sets of valves, and remarkable clashes and conflicts had been the ultimate result which, in course of time, led to the trends of cohesion and compromise. The impact of Muslim rulers and their religion brought terrific influence on the life and living of the people and it also infiltrated into the life and activities of the Bauls.

In this integrated perspective the Bauls try to understand man—the centre of their life long effort to recognise the Ultimate Reality. Thus the Baul sings—

"If you would be a man
then seach out man
    and adore him
O Kshepa[18] continue the daily worship
    at the feet of this man".
Man exists in man
Man exists in sense
Man gets birth and dies out
Look at him through your eyes.

The Bauls understand man in this way. Man is the subject of veneration—his essence of *sadhana*. It is not always easy to reach man. There are many steps to arrive at the threshold of the so-called temple of man.

The Baul is against any form of caste discrimination and for this reason he does not believe in the traditional social stratification of the age-old Indian society. The Baul philosophy is centred round the idea of equality of man not only in India but throughout the world. They believe that the human body with all its precious elements is unique in itself and no society has got any authority to make any sort of differentiation in this domain. Man is in no sense characterised by inequality. In course of his observation on the behaviour-pattern of the general people in the traditional society the Baul pin-points the futility of discrimination according to caste and religion. The Baul presents his partinent question through song—

"Oh my mind there is no justification in the
    caste discrimination

On opening the *puranas* You will find only one
caste known as man.
Purusha[19] and *Prakriti*[20] are the two distinctive
human divisions
They why is so conspicuous eagerness in veda,
Bible, Quaran to prove such differentiation ? Caste in man is never affected by the taking of food Brahmin cannot be recognized only by
examinig sacred thread.
Chacha (uncle) can be recognized by seeing
his beard
Then how would we able to recognize
Chachi (aunt) ?
God, Kali, Ram, Allah reside in church, temple,
shrine and mosque
Rites, rituals, *Jumma, rojah* all are same
Jarusalem, Mecca, Puri, *pani,* water all
indicate the water proper
Thakurdas says, then, on the baseless ground
Why are you quarreling each other ?"

From the remote past period the Bauls have been putting resistance to such behaviour patterns like inequality in human beings. It is highly objectionable to them because of the fact that they can not think man as higher and lower, touchable and untouchable. If the God resides in the inner recess of hearts of each and every person then how a person can be untouchable. If the theory of untouchability is accepted and supported accordingly then it would be the direct insult to the God Himself. Is it desirable to do it ? This partinent question has been raised by the Bauls.

The Bauls are not idol worshippers. Their homage to the deities is not done according to the conventional ways. They do not go to the temples, mosques and churches to have the celebrated *darsan* of the deities. They also do not find any basic difference in various religious sentiments. Rather, they dedicate themselves for religious integration. They try to enter into the central theme of various religious beliefs for understanding the essence of the total religious sentiments. On the basis of their long course of travel through this path they have been able to comprehend the unity of thinking and parallelism of intention in all the religious faiths and beliefs in the world. It is for this reason the Bauls have been engaged in a continuous search for that specific address where all the barriers and prejudices of religious sentiments have been totally dissolved through reciprocal understanding and give and take mentality constituting a specific phenomenon what is known as the religion of man.

On this situation the Baul sings—

> "In order to find out that
> particular shop
> I have become all along impatient
> As I want to find out that holy place
> Where Allah, Hari, Ram, Kali, God
> are engaged in dining in a common plate".

The Bauls are not only the traditional searchers of this celebrated spot where all the religious sentiments have been fused to form concerted whole but also on the basis which they preach the phenomenon of universal brotherhood. The Bauls go the extent of saying global fraternity—a very rare thinking pattern amongst the traditional human communities of the world. People of the world, according to the Bauls, irrespective of nationality, language, religion, customs and belief patterns are tied together in a common sentiment; all are men and this is their one and only recognition. They should evaluate themselves in a brotherly feeling. There must be a mentality of global harmony and if it can be established, the world would be a permanent shelter of eternal peace and continuous happiness. The best creation of the world-man-would live in highest esteem and glorified temperament.

NOTES

1. The ideal of the Baul philosophy. The body of man is regarded as the sacred seat of the Absolute who is beyond the unstanding through the implication of knowledge and intellect. This absolute can be perceived only through deep-based enquiry of the mind.
2. It is a course of spiritual practice which can be achieved through well defined rigid producers.
3. The female meditator who substantially help her male counterpart in maintaining mendicant life.
4- The male mendicant dedicated to the Baul way of thinking and who follows systematic principles.

5. An essential rite in the domain of the Baul *sadhana*. It means the piercing of the 'four moons' i. e. the four essential elements of the body—semen, menstrual flow, stool and urine. The *sadhaka* and *sadhika* are to exchange these elements between each other in course of *sadhana*.
6. The preceptor who gives initiation to the Bauls and provides all sorts of instructions in the performance of *sadhana*.
7. It is the nerve current situated along the left side of the spine.
8. It is the nerve current that flows inside the right side of the spine.
9. It is the nerve current that flows in the centre of the spine.
10. The Bauls who follow the rigid pattern of mendicant life in the Ashram.They follow *sannyasa* way of life.
11. The Bauls staying in the family of procreation after their imitiation.
12. It is a hermitage of the mendicants.The Ascetic—Bauls must perform their *sadhana* inside this hermitage.
13. It is the celebrated begging by the Bauls from door to door in the village society.
14. The consecrated food that has been offered to the deities. Taking of the type of food is considered as a holy act by the devotees.
15. It means the great festival. During this festival devotional songs are sung continuously and the *prasad* is offered to the attending devotees with utmost sincerity.
16. A large cane-made measuring basket used for measuring paddy.
17. A specific state in the Baul *sadhana*. It means death while living. During the deepest *sadhana* the Baul loses his mental existence and his outward movement stops for sometime.
18. Literally it means mad. During *sadhana* the Baul becomes made to get the feet of the Man of the Heart.
19. It means male person. This *purush* when unites with *prakriti* gives the shape of the living world.
20. It means nature. Here *prakriti* signifies the female consort on the male Baul.

References

Bandyopadhyay Upendranath	1388 B.S.	*Banglar Baul O Baul gan* (The Bauls and the Baul songs of Bengal), in Bengali, Calcutta, Orient Book Company.
Bhattacharya, D.	1969	*The Mirror of the Sky : Songs of the Bauls from Bengal*, London, George Allen and Unwin Ltd.
Chakraborty, S. C.	1980	*The Bauls—The spiritual Vikings*, Calcutta, Firma K L M.
Dasgupta A. R. & M. A. Dasgupta	1977	*Roots in the void : Baul songs of Bengal*, Calcutta, K. P. Bagchi & Co.
Dorson R. M.	1972	*Folklore and Folklife—An Introduction*, Chicago, The University of Chicago Press.
Sarkar, R. M.	1984	Conflict-Compromise and Diversity. Unity Oriented Life philosophy of a wandering community, *Indian Musleum Bulletin*, Calcutta. Vol. XIX, pp. 48-55.
Sarkar,R. M.	1988	The Bauls of Bengal—Their Diverse Nature and Patterns of Thinking, *Man in India*, Ranchi, Vol. 68, No. 1, 1988, pp. 1-44
	1990	*Bauls of Bengal : In the Quest of Man of the Heart*, New Delhi, Gian Publishing House.
Singer, Milton (Ed)	1969	*Traditional India*, Philadadlphia, The American Folklore Society.

B.N. Bordoloi

TRIBAL ETHNICITY IN NORTH EAST INDIA AND ITS IMPACT ON NATIONAL INTEGRATION

NORTH EAST TRIBAL INDIA—ITS HISTORICAL BACKGROUND

When we speak of the present North East India, we refer to seven States in this region, viz., Arunachal Pradesh, Assam, Manipur, Meghalaya, Mizoram, Nagaland and Tripura. These States have in total 25,5083 sq. kms. geographical area, and the total area constitutes 8.74 per cent of the total geographical area of the country. The total population inhabiting these seven States of North East India is 3,15,47,314 as per 1991 Census out of which 81,42,624 are tribals constituting 25.71 percent of the total population. Geographical distribution of the Scheduled Tribes population in the North Eastern States as per 1991 Census is given below :

Name of State	*Total population*	*Total S.T. Population*	*Percentage*
1. Arunachal Pardesh	8,64,558	5,50,351	63.66
2. Assam	2,24,14,322	28,74,441	12.87
3. Manipur	18,37,149	6,32,173	34.41
4. Meghalaya	17,74,778	15,17,927	85.53
5. Mizoram	6,89,756	6,53,565	94.75
6. Nagaland	12,09,546	10,60,822	87.70
7. Tripura	27,57,205	8,53,345	30.95
Total	3,15,47,314	81,42,624	25.71

(*Source*—Aspects of population profile of Assam,, 1991 Census).

As per Constitution (Scheduled Tribes) Order 1950 amended up-to-date, 119 communities have been enlisted as scheduled tribes in the seven States of North East India as shown below[1] :

Sl. No.	Name of State	No. of Communities
1.	Arunachal Pradesh	12
2.	Assam	23
3.	Manipur	29
4.	Meghalaya	17
5.	Mizoram	14
6.	Nagaland	5
7.	Tripura	19
	Total	119

An examination of the lists of the Scheduled Tribes in these States, however, reveals two important facts. First, there are many communities who are enlisted as the Scheduled Tribes in more than one state. As for example, the Kukis are enlisted as the Scheduled Tribes in Assam, Manipur, Meghalaya, Mizoram and Tripura. Similarly, the Nagas are enlisted as the Scheduled Tribes in Arunachal Pradesh, Assam, Manipur, Meghalaya and Mizoram. Secondly, a few communities are grouped together sometimes under one head. As for example, under the head 'Any Kuki Tribes', altogether 37 sub-groups are brought together.

Now if we avoid repeatition and also take into account the sub-groups or tribes put under one head, the total number of tribal communities found to inhabit North East India would be 201 as against 430 for all India. This clearly shows that North East India is inhabited by 46.74% of the Scheduled Tribe communities of India. Thus from the point of view of tribal concentration, this area may be regarded as a mini Tribal India.

These tribes with their individual distinct identity marked by their culture, languages/dialects, religions, manners and customs, cultural values and ethos, traditional socio-political organisations and so on have their own history to tell. Unless we have a comparative picture of their historical background, it would rather be difficult to make a correct assessment as to why and how the ethnic movements among the tribal communities of North East India have been gaining such a momentum during last few decades.

For the purpose of this article I propose to make a beginning from the Ahom period since the written history made its appearance so far Assam is concerned during the Ahom era.

Ahom Period

The Ahoms evolved a distinct policy so far their relations with tribal communities, some of which has been living within the territorial jurisdiction and some of which had been living in the border areas of their kingdom, are concerned. This policy had three main aspects. The first aspect could be termed as the non-interference with the internal affairs of the tribes. The second aspect was connected with the maintenance of regular supply line of essential commodities which were of day to day use for the tribes. And the last aspect was connected with the regulation of trades between the hill tribes and the plains people through the 'Dooars' or trade posts on the border of the Ahom kingdom. (Dutta, 1988).

The hill tribes, of course, violated the trade agreements and sometimes committed raids in the plains within the jurisdiction of the Ahom kingdom. The Ahoms immediately punished such tribes by sending soldiers under capable captains.

Hostilities between the Ahoms and the Kacharis were very frequent which resulted in the annexation of the Kachari kingdom to the Ahom kingdom. Similarly there were battles between the Ahoms and the Jaintias (a tribal community of present Meghalaya). Although the Jaintias were defeated, nonetheless, their kingdom was not annexed by the Ahoms and later on cordial relations were established between these two peoples.

It may now be summarised that the Ahoms had cordial relationships with the tribes living within their kingdom and tribes bordering their kindom and the latter had been independently managing their own affairs under their own chieftains.

British Period

The British period is much more important for the purpose of this paper since during the period the seeds of ethnic movements were shown as would be evident subsequently in this very section.

The British policy towards the tribes, specially the hill tribes, was fundamentally different from that of the Ahoms. They followed the policy of annexation in respect of some tribes like the Garos, Lushais (now called Mizos), Nagas, Kukis, Khasis, Jaintias and some other and the policy of non-interference in their internal affairs in respect of some farocious tribes like the Akas, Daflas (now called Nishis), hill Miris, Abors, Mishmis, Khamptis, Singphos and some such tribes in spite of the fact that their small king-doms were physically annexed to the British empire without administrative annexation. They were in fact more or less independent. Another important fact that requires our attention is that while during the Ahom rule intercourse between the people of the hills and plains were free and the relations were cordial, the introduction of the Inner Line Regulation Act 1873 by the British Government restricted free intercourse between these two peoples—meaning the hill people and the plains people, resulting in isolation of the hill people from the plains people and creation of a feeling of distrust (Bordoloi, 1991).

During the British days there were kings in Manipur and Tripura who had definite territorial jurisdiction. There were tribal chiefs among the different tribal communities known by different names. In the earliest days of the British rule, present North East India (the hill areas) excluding Tripura formed a part of the Rangpur District. These areas were separated later on from the Rangpur District and were placed under an officer called Civil Commissioner of North East Rangpur who was given the responsibilities of a Collector, a Magistrate and a Judge. This newly conceived administration was called 'Non-Regulated System' and the areas brought under this system of administration were called 'Non-Regulated Areas'.

The Government of India Act 1919 rechristened these areas as 'Backward Tract'. These areas, according to the opinion of the British Government, being most backward were required to be excluded from the normal system of administration as well as administrative reforms banning the Central and Provincial Legislatures from enacting any laws for these areas. Administration of these 'Backward Tracts' was vested with the Governor in Council or the Governor of the Province. In the North-Eastern Hill Areas, of course, some of the 'Backward Tracts' were not wholly excluded from the applicability of any Act of the Provincial Government. But this would be determined by the Governor in Council and the Governor of the Province.

The Indian Statutory Commission, commonly known as the Simon Commission, had recommended the same line of administration as contemplated under the Government of India Act 1919. It had, of course, done away with the terminology of 'Backward Tract' and replaced it with 'Excluded Areas' and 'Partially Excluded Areas'. The Government of India Act 1935, based on the recommendation of the Simon Commission, declared the following areas as 'Excluded Areas' and 'Partially Excluded Areas':

Excluded Areas

1. North East Frontier (Sadia, Balipara and Lakhimpur)

Districts.

2. Naga Hills District.

3. Lushai Hills District.

4. North Cachar Hills Subdivision of Cachar District.

Partially Excluded Areas

1. Garo Hills District.

2. Mikir Hills in Nagaon and Sibsagar District.

3. The British portion of the Khasi and Jaintia Hills District other than Shillong Municipality and Cantonment Areas.

The hill areas of the North Eastern region were fully or partially excluded from the regular administrative system of the British Government because of the fact that situations—political, economic, and social—obtaining in these areas were quite different from those prevalent in the rest of the country. Secondly, people inhabiting these areas were more concerned with the security and management of their land.

The 'Excluded Areas' were completely outside the purview of the provincial legislature and these areas were administered by the Governor of the Province himself at his discretion. So far as the 'Partially Excluded Areas' were concerned the administration of these areas was the special responsibility of the Governor of the Province. He might accept or reject the advice of the concerned Minister on the administration of 'Partially Excluded Areas' in his individual judgement. Without his prior approval no law of the Central or Provincial Legislature could be applied in these areas. The Governor of the province could make regulations for the peace and good Government in these areas.

The British Government did not formulate any rational policy for the development of the tribal communities of North East India, and as such they did not have any development strategies for them in the true sense of the term. The areas inhabited by the tribals being either excluded or partially excluded ones, the British Government allowed the tribals to manage their own affairs and did not interfere unless it was absolutely necessary. Their 'Laissez Faire" policy or policy of segregation and isolation paid them good dividends. The main intention of the British Government was to keep the tribal people as far as practicable at a long distance from the rest of the population. They followed this policy to suit the needs of the administration and found that it had been working well in serving their interest to the fullest extent.

It would, however, be quite injustice to say that during the British day nothing had been done for the development of the tribal people of the North East India because of the lack of a clear-cut policy for tribal development. But we shall have to remember that whatever development activities were performed by the British Government for the development of the tribal people of this region, they were undertaken not in the interest of the tribal people but to serve the interests, both administrative and commercial, of the rulers. New railway lines were opened to carry coals, timbers, oils, tea, etc. from this region to outside. Roads were constructed to connect district and subdivisional headquarters so that soldiers and police personnel could be sent quickly as soon as some tribal uprisings were reported. To offer basic amenities to the Government employees, serving specially at the district and subdivisional headquarters, opening up of educational institutions, hospitals and dispensaries, provisions for drinking water supply, opening up of commercial establishments, trade centres, markets, etc., were considered absolutely essential. The tribal people living in the North East region had reaped some of the benefits of development schemes primarily meant for providing basic amenities to the employees of the British rulers and other infrastructural facilities created for smooth running of the administration and also for serving the commercial interests of the rulers.

Under the patronage of the British rulers, the Christian Missionaries had a very important service in spreading education and offering medical and other social welfare facilities to the tribal people of North East India. The high percentage of literacy among some of the tribal communities of North East India could be ascribed to this.

To supply essential commodities and other consumption goods to the personnel connected with administration, maintenance of law and order, etc., the British rulers allowed traders and merchants, mostly from outside the North East India, to make an inroad to the tribal areas. These people in course of time settled in the tribal areas permanently and started exploiting the people in various ways. They at the same time, tried to establish a bond of friendship with the tribal people and the trading community became their (tribals') friends, philosophers and guides in due course. By taking of the tribal people's simplicity, truthfulness and ignorance, these traders exploited them to the highest possible extent.

The British rulers, however, kept a close contact with the

tribal chiefs of the different ethnic groups in North East India and through them House Tax or *Chang Khajana* and *Dao* Tax were collected. These tribal chiefs who had a good command over their community members were like petty kings with their small kingdoms and subjects. The British Government always tried their best to have a friendly relationship with these tribal chiefs by following the policy of least interference. But even then, during the early period of the British rule there were frequent uprisings against the British among the hill tribal communities of North East India. Sometimes the entire British encampment was ravaged to the ground at night killing all the inmates. Thus to keep the tribes of North East India under control was rather a very critical problem for the British rulers as there had been a feeling of distrust between the rulers and the ruled. The British Government's approach towards the tribals of the North East India to make them feel impact of administration was very gradual (Bordoloi, 1985).

It is, of course, a fact that a good number of administrators like Mills, Hutton, Gurdon, Hunter, Mackenjie, Playfaire, Soppit, and others, had written books on tribes and travel accounts which had rather exposed the tribes of North East India to the outside world. However, these books were written primarily to facilitate the running of the administration rather than to fulfil academic interest. An understanding of their way of life, customs, socio-political institutions, economic activities, sentiments, feelings, etc. was very much essential for the alien rulers.

POST INDEPENDENCE PERIOD

A. CONCEPT OF SELF-MANAGEMENT

While administration of the tribal areas in the rest of the country excepting the North East has been governed by the provisions of the Constitution, in the Hill Areas of the North East, namely, Assam, Meghalaya, Mizoram and Tripura, the administration is governed by the provisions to the Sixth Schedule of the Constitution which are infact the principles of self-management in a broader sense.

The Constituent Assembly of India has set up an Advisory Committee of Fundamental Rights, Minorities, Tribal and Excluded Areas under the chairmanship of Sardar Bhallavbhai Patel. For the North East Frontier Tribal Areas and Assam Excluded and Partially Excluded Areas, a Sub-Committee with five members, was set up under the chairmanship of Gopinath Bordoloi, the then Chief Minister of Assam, called Prime Minister at that time.

The other four members of the Sub-Committee were Mr. J. J. M. Nichols Roy. Mr. A. V. Thakkar, Mr. Rup Nath Brahma and Mr. Illba Imti. Mr. Imti later on opted to remain outside the Sub-Committee.

This Sub-Committee had submitted its report on 28th July, 1947. Since the drafting of the Constitution had already begun, the recommendations of the Sub-Committee were directly incorporated in the Draft Constitution (Saxena, 1981).

In the Constituent Assembly debates the Draft Provisions incorporated in the Sixth Schedule were discussed thoroughly. These debates revealed the founding fathers' views clearly and precisely and the reasons for recommending special provisions for the administration of the tribal areas of the North Eastern Hill Regions of the country. In the Constituent Assembly debate Mr. Gopi Nath Bordoloi, the Chairman of the Sub-Committee, explained in clear terms the background in which the draft of the Sixth Schedule was prepared. He stated that the problems of hill areas of Assam which were completely excluded areas in the sense that none could from the plains go there and contact the tribal people, were quite different from the problems of those areas which were brought under the normal administrative measures of the British Government. During the Second World War, some of these areas were under war zones. During war times some military officers engaged in these areas to fight against the Japanese, and the British administrators posted there infused in them a sense of separation and isolation. They assured the tribals that as soon as the war was over, they would have their independent states managing their own affairs according to their own way. Mr. Bordoloi strongly argued that instead of using brute military force, a method should be used in which willing co-operation from the people could be obtained by the Government for the purpose of governing these areas. Drawing the attention of the Hon'ble Members he had also pointed out the manner in which even the murder cases had been decided by the village Panchayat. Democracy prevailing in village administration and the manner in which different community works were distributed among the people of different age groups in the village were simply marvellous according to opinion of Mr. Bordoloi. He strongly agrued that the tribals should be allowed to develop themselves in their own way.[2]

In the debates Mr. Bordoloi was supported by Mr. J. J.M. Nichols Roy and Mr. A.V. Thakkar. Even a politician like Sir Mahammad Saadulla who vehemently opposed the incorporation of the Sixth Schedule to the Constitution had, however, pointed out to the basis qualities of the hill tribals, i.e., (1) practice of democracy and (2) community ownership of land.

In drafting the Sixth Schedule to the Constitution of India, Mr. Gopi Nath Bordoloi and three other Members of the Sub-Committee had conceptualised the following few factors:—

(a) Recognition of the distinctive culture of the hill tribes in respect of their social customs, traditional organisations, religious beliefs, dialects/languages, the mode of their living and methods of cultivation, etc., all of which can be termed as their own way of life.

(b) Adequate protective measures against exploitation by the people from the plains on account of their superior organisations and experiences in business. The hill people are afraid of the fact that if suitable provisions are not made to prevent the plains people from acquiring lands in the hill areas, large number of them would settle down and they would not only occupy land belonging to the hill people but would also exploit them in non-agricultural professions like money-lending.

(c) Assimilation cannot take place by sudden breaking of the traditional tribal institutions and by imposing on them a different alien system. The evolution of growth must be based on old foundations. In other words, evolution should come as far as possible from the tribal people themselves.

(d) Adequate protection on the above quoted matters and such allied ones could only be achieved by transferring the management and administration of these matters entirely to the hands of the people. This itself could be termed as self-governance.

To achieve these objectives, the provisions under the Sixth Schedule to the Constitution of India have provided the Autonomous District/Regional Councils with wide range of legislative, executive, financial and judicial powers. Under the legislative powers, management of land, forests other than reserved forests, shifting cultivation, establishment of village councils, town committees, matters connected with customary laws such as appointment/succession of chief or headman, inheritance of property, marriage, etc., regulation and control of money lending and trading by non-tribals, the Councils have been entrusted with enactment of suitable laws.

Executive powers have been given to the Councils to manage primary education including the language/languages in which primary education is imparted, establishment and management of medical institutions, cattle pounds, ferries, roads, waterways, etc.

Among the financial powers entrusted to the District/Regional Councils mention may be made of the following :—

Assessment and collection of land revenue, collection of taxes on lands and buildings, collection of taxes on trades, profession and callings, a share of royalty on extraction of minerals, etc.

Under the judicial powers, the Councils have been authorised to constitute village councils or courts for the trial of suits and cases between the parties belonging to the scheduled tribe communities only. The powers and functions entrusted to the autonomous District/Regional Councils under the provisions of the Sixth Schedule to the Constitution, in the final analysis, are the principles of self-management by the people themselves.

In the Constituent Assembly debates the question in regard to the administration of the areas in the plains districts of Assam where the plains tribal people have been living was also raised. Mr. Gopi Nath Bordoloi replied that his Sub-Committee was concerned with the North East Frontier Tribal Areas and Assam Excluded and Partially Excluded Areas and as such the plains tribal areas were outside the purview of the Sub-Committee. He further stated that it would be the responsibility of the main committee, that is to say, the Advisory Committe on Fundamental Rights, Minorities, Tribal Areas and Excluded Areas of the Constituent Assembly, headed by Sardar Ballavbhai Patel to deal with this aspect.

NATIONAL PERSPECTIVES

(I) Constitutional Frame

The emergence of tribal ethnicity in North East India cannot be understood in isolation and the national perspectives are to be kept in view. In fact our Constitution has provided so many safeguards to protect tribals' interests and measures for welfare and development, direct or indirect, that their brief mention is considered essential to understand the gamut of the emergence of tribal ethnicity.

A. Article 15 (4) of the Constitution of India gives direction to the State in making any special provisions for the advancement of any socially and educationally backward classes or for the scheduled castes and scheduled tribes, although the general provision as laid down in Article 15 (1) is that the State shall not discriminate against any citizen on the grounds only of religion, race, caste, sex, place of birth or any of them.

B. Article 16 (4) of the Constitution of India gives discretion to the State to make provision for the reservation for appointments or posts in favour on any backward classes of citizen which, in the opinion of the State, is not adequately represented in the services under the State although the general provision as laid down in Article 16 (1) of the Constitution is that there shall be equality of opportunity for all citizens in matters relating to employment or appointment to any office under the State.

C. Article 17 of the Constitution of India deals with the fundamental rights.

But under Proviso(s) of this Article the State has been authorised to make reasonable restrictions on the exercise of the Fundamental Right stated in Article 17 (d), namely, to reside and settle in any part of the territory of India and Article 17 (e), namely, to acquire land and dispose of property in any part of the territory of India.

D. Article 46, which is otherwise known as the Directive Principles of State Policy, lays down that the State shall promote with special care the educational and economic interests of the weaker sections and in particular of the Scheduled Castes and Scheduled Tribes. The State shall also protect them from social injustice and all forms of exploitation.

E. While Article 244 (1) relates to the provision as to the administration and control of scheduled areas, Article 244 (2) relates to the provision of the administration of the Sixth Scheduled Areas.

In the seven North Eastern States we do not have any Fifth Scheduled Areas. We have Sixth Scheduled Areas in Assam, Meghalaya, Mizoram and Tripura.

F. Article 244 (2) provides for the creation of Autonomous District/Regional Councils in the Sixth Scheduled Areas with legislative, judicial, executive and financial powers.

G. Article 275 (1) povides for financial assistance to the States for implementation of schemes of development for the Scheduled Tribes and raising the level of administration in the scheduled areas.

H. Article 330 of the Constitution of India provides for the reservation of seats for the members of the Scheduled Castes and Scheduled Tribes in Lok Sabha.

I. Article 332 provides for reservation of seats for the members of the Scheduled Castes and Scheduled Tribes in the assemblies of the concerned States.

J. Although according to the Article 334 of the Constitution of India, reservation of seats and special representation in the Lok Sabha and the State Legislature was to cease after 10 years from the commencement of the Constitution, it was extended upto 1970 first and then subsequently extended to 1980, then upto January 1990 and it now stands extended further upto 2000.

K. Article 335 of the Constitution of India provides for the safeguards to the claims of the Scheduled Castes and Scheduled Tribes in respect of recruitment to the posts and services under the State Governments and the Union Governments. But such claims shall be taken into consideration consistently with the maintenance of efficiency of administration in making appointments to services and posts in connection with the affairs of the Union or of a State.

L. Article 338 of the Constitution of India provides for the appointment of a Special Officer for Scheduled Castes and Scheduled Tribes. This Officer has to oversee as to whether the Constitutional guarantees have been properly implemented. He makes an Annual Report to the President of India and this report is presented to the Parliament so that the members can have an idea regarding the progress in the tribal areas. The Special Officer is designated as the Commissioner for the Scheduled Castes and the Scheduled Tribes.

However, it would be very much pertinent to mention here that by amending the Constitution a National Commission for Scheduled Castes and Scheduled Tribes was constituted and as such the Commissioner for Scheduled Castes and Scheduled Tribes has no *locus-standi* now.

M. The founding fathers of the Constitution of India under Article 339 provide for the setting up of a Commission at the end of 10 years of the commencement of the Constitution to review the tribal situations and recommend measures for their development. The First Commission set up under the chairmanship of Mr. U.N. Dhebar made extensive recommendations for welfare and development of the tribal people of the country.

N. Article 339 (2) lays down that the executive powers of the Union extend to the giving of direction to a State as to the drawing up and execution of schemes for welfare of the Scheduled Tribes in the State.

PANCHASHEEL FOR TRIBAL DEVELOPMENT

In July 1958 our Late Prime Minister Jawaharlal Nehru explicitly enunciated the strategies for tribal development in more clear terms summarising them in five fundamental principles which are commonly known as 'Panchsheel' for tribal development. They are quoted below :

1. People should develop along the lines of their own genius and we should avoid imposing anything on them. We should try to encourage in every way their own traditional arts and culture.

2. Tribals' right to land and forests should be respected.

3. We should try to train and build up a team of their own people to do the work of administration and development. Some technical personnel from outside will no doubt be needed especially in the beginning. But we should avoid too many out-siders into the tribal territory.

4. We should not over administer these areas or overwhelm them with a multiplicity of schemes. We should rather work through, and not in rivalry, to their own social and cultural institutions.

5. We should judge results, not by statistics or the amount of money spent, but the quality of human character that is evolved.

The above five principles may be regarded as an integrated approach to tribal development. The strategies and objectives laid down in different five year plans for the welfare and development of the Scheduled Tribes reflect the underlying ideas of the 'Panchsheel' for tribal development.

EMERGENCE OF TRIBAL ETHNICITY IN THE NORTH EAST

In this part we now propose to discuss the causes and nature of emergence of tribal ethnicity in the North East during the post independence period. The emergence of ethnicity is the direct result of a community's assertion for the establishment of its own ethnic identity which is considered to be on the verge of disappearance according to the perception of the community itself. Various steps—political, economic, social, educational and even religious—are being adopted by the tribal communities as well as other to assert and also to revive their own ethnic identities through movements at various stages and time frame.

In fact the emergence of ethnicity or for that matter the assertion of ethnic identity by small communities have become a global phenomenon not only in the Third World Countries but also in Europe. So far as Europe is concerned, the best examples are United Socialist Republic of Soviet Russia and Yugoslavia.

The International Labour Organisation in its Convention 107 of 1957 and Convention 169 of 1989 concerning the protection and integration of indigenous and tribal peoples, recognises the tribal and indigenous peoples in independent countries as less developed socially and economically than those of the general people and emphasises at the same time their viability and distinctiveness as social and historical entities (Roy Burman, 1992). Although the proceeding of these two Conventions have either no impact or have a very little impact on the tribals and indigenous peoples in the emergence of their ethnicity or the establishment of their ethnic identities since the proceedings of the ILO Conventions are hardly known to these peoples. However, the very fact that an institution like the International Labour Organization recognises the need for protection as well as integration of the tribals and indigenous peoples indicates the phenomenon of emergence of ethnicity or establishment of ethnic identity of these groups.

NATURE OF ETHNIC ASSERTION

In this part of this article we propose to discuss the nature of ethnic assertion and the process through which such assertion is tried to be achieved. The different types of movements that we find among the various tribal communities and groups in the North East are manifested in so many ways that it is very difficult to categorise them. Some of the processes are like the under-current of a river surfacing sometimes to make their presence felt.

Some of the movements like those led by the Naga National Council, Mizo National Front, Tripura National Volunteers, People's Liberation Army of Manipur, People's Revolutionary of Kangleipak and Kuki National Front of Manipur, etc., are originally cessationist in nature since they wanted to go out of India and thus these movements have been a threat to the integration of the country. Although the Naga problem is appeared to be solved, the National Socialist Council of Nagaland has been carrying out its cessationist activities.

Some movements like those of Zeliangrong movement led by Rani Gaidilinu (since her death the movement remains dormant berefet of a leader) for the purpose of carving out a state for three akin Naga groups, namely the Zemei, Longmei and the Rongmei, Hmar People's Convention for a Hmar state, Karbi

Anglong and North Cachar Hills Autonomous State Demand Committee, Bodoland movement for a separate state (the Bodo people now have a Bodoland Autonomous Council in accordance with the accord signed between the Government of Assam and the All Bodo Students' Union and Bodo People's Action Committee), Mising Autonomous State Demand Committee (now the demand is for an Autonomous Council), Rabha Autonomous Council Demand Committee, etc., are not cessationist in nature and hence they are not a threat to the national integration of the country.

There have also been movements for ethnic assertion of smaller tribal communities for the preservation of their socio-cultural and linguistic identities when according to their own perception they feel that their very existence is jeopardised due to the various external factors. These communities have been trying to assert their ethnicity by peaceful means. Their own socio-cultural organisations including the students' unions/associations have been spear heading such movements. Some of such groups have tried to delink their relations with the greater group. An example may be cited here. The Dimasa Students' Union of the Karbi Anglong District and the Dimasa Students' Union of North Cachar Hills District of Assam, while submitting their memoranda to the Expert Committee on Bodo Issues constituted by the Government of India under the Chairmanship of Dr. Bhupinder Singh, clearly stated that they were never Bodos and the Dimisas have been a distinct tribal community having no links with the Bodos. Similar is the case with the Deoris, a Scheduled Tribe of Assam, who now claim that they were the priests of the Chutiyas once upon a time but they were never the Chutiyas.

PRINCIPAL CAUSES OF EMERGENCE OF TRIBAL ETHICITY IN THE NOTRH EAST

There are many causes which are responsible for emergence of tribal ethnicity in the North East. Here I would like to mention only the principal ones without establishing their relationship to different ethnic movements. I would rather try to have a general view based on realistic perspectives.

We have already seen that the Constitution of India has provided adequate safeguards and welfare measures for the Scheduled Tribes. But our question is—why then ethnicity has emerged among the tribal communities at so fast a rate not only among the tribes of North East but also in other parts of our country ? Now let us look at the major causes.

(a) I feel that the main cause of assertion of ethnic identities is their fear for the loss of command over their resources like land and forests. The State has rather become a rival in respect of their traditional command over land and forest. They find that the management of land and forest which had been in their hand for centuries together, has now been taken over by the State so suddenly that the feeling of their own existence is at stake. Nehru's second principal of *Panchsheel* for tribal development that tribals' right to land and forest should be respected is hardly respected. Together with the fear psychosis of losing their traditional command over land and forest. There has been alienation of their land to the non-tribals. In Tripura the percentage of tribal population which was more than 50 percent prior to independence has now been reduced to about 31 per cent (30.95) in 1991 due to heavy influx of refugees from the then East Pakistan (now Bangladesh) after partition of the country. The growth rate of population during the decade 1951-61 was 78% as against 21% in the neighbourhood and this was mainly due to heavy influx for immigrants immediately following partition (Das, 1990).

The landless immigrants naturally wanted land since most of them were cultivators. Then on whose land would they fall back upon ? Naturally it was tribals' land. Tribals' resentment finds its way in their assertions as distinct ethnic identities. In Assam a survey carried out by the author in 1987 reveals that within the protected belts and blocks, popularly known as the tribal belts and blocks, about 10 per cent of *patta* land belonging to the tribals was transferred and alienated to non-eligible persons in spite of existence of the law prohibiting transfer of land from the tribals and other protected classes to non-eligible persons. (Bordoloi, 1991).

(b) Manipur and Tripura, in the true sense of the term, were never Parts of British India since they were princely states. Their merging with the Republic of India was a voluntary action. It is, therefore, cannot but be natural if some of the tribal communities living in these two states want to declare these two states as independent ones thinking that by doing so they would be in a position to manage their own affairs in a better way.

(c) The British policy of isolation or *Laissez Faire* of the hill tribes of North East which had paid them good dividends, has now been paying rather no dividends at all to the Government of India. The seeds sown by the administrators among the tribal leaders that they were never dependent and that they were subjects of the British empire only in a marginal way and that they would be given independence when the IInd World War would be over, have now grown into full-fledged trees. On the basis of these ideas some dissident groups among a few tribal communities of North East India living in the hills are still continuing their cessationist movements.

(d) Although in the first principle of tribal development Nehru has stated that nothing should be imposed on the tribals, nevertheless, things are imposed on them to their great dislikings and resentment which ultimately result in their self-assertion. As for example—making Assamese a State Language in undivided Assam, which was and which is still a multi-lingual State, was nothing but an imposition of the language of the majority on the other linguistic groups, especially the tribal groups, without ascertaining whether the linguistic minorities, especially the tribal groups, would accept such an imposition voluntarily or not. The same was the case with the introduction of Assamese as the medium of instructions at the college level although provision has also been made to retain English also as a medium of instruction. The Assamese intellectuals, not all of course, and the organisations like the Asom Sahitya Sabha were so impatient that they could no longer wait and see as to whether the tribal groups would be willing partners in such exercises. Actions like the issuance of the Assam Board of Secondary Education Circular making Assamese a compulsory subject in all secondary schools in Assam, making the knowledge of Assamese compulsory as one of the entry qualifications for Assam Secretariat Ministerial Service, etc., had created a feeling of bitterness among the different tribal ethnic groups in Assam. Thank God, these two are not in operation now. We have, however, become wise only after the events.

(e) In a pond or in a tank if we keep a canivorous fish, it will surely davour the small fishes. Similar is the case with the smaller tribal ethnic groups surrounded by bigger cultural groups. A small ethnic group always fears that its culture, language, religion and socio-ethical values cannot be retained and preserved since the bigger language-cultural groups would like to assimilate them in the long run. A minority group, therefore, feels that it does not get proper opportunities to preserve its culture and develop its language in spite of the fact that the Constitution of India provides equal opportunities to all such groups. Thus the emergence of tribal ethnicity in the North East is essentially minority movements based on ethnic identity asserting their rights as ethnic minorities.[3]

(f) One of the important factors of emerging tribal ethnicity in the North East is the inadequate or nil representation in the Government jobs by some of the communities although Article 16 (4) of the Constitution of India provides for such representation. Even in the tribal predominated states like Arunachal, Meghalaya, Mizoram and Nagaland the most advanced groups are amassing such benefits depriving the backward groups. Not to speak of representation in the Government services, even in the higher educational institutions allotment of seats to the most backward groups is negligible since the students of the latter groups could hardly compete with those of the advanced groups.

(g) There are many other factors like acquiring political leadership and powers, personal aspirations, exploitation by the larger groups in trade, commerce, industry, a feeling of negligence and so on which are also responsible for the emergence of tribal ethnicity in the North East. Moreover, the tribal ethnic groups have become alive to the recent happenings in the neighbouring countries like Myanmar, Bangladesh, etc. and movements like Khalistan, Liberation of Kashmir from India, Jharkhand, Uttarakhand, Telengana, etc. within the country. Action in one part of the country has a chain of reactions in other parts.

Whatever might be the causes of the emergence of ethnicity among the tribal communities of the North East, such emergence begins with the idea of developing unity among the members of a community with the common objectives of welfare and development as well as preservation of culture and language initially. Later on such ethnicity finds its manifestation in political demands for separate administrative units and very often territorial independence.

EMERGENCE OF TRIBAL ETHNICITY AND NATIONAL INTEGRATION

Now in the last part of this article we propose to examine whether the emergence of tribal ethnicity in the North East is detrimental to national integration.

However a few question always baffle me when we speak of national integration and the North East. Why do we very frequently in the academic and intellectual forums and even in political parlance single out North East for national integration ? According to my own perception this might be due to the fact that this area, meaning the seven State comprising North East India, is situated on the international border. It is surrounded by foreign countries like Bhutan, China, Mynmar and Bangladesh. Anything that happens in this part of the country in the form of an ethnic movement, whatever might be its stage, has a strategic importance. The academicians, intellectuals and the politicians, who are in fact policy makers, cannot remain as silent spectators towards these happenings in the shape of ethnic movements. They, therefore, try to study and analyse the causes and try to formulate remedial measures.

There is another important question. When we speak of tribals and tribal development we always state that they should be brought to the 'main stream of national life'. But nobody has so far defined or described what this 'main stream of national life' is. Is it the stream of the Brahmaputra or the Ganges or the Godavari or the Narmada or the stream of the Aryan civilization.

The Anthropological Survey of India is going to present us with the write-ups of 4635 Indian communities in its book "The People of India". Thus in a country like India with thousands of communities belonging to different races, cultures, religions and creeds there cannot be a single main streams. We shall have to take into account the small streams also if we actually want to have unity in the true sense of the term among diversity.

The very concept or idea of bringing the tribals into the main stream of national life presupposes that the tribals are not an integral part of the Indian nationhood. A time has now come for the social scientists, politicians and the administrators at the highest level to abandon such concepts or for that matters misconcepts.

Another important fact is that we do not have a comprehensive definition of 'National Integration'. 'National Integration' has been interpreted in various ways since there are so many types of integration like social integration, cultural integration, political integration, economic integration, territorial integration, etc. We ourselves are not clear the type or types of integration that we are advocating.

Admist so much confusions I, however, feel that the main ingredient of national integration is an inner feeling of social consciousness that we are all Indians and under all situations we are one. This kind of feeling cannot be brought by brute force. It depends on tolerance, sympathy and respect to all cultural and linguistic groups whatever might be the size of the population of each group. This can be achieved by removing the causes of the feeling of negligence and regional imbalance in the field of economy, trade and commerce. Judicious exploitation of natural resources at the command of the tribal communities is a pre-requisite for national integration. How to involve the tribal people and also to obtain their active co-operation in all matters concerning their development and welfare are two major issues which require immediate attention from all quarters at micro as well macro levels. Live and let others also live as equal partners should be the motto.

Notes

1. Brochure containing the list of Scheduled Castes and Scheduled Tribes and Guidelines for Verification of Claims for Issuing Scheduled Castes and Scheduled Tribes Certificates. Government of India, Ministry of Home Affairs, New Delhi, 1984.
2. Constituent Assembly Debates, Official Report, Lok Sabha Secretariat, New Delhi, 1989 (Reprint).
3. Majumdar, D.N. and Nath Alakananda—Ethnic Movements in North East India, (Seminar Paper).

Reference

Bordoloi, B.N. 1985 Strategies for Tribal Development in North East India with special reference to Assam, *in Bulletin of the Tribal Research Institute, Assam*, Vol. 3.

1991 *Transfer and Alienation of Tribal Land in Assam*, Guwahati.

Dutta, P.N. 1988 *Glimpses into the History of Assam*, Shillong.

Roy Burman, B.K. 1922 Indigenous and Tribal Peoples, Gloval hegemonies and Government of India, in *Mainstream*, September 5.

Saxena, H.C. 1981 *Safeguards for Scheduled Castes and Tribes-Founding Fathers' view*, Delhi.

Mamata Desai

HUMAN CONTRIBUTION IN CHANGING HIMALAYAN ENVIRONMENT

Man has been the maker of deserts in past ages, in the name of development. About a third of the earth's land surface, i.e., the mountain regions, seemingly permanent, are among the most fragile elements. A mountain region is characterised by a third dimension on the land surface. This dimension produces a major ecological contrast within a short linear distance and special biological adaptation to meet the conditions of low temperature, high radiation and strong winds characterizing these areas. These regions show particularly the existence of an altitudinal gradient in the distribution of barometric pressur, radiation temperatures and precipitation. This gradient results in vertical zonation of soils, flora, fauna, and ecosystem type. Accordingly, man's way of life, his habit and land-use and exploitation patterns are differentiated vertically. Furthermore in mountain areas man is especially confronted by problems of isolation and special difficulties in communication. Generally speaking, man's impact on mountain ecosystem are producing critical situations at a faster rate, than in many other types of ecosystems. The inclination of the slopes accelerates and aggravates all processes of site destruction, such as soil erosion and landslides. Mountain ecosystem therefore must be treated in an especially careful way.

The Himalayas, the highest and youngest mountain system of the world, on the northern edge of the Indian subcontinent, extends for 2,400 km from the bend of the Indus river in the west to that of the Brahmaputra in the east. The width of this mountain system is variable being broadest in Kashmir and narrowest in Sikkim, approximately 400 km and 160 km respectively. Based on its geological and geomorphological history, the whole system is divided into three distinct sectors, i.e. Western Himalayas (between the Indus and the Sutlej rivers), Central Himalayas (between the Sutlej and the Singalita range), and Eastern Himalayas (from Sikkim to Arunachal Pradesh).

Structurewise and topographically the Himalayas are divided into three sectors from south to north, i.e., the Siwalik zone, the Middle Himalayas and the High or Greater Himalayas.

Physical Systems

Geologically, the Siwaliks are the youngest in age, having been formed in its third and the last major folding event. Structurally these are made of fresh water deposits, composed mostly of clays, sandstones, grits and conglomerates, and show only variable degrees of consolidation and yield considerable sediments during heavy rains.

The Middle Himalayas are a mass of intricate folding and faulting. The rocks mainly belong to igneous, sedimentary and metamorphic types. There are large scale granitic intrusions in this region for which the region is well dissected.

The High or Greater Himalayas rising above the Middle Himalaya zone and separated by an escarpment, known as Central Thrust, which form the axis of this mountain system. Structurally, the Greater Himalayas are formed of igneous and ultra-basic rocks. Beyond the High Himalayan zone, lie the Zanskar, Ladakh and Karakoram ranges in Kashmir, and the trans-Himalayan ranges in Tibet.

Climatically, the Himalayas present an extremely wide variation from the tropical to the Alpine and even Arctic. There is a great variation in temperature and precipitation from the foot hills to the Alpine peaks and from the western to the eastern ends. But in general the entire western Himalayan region tends to be semi-arid or sub-humid. The Central Himalayan sector is wetter than the western with an average precipitation ranging from 2000 mm to 2500 mm. The slopes exposed to monsoon winds receive copious rainfall.

The abundance of low north-south valleys in the Eastern Himalayas take the monsoon winds right-up to the foot of the Great Himalayas making it an area of warmth and very heavy rainfall (ranging from 2,500 mm to 5,000 mm).

The three major river systems of the subcontinent i.e., the Indus, the Ganges and the Brahmaputra come out of this lofty mountain systems. The three river systems collectively supply water to the northern part of the sub-continent. The innumerable streams that unite to form these river systems, get their water supply from snows, glaciers, springs and rainfall in the Himalayas.

Richness of variety of habitats in the Himalayas resulting from topographical and climatic conditions leads to a large variety of plants and vegetation types lying in close juxtaposition to each other. In the case of the Himalayas, it is possible to discern a zonal pattern of vegetation with changes in elevation. Generally subtropical vegetation scrub and trees are found from 900 m to 2000 m. Whereas below 900 m tropical vegetations are found. Lower and middle temperate forests lie between 2000 to 3000 m. A sub-alpine zone of lower trees and bushes succeeds the latter, giving way to the alpine vegetation from 4000 m to 4,900 m in different localities. The Himalayan vegetation is characterized by a great richness of species. There is very little information available on the state of natural vegetation at present, because they have undergone rapid changes due to large scale removal and deterioration of vegetation for different purposes.

Man vs Mountain

As human population expands in the hills, forests are being depleted. The water retaining capacity of the soil is reduced and run-off is increased. Man's presence in the region makes itself felt in two ways, first by increasing number and second by his behaviour. So regarding number, there is need to analyse the causes and bio-social consequences of population growth, determination of the human carrying capacity of the existing man-environment systems. The density of population, especially, in the mountainous terrain like the Himalayas, reflects the environment of the area and man's ability to use it. In 1981, the Himalayas as a whole had a density of about 110 persons per sq km as compared with 221 persons for India as a whole. The zone with the highest population density was the Siwaliks, with nearly 234 per sq. km. and least was the High Himalaya with 18 persons per sq. km. The Middle Himalayas had a density of 75 persons per sq. km. Sectorwise the Western Himalayas had 151 persons per sq. km. while the Eastern Himalayas had only 6 persons per sq. km.

Population growth in the Himalayan regions has been on the rise since 1951. The population growth during last eighty years as studied in the Sikkim is give below :

Table-1 Growth of Population in Sikkim (From 1901-1981)

Census year	*Total population*
1901	59,014
1911	87,920
1921	81,721
1931	1,09,808
1941	1,21,520
1951	1,37,725
1961	1,62,189
1971	2,09,843
1981	3,14,999

It is clear from the above Table 1, that the population growth in the region has been on the rise since 1951, as compared with the first half of the century, and with the last two decades having really gathered momentum.

On the basis of the geological structure altitude and climate, land-use pattern in the Himalayas varies a great deal from the plains. But for the region as a whole, it appears from the landuse classification survey conducted during 1980-81, 28.8 per cent as cultivated land and 7.2 per cent as potentially cultivable, 32.2 per cent was under forest, 13.7 per cent as pasture land, 8.2 per cent as barren land, and 7.2 per cent was listed under 'other use'. The man-land ratio in the Himalayan region was 5 : 9 hectares per persons in 1981, with 0.84 for India as a whole.

The agricultural systems in the Himalayas are divided into two distinct groups, i.e., (i) intensive terrace cultivation, and (ii) shifting cultivation.

The latter is largely confined to the eastern part of the region, gradually increasing eastwards till it is the only method in Eastern Arunachal Pradesh. It is observed that land under tree crops is on increase in the Higher Himalayas. In the Eastern Himalayas agriculture is a year round-affair, whereas in the Western and Central Himalayas it works round up to 10 months.

The natural resources in the Himalayas have been utilized since the ancient time, both by the local people and by the plain's people. History says that before the Muslim era, there has been a lot of interaction between the hills and the plains. Many Himalayan kingdoms were extended southward. Many people from north

Indian plains fled to the Western and Central Himalayan sectors during the advent of the Muslims. At the same time, people belonging to the Mongoloid origin moved southward from Tibet and China to the Eastern Himalayan sector.

As the population grew, the lateral expansion of the human settlements started in the Himalayas. Thus by the beginning of the 19th century, there was considerable pressure on the basic natural resources like land and water, especially in the thickly populated pockets in the Middle Himalayas.

The East India Company established summer capitals in Eastern and Central Himalayas, and developed tourism. Along with tourists the traders began to settle in the Himalayas.

"Post-independence" development of the Himalayan resources started on the basis of the above settings. The only new dimensions which were added (i) resource development in terms of raw materials, (ii) development of hydroelectricity for industrialisation. This modern "resource based developments" got under way actually from 1960s onwards. As such different policies were framed to develop commercial agriculture, horticulture, animal-husbandry, small scale industries, mining and tourism. Especially under the different multipurpose schemes, commercial, agricultural and industrial productions are increasing by leaps and bounds. Again for the transportation of these products to the big cities of the Indian plains, where the demands for these products are increasing, road-ways are to developed. At present the total road length in the Himalayas is over 80,000 km. As per 1976 report, the density of road in the Himalayas was 8.39 km per 100 km^2 (as against 16.5 km average for India). The above mentioned figures would have increased considerably in the past 15 years. Big and multipurpose hydroelectric projects which came in the Himalayan picture during this period are mainly located in the southern edge of the Middle Himalayas. Hundred of Kilometres of roads are being constructed to supply food, equipments and other essentials, to maintain contacts with plains to the project sites, or for the development of settlements to cater the employees of these projects.

Thus infrastructural developments have quickened the growth of urban centres as well as population in the Himalayan region. Thus the two prime results of these infrastructural development are, rapid growth of population and consequent pressure on forests and land of the Himalayan belt. As is said earlier, the cumulative growth of population during the last three decades was 73.1 per cent (1951-1981). The cumulative effect of what has been going on in the Himalayan region is the tremendous demand on forest and grazing lands. Because and is required for each and every human activities, i.e., living space, roads, different development projects industrial estates etc. Commercial demand for timber and other forest resources in another reason for fast depletion of forest cover. The local people's rights to use timber and other forest produces incorporated in the Forest Act have brought in some malpractices.

Changing Ecological Scenario

When we talk about the ecological change in the Himalaya, that refers to the natural resources, deteriorating condition of the watershed, forest resources, agricultural output, frequency of landslides, droughts, floods, problems of soil erosion etc.

The deforestation in the name of development has greatly affected the Himalayan climate, the amount of snow and also the volume of glaciers. The glaciers are shrinking rapidly and the volume of ice is decreasing fast. It is observed that the Gangotri glacier in the Central Himalayas has been shrinking continuously in the current century. According C.P. Vohra (1985) the rates of retreat of some important glaciers are as follows :

Table-2

	Glacier	*Retreat in metre per year*
1.	Pindari	23.5
2.	Siachen	31.5
3.	Gangotri	14.1

What will be effect of such retreat ?

The rapid shrinkage of the Himalayan glaciers has resulted in the development of huge barren surfaces. Again the enormous erosion caused by the large scale deforestation is producing a vast quantity of debris and silt, for which river basins are gradually shrinking. The ultimate result is flood in the plains.

The accelerated erosion of mountain slopes has removed the top soil and the productive capacity of the terrain for which, it is estimated that about 1.5 m hectares of good forest land is lost every year. The eroded soil can neither hold water nor nutrients. The absence of vegetable cover is also responsible for promoting the quick run-off of water and a very little amount seeps into the ground to re- appear in the form of springs.

As the forest coverage is gradually decreasing, the state of wild life in the Himalayan region is also in critical stage. Again, indiscriminate poaching the illegal trade are rapidly increasing. A kilo of rhino horn fetches about Rs. 2,50,000 in the international market.

The Himalayan belt supports 20 m cattle, 10 m buffaloes, about 10 m sheeps, goats and horses etc.

In the Himalayan belt, the unplanned management of livestock is resulting in deteriorating their quality, and causing a great ecological crises. Due to ever increasing grazing, the temperate grassland of the region is diminishing very rapidly. Generally a livestock holders has to get a permit from the concerned authority for grazing cattle in the hill forests, but unfortunately grazing on the steeper slopes in the Himalayan belt is a very common feature. Again usually upto 33 degrees of slopes is recommended for agriculture with bench terracing, but the land above 50 degrees is cultivated at many places.

What is the effect?

As the result, due to steep gradient and heavy rainfall, soil erosion and landslides are very common features at many places. These are mainly due to the sudden increase of population.

As a result, in large parts of the Himalayan region, the soils are in the process of being rapidly damaged. Their fertility is being reduced, along with their water-holding capacity. Low crop yields are often reflected here by the number of cattle kept by the rural families. In recent years, it is observed that the soil yield has decreased, while the number of animals increased. In many parts of the High Himalayan regions, especially in Lahul-Spiti region, the top soil is already lost, and cultivation is being done on ground moraine left by hanging glaciers. In the Terai region of Nepal, in almost all south facing cultivable land, the top soil is lost, and the load of top soil carried to India by Nepalese rivers is estimated at six million tonnes per ha./year. It is examined that soil loss from 1 to 10 tonnes/per ha/year under natural conditions, is taken as normal. But at present due to intense human interferences the average rate of soil erosion ranges from 20 to 50 tonnes per ha/ year. As a result 38 per cent of the total land area of the most populated "Eastern hills" (Middle Himalayas) of the Nepal Himalayas are abondoned fields, which is a serious indication of lost soils. The unplanned growth in human population in relation to available renewable and non-renewable resource base is the greatest threat to healthy life and environment. About 250 tribal communities inhabiting the Himalayas, and the forests are meaningfully linked with their socio-cultural life which still nurtures an ancient civilisation.

The new Forest Act of 1953 did little to change actions of local people. Then started Chipko movement. Inspite of the pressure applied by the Chipko leaders, the situation has not really changed. On the one hand felling of trees continues unchecked and unabated, on the other hand the Forest Act of 1980 places such impediments before the common man that even minor developmental projects have become impossible. The useful broad-leafed trees are being replaced by other commercially viable species. The issue of the social ownership of forests is always being neglected to the background. Big business people are able to procure raw materials at very low prices for their paper mills or other forest oriented factories while the villagers are unable to get even firewood, fodder or raw material for their houses and huts. Various forest Acts do not affect in any way the large scale developmental projects, ranging from dolomite mining in North Bengal to a big dam at Tehri, while smaller projects have to face obstacles at every step. Various multipurpose projects have been started, among them the Tehri dam project and others of its kind, obviously without proper evaluation and assessment. It is found that within ten years of the construction of these dams, their life expectencies have shrunk to a half or a quarter. But it is needless to mention that there is need for water resources development in the Himalayan region for ever increasing agricultural production to meet the demands of a rapidly growing population. The next few decades will therefore see a large number of reservoirs are likely to come up in the region, which lead to an all round development in the region.

On 20th October 1991, a massive earthquake hit the Tehri Garhwal region, where the gigantic Tehri dam is being built. For the past fifteen years, local people have been protesting against the dam, both on grounds of displacement of 80 thousand inhabitants from Tehri town and surrounding villages as well as on the basis of earth quake hazards, as the dam is being built on a geological fault in a highly seismic zone. The October earthquake proved that the fears of earthquake hazards were not gossips. After the earthquake the nature of the movement against the Tehri dam has undergone a dramatic change. It is no longer largely a movement of people threatened by displacement supported by some environmentalists, but it has become a movement of all potential victims of future disaster, in the form of reservoir induced seismicity and consequent floods. But again the question is not of dam alone. The bigger issue is that of the development strategy in the hills which needs to be fully overhauled.

Another recent hazard in the hills has come with the tourism and mountaineering is the horror of the plastic bags. The bags lie littered over hill sides, block drains and sewers and even reach the streams in the valleys. These innocuous little things may one day become a major destructive force. This is mainly because of the increased tourists traffic. During last two decades tourist traffic has increased enormously far exceeding the actual carrying capacity. Political instability in many regions, has diverted the tourists to Himalayan regions, and this unprecedented growth of tourism has caused the desecration of the environment, uncontrolled urban growth, indiscriminate felling of trees leading to soil erosion. During peak seasons i.e., summer and autumn, all round chaos pervades the entire region, leading to disturbance of community facilities, shortage of essential commodities, soaring prices etc. The boom in tourist trade has augmented the creation of new hotels. Even some times it is observed that tourists are responsible for undetermining and destroying local cultural and way of life. Again rapid revolution in automobiles is responsible for air pollution.

Lastly, the mention should be made about the mountaineering in addition to the act of traditional climbing, it relates to the preservation conservation and development of the mountains without whose proper existence the prospect of climbing itself becomes impossible. Thus the physical well being of the mountains is entirely dependent on the health of the biological system whose habitat is the mountain earth itself.

Note

1. Centre for Science and Environment: The State of India's Environment. A Citizen's Report I and II, *1982* and *1984-85*.
2. Forest Research Institute *1980* "Himalayan Eco-Systems, Consequences of Development and Population Growth" Dehra Dun.

References

Chaube, S.K. 1985 *The Himalayas—Profiles of Modernization and Adoption*—Sterling Publishers Pvt. Ltd. New Delhi.

Dewan, M.L. 1990 *People's Participation in Himalayan Ecosystem Development*—Concept Publishing Company, New Delhi.

Desai, Mamata 1985 "Urban Population and Ecological Balance—A Study on Sikkim Himalayas—*Asian Studies*, Vol. 3, No. 1 and 2, NIAS.

Manis Kumar Raha
Sumitabha Chakravarty

TRIBAL ECONOMY IN THE HIMALAYAS : PERSISTENCE AND CHANGE

Introduction

"Economy" may be considered as the foundation stone of every established society. Only the human being have acquired the power of regulating the wealth. As like with the non-tribal societies, "economy" is one of the major factors to stimulize the essential needs of the tribal people also. The study of the economy of tribal people is not a recent approach to the social science. It has already been studied by a number of eminent scholars like Thurnwald, Herskovitz, Malinowski, Firth and so on. According to their opinion "The tribal economy is the nexus of relationship between the human being and material goods and services" (Thurnwald, 1965; Herskovitz, 1952; Malinowski, 1961; Firth, 1963). But as things have begun to change, the ideas about "tribal economy" also improved and interpreted in various ways. In recent time, the economy of the tribe or "tribal economy" is defined as a projection of the tribal society, a response to the ecosystem in which it is placed through the function of production, consumption and distribution (Singh, 1982). Few Indian social scientist also opined that the "tribal economy is a concept, which have seen in a state of flux with varied ecological niche" (Nag, 1958; Saxena, 1964; Shah, 1967; Mukherjee, 1982). Because, exploitation of nature is one of the most important characteristics of it. Their production, consumption and distribution are solely depended on the environmental condition. But now-a-days with the advent of modern technology, the tribal economy is co-existing and interacting with "superior" socio-economic system, neglecting all sorts of ecological influences.

From the classification point of view, the tribal economy of bygone days was only based on the simple mode of hunting, gathering, animal herding etc. But now-a-days it has been classified in various ways. One of the earlier classification is of Daryll Forde who made five classifications viz. food gathering, hunting and fishing, animal herding, farming and industrial economy (Forde, 1934). Thereafter, a number of scholars also classified "tribal economy" in a number of categories.

But this kind of classification is not quite appropriate for the tribal people inhabiting in the Great Himalayan region. Here these people are influenced by both, the need based and ecology based factors and so their economy may be classified into four categories. The Bhotia, the Bhot, Bhot-pa, Boto, the Kinnaurese and the people of Spiti are engaged with the interdependent economy of agriculture, trade and pastoralism. The pastoralism and agriculture are also the economic pursuits of the Gaddi and the Gujjar while the Bakarwals are totally busy with their large flock of goats and sheep. The Raji people, on the other hand are involved in their traditional hunting and gathering economy.

In the foregoing pages we have attempted to describe the interdependent economic structure of the tribal people of the Himalayas, how they adjust their interlinked economy with ecological condition, are there any modern influences playing important role for removing these interdependency of economy.

Area : Ecology : People

Occupying the entire northern part of India, the Himalayan region covers a long distance from west to east. The total Himalayan area can broadly be divided into three parts, namely, the Western Himalaya; the Central Himalaya and the Eastern Himalaya. According to the statewise distribution, the Western Himalaya covers Jammu and Kashmir and Himachal Pradesh while the Central Himalaya includes the eight hill districts (Tehri, Pouri, Chamoli, Uttarkashi, Dehra Dun, Nainital, Almora and Pithoragarh) of Uttar Pradesh. The Eastern Himalaya, on the other hand, covers the States/Union Territories of Assam, Meghalaya, Arunachal Pradesh, Sikkim, Manipur, Mizoram, Nagaland and Tripura (Census, 1981).

As the present study is restricted among the tribal people of the Western and Central Himalayas, we have given emphasis on these areas of the Great Himalayan Ranges. The Western part of the Himalayas is extended from Indus Valley to Sutlej and the Central part is from Sutlej to Kali basin. A large area of 3,29,013 sq. kms. of Western and Central parts are the motherland of a number of various tribal groups, who are inhabiting in the districts of Jammu and Kashmir; Himachal Pradesh and Uttar Pradesh. Physiographically, the Central and Western Himalayas are the result of thrusts and vertical upheavals (cymatogenic activity) of the late tertiary times. The thrust sheets and overfolds are overridden by relicts of earlier "smoother plantation" of mid tertiary age (Law, 1968). Almost all districts of the Central and Western Himalayas are encompassed by a number of great mountain ranges and valleys. The Zaskar range, the Pir Panjal, the Dhaula Dhar, the Nanga Parbat, the Nanda Devi etc. are the most important mountain ranges in this region. The general features of the mountain systems are usually jagged and shaffy covered with thick unkemp vegetation, while the opposite side is more gently sloped with less developed timbers but with rich pasture land (Raha, 1992).

From snowy, highest peak down to the foothills, everywhere an extreme variable climate has been observed. The temperature usually falls down from the month of September. The months of December, January are the coldest in the year. Again the temperature starts rising after the month of March. The months of June-July are the peak summer season with hot temperature.

Though the annual rainfall is very low in quantity, but yet it varies from one region to other. The snowfall is comparatively higher than rainfall. In some of the regions viz. the high altitude of Ladakh, upper part of Kinnaur and Lahaul and Spiti, there is no major rainfall. These regions have almost semi-arid climate.

The natural vegetation usually found from the sub-tropical dry forest to the alpine pastures. The maximum temperate forest with *deodar*, fir, spruce are found almost everywhere. The extensive alpine pastures are the main feature of the semi-arid zone, which is only found above 5000 metre. Most of the habitations are lying on the bank of the rivers. The villages with maximum number of populations are generally situated in the higher altitude, above 5000 ft. to 14000 ft. (Gupta, 1992).

A large number of tribal populations are found to reside in this high altitude. According to populationwise distribution, the districts of Jammu and Kashmir are the cradle land of Bhot, Boto and Bhot-pa and Bakarwais; the districts of Himachal Pradesh are that of Kinnaurese and Gaddi tribal people. The Bhotia and the Raji are mainly concentrated in the hill districts of Uttar Pradesh, and the Gujjar who are found in all the three states (Jammu and Kashmir, Himachal Pradesh and eight hill districts of U.P.). The population number vary regionwise.

Ladakh—a northwestern most district of Jammu and Kashmir is inhabited by the Ladakhi (Bhot, Bhot-pa) people. The total Ladakhi population within this district is 1,05,291 (Census, 1971). Alongwith many other tribal people the Bhot, Bhot-pa are also declared as the Scheduled Tribe very recently in the year 1989, as per the notification under Article 342 (1) of the Constitution of India. Socio-culturally, the family, *gyut* (more like a lineage group) and *phasphum* are the three important social groups of which the family and *gyut* based on kinship and the *phasphum* is on common brotherhood (Mann, 1992). Though polyandrous type of family with polyandrous marriage is the preferred one, the nuclear family with minor children also exist. In vertically extended family, the oldest person generally takes the whole responsibility of the family. The position of the women in the family is quite sound. Marriage by negotiation is the general rule. In case of the polyandrous family there is no special procedure of determining the social fatherhood. Generally the eldest brother has the social obligation. The "*gyut*" is a social group, whose members believe to be descended from a common ancestor. It is a kin based exogamous group *(ibid)*.

Beyond family and *gyut*, the next bigger social group is "*phasphum*" consisting of few families whose members worship a common God (la). Though patrilineal system is strong, yet the maternal uncle's position is not less important (Mann, 1986).

Their society is widely related with religious organization. Buddhism is the chief religion followed by Muslim, Hindu, Christian etc. (Tyagi, 1992). Monastary or the monastic organization plays a vital role in every sphere of the Ladakhi life. The *lamas* (monk) and the *chomos* (nuns) are the chief mediator who are regarded as most learned persons as they regulate the socio-religio-political organization of the Ladakhi society (Mann, 1992).

The Kinnaurese or Kinnaura are the inhabitants of Kinnaur, the north-eastern most district of Himachal Pradesh with a population of 49,835 (Census, 1971) persons. The Rajput, Khosia or Kanet are the most dominant group, a Scheduled Tribe. The caste groups, the Koli, the Lohar, the Badhi and the Nangalu are the scheduled castes. At present the whole Kinnaura society are divided into two broad groups viz. *Khosia* and *beru*. The *Khosia* includes the dominant group of people, Rajput or Kanet followed by the four castes of *beru* groups (Raha and Mahato, 1985; Raha 1987). The *beru* is again sub-divided into *domang, chamang,* and *chanalas*. On the other hand, the *Khosia* is sub-divided into thre

Khel or the status groups and each *Khel* is further divided into a number of *Khandan* or lineage, which cover a number of household or *Kim* (Raha, 1987).

Socio-culturally, the *Kim* (family) is the basic functional unit which is regulated by the polyandrous marriage. The nuclear and extended type is the major type of family prevalent among them. The rule of descent, residence and authority are followed on the paternal line. The monogamous marriage is the root cause of nuclear family. In polyandrous marriage the eldest brother is the only responsible person to perform different marital ties and rituals. Cousin marriage is totally absent while sororate is permissible in a few cases. Members of same status group but different lineage can matrimonially be affiliated.

In case of religion, it has been found that both Buddhism and Hinduism are practised by them in this district. Some of them started to have faith in the Devi-Devta complex of Hinduism while some others have Lakhan-Labrang complex of Buddhism. The Kinnauras those are living in the central part have faith in both (Raha, 1992).

The famous trading group, the Bhotias are residing in the Eastern, Central and Trans-Himalayan areas. In the Central Himalayas their major concentration are in the districts (Pithoragarh, Chamoli and Uttar Kashi) of Uttar Pradesh with a considerable number of 32,311 (Census, 1981) populations. They are divided into eight exogamous groups, viz. the Jad, Tolchcha, Marchha, Johari, Jethora, Darmi, Chandansi and the Byansi, which are again sub-divided into several clans and lineages (*rathu/ sora/dhada*) (Prasad, 1989).

Socio-culturally, the Bhotias prefer to live in a joint family, but the simple nuclear families are also prevalent amongst them. Monogamy is the rule of marriage, while polygamy, polyandry are absent. The members of Bhotia society follow the strict rule of exogamous clan system *(Rathu)*. The members of a clan are believed to be descended from a single common ancestor. In case of different economic activities, the Bhotia females always ready to co-operate with their male folk. Absence of dowry clearly reveals the status of women. The dormitory system *(rang-bang)* was found to exist in each Bhotia village. Now they do not have such system. Marriage by negotiation is the general rule, but marriage by capture, love marriage, widow remarriage etc. are still practised. Every aspect of crisis of life is followed by them with their kith and kin (Raypa, 1992).

The Bhotias follow Hinduism. They worship the Hindu gods and goddesses. But side by side they worship different spirits, natural and supernatural powers. The most important deities among them, are *Byasirkhi* (Vyas Rishi), Shyang Se, Gabla etc. Socio-politically they have become more conscious than before (Das, 1982).

The semi pastoral and semi-agriculturist Gaddis are denoted as Schedule Tribe under the provisions of Article 342 (2) of the Constitution, in the year 1991. They scattered all over the Himachal Pradesh, but their major concentration is in the Chamba and Kangra districts. According to census report of 1981 the total number of the Gaddis are 76,860 souls. Their history of origin is still dubious, but mythology and folktales reveal that they were the Rajputs migrated from the plains of Lahore (Pakistan) to avoid forcible preselytization of the Muslim invaders (Sarkar and Sarkar, 1992).

Socio-culturally, the Gaddis prefer to make the nuclear household very much but the extended type of family also prevalent in those cases where the oldest male becomes the head of the household. The rules of inheritance and the rules of residence are traced through paternal line only. Though the monogamous marriage is strictly followed one, but polygamous marriages are very few in number. There are various forms of marriage among the Gaddis viz. regular marriage *(byah)*, exchange marriage *(bata sata)*, widow remarriage *(kamash)*, marriage by service *(khewat)*, marriage by elopment *(jhind phunk)* with the modern trend of love marriage. The clan *(gotra)* is the largest exogamous unit for the determination of marriage. They follow the caste endogamy strictly. One pure person can never choose his spouse from an impure category. The caste endogamy plays a dominant role in their socio-economic and religious life also (Newell, 1987).

They follow Hinduism and worship Hindu gods and goddesses. They take part in different colourful religious *yatras*, festivals, fairs etc. As pointed out that "in Bharmour, every year the famous *yatra* starts in the late August or early September for *Manimahesh* (abode of Lord Shiva) (Sarkar and Sarkar, 1992)." Except this they also worship their traditional deities and spirits.

The "natural nomad" (Mishra, 1982) Bakarwals are another most dominant nomadic pastoral group of north-western part of our country. Except the district of Kargil and Leh they are ascendantly concentrated in the districts of Poonch, Rajauri,

Udhampur, Kathua, Dola, Wangat valley etc. with a sizeable population of about six lakhs (Census, 1981). The historical encounters reveal that the name "Bakarwal" is originally derived from "bakri-chayana" i.e. grazing of goats and originated from a part of Gujjar, who depends on the rearing of goats, sheep and horses.

Family is the basic functional unit of their society which is generally nuclear, but the extended type with a group of members is also prevalent. Monogamous marriage is the general rule. Being Islamic in faith they also practise parallel cousin marriage. They strictly follow the patrilineal line of descent with patrilocal residence. But where the parallel cousin marriage takes place, the female remains in her natal family (Maiti, 1992). Both type of exogamous and endogamous marriages are practised by them. The unilineal clans are sub-divided into several sub-clans viz. Khatana, Basir, Ahmed, Ali, Nisa, Nazir, Rasid, Aziz, Baksh and Safi. They do not believe the clan stratification. The social groups are formed on the basis of their clan. In case of marriage, they prefer exogamy. Though monogamous marriage is the general rule but polygynous marriage is also practised. One Bakarwal male is never permitted to have more than four wives at a time. Being a Muslim group they follow the Muslim way of marriage ceremonies and ritual of deities.

The semi-pastoral and semi-agricultural group, the Gujjars are scattered over a large area including Jammu and Kashmir, Himachal Pradesh, Punjab, Haryana and Western Uttar Pradesh. The name Gujjar is a derivation of the Sanskrit word "Gujara". At present, their large concentration is in the whole state of Himachal Pradesh with a considerable number of population (28,121) according to Census, 1981. Most of them were Hindus but a sizeable number of them was converted into Muslim during the Moghul regime. Under the constitutional amendment Act 341 (2), the Gujjars are also treated as Scheduled Tribe all over the country in the year 1991. Once upon a time they were mainly inhabited in the western part of India. But due to the search of ample pasture land they migrated towards the north and north-western part of India.

Cohabiting with the Bhotias in the same region of Pithoragarh, Kumaon Hills, the Raji people are still persisting their nomadic way of life and remain engaged in hunting, gathering and clearing of forest. They themselves claim to have descended from feudal royalty of Ashkote and called as "Raji" i.e. the Royal people, who are still inhabiting in the caves and rock shelters (Negi, *et. al.*

1982). At present their distribution is confined only to the nine villages especially in Dharchula, Askot and Champhawat region of Pithoragarh district. Though actual enumeration is difficult, yet it is estimated that they are only 350 individuals inhabiting in the 70 households *(Ibid)*. They are divided into a number of exogamous patri-lineage called *rath*. They use "Singh" as their surname. Monogamy is the general rule. The rule of inheritance is male equigeniture. They prefer to make nuclear type of family.

Economic pursuits : Strategies and interrelationships

As economy is considered a part and parcel of a society, the tribal people of the Great Himalayan Ranges also perform certain economic activities for fulfilling their regular needs. Some of them performed a number of activities simultaneously and some others are satisfied by only single economic pursuit. According to this varied nature, the total economy of this region may be classified into four broad categories, viz. the tribal groups possessing trade, agriculture, pastoralism with woolen works; as for example—the Bhotia, the Bhot, Bhotpa; and the Kinnaurese. The second group is semi-agro-pastoral including partly agriculturists and partly pastoralism, for example—the Gaddi and the Gujjar, while the third group completely depends on pastoralism with a large flock of animals, example—the Bakarwal. And the last one is a complete nomadic group including hunting, gathering and collecting economy. The best example is the Raji people.

These are the varieties of economy of the highland tribals of the Himalayas which are somewhat different from the plain land economy. This is because, ecological constraints always play a dominant role in this region against their economy. So their economy depends on some need based factors in one hand and some ecology based factors on the other. But even then, neglecting all environmental hazards they have to perform the regular course of economic activities for their survival.

Agriculture

The terraced cultivation is the primary important method of agriculture of these inhabitant groups. The terraced land is situated on the mountain slopes and valleys. The land is definitely infertile. Irrigation facilities is not at all satisfactory. Most of the time they depend on the snowfall for irrigation, of course, the rain water partially meets up the demand for irrigation of the tribal people of lower part of the Himalaya. Though most of them, except the Bakarwal and the Raji, perform agriculture once in a year but very few of low land tribals perform the same twice in a year. In general, the most favourable time for agriculture in this region is from April to middle of October. They accomplish a laborious course of tilling, sowing and harvest to produce maximum yield, but unfortunately due to the ecological constraints, they can only produce the low quality of yields, like wheat, *china, phapher*, beans, *ogla*, potatoes etc. which alone were definitely inadequate to meet up their hunger. Before the Chinese aggression of 1962, the tribals of bordering areas were engaged with famous Indo-Tibetan Trade alongwith their agriculture. At that time, agriculture was secondary, but when the Indo-Tibetan Border route was concealed they are shifted to agriculture pastoralism etc. Traditionally, the Gujjars, the Bakarwals practised pastoralism and the Raji were with their hunting and gathering. After 1962, even the Bhotia also took up agriculture with all interest. In recent time, Gujjar perform pastoralism with agriculture but the Bakarwal and Raji maintain their traditional profession of nomadicism and hunting gathering respectively.

Trade

Possibly, because of agricultural failure to produce sufficient food, some of them were compelled to choose the subsistence economy—trade and animal husbandry. As excellent traders the name of the Bhotia, Bhot, Bhot-pa and the Kinnaurese may be mentioned first, who were "almost extensively the commerical couriers between Hindustan and Tartary and also between Tartary and Cashmere" (Frazer, 1820). A number of valuable trade items were exchanged between the merchants of India and Tibet. The Bhotia traders used to collect different items like medicinal herbs, valuable stones, yak tails, furs, sugar, iron implements from the native place and sell these to different trade centres across the border. In exchange they used to bring high quality wool, high breed sheep, borax, *pasmina* from Tibetan traders (Prasad, 1989). Similarly the Bhot, Bhotpa of Ladakh and the Kinnaurese of Himachal Pradesh used to maintain their trade relation with Tibetan merchants. Tobacco, sugar, copper powder, paper, grains, iron implements were exchanged by salt, wool, gold dust, tea, borax, pasmina etc. from the Tibetan traders (Raha and Mahato, 1985; Mann, 1986). The total operation of such kind of trans-Himalayan trade was performed by means of barter. But finally the age old trade relationship with Tibet had also been disrupted. It was in the year 1962, after the Chinese aggression the trade route between India and Tibet was totally closed down. The people of this region were again over-thrown into a great economic despire. Their life started afresh with other subsistence economy and also timely assistance by the Government who came out with a number of development programmes.

Pastoralism

As already mentioned that the pastoralism was another mode of subsistent economy which would also be regulated by ecology, especially the height of the mountains and availability of rich grazing grounds. Mann points out that "the number of animals reared by a family indicate the economic status of its members. The consideration is that more the number of animals in a house, the better the economic position of that house" (Mann, 1986), the goat, sheep, yak are the common varieties of animals for herding. But every community has a specific one. The Bhot, Bhotpa (Ladakh) and the Kinnaurese kept *soorajee*, dzo, dzomo (cross breed of yak and cow), ponies etc. while the Gaddi and the Gujjar have a large flock of buffaloes and other milching animals. The Bhotias have yak, ponies, horse, sheep, goats; while the Bakarwal have only sheep and large flock of goats. As good pastoralists, the Gaddi, the Gujjar and the Bakarwal undertook the two encampments e.g. the summer and the winter encampments. During summer encampment (May-October) they usually go to the high altitude alpine pasture land with their flock of animals for grazing purpose, and come back to the downward region with them (cattle) during the time of winter encampment (November-April). Such kind of continuous movement from one place to the other had renowned themselves as "natural nomad". The profession of pastoralism generally meet up their basic needs of milk, flesh etc. These animals also help in tidious and adverse transportation in the mountain ranges. The people protect themselves from severe cold by woolen garments which they get only from sheep and goats. This profession of pastoralism also cannot be performed at a full swing against all environmental odds and hazards.

Hunting and Gathering

From less economic records it has been found that the Raji people were a traditional hunters and gatherers. They used to collect honey, wood, leaves, roots and tubers, fruits etc. from the jungle and made different wooden article of various size and shapes. The wooden bowls, wooden pots of different sizes, ropes of wild grass etc. are the important varieties of their handicrafts. After collecting all these things from the forest they used to gather these all in a place near to the forest and returned to the forest again. The local people come and see these articles, if they are satisfied, they collect these in exchange of salt, foodgrains etc. The local people also leave these articles on that spot in a same fashion. After a couple of hours the Raji people came and collected those articles. The whole operation was going on under the shadow of dark night. So they had been treated as "invisible traders" (Majumdar, 1973) and their trade as "silent trade".

Whatever the economic structure, varieties and strategies were, it may be considered from the above discussion that the every economic pursuit in the Great Himalayan region was interdependent and inter-linked with each other. No alone economic pursuit could subsist their need for survival for a long period of time. Because the environment always plays a key role against their economy. Their agriculture, trade, pastoralism, woolen industry were interdependent with each other. The economic insufficiencies and inadequacies are the root cause behind it.

Ecology and Economy : A correlationship

Man's relation with his environment and man's acceptance of the influence of it, established from the day man was born (Raha, 1992). Alongwith many other factors which directly and indirectly contribute in shaping the pattern of livelihood of a person, the role of ecology is unquestionably a vital one. Because ecology and economy inextricably involve with each other. As economy is considered as the base of every society, any kind of its change is reflected throughout the whole society. This kind of correlationship between ecology and economy has been focussed in a number of studies conducted in various parts of the world. The pastoral-horticultural pursuits of the African Nuers are transhumant too (Evans Pritchard, 1940). The environmental perception and the ecological constraints in Western Jamaica, in the same manner, have largely been responsible for the two fold adaptation in the livelihood pattern of the immigrants East Indians who were initially brought by the colonial administration, as indentured servants (Ehrlich, 1974).

Same condition also prevails within the various ethnic groups living in the different areas of the Great Himalayan ranges, especially the central and western parts of Himalayas. A number of economic pursuits like agriculture, trade, pastoralism, hunting and gathering etc. are influenced very much by the hazardous environment. According to the distribution, the tribal people in this area, inhabit either in the wet climatic zone of lower altitude, or in the high mountains arid zone above seven thousand feet. Naturally, they have to face a diverse ecology in this area. In the wet climatic zone of lower altitude, a wide area has occupied under the cover of a thick vegetation. There is a considerable amount of snowfall and rainfall and people of that area are more akin to profess cultivation rather than any other occupations. A quite opposite picture is noticed in the high altitude (above 7000 ft.) arid zone, where rainfall is almost absent and snowfall is extremely meagre. The tribals of that area show their interest in animal husbandry, trade, etc. other than agriculture. So, one portion of the Bhotia, the Bhot-Bhotpa, the Kinnaurese, the Gaddis and the Gujjars, who reside in the wet climatic zone, profess agriculture as their main profession, while the rests of arid zone involve in pastoralism, trade, woolen industry etc.

In case of the famous Trans-Himalayan trade with Tibet of pre-Chinese aggression (1962), the ecological and regional, both factors played an important role. The tribals (Bhotia, Bhot, Bhotpa, Kinnaurese) of bordering high altitude areas had much affiliation in trade with the Tibetan merchants because of some reasons. At first, due to the hazardous climate and environmental strains, the agricultural yield from their cultivable land, was very insufficient to meet up their regular requirements. Secondly, due to pastoralism, the tribal people, specially the people of bordering areas, used to go to the alpine pasture land for herding of their large flock of animals. Gradually the regular interaction of the people of these two areas turned into a "mitra" relationship which helped them to develop the famous age-old trade. Finally, at that time the trade was considered as a major economic resource of their livelihood because of its economic stability.

The other economic resource, animal husbandry also received a moderate response of environment. It is also influenced by the ecological diversities. It cannot possible to tend the animals in the high Alpine pasture during the winter months. So, the profession of pastoralism is undertaken with two different encampments, summer encampment and winter encampment.

Another important example of environmental influences with their economic pursuit is the development of woolen industry. The tribal people are inhabited in such a high altitude mountainous areas of the Great Himalayan region, where winter lasts for six months from November to April. During that particular period, the whole area remains under the grip of severe cold with snowfall. During this period, to protect themselves from the biting cold, they felt the need to have more and more woolen garments. But, in the past, the production of good quality wool was definitely not sufficient in comparison to their demand. They used to import good variety of wool and high breed sheep and goats from Tibetan trade centres. But now-a-days, with the gradual increase of their own livestocks (goats and sheep) and also of the availability of the high breed varieties from Government sources, they develop the household woolen industry. In this way, these flocks of livestocks help themselves to protect from the environment in one hand and to carry their transporting goods from one place to another on the other hand.

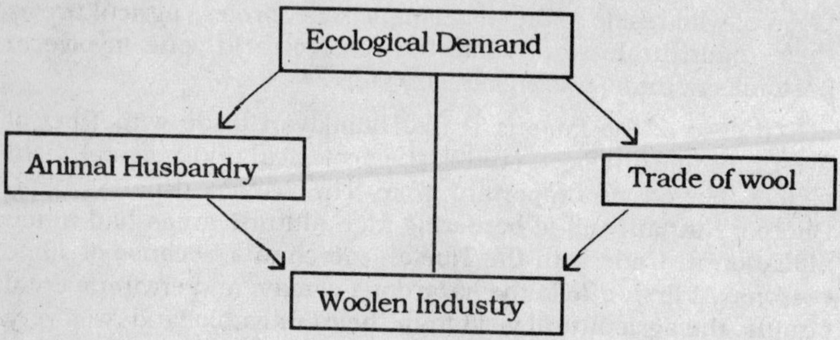

Ecological Factor and Development of Woolen Industry : Correlation

Source : Economic Strategies, Religious Dualism etc. by Dr. M.K. Raha in *Himalayan and the Himalayas.*

From the above mentioned diagram, it is clearly revealed that in the Great Himalayan region, the ecological demand is the root of all influences which regulates the every kind of economic pursuits. Due to the ecological demand only animal husbandry in one hand and trade of wool on the other have come up. Because, in the severe biting cold weather they have to eat meat and to wear the woolen garments. The good quality of wool was available in Tibet wherefrom the Himalayan tribals used to procure the good quality of wool and high breed sheep and goat. Slowly, those tribals became the owner of a good number of livestock which forced them to adopt a good knowledge of animal husbandry. In this way, with the help of these profession (animal husbandry and trade of wool), the woolen industry, another important economy was developed.

The primary important method of agriculture of this region—the terraced cultivation is affected very much by the Himalayan environment. First of all the terraced cultivable land is definitely infertile and full of stones, and pebbles. Secondly, the rainfall is extremely meagre in the lower altitude and very little or almost absent in the high altitude area. Irrigation facilities is not at all satisfactory. Most of the time they depend on the snowfall for irrigation. During the winter months agricultural operations cannot be possible, because most of the high altitude areas of the Great Himalayas remain embeded under the thick layer of snow. That is why the most favourable time for agriculture is from April to October, once, somewhere twice in a year. Due to such kind of severe environment the agricultural yield is below quality and insufficient.

The hazardous environment, like, sudden snowfall, extreme cold etc. also affect the hunting, gathering making of wooden bowls and the preparation of the water channels in the mountain etc. of the Raji people. But yet then they persist those traditional economy with some modern measures of recent years.

Last of all, it is better to say that the Himalayan ecosystem has not only the negative impression, it has positive impression also. Terracing the hilly land, agricultural cycle, yield of high altitude crops, agricultural operations, etc. all these activities are influenced by the Himalayan environment (Raha, 1992).

Modern economy with various developmental measures

It was the year of 1950, the hightime of tribal transformation throughout the country. The tribal people, all over India were being transformed because of the implementation of different governmental and non-governmental development schemes. In the course of development, in recent years, they are adopting different modern economic measures. The similar picture of development has also been noticed in the Great Himalayan areas. But actual development had started in this region after sealing of the Indo-Tibetan border trade in the year of 1962. At that time, the tribal people viz. the Bhotia, Bhot, Bhotpa, Kinnaurese, Gaddi, Gujjar, Bakarwal and the Raji were compelled to satisfy their regular hunger by traditional occupation. From that time till today, government and many other private welfare associations have taken up various measures for economic development to emancipate their severe economic disparities. With the help of the Government they started horticulture in a larger way than before. It was only practised for domestic purpose during the bygone days. In recent years, the rich quality of apple, apricot, walnut, cherry etc. have created a good market throughout the country. They practise horticulture to a large extent.

The major development activities in the great Himalayan region have been provided by the Government under three tier development programmes (Sarkar, Sarkar, Raha, 1992). For agriculture development, many of these people have been provided by improved implements for hilly areas, improved varieties of hybrid high yielding seeds, appropriate varieties of chemical fertilizers etc. As a result, the people practise cultivation more than before to earn a good amount of yield.

The Government also imported the improved knowledge of scientific herding to the tribal people with a special arrangement of co-operative dairy farming etc. *(ibid)*. The groups of people, who profess pastoralism, are benefitted very much by this revised Government provision. They adopt the opportunities of selling milk and various milk products through the co-operatives in exchange of money.

To develop their household woolen industry to a great extent, the Government has taken up several steps, such as, providing good quality raw wool at a subsidized rate, imparting the knowledge of modern spinning and weaving at different centres of this area, procuring the manufactured woolen goods in the different woolen industries and the like. As a result their woolen industry became more improved and a large percentage of women folks remain engaged with their male partners in this industry. After sealing of the Indo-Tibetan border trade route, the fine quality of woolen products are procured now-a-days through different industrial departments.

With the closure of the Indo-Tibetan trade routes after the Chinese aggression (1962), a number of security departments, like the Border Security Force, ITBP (Indo-Tibetan Border Petrol), the police department etc. are posted there. Due to the undeveloped transportation in that region, the pack animals of tribal people are extensively used for transporting their goods at the station situated in the remote corners in exchange of some amount of money. The animals (sheep, goats) only have the capacity to cross such kind of rocky, mountainous, narrow, zig-zag mule track (Das, 1982). But gradually, the transportation system developed with newly constructed roads and bypasses which employ a number of tribal people as a wage labour. It is true to say that, this is the develop transport system which can motivate the economic aspects of the Himalayan tribes in the recent years. A number of government, semi-government, and private sector offices have been set up which provide a good strength of local tribals as the wage earners. These people became more mobile. Now-a-days unhesitingly they cross over a large distance for a better job.

As we are all aware, that the Himalayan region itself is a tourist industry, because of its close attachment with nature. This region is lying on the lap of nature, with a number of tourist spots. Under developed transport system, these tourist spots have been connected, which directly or indirectly influence the tribal people to get their job as helper-cum-guide and earn a good livelihood.

The same kind of new, improved development measures have also been provided to the Raji people. As they have a good knowledge of forestry and wooden works, they are given training in the manufacturing of agricultural implements and vessels of different shape and size. They are permitted to occupy the forest land. They are employed as forest labourers in various labour works by the Forest and the Irrigation Departments. Nowadays, a very few of them are involved in different training programmes related to the sedentary agriculture (Negi, *et. al.* 1982).

Gradually, a number of business centres, shopping complexes, regular or weekly markets have set up in different places which improve their economic condition. Their age old barter system has been transformed into cash economy, which motivate the tribal life.

From the above discussion, it clearly reveals that although those ethnic group are modified by a number of modern developed measures and new economic set-up, but they still practise some of their age-old professions, like animal husbandry, agriculture, hunting, gathering etc. One thing is very interesting that in the bygone days, all of their economic resources were interdependent with one another but nowadays, the economic interdependency is removed. Under the development programmes, the people also get the modern educational facilities which will increase their overall knowledge and provide them into different white collar jobs.

It is a matter of great hope that the Indo-Tibetan Border trade again comes into action. After a long term interval, the age-old border trade is getting materialized recently, by the diplomatic dealings of India and China. Both the countries flashed a green signal for the trade run immediately after the protocol was signed on July 1st, 1992 (India Today, 1992). The reopening of Lipu Lekh routes linking Dharchula Tehsil of Pithoragarh district with the Purang district of China's Tibet, autonomous region, has already started luring people back into trade once again *(ibid)*. It is undoubtedly a great achievement for the development of total Himalayan economy.

Change

With the advent of various development measures, taken up by the government and private agencies, the overall socio-economic and cultural condition of Himalayan tribes has changed to a greater extent. The developed transport system has motivated the tribal life as a whole. They become mobile, the inter-relationship between the neighbouring tribal and non-tribal groups has increased and various socio-economico-religious ties have been established with the neighbouring people. Overall, it can be said that the age-old "isolation" has been removed. In the social sphere, family pattern transformed from polyandry and polygyny to nuclear family instead of extended type. In case of marriage rules, monogamy is the preferred rule other than polygynous and polyandrous type. Perhaps the basic reason of that is social mobility. The groups of people move from one place to other for a better economy. The markets, business centres, shopping complexes of various places, in this region has generated the idea of cash economy into their mind. All these factors have shifted their economic interdependency of bygone days to somewhat independent economy. Both male and female folks have been attracted by the various modern fashionable goods. The recent involvement in modern education and different white collar jobs, have increased their knowledge about their political rights. Though change is a slow going process, but it is still going on amongst them even today. Even then, a number of questions arise, how many tribal people of this area will actually get the opportunities and facilities provided by the government, how far they will be evolved against our modern economic parlance, will their poverty be at least partially removed, these all are a matter of great querries.

Summing up

From the foregoing pages it has been revealed that the environment and its influences are very much responsible for the economic set up of the tribal people of the Great Himalayan region. In spite of all environmental hazards and ecological constraints, they perform the courses of economic activities according to the dictates of the diverse eco-systems of the Himalayas.

The next worthmentioning feature is that of their changing economic condition. During the bygone days, the tribals performed various economic pursuits like pastoralism, trade, woolen industry etc, which were interdependent and supplimented by agriculture. Due to the environmental hazards, the agriculture alone could not satisfy their regular demands. But with the continuous advancement in the economic field, in recent years, they overcome such kind of interdependency by means of various improved measures.

Finally, following the closure of the border route with Tibet, the economic set up of the tribals of the Himalayan region has undergone some modifications. However, the patterns of livelihood continued to be largely dominated by animal husbandry, despite the changing conditions, although the partial reliance on agriculture cannot be overlooked in the present context. With the closure of the border with Tibet, it is true that the various development programmes, mechanical transport system, development of market economy etc, eventually, modified the life style and the economic habit of the tribal people of this region. The shortage of income has been minimized by both the traditional and modern economic pursuits. The Sino-Indian diplomatic assignment of very recent time opens again the Indo-Tibetan border route which undoubtedly is a major step forward to boost up livelihood pursuits and to maintain the equilibrium under the changing condition.

References

Das, J.C. 1982 From Trade to Agriculture : A case study to the Bhotias of Pithoragarh in *Economies of The Tribes And Their Transformation* edited by Dr. K.S. Singh, Concept Publishing, New Delhi.

Das, J.C. and M.K. Raha 1976 Ecology, Economy And Transhumance : A study of Immigrant Society in Himalayas. *Bull. of the Anthropological Survey of India;* Vol. XXV; Nos. 3 and 4, Calcutta.

Ehrlich, A.S. 1974 Ecological Perception And Economic Adaptation in Jamaica. *Human Organization*, Vol. 33, No. 2.

Evans Pritchard, E.E. 1940 The Nuer. Oxford University Press, London.

Firth, Raymond 1967 Themes in Economic anthropology, Tavistock, London.

Forde, Daryll 1934 Habitat, Economy And Society. Methuen and Co. Ltd., London.

Frazer, J.B. 1820 Journal of a Tour Through part of the

Snow Range of the Himalayan Mountain and to the sources of Jumna and Ganges, London.

Gupta, Ramji 1992 Ecological Setting of the Central and Western Himalayas in *The Himalayas and the Himalayans* edited by Dr. M.K. Raha, Anthropological Survey of India, Calcutta.

Herskovitz, M.J. 1952 Man and His Works. Knopf. New York.

India Today 1992 *Indo-China Border Trade : Trading on Top of the World.* Vol. XVII, No. 18, September.

Law, B.C. 1968 *Mountains and Rivers of India;* National Committee for Geography, Calcutta.

Maiti, Subhrendu 1992 Pastoral Economy And Territorial Organizations among the Bakarwals of Jammu and Kashmir in *The Himalayas and the Himalayans* edited by Dr. M.K. Raha, Anthropological Survey of India, Calcutta.

Majumdar, D.N. 1973 Races and Cultures of India Asia Publishing House; Bombay.

Malinowski, Bronislaw 1961 Argonants of the Western Pacific, Routledge and Kegan Paul; London.

Mann, R.S. 1986 The Ladakhi : A study in Ethnography and Change; Anthropological Survey of India, Calcutta.

1992 Intra and Inter family relation among the Ladakhis of Ladakh in *The Himalayas and the Himalayans* edited by Dr. M.K. Raha, Anthropological Survey of India, Calcutta.

Mishra, P.K. 1982 Nomads in India; Anthropological Survey of India, Calcutta.

Mukherjee, Ramkrishna 1982 Tribal Economy or Economies of the Tribes in *Economics of the Tribes and their Transformation,* edited by Dr. K.S. Singh, Concept Publishing Company; New Delhi.

Nag, D.C. 1958 Tribal Economy—An Economic Study of the Baiga; Bharatiya Adimjati Sevak Sangha, Kingsway; New Delhi.

Negi, R.S.; M.K. Raha 1982 The Raji and their Economy in *Econo-*

and J.C. Das		mies of the Tribes and Their *Transformation* edited by Dr. K.S. Singh Concept Publishing Company, New Delhi.
Newell, William Hare	1987	The Gaddis of the Upper Ravi as an example of a traditional Hindu Kingdom in *Himalayan Heritage* edited by Dr. M.K. Raha, Gian Publishing House, New Delhi.
Prasad, R.R.	1989	*Bhotia Tribals of India;* Gian Publishing House, New Delhi.
Raha, M.K.	1978	Stratification and Religion in Himalayan Society in *Himalayan Anthropology* edited by James Fisher, The Hague, Mouton Publisher.
	1987	The Khandan System of the Kinnaura of the Western Himalaya in *Himalayan Heritage* edited by Dr. M.K. Raha, Gian Publishing House, New Delhi.
Raha, M.K. and S.N. Mahato	1985	The Kinnaurese of Himalayas Anthropological Survey of India; Calcutta.
Raha, M.K.	1992	Economic strategies, Religious Dualism and Change in Diverse Cultural and Ecological Settings : A case from the Western Himalayas in *The Himalayas and the Himalayans,* edited by Dr. M.K. Raha, Anthropological Survey of India, Calcutta.
Raypa, R.S.	1992	Ecological Adaptation of the Bhotias of Kali Basin of U.P. Hills in *The Himalayas and the Himalayans* edited by Dr. M.K. Raha, Anthropological Survey of India, Calcutta.
Sarkar, V and R. Sarkar	1992	The Changing Horizons of marriage and family among the Gaddis of Himachal Pradesh in *The Himalayas, and the Himalayans* edited by Dr. M.K. Raha, Anthropological Survey of India, Calcutta.
Sarkar, V, R. Sarkar and M.K. Raha	1992	Caste and Cohesion in a Western Himalayan Village in *The Himalayas and the Himalayans,* edited by Dr. M.K. Raha, Anthropological Survey of India, Calcutta.

Saxena, R.P. 1964 Tribal Economy in Central India, Firma, K.L.M.; Calcutta.

Shah, Vimal 1967 Tribal Economy in Gujarat; *Tribal;* Vol. IV; No. 2; Tribal Cultural Research and Training Institute, Hyderabad.

Singh, K.S. 1982 Economies of the Tribes and Their Transformation; Concept Publishing Company, New Delhi.

Thurnwald, Richard 1965 Economics in Primitive Communities; Anthropological Publications; Oosterhout.

Tyagi, D. 1992 Ladakh, Some Demographic aspects in *The Himalayan and the Himalayas;* edited by Dr. M.K. Raha; Anthropological Survey of India, Calcutta.

Index